1–35
68
100
131
164
181

236– 276
318
360

181–236

361–411   (Reference only → 421–456)

NEGOTIABLE INSTRUMENTS, PAYMENTS AND CREDITS

FOURTH EDITION

by

ROBERT L. JORDAN
University of California, Los Angeles

WILLIAM D. WARREN
University of California, Los Angeles

WESTBURY, NEW YORK

THE FOUNDATION PRESS, INC.

1997

COPYRIGHT © 1992 THE FOUNDATION PRESS, INC.
COPYRIGHT © 1997 By THE FOUNDATION PRESS, INC.
615 Merrick Ave.
Westbury, N.Y. 11590–6607
(516) 832–6950
ISBN 1–56662–550–5

 TEXT IS PRINTED ON 10% POST
CONSUMER RECYCLED PAPER

PREFACE

We offer this book for use in courses devoted primarily to study of Articles 3, 4 and 4A of the Uniform Commercial Code. We also include chapters on letters of credit (Article 5) and documents of title (Article 7). Owing to the incredible growth of standby letters of credit over the past two decades, we believe it imperative that this subject matter be taught at some point in the series of commercial law courses and this is as good a place as any.

In recent years the Uniform Commercial Code has undergone substantial revision. Article 3 (Negotiable Instruments) (1990) has been completely redrafted and Article 4 (Bank Deposits and Collections) (1990) has been significantly revised. Both statutes have been widely adopted and promise to become the law of the land; case law on these articles is beginning to come down. Article 4A (Funds Transfers) (1989) has now been enacted in all jurisdictions and incorporated into federal law; here again, case law is appearing. Article 5 (Letters of Credit) (1995) has been completely redrafted and is currently in the enactment process. Important developments are taking place in payment methods and in federal laws regulating bank-customer relations. This fourth edition is intended to catch up with these major changes.

Throughout this book we cite two treatises many times, and, for convenience, they will be cited without repeating the first names and initials of the authors. These are:

Barkley Clark and Barbara Clark, The Law of Bank Deposits, Collections and Credit Cards (Rev.ed. 1995).

James J. White & Robert S. Summers, Uniform Commercial Code (4th ed. 1995). Reference will also be made to the authors' three volume practitioner's edition.

I regret that my friend, colleague and collaborator of over 30 years, Robert L. Jordan, did not participate in this edition. I am deeply grateful to James Joseph Rubin who prepared the manuscript for publication with intelligence, skill and dedication.

WILLIAM D. WARREN

May 1997

*

ACKNOWLEDGMENTS

We gratefully acknowledge the permission extended to reprint excerpts from the following works:

Douglas G. Baird, Standby Letters of Credit in Bankruptcy, 49 University of Chicago Law Review 130, 133-135 (1982). Reprinted with the permission of the author and the University of Chicago Law Review.

Barkley and Barbara Clark, Regulation CC, Funds Availability and Check Collection (1988), portions of page 1-10. Reprinted with the permission of the authors and publisher, Warren, Gorham & Lamont, Inc.

John F. Dolan, Good Faith Purchase and Warehouse Receipts: Thoughts on the Interplay of Articles 2, 7 and 9 of the UCC, reprinted from Hastings Law Journal, Vol. 30, No. 1 (1978), pages 2-3, by permission.

Grant Gilmore, Formalism and the Law of Negotiable Instruments, 13 Creighton Law Review 441, 446-450 (1979). Copyright © 1979 Creighton University School of Law. Reprinted from the Creighton Law Review by permission.

Albert J. Givray, UCC Survey, Letters of Credit, 44 Business Lawyer 1567, 1589 (1989). Reprinted with permission of the author.

Albert J. Givray, UCC Survey, Letters of Credit, 45 Business Lawyer 2381, 2404 (1990). Reprinted with permission of the author.

Restatement of the Law Property (Mortgages) Tentative Draft No. 5, § 5.5 and portions of Comment a. of § 5.5 (1996). Copyright © 1996 by the American Law Institute. Reprinted with permission.

Albert J. Rosenthal, Negotiability—Who Needs It? 71 Columbia Law Review 375, 378-381, 382-385 (1971). Copyright © 1971 by the Directors of the Columbia Law Review Association, Inc. All Rights Reserved. This article originally appeared at 71 Columb. L.Rev. 375 (1971). Reprinted by permission.

Craig Winchester, Electronic Commerce on the Internet: The Rise of Anonymous Digital Coin Transfer (1996) (unpublished manuscript). Reprinted with permission.

*

SUMMARY OF CONTENTS

*

TABLE OF CONTENTS

*

TABLE OF CASES

Principal cases are in bold type. Non-principal cases are in roman type. References are to Pages.

*

NEGOTIABLE INSTRUMENTS, PAYMENTS AND CREDITS

*

CHAPTER 1

NEGOTIABILITY AND HOLDERS IN DUE COURSE

A. INTRODUCTION

We introduce the materials on negotiable instruments and payments by a treatment in this Chapter of two traditional doctrines unique to negotiable instruments. We will refer to these as the merger doctrine (the instrument reifies the obligation to pay; the holder of the instrument is entitled to payment) and the holder-in-due-course doctrine (the holder of an instrument may take free of claims and defenses on the instrument). As we shall see, the holder-in-due-course doctrine, conceived long ago under different social and economic conditions, has been under attack for years by courts, legislatures and commentators. The policy justification for this harsh doctrine is so questionable that there was debate on whether what now remains of the doctrine should be retained in revised Article 3. However, under the drafting-by-consensus regime that prevails in the writing of uniform state laws the doctrine was retained. In recent years the merger doctrine has come under criticism for the results it yields in real estate transactions which participants in that field believe are unjust. We will be inquiring throughout this Chapter whether the decision to retain these doctrines in revised Article 3 was sound. Whatever the merit of these rules, an understanding of them is essential to those planning and executing payment and credit transactions, and we give them full treatment in this Chapter.

The law of negotiable instruments is based in large part on common law doctrine developed primarily in the last half of the eighteenth century and the first half of the nineteenth century. This law was codified in Great Britain in 1882 in the Bills of Exchange Act and in 1896 in the United States in the Uniform Negotiable Instruments Law, usually referred to as the NIL. In 1952 the American Law Institute and the National Conference of Commissioners on Uniform State Laws promulgated the Uniform Commercial Code. Article 3 of the Code eventually displaced the NIL as the primary statute governing negotiable instruments. Article 4 of the Code complements Article 3 with respect to collection of negotiable instruments by banks and also governs the bank-customer relationship with respect to some matters relating to instruments. In 1990 a revised Article 3 was promulgated to take the place of the original Article 3. At the same time conforming amendments to Articles 1 and 4 were promulgated. Revised Article 3 and the conforming amendments to Articles 1 and 4 have been enacted in 44 states and it is anticipated that revised Article 3 will eventually displace the original Article 3. Revised Article 3 is not a radical departure from the earlier statute; the principal concepts of traditional negotiable instruments law have been preserved. But revised Article 3 differs from the original Article 3 with respect to a number of important substantive areas. In addition, no attempt was made to preserve the language of the original Article 3. As a result, the drafting style reflected in revised Article 3 is quite different from that of the previous statute.

Since almost all of the negotiable instruments cases reprinted in this book were decided under the original Article 3 or 4, we include the text of the particular section involved to the extent reference to the statutory language is necessary to understand the point at issue. Revised Article 3 is accompanied by a "Table of Disposition of Sections in Former Article 3" that indicates the section of revised Article 3 which governs the issue addressed by a section of the original Article 3. In reading cases reprinted in this book, this table should be consulted because the result reached in the case may be different if the same facts are governed by revised Article 3. In the text of this book other than the reprinted cases, references to sections of Article 3 or 4 are to revised Article 3 or 4 unless the contrary is stated.

B.   CONCEPT OF NEGOTIABILITY

1.   HISTORICAL ORIGIN

Professor Gilmore sketches the background of negotiable instruments law in the following quotation from his article "Formalism and the Law of Negotiable Instruments," 13 Creighton L.Rev. 441, 446–450 (1979)

Our law of negotiable instruments dates from the late eighteenth century. * * * Lord Mansfield and his colleagues in the late eighteenth century were faced with radically new problems for which they devised radically new solutions.

The radically new problems all stemmed from the industrial revolution and the vastly increased number of commercial transactions which it spawned. When goods were shipped, they had to be paid for. The idea that the payments could be made in metallic currency, chronically in short supply, was ludicrous. The primitive banking system could not cope with the situation: the bank check which—a hundred years later—became the universal payment device was unknown. In effect the merchants and the bankers invented their own paper currency. The form which they used was an old one: the so-called bill of exchange which was an order issued by one person (the drawer) to a second person (the drawee) directing the drawee to pay a specified sum of money at a specified time to a third person (the holder). Frequently these bills, drawn by sellers on buyers, represented the purchase price of goods sold. In a more sophisticated and somewhat later variant a mercantile banking house issued what came to be called a letter of credit to a customer. The letter authorized the customer to draw on the bankers for the purchase price of goods which he intended to buy: Through the first half of the nineteenth century Yankees trading out of Boston, armed with their letters of credit which were frequently issued by English houses, roamed the Far East assembling their precious and fabulously profitable cargoes of silks and teas and spices, paying for them with drafts on London. For half a century these bills or drafts were an indispensable supplement to the official currencies and were indeed used as currency: the bills which showed up in litigation had, as the case reports tell us, passed from hand to hand in a long series of transactions. And a draft on a ranking London house was a much safer as well as a much more convenient thing to have than a bag-full of clipped Maria Theresa dollars. These bills moved in a world-wide market, typically ending up in the possession of people who knew nothing about the transaction which had given rise to the bill, had no way of finding out anything about the transaction and, in any case, had not the slightest interest in it.

Against that background, the courts, English and American, put together, in not much more than half a century, the law of negotiable instruments almost exactly as we know it today. Indeed anyone who has mastered the current American formulation of the subject in Article 3 of the Uniform Commercial Code will have a startling sense of *deja vu*—I suppose this is *deja vu* in reverse—if he then goes back to the mid-nineteenth century treatises: time seems to have been suspended, nothing has changed, the late twentieth century law of negotiable instruments is still a law for clipper ships and their exotic cargoes from the Indies. The *deja vu* is false, a sort of floating mirage—but I will return to that later.

In putting together their law of negotiable instruments, the courts assumed that the new mercantile currency was a good thing whose use should be encouraged. Two quite simple ideas became the foundation pieces for the whole structure. One was the good faith purchase idea. The stranger who purchased the bill in the market was entitled to do so without inquiry into the facts of the underlying transaction or of previous transfers of the bill and without being affected by them: if he bought the bill for value, in good faith and in the ordinary course of business, he held it free both of underlying contract defenses and of outstanding equities of ownership. The other idea which, the first time you run into it, sounds like nonsense—the legal mind at its worst—was even more basic to the structure and indeed was what gave the completed edifice its pure and almost unearthly beauty. That was the idea that the piece of paper on which the bill was written or printed should be treated as if it—the piece of paper—was itself the claim or debt which it evidenced. This idea came to be known as the doctrine of merger—the debt was merged in the instrument. At one stroke it drastically simplified the law of negotiable instruments, to the benefit of both purchasers and the people required to pay the instruments. Under merger theory the only way of transferring the debt represented by the bill was by physical delivery of the bill itself to the transferee.

The courts also worked out an elaborate set of rules on when the transferor was required to endorse, as well as deliver, the bill and on what liabilities to subsequent parties he assumed by endorsing. When these formalities—delivery and endorsement—had been accomplished—but not until then—the transfer became a negotiation and the transferee a holder. Only the holder—the person physically in possession of the bill under a proper chain of endorsements—was entitled to demand payment of the bill from the party required to pay it; only payment to such a holder discharged the bill as well as the underlying obligation. Merger theory was also of immense importance from the point of view of the paying party: not only did he know whom he was supposed to pay—the holder—but, under another aspect of the theory, he was entitled to pay (and get his discharge) even if he knew, to state an extreme case, that the holder he paid had acquired the bill by fraud or trickery from a previous holder. Parties with claims adverse to the holder were required to fight their own battles; they could not involve the payor by serving notice on him not to pay.

See also James S. Rogers, The Early History of the Law of Bills and Notes (1995).

2.   MERGER DOCTRINE

a.   NEGOTIATION AND TRANSFER

(i) *Negotiation*

Under the merger doctrine described by Professor Gilmore the right to enforce or receive payment of an instrument is the exclusive right of the holder of the instrument. Although the notion that the right to enforce an instrument results from possession by a holder remains a central concept of Article 3, merger doctrine is attenuated in some cases. This is reflected in § 3–301 which defines "person entitled to enforce" to include some non-holders. The following cases illustrate § 3–301 and some basic concepts and terminology regarding negotiation and transfer of instruments.

Case # 1. John signs a note and delivers it to Rachel. The note reads as follows:

I promise to pay $1,000 on April 1, 1997 to the bearer of this note.

The note is "issued" by John, the "maker," when it is delivered to Rachel. § 3–105(a) and § 3–103(a)(5). The note is "payable to bearer." § 3–109(a). When Rachel receives possession, she becomes the bearer of the note as well as its holder. § 1–201(5) and (20). Normally, Rachel is also the owner of the note. But the right of Rachel to receive or enforce payment is based on the fact that Rachel is the holder of the note, not on Rachel's ownership. § 3–301.

Suppose Rachel loses the note and it is found by Peter who takes possession of it. By obtaining possession Peter does not become the owner of the note, but Peter becomes the holder of the note and thereby obtains the right to enforce it. § 3–301. The transfer of possession which resulted in Peter's becoming a holder is described in § 3–201(a) as a negotiation of the note. Typically, negotiation is the result of a voluntary transfer of possession, but § 3–201(a) applies to any transfer of possession, voluntary or involuntary.

Case # 2. John signs a note and delivers it to Rachel. The note reads as follows:

> I promise to pay $1,000 on April 1, 1997 to the order of Rachel.

In this case the note is not payable to bearer. Rather, it is "payable to order" because it is "payable to the order of an identified person." § 3–109(b). Upon delivery of the note to Rachel, she becomes its holder because she has possession and she is the person identified in the note as its payee. § 1–201(20). In Case # 1 we saw that a finder or thief can obtain the right to enforce a note payable to bearer simply by obtaining possession of it. That rule does not apply if an instrument is payable to an identified person. Negotiation of such an instrument also requires transfer of possession, but an indorsement by the holder is necessary as well. § 3–201(b). Thus, the note payable to Rachel cannot be negotiated, i.e. nobody else can become its holder, unless she indorses it.

Suppose Rachel does not lose the note. Rather, she sells it to Peter for cash and delivers the note to him. In this case no negotiation to Peter occurs unless Rachel indorses the note. Indorsement is defined in § 3–204(a) and can be made for several purposes. The most important purpose is to negotiate the instrument. An indorsement is normally made on the reverse side of the instrument and can consist of a signature alone or a signature accompanied by other words. An indorsement by Rachel consisting of her signature preceded by the words "Pay to Peter" identifies a person to whom it makes the note payable and is called a "special indorsement." § 3–205(a). An indorsement by Rachel consisting solely of her signature does not identify a person to whom it makes the note payable and is called a "blank indorsement." § 3–205(b). The effect of a blank indorsement is to make the note payable to bearer. § 3–205(b) and § 3–109(c). If either indorsement is made, Peter becomes the holder when he obtains possession of the note (§ 1–201(20)) and may enforce the note as holder. If Rachel indorses in blank, Peter can negotiate the note to somebody else either by delivery alone or by delivery plus Peter's indorsement. § 3–205(b) and § 3–109(c). If Rachel indorses specially, Peter must indorse the note in order to negotiate it and may indorse either specially or in blank. § 3–205(a).

(ii) Transfer

Although the right to enforce an instrument is normally obtained as a result of negotiation, the right to enforce an instrument can also be obtained in some transactions in which negotiation does not occur. Suppose Rachel delivers the note in Case #2 to Peter without indorsing it. What rights does Peter obtain? Because Rachel's purpose in delivering the note is to give Peter the right to enforce it, Rachel has "transferred" the note to Peter. § 3–203(a). Transfer means that there has been a conveyance by the transferor to the transferee of the transferor's right to enforce the instrument. This transfer can occur only by "delivery," a voluntary transfer of possession (Section 1–201(14)), plus an intent by the transferor to give to the transferee the right to enforce. Since the note was not indorsed by Rachel, Peter cannot enforce the note in his own right as holder and cannot negotiate the note to somebody else. But as a result of the transfer from Rachel, Peter obtains Rachel's right as holder to enforce the note. § 3–203(b). This result is commonly referred to as the "shelter doctrine." Armed with that right and possession of the note, Peter becomes a person entitled to enforce the note under clause (ii) of the first sentence of § 3–301. In addition Peter, as a buyer of the note for value, obtains a specifically enforceable right to have Rachel indorse the note so that Peter can become its holder. § 3–203(c).

If, by transfer, Peter acquires Rachel's right as holder to enforce the note, why is it important whether Peter, in enforcing the note, is asserting his own right as holder or a right to enforce derived from Rachel's right as holder? Read Comments 2 through 4 to § 3–203 as well as § 3–308(b) and the first two paragraphs of Comment 2 to § 3–308.

PROBLEMS

1. Mark signed a note and delivered it to Patricia for value; she, in turn, delivered it to Teresa for value. The note reads as follows:

> I promise to pay $1,000 to the order of Patricia on November 1, 1997.

Mark defaulted on the note and Teresa brought an action to enforce the note against him. In his pleadings Mark did not deny the authenticity of his signature or raise any defense to his liability on the note. Teresa introduced the note into evidence and rested. Mark sought a directed verdict. Is he entitled to one under §§ 3–203, 3–301 and 3–308 if

a. When Patricia delivered the note to Teresa she indorsed the instrument?

b. When Patricia delivered the note to Teresa she intended to pass ownership to Teresa but failed to indorse the instrument?

White & Summers, Uniform Commercial Code § 13–4b (burden of proof) (4th ed.1995).

2. Pete fraudulently induced Maria to issue a note to him. The note reads as follows:

> I promise to pay $1,000 to the order of Pete on July 1, 1997.

In May 1997 Pete indorsed and delivered the note to Helen who gave value, was in good faith and had no notice of any claims or defenses on the instrument. In June Maria discovered that she had been defrauded, notified Helen of the fraud, and stated her intention to refuse payment of the note. Helen, a busy executive, had no interest in incurring the litigation expenses needed to enforce the note, and, in August 1997, out of sympathy, gave the note, without indorsement, to her former husband, David, now an impecu-nious law student and desperate for money. She told him the circumstances surrounding the note and said that if he could recover anything on the note he could keep the recovery "for old times sake." May David recover on the note from Maria free of her defense of fraud? § 3–203(b). What policy is furthered by Article 3 in this case? Comment 2 to § 3–203.   *cont wash it clean by passing it from to someone else.*

b. DISCHARGE

A corollary to the merger doctrine that the right to enforce an instrument is the exclusive right of the holder is that the person obliged to pay the instrument discharges the obligation by paying the holder. Revised Article 3 reflects this corollary in a modified form in § 3–602(a). The obligor who pays the holder is assured that nobody else can obtain a right to enforce the instrument if the obligor obtains surrender of the instru-ment from the holder at the time of payment. § 3–501(a) and (b)(2). But there is also a corollary to the discharge rule: payment to a person who is not the holder might not result in discharge. This corollary is considered in *Lambert* which follows.

Lambert v. Barker

Supreme Court of Virginia, 1986.
232 Va. 21, 348 S.E.2d 214.

■ COCHRAN, JUSTICE.

The central question in this appeal is whether payment by the obligors of a note to a party not in possession of the note discharged the obligation of the makers and precluded recovery on the note by the party in posses-sion.

The facts surrounding the underlying transactions are substantially undisputed. In May 1978, William K. Barker and Barbara R. Barker acquired from Robert O. Davis, Jr., property located at 2610 Monument Avenue, Richmond. As part of the consideration for their purchase, the Barkers executed a note, secured by a second deed of trust on the property, in the principal amount of $20,300 payable to Davis, or order, in monthly installments.

In December 1978, the Barkers conveyed the property to S. David Beloff, who in turn conveyed it to Charles P. Harwood, Jr., and Ann G. Harwood in January 1979. The Harwoods, uniting in the deed from Beloff, expressly agreed to pay the Barker note. Pursuant to a loan agreement dated November 1, 1979, Davis transferred this note, along with certain other notes, to Katherine W. Lambert (who signed her name as Kathleen), Trustee for Cecil–Waller & Sterling, Inc. (Lambert), to secure a loan from Cecil–Waller & Sterling to Davis in the amount of $197,234.72. The loan agreement between Davis and Lambert provided that the monthly install-ments on the Barker note would continue to be payable to Davis, while any prepayment was to be made to Lambert.

In February 1980, the Harwoods conveyed the property to Bryce A. Bugg and Nancy S. Bugg. At closing, Davis provided an affidavit in which he falsely asserted that he was the noteholder but that the Barker note was lost. The sum of $18,446.17 was withheld from the sale proceeds and paid to Davis, purportedly in satisfaction of the note.

In 1981, Lambert instituted this action against the Barkers and the Harwoods to recover $18,497.94 on the note, together with interest, costs, and attorney's fees. Alleging the note was in default and this amount represented the unpaid balance, Lambert claimed she was entitled to payment as the holder of the note.

The Barkers and Harwoods filed their separate grounds of defense denying liability on the ground that the Harwoods' payment to Davis satisfied the note in full. They also filed third-party motions for judgment against the attorney who represented the Buggs in their purchase from the Harwoods and against his law firm, alleging negligence and breach of fiduciary duty in failing properly to discharge the obligation of the note by paying the holder.

After a hearing at which Lambert tendered the note in her possession indorsed by Davis, the trial court granted a motion for summary judgment filed by the Barkers and the Harwoods and dismissed a motion for summary judgment filed by Lambert. The court ruled that UCC § 9–318(3) was controlling and required Lambert to give notice to both the Barkers and the Harwoods of the pledge of the note. Finding no such notice had been given, the court ruled that Lambert could not "question" payments by the Barkers or the Harwoods made directly to Davis. Accordingly, the court dismissed both the principal action and the third-party motions for judgment. Lambert appealed the court's dismissal of her action against the Barkers.

[Omitted is the part of the opinion in which the Court held that UCC § 9–318(3) was inapplicable.]

The Barkers contend, as they did below, that payment to Davis discharged their liability as makers of the note. The right of a party to payment, however, depends upon his status as a holder. UCC § 3–301. A holder is one who is in possession of an instrument issued or indorsed to him or his order, to bearer, or in blank. UCC § 1–201(20) * * *. Payment or satisfaction discharges the liability of a party only if made to the holder of the instrument. * * * Because payment in satisfaction of the instrument must be made to a party in possession in order to discharge the payor's liability, no notice is required for the protection of the payor. Rather, the payor may protect himself by demanding production of the instrument and refusing payment to any party not in possession unless in an action on the obligation the owner proves his ownership.

Payment to an authorized agent of the holder will also satisfy the requirement of payment to the holder, resulting in discharge. UCC § 1–103 (agency principles supplement UCC provisions); American Security Company v. Juliano, Inc., 203 Va. 827, 833, 127 S.E.2d 348, 352 (1962) * * *. But the burden of proving an agency relationship rests on the party claiming payment as a defense.

> One making payment to an agent has the burden of showing that the agent has either express or apparent authority to receive such payment upon behalf of his principal, and the evidence to that effect must be clear and convincing. If payment is made to a party who does not have in hand the obligation, the debtor takes the risk of such party having the authority to make collection.

Security Company, 203 Va. at 833, 127 S.E.2d at 352 * * *.

It is clear that Davis was not the holder of the Barker note at the time of payment, as the note was not in his possession. By delivering the note, indorsed in blank, to Lambert, Davis negotiated the instrument and made Lambert the holder. * * * Payment to Davis could therefore discharge the Barkers' liability only if Davis were the authorized agent of Lambert. Moreover, it was the Barkers' responsibility to raise and establish this affirmative defense. *Security Company,* 203 Va. at 833, 127 S.E.2d at 352. The Barkers, however, never asserted payment to Lambert; nor did they allege that payment to Davis constituted payment to Lambert under an actual or implied agency theory. Having failed properly to assert a defense of payment to Lambert, the noteholder, the Barkers were not entitled to summary judgment. To the contrary, Lambert was entitled to judgment against the Barkers upon their failure to raise a valid defense.

The Barkers contend that, even if Lambert were the holder of the note, she was not a holder in due course under UCC § 3–302 and therefore did not take the instrument free from defenses under UCC § 3–305. Because the Barkers failed properly to assert the defense of payment to Lambert, Lambert's status—whether as a holder in due course or not in due course— does not affect this result.

The amount payable on the note is not controverted. Accordingly, we will reverse the judgment of the trial court and enter final judgment in favor of Lambert.

NOTE

The doctrine of § 3–602(a) is disapproved in Restatement of the Law Property (Mortgages) § 5.5 (1996). It states:

§ 5.5 Effect of Performance to the Transferor After Transfer of an Obligation Secured by a Mortgage

After transfer of an obligation secured by a mortgage, performance of the obligation to the transferor is effective against the transferee if rendered before the obligor receives notice of the transfer.

Comment:

a. Introduction. When a mortgage debt is transferred by the original mortgagee to another investor, the mortgagor may or may not be informed of the transfer. In many cases, failure to advise the mortgagor is innocuous, since the investor-transferee often designates the original mortgagee as its servicing agent for purposes of collecting the obligation. Hence, the mortgagor may simply continue to perform the obligation to the mortgagee as in the past; the transferee, by virtue of the agency relationship, will be bound to give credit for performance to its agent.

However, in some cases the mortgagee is not made the transferee's agent. Nonetheless, if the mortgagor is not informed of the transfer, the mortgagor may continue to perform to the original mortgagee. In theory the mortgagor could discover the transfer by demanding that the mortgagee exhibit the evidence of the obligation (typically a promissory note) before making each payment, but such a demand would be extremely cumbersome for both mortgagor and mortgagee, and is an entirely unrealistic expectation.

This section protects the innocent mortgagor who continues to make such payments. It provides that they are effective against the transferee until the mortgagor receives notice of the transfer. See Illustration 1. The contrary rule, giving the mortgagor no credit for payments innocently made to the mortgagee after the transfer, is usually (although not exclusively) followed in the cases. However, that rule is old, ill-considered, and has the potential for great injustice to mortgagors. It has been abandoned by all modern model acts that deal with the issue, including the Uniform Commercial Code (with respect to obligations secured by accounts, chattel paper, or general intangibles), the Uniform Land Security Interest Act, the Uniform Land Transactions Act, and the Uniform Consumer Credit Code.

Illustration:

1.   Mortgagor borrows money from Mortgagee and gives Mortgagee a promissory note for the amount borrowed and, as security for payment of the note, a mortgage on Blackacre. The note requires Mortgagor to make monthly payments of principal and interest. Mortgagee subsequently indorses the promissory note to Assignee and executes an assignment of the mortgage to Assignee. Mortgagor has no notice of this transfer, and continues to make monthly payments to Mortgagee. These payments are effective against Assignee.

While Illustration 1 involves the making of regular monthly payments on the mortgage debt, the principle of this section is not so limited; it applies as well to acceptance by the mortgage transferor of final payments, balloon payments, and prepayments.

Which policy is more sound, that of § 3–602 or of the Restatement?

PROBLEM

Mary Ann and her husband, Curtis, borrowed $75,000 from a family friend, Frank, in order to start a business. They delivered a negotiable note to Frank which promised to repay this amount with interest. After Mary Ann and Curtis divorced and Curtis departed for parts unknown, Mary Ann found what appeared to be the original note in a file in the basement of the house she had shared with Curtis. Later Frank sued Mary Ann on the note. At the time of the trial the note bore the word "Paid" written across the face of it. Frank had a copy of the note that was not marked paid. At trial Mary Ann testified that she had assumed that Curtis, who had operated the failed business, had paid the note, and that she could not recall whether the note was marked paid when she found it. She based her defense on § 3–604(a) which provides that "A person entitled to enforce an instrument, with or without consideration, may discharge the obligation of a party to pay the instrument (i) by an intentional voluntary act, such as surrender of the instrument to the party * * * ." Frank testified that the note had not been paid, that he didn't know how she received possession of it and that he had no intention of discharging Mary Ann and Curtis from their obligation on the note. 2 White & Summers, Uniform Commercial Code § 16–13 (4th prac.ed.1995), says: "When the obligor has possession, the party suing on the instrument has to overcome a presumption that the instrument was discharged." Has Frank overcome the presumption in this case? The facts of this case are loosely based on those of Gardner v. McClusky, 647 N.E.2d 1 (Ind.App.1995). *No. When the note is in the hands of the maker after the due date it is presumed at law to have been discharged. Fact finder determines is presumption is overcome.*

3.   GOOD FAITH PURCHASE: FREEDOM FROM CLAIMS AND DEFENSES ·

a.   CLAIMS OF OWNERSHIP

The doctrine that a good faith purchaser for value takes an instrument free both of defenses arising from the transaction giving rise to the instrument and claims of ownership to the instrument can be traced to two seminal cases. The first, Miller v. Race, 1 Burr. 452, 97 Eng.Rep. 398 (K.B. 1758), presented the question of title to a stolen promissory note issued by the Bank of England for the payment of 21 pounds ten shillings to "William Finney or bearer, on demand." On December 11 Finney mailed the note to one Odenharty but that night the note was stolen from the mails by a robber. The next day, in the words of Lord Mansfield, "an innkeeper took it, bona fide, in his business from a person who made an appearance of a gentleman. Here is no pretence or suspicion of collusion with the robber: for this matter was strictly inquired and examined into at the trial; and is so stated in the case 'that he took it for a full and valuable consideration, in the usual course of business.' Indeed if there had been any collusion, or any circumstances of unfair dealing; the case had been much otherwise. If it had been a note for 1000 [pounds] it might have been suspicious: but this was a small note for 21 [pounds] 10 [shillings] only: and money given in exchange for it." On December 13 Finney, having learned of the robbery, "applied to the Bank of England 'to stop the payment of this note:' which was ordered accordingly, upon Mr. Finney's entering into proper security 'to indemnify the bank.'" Plaintiff then delivered the note for payment to defendant, a clerk of the Bank of England. Defendant refused to pay or to redeliver the note to Plaintiff. In an action in trover judgment for the amount of the note was given to Plaintiff. Lord Mansfield in holding that Plaintiff, the good faith purchaser, had acquired good title to the note superior to that of Finney said "A banknote is constantly and universally, both at home and abroad, treated as money, as cash; and paid and received, as cash; and it is necessary, for the purposes of commerce, that their currency should be established and secured."

Notes of the kind involved in Miller v. Race were the ancestors of modern English currency and similar in form. A modern ten-pound note reads as follows "I promise to pay the bearer on demand the sum of ten pounds." The promise to pay is signed by the Chief Cashier of the Bank of England "For the Governor and Company of the Bank of England." Commercial transactions would be seriously impeded if money, or its equivalent, could not be accepted without question as to whether the taker was acquiring good title to it. The rule of Miller v. Race might have been explained as being simply a recognition of this fact in the case of certain bank obligations which, de facto, were taken as the equivalent of money. But the rule was also applied to the obligations of individuals to which the rationale of "money equivalent" was less persuasive.

The second case, Peacock v. Rhodes, 2 Doug. 633, 99 Eng.Rep. 402 (K.B. 1781), involved a bill of exchange, payable on issue to "William Ingham, or order" and subsequently indorsed by Ingham in blank. Neither the drawer nor the drawee was a bank. The bill, indorsed in blank, was stolen and negotiated to plaintiff, a mercer who "received the bill from a man not known, who called himself William Brown, and, by that name, indorsed the bill to the plaintiff, of whom he bought cloth, and other articles in the way of the plaintiff's trade as a mercer, in his shop at Scarborough, and paid him that bill, the value whereof the plaintiff gave to the buyer in cloth and other articles, and cash, and small bills."

Lord Mansfield stated that the case was within the rule of Miller v. Race. "The holder of a bill of exchange, or promissory note, is not to be considered in the light of an assignee of the payee. An assignee must take the thing assigned, subject to all the equity to which the original party was subject. If this rule applied to bills and promissory notes, it would stop their currency. The law is settled, that a holder, coming fairly by a bill or note, has nothing to do with the transaction between the original parties; unless, perhaps, in the single case (which is a hard one, but has been determined) of a note won at play. I see no difference between a note indorsed blank, and one payable to bearer. They both go by delivery, and possession proves property in both cases. The question of mala fides was for the consideration of the jury. The circumstances, that the buyer and also the drawers were strangers to the plaintiff, and that he took the bill for goods on which he had a profit, were grounds of suspicion, very fit for their consideration. But they have considered them, and have found it was received in the course of trade, and, therefore, the case is clear, and within the principle of * * * Miller v. Race * * *."

Miller v. Race and Peacock v. Rhodes both involved good faith purchasers for value who took free of claims of ownership, but the words of Lord Mansfield in Peacock v. Rhodes—"the holder * * * has nothing to do with the transaction between the original parties"—applied as well to defenses that the drawer of the bill may have had against the original payee of the bill. Thus, the good faith purchaser took free of defenses as well.

The common law doctrine of these cases was codified in the NIL and in Article 3 with different terminology. The early cases spoke of a holder who was a good faith purchaser for value. In Article 3 this holder is referred to as a "holder in due course," a term defined in § 3–302(a). This definition is discussed in Comments 1 and 2 to § 3–302. The rule of Miller v. Race is restated in § 3–306. A person taking an instrument, other than a person with rights of a holder in due course, is subject to a "property or possessory right" in the instrument or its proceeds. Thus, if a check is stolen from the payee of the check or possession is obtained from the payee by fraud, the payee has a claim to the check or, if the check is paid, to the proceeds of the check. But that claim cannot be asserted against a person having rights of a holder in due course.

b.   ORDINARY DEFENSES

The extent to which a holder takes free of defenses is governed by § 3–305(a) and (b). Subsection (a) states that the right to enforce an instrument is subject to defenses described in paragraphs (1) and (2) of that subsection and claims in recoupment described in paragraph (3). Subsection (b) of § 3–305 is a limitation on subsection (a). The right of a holder in due course to enforce an instrument is subject to the defenses stated in subsection (a)(1)—the so-called "real defenses"—but is not subject to the "ordinary" defenses stated in subsection (a)(2) or claims in recoupment described in subsection (a)(3).

Section § 3–305(a)(2) refers to defenses that are specifically stated in other sections of Article 3. Those defenses and the sections in which they are found are listed in the first paragraph of Comment 2 to § 3–305. Subsection (a)(2) also refers to the common law defenses applicable to simple contracts which are not enumerated. The principal common law defenses are fraud, misrepresentation, and mistake in the issuance of the instrument.

c.   REAL DEFENSES

Section § 3–305(a)(1) lists the defenses that may be asserted against even a holder in due course. These defenses are discussed in Comment 1 to § 3–305. With the exception of the defense of discharge in an insolvency proceeding, all of the real defenses refer to an instrument that is made unenforceable in order to carry out some public policy of the state not related to the law of negotiable instruments, or to an instrument which does not represent a contract of the person who signed the instrument.

d. CLAIMS IN RECOUPMENT

Restatement (Second) of Contracts § 336(2) (1981) states: "The right of an assignee is subject to any defense or claim of the obligor which accrues before the obligor receives notification of the assignment, but not to defenses or claims which accrue thereafter * * *." Suppose A promises to pay $1,000 to B in return for a promise by B to deliver goods to A. B assigns to C the right of B to receive $1,000 from A. A receives no notification of the assignment. If A's promise to pay B was induced by B's fraud or if B failed to deliver the goods as promised, A has a defense to the obligation to pay B. The defense can be asserted against C, the assignee. Change the facts. Suppose there was no fraud by B and B tendered the goods to A, who accepted them. A has no defense to the obligation to pay for the goods. But suppose A has a claim against B to receive $600. If C demands payment of $1,000 from A, A can assert the $600 claim as a reduction of the amount owing to C from $1,000 to $400.

If A's promise to pay is a negotiable instrument and the instrument is negotiated to C, § 3–305 rather than the Restatement governs the rights of A and C. Subsection (a)(2) of § 3–305 applies to the defense of fraud or failure to deliver the goods. Subsection (a)(3) applies to A's $600 claim against B if A's claim arose from the transaction that gave rise to the instrument and is therefore a claim in recoupment. Furthermore, the rights of C depend upon whether C is a holder in due course. § 3–305(b). Claims in recoupment are discussed in Comment 3 to § 3–305.

PROBLEM

Merchant sold and delivered goods to Plumber who accepted them and, as payment of the price, delivered to Merchant a negotiable note of Plumber to pay $10,000 to the order of Merchant. The note was payable one year after the date it was issued. Merchant immediately negotiated the note to Finance Co. A month after the sale and delivery of the goods by Merchant, Plumber, at the request of Merchant, repaired and replaced water pipes and plumbing fixtures at Merchant's place of business. Plumber's bill for this work was $8,000. When Plumber's note became due Finance Co. demanded payment. Plumber refused to pay for the following reasons: (1) Merchant had not paid the $8,000 owed for the work performed by Plumber; (2) some of the goods sold by Merchant to Plumber were defective and, as a result of the defects, Plumber incurred losses of over $4,000. How much is Finance Co. entitled to recover from Plumber if Finance Co. is a holder in due course? How much is Finance Co. entitled to recover if Finance Co. is not a holder in due course?

C. FORMAL REQUISITES OF NEGOTIABLE INSTRUMENTS

Merger theory and the ability of a good faith purchaser for value to take free of claims and defenses with respect to the instrument were based on a separation of the right to payment represented by the instrument from the transaction giving rise to the instrument. But merger theory assumed that the terms of the instrument were not inconsistent with separation from the underlying transaction, and that the terms of the right to receive payment could be determined simply by examination of the instrument itself. Thus the consequences of negotiability were applied by the common law courts only if the instrument met certain criteria that satisfied these assumptions. The definition of negotiable instrument is found in Article 3 in § 3–104(a), and this definition differs only slightly from the requisites for negotiability stated in the NIL and the original Article 3.

The definition of negotiable instrument in § 3–104 defines the scope of Article 3. § 3–102(a). The most important elements of that definition can be briefly described. Only an "order" or "promise" can qualify as a negotiable instrument. "Order" is defined in § 3–103(a)(6) as a written instruction to pay money signed by the person giving the instruction. "Promise" is defined in § 3–103(a)(9) as a written undertaking to pay money signed by the person undertaking to pay. Thus, a negotiable instrument is always a signed writing that promises or orders payment of money. Negotiable instruments fall into two categories: drafts and notes. An instrument is a draft if it is an order and is a note if it is a promise. § 3–104(e). Checks are the most common examples of drafts. § 3–104(f). Certificates of deposit are considered to be notes. § 3–104(j).

Because the rules applicable to negotiable instruments and the rules applicable to ordinary contracts can produce dramatically different results in some cases, it is imperative that both the person issuing a promise or order to pay money and the person to whom the promise or order is issued be able to know in advance whether Article 3 or ordinary contract law will apply. The various requirements of § 3–104(a) are designed to provide mechanical tests to allow that determination to be made. One particularly important requirement is that the order or promise be "payable to bearer or to order," a term explained in § 3–109. Thus, a technical and wholly formal distinction is made between a promise to pay "to John Doe" and a promise to pay "to the order of John Doe." The second promise may be a negotiable instrument if it otherwise qualifies under § 3–104. The first promise cannot be a negotiable instrument. Because of this distinction, the issuer of a promissory note payable to an identified person can easily avoid the consequences of negotiability by avoiding use of the words of negotiability: "to order" or "to bearer." Another device for avoiding the effects of Article 3 is provided by § 3–104(d). These devices for excluding an order or promise from Article 3 are discussed in Comments 2 and 3 to § 3–104.

Three of the requisites of a negotiable instrument relate to the certainty of the obligation to pay. First, the order or promise to pay must be "unconditional," a term explained in § 3–106. An examination of that provision discloses that some promises or orders that are in fact conditional are deemed to be unconditional while others that are in fact unconditional are deemed to be conditional for the purposes of § 3–104(a). The Comment to § 3–106 is a guide to the rather arbitrary distinctions and refinements of § 3–106. Second, the order or promise must be payable on demand or at a definite time, a requirement explained in § 3–108. Third, the order or promise must be to pay a "fixed amount of money, with or without interest or other charges described in the promise or order." § 3–104(a). The quoted language differs from § 3–104(1)(b) of the original Article 3 which used the phrase "sum certain in money." Taylor v. Roeder, which follows, discusses the problem of variable interest rates under the original Article 3. How is this issue resolved under revised Article 3? § 3–112(b).

Taylor v. Roeder

Pre - Art 3 - problem w/ variable interest rate

Supreme Court of Virginia, 1987.
234 Va. 99, 360 S.E.2d 191.

■ RUSSELL, JUSTICE.

The dispositive question in this case is whether a note providing for a variable rate of interest, not ascertainable from the face of the note, is a negotiable instrument. We conclude that it is not.

The facts are undisputed. VMC Mortgage Company (VMC) was a mortgage lender in Northern Virginia. In the conduct of its business, it borrowed funds from investors, pledging as security the notes secured by deeds of trust which it had obtained from its borrowers. Two of these transactions became the subject of this suit. Because they involve similar facts and the same question of law, they were consolidated for trial below and are consolidated in a single record here * * *.

In the first case, Olde Towne Investment Corporation of Virginia, Inc., on September 11, 1979, borrowed $18,000 from VMC, evidenced by a 60–day note secured by a deed of trust on land in Fairfax County. The note provided for interest at "[t]hree percent (3.00%) over Chase Manhattan Prime to be adjusted monthly." The note provided for renewal "at the same rate of interest at the option of the makers up to a maximum of six (6) months in sixty (60) day increments with the payment of an additional fee of [t]wo (2) points." The note was renewed and extended to November 11, 1980, by a written extension agreement signed by Olde Towne and by VMC.

In May 1981, Frederick R. Taylor, Jr., as trustee for himself and other parties, entered into a contract to buy from Olde Towne the land in Fairfax County securing the $18,000 loan. Taylor's title examination revealed the VMC deed of trust. He requested the payoff figures from VMC and forwarded to VMC the funds VMC said were due. He never received the cancelled Olde Towne note, and the deed of trust was not released.

In the second case, Richard L. Saslaw and others, on December 31, 1979, borrowed $22,450 from VMC evidenced by a 12–month note secured by deed of trust on Fairfax County land. This note also bore interest at "3% over Chase Manhattan prime adjusted monthly." Interest was to be "payable quarterly beginning April 1, 1980." In November 1980, Virender and Barbara Puri entered into a contract to purchase from Saslaw, et al., the land subject to the last-mentioned deed of trust. The Puris designated the same Frederick R. Taylor, Jr., as their settlement attorney. Taylor's title examination revealed VMC's deed of trust. Taylor again requested a payoff figure from VMC. At settlement, Saslaw objected to the figure, communicated with VMC and received VMC's agreement to an adjusted figure. Taylor paid the adjusted amount to VMC. Again, Taylor failed to receive the cancelled Saslaw note, and the Saslaw deed of trust was not released.

Cecil Pruitt, Jr., was a trustee of a tax-exempt employees' pension fund. He invested some of the pension fund's assets with VMC, receiving as collateral pledges of certain secured notes that VMC held. The Saslaw note was pledged and delivered to him on January 25, 1980; the Olde Towne note was pledged and delivered to him on September 12, 1980. No notice was given to the makers, or to Taylor, that the notes had been transferred, and all payments on both notes were made to and accepted by VMC.

VMC received and deposited in its account sufficient funds to pay both notes in full, but never informed Pruitt of the payments and made no request of him for return of the original notes. In February 1982, VMC defaulted on its obligation to Pruitt for which both notes had been pledged as collateral. In May 1982, VMC filed a bankruptcy petition in federal court.

Learning that the properties securing both notes had been sold, Pruitt demanded payment from the respective original makers as well as the new owners of the properties, contending that he was a holder in due course. The makers and new owners took the position that they had paid the notes in full. Pruitt caused William F. Roeder, Jr., to qualify as substituted trustee under both deeds of trust and directed him to foreclose them. Taylor and the Puris filed separate bills of complaint against Roeder, trustee, seeking to enjoin the foreclosure sales. The chancellor entered a temporary injunction to preserve the *status quo* and heard the consolidated cases *ore tenus*. By letter opinion incorporated into a final decree entered February 3, 1984, the chancellor found for the defendant and dissolved the injunctions. We granted the complainants an appeal. The parties have agreed on the record that foreclosure will be withheld while the case is pending in this Court.

Under the general law of contracts, if an obligor has received no notice that his debt has been assigned and is in fact unaware of the assignment, he may, with impunity, pay his original creditor and thus extinguish the obligation. His payment will be a complete defense against the claim of an assignee who failed to give him notice of the assignment. * * *

Under the law of negotiable instruments, continued in effect under the Uniform Commercial Code, the rule is different: the makers are bound by their contract to make payment to the *holder*. * * * Further, a holder in due course takes the instrument free from the maker's defense that he has made payment to the original payee, if he lacks notice of the payment and has not dealt with the maker. UCC § 3–305. Thus, the question whether the notes in this case were negotiable is crucial.

UCC § 3–104(1) provides, in pertinent part:

> Any writing to be a negotiable instrument within this title must

> * * *

> (b) contain an unconditional promise or order to pay a sum certain in money * * *.

The meaning of "sum certain" is clarified by UCC § 3–106:

> (1) The sum payable is a sum certain even though it is to be paid

> (a) with stated interest or by stated installments; or

> (b) with stated different rates of interest before and after default or a specified date; or

> (c) with a stated discount or addition if paid before or after the date fixed for payment; or

> (d) with exchange or less exchange, whether at a fixed rate or at the current rate; or

> (e) with costs of collection or an attorney's fee or both upon default.

> (2) Nothing in this section shall validate any term which is otherwise illegal.

Official Comment 1, which follows, states in part:

> It is sufficient [to establish negotiability] that at any time of payment the holder is able to determine the amount then payable *from the instrument itself* with any necessary computation * * *. The computation must be one which can be made *from the instrument itself without reference to any outside source,* and this section does not make negotiable a note payable with interest "at the current rate."

(Emphasis added.) UCC § 3–107 provides an explicit exception to the "four corners" rule laid down above by providing for the negotiability of instruments payable in foreign currency.

We conclude that the drafters of the Uniform Commercial Code adopted criteria of negotiability intended to exclude an instrument which requires reference to any source outside the instrument itself in order to ascertain the amount due, subject only to the exceptions specifically provided for by the U.C.C. * * *

The appellee points to the Official Comment to UCC § 3–104. Comment 1 states that by providing criteria for negotiability "within this Article," * * * "leaves open the possibility that some writings may be made negotiable by other statutes or by judicial decision." The Comment continues: "The same is true as to any new type of paper which commercial practice may develop in the future." The appellee urges us to create, by judicial decision, just such an exception in favor of variable-interest notes.

Appellants concede that variable-interest loans have become a familiar device in the mortgage lending industry. Their popularity arose when lending institutions, committed to long-term loans at fixed rates of interest to their borrowers, were in turn required to borrow short-term funds at high rates during periods of rapid inflation. Variable rates protected lenders when rates rose and benefitted borrowers when rates declined. They suffer, however, from the disadvantage that the amount required to satisfy the debt cannot be ascertained without reference to an extrinsic source—in this case the varying prime rate charged by the Chase Manhattan Bank. Although that rate may readily be ascertained from published sources, it cannot be found within the "four corners" of the note.

Other courts confronted with similar questions have reached differing results. See, e.g., A. Alport & Son, Inc. v. Hotel Evans, Inc., 65 Misc.2d 374, 376–77, 317 N.Y.S.2d 937, 939–40 (1970) (note bearing interest at "bank rates" not negotiable under U.C.C.); Woodhouse, Drake and Carey, Ltd. v. Anderson, 61 Misc.2d 951, 307 N.Y.S.2d 113 (1970) (note providing for interest at "8½% or at the maximum legal rate" was not usurious. Inferentially, the note was negotiable.); Farmers Production Credit Ass'n v. Arena, 145 Vt. 20, 23, 481 A.2d 1064, 1065 (1984) (variable-interest note not negotiable under U.C.C.).

The U.C.C. introduced a degree of clarity into the law of commercial transactions which permits it to be applied by laymen daily to countless transactions without resort to judicial interpretation. The relative predictability of results made possible by that clarity constitutes the overriding benefit arising from its adoption. In our view, that factor makes it imperative that when change is thought desirable, the change should be made by statutory amendment, not through litigation and judicial interpretation. Accordingly, we decline the appellee's invitation to create an exception, by judicial interpretation, in favor of instruments providing for a variable rate of interest not ascertainable from the instrument itself.

In an alternative argument, the appellee contends that even if the notes are not negotiable, they are nevertheless "symbolic instruments" which ought to be paid according to their express terms. Those terms include the maker's promises to pay "to VMC Mortgage Company *or order*," and in the event of default, to make accelerated payment "at the option of the *holder*." The emphasized language, appellee contends, makes clear that the makers undertook an obligation to pay any party who held the notes as a result of a transfer from VMC. Assuming the abstract correctness of that argument, it does not follow that the makers undertook the further obligation of making a monthly canvass of all inhabitants of the earth in order to ascertain who the holder might be. In the absence of notice to the makers that their debt had been assigned, they were entitled to the protection of the rule in *Evans v. Joyner* in making good-faith payment to the original payee of these non-negotiable notes.

Accordingly, we will reverse the decree and remand the cause to the trial court for entry of a permanent injunction against foreclosure.

■ COMPTON, JUSTICE, dissenting.

The majority views the Uniform Commercial Code as inflexible, requiring legislative action to adapt to changing commercial practices. This overlooks a basic purpose of the Code, flexibility and adaptability of construction to meet developing commercial usage.

According to § 1–102(1), the UCC "shall be liberally construed and applied to promote its underlying purposes and policies." One of such underlying purposes and policies is "to permit the continued expansion of commercial practices through custom, usage and agreement of the parties." § 1–102(2)(b). Comment 1 to this section sets out clearly the intention of the drafters:

> "This Act is drawn to provide flexibility so that, since it is intended to be a semi-permanent piece of legislation, it will provide its own machinery for expansion of commercial practices. *It is intended to make it possible for the law embodied in this Act to be developed by the courts in light of unforeseen and new circumstances and practices.* However, the proper construction of the Act requires that its interpretation and application be limited to its reason." (Emphasis added).

The majority's rigid interpretation defeats the purpose of the Code. Nowhere in the UCC is "sum certain" defined. This absence must be interpreted in light of the expectation that commercial law continue to evolve. The § 3–106 exceptions could not have been intended as the exclusive list of "safe harbors," as the drafters anticipated "unforeseen" changes in commercial practices. Instead, those exceptions represented, at the time of drafting, recognized conditions of payment which did not impair negotiability in the judgment of businessmen. To limit exceptions to those existing at that time would frustrate the "continued expansion of commercial practices" by freezing the Code in time and requiring additional legislation whenever "unforeseen and new circumstances and practices" evolve, regardless of "custom, usage, and agreement of the parties."

> "The rule requiring certainty in commercial paper was a rule of commerce before it was a rule of law. It requires commercial, not mathematical, certainty. An uncertainty which does not impair the function of negotiable instruments in the judgment of business men ought not to be regarded by the courts * * *. The whole question is, do [the provisions] render the instruments so uncertain as to destroy their fitness to pass current in the business world?" *Cudahy Packing Co. v. State National Bank of St. Louis,* 134 F. 538, 542, 545 (8th Cir.1904).

Instruments providing that loan interest may be adjusted over the life of the loan routinely pass with increasing frequency in this state and many others as negotiable instruments. This Court should recognize this custom and usage, as the commercial market has, and hold these instruments to be negotiable.

The majority focuses on the requirement found in Comment 1 to § 3–106 that a negotiable instrument be self-contained, understood without reference to an outside source. Our cases have interpreted this to mean that reference to terms in another agreement which materially affect the instrument renders it nonnegotiable. See, e.g., McLean Bank v. Nelson, Adm'r, 232 Va. 420, 350 S.E.2d 651 (1986) (where note was accepted "pursuant" to a separate agreement, reference considered surplusage and the note negotiable); Salomonsky v. Kelly, 232 Va. 261, 349 S.E.2d 358 (1986) (where principal sum payable "as set forth" in a separate agreement, all the essential terms did not appear on the face of the instrument and the note was nonnegotiable).

The commercial market requires a self-contained instrument for negotiability so that a stranger to the original transaction will be fully apprised of its terms and will not be disadvantaged by terms not ascertainable from the instrument itself. For example, interest payable at the "current rate" leaves a holder subject to claims that the current rate was established by one bank rather than another and would disadvantage a stranger to the original transaction.

The rate which is stated in the notes in this case, however, does not similarly disadvantage a stranger to the original agreement. Anyone coming into possession could immediately ascertain the terms of the notes; interest payable at three percent above the prime rate established by the Chase Manhattan Bank of New York City. This is a third-party objective standard which is recognized as such by the commercial market. The rate can be determined by a telephone call to the bank or from published lists obtained on request. * * *

Accordingly, I believe these notes are negotiable under the Code and I would affirm the decision below.

NOTES

1. Since the scope of Article 3 (§ 3–102(a)) is determined by the definition of negotiable instrument in § 3–104, it is not surprising that this definition was the subject of a great deal of debate in the revision of Article 3. There were a number of proposals either to restrict or enlarge the kinds of instruments to which the harsh doctrine of negotiability would apply by changes in the definition of negotiable instrument. At one extreme was the view that the concept of negotiability was no longer needed; let the parties contract for whatever terms they can agree on for credit and payment instruments. A recurring suggestion for reform was to discard the "magic words"—order and bearer—as prerequisites of negotiability. Then too, a number of proposals were made to junk the traditional formal requirements of negotiability in favor of a functional test along the lines of that suggested in Fred H. Miller and Alvin C. Harrell, The Law of Modern Payment Systems and Notes 37 (1985):

> (1) Any writing to be a negotiable instrument within this article must
>
>> (a) be signed by the maker or drawer;
>>
>> (b) be for the payment, or evidence a right to the payment, of money; and

(c) be of a type which in the ordinary course of business is transferred by delivery with any necessary endorsement or assignment.

This is similar to the definition of "instrument" in § 9–105(1)(i).

After five years of discussion, the Drafting Committee decided to retain the traditional, somewhat mechanical tests similar to those developed at common law and codified in both the NIL and the 1962 version of Article 3. The strongest reason for this was the elusive quest for a "bright line." Comment 2 to § 3–104 explains: "Total exclusion from Article 3 of other promises or orders that are not payable to bearer or order serves a useful purpose. It provides a simple device to clearly exclude a writing that does not fit the pattern of typical negotiable instruments and which is not intended to be a negotiable instrument. If a writing could be an instrument despite the absence of 'to order' or 'to bearer' language and a dispute arises with respect to the writing, it might be argued that the writing is a negotiable instrument because the other requirements of subsection (a) are somehow met. Even if the argument is eventually found to be without merit it can be used as a litigation ploy. Words making a promise or order payable to bearer or to order are the most distinguishing feature of a negotiable instrument and such words are frequently referred to as 'words of negotiability.' Article 3 is not meant to apply to contracts for the sale of goods or services or the sale or lease of real property or similar writings that may contain a promise to pay money. The use of words of negotiability in such contracts would be an aberration. Absence of the words precludes any argument that such contracts might be negotiable instruments."

2. Why then is a check which says "Pay to Payee" a negotiable instrument under § 3–104(c) while a promissory note with this language is not? The reason for this distinction is that, as we shall see, banks deal with the billions of checks issued each year almost entirely on an automated basis. They pay checks drawn on them largely on the basis of machine-readable information encoded on the bottom of the check. Virtually all checks are printed with the words "Pay to the order of." If a drawer scratches out the word "order," the depositary and drawee banks have no feasible way of detecting that they are taking a nonnegotiable instrument. Section 3–104(c) largely relieves them of the burden of having to look at the face of each check to know whether it is negotiable. Comment 2 to § 3–104.

3. The justification for retaining the "words of negotiability"—bearer or order—stated in Note 1 is that they give us a bright line test for negotiability. Certainly most creditors know what these words mean, but is this true of debtors? There is nothing about this 18th century formalism which would indicate to an unsophisticated debtor that its inclusion means that the debtor who is defrauded by a payee is, nevertheless, liable to a good faith purchaser of the instrument. This is a harsh consequence to visit upon a debtor who has no way of learning what these words mean short of consulting a lawyer. During the Drafting Committee discussions, a strong view was pressed that if we are to retain the doctrine of negotiability (and not all were in favor of doing so), then any note that purported to be negotiable should bear a legend warning of the consequences of negotiability. Such a provision was carried in a number of drafts until late in the drafting process. When it was finally dropped in the last year of the project, the justification for doing so was that business debtors should be held to know what business documents mean and, as we shall see, the doctrine of negotiability has been severely circumscribed in consumer transactions.

D.   REQUIREMENTS FOR STATUS AS HOLDER IN DUE COURSE
1.   GOOD FAITH AND NOTICE

To qualify as a holder in due course under § 3–302 a holder must, among other requirements, have taken the instrument in good faith and without notice of any defense against or claim to it on the part of any person. The meaning of good faith as applied to negotiable instruments has varied over the years. The law prior to the adoption of the NIL is traced by the Court in Howard National Bank v. Wilson, 96 Vt. 438, 120 A. 889 (1923):

> Prior to the Negotiable Instruments Act, two distinct lines of cases had developed in this country. The first had its origin in Gill v. Cubitt, 3 B. & C. 466, 10 E.C.L. 215, where the rule was distinctly laid down by the court of King's Bench that the purchaser of negotiable paper must exercise reasonable prudence and caution, and that, if the circumstances were such as ought to have excited the suspicion of a prudent and careful man, and he made no inquiry, he did not stand in the legal position of a bona fide holder. The rule was adopted by the courts of this country generally and seem to have become a fixed rule in the law of negotiable paper. Later in Goodman v. Harvey, 4 A. & E. 870, 31 E.C.L. 381, the English court abandoned its former position and adopted the rule that nothing short of actual bad faith or fraud in the purchaser would deprive him of the character of a bona fide purchaser and let in defenses existing between prior parties, that no circumstances of suspicion merely, or want of proper caution in the purchaser, would have this effect, and that even gross negligence would have no effect, except as evidence tending to establish bad faith or fraud. Some of the American courts adhered to the earlier rule, while others followed the change inaugurated in Goodman v. Harvey. The question was before this court in Roth v. Colvin, 32 Vt. 125, and, on full consideration of the question, a rule was adopted in harmony with that announced in Gill v. Cubitt, which has been adhered to in subsequent cases, including those cited above. Stated briefly, one line of cases including our own had adopted the test of the reasonably prudent man and the other that of actual good faith. It would seem that it was the intent of the Negotiable Instruments Act to harmonize this disagreement by adopting the latter test. That such is the view generally accepted by the courts appears from a recent review of the cases concerning what constitutes notice of defect. Brannan on Neg.

Ins.Law, 187–201. To effectuate the general purpose of the act to make uniform the Negotiable Instruments Law of those states which should enact it, we are constrained to hold (contrary to the rule adopted in our former decisions) that negligence on the part of the plaintiff, or suspicious circumstances sufficient to put a prudent man on inquiry, will not of themselves prevent a recovery, but are to be considered merely as evidence bearing on the question of bad faith. 96 Vt. at 452–453, 120 A. at 894.

Gill v. Cubitt, referred to in the above quotation and decided by the Court of King's Bench in 1824, is reminiscent of Miller v. Race. It involved a stolen bill of exchange purchased by plaintiff without any inquiry about the title of the transferor. The court decided that the circumstances under which the purchase was made should have caused plaintiff to be suspicious about the transferor. Because plaintiff did not make inquiries about the title of the transferor, he did not qualify as a bona fide purchaser and was subject to the defense of theft pleaded by defendants who were the acceptors of the bill. Thus, good faith and notice of the claim to the instrument were part of one package. The NIL and the UCC, however, both treat good faith and notice as two separate concepts, and this has caused some difficulties of analysis. The NIL required that a taker to be a holder in due course must take in "good faith" and without "notice of any infirmity or defect in the title of the person negotiating it." (Section 52.) Good faith was not defined but notice was defined in Section 56: "To constitute notice of an infirmity in the instrument or defect in the title of the person negotiating the same, the person to whom it is negotiated must have had actual knowledge of the infirmity or defect, or knowledge of such facts that his action in taking the instrument amounted to bad faith." Professor Britton agrees with the conclusion in *Howard National Bank,* that the effect of the NIL provisions, as interpreted by the courts, was to reject Gill v. Cubitt and to adopt a test of subjective good faith. Britton, Bills and Notes 246 (2d ed. 1961).

The UCC, during its development, at first departed from the NIL approach and then, in part, returned to it. Section 1–201(19), the general definition applicable to all articles of the UCC, defines "good faith" as "honesty in fact in the conduct or transaction concerned." This is a purely subjective standard. The 1952 draft of the UCC in § 2–103(1)(b) applicable to sale of goods transactions added an objective standard of conduct by merchants. It stated that "'Good faith' in the case of a merchant includes observance of reasonable commercial standards." The 1952 draft also added an objective standard of conduct for purchasers of instruments. Section 3–302(1)(b) of that draft provided as follows: "in good faith including observance of the reasonable commercial standards of any business in which the holder may be engaged." The apparent purpose was to return to the rule of Gill v. Cubitt which required the exercise of reasonable prudence and caution in taking an instrument with respect to which there may be indications of a possible defense or claim. The comment to this section said: "The 'reasonable commercial standards' language added here and in comparable provisions elsewhere in the Act, e.g., Section 2–103, merely makes explicit what has long been implicit in case-law handling of the 'good faith' concept. A business man engaging in a commercial transaction is not entitled to claim the peculiar advantages which the law accords the good faith purchaser—called in this context holder in due course—on a bare showing of 'honesty in fact' when his actions fail to meet the generally accepted standards current in his business, trade or profession. The cases so hold; this section so declares the law.''

But in the later versions of the UCC the objective standard of good faith in both Article 2 and Article 3 was changed. With respect to Article 2, in the 1962 Official Text, § 2–103(1)(b) was changed to read as follows: "Good faith'' in the case of a merchant means honesty in fact and the observance of reasonable commercial standards of fair dealing in the trade. Although this definition is an objective standard of good faith it relates to fairness rather than prudence and caution which were the focus of the 1952 draft of § 2–103(1)(b). In the 1962 Official Text, § 3–302(1)(b) was amended to drop the words "including observance of the reasonable commercial standards of any business in which the holder may be engaged.'' The apparent purpose of this change in § 3–302(1)(b) was to return to the subjective standard of the NIL, the so-called "pure heart'' doctrine. But this purpose was not achieved. The 1962 Official Text of § 3–302(1)(c) provided: "without notice * * * of any defense against or claim to [the instrument] on the part of any person.'' The NIL applied the good or bad faith standard to the concept of "notice.'' The purchaser had notice of a defense or claim to the instrument only if the purchaser had "knowledge of such facts that his action in taking the instrument amounted to bad faith.'' The UCC has always had an objective standard of notice. Section 1–201(25) states that a person has notice of a fact when "from all the facts and circumstances known to him at the time in question he has reason to know that it exists.'' Thus, through § 3–302(1)(c) and § 1–201(25) the result reached in Gill v. Cubitt, on the same facts can easily be reached under the 1962 Official Text of Article 3. From 1962 until adoption of Revised Article 3 in 1990, no changes to the Official Text of Article 3 were made with respect to this issue. Most cases probably involve situations in which the facts relevant to the issue of good faith are the same facts giving rise to notice of a defense or claim. In those cases the issue of whether good faith is subjective or objective seems academic. See Neil O. Littlefield, Good Faith Purchase of Commercial Paper: The Failure of the Subjective Test, 39 S.Cal.L.Rev. 48 (1966).

Revised Article 3 adopts a new definition of good faith in § 3–103(a)(4). This definition applies to both Article 3 and Article 4. It differs from the definition of good faith in § 1–201(19) by referring not only to honesty in fact but also to "observance of reasonable commercial standards of fair dealing.'' Although the quoted words may have importance with respect to other sections of Article 3 or Article 4 in which good faith is an issue, these words do not change the standard of the original Article 3 for determining holder-in-due-course status. Section 3–302(a)(2) continues the previous Article 3 requirement that the instrument be taken both in good faith and without notice of claims or defenses. Good faith does not relate to the issue of notice of claims and defenses. Since § 1–201(25), which defines notice, has not been amended, the result reached in Gill v. Cubitt would also be reached under revised Article 3 on the same facts.

Kaw Valley State Bank & Trust Co. v. Riddle

Supreme Court of Kansas, 1976.
219 Kan. 550, 549 P.2d 927.

■ FROMME, JUSTICE. This action was brought by The Kaw Valley State Bank and Trust Company (hereinafter referred to as Kaw Valley) to recover judgment against John H. Riddle d/b/a Riddle Contracting Company (hereafter referred to as Riddle) on two notes and to determine the priority of conflicting security agreements. The two notes were covered by separate security agreements and were given to purchase construction equipment. The Planters State Bank and Trust Company (hereinafter referred to as Planters) held a note and security interest on the same and other construction equipment acquired by Riddle. Kaw Valley had acquired the two notes and the security agreements by assignment from Co–Mac, Inc. (hereinafter referred to as Co–Mac), a dealer, from whom Riddle purchased the construction equipment.

In a trial to the court Kaw Valley was found not to be a holder in due course of one of the notes. Its claim on said note, totaling $21,904.64, was successfully defended on the grounds of failure of consideration. It was stipulated at the trial that none of the construction equipment for which the note was given had ever been delivered by Co–Mac. Kaw Valley has appealed.

* * *

Prior to the transactions in question Riddle had purchased construction equipment and machinery from the dealer, Co–Mac. A number of these purchases had been on credit and discounted to Kaw Valley by Co–Mac. Including the Riddle transactions, Kaw Valley had purchased over 250 notes and security agreements from Co–Mac during the prior ten year period. All were guaranteed by Co–Mac and by its president personally.

In May, 1971, Riddle negotiated for the purchase of a model 6–c Caterpillar tractor, a dozer and a used 944 Caterpillar wheel tractor with a two yard bucket. Riddle was advised that this machinery could be delivered but it would first be necessary for Co–Mac to have a signed note and security agreement to complete the transaction. An installment note, security agreement and acceptance of delivery of the machinery was mailed to Riddle. These were signed and returned to Co–Mac. Ten days later, the machinery not having been delivered, Riddle called Co–Mac and inquired about purchasing a D–8 Caterpillar and a #80 Caterpillar scraper in place of the first machinery ordered. Co–Mac agreed to destroy the May 11, 1971 papers and sell this larger machinery to Riddle in place of that previously ordered.

The sale of this substitute machinery was completed and the machinery was delivered after the execution of an additional note and security agreement. However, the May 11, 1971 papers were not destroyed. The note had been discounted and assigned to Kaw Valley prior to the sale of the substitute machinery. Thereafter Co–Mac, who was in financial trouble, made regular payments on the first note to Kaw Valley. The note was thus kept current by Co–Mac and Riddle had no knowledge of the continued existence of that note. The 6–c Caterpillar tractor, dozer and the used 944 Caterpillar wheel tractor were never delivered to Riddle. Riddle received no consideration for the May 11, 1971 note and no lien attached under the security agreement because the machinery never came into possession of Riddle. (See UCC § 9–204.) The debtor never had rights in any of the collateral.

On February 24, 1972, representatives of Riddle, Co–Mac and Kaw Valley met for the purpose of consolidating the indebtedness of Riddle on machinery notes held by Kaw Valley and guaranteed by Co–Mac. Riddle was behind in some of his payments and wanted to consolidate the notes and reduce his monthly payments to $4,500.00. Kaw Valley disclosed eight past due machinery notes, each representing separate purchase transactions by Riddle. Riddle objected to one of these notes dated July 16, 1971, because the machinery purchased under this particular transaction had been previously returned to Co–Mac.

It was agreed by Kaw Valley that Riddle did not owe for this machinery because of the previous settlement between Co–Mac and Riddle. Kaw Valley cancelled the $5,000.00 balance shown to be due from Riddle.

Thereupon a renewal note and security agreement for $44,557.70 dated February 24, 1972, was drawn consolidating and renewing the seven remaining notes. Riddle then asked Kaw Valley if this was all that it owed the bank and he was assured that it was. The renewal note was then executed by Riddle.

It was not until March 12, 1972, that Riddle was advised by Kaw Valley that it held the note and security agreement dated May 11, 1971, which Riddle believed had been destroyed by Co–Mac. This was within a week after a receiver had been appointed to take over Co–Mac's business affairs. Riddle explained the machinery had never been delivered and Co–Mac promised to destroy the papers. No demand for payment of the May 11, 1971 note was made on Riddle until this action was filed.

Prior to the time this action was filed, Riddle executed a note and granted a security agreement in all of its machinery and equipment to Planters. This included the machinery covered in the previous consolidation transaction of February 24, 1972, with Kaw Valley and Co–Mac.

Subsequently Kaw Valley obtained possession of the machinery covered by the February 24 transaction by court order. Thereupon by agreement in writing between Kaw Valley, Planters and Riddle an immediate sale of the collateral covered in the February 24 transaction was held. By the terms of this agreement the first $22,200.00 in proceeds was to be paid to Kaw

Valley in full satisfaction of the note of February 24, 1972. The money received from the sale in excess of this amount was to be paid to the Merchants National Bank to hold as escrow agent, awaiting a determination of entitlement by the court.

At the time of the trial the $22,200.00 had been received by Kaw Valley and the balance of the proceeds of the agreed sale amounting to $25,371.15 was in the hands of the escrow agent.

In the court's memorandum of decision filed November 19, 1974, the court found:

> "That the proceeds remaining in plaintiff's possession from the agreed equipment sale are $25,371.15. The plaintiff claims $21,904.64 of same is due on the transaction of May 11, 1971. The parties agree that the excess of $3,466.51 should be paid to defendant Planters State Bank to apply on its August 28, 1972 claim;"

On December 20, 1974, the court entered the following pay-out order:

"TO THE CLERK OF THE DISTRICT COURT:

> "Now on this 20th day of December 1974, you are ordered to pay to The Planters State Bank and Trust Company the sum of $3,466.51 now in your hands, having been paid by the Kaw Valley State Bank and Trust Company, pursuant to the Journal Entry of Judgment entered herein on November 19, 1974."

Although it does not appear who initiated the order, the $3,466.51 was paid to and accepted by Planters leaving the disputed proceeds of the sale ($21,904.64) in the hands of either the escrow agent or the court.

* * *

The primary point on appeal questions the holding of the trial court that Kaw Valley was not a holder in due course of the note and security agreement dated May 11, 1971.

UCC § 3–306 provides that unless a holder of an instrument is a holder in due course he takes the instrument subject to the defenses of want or failure of consideration, nonperformance of any condition precedent, nondelivery or delivery for a special purpose. It was undisputed in this case that Riddle received no consideration after executing the note. The machinery was never delivered and he was assured by Co–Mac that the papers would be destroyed. The parties so stipulated. If Kaw Valley was not a holder in due course the proven defense was a bar to recovery by Kaw Valley.

UCC § 3–302 states that a holder in due course is a holder who takes the instrument (1) for value, (2) in good faith and (3) without notice of any defense against it. It was not disputed and the court found that Kaw Valley took the note for value so the first requirement was satisfied. The other requirements were subject to dispute. The trial court concluded:

> "Kaw Valley State Bank and Trust Company is not a holder in due course of the note and security agreement, dated May 11, 1971 for the

reason that it did not establish in all respects that it took said instruments in good faith and without notice of any defense against or claimed to it on the part of John H. Riddle, and Kaw Valley State Bank and Trust Company therefor took said instruments subject to the defense of failure of consideration. [Citations omitted.]"

So we are confronted with the question of what is required for a holder to take an instrument "in good faith" and "without notice of defense." We will consider the two parts of the question in the order mentioned.

"Good faith" is defined in UCC § 1–201(19) as "honesty in fact in the conduct or transaction concerned." The first draft of the Uniform Commercial Code (U.C.C.) as proposed required not only that the actions of a holder be honest in fact but in addition it required the actions to conform to *reasonable commercial standards*. This would have permitted the courts to inquire as to whether a particular commercial standard was in fact reasonable. (See Uniform Commercial Code, Proposed Final Draft [1950], § 1–201, 18, p. 30.) However, when the final draft was approved the test of reasonable commercial standards was excised thus indicating that a more rigid standard must be applied for determining "good faith." * * *

From the history of the Uniform Commercial Code it would appear that "good faith" requires no actual knowledge of or participation in any material infirmity in the original transaction.

The second part of our question concerns the requirement of the U.C.C. that a holder in due course take the instrument without notice of any defense to the instrument. UCC § 1–201(25) provides:

"A person has 'notice' of a fact when

"(a) he has actual knowledge of it; or

"(b) he has received a notice or notification of it; or

"(c) from all the facts and circumstances known to him at the time in question he has reason to know that it exists. A person 'known' or has 'knowledge' of a fact when he has actual knowledge of it. 'Discover' or 'learn' or a word or phrase of similar import refers to knowledge rather than to reason to know. The time and circumstances under which a notice or notification may cease to be effective are not determined by this act."

As is apparent from reading the above statute the standard enunciated is not limited to the rigid standard of actual knowledge of the defense. Reason to know appears to be premised on the use of reasonable commercial practices. * * * Since "good faith" and "no notice of defense" are both required of a holder to claim the status of a holder in due course it would appear that the two standards are not in conflict even though the standards of conduct may be different.

There is little or no evidence in the present case to indicate that Kaw Valley acted dishonestly or "not in good faith" when it purchased the note of May 11, 1971. However, as to "notice of defense" the court found from all the facts and circumstances known to Kaw Valley at the time in question it had reason to know a defense existed. The court found:

"During the period 1960 to May, 1971, plaintiff purchased from Co–Mac over 250 notes and secured transactions and held at any given time between $100,000.00 and $250,000.00 of such obligations. All of which were guaranteed by Co–Mac and personally guaranteed by D. J. Wickern, its president. Conant Wait personally handled most if not all of such transactions for plaintiff. Mr. Wait was aware that Co–Mac was making warranties and representation as to fitness to some purchasers of new and used equipment. Mr. Wait further knew that some transactions were in fact not as they would appear to be in that the money from Kaw Valley would be used by Co–Mac to buy the equipment that was the subject matter of the sale. Further, that delivery to the customer of said purchased equipment was sometimes delayed 60 to 90 days for repairing and/or overhauling of same. The plaintiff obviously on many transactions was relying on Co–Mac to insure payment of the obligations and contacted Co–Mac to collect delinquent payments. Some transactions involved delivery of coupon books to Co–Mac rather than the debtor so Co–Mac could bill service and parts charges along with the secured debt. Co–Mac collected payments directly from debtors in various transactions and paid plaintiff. Plaintiff did not concern itself with known irregularities in the transactions as it clearly was relying on Co–Mac;

"The coupon book on the May 11, 1971 transaction was not sent to defendant Riddle; no payments on same were made by defendant Riddle; the payments were made by Co–Mac until January 25, 1972; prior to early March, 1972, defendant Riddle did not know plaintiff had the May 11, 1971 secured transaction; knowledge of said transaction came to defendant Riddle on March 12, 1972 when Mr. Wait contacted defendant Riddle's manager; that Co–Mac had shortly before been placed in receivership; that no demand for any payment on said transaction was made by plaintiff to defendant Riddle until September 1972."

To further support its holding that Kaw Valley had reason to know that the defense existed the court found that when Kaw Valley, Co–Mac and Riddle met on February 24, 1972, to consolidate all of Riddle's past due notes Kaw Valley recognized Co–Mac's authority to act for it. Co–Mac had accepted return of the machinery on one of the eight transactions and Kaw Valley recognized its authority as their agent to do so and cancelled the $5,000.00 balance remaining due on the note held by the bank.

The cases dealing with the question of "reason to know a defense exists" seem to fall into four categories.

The first includes those cases where it is established the holder had information from the transferor or the obligor which disclosed the existence of a defense. In those cases it is clear if the holder takes an instrument having received prior or contemporaneous notice of a defense he is not a holder in due course. (Billingsley v. Mackay, 382 F.2d 290 [5th Cir. 1967].)

Our present case does not fall in that category for there is no evidence that Co–Mac or Riddle informed Kaw Valley that the machinery had not been delivered when the note was negotiated.

The second group of cases are those in which the defense appears in an accompanying document delivered to the holder with the note. For example, when a security agreement is executed concurrently with a note evidencing an indebtedness incurred for machinery to be delivered in the future. In such case the instrument may under certain circumstances disclose a defense to the note, such as nondelivery of the machinery purchased. (See also Commerce Trust Company v. Denson, 437 S.W.2d 94 [Mo.App.1968], and HIMC Investment Co. v. Siciliano, 103 N.J.Super. 27, 246 A.2d 502, for other examples.) Our present case does not fall in this category because Riddle had signed a written delivery acceptance which was handed to Kaw Valley along with the note and security agreement.

A third group of cases are those in which information appears in the written instrument indicating the existence of a defense, such as when the note on its face shows that the due date has passed or the note bears visible evidence of alteration and forgery or the note is clearly incomplete. (See E. F. Corporation v. Smith, 496 F.2d 826 [10th Cir. 1974]; Srochi v. Kamensky, 118 Ga.App. 182, 162 S.E.2d 889; and Winter & Hirsch, Inc. v. Passarelli, 122 Ill.App.2d 372, 259 N.E.2d 312.) In our present case the instrument assigned bore nothing unusual on its face and appeared complete and proper in all respects.

In the fourth category of cases it has been held that the holder of a negotiable instrument may be prevented from assuming holder in due course status because of knowledge of the business practices of his transferor or when he is so closely aligned with the transferor that transferor may be considered an agent of the holder and the transferee is charged with the actions and knowledge of the transferor.

Under our former negotiable instruments law containing provisions similar to the U.C.C. this court refused to accord holder in due course status to a machinery company receiving notes from one of its dealers because of its knowledge of the business practices of the dealer and the company's participation and alignment with the dealer who transferred the note. (International Harvester Co. v. Watkins, 127 Kan. 50, Sly. C7 3, 272 P. 139, 61 A.L.R. 687.)

In Unico v. Owen, 50 N.J. 101, 232 A.2d 405, the New Jersey court refused to accord holder in due course status to a financing partnership which was closely connected with the transferor and had been organized to finance the commercial paper obtained by the transferor and others. The financing partnership had a voice in setting the policies and standards to be followed by the transferor. Under such circumstances the court found that the holder must be considered a participant in the transaction and subject to defenses available against the payee-transferor. In United States Finance Company v. Jones, 285 Ala. 105, 229 So.2d 495, it was held that a finance company purchasing a note from a payee for fifty percent of its face value did not establish holder in due course status and must be held subject to defenses inherent in the original transaction. Other jurisdictions have followed the rationale of Unico. See American Plan Corp. v. Woods, 16 Ohio App.2d 1, 240 N.E.2d 886, where the holder supplied forms to the payee, established financing charges and investigated the credit of the maker of the note; Calvert Credit Corporation v. Williams, 244 A.2d 494 (D.C.App. 1968), where the holder exerted total control over payee's financial affairs; and Jones v. Approved Bancredit Corp., 256 A.2d 739 (Del.1969), where ownership and management of the holder and payee were connected.

In the present case Kaw Valley had worked closely with Co–Mac in over 250 financing transactions over a period of ten years. It knew that some of these transactions were not for valuable consideration at the time the paper was delivered since the bank's money was to be used in purchasing the machinery or equipment represented in the instruments as already in possession of the maker of the note. Kaw Valley had been advised that delivery to Co–Mac's customers was sometimes delayed from 60 to 90 days. Kaw Valley continued to rely on Co–Mac to assure payment of the obligations and contacted it to collect delinquent payments. Some of these transactions, including the one in question, involved the use of coupon books to be used by the debtor in making payment on the notes. In the present case Kaw Valley did not notify Riddle that it was the holder of the note. It delivered Riddle's coupon book to Co–Mac as if it were the obligor or was authorized as its collection agent for this transaction.

Throughout the period from May 11, 1971, to February 25, 1972, Kaw Valley received and credited the monthly payments knowing that payments were being made by Co–Mac and not by Riddle. Then when Riddle's loans were consolidated, the May 11, 1971 transaction was not included by Kaw Valley, either by oversight or by intention, as an obligation of Riddle. Co–Mac occupied a close relationship with Kaw Valley and with its knowledge and consent acted as its agent in collecting payments on notes held by Kaw Valley. The working relationship existing between Kaw Valley and Co–Mac was further demonstrated on February 24, 1972, when the $5,000.00 balance due on one of Riddle's notes was cancelled when it was shown that the machinery for which the note was given had previously been returned to Co–Mac with the understanding that no further payments were due.

UCC § 3–307(3) provides:

"After it is shown that a defense exists a person claiming the rights of a holder in due course has the burden of establishing that he or some person under whom he claims is in all respects a holder in due course."

In the present case the court found that the appellant, Kaw Valley, had not sustained its burden of proving that it was a holder in due course. Under the evidence in this case the holder failed to advise the maker of the note of its acquisition of the note and security agreement. It placed the payment coupon book in the hands of Co–Mac and received all monthly payments from them. A close working relationship existed between the two companies and Co–Mac was clothed with authority to collect and forward all payments due on the transaction. Agency and authority was further shown to exist by authorizing return of machinery to Co–Mac and terminating balances due on purchase money paper. We cannot say under the facts and circumstances known and participated in by Kaw Valley in this transaction it did not at the time in question have reason to know that the defense existed. This was a question of fact to be determined by the trier of fact which if supported by substantial competent evidence must stand.

* * *

The judgment is affirmed.

NOTE

Is the court telling us that the doctrine of holding in due course performs no legitimate function in inventory and sales financing?

PROBLEMS

1. On October 16, 1969, $8,000,000 of United States Treasury Bills in bearer form were stolen from Morgan Bank. On October 28, 1969, when the theft was discovered, Morgan Bank sent a "notice of lost securities," describing the stolen bills by serial number, to bankers and brokers throughout the country. Third Bank, upon receiving the notice placed the notice in its lost securities file. On January 30, 1970 Third Bank made loans totalling $82,000 to Bialkin. As collateral for the loans it took two treasury bills each with a face amount of $50,000. The two bills were among those stolen from Morgan Bank and were listed in the notice of lost securities. The officer of Third Bank who approved the loan to Bialkin did not check the lost securities file of Third Bank. He testified that he was not aware of its existence. Third Bank later discovered that the treasury bills had been stolen and reported it to law enforcement authorities. Morgan Bank then sued to recover the bills.

Treasury bills come within the definition of "security" (§ 8–102(a)(15)) that are governed by Article 8 of the UCC rather than Article 3. § 3–102(a). In this case Third Bank would defeat the claim of Morgan Bank if it qualified as a "protected purchaser." § 8–303. The treasury bills in this case are now known as "security certificates." § 8–102(d)(16). A protected purchaser of a security certificate is essentially the same as a holder in due course of a negotiable instrument. Although the 1995 revision of Article 8 changed the notice test under that statute (§ 8–105), would Third Bank have notice of the claim of Morgan Bank under § 1–201(25), (26), and (27)? This problem is based on the facts, slightly modified, of Morgan Guaranty Trust Co. of New York v. Third National Bank of Hampden County, 529 F.2d 1141 (1st Cir.1976).

2. In December 1957 Fazzari was induced by fraud to sign a promissory note for $400 payable to the order of Wade. After discovering the fraud, in January 1958, Fazzari notified all of the local banks of the fraud. He personally spoke to the cashier of Odessa Bank and advised him not to purchase the note because he had been "tricked" by Wade. Three months later Odessa Bank, acting through its cashier, purchased the note. The cashier admitted that Fazzari had told him about the note in January but testified that at the time the note was purchased in April he had forgotten the incident. Did Odessa Bank take the note as a holder in due course? § 1–201(25) and the Comment to that provision. This problem is based on the facts of First National Bank of Odessa v. Fazzari, 10 N.Y.2d 394, 223 N.Y.S.2d 483, 179 N.E.2d 493 (1961).

2.   OVERDUE OR IRREGULAR INSTRUMENTS

Section 3–302(a) incorporates two traditional rules: holder in due course status cannot be attained if the instrument is taken with notice that it is overdue or if the instrument is so irregular or incomplete as to call into question its authenticity. These doctrines are rooted in the law of good faith and may be viewed as special applications of the suspicious circumstances rule of Gill v. Cubitt. But for a long time they have enjoyed independent status, and NIL § 52 adopted them as separate requirements for holder in due course status in addition to the good faith requirement.

Under the common law view, the fact that an instrument was overdue or irregular or incomplete was notice that something was wrong. But the fact that an instrument is overdue does not point to any particular defense or claim or, for that matter, to the existence of any defense or claim at all. Most notes are probably overdue because the makers can't pay them. Most checks that are still out more than 90 days (§ 3–304(a)(2)) have not been collected because the holder hasn't deposited them. In the range of possibilities raised in the mind of one purchasing an overdue instrument, it is doubtful that the likelihood of a defense rises very high or that the possibility of a claim of ownership by a prior party is considered at all. The fact that an instrument bears an obvious alteration does warn a taker of the possibility of a fraudulent alteration but not of defenses or claims wholly unrelated to the alteration.

Why shouldn't a purchaser who is willing to pay good money for an overdue or irregular or incomplete instrument be entitled to holder in due course status? Perhaps the question is better phrased in terms of why should such a holder be accorded that status. The answer to these questions may depend upon whether one looks upon holder in due course status to be the norm or whether it should be seen as something unusual to be given only when a clear commercial benefit is achieved. If negotiability is a doctrine to promote the free flow of instruments, what social or economic gain is achieved by encouraging the currency of stale, irregular or incomplete instruments?

PROBLEMS

1. S agreed to sell real property to B for $58,000, of which $6,500 was to be a down payment. When making the down payment, B insisted that S execute a promissory note to B's order for the amount of $6,500 as evidence of indebtedness for any sums B might be called upon to expend to pay off any claims or liens with respect to the property of which B was not aware. In time B expended $4,244 in paying these claims. The note, which was executed by S on March 25 and due 75 days after date, was indorsed without recourse to Plaintiff on September 1 for a total consideration of $3,067. S refused to pay the note and Plaintiff brought suit. How much is Plaintiff entitled to recover—$6,500, $4,244, or $3,067? § 3–203(b), § 3–302(a), § 3–117, and § 3–305(a). See also Brock v. Adams, 79 N.M. 17, 439 P.2d 234 (1968).

2. Payee sold a house to Maker and as partial payment of the price took a promissory note for $5,000 payable in monthly installments over a five year period. When Payee's reserve army unit was called to active duty Payee asked Banker to collect the note during Payee's indefinite absence. Banker insisted that Payee indorse the note in blank and turn over possession of both the note and mortgage. Later Maker fell in default on the payments and Banker, who was also in financial difficulties, sold the note to Purchaser for value. Purchaser knew that four payments had not been made but had no knowledge of the circumstances under which Banker had taken the note. After Payee returned and learned of Banker's actions, Payee asserted a claim of ownership against Purchaser and sued to retake possession of the note. What result? Justice v. Stonecipher, 267 Ill. 448, 108 N.E. 722 (1915). § 3–304(b)(1) and § 3–306.

3. In payment of goods, Maker signed a negotiable note in the amount of $10,000 and mailed it to Payee. The note should have been payable in the amount of $20,000. Payee noticed the discrepancy and called Maker's attention to it. Maker told Payee to change the $10,000 to $20,000. Payee did so by erasing and typing over. The alteration was crudely done and very obvious. Payee then sold the note to Holder. Holder noticed the alteration but accepted Payee's truthful explanation of the circumstances under which it was made. When Holder demanded payment Maker refused, stating that Payee never delivered the goods for which the note was given. Is Holder subject to the defense of Maker? Suppose Holder, before completing the transaction, had called Maker and that Maker had verified that the $20,000 figure was correct. How does this affect your answer? § 3–302(a)(1) and § 3–305(a).

3. NEGOTIABILITY IN CONSUMER TRANSACTIONS

a. INTRODUCTION

Whether the doctrine of negotiability in all its vigor is necessary or even desirable when applied to modern negotiable instruments such as promissory notes and checks has been challenged. See Gilmore, The Good Faith Purchase Idea and the Uniform Commercial Code: Confessions of a Repentant Draftsman, 15 Ga.L.Rev. 605 (1981). Consider the following observations of Professor Albert J. Rosenthal taken from his article, Negotiability—Who Needs It? 71 Colum.L.Rev. 375, 378–381 (1971):

The negotiable promissory note of today is quite a different instrument, serving different purposes, and the consequences of its negotiability are quite different in impact. By far the most commonly employed variety of the species today is the note given by the installment purchaser of goods to reflect the unpaid portion of the purchase price. Typically, such a note is transferred just once, from the dealer to the lender (usually either a finance company or a bank), and thereafter remains in the possession of the latter or its lawyers until it is either paid off or offered in evidence in court. Its negotiable character is of no importance with respect to claims of ownership, as it is unlikely to be lost or stolen. Even if it is, the last indorsement will have been a special indorsement to the order of the lender; without the genuine further indorsement of the latter there can be no subsequent holder, much less a holder in due course.

The only significant consequence of the negotiability of such a note is that it cuts off the defenses of the maker. If, for example, the purchaser gives the note in payment for a refrigerator, the finance company is entitled to full payment regardless of whether the refrigerator fails to work or whether its sale was accomplished through fraudulent misrepresentations or, indeed, whether it was ever delivered at all. And it may be small comfort to the buyer, forced to pay the finance company in full, to know that he has a cause of action against the seller, which may at best be collectible with difficulty and may in many cases be worthless because the seller is insolvent or has left town.

A promissory note of this kind, and a consequence of negotiability that works in this fashion, are a far cry from the stolen Bank of England note, and the protection accorded its purchaser, in Miller v. Race. Whether the finance company should be allowed to prevail free of the maker's defenses raises questions that ought to be decided on their own merits, and not merely through the absent-minded application of a doctrine created to meet an entirely different situation.

The social evils flowing from negotiability in this circumstance have become manifest, and there has been a clear trend in both the courts and the legislatures toward amelioration of its consequences. In particular, the unfairness to the poorest members of the community of the law governing consumer installment purchases has generated a reaction that is giving rise to a major alteration in it. This departure is being accomplished, not by modification of the provisions of Article 3 of the Code, but by legislative action forbidding the use of negotiable instruments in consumer installment transactions and by judicial attempts to stretch the facts to deny holder in due course status to finance companies. Since the installment buyer can be similarly harmed even without a negotiable instrument if there is a clause in his purchase contract waiving, as against an assignee of his obligation, any defenses on the contract that he may have, legislatures and courts have also been moving in the direction of declaring such clauses invalid.

It is not clear whether the apparent weakness in the opposition to these changes springs from a lack of genuine need on the part of sellers or lenders for continuation of the power to cut off buyers' defenses. While there has been ground to believe that where this protection is denied, credit nevertheless will remain available, a recent study suggests that this may not be so.

If an exception is carved out, should it be limited to consumer paper, or should it be applied to promissory notes across the board? Thus far, the demand for reform has been confined largely to the former. While there may be small commercial purchasers also in need of similar protection, and while there may be other situations in which unfair advantage seems to be taken of makers of promissory notes, there does not appear in such cases to be a resulting social problem of comparable dimension. On the other hand, we need to know more about the range of other uses to which promissory notes are put in today's economy, and about the circumstances in which the cutting off of claims and defenses in connection with such notes serves legitimate needs or works undue hardship.

* * *

b. THE JUDICIAL RESPONSE

Unico v. Owen

Supreme Court of New Jersey, 1967.
50 N.J. 101, 232 A.2d 405.

■ FRANCIS, J. The issue to be decided here is whether plaintiff Unico, a New Jersey partnership, is a holder in due course of defendant's note. If so, it is entitled to a judgment for the unpaid balance due thereon, for which this suit was brought. The District Court found plaintiff was not such a holder and that it was therefore subject to the defense interposed by defendant, maker of the note, of failure of consideration on the part of the payee, which endorsed it to plaintiff. Since it was undisputed that the payee failed to furnish the consideration for which the note was given, judgment was entered for defendant. The Appellate Division affirmed, and we granted plaintiff's petition for certification in order to consider the problem. 47 N.J. 241, 220 A.2d 114 (1966).

The facts are important. Defendant's wife, Jean Owen, answered an advertisement in a Newark, N.J. newspaper in which Universal Stereo Corporation of Hillside, N.J., offered for sale 140 albums of stereophonic records for $698. This amount could be financed and paid on an installment basis. In addition the buyer would receive "without separate charge" (as plaintiff puts it) a Motorola stereo record player. The plain implication was that on agreement to purchase 140 albums, the record player would be given free. A representative of Universal called at the Owens' home and discussed the matter with Mr. and Mrs. Owen. As a result, on November 6, 1962 they signed a "retail installment contract" for the purchase of 140 albums on the time payment plan proposed by Universal.

Under the printed form of contract Universal sold and Owen bought "subject to the terms and conditions stipulated in Exhibit 'A' hereto annexed and printed on the other side hereof and made part hereof, the following goods * * * : 12 stereo albums to be delivered at inception of program and every 6 months thereafter until completion of program," a "new Motorola consolo [sic]" and "140 stereo albums of choice * * * ." The total cash price was listed as $698; a downpayment of $30 was noted; the balance of $668, plus an "official fee" of $1.40 and a time price differential of $150.32, left a time balance of $819.72 to be paid in installments. Owen agreed to pay this balance in 36 equal monthly installments of $22.77 each beginning on December 12, 1962, "at the office of Universal Stereo Corp., 8 Hollywood Avenue, Hillside, N.J., or any other address determined by assignee." The contract provided:

"If the Buyer executed a promissory note of even date herewith in the amount of the time balance indicated, said note is not in payment thereof, but is a negotiable instrument separate and apart from this contract even though at the time of execution it may be temporarily attached hereto by perforation or otherwise."

It was part of Universal's practice to take notes for these contracts, and obviously there was no doubt that it would be done in the Owen case. Owen did sign a printed form of note which was presented with the contract. The name of Universal Stereo Corporation was printed thereon, and the note provided for the monthly installment payments specified. On the reverse side was an elaborate printed form of endorsement which began "Pay to the order of Unico, 251 Broad St., Elizabeth, New Jersey, with full recourse;" and which contained various waivers by the endorser, and an authorization to the transferee to vary the terms of the note in its discretion in dealing with the maker.

Exhibit "A", referred to as being on the reverse side of the contract, is divided into three separate parts, the body of each part being in very fine print. The *first* section sets out in 11 fine print paragraphs the obligations of the buyer and rights of the seller. Under paragraph 1 the seller retains title to the property until the full time price is paid. Here it may be noted that Universal recorded the contract in the Union County Register's Office a few days after its execution. Paragraph 2 says that the term "Seller" as used shall refer to the party signing the contract as seller "or *if said party has assigned said contract, any holder of* said contract." (Emphasis added). It is patent that Universal contemplated assigning the contract forthwith to Unico, and it was so assigned. Of course, it was a bilateral executory contract, and since under the language just quoted "assignee" and "seller" have the same connotation, the reasonable and normal expectation by Owen would be that performance of the delivery obligation was a condition precedent to his undertaking to make installment payments. * * * Universal sought under paragraph 5 to deprive Owen of his right to plead failure of consideration against its intended assignee, Unico. The paragraph provides:

"Buyer hereby acknowledges notice that the contract may be assigned and that assignees will rely upon the agreements contained in this paragraph, and agrees that the liability of the Buyer to any assignee shall be immediate and absolute and not affected by any default whatsoever of the Seller signing this contract; and in order to induce assignees to purchase this contract, the Buyer further agrees not to set up any claim against such Seller as a defense, counterclaim or offset to any action by any assignee for the unpaid balance of the purchase price or for possession of the property."

The validity and efficacy of this paragraph will be discussed hereinafter. At this point it need only be said that the design of Universal in adopting this form of contract and presenting it to buyers, not for bargaining purposes but for signature, was to get the most and give the least. Overall it includes a multitude of conditions, stipulations, reservations, exceptions and waivers skillfully devised to restrict the liability of the seller within the narrowest limits, and to leave no avenue of escape from liability on the part of the purchaser.

The *second* part of Exhibit "A" is entitled in large type, "Assignment and dealer's recommendation. This must be executed by the dealer." There follows an elaborate fine-print form of assignment of the contract and the rights thereunder to Unico, which name is part of the printed form. It is signed by Murray Feldman, President of Universal.

The *third* part of Exhibit "A" is entitled "Guaranty." It is a printed form signed by Murray Feldman, as President, and Rhea M. Feldman, as Secretary, of Universal, and also as individuals guaranteeing payment of the sums due under Owen's contract to Unico.

As Exhibit "A" appears in the appendix, the Owen note referred to above is not now attached to the contract. The record is not clear as to just how it was attached originally, i.e., by a perforated line or otherwise; indication from the agreement itself is that it was attached, and was removed after execution and after or upon endorsement to Unico. In any event it was presented to and executed by Owen with the contract, and in view of the result we have reached in the case, whether it was attached or simply presented to Owen for signature with the contract is of no particular consequence.

At this point the hyper-executory character of the performance agreed to by Universal in return for the installment payment stipulation by Owen must be noted. Owen's time balance of $819.72 was required to be paid by 36 monthly installments of $22.77 each. Universal's undertaking was to deliver 24 record albums a year until 140 albums had been delivered. Completion by the seller therefore would require 5⅚ years. Thus, although Owen would have fully paid for 140 albums at the end of three years, Universal's delivery obligation did not have to be completed until 2⅚ years thereafter. This means that 40% of the albums, although fully paid for, would still be in the hands of the seller. It means also that for 2⅚ years Universal would have the use of 40% of Owen's money on which he had been charged the high time-price differential rate. In contrast, since Universal discounted the note immediately with Unico on the strength of Owen's credit and purchase contract, the transaction, so far as the seller is concerned, can fairly be considered as one for cash. In this posture, Universal had its sale price almost contemporaneously with Owen's execution of the contract, in return for an executory performance to extend over 5⅓ years. And Unico acquired Owen's note which, on its face and considered apart from the remainder of the transaction, appeared to be an unqualifiedly negotiable instrument. On the other hand, on the face of things, by virtue of the ostensibly negotiable note and the waiver or estoppel clause quoted above which was intended to bar any defense against an assignee for the seller's default, Owen had no recourse and no protection if Universal defaulted on its obligation and was financially worthless.

Owen's installment note to Universal for the time balance of $819.72 is dated November 6, 1962. Although the endorsement on the reverse side is not dated, Unico concedes the note was received on or about the day it was made. The underlying sale contract was assigned to Unico at the same time, and it is admitted that Owen was never notified of the assignment.

Owen received from Universal the stereo record player and the original 12 albums called for by the contract. Although he continued to pay the monthly installments on the note for the 12 succeeding months, he never received another album. During that period Mrs. Owen endeavored unsuccessfully to communicate with Universal, and finally ceased making payments when the albums were not delivered. Nothing further was heard about the matter until July 1964, when the attorney for Unico, who was also one of its partners, advised Mrs. Owen that Unico held the note and that payments should be made to it. She told him the payments would be resumed if the albums were delivered. No further deliveries were made because Universal had become insolvent. Up to this time Owen had paid the deposit of $30 and 12 installments of $22.77 each, for a total of $303.24. Unico brought this suit for the balance due on the note plus penalties and a 20% attorney's fee.

Owen defended on the ground that Unico was not a holder in due course of the note, that the payment of $303.24 adequately satisfied any obligation for Universal's partial performance, and that Universal's default and the consequent failure of consideration barred recovery by Unico. As we have said, the trial court found plaintiff was not a holder in due course of the note and that Universal's breach of the sales contract barred recovery.

I.

This brings us to the primary inquiry in the case. Is the plaintiff Unico a holder in due course of defendant's note?

The defendant's note was executed on November 6, 1962. The Uniform Commercial Code was adopted by the Legislature in 1961 (L.1961, c. 120), but it did not become operative until January 1, 1963. The note, therefore, is governed by the Uniform Negotiable Instruments Law. Section 52 thereof defined a holder in due course as one who (among other prerequisites) took the instrument "in good faith and for value." If plaintiff is not a holder in due course it is subject to the defense of failure of consideration on the part of Universal, both under the Negotiable Instruments Law, § 58, and the Uniform Commercial Code, § 3–306(c).

In the field of negotiable instruments, good faith is a broad concept. The basic philosophy of the holder in due course status is to encourage free negotiability of commercial paper by removing certain anxieties of one who takes the paper as an innocent purchaser knowing no reason why the paper is not as sound as its face would indicate. It would seem to follow, therefore, that the more the holder knows about the underlying transaction, and particularly the more he controls or participates or becomes involved in it, the less he fits the role of a good faith purchaser for value; the closer his relationship to the underlying agreement which is the source of the note, the less need there is for giving him the tension-free rights considered necessary in a fast-moving, credit-extending commercial world.

We are concerned here with a problem of consumer goods financing. Such goods are defined in the Uniform Commercial Code as those used or bought for use primarily for personal, family or household purposes. § 9–109(1). Although the Code as such is not applicable in this case, the definition is appropriate for our purposes. And it is fair to say also that in today's society, sale of such goods and arrangements for consumer credit financing of the sale are problems of increasing state and national concern. The consumer-credit market is essentially a process of exchange, the general nature of which is shaped by the objectives and relative bargaining power of each of the parties. In consumer goods transactions there is almost always a substantial differential in bargaining power between the seller and his financer, on the one side, and the householder on the other. That difference exists because generally there is a substantial inequality of economic resources between them, and of course, that balance in the great mass of cases favors the seller and gives him and his financer the power to shape the exchange to their advantage. Their greater economic resources permit them to obtain the advice of experts; moreover, they have more time to reflect about the specific terms of the exchange prior to the negotiations with the consumer; they know from experience how to strengthen their own position in consumer-credit arrangements; and the financer-creditor is better able to absorb the impact of a single imprudent or unfair exchange. See Curran, Legislative Controls as a Response to Consumer–Credit Problems, 8 B.C.Ind. and Com.L.Rev. 409, 435–437 (1967).

Mass marketing in consumer goods, as in many other commercial activities, has produced standardized financing contracts. Henningsen v. Bloomfield Motors, Inc., 32 N.J. 358, 389, 161 A.2d 69, 75 A.L.R.2d 1 (1960). As a result there is no real arms-length bargaining between the creditor (seller-financer) and the consumer, beyond minimal negotiating about amount of credit, terms of installment payment and description of the goods to be purchased, all of which is accomplished by filling blanks left in the jungle of finely printed, creditor-oriented provisions. In the present case the purchase contract was a typical standardized finely printed form, focused practically in its entirety upon the interests of the seller and its intended assignee. Little remained to be done but to describe the stereo record player and to fix the price and terms of installment payment by filling in the blanks. Even as to the matter inserted in the blanks, it cannot be said that there was any real bargaining; the seller fixed the price of the albums, and, as we shall see, the plaintiff Unico as the financer for Universal established the maximum length of the installment payment period under its contract with Universal. The ordinary consumer goods purchaser more often than not does not read the fine print; if he did it is unlikely that he would understand the legal jargon, and the significance of the clauses is not explained to him. This is not to say that all such contracts of adhesion are unfair or constitute imposition. But many of them are, and the judicial branch of the government within its sphere of operation in construing and applying such contracts must be responsive to equitable considerations. As the late Mr. Justice Frankfurter said in United States v. Bethlehem Steel Corp., 315 U.S. 289, 326, 62 S.Ct. 581, 599, 86 L.Ed. 855, 876 (1942):

> "But is there any principle which is more familiar or more firmly embedded in the history of Anglo–American law than the basic doctrine that the courts will not permit themselves to be used as instruments of inequity and injustice? Does any principle in our law have more universal application than the doctrine that courts will not enforce transactions in which the relative positions of the parties are such that one has unconscionably taken advantage of the necessities of the other?"

And see, Henningsen v. Bloomfield Motors, 32 N.J. at 388, 390, 161 A.2d 69; 1 Corbin on Contracts, § 128 (1963). Just as the community has an interest in insuring (usually by means of the legislative process) that credit financing contracts facilitating sales of consumer goods conform to community-imposed standards of fairness and decency, so too the courts, in the absence of controlling legislation, in applying the adjudicatory process must endeavor, whenever reasonably possible, to impose those same standards on principles of equity and public policy. An initial step in that direction of unquestioned need, and fortunately of common judicial acceptance, is the view that consumer goods contracts and their concurrent financing arrangements should be construed most strictly against the seller who imposed the contract on the buyer, and against the finance company which participated in the transaction, directly or indirectly, or was aware of the nature of the seller's consumer goods sales and installment payment operation.

The courts have recognized that the basic problem in consumer goods sales and financing is that of balancing the interest of the commercial community in unrestricted negotiability of commercial paper against the interest of installment buyers of such goods in the preservation of their normal remedy of withholding payment when, as in this case, the seller fails to deliver as agreed, and thus the consideration for his obligation fails.

Many courts have solved the problem by denying to the holder of the paper the status of holder in due course where the financer maintains a close relationship with the dealer whose paper he buys; where the financer is closely connected with the dealer's business operations or with the particular credit transaction; or where the financer furnishes the form of sale contract and note for use by the dealer, the buyer signs the contract and note concurrently, and the dealer endorses the note and assigns the contract immediately thereafter or within the period prescribed by the financer. * * * Other courts have said that when the financer supplies or prescribes or approves the form of sales contract, or conditional sale agreement, or chattel mortgage as well as the installment payment note (particularly if it has the financer's name printed on the face or in the endorsement), and all the documents are executed by the buyer at one time and the contract assigned and note endorsed to the financer and delivered to the financer together (whether or not attached or part of a single instrument), the holder takes subject to the rights and obligations of the seller. The transaction is looked upon as a species of tripartite proceeding, and the tenor of the cases is that the financer should not be permitted "to isolate itself behind the fictional fence" of the Negotiable Instruments Law, and thereby achieve an unfair advantage over the buyer * * *.

Before looking at the particular circumstances of the above cases, it seems advisable to examine into the relationship between Universal and the financer Unico.

Unico is a partnership formed expressly for the purpose of financing Universal Stereo Corporation, and Universal agreed to pay all costs up to a fixed amount in connection with Unico's formation. The elaborate contract between them, dated August 24, 1962, recited that Universal was engaged in the merchandising of records and stereophonic sets, and that it desired to borrow money from time to time from Unico, "secured by the assignment of accounts receivable, promissory notes, trade acceptances, conditional sales contracts, chattel mortgages, leases, installment contracts, or other forms of agreement evidencing liens." Subject to conditions set out in the agreement, Unico agreed to lend Universal up to 35% of the total amount of the balances of customers' contracts assigned to Unico subject to a limit of $50,000, in return for which Universal submitted to a substantial degree of control of its entire business operation by the lender. As collateral security for the loans, Universal agreed to negotiate "to the lender" all customers' notes listed in a monthly schedule of new sales contracts, and to assign all conditional sale contracts connected with the notes, as well as the right to any monies due from customers.

Specific credit qualifications for Universal's record album customers were imposed by Unico; requirements for the making of the notes and their endorsement were established, and the sale contracts had to be recorded in the county recording office. All such contracts were required to meet the standards of the agreement between lender and borrower, among them being that the customer's installment payment term would not exceed 36 months and "every term" of the Unico–Universal agreement was to "be deemed incorporated into all assignments'' of record sales contracts delivered as security for the loans. It was further agreed that Unico should have all the rights of Universal under the contracts as if it were the seller, including the right to enforce them in its name, and Unico was given an irrevocable power to enforce such rights.

In the event of Universal's default on payment of its loans, Unico was authorized to deal directly with the record buyers with respect to payment of their notes and to settle with and discharge such customers. Unico was empowered to place its representatives on Universal's premises with full authority to take possession of the books and records; or otherwise, it could inspect the records at any time; and it was given a "special property interest" in such records. Financial statements were required to be submitted by Universal "at least semiannually"; and two partners of Unico were to be paid one-quarter of one per cent interest on the loans as a management service charge, in addition to the interest to be paid Unico. Significant also in connection with the right to oversee Universal's business is a warranty included in the contract. It warrants that Universal owns free and clear "all merchandise referred to and described in [the sales] contracts, * * * at the time of making the sale creating such contracts." Obviously this was not the fact, otherwise Universal would not have discontinued shipping records to its customers, such as Owen. If Universal did not have such a store of records, as warranted, Unico might well have had reason to suspect its borrower's financial stability.

This general outline of the Universal–Unico financing agreement serves as evidence that Unico not only had a thorough knowledge of the nature and method of operation of Universal's business, but also exercised extensive control over it. Moreover, obviously it had a large, if not decisive, hand in the fashioning and supplying of the form of contract and note used by Universal, and particularly in setting the terms of the record album sales agreement, which were designed to put the buyer-consumer in an unfair and burdensome legal strait jacket and to bar any escape no matter what the default of the seller, while permitting the note-holder, contract-assignee to force payment from him by enveloping itself in the formal status of holder in due course. To say the relationship between Unico and the business operations of Universal was close, and that Unico was involved therein, is to put it mildly. There is no case in New Jersey dealing with the contention that the holder of a consumer goods buyer's note in purchasing it did not meet the test of good faith negotiation because the connection between the seller and the financer was as intimate as in this case. * * *

There is a conflict of authority in other jurisdictions (Annotation, 44 A.L.R.2d 8 (1955)), but we are impelled for reasons of equity and justice to join those courts which deny holder in due course status in consumer goods sales cases to those financers whose involvement with the seller's business is as close, and whose knowledge of the extrinsic factors—i.e., the terms of the underlying sale agreement—is as pervasive, as it is in the present case. Their reasoning is particularly persuasive in this case because of the unusual executory character of the seller's obligation to furnish the consideration for the buyer's undertaking.

In Commercial Credit Corp. v. Orange County Mach. Wks., 34 Cal.2d 776, 214 P.2d 819 (1950), Machine Works was in the market for a press. Ermac Company knew of one which could be purchased from General American Precooling Corporation for $5000, and offered to sell it to Machine Works for $5500. Commercial Credit was consulted by Ermac, and agreed to finance the transaction by taking an assignment of the contract of sale between Ermac and Machine Works. For a substantial period before this time, Ermac had obtained similar financing from Commercial Credit and had some blank forms supplied to it by the latter. By a contract written on one of these forms, which was entitled "Industrial Conditional Sales Contract," Ermac agreed to sell and Machine Works bound itself to purchase the press.

The terms of the contract were very much like those in the case now before us. The purchase price was to be paid in 12 equal monthly installments, "evidenced by my note of even date to your order." As to the note, the contract said:

> "Said note is a negotiable instrument, separate and apart from this contract, even though at the time of execution it may be temporarily attached hereto by perforation or otherwise."

It provided also, as in our case:

> "This contract may be assigned and/or said note may be negotiated without notice to me and when assigned and/or negotiated shall be free from any defense, counterclaim or cross complaint by me."

The note originally was the latter part of the printed form of contract, but could be detached from it at a dotted or perforated line.

Machine Works made the required down payment to Ermac, which in turn under its contract with Commercial assigned the contract and endorsed the note to the latter. Commercial then gave its check to Ermac for $4261. Ermac sent its check to Precooling Corporation, which refused to deliver the press to Machine Works when the check was dishonored. Commercial sued Machine Works as a holder in due course of its note to Ermac. Machine Works contended Commercial was not entitled to the status of such a holder because the sales contract and attached note should be construed as constituting a single document. Machine Works contended also that the finance company was a party to the original transaction rather than a subsequent purchaser, that it took subject to all equities and defenses existing in its favor against Ermac, and that the claimed negotiability of the note was destroyed when it and the conditional sales agreement were transferred together as one instrument.

The Supreme Court of California said the fact that the contract and note were physically attached at the time of transfer to Commercial would not alone defeat negotiability. But the court pointed out that Commercial advanced money to Ermac (with which it had dealt previously and whose "credit had been checked and financial integrity demonstrated"), with the understanding that the agreement and note would be assigned and endorsed to it immediately; and that "[i]n a very real sense, the finance company was a moving force in the transaction from its very inception, and acted as a party to it." In deciding against Commercial, the court said:

> "When a finance company actively participates in a transaction of this type from its inception, counseling and aiding the future vendor-payee, it cannot be regarded as a holder in due course of the note given in the transaction and the defense of failure of consideration may properly be maintained. Machine Works never obtained the press for which it bargained and, as against Commercial, there is no more obligation upon it to pay the note than there is to pay the installments specified in the contract."

In the case before us Unico was brought into existence to finance all Universal's sales contracts, and it was a major factor in establishing the terms upon which the financing and installment payment of the resulting notes and installment delivery of the record albums were to be engaged in. As in the case just cited, it too was "in a very real sense" a party not only to the Owen contract, but to all others similarly procured by Universal.

* * *

The *Martin* case, decided by the Supreme Court of Florida, is frequently cited by the courts of other states. Martin purchased a deep freezer and meat saw from an appliance dealer on an installment payment conditional sale agreement. He executed the agreement and a note (attached thereto by perforations) for payment of the balance due in monthly installments. On the following day the sale agreement and note were assigned and endorsed respectively to the plaintiff-finance company. The freezer turned out to be an outmoded model and otherwise totally unfit for Martin's purposes, and when neither the dealer nor the financer remedied the defects he declined to make further payments on the note.

The finance company prepared and furnished to the dealer the printed forms of conditional sale agreement and promissory note employed in the transaction. The forms designated the financer as the specific assignee of the contract and note; its office was designated as the place of payment of the note installments; it investigated and approved Martin's credit, agreed to purchase his contract and note, and by written assignment took the contract and note contemporaneously from the dealer.

In deciding that the finance company was not a holder in due course, the court declared it saw no reason why the concurrent execution of such a contract along with a promissory note, whether the note is a separate piece of paper or is attached to the contract by perforations, of itself should in any way affect "any of the characteristics of the note which give it commercial value." But, referring to the conflicting decisions in various states, it said that in situations such as the one before it, the better rule is that the note and the contract should be considered as one instrument. It approved the language of the Arkansas Supreme Court in Commercial Credit Co. v. Childs, supra, to the effect that the financer was so closely connected with the entire transaction that it could not be heard to say that it, in good faith, was an innocent purchaser for value; rather, to all intents and purposes it was a party to the agreement and instrument from the beginning.

The finance company in *Martin,* as in this case, contended that to deny it holder in due course status would seriously affect the mode of transacting business in Florida. In answer, the Court said:

> "It may be that our holding here will require some changes in business methods and will impose a greater burden on the finance companies. We think the buyer—Mr. & Mrs. General Public—should have some protection somewhere along the line. We believe the finance company is better able to bear the risk of the dealer's insolvency than the buyer and in a far better position to protect his interests against unscrupulous and insolvent dealers." 63 So.2d at p. 653.

In our judgment the views expressed in the cited cases provide the sound solution for the problem under consideration. Under the facts of our case the relationship between Unico and Universal, and the nature of Unico's participation in Universal's contractual arrangements with its customers, if anything are closer and more active than in any of those cases, and in justice Unico should not be deemed a holder in due course of the Owen note. Adoption of such a rule is consistent in theory with the Court of Errors and Appeals' holding in General Contract etc. Corp. v. Moon Carrier Corp., 129 N.J.L. 431, 435, 29 A.2d 843 (E. & A.1943), where it was said that where a note refers to or is accompanied by a collateral contemporaneous agreement, or the purchaser has actual knowledge of the collateral agreement, he takes subject to its contents and conditions. Moreover, although as we have already noted, the Uniform Commercial Code is not applicable because its effective date was subsequent to Owen's note, the principle we now espouse is consistent with § 3–119 thereof. That section provides that:

> "As between the obligor and his immediate obligee or any transferee the terms of an instrument may be modified or affected by any other written agreement executed as a part of the same transaction, except that a holder in due course is not affected by any limitation of his rights arising out of the separate written agreement if he had no notice of the limitation when he took the instrument."

For purposes of consumer goods transactions, we hold that where the seller's performance is executory in character and when it appears from the totality of the arrangements between dealer and financer that the financer has had a substantial voice in setting standards for the underlying transaction, or has approved the standards established by the dealer, and has agreed to take all or a predetermined or substantial quantity of the negotiable paper which is backed by such standards, the financer should be considered a participant in the original transaction and therefore not entitled to holder in due course status. We reserve specifically the question whether, when the buyer's claim is breach of warranty as distinguished from failure of consideration, the seller's default as to the former may be raised as a defense against the financer. Cf. Eastern Acceptance Corp. v. Kavlick, 10 N.J.Super. 253, 77 A.2d 49 (App.Div.1950).

II.

Plaintiff argues that even if it cannot be considered a holder in due course of Owen's note, it is entitled to recover regardless of the failure of consideration on the part of Universal, because of the so-called waiver of defenses or estoppel clause contained in the sale contract. The clause says:

> "Buyer hereby acknowledges notice that this contract may be assigned and that assignees will rely upon the agreements contained in this paragraph, and agrees that the liability of the Buyer to any assignee shall be immediate and absolute and not affected by any default whatsoever of the Seller signing this contract; and in order to induce assignees to purchase this contract, the Buyer further agrees not to set up any claim against such Seller as a defense, counterclaim or offset to any action by any assignee for the unpaid balance of the purchase price or for possession of the property."

This provision is the fifth of 11 fine print paragraphs on the reverse side of the sale contract. The type is the same as in the other clauses; there is no emphasis put on it in the context, and there is no evidence that it was in any way brought to Owen's attention or its significance explained to him. But regardless, we consider that the clause is an unfair imposition on a consumer goods purchaser and is contrary to public policy.

The plain attempt and purpose of the waiver is to invest the sale agreement with the type of negotiability which under the Negotiable Instruments Law would have made the holder of a negotiable promissory note a holder in due course and entitled to recover regardless of the seller-payee's default.

In our judgment such a clause in consumer goods conditional sale contracts, chattel mortgages, and other instruments of like character is void as against public policy for three reasons: (1) it is opposed to the policy of the Negotiable Instruments Law which had established the controlling prerequisites for negotiability, and provided also that the rights of one not a holder in due course were subject to all legal defenses which the maker of the instrument had against the transferor. § 58; (2) it is opposed to the spirit of N.J.S. 2A:25–1, N.J.S.A., which provides that an obligor sued by an assignee "shall be allowed * * * all * * * defenses he had against the assignor or his representatives before notice of such assignment was given to him." (It is conceded here that plaintiff gave no notice of the assignment to defendant); and (3) the policy of our state is to protect conditional vendees against imposition by conditional vendors and installment sellers.

Section 9–206(1) of the Uniform Commercial Code (Secured Transactions) deals with this problem. It provides:

> "Subject to any statute or decision which establishes a different rule for buyers of *consumer goods,* an agreement by a buyer that he will not assert against an assignee any claim or defense which he may have against the seller is enforceable by an assignee who takes his assign-

ment for value, in good faith and without notice of a claim or defense, except as to defenses of a type which may be asserted against a holder in due course of a negotiable instrument under the Chapter on Commercial Paper (Chapter 3). A buyer who as part of one transaction signs both a negotiable instrument and a security agreement makes such an agreement." (Emphasis ours).

In this section of the Code, the Legislature recognized the possibility of need for special treatment of waiver clauses in consumer goods contracts. Such contracts, particularly those of the type involved in this case, are so fraught with opportunities for misuse that the purchasers must be protected against oppressive and unconscionable clauses. And section 9–206 in the area of consumer goods sales must as a matter of policy be deemed closely linked with section 2–302 which authorizes a court to refuse to enforce any clause in a contract of sale which it finds is unconscionable. We see in the enactment of these two sections of the Code an intention to leave in the hands of the courts the continued application of common law principles in deciding in consumer goods cases whether such waiver clauses as the one imposed on Owen in this case are so one-sided as to be contrary to public policy. Cf. Williams v. Walker–Thomas Furniture Co., 121 U.S.App.D.C. 315, 350 F.2d 445, 448–449 (1965). For reasons already expressed, we hold that they are so opposed to such policy as to require condemnation. As the New Jersey Study Comment to section 2–302 indicates, the practice of denying relief because of unconscionable circumstances has long been the rule in this state. * * *

For the reasons stated, we hold the waiver clause unenforceable and invalid against Owen.

III.

We agree with the result reached in the tribunals below. Plaintiff offered no proof in the trial court to show that the value of the 12 albums Owen received before breach of the contract by Universal, together with that of the record player at the time of the breach (assuming its value was material in view of the seller's representation that there was to be no charge for it), was in excess of the $303.24 paid by Owen under the contract. Moreover, there has been no suggestion throughout this proceeding that plaintiff is entitled to a partial recovery on the note in its capacity as an assignee thereof. Accordingly, the judgment for the defendant is affirmed.

NOTE

Cases such as *Unico* are given effect under revised Article 3. § 3–302(g) and Comment 7 to § 3–302.

c. THE LEGISLATIVE RESPONSE

Consumer Credit Sales

By the early 1960s the handwriting was on the wall with respect to the judicial enforceability of notes against consumers who had valid defenses.

One way or another, courts allowed consumers to assert their defenses. Indeed, many creditors had long since given up the use of negotiable instruments and contract clauses cutting off defenses upon assignment. Nevertheless, the issue of negotiability occupied more time and caused more rancor in the drafting of the Uniform Consumer Credit Code (1964–74) than any other issue. Creditor representatives saw negotiability as an issue of freedom of contract and wanted the UCCC to turn back the clock. To consumer advocates negotiability was a symbol of creditor overreaching, and they saw the UCCC as the instrumentality for finally driving a stake through the heart of negotiability in consumer cases. As we see below, the consumers won, but not before years of wrangling and equivocation. While these bitter debates were going on as late as the early 1970s, consumer credit was being revolutionized by the growth of the bank credit card which, in all but the largest consumer purchases, replaced promissory notes and rendered the negotiability issue irrelevant.

Consumer credit sales are regulated in most states by statute. Most states have taken the position that the holder in due course doctrine should be abrogated with respect to notes given by buyers to sellers of consumer goods or services. One approach taken is to prohibit the taking of a negotiable note from the buyer and to invalidate waiver of defenses clauses in the installment sale contract. The Uniform Consumer Credit Code, in effect in 11 jurisdictions, is an example of this kind of legislation. The 1974 Official Text provides as follows:

Section 3.307 [Certain Negotiable Instruments Prohibited]

With respect to a consumer credit sale or consumer lease, [except a sale or lease primarily for an agricultural purpose,] the creditor may not take a negotiable instrument other than a check dated not later than ten days after its issuance as evidence of the obligation of the consumer.

Section 3.404 [Assignee Subject to Claims and Defenses]

(1) With respect to a consumer credit sale or consumer lease [, except one primarily for an agricultural purpose], an assignee of the rights of the seller or lessor is subject to all claims and defenses of the consumer against the seller or lessor arising from the sale or lease of property or services, notwithstanding that the assignee is a holder in due course of a negotiable instrument issued in violation of the provisions prohibiting certain negotiable instruments (Section 3.307).

(2) A claim or defense of a consumer specified in subsection (1) may be asserted against the assignee under this section only if the consumer has made a good faith attempt to obtain satisfaction from the seller or lessor with respect to the claim or defense and then only to the extent of the amount owing to the assignee with respect to the sale or lease of the property or services as to which the claim or defense arose at the time the assignee has notice of the claim or defense. Notice of the claim or defense may be given before the attempt

specified in this subsection. Oral notice is effective unless the assignee requests written confirmation when or promptly after oral notice is given and the consumer fails to give the assignee written confirmation within the period of time, not less than 14 days, stated to the consumer when written confirmation is requested.

* * *

(4) An agreement may not limit or waive the claims or defenses of a consumer under this section.

The Federal Trade Commission has promulgated rules (16 C.F.R. Part 433—Preservation of Consumers' Claims and Defenses) designed to prevent the use of the holder-in-due-course doctrine in sales of consumer goods or services. The rules also apply to leases of consumer goods. References to "seller" also include a lessor. Any "consumer credit contract," a term which includes a promissory note, arising out of such a sale or lease must contain a bold-faced legend stating in effect that any holder of the contract is subject to all claims and defenses that the debtor has against the seller of the goods or services. The effect of the legend is to cause any assignee of the note or sales contract to take subject to the buyer's claims and defenses against the seller. Failure by a seller to include the legend is an unfair or deceptive act or practice under Section 5 of the Federal Trade Commission Act. Under that Act, the seller is subject to a civil suit by the FTC in which the court may "grant such relief as the court finds necessary to redress injury to consumers * * * resulting from the rule violation * * *. Such relief may include, but shall not be limited to, rescission or reformation of contracts, the refund of money or return of property, the payment of damages, and public notification respecting the rule violation * * * except that nothing in this subsection is intended to authorize the imposition of any exemplary or punitive damages." 15 U.S.C. § 57b(a)(1) and (b). Under revised Article 3, a promissory note bearing the FTC legend can be a negotiable instrument if it otherwise complies with § 3–104(a) but there cannot be a holder in due course of the note. § 3–106(d) and Comment 3 to § 3–106.

[handwritten margin note: FTC legend / doesn't work w/ direct loans (direct loan exception)]

Purchase Money Loans

Under traditional law, a financer who loans money directly to a debtor for the purpose of buying goods or services is not subject to claims or defenses the buyer may have against the seller. However, the purchase money loan transaction bears a close functional resemblance to the assigned paper transaction discussed above. In both cases the seller desires to be paid as soon as possible; the buyer has no cash to pay; and the financer is willing to provide the money. In the purchase money loan, the financer makes a direct loan to the buyer; in the assigned paper case, the financer buys the buyer's credit contract from the seller. Customs differ among the states: in some, consumer goods financing is done by purchase money loans, but in most the assigned-paper transaction predominates.

If financers are subject to consumer defenses in assigned-paper trans-actions, incentive is present to convert to purchase money loans to free financers of consumer defenses. By the latter part of the 1960s consumer representatives began to advocate subjecting purchase money lenders to consumer claims and defenses in situations in which there was a sufficiently close relationship between the seller and the lender to warrant doing so. But how close must this relation be? The task of defining the requisite relationship has been difficult.

Under the FTC rule referred to above the seller is guilty of an unfair or deceptive act if it accepts the proceeds of a purchase money loan (§ 433.2(b)) unless the loan agreement between the debtor and the pur-chase money lender contains the requisite notice. If the loan agreement contains the notice, the lender thereby subjects itself to defenses arising out of the sale. Section 433.1(d) defines purchase money loan to include two cases: (1) the seller refers the buyer to the lender, or (2) the seller is affiliated with the lender by common control, contract or business arrange-ment (defined in Section 433.1(f) as "any understanding, procedure, course of dealing, or arrangement, formal or informal, between a creditor and a seller, in connection with the sale of goods or services to consumers or the financing thereof"). It is not at all clear what constitutes affiliation by business arrangement. In the very common case of the secured loan the loan is made for a particular purpose and the lender will be aware that a particular seller is involved in the transaction, but, without more, this should not mean that the lender's right to repayment is subject to any defenses that the borrower has against the seller. There is no problem in the case in which the seller steers the buyer to the lender or the case in which the lender will make loans only if the proceeds are used to purchase from the particular seller. Suppose the buyer of an automobile from a dealer shows that the lender has made numerous loans to borrowers who used the proceeds to purchase automobiles from the same dealer. Have the lender and the dealer become affiliated by an informal course of dealing? Must the seller in each case inquire about the buyer's source of funds to determine whether the required legend was required and was in fact made? 2 White & Summers, Uniform Commercial Code § 17–9 b. (4th prac.ed. 1995).

Compare the following provision of the Uniform Consumer Credit Code (1974 Official Text) dealing with the same problem.

Section 3.405 *[Lender Subject to Claims and Defenses Arising from Sales and Leases]*

(1) A lender, except the issuer of a lender credit card, who, with respect to a particular transaction, makes a consumer loan to enable a consumer to buy or lease from a particular seller or lessor property or services [, except primarily for an agricultural purpose,] is subject to all claims and defenses of the consumer against the seller or lessor arising from that sale or lease of the property or services if:

(a) the lender knows that the seller or lessor arranged for the extension of credit by the lender for a commission, brokerage, or referral fee;

(b) the lender is a person related to the seller or lessor, unless the relationship is remote or is not a factor in the transaction;

(c) the seller or lessor guarantees the loan or otherwise assumes the risk of loss by the lender upon the loan;

(d) the lender directly supplies the seller or lessor with the contract document used by the consumer to evidence the loan, and the seller or lessor has knowledge of the credit terms and participates in preparation of the document;

(e) the loan is conditioned upon the consumer's purchase or lease of the property or services from the particular seller or lessor, but the lender's payment of proceeds of the loan to the seller or lessor does not in itself establish that the loan was so conditioned; or

(f) the lender, before he makes the consumer loan, has knowledge or, from his course of dealing with the particular seller or lessor or his records, notice of substantial complaints by other buyers or lessees of the particular seller's or lessor's failure or refusal to perform his contracts with them and of the particular seller's or lessor's failure to remedy his defaults within a reasonable time after notice to him of the complaints.

* * *

4.   PAYEE AS HOLDER IN DUE COURSE

We don't usually think of a payee as being a holder in due course because the defenses that a maker or drawer raises are commonly based on the conduct of the payee such as fraud, misrepresentation, lack of consideration and the like. Since the payee perpetrated these wrongs on the obligor, the payee can hardly qualify as one who takes the instrument in good faith and without knowledge of the defense. But there are a few situations in which a payee should be allowed holder-in-due-course status; these involve more than two parties. Old § 3–302(2) expressly stated: "A payee may be a holder in due course." This provision was omitted in the revision of Article 3. Comment 4 to § 3–302 states: "Former Section 3–302(2) has been omitted in revised Article 3 because it is surplusage and may be misleading. The payee of an instrument can be a holder in due course, but use of the holder-in-due-course doctrine by the payee of an instrument is not the normal situation." We will look at two situations, one involving recoupment and one a defense.

Recoupment. Seller (S) sold goods to Buyer (B). B issued a promissory note payable to the order of S to evidence B's obligation to pay for the goods. At the time S took the note, it had no reason to believe that there were any defects in the goods. Later it was clear that the goods were defective and that B had a claim in recoupment against S for breach of warranty. S sued B on the note claiming that it had been in good faith at the time the note was taken and had no reason to believe at that time that there was anything wrong with the goods, and, therefore, was a holder in due course. It would be absurd in this case to allow S to take free of B's claim based on breach of warranty on the ground that S was a holder in due course. Section 3–305(b) states that a the right of a holder in due course to enforce an obligation is not subject to "claims in recoupment * * * against a person other than the holder." Here the claim of recoupment can be asserted because it is against the holder. Comment 3 to § 3–305 states: "It is obvious that the holder-in-due-course doctrine cannot be used to allow Seller to cut off a warranty claim that Buyer has against Seller."

Defenses. In Kane v. Kroll, 196 Wis.2d 389, 538 N.W.2d 605 (Wis.App. 1995), the facts, somewhat altered, were these. Seller (S) sold cows to Buyer (B) on credit. B induced his Mother (M) to pay his debt to S by falsely representing to her that he was about to sell enough hay to come up with the money. M wrote a check to S for the debt. The next day B disclosed his fraud to M and she promptly stopped payment on the check. When S presented the check to the drawee bank it was dishonored because of the stop order. S sued M on the check, claiming to be a holder in due course because S had no reason to know of the fraud that B had perpetrated on M.

(1) Under the old law we would need more facts to decide the case. Old § 3–305(2) provided that a holder in due course "takes the instrument free from all defenses of any party to the instrument with whom the holder has not dealt." Thus if M had given the check to B and B had delivered the check to S, S would be a holder in due course because there were no dealings with M. But if M had delivered the check to S, S would most likely not be a holder in due course because S had dealt with M. This distinction makes no sense; in both cases S knew nothing of B's fraud on M. Why make a distinction based on such an irrelevant fact (i.e., which party handed the check to S) determinative of S's status as a holder in due course?

(2) Under revised Article 3, the language in old § 3–305(2) is deleted. Comment 2 to § 3–305 explains: "The meaning of this language was not at all clear and if read literally could have produced the wrong result." Examples of cases in which payees may be holders in due course are set out in Comment 4 to § 3–302. Case #1 is comparable to *Kane.* Comment 2 to § 3–305 concludes: "The [holder-in-due-course] doctrine applies only to cases in which more than two parties are involved. Its essence is that the holder in due course does not have to suffer the consequences of a defense of the obligor on the instrument that arose from an occurrence with a third party." Although it is quite clear from the comments to §§ 3–302 and 3–305 that payees can be holders in due course in three-party transactions coming within the ambit of the language quoted in the previous sentence, it is not so clear whether Article 3 offers specific guidance on cases in which payees cannot become holders in due course, other than the general rule

that a taker with notice of a defense cannot qualify as a holder in due course. Comment 2 to § 3–305 says that the "with whom the holder has not dealt" language of old § 3–305(2) was dropped because "It is not necessary." White & Summers, Uniform Commercial Code § 14–9 (4th ed. 1995), contends that § 3–305(b) serves the function of determining when payees cannot become holders in due course. It provides that the rights of a holder in due course are not subject "to defenses of the obligor stated in subsection (a)(2) or claims in recoupment stated in subsection (a)(3) against a person other than the holder." If the "against" clause at the end of the section applies to defenses as well as recoupment, the implication is that even if the payee is a holder in due course that person cannot take free of the defenses that a maker or drawer has against the payee-holder. This interpretation gives a sensible result, but nowhere do the voluminous comments to §§ 3–302 and 3–305 refer to the "against" clause as applying in any case but recoupment.

5.   TRANSACTIONS WITH FIDUCIARIES

Under § 3–306 a holder in due course of an instrument takes free of "a claim of a property or possessory right in the instrument or its proceeds." For example, a claim to the instrument or its proceeds may arise if a fiduciary, in breach of fiduciary duty, negotiates the instrument for value. The negotiation of the instrument may be the means used by the fiduciary to misappropriate funds of the person to whom the fiduciary duty is owed. The claim of that person falls within the language of § 3–306. Under § 3–302(a)(2), the person to whom the instrument is negotiated cannot be a holder in due course if the instrument was taken with notice of the claim. Section 3–307 governs cases of negotiation of instruments in breach of fiduciary duty. It states rules for determining when the person taking the instrument has notice of breach of fiduciary duty. It also states that notice of breach of fiduciary duty is notice of the claim of the person to whom the fiduciary duty was owed. Consider how the following case would have been decided if revised Article 3 had been in effect when the transactions occurred.

Smith v. Olympic Bank

Supreme Court of Washington, 1985.
103 Wn.2d 418, 693 P.2d 92.

■ DORE, JUSTICE.

We hold that, where a bank allows a check that is made payable to a guardian to be deposited in a guardian's personal account instead of a guardianship account, the bank is not a holder in due course under the Uniform Commercial Code (UCC) because it has notice that the guardian is breaching his fiduciary duty.

Facts

Charles Alcombrack was appointed guardian for his son Chad Stephen Alcombrack who was then 7 years old and the beneficiary of his grandfather's life insurance policy. The insurance company issued a check for $30,588.39 made payable to "Charles Alcombrack, Guardian of the Estate of Chad Stephen Alcombrack a Minor". The attorney for the son's estate directed the father to take the check, along with the letters of guardianship issued to the father, to the bank and open up a guardianship savings and checking account. The father, however, did not follow the attorney's instructions. Instead, he took the check, without the letters of guardianship, to the bank and opened a personal checking and a personal savings account. The following was printed on the back of the check:

> By endorsement of this check the payee acknowledges receipt of the amount thereof in full settlement of all claims resulting from the death of Roy Alcombrack, certificate holder under Group Life Policy No. 9,745,632

/s/ Charles Alcombrack

Guardian of the Estate of Chad Stephen Alcombrack, a minor

Despite the above written notice that the check was payable to the father in his guardianship capacity, the bank allowed the father to place the entire amount in newly opened personal accounts. On the same day that the father opened his accounts, the attorney for the guardian called a trust officer from Olympic Bank and inquired as to the fees the bank charged for maintaining guardianship accounts. Responding to the attorney's questions, the trust officer wrote the attorney, specifically mentioning the "Estate of Chad Alcombrack".[1]

The father, and later his new wife, used all but $320.60 of the trust money for their own personal benefit. Bank records disclosed how the estate money was withdrawn: five withdrawals were made to cash or into the father's checking account (total—approximately $16,000); one withdrawal paid off an unsecured personal loan made by the bank to the father (approximately $3,000); seven debits to the account were made by the bank exercising its right of offset to make payments on or pay off personal loans by the bank to the father (total—approximately $12,500).

After the depletion of the son's estate, J. David Smith was appointed successor guardian. He received a judgment against the father and institut-

---

1. The following is the letter sent by the trust officer to the guardian's attorney:

"October 30, 1975

"Mr. Charles A. Schaaf, Attorney

"Reference: Estate of Chad Alcombrack

"Dear Mr. Schaaf:

"This is a follow up to our telephone conversation of October 28, 1975. The information you requested on the performance of our common trust funds will be available in about four weeks. October 31st is the end of our fiscal year. If this is not too long for you to wait, please let me know and I will send you a copy of our annual report.

"Our fee for handling a Guardianship account is, eight tenths (8⁄10) of one percent (1%), minimum of $350.00 per year."

ed this suit against the bank. The trial court granted summary judgment in favor of the bank. The Court of Appeals reversed and remanded, holding that the trial court should determine the factual issue whether the bank was a holder in due course.

Argument

Olympic Bank claims that it is a holder in due course (HIDC) and, as such, is not subject to the claims of the petitioner. In order to qualify as a HIDC, the bank must meet five requirements. It must be (1) a holder (2) of a negotiable instrument, (3) that took the instrument for value (4) in good faith and (5) without notice that it was overdue, dishonored, or of any defense or claim to it on the part of any person. * * * We need not decide whether the bank met the first four conditions as we hold that the bank took the check with notice of an adverse claim to the instrument and, therefore, is not a holder in due course. Consequently, the bank is liable to the petitioner.[4]

A purchaser has notice of an adverse claim when "he has knowledge that a fiduciary has negotiated the instrument in payment of or as security for his own debt or in any transaction for his own benefit or otherwise in breach of duty." UCC § 3–304(2). Thus, the issue raised by this case is whether the bank had knowledge that the guardian was breaching his fiduciary duty when it allowed him to deposit a check, made payable to him in his guardianship capacity, into his personal accounts. As to this issue, Von Gohren v. Pacific Nat'l Bank, 8 Wash.App. 245, 505 P.2d 467 (1973) is persuasive and controlling. In *Von Gohren*, it was held that a bank had notice that an employee was breaching her fiduciary duty when it allowed her to deposit third-party checks payable to her employer in her personal account. The bank was put on notice despite the fact that the employer had authorized the employee to draw checks against his account and also to endorse checks made payable to him and deposit such checks into his account. The court held that notice need not always consist of actual knowledge of a breach of a fiduciary duty, but can be predicated upon reasonable commercial standards. The court concluded by stating:

> It is our view that since defendant had notice of the claim by virtue of UCC § 3–304(2), and since it is undisputed that defendant did nothing to investigate Mrs. Martin's authority to negotiate checks payable to her employer, we must hold as a matter of law it did not act in accordance with reasonable commercial standards.

Von Gohren, at 255, 505 P.2d 467. The same conclusion is mandated in the present case.

---

4. UCC § 3–306 sets forth the liabilities of one who accepts a check and who is not a holder in due course.

"Unless he has the rights of a holder in due course any person takes the instrument subject to

"(a) all valid claims to it on the part of any person; and

"(b) all defenses of any party which would be available in an action on a simple contract; * * * "

Here, the bank knew it was dealing with guardianship funds. The check was payable to the father as guardian and not to him personally. The father endorsed it in his guardianship capacity. The bank received a call from the guardian's attorney inquiring about the fee the bank charged for guardianship accounts, and a trust officer for the bank replied in a letter referring to the "Estate of Chad Alcombrack".

Reasonable commercial practices dictate that when the bank knew that the funds were deposited in a personal account instead of a guardianship account, it also knew that the father was breaching his fiduciary duty. The funds lost the protection they would have received in a guardianship account when they were placed in a personal account. If the funds had been placed in a guardianship account, the bank would not have been allowed to exercise its set-off rights which amounted to approximately $12,500. * * * Nor would it have been permitted to accept a check, drawn on the guardianship account, from the father in satisfaction of the father's unsecured personal loan in the amount of approximately $3,000. Nor could the father, or bank, have authorized his new wife to write checks against the guardianship account without court approval. * * * A fiduciary has a duty to ensure that trust funds are protected. * * * Here, the father breached his duty.

While this is the first time, under the Uniform Commercial Code, that we have held a bank liable for allowing a guardian to deposit trust funds in a personal account, we have held a bank liable in a pre-Code case for allowing a trustee to breach his fiduciary duty. * * * In addition, other jurisdictions have held banks liable under similar circumstances using the Code * * * and without using the Code * * *. The policy reasons for holding a bank liable are compelling—especially in the situation presented in this case. The ward has no control of his own estate. He must rely on his guardian and on the bank for the safekeeping of his money. In order to protect the ward, the guardian and bank must be held to a high standard of care. For the guardian, this means that he must deposit guardian funds in a guardianship account. For the bank, it means that when it receives a check made payable to an individual as a guardian, it must make sure that the check is placed in a guardianship account. This will not place an undue burden on either banks or guardians and will have the beneficial effect of protecting the ward.

policy

* * *

NOTES

1. A view contrary to Smith v. Olympic Bank is expressed in Matter of Knox, 64 N.Y.2d 434, 488 N.Y.S.2d 146, 477 N.E.2d 448 (1985), a case also involving a father who was guardian of the property of a minor son. Robert, the son, was injured when he was four years old. An action brought on behalf of Robert for damages was settled and a check was issued to the father as guardian of the property of the son. The check was negotiated to a bank and $11,000 of the proceeds of the check was deposited in the personal account of the father in the bank. The amount deposited in the account was eventually spent in the purchase of a house for the family and for other family expenses. The family included three other children besides Robert and the parents. The family was impoverished and the father stated that the money was spent to "give Robert as well as the rest [of the family] the same kind of normal life that any family enjoys." Eventually an action was brought against the father by a guardian ad litem appointed for Robert to recover the funds that had been misappropriated by the father. The bank was joined in the action and the trial court entered judgment against both. The bank appealed and the Appellate Division reversed the judgment against the bank. In affirming the Appellate Division, the Court of Appeals, one judge dissenting, stated:

> In Bradford Trust Co. v. Citibank, 60 N.Y.2d 868, 470 N.Y.S.2d 361, 458 N.E.2d 820, we held that "there is no requirement that a check payable to a fiduciary be deposited to a fiduciary account, and the fact that the instrument was not so deposited may not, without more, be relied upon as establishing a wrongful payment on the part of the depositary bank" * * *. Our decision was grounded upon the Uniform Commercial Code which provides that "[a]n instrument made payable to a named person with the addition of words describing him * * * as [a] fiduciary for a specified person or purpose is payable to the payee and may be negotiated, discharged or enforced by him" (Uniform Commercial Code § 3–117[b]), and that mere knowledge that the "person negotiating the instrument is or was a fiduciary" does not of itself give the purchaser of a negotiable instrument notice of any claims or defenses (Uniform Commercial Code § 3–304[4][e]). The conduct with which [the bank] is charged—having negotiated a check payable to [the father] in a fiduciary capacity without requiring deposit of the check in a fiduciary account—is thus permissible.

> In general, a bank may assume that a person acting as a fiduciary will apply entrusted funds to the proper purposes and will adhere to the conditions of the appointment * * *. A bank is not in the normal course required to conduct an investigation to protect funds from possible misappropriation by a fiduciary, unless there are facts—not here present—indicating misappropriation * * *. In this event, a bank may be liable for participation in the diversion, either by itself acquiring a benefit, or by notice or knowledge that a diversion is intended or being executed * * *. No facts are before this court suggesting that [the bank] had notice that [the father] intended to, or did in fact, use the settlement proceeds for improper purposes. Consequently, [the bank] cannot be charged with the misappropriation.

2. When the National Conference approved the final draft of revised Article 3, the Commissioners did so knowing that § 3–307 took positions contrary to those of another uniform act, the Uniform Fiduciaries Act, that had been promulgated by the National Conference in the 1920s and adopted in about half of the states. The inconsistency between the two acts was before the court in County of Macon v. Edgcomb, 274 Ill.App.3d 432,

211 Ill.Dec. 136, 654 N.E.2d 598 (Ill.App.1995), in which a county treasurer, Edgcomb, embezzled over $400,000 in county funds by stealing checks made to the county, endorsing them and depositing them in his personal account in Bank. Under UFA § 9, Bank had no liability in the absence of knowledge of the breach of fiduciary obligation or bad faith, but under § 3–307(b)(2) Bank would be liable. Conceding that when choosing between conflicting statutes the more recent enactment will prevail as the later expression of legislative intent, the court applied the UFA to the case because revised Article 3 was not in effect at the time of the embezzlement and amendatory acts should be construed as prospective unless the act indicates otherwise. The National Conference has issued an "Addendum to Revised Article 3, Notes to Legislative Counsel. * * * 2. If revised Article 3 is adopted in your state and the Uniform Fiduciaries Act is also in effect in your state, you may want to consider amending Uniform Fiduciaries Act § 9 to conform to Section 3–307(b)(2)(iii) and (4)(iii). See Official Comment 3 to Section 3–307."

PROBLEM

Little Corporation has about 100 stockholders and conducts its manufacturing operations in Centerville, a small city. Little has a checking account in Centerville Bank. The agreement between Little and the bank provides that the bank is authorized to honor checks drawn on the account if signed in the name of Little by either the president or treasurer of Little. Della, the president of Little, was involved in the following transactions:

Case # 1. Della's personal credit card was used to pay for automobile rentals, restaurant meals, and hotel accommodations. All of the credit card charges were incurred for her personal benefit and were not related to any business purpose of Little. Della wrote a check drawn on Little's checking account and sent it to the issuer of the credit card to pay the monthly bill that included the charges.

Case # 2. Della bought a small but expensive rug from Merchant and paid for it by writing a check drawn on Little's checking account. The rug was delivered to Della at the store.

Case # 3. Della went to Clothier's store and ordered several dresses that were to be custom made for her. Della paid by writing a check drawn on Little's checking account. Before accepting the check, Clothier asked her why a check of the corporation was being used to pay for the clothing. She answered, "The dresses are a present from a grateful employer for five years of faithful service by yours truly."

Case # 4. Della wrote a $1,000 check drawn on Little's account payable to her. She indorsed the check in blank and deposited it to her account in Depositary Bank by delivering it to a teller who knew her personally and knew that she was president of Little.

In each of the foregoing cases, Della committed a breach of fiduciary duty to Little in writing the check on Little's account. When Little discovered the defalcations it brought actions to recover the proceeds of the checks written by Della and paid from Little's account. The actions were brought against the issuer of the credit card in Case # 1, against Merchant in Case # 2, against Clothier in Case # 3, and against Centerville Bank in Case # 4. State your opinion whether Little is entitled to recover in each case. § 3–306, § 3–307, § 1–201(25) and (27), and Comment 2 to § 3–307.

6. THE FEDERAL HOLDER–IN–DUE–COURSE DOCTRINE

Section 3–302(c) provides that a person does not acquire rights as a holder in due course by purchasing instruments as "part of a bulk transfer not in ordinary course of business." However, in one familiar class of cases involving bulk transfers, the transferee may gain the rights of a holder in due course even though the transaction is clearly not in the ordinary course of business. This is the case in which the Federal Deposit Insurance Corporation takes over an insolvent bank. Here § 3–302(c) is preempted by federal law as explained in the following case. Comment 5 to § 3–302. The subject is extensively discussed in 2 White & Summers, Uniform Commercial Law § 17–13 (4th prac.ed.1995).

Campbell Leasing, Inc. v. Federal Deposit Insurance Corp.

United States Court of Appeals, Fifth Circuit, 1990.
901 F.2d 1244.

■ CLARK, CHIEF JUDGE:

I.

Appellants Campbell Leasing, Inc., Eagle Airlines, Inc., and George A. Day challenge the district court's entry of summary judgment on a promissory note in favor of the Federal Deposit Insurance Corporation (FDIC) and NCNB Texas National Bank (NCNB). We affirm in part, vacate in part, and remand for further proceedings.

II.

On February 16, 1984, Campbell Leasing, Inc. (Campbell Leasing) executed a promissory note in the amount of $136,804.24, plus interest, payable to RepublicBank Brownwood (RepublicBank). To secure payment of the note, Campbell Leasing granted RepublicBank a security interest in a 1979 Piper airplane. RepublicBank also obtained the personal guarantee of George A. Day (Day).

In May of 1986, Campbell Leasing defaulted on the note. RepublicBank accelerated the maturity of the note after Campbell Leasing failed to cure its default. On June 12, 1986, RepublicBank seized the airplane but did not gain possession of its maintenance records or flight logs. The seizure prompted appellants to file this lawsuit. RepublicBank counterclaimed for payment of the note, plus interest, costs, and attorneys' fees.

On July 29, 1988, the successor to RepublicBank, First RepublicBank Brownwood, N.A. (First RepublicBank), was declared insolvent and closed. The Comptroller of Currency appointed the FDIC as receiver. The FDIC entered into a purchase and assumption agreement with a federally established bridge bank, which purchased the promissory note, security agreement, and guarantee at issue in this case. The bridge bank became NCNB Texas National Bank.

In August of 1988, the FDIC and NCNB removed the case to federal court and filed a motion for summary judgment. The district court subsequently permitted the parties to amend their pleadings. In their amended complaint, the appellants asserted: (1) that prior to seizing the airplane RepublicBank had agreed to a novation wherein Tex–Star Airlines, Inc. (Tex–Star) executed a note to RepublicBank for the purchase of the plane, thereby relieving Campbell Leasing and Day of their obligations under the Campbell Leasing note; (2) that RepublicBank was guilty of trespass and conversion in connection with the seizure of the airplane; (3) that after seizing the plane, RepublicBank failed to deal with the appellants fairly and in good faith and tortiously interfered with their attempts to lease the plane to a third party; (4) that RepublicBank failed to maintain the plane and dispose of it in a commercially reasonable manner; (5) that Republic-Bank had elected to retain the plane in satisfaction of Campbell Leasing's debt, and (6) that RepublicBank had caused Day to suffer mental and emotional distress.

The district court granted summary judgment for NCNB and the FDIC, concluding that all of the appellants' claims and affirmative defenses were barred by the federal common-law doctrine announced in D'Oench, Duhme & Co. v. Federal Deposit Insurance Corporation, 315 U.S. 447, 62 S.Ct. 676, 86 L.Ed. 956 (1942) and the holder in due course doctrine announced in Federal Deposit Insurance Corporation v. Wood, 758 F.2d 156 (6th Cir.), cert. denied, 474 U.S. 944, 106 S.Ct. 308, 88 L.Ed.2d 286 (1985). The court entered judgment against Campbell Leasing and Day jointly and severally for the amount due on the note, plus interest, and awarded the FDIC and NCNB costs and attorneys' fees. The court also foreclosed the lien on the plane and its attachments and directed the appellants to deliver the maintenance records and log books to the FDIC and NCNB. Finally, the court ordered the airplane sold and the amount of the judgment reduced by the proceeds.

The appellants now challenge the district court's entry of summary judgment. At oral argument, the appellants waived all but the following contentions: (1) the *D'Oench, Duhme* doctrine is unconstitutional; (2) the federal holder in due course doctrine does not bar their claims against RepublicBank, and if it does bar those claims it is unconstitutional; and (3) the FDIC and NCNB have not acted in a commercially reasonable manner regarding the maintenance and sale of the airplane. We affirm in part, vacate in part, and remand.

III.

A. The D'Oench, Duhme Doctrine.

The appellants concede that the *D'Oench, Duhme* doctrine bars their claim that the promissory note was extinguished in a transaction involving Tex–Star, because the transaction was not documented in RepublicBank's records. They argue instead that the *D'Oench, Duhme* doctrine violates their rights under the fifth amendment by depriving them of valuable property—their defense to liability on the note—without just compensation or due process of law. We disagree.

The *D'Oench, Duhme* doctrine is "a common law rule of estoppel precluding a borrower from asserting against the FDIC defenses based upon secret or unrecorded 'side agreements' that alter the terms of facially unqualified obligations." Bell & Murphy & Assoc. v. Interfirst Bank Gateway, N.A., 894 F.2d 750, 753 (5th Cir.1990). Even borrowers who are innocent of any intent to mislead banking authorities are covered by the doctrine if they lend themselves to an arrangement which is likely to do so. Id. at 753–54. The doctrine thus "favors the interests of depositors and creditors of a failed bank, who cannot protect themselves from secret agreements, over the interests of borrowers, who can." Id. at 754.

In this case, the appellants were in a position to protect themselves by ensuring that the alleged Tex–Star transaction was adequately documented in RepublicBank's records. They failed to do so. Because the absence of documentation was likely to mislead banking authorities as to the value of the Campbell Leasing note, the appellants are estopped from asserting against the FDIC and NCNB any claims relating to the Tex–Star transaction. Id.

The *D'Oench, Duhme* doctrine does not deprive the appellants of property without just compensation. The appellants have simply deprived themselves of certain defenses to liability by failing to protect themselves in the manner required by the *D'Oench, Duhme* doctrine. See United States v. Locke, 471 U.S. 84, 107–08, 105 S.Ct. 1785, 1799, 85 L.Ed.2d 64 (1985) (upholding a federal provision extinguishing mineral interests for failure to make a timely annual filing). The government has never been required "to compensate [property owners] for the consequences of [their] own neglect." Texaco, Inc. v. Short, 454 U.S. 516, 530, 102 S.Ct. 781, 792, 70 L.Ed.2d 738 (1982).

Nor have the appellants been denied due process. The *D'Oench, Duhme* doctrine is a federal common law rule of general applicability that was established long before the appellants' claims arose. Because the appellants had "a reasonable opportunity both to familiarize themselves with [its] general requirements and to comply with those requirements," due process has been satisfied. *Locke,* 471 U.S. at 108, 105 S.Ct. at 1799. We conclude that the *D'Oench, Duhme* doctrine does not violate the takings clause or the due process clause of the fifth amendment.

B.   The Federal Holder In Due Course Doctrine.

The federal holder in due course doctrine bars the makers of promissory notes from asserting various "personal" defenses against the FDIC in connection with purchase and assumption transactions involving insolvent banks. *Wood,* 758 F.2d at 161; see also FSLIC v. Murray, 853 F.2d 1251, 1256 (5th Cir.1988). The protection extends to subsequent holders of the notes. See id.

policy

This doctrine is grounded in the federal policy of "bringing to depositors sound, effective, and uninterrupted operation of the [nation's] banking system with resulting safety and liquidity of bank deposits." S.Rep. No. 1269, 81st Cong., 2d Sess., *reprinted in* 1950 U.S.CODE CONG. & ADMIN.NEWS 3765, 3765–66. The most effective way for the FDIC to implement this policy when a bank becomes insolvent is by arranging a purchase and assumption transaction rather than by liquidating the bank. *Wood,* 758 F.2d at 160–61; see also Murray, 853 F.2d at 1256–57. If the FDIC were required to determine the value of the bank's notes in light of all possible "personal" defenses, a purchase and assumption transaction could not take place in the timely fashion necessary to ensure "uninterrupted operation" of the bank and the "safety and liquidity of deposits." Thus, the FDIC as a matter of federal common law enjoys holder in due course status in order to effectively perform its congressionally mandated function.

In this case, the appellants assert various defenses and counterclaims to liability on the note. They contend that RepublicBank tortiously interfered with their efforts to lease the Piper airplane to a third party and delayed too long after the plane's seizure before attempting to sell it. They maintain that the note could have been completely discharged absent RepublicBank's wrongful actions. They also claim that RepublicBank elected to keep the airplane in full satisfaction of the note and caused Day to suffer mental and emotional distress. Because these are "personal" rather than "real" defenses to liability on the note, * * * the FDIC and NCNB as holders in due course acquired the note free of these claims. * * *

The appellants challenge this conclusion, contending that the federal holder in due course doctrine does not apply to this case because the FDIC was not acting in its corporate capacity. See *Wood,* 758 F.2d at 161. They also argue that the FDIC and NCNB do not qualify as holders in due course under Texas law because they acquired the note in a bulk transaction by legal process and had notice that the note was overdue. * * * We reject these contentions.

We find no logical reason to limit federal holder in due course protection to the FDIC in its corporate capacity, to the exclusion of its receivership function. In its corporate capacity, the FDIC is obligated to protect the depositors of a failed bank, while the FDIC as receiver must also protect the bank's creditors and shareholders. Gilman v. FDIC, 660 F.2d 688, 690 (6th Cir.1981); see generally 12 U.S.C. § 1821. In both cases, the holder in due course doctrine enables the FDIC to efficiently and effectively fulfill its role, thus minimizing the harm to depositors, creditors, and shareholders.

See *Wood,* 758 F.2d at 160–61; *Murray,* 853 F.2d at 1256. For example, the doctrine prevents note makers from gaining absolute priority over a failed bank's assets, by asserting "personal" claims as defenses or setoff to their notes, to the detriment of the bank's other creditors and potentially its depositors. *Wood,* 758 F.2d at 160–61; see also *Murray,* 853 F.2d at 1256–57. We conclude that the FDIC enjoys holder in due course status as a matter of federal common law whether it is acting in its corporate or its receivership capacity. * * *

In addition, the FDIC and subsequent note holders enjoy holder in due course status whether or not they satisfy the technical requirements of state law. The court in *Wood* assumed that the FDIC did not qualify as a holder in due course under state law, yet it still held that the FDIC was entitled to the protections of a holder in due course as a matter of federal common law. See 758 F.2d at 158. We reached the same conclusion with respect to the FSLIC. *Murray,* 853 F.2d at 1256. This rule "promotes the necessary uniformity of law in this area while it counters individual state laws that would frustrate [basic FDIC objectives]." Id.

However, the district court erred in granting summary judgment against the appellants on all their claims. The appellants have a statutory right to continue their action against the FDIC as receiver for First RepublicBank on their claims of tortious interference with contract, breach of the Campbell Leasing security agreement, and intentional infliction of mental and emotional distress. 12 U.S.C. § 1821(d)(6)(A). While the holder in due course doctrine prevents the appellants from asserting these claims as a set-off to liability on the note, it does not prevent the appellants from trying these claims to the district court, liquidating the amount of damages, and subsequently receiving a pro-rata share of First RepublicBank's remaining assets along with the bank's other creditors. See id. § 1821(d)(11)(A)(ii). We therefore must vacate that part of the district court's judgment dismissing the appellants' breach of contract and tort claims and remand for additional proceedings.

In light of these statutory provisions, we reject the appellants' further contention that application of the holder in due course doctrine violates due process or amounts to an unconstitutional taking of property without just compensation.

> A negotiable instrument is subject to transfer at any time, and the maker must always be aware that the transferee may be a holder in due course. From the maker's view, there is no difference between his bank failing and the note going to the * * * FDIC, and his bank failing after selling the note to a holder in due course.

Wood, 758 F.2d at 161. The appellants have not been denied the opportunity to assert their claims because they may pursue them against the FDIC as receiver for First RepublicBank. The appellants have "therefore suffer[ed] no prejudice." *Murray,* 853 F.2d at 1256–57.

* * *

NOTE

The *D'Oench* doctrine is federal common law. In 1950, eight years after *D'Oench* was decided, Congress enacted the Federal Deposit Insurance Act, 12 U.S.C. § 1811 et seq., which bars anyone from asserting against the FDIC any agreement not properly documented in the records of the bank that would diminish the value of an asset held by the FDIC. In 1989 this provision was modified by the Financial Institutions Reform, Recovery, and Enforcement Act (FIRREA) in 12 U.S.C. § 1823(e)(1). Though this provision could be viewed as a rather narrow codification of *D'Oench*, most courts either expressly or impliedly have held that it did not preempt the common law *D'Oench* doctrine, which has grown far beyond the limits of § 1823(e)(1) to bar many claims against failed banks that were not based on written records of the bank. But in O'Melveny & Myers v. FDIC, 512 U.S. 79, 114 S.Ct. 2048, 129 L.Ed.2d 67 (1994), the Court held in general terms, with no mention of *D'Oench*, that FIRREA preempts federal common law on any issue expressly covered by the statute. And in Murphy v. FDIC, 61 F.3d 34 (D.C.Cir.1995), the court held that under *O'Melveny*, § 1823(e)(1) preempted *D'Oench* and requires that for the unrecorded claim to be barred it must diminish the interest of the FDIC in a specific asset. An unrecorded claim that merely diminishes the value of the failed bank in general (e.g. a tort claim) is not barred by FIRREA.

Does § 1823(e)(1) preempt the federal holder-in-due-course doctrine under *O'Melveny* and *Murphy*? Courts have generally viewed the federal holder-in-due-course doctrine as separate from the *D'Oench* doctrine. *Campbell Leasing* and 2 White & Summers, § 17–13 b. (4th prac.ed.1995), take this view. Section 1823(e)(1) provides: "No agreement which tends to diminish or defeat the interest of the [FDIC] in any asset acquired by it * * * " is valid unless it is in writing, approved by the bank and is an official record of the bank. Although claims and defenses raised on an instrument would seem to meet the test of diminishing the value of a specific asset (e.g., the note obligation), the question is whether they involve "agreements" under that provision. It might be argued that although this provision could be considered a narrow codification of *D'Oench*, which safeguards the FDIC from secret agreements, it should not be viewed as a preemption of the broad federal holder-in-due-course doctrine. White & Summers, supra, questions whether a fair reading of "agreements" would include such defenses as fraud or failure of consideration; however, some courts have given the term an expansive reading.

7. VALUE

a. INTRODUCTION

If Thief steals a negotiable instrument from Owner and sells it to unsuspecting Holder, it may make sense to give Holder rights in the instrument at the expense of Owner. One or the other must bear a loss. Although each is equally innocent, the negotiability doctrine tips the scales in favor of Holder in order to carry out a policy objective of encouraging free commerce in instruments. But if Holder has paid nothing for the instrument, denial of the right to defeat Owner's title results in no loss to Holder except the loss of a windfall. Thus, if Thief makes a gift of the instrument to Holder it seems unfair to allow Holder to profit at the expense of Owner. Since it is not necessary to impose a loss on Owner in order to carry out the objective of encouraging free commerce in instruments, Holder loses. Section 3–302(a)(2)(i) provides that only a holder who takes the instrument for value can be a holder in due course. Taking for value is defined in § 3–303(a). Although the taking for value requirement can be explained in part by distinguishing between loss and windfall, this distinction is not always clearly apparent in the cases covered by § 3–303(a). The problems that follow illustrate the cases covered by that section. In each problem, and the cases that follow, you might ask yourself the question whether the holder-in-due-course doctrine is necessary in order to protect some interest of the holder or whether the doctrine simply confers on the holder a windfall. If there is a windfall, is the result justified by commercial necessity? You might also ask the question whether, if the doctrine did not exist, the taking of the instrument in the particular transaction would have been discouraged.

PROBLEMS

In each of the following problems make these assumptions: Maker gave to Payee a negotiable note in the amount of $1,000 payable on a stated date. Maker's issuance of the note was induced by Payee's fraudulent promise to deliver goods which were never delivered. In each case, Payee, prior to the due date, negotiated the note to Holder who had no notice of the fraud. On the due date Holder demanded payment of Maker who refused and asserted the defenses of fraud and failure of consideration.

1. Payee negotiates the note to Holder in consideration of Holder's agreement to perform services for Payee. Before Holder is obligated to begin performance of the promised services the note falls due. Was there consideration for the transfer of the note from Payee to Holder? Was the note taken for value by Holder? § 3–303(a)(1).

2. Payee negotiates the note to Holder who pays $900 cash for the note. Is Maker's defense good against Holder? If Maker is liable, how much can Holder recover? § 3–302(a)(2). Suppose Holder paid $600 cash for the note and promised to pay an additional $300 cash in 60 days. After paying the $600, Holder learned of the fraud and paid no more. How much can Holder recover? See O. P. Ganjo, Inc. v. Tri–Urban Realty Co., 108 N.J.Super. 517, 261 A.2d 722 (1969). § 3–302(d). Comment 6, Case #5.

3. Payee was indebted to Holder on a loan past due. Holder demanded payment but Payee was unable to pay. In order to forestall legal action by Holder, Payee negotiated Maker's note to Holder as collateral for payment of Payee's loan. When the note became due Payee was still unable to repay the loan. Holder thereupon demanded payment of the note by Maker. Is Maker's defense good against Holder? § 3–303(a)(3).

b.   RIGHTS OF DEPOSITARY BANK IN DEPOSITED CHECK

Checks are usually deposited by the payee in the payee's bank. That bank is referred to in § 4–105(2) as the "depositary bank." The payee's bank is also referred to as a "collecting bank" if the check is not drawn on the payee's bank. § 4–105(5). The depositary bank normally credits the account of the depositor in the amount of the check and forwards the check to the drawee for payment. The drawee is referred to in § 4–105(3) as the "payor bank." The depositary bank is considered to be acting as the agent of the depositor in obtaining payment of the deposited check. § 4–201. The credit to the depositor's account is normally provisional in nature. When the check is paid by the payor bank, this provisional credit becomes final, i.e., the credit represents a debt owed by the depositary bank to the depositor, § 4–215(d). If the check is not paid by the payor bank, the depositary bank has the right to "charge back," i.e., cancel the provisional credit. § 4–214(a).

Frequently, the depositary bank will also be a creditor of the depositor because of a past transaction such as a loan. If a debt owing by the depositor to the depositary bank is past due, the depositary bank may exercise a common law right to set off against the debt any amounts which the bank owes the depositor. For example, if the depositor owes the depositary bank $1,000 on a past-due loan and there is an $800 final credit balance in the depositor's checking account, the depositary bank may simply wipe out the $800 balance by applying it to reduce the $1,000 loan balance.[1] In addition to this right of setoff a depositary bank has a closely-related common law right known as a banker's lien.[2] For example, if the

---

1. The bank's right of setoff may be limited by statute. For example, Calif. Financial Code § 864 limits setoffs with respect to certain consumer-type installment debt owed to the bank.

2. Restatement, Security § 62 provides as follows: "General possessory liens exist in favor of * * * (c) a banker, as security for the general balance due him from a customer, upon commercial paper and other instruments which can be used as the basis of credit and which are deposited with him in the regular course of business." Some states have codified the common-law lien. For example, a California statute provides: "A banker, or a savings and loan association, has a general lien, dependent on possession, upon all property in his or her hands belonging to a customer, for the balance due to the banker or savings and loan association from the customer in the course of the business." Civil Code § 3054(a). The lien may be important to the bank in the event of the depositor's insolvency. In Goggin v. Bank of America, 183 F.2d 322 (9th Cir.1950), the depositor owed the bank $600,000 on a loan. At the time of the depositor's bankruptcy the bank held commercial paper delivered by the depositor for collection and credit to its general deposit account. After bankruptcy and after written notice by the depositor attempting to terminate the authority of the bank to act as agent for collection, the bank collected the commercial paper. In an action by the receiver of the depositor's estate in bankruptcy to recover the proceeds for the estate, it was held (a) that the bank had a banker's lien on the commercial paper at the date of bankruptcy, (b) that the authority of the bank to collect the paper was not affected by either bankruptcy or the attempt of the depositor to revoke the bank's authority, and (c) that the bank was entitled to apply the proceeds to reduction of the loan balance. This case was decided under the Bankruptcy Act. Under the present Bankruptcy Code the right of the bank to enforce its lien after bankruptcy would be affected by the automatic stay pursuant to Bankruptcy Code § 362(a)(7). If the bank had collected the paper before bank-depositor owes the depositary bank $1,000 on a past-due loan and deposits a check to the depositor's account in the regular course of business, the depositary bank has a lien in the check as security for the $1,000 debt. Although the bank when it forwards the check to the payor bank for payment acts as agent for the depositor, it also has a property interest in the check represented by the lien. Thus, the depositary bank can collect the check and apply the proceeds to the debt owed by the depositor. Since the taking of an instrument for an antecedent debt is value, the depositary bank could attain the rights of a holder in due course. These two related but separate common law rights—setoff and banker's lien—are preserved under § 1–103. Comment 1 to § 4–210. The two common law rights are frequently confused. It is not uncommon for a court to refer to the banker's lien as a right of setoff or to refer to the right of setoff as a banker's lien. When a depositary bank is asserting a right in an uncollected check it is relying on a lien. A setoff can occur only if there are mutual debts. There can be no present right of setoff with respect to an uncollected check because until collected the check does not represent a debt of the depositary bank to the depositor.

Depositary banks may acquire rights as holders in due course under other provisions of the UCC. Suppose there is no debt owing by the depositor when the check is deposited. Whether the depositary bank has given value for the check is determined under § 4–211 which states that the bank has given value to the extent it has a security interest in the check. Section 4–210 states rules for determining when a security interest

ruptcy it would have had in bankruptcy a right of setoff with respect to the mutual debts existing at the time of bankruptcy. This right of setoff is subject to certain limitations. Bankruptcy Code § 553. In *Goggin* the setoff after bankruptcy was based on the bank's lien existing at the time of bankruptcy.

The banker's lien may also be the basis for cutting off claims of third parties to the paper deposited by the depositor. In Wyman v. Colorado National Bank, 5 Colo. 30 (1879), plaintiff drew a draft on a drawee in London payable to the order of First Bank with which plaintiff had an account. Plaintiff's intent was to have First Bank collect the draft and deposit the proceeds to plaintiff's account. First Bank indorsed the draft and sent it to Second Bank with orders to collect it. At that time First Bank was indebted to Second Bank on an overdraft. Second Bank sent the draft to London for collection. After the draft was paid but before Second Bank was paid the proceeds Second Bank was notified that the draft was the property of plaintiff and that First Bank had failed. The court held that Second Bank got a lien on the draft immediately upon receipt of the draft and

became a holder for value without notice of plaintiff's claim, thereby cutting off the claim. In effect Second Bank took the draft as security for the antecedent debt represented by the overdraft. Compare UCC § 3–303(a)(2) and (3). The issue in cases like *Wyman* is whether the deposited paper "belongs" to the customer making the deposit. For example, if Second Bank had been aware that First Bank was acting solely as collecting agent with respect to the draft the lien would not have attached. But in cases of undisclosed agency there is no notice of the claim of the owner of the item and the apparent ownership of the paper by the depositor has been recognized by some courts as sufficient to allow the lien to attach.

A rationale for the banker's lien is stated in Gibbons v. Hecox, 105 Mich. 509, 513, 63 N.W. 519, 520 (1895). "The reason for allowing the lien is that any credit which a bank gives by discounting notes or allowing an overdraft to be made is given on the faith that money or securities sufficient to pay the debt will come into the possession of the bank in the due course of future transactions."

arises. This security interest is in addition to the bank's common law banker's lien. Comment 1 to § 4–210. By virtue of § 4–210 the depositary bank has a security interest under subsection (a)(1) if the check is deposited and the resulting credit is withdrawn, under subsection (a)(2) if the check is deposited and the depositor is given the right to withdraw the credit, and under (a)(3) if the bank makes a loan or cash payment based on the check. In these cases the bank is treated as though it were a lender to the depositor taking as security a security interest in the check. In the case in which the depositor is not allowed to withdraw the funds, the bank does not have a security interest and is not a holder in due course. It has committed no funds and is fully protected by its ability to charge back the depositor's account in the event the check is not paid by the payor bank.

In most cases the depositor has an existing credit balance in the account when a deposit is made and there may be a series of deposits and withdrawals from the account. In those cases, whether credit for a particular check has been withdrawn cannot be determined except by applying some mechanical tracing rule. Such a rule is provided by the last sentence of § 4–210(b) which states that "credits first given are first withdrawn." This rule is usually referred to as the first-in-first-out or FIFO rule.

PROBLEM

The table shows debits and credits made to Depositor's checking account in Depositary Bank. Withdrawals were made by payment by Depositary Bank of checks drawn by Depositor on the account. Deposits were made either in cash or by third-party checks payable to Depositor as indicated.

Date		Debit	Credit	Balance
Nov. 1	Existing balance			4,000
Nov. 2	Deposit by check		5,000	9,000
Nov. 3	Withdrawal	4,000		5,000
Nov. 4	Deposit in cash		6,000	11,000
Nov. 5	Withdrawal	5,000		6,000
Nov. 6	Received notice of dishonor of check deposited on Nov. 2			
Nov. 7 (A.M.)	Withdrawal	3,000		3,000
`Nov. 7 (P.M.)	Charge-back of Nov. 2 credit	5,000		(2,000)

The check deposited on November 2 was not paid by the payor bank because the drawer had stopped payment. § 4–403(a). Depositary Bank received notice of dishonor of the check on November 6. Depositor is insolvent. Depositary Bank brings an action against the drawer of the November 2 check to recover the amount of the check. § 3–414(b). The drawer defends by asserting that no consideration was given for the check. § 3–303(b). Assume that Depositary Bank is a holder in due course if it gave value for the check. Did Depositary Bank give value? § 4–210(a)(1) and (b). Is the result in this problem consistent with the case discussed in Comment 2 to § 3–303? That case is governed by § 3–303(1)(a), under which the unperformed promise of performance is not value. The rationale is that until performance is made the promisor will not suffer any out-of-pocket loss and dishonor of the check excuses performance by the promisor. In this problem, is holder-in-due-course status necessary to protect Depositary Bank against an out-of-pocket loss when Depositary Bank received notice of dishonor on November 6? § 4–214(a).

Section 4–210(a)(1) refers not only to cases in which a credit has been withdrawn, but also to cases in which the credit has been "applied." The latter term refers to cases in which the credit has been used by the bank to pay an obligation to itself or to make a payment to a third party. This provision is considered in the cases that follow. When these cases were decided, the current § 4–210(a)(1) and § 4–211 appeared in slightly different form as § 4–208(1)(a) and § 4–209 of the pre–1990 Article 4.

Laurel Bank & Trust Co. v. City National Bank of Connecticut

Superior Court of Connecticut, Appellate Session, 1976.
33 Conn.Sup. 641, 365 A.2d 1222.

* * *

■ SPONZO, JUDGE. * * *

[Summary by Eds. Maisto had two checking accounts in Plaintiff Bank: Account #1, "Tony's Sunoco" and Account #2, "B & D Automotive." On March 27 Maisto bought a cashier's check from Defendant Bank in the amount of $3,446. He paid for the check by giving some cash and two checks, one of which was a $2,500 check drawn on Account #1 in Plaintiff Bank. A few hours later he indorsed and deposited the cashier's check in Account #2 in Plaintiff Bank, along with other checks making a total deposit of $9,501. Account #2 was provisionally credited with the amount of the deposit, but since there was a $21,000 overdraft in the account, the effect of the deposit was merely to reduce the overdraft in Account #2 by the amount of the deposit. The next day the $2,500 check drawn on Account #1 was presented to Plaintiff Bank for payment and was returned to Defendant Bank because drawn on insufficient funds. Later that day the $3,446 cashier's check was presented to Defendant Bank for payment, and Defendant Bank refused to pay it because it had been purchased in part by a check that bounced. Since a cashier's check is the obligation of the issuing bank, Plaintiff Bank sued Defendant Bank, claiming to be a holder in due course who took free of the defense of absence of consideration that Defendant Bank had against Maisto on the cashier's check which it had issued to him.]

* * *

* * * The principal issue in this case is whether the provisional credit made by the plaintiff against the B & D Automotive account, which was overdrawn in the amount of $21,079.43, constituted value * * *. The credit entered was subject to a later withdrawal or reversal of the credit by the plaintiff. The trial court concluded that no value was given because the credit was not extended irrevocably. That conclusion was erroneous.

UCC § 3–303(b) provides that a holder takes for value "when he takes the instrument in payment of or as security for an antecedent claim against any person whether or not the claim is due * * * ." UCC § 4–208(1)(a) elaborates on that concept and provides that "[a] bank has a security interest in an item and any accompanying documents or the proceeds of either * * * in case of an item deposited in an account to the extent to which credit given for the item has been withdrawn or applied * * * ." UCC § 4–209 completes that thought, stating that "[f]or purposes of determining its status as a holder in due course, the bank has given value to the extent that it has a security interest in an item provided that the bank otherwise complies with the requirements of section 3–302 on what constitutes a holder in due course."

In order to comprehend how the plaintiff became a holder for value under the provisions of the statutes referred to, it is necessary to state the parameters of the security interest with relation to the value concept. It is clear that if a depositor's account is not overdrawn and he deposits a check which is credited to his account but not drawn on, then no value is given. * * * It is clear under UCC § 4–208(1)(a) that a bank has given value and is a holder in due course to the extent that a depositor actually draws against a check given for collection, even if the check is later dishonored. It is immaterial that the bank takes the check for collection only and can charge back against the depositor's account the amount of the uncollected item. * * *

The reason for that rule is to prevent the hindrance to commercial transactions which would result if depository banks refused to permit withdrawal prior to clearance of checks. By giving the bank a security interest in the amount credited prior to notice of a stop payment order or other notice of dishonor, UCC §§ 4–208 and 4–209 allow continuation of that common practice while protecting the bank as a holder in due course. * * *

While Maisto did not draw upon the deposit of $9501, the deposit was applied to his overdraft or antecedent debt on a provisional basis. Under the circumstances it appears that where the plaintiff applied the deposit, even provisionally, to Maisto's overdrawn account, it gave value and thus cut off the defense of want of consideration. In a leading case, Bath National Bank v. Sonnenstrahl, Inc., 249 N.Y. 391, 394, 164 N.E. 327, 328, it was stated: "Though title to a draft left by a depositor with the bank for collection does not pass absolutely to the bank where the full amount of the draft was credited to the depositor, 'for convenience and in anticipation of its payment,' and 'the bank could have cancelled the credit, as it clearly accepted no risk on the paper,' yet if the depositor 'had overdrawn, and this draft had been credited to cover the overdraft, or if the company had drawn against the draft, the bank could hold the paper until the account was squared.' It would then be a holder for value. St. Louis & San Francisco Ry. Co. v. Johnston, 133 U.S. 566, 10 S.Ct. 390, 33 L.Ed. 683.''

UCC § 4–201(1) provides, in part, that "[u]nless a contrary intent clearly appears and prior to the time that a settlement given by a collecting bank for an item is or becomes final as provided in subsection (3) of section 4–211 and sections 4–212 and 4–213 the bank is an agent or subagent of the owner of the item and any settlement given for the item is provisional. * * * [A]ny rights of the owner to proceeds of the item are subject to rights of a collecting bank such as those resulting from outstanding advances on the item and valid rights of setoff." That provision, which makes the bank an agent of its customer, is to be construed harmoniously with UCC § 4–208(1) which does not derogate from the banker's general common-law lien or right of setoff against indebtedness owing in deposit accounts.

In the present case, the plaintiff's action in provisionally crediting a $9501 deposit to the antecedent debt of the depositor was an exercise of its common-law right of setoff, UCC § 4–208(1) and also gave the plaintiff a security interest sufficient to constitute value. In Sandler v. United Industrial Bank, 23 A.D.2d 567, 256 N.Y.S.2d 442, a check was deposited in an account which was overdrawn and the bank credited the deposit in part to repay the overdrawn account and applied the balance to a new item presented for payment. The maker of the check died that evening and his bank returned his check unpaid. The court held that the collecting bank became a holder for value prior to the maker's death. See Bowling Green, Inc. N. H. v. State Street Bank & Trust Co. of Boston, 307 F.Supp. 648, 654–55 (D.Mass.).

To make a collecting bank a holder for value where it applies a deposit to an overdrawn account is a result consistent with logic and good banking practice. If an account is overdrawn, it is highly doubtful that a bank would pass over an opportunity to erase or reduce the overdraft. That opportunity arises when the customer makes a deposit. The bank credits or sets off the overdraft and waits for final settlement as a holder for value. If the check is dishonored, the bank may then reverse the provisional granting of credit to the overdraft and proceed not only against its customer but also against the drawee bank. If it can proceed against the drawee bank, the latter can then recover from its customer.

The trial court erred in concluding that the plaintiff was not a holder for value when it applied Maisto's deposit, which included the cashier's check in the amount of $3446, to an overdraft in his account, subject to reversal upon dishonor.

There is error, the judgment is set aside and the matter is remanded for a trial limited to the issue of whether the plaintiff took the cashier's check in good faith and without notice that it was overdue, dishonored or that there was any defect or defense.

NOTES

1. *Laurel Bank* represents an orthodox analysis of former § 4–208(1)(a) (now § 4–210(a)(1)). A contrary analysis of that provision was made by the New York Court of Appeals in Marine Midland Bank–New York v. Graybar Electric Co., Inc., 41 N.Y.2d 703, 395 N.Y.S.2d 403, 363 N.E.2d 1139 (1977). Dynamics was indebted to the bank on a loan. A check of Graybar payable to Dynamics was deposited in Dynamics' account with the bank which forwarded it for collection. On the day of the deposit the credit given for the check was "set off" against Dynamics' loan debt to the bank. The check was not paid because Graybar had stopped payment. The bank then brought an action against Graybar as drawer of the check. Under the court's analysis of the case the bank's rights to recover the amount of the check depended upon whether it was a holder in due course and this in turn depended upon whether the bank took the check for value. The court analyzed this issue as follows:

> As to value, the bank contends that it took the July 25 check for value because under the Uniform Commercial Code "A holder takes the instrument for value (a) to the extent that * * * he acquires a *security interest in or a lien on the instrument* * * * or (b) when he takes the instrument in *payment of or as security for an antecedent claim* against any person whether or not the claim is due" (Uniform Commercial Code, § 3–303; emphasis added). Further, the bank notes that the Uniform Commercial Code accords to it a "security interest" in a check "to the extent to which credit given for the item is withdrawn or *applied*" * * *. Thus, the bank's position is that, by its setoff, it took the check in payment of its antecedent loan, and also that by applying the credit for the check to the loan, the bank acquired a security interest therein. For these reasons, the bank argues that it has given value under the Uniform Commercial Code * * *.

> Dynamics argues that a bank and its depositor must "bilaterally" agree, either expressly or impliedly, to the creation of a security interest in an item. Examples of an implied agreement are said to be participating in the withdrawal of funds, or applying the credit which the bank has given for the item prior to collection. Furthermore, Dynamics argues, the bank must give value unconditionally and irrevocably by actually extinguishing the depositor's debt upon receipt of the check, even though not yet collected. Dynamics is thus arguing that under the circumstances presented here the bank has not given value.

> A bank, of course, gives value to the extent that a credit given for an item is withdrawn by the party whose account was credited * * *. Value is also given by a holder when it takes a check in payment of, or as security for, an antecedent debt * * *. Long before the enactment of the Uniform Commercial Code, however, the entry of a credit on a bank's books was held not to be parting with value under circumstances manifesting that the pre-existing debt or a part thereof was not, in fact, extinguished in consideration for the item for which the credit was given (see Sixth Nat. Bank of City of N. Y. v. Lorillard Brick Works Co., Sup., 18 N.Y.S. 861, affd., 136 N.Y. 667, 33 N.E. 335). The basis for that decision was that the bookkeeping entry of the credit was not a parting with value * * *.

These events present somewhat of a hybrid situation in that the bank first gave Dynamics a credit for the Graybar check and then applied this credit, by way of setoff, to Dynamics' indebtedness to it. A literal reading of the Uniform Commercial Code suggests that under § 4–208(1)(a) the net result of the credit followed by the setoff is that the bank had taken the check for value. The difficulty with this analysis is, however, that the credit given to Dynamics' account was provisional because the bank could and did reverse the credit after notice of the stop payment order, thereby reinstating that portion of the loan against which the credit was set off.

Considering first the credit given to Dynamics' account for the Graybar check, it is established that the giving of a provisional credit is not a parting with value under the Uniform Commercial Code. In discussing the notion that it is not necessary to give holder in due course status to one who has not actually paid value, the Official Commentary to the Uniform Commercial Code cites as an illustration "the bank credit not drawn upon, which can be and is revoked when a claim or defense appears" * * *.

* * *

Turning then to the argument that by applying the credit by way of setoff to Dynamics' indebtedness the bank gave value, the following is relevant. The clearest instance of giving value in this sort of case is where a bank actually extinguishes a debt by, for example, parting with a note in exchange for a check and then seeking to collect on the check * * *. With respect to UCC § 4–208(1)(a), however, one text has suggested that its purpose was to give "the bank protection in any case in which it is not clear that the bank purchased the item outright, but in which it is clear that the bank has done something, of advantage to the depositor, more than giving the depositor a mere credit on the bank's books" (Clarke, Bailey & Young, Bank Deposits and Collections [1963], p. 56). Here, the bank argues that by applying the credit to Dynamics' indebtedness it was giving value as contemplated under UCC § 4–208.

This argument should be rejected. To say that the bank was doing something of advantage to Dynamics by applying the credit to that depositor's indebtedness is to ignore what actually occurred. The bank was merely seeking to protect itself and not giving value, in any traditional sense, or under the Uniform Commercial Code. Since the credit given to the Dynamics account was not, as noted, available to Dynamics, there is no reason for allowing the bank to benefit from this credit, particularly since the bank reinstated that portion of the debt against which the credit was applied upon learning that payment was not to be forthcoming on the check. Under this analysis the bank is in no worse position than any other creditor, and the bank's unilateral agreement to take the credit for the indebtedness, conditioned on payment of the check for which the credit was given, is recognized for what it was—an attempt to recoup its losses.

This is not to diminish the bank's right of setoff of mutual debts in a bankruptcy situation * * *. Nor is this holding intended to suggest that the setoff was impermissible simply because the check was uncollected at the time of the setoff * * *. Rather, this determination is based on the conclusion that what the bank did was merely give a provisional credit for the Graybar check. That the bank unilaterally agreed to apply this provisional credit to Dynamics' indebtedness should not elevate the transaction to the level of those instances where value is considered to be given under the Uniform Commercial Code. Therefore, since the bank did not give value, it is not a holder in due course and cannot recover on the check.

The Court of Appeals suggests that an antecedent debt can constitute value only in cases in which the debt was "extinguished" in consideration of the instrument for which the credit was given. Taking a personal check for an underlying obligation does not normally "extinguish" the obligation. Under § 3–310(b) the underlying obligation is suspended until the check is presented; if the check is dishonored the obligation revives. It is a rare case indeed in which a personal check is accepted in absolute payment of an obligation. Thus, in the normal case, the check is taken as provisional payment. This is similar to the provisional credit given by the depositary bank for an uncollected check. In both cases the credit given for the check is reversed if the check is not paid. But, under § 3–310(b), the person taking the check may sue on it and there is no indication in the UCC that the fact that the debt was not extinguished affects the taking-for-value question. One of the arguments against recognizing an antecedent debt as value is that the creditor taking the instrument is often given a windfall. The creditor may not have made any detrimental reliance and if the instrument is not enforceable the creditor is in no worse position than before taking the instrument. This argument was rejected by the drafters of the NIL and the UCC. Before New York adopted the NIL, the common law rule in that state did not recognize an antecedent debt as value for holder-in-due-course purposes. See Kelso & Co. v. Ellis, 224 N.Y. 528, 121 N.E. 364 (1918). *Marine Midland* appears to be a step backward in the direction of the old New York doctrine.

2. Earlier, when we were discussing the concept of negotiability, we quoted from Professor Rosenthal's article questioning the desirability of the doctrine of negotiability. Here we include another section of that article in which he considers the negotiability of checks. This is from Negotiability—Who Needs It? 71 Colum.L.Rev. 375, 382–385 (1971).

To begin with, negotiability normally plays almost no part with respect to checks. While some checks are cashed at a grocery store or across the counter at a bank, the overwhelming majority of checks are deposited by the payee for collection at his own bank, which, acting merely as the depositor's agent for that purpose, sends the check through banking channels to the drawee bank where it is presented for payment. If paid, the check is so marked and is ultimately returned to the drawer along with his monthly statement; if the check is dishonored, a slip setting forth the reason is attached to it and goes with it back through banking channels to the payee.

There is no holder in due course (except perhaps the payee himself) of such a check since, even though such other requirements as good faith and lack of notice may be met, the bank would not have given value for the check. Any dispute between drawer and payee will, therefore, simply be between themselves, with no one else in a position to assert special rights.

Let us now modify the case of a relatively poor buyer purchasing a refrigerator on installments, and substitute a middle-class consumer paying for it with his personal check. If the refrigerator fails to work properly, if its defect is immediately apparent, if the buyer's attempts to get redress from the seller prove unavailing, and if the buyer moves with sufficient alacrity, he can often stop payment on his check before it has cleared through his own bank. The buyer and seller will then be in a position themselves to resolve their dispute on the merits, with the buyer having the tactical advantage that the seller will have to bring suit in order to collect if the matter cannot be resolved without litigation.

Suppose, however, the bank in which the seller-payee deposits the check allows him to draw against it before it has been collected. This is not standard practice, but it does occur with some frequency. When the check is presented to the drawee bank for payment, it is dishonored because of the stop payment order. This time, however, the depositary bank is given the status of holder in due course "to the extent to which credit for the item has been withdrawn or applied," or "if it makes an advance on or against the item." To this extent, the drawer cannot assert against the bank the defense that the sale of the refrigerator was fraudulent. Although the stop payment order is effective, its utility to the drawer is defeated, since he is liable to the depositary bank.

* * *

If the depositary bank were to grant credit to the payee by allowing withdrawals before collection, and if it were to do this in reliance upon its knowledge of the *drawer's* financial standing or reputation, there might be good reason to protect the depositary bank in this fashion. Typically, however the depositary bank pays no attention to the identity of the drawer; in fact, it does not even know whether the drawer's signature is genuine. It will often allow or refuse to allow withdrawals against the check before collection solely on the basis of its relations with and knowledge of the creditworthiness of its own customer, the payee. If payment is stopped, and the depositary bank cannot recover its advances by charging the amount back against the payee's account, but is permitted to hold the drawer liable, the bank receives a windfall: in such cases, it picks up the liability of the drawer, which by hypothesis it had not counted upon when it made its decision to allow withdrawals before collection.

The fact that the depositary bank would not normally be relying upon the drawer's credit may be seen in the improbable combination of circumstances that have to coincide for the drawer's liability to matter. First, the bank's customer, the payee, must have allowed his account to drop to the point at which some of his withdrawals cannot be charged against other funds in the account but must be regarded as advances against the uncollected check. Second, the payee must be insolvent, or at least his assets must not be readily amenable to collection. Third, the drawer has to be solvent and available, and his signature genuine. Fourth, the check must be dishonored. Finally, for the doctrine to make any ultimate difference, the drawer must have a legitimate defense on the check that is good against the payee, but is not of a type that can be asserted against a holder in due course. Only if all of these elements coincide is the bank's position improved by virtue of its becoming a holder in due course. It must therefore be a rare case indeed in which the bank's decision to extend credit before the check is collected can be regarded as having been made in reliance upon its ability to cut off the defenses of the drawer. Neither banks specifically, nor commerce in general, seem to need the rule declaring the bank to be a holder in due course. Where the bank relies entirely on the identity and credit of the payee in allowing withdrawals, it should shock no one's conscience if the bank were limited to the payee as a source of reimbursement.

* * *

Bowling Green, Inc. v. State Street Bank & Trust Co.

United States Court of Appeals, First Circuit, 1970.
425 F.2d 81.

■ COFFIN, CIRCUIT JUDGE. On September 26, 1966, plaintiff Bowling Green, Inc., the operator of a bowling alley, negotiated a United States government check for $15,306 to Bowl–Mor, Inc., a manufacturer of bowling alley equipment. The check, which plaintiff had acquired through a Small Business Administration loan, represented the first installment on a conditional sales contract for the purchase of candlepin setting machines. On the following day, September 27, a representative of Bowl–Mor deposited the check in defendant State Street Bank and Trust Co. The Bank immediately credited $5,024.85 of the check against an overdraft in Bowl–Mor's account. Later that day, when the Bank learned that Bowl–Mor had filed a petition for reorganization under Chapter X of the Bankruptcy Act, it transferred $233.61 of Bowl–Mor's funds to another account and applied the remaining $10,047.54 against debts which Bowl–Mor owed the Bank. Shortly thereafter Bowl–Mor's petition for reorganization was dismissed and the firm was adjudicated a bankrupt. Plaintiff has never received the pin-setting machines for which it contracted. Its part payment remains in the hands of defendant Bank.

Plaintiff brought this diversity action to recover its payment from defendant Bank on the grounds that the Bank is constructive trustee of the funds deposited by Bowl–Mor. In the court below, plaintiff argued that Bowl–Mor knew it could not perform at the time it accepted payment, that the Bank was aware of this fraudulent conduct, and that the Bank therefore received Bowl–Mor's deposit impressed with a constructive trust in plaintiff's favor. The district court rejected plaintiff's view of the evidence, concluding instead that the Bank was a holder in due course * * * and was therefore entitled to take the item in question free of all personal defenses. Bowling Green, Inc., etc. v. State Street Bank and Trust Co., 307 F.Supp. 648 (D.Mass.1969).

* * *

Plaintiff's first objection arises from a technical failure of proof. The district court found that plaintiff had endorsed the item in question to Bowl–Mor, but there was no evidence that Bowl–Mor supplied its own endorsement before depositing the item in the Bank. Thus we cannot tell whether the Bank is a holder within the meaning of § 1–201(20), which defines holder as one who takes an instrument endorsed to him, or to bearer, or in blank. But, argues plaintiff, once it is shown that a defense to an instrument exists, the Bank has the burden of showing that it is in all respects a holder in due course. This failure of proof, in plaintiff's eyes, is fatal to the Bank's case.

We readily agree with plaintiff that the Bank has the burden of establishing its status in all respects. UCC § 3–307(3), on which plaintiff relies to establish the defendant's burden, seems addressed primarily to cases in which a holder seeks to enforce an instrument, but Massachusetts courts have indicated that the policy of § 3–307(3) applies whenever a party invokes the rights of a holder in due course either offensively or defensively. Cf. Elbar Realty Inc. v. City Bank & Trust Co., 342 Mass. 262, 267–268, 173 N.E.2d 256 (1961). The issue, however, is not whether the Bank bears the burden of proof, but whether it must establish that it took the item in question by endorsement in order to meet its burden. We think not. The evidence in this case indicates that the Bank's transferor, Bowl–Mor, was a holder. Under UCC § 3–201(a), transfer of an instrument vests in the transferee all the rights of the transferor. As the Official Comment to § 3–201 indicates, one who is not a holder must first establish the transaction by which he acquired the instrument before enforcing it, but the Bank has met this burden here.

We doubt, moreover, whether the concept of "holder" as defined in § 1–201(20) applies with full force to Article 4. Article 4 establishes a comprehensive scheme for simplifying and expediting bank collections. Its provisions govern the more general rules of Article 3 wherever inconsistent. UCC § 4–102(1). As part of this expediting process, Article 4 recognizes the common bank practice of accepting unendorsed checks for deposit. * * * § 4–201(1) provides that the lack of an endorsement shall not affect the bank's status as agent for collection, and § 4–205(1) authorizes the collecting bank to supply the missing endorsements as a matter of course. In practice, banks comply with § 4–205 by stamping the item "deposited to the account of the named payee" or some similar formula. * * * We doubt whether the bank's status should turn on proof of whether a clerk employed the appropriate stamp, and we hesitate to penalize a bank which accepted unendorsed checks for deposit in reliance on the Code, at least when, as here, the customer himself clearly satisfies the definition of "holder". Section 4–209 does provide that a bank must comply "with the requirements of section 3–302 on what constitutes a holder in due course," but we think this language refers to the enumerated requirements of good faith and lack of notice rather than to the status of holder, a status which § 3–302 assumes rather than requires. We therefore hold that a bank which takes an item for collection from a customer who was himself a holder need not establish that it took the item by negotiation in order to satisfy § 4–209.

Holding [handwritten marginal note]

* * *

This brings us to plaintiff's final argument, that the Bank gave value only to the extent of the $5,024.85 overdraft, and thus cannot be a holder in due course with respect to the remaining $10,047.54 which the Bank credited against Bowl–Mor's loan account. Our consideration of this argument is confined by the narrow scope of the district court's findings. The Bank may well have given value under § 4–208(1)(a) when it credited the balance of Bowl–Mor's checking account against its outstanding indebtedness. See Banco Espanol de Credito v. State Street Bank & Trust Co., 409 F.2d 711 (1st Cir.1969). But by that time the Bank knew of Bowl–Mor's petition for reorganization, additional information which the district court did not consider in finding that the Bank acted in good faith and without notice at the time it received the item. We must therefore decide whether the Bank gave value for the additional $10,047.54 at the time the item was deposited.[5]

Resolution of this issue depends on the proper interpretation of § 4–209, which provides that a collecting bank has given value to the extent that it has acquired a "security interest" in an item. In plaintiff's view, a collecting bank can satisfy § 4–209 only by extending credit against an item in compliance with § 4–208(1). The district court, on the other hand, adopted the view that a security interest is a security interest, however acquired. The court then found that defendant and Bowl–Mor had entered

---

5. Defendant suggests that we can avoid the analytical problems of § 4–209 by simply holding that the Bank's inchoate right to set off Bowl–Mor's outstanding indebtedness against deposits, as they were made constituted a giving of value. See Wood v. Boylston National Bank, 129 Mass. 358 (1880). There are, however, some pitfalls in this theory. First, under prior law a secured creditor could not exercise its right of set-off without first showing that its security was inadequate. Forastiere v. Springfield Institution for Savings, 303 Mass. 101, 104, 20 N.E.2d 950 (1939). Second, although the Uniform Commercial Code forswears any intent to change a banker's right of set-off, § 4–201 does change the presumption that a bank owns items deposited with it. This presumption played a role under prior law in assessing the bank's rights against uncollected commercial paper. Compare Wood v. Boylston National Bank, supra, with Boston–Continental National Bank v. Hub Fruit Co., 285 Mass. 187, 190, 189 N.E. 89 (1934) and American Barrel Co. v. Commissioner of Banks, 290 Mass. 174, 179–181, 195 N.E. 335 (1935).

a security agreement which gave defendant a floating lien on Bowl–Mor's chattel paper. Since the item in question was part of the proceeds of a Bowl–Mor contract, the court concluded that defendant had given value for the full $15,306.00 at the time it received the deposit.[a]

With this conclusion we agree. Section 1–201(37) defines "security interest" as an interest in personal property which secures payment or performance of an obligation. There is no indication in § 4–209 that the term is used in a more narrow or specialized sense. Moreover, as the official comment to § 4–209 observes, this provision is in accord with prior law and with § 3–303, both of which provide that a holder gives value when he accepts an instrument as security for an antecedent debt. Reynolds v. Park Trust Co., 245 Mass. 440, 444–445, 139 N.E. 785 (1923). Finally, we note that if one of the Bank's prior loans to Bowl–Mor had been made in the expectation that this particular instrument would be deposited, the terms of § 4–208(1)(c) would have been literally satisfied. We do not think the case is significantly different when the Bank advances credit on the strength of a continuing flow of items of this kind. We therefore conclude that the Bank gave value for the full $15,306.00 at the time it accepted the deposit.

We see no discrepancy between this result and the realities of commercial life. Each party, of course, chose to do business with an eventually irresponsible third party. The Bank, though perhaps unwise in prolonging its hopes for a prospering customer, nevertheless protected itself through security arrangements as far as possible without hobbling each deposit and withdrawal. Plaintiff, on the other hand, not only placed its initial faith in Bowl–Mor, but later became aware that Bowl–Mor was having difficulties in meeting its payroll. It seems not too unjust that this vestige of caveat emptor survives.

Affirmed.

NOTES

1. The conclusion in *Bowling Green* that a depositary bank could become a holder in due course of a check which did not bear the indorsement of the depositor was very controversial and was not supported by the text of Article 3 and Article 4 then in effect. Some courts refused to follow *Bowling Green*. But the 1990 Official Text of Article 4 follows *Bowling Green* in this regard. Section 4–205 states that a depositary bank receiving a check for collection becomes a holder when it receives the check if the customer was then a holder regardless of whether the check is indorsed by

a. [Eds. The bank secured its loan to Bowl–Mor by a security interest in Bowl–Mor's installment sale contracts (defined as chattel paper by § 9–105(1)(b)). Its security interest applied not only to the chattel paper but also to any proceeds of the chattel paper. § 9–306. Bowling Green's check to Bowl– Mor, since it was in payment of the first installment of its sales contract, was proceeds. Under § 9–306 and § 9–203 the bank automatically obtained a security interest in this check as soon as Bowl–Mor obtained "rights" in the check, which in this case was when Bowl–Mor received the check.]

the customer. It goes on to state that the bank becomes a holder in due course if it satisfies the other requirements of § 3–302.

2. In footnote 5 of *Bowling Green* the court's reference to "the Bank's inchoate right to set off" is apparently meant to apply to the banker's lien. It is clear that a banker's lien is not a security interest under § 4–210, but Comment 1 to that section states that "Subsection (a) does not derogate from the banker's general common law lien or right of set-off against indebtedness owing in deposit accounts." The Comment to § 4–211 states that that section is in accord with the prior law (NIL § 27) and with § 3–303. NIL § 27 states: "Where the holder has a lien on the instrument, arising either from contract or by implication of law, he is deemed a holder for value to the extent of his lien." Section 3–303(a)(2) states that an instrument is transferred for value if the transferee acquires a security interest or other lien in the instrument other than a lien obtained by judicial proceeding. Assuming that the Bowl–Mor loan was due at the time the check was deposited, there is abundant authority, including Wood v. Boylston National Bank, 129 Mass. 358 (1880), cited by the court, which supports the defendant's argument that it acquired a lien in the check when it was deposited. But the Massachusetts courts seem to severely restrict the banker's lien by their reading of the special deposit rule, which is a qualification on a bank's ability to obtain a lien. This qualification states that the banker's lien does not apply to items deposited for a special purpose. Jones on Liens § 251 (3d ed. 1914). Two examples illustrate the doctrine. In Bank of the United States v. Macalester, 9 Pa. 475 (1849), the obligor on interest coupons payable to bearer deposited funds with Bank, which as its agent was to use the funds to pay holders of the coupons who presented them for payment. At the time of the deposit the obligor on the coupons was indebted to Bank. Instead of paying the coupons Bank asserted a lien on the deposited funds to pay the debt owing to it. The court held that because the funds were deposited for a special purpose Bank could not assert a lien against them. In Rockland Trust Co. v. South Shore National Bank, 366 Mass. 74, 314 N.E.2d 438 (1974), the court stated that "it seems at least doubtful" that a depositary bank could assert a lien against a certified check deposited to the account of its customer for the purpose of having the funds represented by the check wired to a third party to whom its customer was indebted. But the Massachusetts courts have also applied the special deposit rule to checks deposited for collection with the effect that a depositary bank acting as agent of its customer to collect the check cannot claim any beneficial interest in the check. Under this reading of the rule the qualification apparently destroys the banker's lien in most of the cases to which it has historically been applied, and the bank is limited to a right of setoff after the check is paid. See Boston–Continental National Bank v. Hub Fruit Co., 285 Mass. 187, 189 N.E. 89 (1934).

3. Acquisition of a lien by a depositary bank does not depend upon the bank's making any accounting entries to "apply" the check to the outstanding debt. See Maryland Casualty Co. v. National Bank of Germantown & Trust Co., 320 Pa. 129, 182 A. 362 (1936). By contrast § 4–210(a)(1) states that the bank gets a security interest in the deposited check at the time that credit given for it is "applied." In *Bowling Green* the court indicates that this refers to the time when Bowl–Mor's deposit account, which had been credited with the amount of the check, was charged $10,047.54 in reduction of the loan. Suppose a check payable to Customer was indorsed by Customer to Depositary Bank and delivered to one of its officers in reply to a demand by Depositary Bank to immediately cover an overdraft. Thereafter, but before the check was deposited to Customer's account the drawer of the check told the officer handling the transaction that the check was issued without consideration. At what time was "credit given for the item * * * applied"? § 4–210(a)(1). At what time did Depositary Bank take the instrument "as payment of, or as security for, an antecedent claim"? § 3–303(a)(3). At what time did Depositary Bank acquire a "lien in the instrument other than a lien obtained by judicial proceeding?" § 3–303(a)(2). Peoria Savings & Loan Association v. Jefferson Trust & Savings Bank of Peoria, 81 Ill.2d 461, 43 Ill.Dec. 712, 410 N.E.2d 845 (1980).

c.   ANTECEDENT CLAIMS AND SECURITY INTERESTS IN GOODS

The depositary bank in *Bowling Green* was able to assert rights in the deposited check as a holder in due course because its Article 9 security interest in the check securing an antecedent debt satisfied the taking-for-value requirement. Thus, without giving any new value and without showing any detrimental reliance, it was able to profit from its customer's fraud against Bowling Green. An analogous problem is raised in the case of goods. Negotiability is provided by § 2–403(1) and value is provided, as in *Bowling Green*, by an antecedent debt and an Article 9 security interest.

CHAPTER 2

LIABILITY OF PARTIES TO NEGOTIABLE INSTRUMENTS

A. LIABILITY OF DRAWER AND DRAWEE

The promissory note is the most simple kind of negotiable instrument. The person primarily obliged to pay is the maker who has expressly agreed to do so. The draft is a more complex form of instrument. The drawer orders the drawee to pay an amount of money to the payee, but nobody has expressly agreed to make the payment. A draft normally arises out of a pre-existing creditor-debtor relationship between the drawer and the drawee. For example, a seller ships goods to a buyer who is located in a distant market. The contract of sale provides for payment of the price of the goods by a draft drawn by the seller on the buyer or the buyer's bank acting on behalf of the buyer. The seller draws a draft ordering the drawee to pay to the order of a named payee a sum of money equal to the price of the goods. The named payee may be the seller's bank which buys the draft from the seller for the face amount less a discount to compensate the bank for its services. In that case, the draft is delivered to the bank, which then becomes its holder. The draft is then "presented" to the drawee for payment. "Presentment" is defined in § 3–501(a). In this case, presentment is simply a demand made on the drawee to pay. Subsection (b) of § 3–501 states rules regarding the place, time, and manner of presentment. In our example, presentment might be made by the bank named as payee of the draft, but often the draft will be negotiated to another bank located near the buyer and that bank will present the draft to the drawee for payment. When the draft is paid the buyer has discharged the obligation to the seller to pay the price of the goods.

The most common example of a draft is the ordinary check which is a draft drawn on a bank and payable on demand. § 3–104(f). Payment of checks is also normally based on a creditor-debtor relationship. A check is drawn by a customer of a bank who has a checking account in the bank; the credit balance in the account represents a debt of the bank to the customer. When the bank pays the check, the bank's debt to the customer is reduced by the amount of the check.

Since the drawee of a draft has made no promise in the instrument to pay the payee or other holder, the holder has no action on the instrument against the drawee to enforce payment. § 3–408. Sometimes the drawee will obligate itself, by a letter of credit or other separate contract, to pay a draft. In that case failure by the drawee to pay the draft may result in liability to the holder for breach of the letter of credit, but there is no liability based on an obligation created by the draft. In the absence of a separate contract of the drawee such as a letter of credit, payment by the drawee will normally depend upon the drawee's obligation to the drawer arising from an express or implied contract between them. For example, in opening a checking account for a customer, the bank incurs an obligation to the customer to pay properly payable checks drawn on the account. Failure to pay a properly payable check may result in liability to the customer for wrongful dishonor (§ 4–402), but the holder of the check has no cause of action against the drawee bank. Before codification of negotiable instruments law by the NIL in the late 19th century a minority of states took the view that a check created a direct liability on the part of the drawee bank to the holder. The theory was that a check amounted to an equitable assignment of the drawer's funds on deposit, but NIL § 189 took the majority view that the check is not itself an assignment. Article 3 follows the NIL in that respect.

Although a draft, by its stated terms, is simply an order of the drawer to the drawee to pay, it is also an obligation of the drawer to pay the draft if the draft is dishonored. § 3–414(b). "Dishonor" occurs if the drawee fails to make timely payment when the draft is presented for payment. Dishonor of ordinary checks and drafts is defined in § 3–502(b) and (e). The drawer of a draft other than a check can avoid liability under § 3–414(b) if the signature of the drawer is accompanied by words which disclaim liability such as "without recourse." § 3–414(e). Disclaimer of the drawer's liability is normally limited to documentary drafts. Comment 5 to § 3–414. With respect to checks, disclaimer is not effective. § 3–414(e). A relatively unimportant limitation on drawer's liability is provided by § 3–414(f). This provision is explained in Comment 6 to § 3–414.

Section 3–408 states that "the drawee is not liable on the instrument until the drawee accepts it." Section 3–409(a) defines "acceptance" as "the drawee's signed agreement to pay a draft as presented." The acceptance "must be written on the draft and may consist of the drawee's signature alone." A drawee that accepts a draft is known as the "acceptor" and is obliged to the holder to pay the draft. § 3–413(a). To better understand the concept of acceptance it is appropriate to distinguish between two types of drafts. The most common type of draft is the demand draft or "sight draft." It contemplates that the amount of the draft will be paid by the drawee upon presentation or "on sight." A draft which does not specify a time of payment is payable on demand. § 3–108(a). A check is the most common example of a demand draft. Another type of draft, called a "time draft" does not contemplate immediate payment by the drawee. For example, suppose the draft reads as follows: "Pay $1,000 to the order of Jane Doe sixty days after presentment of this draft." Here, two steps are contemplated. Jane Doe, or some subsequent holder, will initially present the draft to the drawee to start the running of the 60 days, and when that period of time has passed a second presentment will be made for payment. The first presentment is known as a "presentment for acceptance." Its purpose is to allow the holder to know whether the drawee is agreeable to honoring the draft. Agreement of the drawee is manifested by acceptance, i.e., the drawee's signing of the draft with or without the addition of the word "accepted" or other words indicating an intention to accept. The date of acceptance is normally included but is not required. § 3–409(a) and (c). The drawee's acceptance is equivalent to a promise to pay the amount of the draft to the holder. Thus, the obligation of an acceptor is like that of the maker of a note.

Another example of an accepted draft is the certified check. If the payee of an ordinary check wants assurance of payment, one way of getting it is to insist that the drawer obtain the acceptance of the drawee bank before the check is taken by the payee. This is done by the drawee bank's signing the check in much the same way as described in the case of a time draft. But the terminology differs. The bank's signature is called "certification" but it is identical to acceptance. § 3–409(d). Certification is normally obtained by the drawer before delivery of the check to the payee, but in unusual cases the holder of an uncertified check may prefer to obtain the drawee bank's agreement to pay rather than payment itself. This can be done by asking the drawee bank to certify the check. The drawee of a check may certify it as a courtesy to the drawer or to the holder, but is not obliged to do so. Nor is refusal to certify a dishonor of the check. § 3–409(d). Because certification of a check is treated by the bank as the equivalent of payment insofar as the drawer is concerned, the account of the drawer will be debited in the amount of the check at the time of certification. The effect of certification is to transform the check, which originally represented an order to pay of the drawer, into a promise of the drawee to pay the amount of the check to its holder. This transformation is reflected in § 3–414(c) which states that acceptance of a draft by a bank discharges the drawer's obligation to pay the draft.

B.   LIABILITY OF INDORSER

In Chapter 9 we examined the function of an indorsement in the negotiation of an instrument. Indorsement also has the additional function of causing the indorser to incur liability on the instrument. The obligation of the indorser, stated in § 3–415(a), is to pay the instrument if the instrument is dishonored, but indorser's liability may be avoided by appropriate words accompanying the signature which disclaim liability. The most commonly used words indicating disclaimer are "without recourse." § 3–415(b).

Drafts

The obligation of the indorser to pay an instrument arises upon its dishonor. With respect to unaccepted drafts, dishonor usually requires presentment for payment and a failure of the drawee to pay. § 3–502(b)(1) through (3). With respect to some time drafts, dishonor requires presentment for acceptance and failure of the drawee to accept. § 3–502(b)(4). In some cases, dishonor can occur without presentment. § 3–502(e) and § 3–504(a).

The obligation of an indorser of an unaccepted draft is subject to discharge in two situations. First, if the draft is a check and collection of the check is not initiated within 30 days of the indorsement, the indorser is discharged. § 3–415(e). Second, discharge can occur as the result of a failure to give timely notice of dishonor to the indorser. § 3–415(c) and § 3–503(a). The manner and time for giving notice are stated in § 3–503(b) and (c). Notice of dishonor need not be given if it is excused. § 3–504(b). Delay in giving notice may also be excused in some cases. § 3–504(c).

Indorser's liability with respect to checks has very limited importance because most checks are deposited by the payee with a depositary bank for collection. The depositary bank gives the depositor provisional credit for the check. Under § 4–214(a), if the check is dishonored, the depositary bank may revoke the credit or otherwise obtain refund from the depositor. Normally, the depositary bank will use this remedy rather than the remedy provided by § 3–415(a).

If a draft is accepted by a bank after the draft is indorsed, the indorser is discharged. § 3–415(d). The rule is similar to § 3–414(c) with respect to the liability of a drawer. Thus, with respect to an accepted draft, an indorser has liability under § 3–415(a) only if the indorsement is made after the acceptance or if the acceptor is not a bank. Rules with respect to dishonor of accepted drafts are stated in § 3–502(d).

Notes

Dishonor of a note payable at a definite time does not normally require presentment unless the note is payable at or through a bank. § 3–502(a)(2) and (3). In the case of notes that do not require presentment, indorser's liability under § 3–415(a) arises automatically if the note is not paid when due. If a note is payable on demand, is payable at or through a bank, or the terms of the note require presentment, dishonor requires presentment and a failure to pay by the maker. But the requirements in § 3–502(a) with respect to presentment can be waived. § 3–504(a). Notice of dishonor required by § 3–503(a) also can be waived, and waiver of presentment is also waiver of notice of dishonor. § 3–504(b). Since most promissory note forms contain a clause waiving presentment and notice of dishonor, these formalities have little importance with respect to indorser liability in note cases.

C. LIABILITY OF TRANSFEROR

If goods are sold the law gives to the buyer the benefit of certain warranties of the seller that are implied by reason of the sale and which apply unless they are disclaimed in the contract between the parties. For example, the seller warrants that the buyer is receiving good title to the goods and, if the seller is a merchant, that the goods are fit for the ordinary purposes for which such goods are used. § 2–312(1) and § 2–314. If an instrument is sold the law gives to the buyer the benefit of implied warranties that are comparable to sale of goods warranties, but which are expressed in terms appropriate to what the buyer is buying—a right to receive payment from the person obliged to pay the instrument. These warranties are known as "transfer warranties" and are stated in § 3–416(a).

Two of the transfer warranties relate to the authenticity of the instrument; the transferor warrants that all signatures are authentic and authorized and the instrument has not been altered. § 3–416(a)(2) and (3). The other three warranties relate to the enforceability of the instrument. Under § 3–416(a)(1) there is a warranty that the transferor is a person entitled to enforce the instrument. If the transferor is a person entitled to enforce the instrument, transfer will give the transferee that right. § 3–203(b). The § 3–416(a)(1) warranty, in practice, serves as a warranty that there are no unauthorized or missing indorsements that prevent the transferor from giving to the transferee the right to enforce the instrument. Under § 3–416(a)(4) there is a warranty that the right to enforce the instrument is not subject to defenses that can be asserted against the transferor. Finally, there is a warranty of no knowledge of bankruptcy or other insolvency proceedings initiated against the person obliged to pay the instrument. § 3–416(a)(5).

The transfer warranties are of very limited importance because in most cases the transferor is also an indorser and, as such, guarantees payment of the instrument. § 3–415(a). In those cases the transfer warranties are redundant because the guarantee of payment gives greater rights to the transferee than do the warranties. Thus, the transfer warranties are important only in cases in which the transfer is made without indorsement or there is an indorsement without recourse. If the payee of a note indorsed the note without recourse, the transferee is assured of receiving an authentic and enforceable instrument but takes the risk that the maker will be unwilling or unable to pay the note.

Before going further, test your knowledge of the material in preceding Sections A, B and C by solving the following elementary Problems.

PROBLEMS

1. Dorrie wrote a check on her account in First Bank payable to Paul who indorsed the check and deposited it in his account in Second Bank. When Second Bank presented the check to First Bank for payment, it was dishonored even though Dorrie's account had sufficient funds to pay the check.

    a. When First Bank returned the dishonored check to Second Bank, Second Bank charged the amount of the check against the provisional credit it had entered in Paul's account upon deposit and returned the check to Paul. What rights does Paul have against First Bank? § 3–408. Against Dorrie? § 3–414(b).

b.   How would your answer to "a" change if Dorrie had obtained First Bank's certification of the check before delivering it to Paul? If Paul had obtained certification before deposit of the check? § 3–413(a), § 3–414(c).

c.   What are Dorrie's rights against First Bank? § 4–402(b).

2.   Morris signed and delivered a promissory note payable to the order of Patience one year after date. One month after receiving the note Patience indorsed the note and delivered it to Helen for value. If Patience indorsed the note "without recourse" and Morris failed to pay the note when it was due because he learned that Patience had defrauded him, is Patience liable to Helen? § 3–415(b), § 3–416(a)(4).

D.   CASHIER'S CHECKS AND TELLER'S CHECKS

In this section we give detailed treatment to the rights of parties under cashier's checks and teller's checks. Our objective is to help you deal with one of the contemporary dilemmas facing business lawyers: how to take payment when the deal closes. Since the obligor side is not likely to lug sacks of money to the closing, the obligee should obtain agreement in advance on how payment is to be made. The ordinary uncertificated check leaves the payee vulnerable on several grounds: the drawer may stop payment on the check, thereby placing the burden on the payee to come after the drawer for payment; the drawer may have no money in its account in the bank; or, in rare cases, the bank on which payment is drawn may suspend payments before the check is paid because of insolvency, leaving the payee with a claim against the bank not covered by deposit insurance because the bank has no liability on the check (§ 3–408) and therefore the payee has no "deposit" insured by the Deposit Insurance Act. 12 USC § 1813(*l*) ("deposit"). On the other hand, we will see that no one can stop payment under § 4–403 on a cashier's check; the payee can be sure that a cashier's check will not be returned marked "not sufficient funds"; and, even if the bank fails, the holder of the check is protected, at least to the extent of $100,000, by federal deposit insurance. 12 USC § 1813(*l*)(4). So why is it that in some cases even when the parties are across the street from each other, the obligee will insist on a wire transfer, which we will study in Chapter 11, instead of a cashier's check? But first we have more to learn about cashier's checks.

1.   USE IN PAYMENT OF OBLIGATIONS

In some transactions a creditor is unwilling to take the personal check of the debtor in payment of the obligation owed to the creditor. Instead, the creditor may insist on delivery by the debtor of the obligation of a bank as payment. The debtor can comply by delivering a cashier's check, a teller's check, or a check of the debtor that has been certified by the drawee. We have already discussed the certified check. Some banks have discontinued the practice of certifying checks. Cashier's checks and teller's checks have become the principal means of allowing a debtor to pay a debt with a bank obligation.

A cashier's check is a rather strange instrument. It is always issued by a bank and is in the form of an ordinary check, except that the drawer and the drawee are the same bank. Thus, Bank A orders itself to pay a sum of money to the payee stated in the instrument. One can justly argue that an order to oneself to pay money is fundamentally different from an order by one person to another person to pay money. In fact, the original Article 3, which did not specifically deal with cashier's checks, supports that argument in former § 3–118(a) which states: "A draft drawn on the drawer is effective as a note." An order to oneself to pay money was given effect as a promise to pay money. The approach of revised Article 3 is somewhat different. Section 3–104(f) follows the universal banking practice of referring to a cashier's check as a check. This practice is also reflected in legislation other than Articles 3 and 4. Section 3–103(a)(6) defines "order" as a "written instruction to pay money" and artificially states that the "instruction may be addressed to anyone, including the person giving the instruction." Thus, a cashier's check is an order and, under § 3–104(e) and (f), is a draft and a check. The purpose of the artificiality in the definition of "order" was to allow references to drafts and checks in Article 3 to include cashier's checks. But the liability of the "issuer" (§ 3–105(c)) of a cashier's check is not stated in § 3–414(b) which applies to drawers of drafts. § 3–414(a). Rather, the liability of the issuer of a cashier's check is found in § 3–412 and is identical to the obligation of the maker of a note.

A teller's check, like a cashier's check, is always issued by a bank. The difference between the two is that a cashier's check is drawn on the issuing bank while a teller's check typically is drawn on another bank. In some cases a teller's check is drawn on a nonbank but is payable at or through a bank. § 3–104(h). The issuer of a teller's check is obliged to pay the check as drawer of the check. § 3–414(b). If a teller's check is issued by Bank A and the check is drawn on Bank B, presentment for payment of the check is made to Bank B, the drawee. As in the case of the drawee of an ordinary check, Bank B as drawee of a teller's check has no obligation to the payee to pay the check. § 3–408. If the check is dishonored, the remedy of the payee is against Bank A. Thus, a teller's check represents an obligation of the bank that issues the check, not of the bank on which it is drawn.

One of the aspects in which cashier's checks differ from ordinary checks is the effect of taking a check on the underlying obligation for which the check was given. Section § 3–310(b)(1) provides that if an uncertified check is taken for an obligation, the obligation is suspended "until dishonor of the check or until it is paid or certification." If the check clears, the obligation is discharged; if it is dishonored, the payee has a choice whether to take action against the drawer on the check or on the underlying obligation. Usually, there is no advantage to the payee in being able to pursue the drawer on the underlying transaction, but in a few instances there may be. However, if the obligee takes a cashier's check for an obligation, the obligation is discharged (§ 3–310(a)) and the payee is restricted to its rights on the check against the issuing bank. As we explained above, if the bank has failed, the holder is insured by federal deposit insurance to the extent of $100,000. We treat these issues in the following Problems.

PROBLEMS

1. Buyer wants to buy goods from Seller. Seller insists that Buyer pay for the goods by a check issued by a bank. Buyer purchases a cashier's check issued by Bank A. Bank A issues the check either to the order of Buyer or to the order of Seller. In either case Bank A delivers the check to Buyer, who becomes the owner of the check. If the check is payable to Buyer when issued, Buyer will also become the holder of the check. If the check is payable to Seller, Buyer is the "remitter" of the check rather than its holder. § 3–103(a)(11). In either case, Buyer can negotiate the check to Seller. If the check is payable to Buyer, negotiation requires the indorsement of Buyer and delivery to Seller. If the check is payable to Seller, negotiation occurs by delivery alone. § 3–201.

On April 1, Seller delivers the goods to Buyer immediately after the check is negotiated to Seller. The check is deposited in Seller's account in Seller's bank. On April 2, the check is presented for payment and is dishonored because Bank A suspended payments on that day. § 4–104(a)(12). The dishonored check is returned by Bank A to Seller's bank and then to Seller.

If the cashier's check received by Seller was payable to the order of Buyer when issued, what cause of action does Seller have against Buyer (a) on the dishonored check, and (b) on the obligation of Buyer to pay the price of the goods delivered to Buyer? § 2–607(1) and § 3–310(a).

If the cashier's check received by Seller was payable to the order of Seller when issued, what cause of action does Seller have against Buyer?

2. The facts are the same as in Problem 1, except as follows: The check was not a cashier's check. Rather, it was a teller's check issued by Bank A and drawn on Bank B. The check when issued was payable to the order of Seller. On April 2, the check was presented for payment to Bank B which refused payment because Bank A suspended payments on that day. The dishonored check was returned by Bank B to Seller's bank which then returned the check to Seller.

What cause of action does Seller have against Bank A because of dishonor of the check? What cause of action does Seller have against Bank B because of dishonor of the check? Does Seller have any cause of action against Buyer?

3. The facts are the same as in Problem 1 except as follows: Buyer did not purchase a cashier's check to pay for the goods. Rather, Buyer paid for the goods by delivery of an uncertified personal check of Buyer drawn on Bank A to the order of Seller. The check was dishonored by Bank A and returned by Bank A to Seller's bank which then returned the check to Seller.

What cause of action does Seller have against Buyer (a) on the dishonored check, and (b) on the obligation of Buyer to pay the price of the goods delivered to Buyer? § 3–310(b)(1) and (3).

2. PAYMENT WITH NOTICE OF ADVERSE CLAIM

Suppose a buyer pays for goods by delivering the buyer's uncertified personal check to the seller. Shortly after the goods are delivered, the buyer examines them and decides that they are unsatisfactory. The buyer seeks to return the goods to the seller and obtain return of the check. The seller denies that the goods are defective and refuses to return the buyer's check. Or, suppose there is a fraudulent sale. The seller took the buyer's check after promising to deliver the goods, but the seller had no intention of carrying out the promise. No goods were ever delivered to the buyer. In either of these two cases the best remedy of the buyer is to prevent the drawee of the check from paying the check. Without that remedy the buyer has the burden of bringing an action against the seller. If the buyer can prevent payment of the check, it is the seller who has the burden of bringing an action. The buyer can prevent payment of an uncertified check of the buyer if the buyer can act very quickly. The check issued by the buyer to the seller functions as an order by the buyer to the buyer's bank to pay money to the seller. Section 4–403 allows the buyer to countermand that order by what is referred to as a "stop-payment order," which is simply an instruction to the bank not to pay the check. A stop-payment order may be given orally or in writing and must describe the check with reasonable certainty so that the bank can identify the check. The bank is obliged to carry out the order if it is received in time to allow the bank a reasonable opportunity to act on the order before the check is paid. § 4–403(a). Failure to carry out the order can give rise to an action for damages. § 4–403(c).

The remedy provided by § 4–403 is not available, however, if the buyer pays for the goods with a certified check, cashier's check, or teller's check. Section 4–403 applies only to an "item [check] drawn on the customer's [buyer's] account." What are the rights of the buyer under § 4–403 if a certified check is delivered to the seller? A certified check, in form, is drawn on the customer's account, but it is not treated that way under § 4–403(a). The right of a customer to stop payment of a check is conditioned upon receipt by the bank of a stop-payment order "before any action by the bank with respect to the item described in Section 4–303." One of the actions referred to in § 4–303 is payment of the check. § 4–303(a)(2). Another is certification. § 4–303(a)(1). So far as the rights and obligations of the drawer are concerned, certification of a check is treated as the equivalent of payment. When the check is certified it is treated as an obligation of the certifying bank rather than an item drawn on the drawer's account. Thus, if the buyer delivers a certified check to the seller, no right to stop payment of the check ever arises.

If the buyer delivered a cashier's check or teller's check to the seller, the analysis under § 4–403 is somewhat different. A cashier's check or teller's check is not drawn on the buyer's account even though the buyer may have bought the check from the buyer's bank which obtained payment for it by debiting the buyer's account. Section 4–403 allows the buyer to stop payment of a check of the buyer, but does not allow the buyer to stop payment of a check issued by the buyer's bank. Comment 4 to § 4–403. Section 4–403 does not apply at all to a cashier's check because the obligation of the issuer is the same as the obligation of the issuer of a note. § 3–412. There is no instruction by one person to another that can be countermanded. Section 4–403 does apply to a teller's check. The issuer of a teller's check is like the drawer of an ordinary check. The bank issuing the teller's check draws the check on the account of the issuer in the drawee bank. The issuer is a customer of the drawee bank. § 4–104(a)(5). Thus, under § 4–403, the issuer of the teller's check has a right to stop payment by the drawee bank. But that right belongs only to the issuer of the check; the buyer has no right to stop payment.

The rights of a buyer who has paid a seller with a cashier's check and who either has been defrauded or has received defective goods are considered in the following problem.

PROBLEM

Seller agreed to sell goods to Buyer but insisted on immediate payment by means of a cashier's check. Buyer had an account in Bank. At the request of Buyer, Bank issued a cashier's check payable to the order of Seller and delivered it to Buyer. Bank debited the account of Buyer in the amount of the cashier's check. Buyer delivered the check to Seller, but Seller failed to deliver the promised goods stating that they would be delivered as soon as they became available. Buyer stated that Seller had promised immediate delivery and demanded return of the check. Seller refused.

a.   Immediately before Buyer delivered the check to Seller, was Buyer the owner of the check? At that time was Buyer a "person entitled to enforce" the check? § 3–301. If Buyer had not delivered the check to Seller, would Buyer be entitled to return the check to Bank and obtain refund from Bank of the amount Buyer paid Bank? § 1–103.

b.   After Seller refused to return the check, did Buyer have a claim to the check that could be asserted against Seller? § 3–306, § 3–202(b), § 3–201(a), and Comment 2 to § 3–201. If Buyer had a claim to the check, could that claim be asserted against a holder in due course to whom Seller negotiated the check? § 3–306.

c.   After Seller refused to return the check, Buyer asked Bank to refuse payment of the check. Buyer informed Bank of all of the facts with respect to the negotiation of the check to Seller and asserted that Seller had deceived Buyer in order to obtain possession of the check.

Buyer demanded that Bank return the money that Buyer paid for the check. Does Bank have to return the money it received from Buyer for the check? If Seller presents the check for payment, does Bank satisfy its obligations with respect to the check by paying Seller? § 3–602. If Seller presents the check for payment, may Bank refuse payment on the ground that Buyer has a claim to the check that is enforceable against Seller? § 3–305(c) (first sentence) and Comment 4 to § 3–305. If Seller presents the check for payment and Bank refuses payment, what rights does Seller have against Bank? § 3–412 and § 3–411. If Bank tells Buyer that it intends to pay the check when it is presented for payment, what can Buyer do to prevent Bank from paying? § 3–305(c), § 3–602(b)(1), and § 3–411(c)(iv).

3.   CASHIER'S CHECKS AS CASH EQUIVALENTS

In our inquiry into the question whether you would advise a client to accept a cashier's check in payment, we have seen that the person obtaining a cashier's check has no right to stop payment on the check under § 4–403 and that the issuing bank cannot assert defenses of others (§ 3–305(c)) unless payment has been enjoined (§ 3–602(b)(1)). This leaves a third issue to be resolved: can the issuing bank raise its own defenses when a cashier's check is presented to it for payment? Before enactment of revised Article 3 there was a split of authority in the cases, as well as a lively disagreement among commentators, on the matter. Arline v. Omnibank, N.A., 894 S.W.2d 76, 78 n. 2 (Tex.App.1995), marshals the case law. The initial article on the subject was Lary Lawrence, Making Cashier's Checks and Other Bank Checks Cost–Effective: A Plea for Revision of Articles 3 and 4 of the Uniform Commercial Code, 64 Minn.L.Rev. 275 (1980), which advocated making cashier's checks "cash equivalents" by prohibiting issuing banks from raising any defenses to payment even against non-holders in due course.

Bank One, Merrillville v. Northern Trust Bank/DuPage

United States District Court, N.D. Illinois, E.D, 1991.
775 F.Supp. 266.

■ HOLDERMAN, DISTRICT JUDGE:

Plaintiff, Bank One, Merrillville, NA ("Bank One"), brought this diversity action against defendant, Northern Trust Bank/DuPage ("Northern"), claiming wrongful dishonor of a cashier's check. Northern asserted affirmative defenses and a counterclaim based on fraud, bad faith and misconduct. Bank One has moved, pursuant to Fed.R.Civ.P. 56, for partial summary judgment on the issue of Northern's wrongful dishonor. For the reasons stated in this opinion, Bank One's motion is granted.

FACTS

This case concerns two banks, Bank One of Merrillville, Indiana ("Bank One") and Northern Trust Bank/DuPage of Oak Brook, Illinois

("Northern"), and two of their customers, Zaragoza Motors Inc. ("Zaragoza") and Sakoff Media Enterprises, Inc. ("Sakoff"). In June 1990, Zaragoza had a checking account at Bank One, while Sakoff had one at Northern.

On or before June 7, 1990 Sakoff wrote a check for $98,581.40 ("the Sakoff check") on its account at Northern, payable to the order of Zaragoza. Zaragoza deposited the Sakoff check in its account at Bank One on June 7, 1990. Bank One sent the Sakoff check to Northern for payment. On June 13, 1990, it was returned to Bank One, as the funds in Sakoff's account were insufficient to cover the amount of the Sakoff check.

Kenneth Dykstra, a Bank One employee, telephoned Northern upon receiving the returned Sakoff check on June 13, and was told that Sakoff's account did contain sufficient funds to cover the check. On the same day, Dykstra drove to Northern's offices and exchanged the Sakoff check for a Northern cashier's check for $98,581.40. When Bank One sent the endorsed cashier's check through the Federal Reserve Bank to Northern for payment, however, Northern refused to honor the check.

The reasons for Northern's refusal to pay relate to another check ("the Zaragoza check"), drawn on Zaragoza's account at Bank One, for $103,200, which Zaragoza presumably transferred to Sakoff at about the same time that Zaragoza received the Sakoff check for $98,581.40. At some point before June 12, 1990, Sakoff deposited Zaragoza's check into Sakoff's account at Northern. Northern then sent the Zaragoza check to Bank One for collection. Bank One received the check on June 12 but, on June 13, issued notice to Northern, through the Federal Reserve Bank, that it was dishonoring the Zaragoza check, because of insufficient funds in Zaragoza's account. This notice did not reach Northern until after Dykstra had obtained the cashier's check. As a result of Bank One's rejection of the Sakoff check, the funds in Sakoff's account were insufficient to cover the Sakoff check for which Northern had issued its cashier's check.

DISCUSSION

Under Fed.R.Civ.P. 56(c), summary judgment is proper "if the pleadings, depositions, answers to interrogatories, and admissions on file, together with the affidavits, if any, show that there is no genuine issue as to any material fact and that the moving party is entitled to a judgment as a matter of law." According to Bank One, Illinois law forbids a bank from dishonoring its cashier's checks for any reason. On the basis of this understanding of the law, Bank One contends that it is entitled to summary judgment, since any arguments Northern might make and any factual issues they might raise are immaterial to the issue of wrongful dishonor.

In response, Northern asserts bad faith on the part of Bank One. Northern contends that when Dykstra drove to Northern to obtain the cashier's check, he was aware that his bank was in the process of dishonoring the Zaragoza check. According to Northern, Bank One feared that its dishonor of the Zaragoza check would result in there being insufficient funds to cover the Sakoff check. This fear allegedly prompted Dykstra to hurry to Northern in order to obtain the cashier's check before Northern received notice of Bank One's dishonor. Northern contends that bad faith such as that alleged justifies a refusal to honor a cashier's check, and that the factual issue of Bank One's bad faith precludes summary judgment.

The transaction in this case involved an official of an Indiana bank coming into Illinois and receiving a cashier's check from an Illinois bank. Plaintiff, in its brief, assumed the application of Illinois law. Defendant, while citing cases from other jurisdictions, raised no explicit protest. Because the outcome of the case hinges on the applicability of Illinois law, the court must first confirm the parties' implicit choice of law.

In a diversity case, the court must apply the conflict of law rules of the state in which it sits. Klaxon Co. v. Stentor Electric Mfg. Co., 313 U.S. 487, 61 S.Ct. 1020, 85 L.Ed. 1477 (1941). This case involves a negotiable instrument, so it implicates the Illinois version of the Uniform Commercial Code ("the Code"). Ill.Rev.Stat. ch. 26 P 1–101 et seq. The relevant choice of law provision is therefore § 1–105, which provides that the Illinois Code applies to "transactions bearing an appropriate relation to this state." The cashier's check in this case was issued by an Illinois bank to a person in Illinois. The relation of this transaction to Illinois therefore calls for the application of Illinois law.

Although the Illinois Code does not specifically address the subject of a bank's cashier's checks, the Illinois Appellate Court interpreted the Code's application to the issue in Able & Associates, Inc. v. Orchard Hill Farms of Illinois, Inc., Etc., 77 Ill.App.3d 375, 395 N.E.2d 1138, 32 Ill.Dec. 757 (1st Dist.1979). In *Able & Associates*, the court rejected defendant Union National Bank's argument that a failure of consideration justified its refusal to honor a cashier's check. The court instead employed a line of analysis under the Code which led it to endorse "a rule which prohibits a bank from refusing to honor its cashier's checks." Id., 77 Ill.App.3d at 381–82, 32 Ill.Dec. at 761, 395 N.E.2d at 1142.

Characterizing the bank's issuance of a cashier's check as acceptance of the item, the court in *Able & Associates* applied § 4–303 of the Code, which provides that a stop order on a check is ineffective after acceptance.[1] 77 Ill.App.3d at 380, 32 Ill.Dec. at 761, 395 N.E.2d at 1142. As a consequence, under Illinois law, a bank cannot refuse to pay a cashier's check which it has issued. The court in *Able & Associates* viewed its holding as compelled by policy concerns about the negotiability of cashier's checks:

> A cashier's check circulates in the commercial world as the equivalent of cash ... to allow a bank to stop payment on such a check would ... undermine the public confidence in the bank and its checks and thereby deprive the cashier's check of the essential incident which makes it useful.

---

1. Code § 4–303 provides, in relevant part: "(1) Any knowledge, notice or stop-order received by ... a payor bank, whether or not effective under other rules of law to terminate, suspend, or modify a bank's right or duty to pay an item ... comes too late to so terminate, suspend or modify such right or duty if the knowledge, notice, [or] stop-order is received ... after the bank has ... (a) accepted or certified the item."

Able & Associates, 77 Ill.App.3d at 382, 32 Ill.Dec. at 761, 395 N.E.2d at 1142, quoting National Newark & Essex Bank v. Giordano, 111 N.J.Super. 347, 268 A.2d 327 (1970).

The 1979 ruling in *Able & Associates* relied upon and reflected that of a 1973 Seventh Circuit decision applying Illinois law, Munson v. American National Bank & Trust Co., 484 F.2d 620 (7th Cir.1973). In Munson, the Seventh Circuit ruled, as the Illinois Appellate Court later would in *Able*, that a bank could not assert failure of consideration as an excuse for the dishonor of a cashier's check. The Seventh Circuit applied Code § 4–303, and explained that, as a consequence, a bank has "no more right to countermand its cashier's checks than" it has rights "to refuse to pay cash it has already paid." Id. at 623–24.

In both *Able & Associates* and *Munson*, the courts, while holding that the cashier's checks must be honored, permitted the banks to raise their defenses and issues relating to the underlying transactions as part of their own affirmative claims. *Able & Associates*, 77 Ill.App.3d at 382–83, 32 Ill.Dec. at 761–62, 395 N.E.2d at 1142–43; *Munson*, 484 F.2d at 624. The defendants in both cases had to pay the cashier checks, and then seek to recover the funds from the hands of the plaintiffs just as they would as if they had paid cash.[2]

In the face of this case law which holds that a bank has no right to dishonor its cashier's checks but must instead assert its reason for non-payment as part of its own action to recover the funds, Northern essentially argues for a "bad faith" or "fraud" exception to the general principle. Northern reasons that, while Illinois courts have held that failure of consideration is no excuse for dishonoring a cashier's check, they have never ruled that the procurer's bad faith does not provide a defense.

In support of the distinction, Northern argues that "better authority for the law that governs this particular situation" appears in cases which hold that banks can refuse to honor cashier's checks obtained through fraud. Defendant then cites cases such as Farmers & Merchants State Bank v. Western Bank, 841 F.2d 1433 (9th Cir.1987) and TPO, Inc. v. Federal Deposit Insurance Corp., 487 F.2d 131, 135–36 (3d Cir.1973) as authority for its argument.

These cases interpret the UCC in a way that enables a bank to stop payment on a cashier's check in case of fraud, and thereby support defendant's position. This court, however, could not rely on the authority cited by Northern even if it were persuasive. As stated earlier in this opinion, this diversity case must be decided according to Illinois law. The interpretation of the UCC found in the cases cited by Northern, which grants a bank the power to stop payment on its cashier's checks, is,

---

2. In *Munson*, the bank's counterclaim for a setoff was ripe for summary judgment, which the court granted. The plaintiff's success on the wrongful dishonor issue was therefore empty, since it simultaneously lost on the issue of liability in the underlying transaction. In *Able & Associates*, the court, after resolving the cashier's check issue, remanded for determination of the bank's affirmative claim regarding the underlying transaction.

however, directly and explicitly contrary to the law articulated by Illinois courts.

As previously discussed, Illinois courts view an issued cashier's check as accepted under Code § 4–303 and as the equivalent of cash. In *Farmers & Merchants State Bank*, however, the Ninth Circuit rejected the approach taken in *Able & Associates*, concluding that § 4–303 "had no bearing on the question whether [a bank] may assert its own defenses to liability on its cashier's check," *Farmers & Merchants State Bank*, 841 F.2d at 1451. The Ninth Circuit cited the Seventh Circuit's *Munson* opinion as an opposing view. Id. at 1440 n. 11. Likewise, in TPO, Inc. v. Federal Deposit Insurance Corporation, the Third Circuit expressly spurned the § 4–303 "acceptance" mode of analyzing the issuance of cashier's checks. *TPO*, 487 F.2d at 135–136.

The Ninth Circuit, in *Farmers & Merchants State Bank*, also explicitly eschewed the notion, adopted in Illinois, that certified checks must be viewed as cash equivalents, reasoning that "nothing in the U.C.C. suggests that cashier's checks should be treated differently from other instruments subject to Articles 3 and 4." *Farmers and Merchants State Bank*, 841 F.2d at 1440. Similarly, the Third Circuit, in *TPO*, explained its view that a cashier's check "is equivalent to a negotiable promissory note of a bank. . . . not the same as cash as has been loosely asserted." *TPO*, 487 F.2d at 136.

The rejection by the non-Illinois courts of the "acceptance" and "cash equivalency" treatment of cashier's checks leads directly to their recognition of a bank's ability to stop payment in the case of fraud. Having concluded that issuance of a cashier's check is not acceptance under § 4–303 and that a cashier's check is not necessarily equivalent to cash, the courts, not applying Illinois law, were free to analyze the check as they would any other negotiable instrument, in terms of whether the plaintiff seeking payment was a holder in due course. If the plaintiff in a wrongful dishonor action is guilty of fraud, he would not be a holder in due course. Consequently, under § 3–306, the bank would be entitled to present all defenses which would be available on a simple contract such as lack of consideration or fraud. * * *

The holding and reasoning of *Able & Associates* clearly indicates that Illinois courts have adopted the § 4–303 acceptance and cash equivalency method of analyzing cashier's checks, not the holder in due course analysis exhibited in the cases cited by Northern. Indeed, the Illinois Appellate Court, in *Able & Associates*, explicitly considered and rejected the approach taken by the Third Circuit in *TPO*.[4] *Able & Associates*, 77 Ill.App.3d at

---

4. The diverging approaches taken in the various opinions reflects a wider split of authority regarding the character of cashier's checks, between courts that take the § 4–303 approach, viewing an issued cashier's check as accepted, and those that view cashier's checks as being subject, in the same way as other negotiable instruments, to the defenses of § 3–305 and § 3–306, such as lack of consideration and fraud. See DaSilva v. Sanders, 600 F.Supp. 1008 (D.D.C.1984) (discussing split of authority and citing cases); L. Lawrence, Making Cashier's Checks and Other Bank Checks Cost Effective: A Plea for Revi-

380–82, 32 Ill.Dec. at 759–60, 395 N.E.2d at 1140–41. This court cannot accept Northern's attempt to avail itself of the defenses to dishonor provided by the Third and Ninth Circuit's interpretations of the UCC because Illinois law, which applies in this case, contradicts the theory of cashier's checks upon which they, and Northern, rely.

As a consequence of the application of Illinois law to the subject of cashier's checks, Northern, under § 4–303, can raise no excuse "whether or not effective under other rules of law" justifying its refusal to pay. The proper context for Northern's arguments regarding Bank One's alleged bad faith is its counterclaim rather than as a defense to Bank One's action for wrongful dishonor. Unfortunately for Northern in this case, its claim concerning the underlying transaction is not yet ready for judgment.[6]

Northern therefore must honor its cashier's check and seek to recover the funds in the hands of Bank One, just as it would have to do if it had paid cash. Under Illinois law, Northern assumed the risk of having to pursue litigation to recover improperly paid funds when it issued the cashier's check. This result, which is dictated by Illinois law, serves the interest of preserving the free negotiability of cashier's checks while at the same time affording Northern the opportunity to remedy what it views as a wrong.

CONCLUSION

For the foregoing reasons, plaintiff's motion for partial summary judgment is GRANTED. * * *

NOTE

Whatever the merits of making cashier's checks cash equivalents, there was no basis for doing so in old Article 3 which made no specific reference to cashier's and teller's checks. The accepted draft theory embraced by *Bank One* was not supported by the statute. Old § 3–118(a) stated: "A draft drawn on the drawer is effective as a note." Thus an order to oneself to pay money had the effect of a promise to pay, and promisors may always assert their own defenses. The cash equivalent theory found little support among the Drafting Committee in the revision of Article 3, and § 3–411(c) allows the "obligated bank" to refuse payment with impunity if it "asserts a claim or defense of the bank that it has reasonable grounds to believe is available against the person entitled to enforce the instrument."

PROBLEM

Seller agreed to sell goods to Buyer but insisted on immediate payment by means of a cashier's check before it would deliver the goods. Buyer had

sion of Articles 3 and 4 of the Uniform Commercial Code, 64 Minn.L.Rev. 275, 285–320 (discussing different approaches).

6. As Northern has not yet paid the cashier's check, its counterclaim requests only incidental damages. Now that it must honor the check, Northern may, before the date set for the next status report in the case, amend its counterclaim to allege damages it suffers thereby.

an account in Bank, and, at the request of Buyer, Bank issued a cashier's check payable to the order of Seller and delivered it to Buyer. Buyer delivered the check to Seller who promised delivery of the goods the following day. Over night Buyer developed a common commercial affliction known as "buyer's remorse"; Buyer pleaded with Seller to call the deal off and return the check. When Seller proved unreasonable, Buyer demanded that Bank not pay the check, promising to reimburse it for any litigation expenses if Seller pressed its claim. Buyer assured Bank that Seller probably didn't want a lawsuit and would just drop the whole matter. Assuming that Buyer is a very good customer of Bank, would you advise Bank that in view of passage of § 3–411 Bank should go ahead and pay Seller? If you were Seller, would you ever take a cashier's check again unless you were confident that your buyer was completely trustworthy?

4.   LOST INSTRUMENTS

We have seen that the person obliged to pay an instrument can obtain discharge by paying the holder even if some other person has a claim to the instrument. The discharge can be asserted against anyone other than a person with rights of a holder in due course who took the instrument without notice of the discharge. § 3–601(b). If the instrument is surrendered when payment is made, there is no risk that the instrument will be negotiated to a holder in due course. But we have also seen that in some cases the person entitled to enforce the instrument is not in possession of the instrument. § 3–301. Although payment to a person entitled to enforce who does not have possession results in discharge (§ 3–602(a)), there is the possibility that the instrument is in existence and has or will come into the possession of a holder in due course. Section 3–309 deals with enforcement of lost instruments. Suppose the payee indorses the instrument in blank and then loses it. The payee can enforce the instrument, but § 3–309(b) requires the court to find that the person required to pay the instrument is "adequately protected against loss that might occur by reason of a claim by another person to enforce the instrument." The predecessor of § 3–309 is § 3–804 of the original Article 3 which provided that "the court may require security indemnifying the defendant against loss by reason of further claims on the instrument." The quoted language in § 3–804 was not uniformly adopted. Some states, including New York, changed the language in their versions of Article 3.

Since § 3–309 deals with enforcement, it can be used only by a person entitled to enforce under § 3–301. Although § 3–309 and its predecessor, former § 3–804, apply to any instrument, most lost instrument problems arise with respect to cashier's checks, teller's checks, and certified checks. Section 3–312, which has no predecessor, applies only to these bank obligations and can be used as an alternative to § 3–309. But in some cases a person with rights under § 3–312 does not have rights under § 3–309 because the person is not a person entitled to enforce the instrument. In that category are remitters of cashier's checks or teller's checks and drawers of certified checks who cannot enforce the lost check but who can use § 3–312 to obtain refund from the bank that issued or certified the check.

Diaz, which follows, was decided under the New York version of § 3–804 of the original Article 3. It involved loss of a certified check by the payee of the check.

Diaz v. Manufacturers Hanover Trust Co.

New York Supreme Court, Queens County, Special Term, 1977.
92 Misc.2d 802, 401 N.Y.S.2d 952.

■ MARTIN RODELL, JUSTICE.

The petitioner moves by order to show cause to require the respondent Manufacturers Hanover Trust Company to pay the sum of $37,000 or in the alternative to require the respondent Al Newman to issue a new negotiable instrument to her in the same amount.

The facts are uncontroverted. The petitioner posted the sum of $37,000 as security for a bond in behalf of a defendant in a criminal proceeding. Said security was posted with the respondent Newman, a licensed bail bondsman.

The aforementioned criminal action was concluded on July 20, 1977. Subsequently, the petitioner made demand upon the respondent Newman for the sum of $37,000, which she had heretofore posted with him. On August 4, 1977 the respondent Newman dutifully delivered to the petitioner two certified checks, in the amounts of $12,000 and $25,000, drawn on the respondent Manufacturers Hanover Trust Company. Shortly thereafter, the petitioner lost, misplaced, or was criminally relieved of the said certified checks and has to this date been unable to locate them.

The petitioner notified the respondent Newman, who, in turn, requested that the respondent Manufacturers Hanover Trust Co. stop payment. To this date, the checks have not been presented to Manufacturers Hanover Trust Co. for payment.

The petitioner also contacted an unnamed officer of the respondent Manufacturers Hanover Trust Co., who informed her that the bank would not honor any replacement checks issued by the respondent Newman unless an indemnity bond was posted in twice the amount of the original checks. The petitioner avers that this is an onerous and unjust burden; justifiably so, as it would require the posting of $74,000 as security.

* * * When a bank certifies a check, it accepts that check and has the obligation to pay the amount for which it is drawn. * * * The bank in certifying a check obligates itself to an innocent holder in due course to pay the amount for which the check is drawn. Thus, the respondent Manufacturers Hanover Trust Co., through its act of certification, assumed liability on the instruments.

The owner of an instrument which is lost, whether by destruction, theft or otherwise, may maintain an action in his own name and recover from any party liable thereon upon due proof of his ownership, the facts which prevent his production of the instrument and its terms. The court shall require security, in an amount fixed by the court not less than twice the amount allegedly unpaid on the instrument, indemnifying the defendant, his heirs, personal representatives, successors and assigns against loss, including costs and expenses, by reason of further claims on the instrument, but this provision does not apply where an action is prosecuted or defended by the state or by a public officer in its behalf. L.1962, c. 553; amended L.1963, c. 1003, § 9, eff. Sept. 27, 1964 (Uniform Commercial Code, § 3–804.)

While it is clear that the petitioner has the right to recover the amount of the checks upon sufficient proof that in fact the checks did at one time exist, were payable to her and cannot be produced, the issue to be decided is presented to this court as follows:

May the court order payment on a lost negotiable instrument without requiring the payee to post security as required in Uniform Commercial Code, § 3–804? In 487 Clinton Avenue v. Chase Manhattan Bank, 63 Misc.2d 715, 313 N.Y.S.2d 445 (1970, Supreme Court, Kings County), the payee of a certified check was robbed of same at gun point and offered to pay the proceeds into an account controlled by the certifying bank. The court held that it had discretion to fix the security and that the security offered by the plaintiff was adequate.

The court notes that no appeal has been taken from the above decision, and thus no Appellate Court guidance is available. However, the Supreme Court in New York County in Guizani v. Manufacturers Hanover Trust, N.Y.L.J. October 12, 1971, p. 2, col. 5, held that under New York's version of this section (Uniform Commercial Code, § 3–804), the furnishing of the security is mandatory and not discretionary.

The section, as drawn by the drafters of the Uniform Commercial Code, and found in the Official Text and Official Commentaries, made the requirement for security discretionary with the court by the use of the word "*may.*" The Official Commentaries to the Uniform Commercial Code state as follows:

> "There may be cases in which so much time has elapsed, or there is so little possible doubt as to the destruction of the instrument and its ownership that there is no good reason to require the security."

The court, in 487 Clinton Avenue v. Chase Manhattan Bank, supra, predicated its decision on the above reasoning. However, the New York version of section 3–804 of the Uniform Commercial Code pointedly changed the word "may" to "shall," and the Legislature in 1964 further amended this section to fix the amount of security to be not less than twice the amount allegedly unpaid on the instrument. * * * Thus, our Legislature appears to have considered the matter and amended the statute to make the furnishing of security not only mandatory but has also set the minimal amount at not less than twice the amount allegedly unpaid on the instrument.

* * *

The New York Commission Commentaries on section 3–804 of the Uniform Commercial Code leave little doubt that the express purpose of the Legislature was to make the furnishing of security mandatory rather than discretionary and thus conform to section 333 of the old Civil Practice Act.

* * *

If the court is to have the authority to determine the amount of security to be furnished, it would seem on the basis of the legislative history of this section that the change must come from the Legislature.

The court notes additionally that this section, as enacted by our Legislature, while being most positive in regard to the requirement of security and the amount thereof, fails to set any limit whatsoever as to the amount of time the security shall remain posted. The problem of the longevity of a certified check no doubt rendered the Legislature unable to fix a time limit. There being no legislative scheme to either limit the life of a certified check or the duration of time for which a bond must be posted, an unfortunate gap exists into which the petitioner's prayer must fall. It is the opinion of this court that further revision of this section of the Uniform Commercial Code is mandated, or in the alternative, legislation dealing with the valid life of certified checks must be enacted. Simple justice cries out for remedial legislation at the next session of the Legislature. The petitioner is being deprived of her life savings; the bank receives no benefit from the funds which are necessarily frozen. Under the present posture of the law, the funds will remain in that condition until the end of time or it escheats to the state, whichever comes first.

In light of the above, the court is constrained to reject the petitioner's application for recovery without posting of security as required by section 3–804 of the Uniform Commercial Code.

* * *

PROBLEMS

Section 3–312 was drafted in response to the hardship suffered by people like Diaz who have the misfortune to lose a cashier's, teller's, or certified check or to have such a check stolen from them. How does § 3–312 resolve the following problems? Comment 4 to § 3–312.

Claimant lives in New York and has her life savings amounting to almost $100,000 in First Bank. She decides to retire and move to Miami Beach to be near her sister. In anticipation of the move she obtained a cashier's check, dated January 2, from First Bank for $90,000 payable to her order. Her deposit account was immediately debited for $90,000.

1. Thief stole Claimant's purse on January 5 and it contained the cashier's check. The check was not indorsed by Claimant. She immediately called First Bank and asked that payment be stopped. An employee explained to her that if she would come in and sign a form asserting a claim to the check she could get her money back 90 days after the date of the check, but if she wanted her money immediately she would have to provide a bond to protect the bank. § 3–309. Having no resources to obtain a bond, Claimant went to First Bank on January 6 and signed a form asserting her rights under § 3–312(b). Included in the form was a declaration of loss complying with § 3–312(a)(3). Thief forged Claimant's signature as an indorsement of the cashier's check and deposited the check in his account in Second Bank on January 8. The check was promptly presented to First Bank for payment. First Bank paid the check. Thief withdrew the proceeds of the check from his account in Second Bank and absconded. Ninety days after the date of the check, Claimant demanded payment of $90,000 from First Bank. What are Claimant's rights against First Bank if it refuses to pay? If First Bank pays, what are its rights against Second Bank?

2. Change the facts in Problem 1. When First Bank issued the check to Claimant, she indorsed the check by writing her name on the back. She then mailed the check to her sister in Miami Beach who had agreed to deposit it in her account until Claimant could arrive and open her own account. The check was stolen from the mail by Thief who deposited it in his account in Second Bank. By January 10, Claimant realized that something had happened to the check. On that date she went to First Bank and requested that payment be stopped. She was given the same information that was given in Problem 1 and on January 10 executed the necessary form to claim her rights under § 3–312(b). On January 11 Second Bank presented the check to First Bank for payment. First Bank paid the check. Ninety days after the date of the check, Claimant sought $90,000 from First Bank and it refused to pay. What are Claimant's rights against First Bank?

3. Change the facts in Problem 2 in one respect. The check was deposited by Thief in Second Bank on May 10. Second Bank promptly presented the check to First Bank for payment. At the time the check was presented for payment First Bank had already paid $90,000 to Claimant because 90 days had elapsed since the date of the check. First Bank dishonored the check. What are Second Bank's rights against First Bank and Claimant?

E. Accommodation Parties

1. Liability of Accommodation Party and Rights Against Accommodated Party

A creditor taking the promissory note of a debtor who is not a good credit risk may require that a third party act as guarantor of the debtor's obligation to pay the note. Sometimes this guaranty is expressly stated. In many cases, however, a person who intends to act as guarantor does not expressly state that intention and signs the note as co-maker or indorser. For example, Son wants to buy equipment from Dealer for use in Son's business venture. Dealer is willing to sell to Son on credit only if Mother signs the note as co-maker along with Son. Two people who sign a note as co-makers are jointly and severally liable to pay the note. § 3–412 and § 3–116(a). Thus, if the note is not paid at the due date, Dealer as holder can enforce payment for the full amount against either Son or Mother or both. If two people are jointly and severally liable to pay an obligation and one of the obligors pays the entire amount, the normal rule, in the absence of a contrary agreement between the two obligors, is that the burden is shared equally by the two obligors. This principle of equal sharing is expressed as a right of the obligor who pays the obligation to receive "contribution" from the other obligor. § 3–116(b). The contribution rule is based on the assumption that the joint obligation was incurred for the joint benefit of the two obligors and that each should contribute equally in the payment of the obligation. But this assumption is not true if Mother did not have any property interest either in Son's business venture or in the equipment for which the note was given. There is a suretyship relationship between Son and Mother. Generically, Mother is referred to as the "surety" and Son is referred to as the "principal" or "principal debtor." In Article 3, the terminology is different. Mother is the "accommodation party," Son is the "accommodated party," and the note is signed by Mother "for accommodation." § 3–419(a).

Mother, as accommodation party, has certain rights against Son. If Son doesn't pay the note when due and Mother has to pay, it is only fair that she be entitled to recover from Son the full amount that she paid. He got the full benefit of the transaction that gave rise to the note and therefore should have to bear the full burden. Otherwise, Son would be unjustly enriched at the expense of Mother. Instead of having the normal right of contribution from a co-obligor, Mother has a right of "reimbursement" for the amount she paid and has subrogation rights as well. By subrogation she succeeds to the rights that Dealer had against Son on the note. § 3–419(e). When she pays the note she can require its surrender by Dealer (§ 3–501(b)(2)) and becomes the person entitled to enforce the note. § 3–301. Thus, if a note is secured by a security interest in collateral, the accommodation party who pays the note succeeds to the rights of the creditor with respect to the security interest (§ 9–504(5)) and is entitled to a formal transfer of the note and security interest. Reimann v. Hybertsen, 275 Or. 235, 550 P.2d 436 (1976).

If Son pays the note when due, Son has no right of contribution against Mother because she did not benefit from the transaction. § 3–419(e) and § 3–116(b).

Any type of instrument can be signed for accommodation and an accommodation party could sign as maker, drawer, acceptor, or indorser, but in the typical case the instrument is a note and the accommodation party signs either as maker or indorser. We have examined the function of indorsement in the negotiation of an instrument and that is its primary function, but an indorsement can also be made for the purpose of incurring liability on the instrument. § 3–204(a). In most cases, the negotiation and liability purposes coincide, but in some cases only one is present. For example, if an instrument is payable to an identified person, negotiation requires indorsement by the holder. § 3–201(b). But the holder can negotiate the instrument without incurring liability as an indorser by indorsing without recourse. § 3–415(b). The purpose of the indorsement is negotiation, not liability. An indorsement for accommodation is the converse. Because it is not made by the holder of the instrument, it has no negotiation function and is referred to in § 3–205(d) as an "anomalous indorsement." Its only purpose is to impose liability on the indorser.

The predecessor to § 3–419 is § 3–415 of the original Article 3. It is discussed in the following case.

Fithian v. Jamar

Court of Appeals of Maryland, 1979.
286 Md. 161, 410 A.2d 569.

■ COLE, JUDGE. The dispute in this case involves the rights and liabilities of co-makers of a note in a suit among themselves, where none of the disputants is a holder of the note. We granted certiorari to consider two questions, which simply stated are:

1.   Whether a co-maker of a note was also an accommodation maker of the note and thus not liable to the party accommodated;

2.   Whether the agreement of one co-maker to assume another co-maker's obligation on a note constitutes a defense to the latter when sued for contribution by the former.

In 1967 Walter Fithian (Walter) and Richard Jamar (Richard), who were employed as printers at Baltimore Business Forms, decided to form a partnership to carry on their own printing business. They applied to the People's Bank of Chestertown, Maryland (Bank) for an $11,000 business loan to enable them to purchase some equipment. The Bank agreed to lend the money to Walter and Richard only if Walter's wife, Connie, Richard's wife, Janet, and Walter's parents, Walter William (Bill) and Mildred Fithian would co-sign the note. The Executive Vice–President of the Bank explained that the additional signatures were required to make the Bank more secure. The note, which authorized confession of judgment in the event of default, was signed on its face in the bottom right-hand corner by these six parties. The monies loaned were deposited in Walter and Richard's business checking account and were used to purchase printing equipment.

By 1969, Walter and Richard were encountering business problems. They spoke with Frank Hogans (Hogans) and Gerald Bos (Bos) (who were interested in joining the business) about forming a corporation to be called J–F Printing Co., Inc. and refinancing the note so that it (the note) could become a corporate rather than an individual obligation. The business continued to falter and on March 23, 1972 Walter, Richard, Hogans and Bos met and entered into a written agreement in their individual capacities whereby Richard was to take over management and ownership of the business in exchange for his assumption of liability for the company's outstanding obligations, one of which was the note in question in this case. The agreement also provided that should Richard default in the performance of those obligations, Walter, Hogans, and Bos would have the right to terminate the agreement and resume ownership of the business.

Pursuant to the agreement Richard assumed control of the business but was unable to make any further payments on the note. Consequently, the Executive Vice–President of the Bank requested that Bill and Mildred Fithian pay the note in full. They did and the Bank assigned the note to them for whatever disposition they might choose. Bill demanded that Richard indemnify him for the total amount Bill paid on the note.

Receiving no satisfaction from Richard, Bill and Mildred sought judicial relief. On November 10, 1976, a confessed judgment against Richard and Janet of $8,953.95, the balance on the note paid by Bill and Mildred, with interest from January 18, 1974 * * * was entered in the Circuit Court for Kent County. Richard and Janet filed a motion to vacate the judgment, which the circuit court granted and ordered a hearing on the merits. Prior to trial, Richard and Janet filed a third party claim against Walter and Connie averring that as co-makers of the note, Walter and Connie were liable to Richard and Janet for any judgment that Bill and Mildred might recover against Richard and Janet. Walter and Connie counterclaimed contending that the agreement barred Richard's recovery.

The matter was brought to trial on August 25, 1977 before the circuit court, sitting without a jury. The court found that the J–F Printing Company, Inc. was never a de jure corporation and that those who attempted to act under that name were merely acting in their individual capacities; that the March 23, 1972 agreement was not material to the determination of the case; that Bill and Mildred were accommodation makers for Richard, Janet, Walter and Connie and were entitled to collect from any one of the four.

Final judgment was entered on September 6, 1977 for Bill and Mildred against Richard and Janet in the amount of $8,953.95, the principal sum due, plus $2,288.95, representing interest from January 18, 1974 to August 25, 1977. The court * * * entered a judgment for Richard and Janet on Walter and Connie's counterclaim. In the third party claim of Richard and Janet against Walter and Connie, judgment was entered for Richard and Janet in the amount of $5,621.45, fifty percent of the total judgment. * * *

In an unreported per curiam decision * * *, the Court of Special Appeals affirmed the circuit court's finding that Connie Fithian was a co-maker of the note, and not an accommodation party. The Court of Special Appeals also affirmed the trial court's finding that the March, 1972 agreement was not material to the case because it was "a private agreement between only two (2) of the six (6) makers of the note."

Walter and Connie requested review of these rulings in this Court, and we granted their petition for certiorari on June 21, 1978 to consider the two questions presented: whether Connie Fithian was an accommodation maker of the note and thus not liable to the party accommodated; and whether the March, 1972 agreement constitutes a defense to Richard and Janet's third party claim against Walter and Connie.

Our disposition of the questioned rulings requires us to reverse and remand. The error which occurred in the court below was caused in part by a failure to fully analyze the individual rights and obligations of Connie, Walter, Janet and Richard. Therefore, in the discussion which follows, in addition to examining the two questions presented, we will clarify the resulting rights and obligations of these parties.

Richard v. Connie

Since there is no dispute that Connie signed the note, the answer to the first question depends on her purpose in doing so. This is made clear by * * * § 3–415(1) of the Uniform Commercial Code which provides that an accommodation party is "one who signs the instrument in any capacity for the purpose of lending his name to another party to it." The undisputed evidence as presented by the Executive Vice–President of the Bank was to the effect that the wives' signatures were required before the Bank would make the loan to Walter and Richard. Such practices are common among lending institutions which recognize that

> [o]ne with money to lend, goods to sell or services to render may have doubts about a prospective debtor's ability to pay. In such cases he is likely to demand more assurance than the debtor's bare promise of payment. The prospective creditor can reduce his risk by requiring some sort of security. One form of security is the Article 9 security interest in the debtor's goods. Another type of security takes the form of joining a third person on the debtor's obligation. [J. White and R. Summers, Uniform Commercial Code § 13–12, at 425 (1972)].

It is readily apparent, therefore, that Connie lent her name to facilitate the loan transaction. As such she lent her name to two parties to the instrument, Richard and Walter, to enable them to receive a *joint* loan for the purchase of equipment for their printing business, thereby giving the Bank the added assurance of having another party to the obligation. Connie signed as an accommodation party as to both Walter and Richard.

Nor is there any merit in the argument advanced by Richard that Connie must be either a co-maker or an accommodation party, that she cannot be both. The actual language of § 3–415(1) indicates that an accommodation party also signs in a particular capacity, as maker, acceptor or indorser of an instrument. The Official Comment 1 to § 3–415 explains that

> [s]ubsection (1) recognizes that an accommodation party is always a surety (which includes a guarantor), and it is his only distinguishing feature. He differs from other sureties only in that his liability is on

the instrument and he is a surety for another party to it. His obligation is therefore determined by the capacity in which he signs. An accommodation maker or acceptor is bound on the instrument without any resort to his principal, while an accommodation indorser may be liable only after presentment, notice of dishonor and protest.

Moreover, § 3–415(2) refers specifically to the liability of an accommodation party "in the capacity in which he has signed." It follows, therefore, that the fact that Connie was a co-maker of the note does not preclude her from also being an accommodation party.

Section 3–415(5) states that "[a]n accommodation party is not liable to the party accommodated"; thus, Connie is not liable to Richard. Our predecessors, prior to Maryland's adoption of the Uniform Commercial Code, explained the reasons for this proposition in Crothers v. National Bank, 158 Md. 587, 593, 149 A. 270, 273 (1930):

> Since the accommodating party lends his credit by request to the party accommodated upon the assumption that the latter will discharge the debt when due, it is an implied term of this agreement that the party accommodated cannot acquire any right of action against the accommodating party.

Richard contends, however, that Connie intended to accommodate only her husband, Walter. Even if there were evidence to this effect (and there is none), the subjective intent of a co-maker of a note is of little weight when objective facts and circumstances unambiguously demonstrate the capacity in which the note was signed. * * * It is clear to us that the signatures of both wives were required to effect this joint business venture and thus Connie's signature was as much an accommodation to Richard as it was to Walter. We hold that Connie was an accommodation maker and that she cannot be liable to Richard, the party accommodated. The Court of Special Appeals erroneously held to the contrary.

Janet v. Connie

The preceding discussion of Connie's status demonstrates that each of the four parties, Walter, Connie, Richard, and Janet, has certain rights and obligations with respect to this note which are not affected by his or her marital status. The court below erred in not fully analyzing these separate rights and obligations. It follows that our finding that Connie has no liability to Richard in no way changes any obligation she may have to Janet. Janet, as well as Connie, is a co-accommodation maker on this note.

The question is therefore whether one co-accommodation maker who pays more than her proportionate share of the debt has a right of contribution against another co-accommodation maker. The Uniform Commercial Code contains no provision expressly dealing with the right of an accommodation party to contribution from another accommodation party. However, § 1–103 of the Code does provide that the principles of the common law remain applicable "[u]nless displaced by the particular provisions" of the Code.

That an accommodation maker has a right of contribution from a co-accommodation maker is a settled principle of the law. The Restatement of Security provides

A surety who in the performance of his own obligation discharges more than his proportionate share of the principal's duty is entitled to contribution from a co-surety. [Restatement of Security § 149 (1941)].

* * *

This Court has not addressed this question in regard to a note controlled by the U.C.C. Our research revealed only one case which directly confronted the effect of the U.C.C. on the common law rule. The court stated that the U.C.C. does not change the rule of suretyship law permitting contribution by one surety from a co-surety. McLochlin v. Miller, 139 Ind.App. 443, 217 N.E.2d 50 (1966).

Accordingly Janet has a right of contribution against Connie. But this right to contribution is an inchoate claim which does not ripen into being unless and until Janet pays more than her proportionate share to Bill and Mildred. * * * Judgment can be entered on behalf of Janet against Connie, but it must be fashioned so that it may not be enforced until Janet proves she actually paid more than her proportionate share to Bill and Mildred.[1]
* * *

Richard v. Walter

[Omitted is the portion of the opinion in which the court held that Richard's agreement in 1972 to assume all liabilities of the printing business, including the note, precluded any right of contribution that Richard would otherwise have against Walter, his joint obligor on the note.]

Janet v. Walter

That the 1972 agreement serves as a defense by Walter against Richard in no way serves to insulate Walter against Janet. Janet's status as an accommodation maker is unaffected by the agreement. As an accommodation maker, Janet has a right to look to any principal, including Walter for any amounts she actually pays. * * * Janet's status as Richard's wife does not affect her status as an accommodation maker. She is entitled to judgment from either principal when she actually pays any amount of the debt.

In summary, Richard is not entitled to judgment against Walter because of the agreement. Rather, Walter is entitled to indemnification from Richard for any amount Walter is forced to pay. Richard is not entitled to judgment against Connie because an accommodation party is not liable to the party accommodated. Janet is entitled to contribution from her

---

1. A surety who is called upon to pay more than his proportionate share of the debt has a right of contribution from his co-sureties in an amount not to exceed each co-surety's proportionate share of the debt.

* * * Here the note was signed by four sureties (Bill, Mildred, Connie and Janet); Janet's proportionate share of indebtedness to her co-sureties is 25% of the debt.

co-surety, Connie, the judgment being unenforceable unless and until Janet proves she actually has paid more than her proportionate share of the debt to Bill and Mildred. Similarly, Janet as a surety is entitled to judgment against Walter as a principal for any amount of the debt for which Janet proves payment.[3]

NOTES

1. In footnote 3 the court states that it does not decide whether Bill and Mildred were entitled to recover the full amount of the debt from Janet. How much were Bill and Mildred entitled to recover from Janet?

2. How would the result in this case change in a jurisdiction in which all property acquired during marriage is community property?

PROBLEM

X owned 50% of the capital stock of Corporation and was its President. Y and Z each owned 25%. Corporation needed money for working capital and borrowed it from Bank which insisted as a condition to the loan that X sign the note because of the precarious financial condition of Corporation. The note was signed as follows:

Corporation

By X, President

X, individually

The loan, which is unsecured, was made by crediting the entire principal amount to Corporation's account with Bank and was used entirely for corporate purposes. Corporation has defaulted on the loan. After Corporation's default on the loan to Bank, X paid Bank the entire unpaid balance amounting to $10,000. Is X an accommodation party? Is X entitled to reimbursement from Corporation for the $10,000 paid to Bank or are X's rights limited to a claim for contribution? Would X's rights be any different if X owned 100% of the stock of Corporation rather than 50%?

2. SURETYSHIP DEFENSES

A surety, in addition to having rights against the principal debtor, also has certain rights which can be asserted against the creditor seeking enforcement of the surety's obligation to pay the debt. These rights are usually referred to as "suretyship defenses." Suretyship defenses relate to changes in the obligation of the principal debtor without the consent of the surety. For example, a surety guarantees performance of the principal debtor as buyer under a contract of sale of coal to be supplied on credit by a seller. The seller and the principal debtor agree to amend the contract so that it refers to fuel oil rather than coal. The surety didn't agree to the

3. Whether Bill and Mildred were entitled to judgment in the full amount of the debt against Janet we do not decide because Janet did not appeal from that judgment.

amendment. If the principal debtor fails to pay for fuel oil purchased under the amended contract and the seller demands payment, the surety has a complete defense. The surety's obligation related to a contract of the principal debtor to buy coal not fuel oil. The seller and the principal debtor cannot impose a new contract on the surety. Restatement, Security § 128(b).

However, in some cases it cannot be said that the creditor and the principal debtor have attempted to impose an entirely new contract on the surety. There might be only some modification of the contract. In those cases the existence of a defense may be justified only if the modification causes loss to the surety. A few examples illustrate the problem. The principal debtor borrows money from a lender. The debt is payable with interest and is secured by a security interest in personal property of the principal debtor. After the suretyship relationship arises, the lender agrees with the principal debtor to an amendment of the debt obligation as follows: (1) the amendment changes the interest rate; or (2) it extends the due date of the debt; or (3) it releases some of the collateral that secures the debt; or (4) it releases the principal debtor from any personal obligation to pay the debt. In each of these cases, if the surety does not agree to the change it may be unfair to allow the lender to enforce the surety's obligation to pay if, at the time the change was made, the lender had knowledge of the suretyship relationship. The suretyship defenses are intended to protect the surety by providing that in some cases a change in the terms of the debt may result in a total or partial discharge of the surety.

The suretyship defenses with respect to negotiable instruments are stated in § 3–605. These defenses are not identical to suretyship defenses that may apply under the general law of suretyship with respect to obligations other than negotiable instruments. Section 3–605 gives defenses to accommodation parties and to indorsers whether or not they are accommodation parties. Subsection (f) of § 3–605 gives a defense to a co-maker of a secured note in some cases even if the co-maker is not an accommodation party.

PROBLEM

In each of the following cases Corporation borrowed money from Bank and the proceeds of the loan were paid to Corporation and used solely in the conduct of the business of Corporation. Corporation has three stockholders, Doe, Roe, and Poe, each of whom owns one-third of the stock. Doe and Roe manage the business of Corporation. Poe is a passive investor who takes no part in managing Corporation. The loan was made to Corporation by Bank in exchange for a negotiable note payable to the order of Bank and signed by Corporation as maker. Doe and Roe signed on behalf of Corporation as its authorized officers. Poe also signed the note as co-maker at the request of Bank.

Case # 1

Assume the following facts. The note was not secured by a security interest. $50,000 was owed on the note when it became due. At that time Doe and Roe informed Bank that Corporation was unable to pay the full amount. They also informed Bank that if Bank initiated any proceedings to collect the note, Corporation would file in bankruptcy. Doe and Roe explained that they wanted to avoid bankruptcy and were willing to settle the obligation of Corporation on the note by paying a part of the amount owed. Bank and Corporation then signed an agreement providing for payment by Corporation to Bank of $20,000 in full satisfaction of Corporation's obligation on the note. The payment was made and Bank executed a release of all rights of Bank against Corporation on the note. Poe did not consent to this transaction. Bank then demanded that Poe pay the remaining $30,000 due on the note.

If Poe pays $30,000 to Bank, what rights does Poe have against Corporation? § 3–419(e) and § 3–604(a). If Poe refuses to pay Bank, is Bank entitled to recover from Poe the amount due on the note? § 3–419(b), § 3–412, § 3–605(b), Comment 3 to § 3–605.

Case # 2

Assume the following facts: The note was secured by a perfected security interest in collateral owned by Corporation. The collateral consisted of two pieces of equipment (Machine # 1 and Machine # 2) used in the business of Corporation. On behalf of Corporation, Doe and Roe asked Bank to release its security interest in Machine #2 and to permit Corporation to sell Machine # 2 for cash. They explained to Bank that they intended to use the proceeds of the sale to buy a more modern piece of equipment which would be substituted for Machine # 2 as collateral for the loan. Bank agreed. Poe did not consent to the release of the security interest by Bank or to the sale of Machine #2. Corporation made the sale for $40,000 cash, but the $40,000 was not used to buy substitute equipment. Rather, it was used to pay various debts of Corporation. No substitute for Machine # 2 was ever acquired by Corporation. Later, Corporation filed in bankruptcy. At that time $50,000 was owed on the note and Machine # 1 had a net resale value of $30,000. Corporation is insolvent and no money will be available for payment of unsecured claims in the bankruptcy. Bank demanded that Poe pay the $50,000 due on the note.

If Poe pays $50,000 to Bank and then files a claim in the bankruptcy, how much will Poe receive in the bankruptcy? § 3–419(e) and § 9–504(5). If Poe refuses to pay Bank and Bank brings an action against Poe to enforce the note, how much is Bank entitled to recover from Poe? § 3–419(b), § 3–412, § 3–605(e) and (g), § 9–306(2), Comment 6 to § 3–605. How much is Bank entitled to recover from Poe if the note included a clause as follows: "All signers of the note are principals and not accommodation parties, guarantors, or other sureties?" § 3–605(i) and Comments 2 and 8 to § 3–605.

Case # 3

Assume the following facts: The note was not secured by a security interest. The note had a stated due date which was one year after the date it was issued. Shortly before the due date, Doe and Roe informed Bank that Corporation did not have sufficient cash to pay the note on the due date. They also stated that if Bank initiated any proceedings to collect the note, Corporation would file in bankruptcy. Doe and Roe asked Bank to extend the due date of the note. Corporation and Bank then signed an agreement under which the due date of the note was extended for a period of two years in return for an agreement by Corporation to pay interest during the two-year period at a rate higher than the rate stated in the note. Poe did not consent to the agreement between Bank and Corporation. About a year after this agreement was signed Corporation filed a petition in bankruptcy. No money will be available for payment of unsecured claims in bankruptcy. At the time of the bankruptcy the note was unpaid. Bank demanded payment from Poe.

Does Poe have any defense against Bank? § 3–605(c), § 3–605(d), and Comments 4 and 5 to § 3–605.

F.   SIGNATURES BY REPRESENTATIVES

A person is not liable on an instrument unless the instrument is signed personally by that person or by a representative who is authorized to sign for that person. § 3–401(a). Whether a representative is authorized to sign for a represented person is determined by general principles of the law of agency. § 3–402(a). Consider this case: Employer, an individual, has a checking account in Bank which is used to pay obligations incurred in Employer's business. Employer follows the practice of personally signing all checks, except that Employer authorizes Employee to sign Employer's name to checks during extended absences of Employer. Bank has paid all checks drawn on Employer's account whether Employer's name was written in Employer's handwriting or that of Employee. Employer never objected to the payment by Bank of any check on which Employer's name was written by Employee. On one occasion Employer was about to leave town and instructed Employee to pay all invoices arriving during Employer's absence except invoices of John Doe. In violation of these instructions Employee writes a check on Employer's account to John Doe in payment of a bill that Doe submitted. Employee's act of signing Employer's name to that particular check is not authorized by Employer in the sense that Employer never assented to it, but Employer nevertheless may be bound by the signature. The question of whether the signature is binding on Employer is determined by the law of agency. In our example, the probable result under agency law is that Employer is bound because Employee, although lacking actual authority to sign the Doe check, had apparent authority to do so because Employee had general authority to sign checks. In that event, under § 3–401(a) and § 3–402(a), the signature by Employee is effective as the authorized signature of Employer.

Signatures by agents on behalf of principals occur most often with respect to the obligations of organizations such as corporations whose signatures are made by its officers or employees. Two problems arise. First, there is the question of whether the corporation is bound by the signature of the officer or employee. Second, there is the question of whether the officer or employee also becomes a party to the instrument by signing it on behalf of the principal. If it is clear that an agent is signing on behalf of a named principal, only the principal is bound. But sometimes it is not clear whether the agent's signature is in behalf of the principal or whether it is made to impose liability on the officer as an accommodation party.

1.   LIABILITY OF AGENT ON NOTES

The problem of ambiguous signatures by representatives is governed by § 3–402(b) and (c). The following case considered the problem under § 3–403(2) of the original Article 3.

Wang v. Wang

Supreme Court of South Dakota, 1986.
393 N.W.2d 771.

■ MORGAN, JUSTICE.

Plaintiff, Robert L. Wang (Robert), appeals from a judgment entered on a jury verdict in favor of defendant Albert Schramm (Schramm) in Robert's suit to recover on a promissory note. Robert raises three issues: (1) the trial court improperly admitted parol evidence regarding the parties' intentions at the time they executed the note and assignment documents; (2) the trial court erred in giving certain instructions; and (3) the trial court erred in refusing to recuse itself prior to trial. We reverse and remand.

One of the documents that is the subject of this litigation is a promissory note executed by Victor Wang (Victor) to the Rosebud Federal Credit Union (RFCU) on January 18, 1978, in the amount of $97,425.09 with interest at nine percent per annum and due and payable on January 18, 1979. Victor is Robert's brother.

At this point we must digress for some background information. The RFCU was affiliated with the Farmer's Cooperative Oil Company (Coop) of Winner, South Dakota. There was an agreement between these entities that the Coop would guarantee patrons' notes to RFCU to the extent that the proceeds were used for Coop's purchases. This agreement had been formalized in writing and the practice was that after a note was signed by the patron, the Coop would co-sign the note. Schramm, an officer in both organizations, testified that after the patron had signed the note on the RFCU side of the office it would come to the Coop. The usual procedure would be for Schramm to first sign and then a stamp bearing the words:

"Farmer's Cooperative Oil Association of Winner by _____"

would then be affixed over his signature by someone else to designate the Coop as the comaker. There was no other notation on the instrument to indicate that the Coop was anything but a comaker on the note. Furthermore, it appears that in most instances, the patron-comaker was not even aware of the Coop's action until he would receive the cancelled instrument after it was discharged. In this instance, however, the stamp was not affixed to Victor's note and Schramm's signature as comaker was left bare.

The note was executed as a renewal of Victor's obligation under a prior note that was due and, in addition, Victor obtained additional funding to repair his equipment in preparation for a sale. The note was secured by financing agreements on various items of Victor's property and when the sale was completed the net proceeds were apparently deposited in an escrow account with the RFCU. Some of the property apparently was not sold, but was traded off, or was not otherwise accounted for. RFCU permitted Victor to pay out a considerable part of the escrow account for other obligations. On January 18, 1979, when the note became due, Victor was unable to meet his obligation. On demand by RFCU, the Coop paid $43,344.00 under the terms of the guaranty agreement previously discussed.

Robert first became involved when he was contacted at his home in Sturgis by Schramm who was looking for Victor to discuss the delinquent note. Robert indicated some interest in acquiring some of the collateral listed on RFCU's security agreement that had not been disposed of at Victor's sale. On July 3, 1980, Robert traveled to Winner and entered into negotiations with Larry Meiners (Meiners), the manager of RFCU, that culminated in an agreement to sell Robert the note and security agreements for the sum of $8,000.00. An assignment agreement was prepared that same day by a local attorney who had not even seen the note. Schramm, as president of the board of directors of RFCU, was called to the attorney's office to sign the assignment agreement on behalf of RFCU. He did so without reading the assignment or viewing the note. Meiners, was also present and signed as a witness. Robert paid the $8,000.00, took his note and assignment, returned to Sturgis, and shortly thereafter made demand upon Schramm as comaker to pay the principal and interest then claimed due on the note in the amount of $106,193.33. This was obviously the first time Schramm was made aware of his precarious position. The RFCU sought to secure a cancellation of the assignment by refunding the $8,000.00 to Robert. He refused and this suit followed.

Schramm interposed a number of defenses by answer and by motion to amend at the close of all the testimony. The trial court ultimately instructed the jury on three defenses: (1) signature in a representative capacity; (2) unjustifiable impairment of collateral; and (3) lack of mutuality with respect to the assignment by reason of mistake of fact or mistake of law. The jury returned a verdict in favor of Schramm.

The various aspects of the pleadings and trial will be included where pertinent in the discussion of the issues raised by Robert, which were three in number, as follows: (1) Whether the trial court committed reversible error by allowing parol evidence to be considered by the jury regarding the parties' intentions at the time they executed the note and assignment documents? (2) Whether the trial court committed reversible error in giving Instructions 6, 9 and 10 to the jury and denying Robert's Proposed Instructions 1, 2, 3 and 4? (3) Whether the trial court committed reversible error in refusing to recuse itself from the case prior to trial? Because issues (1) and (2) are clearly related and intertwined, they will be discussed conjunctionally. Issue (3) will be dealt with separately.

Robert brought suit on the note by virtue of the assignment. His first issue relates to admission of parol evidence regarding the intentions of the parties at the time of the execution of both instruments. His second issue relates to jury instructions in relation to both instruments. For the purpose of clarity, we will first address those issues with respect to the promissory note and then with respect to the assignment.

The issues related to the promissory note all fall within the purview of the Uniform Commercial Code, particularly Article 3, Commercial Paper. Robert first argues that Schramm is personally obligated on the note under the provisions of § 3–403(2) which provides, in pertinent part:

> (2) An authorized representative who signs his own name to an instrument (a) Is personally obligated if the instrument neither names the person represented nor shows that the representative signed in a representative capacity. . . .

Inasmuch as Schramm's signature on the note was "bare," i.e., without any showing that he signed in a representative capacity, Schramm was indeed personally liable as a comaker. On this point, Robert proposed an instruction: "A signature may be made by an agent or other representative, however, an authorized representative who signs his name to an instrument is personally obligated if the instrument neither names the person represented nor shows that the representative signed in a representative capacity." This proposed instruction accurately sets out the essence of § 3–403(2). In rejecting Robert's proposed instruction, the trial court gave an instruction which exactly stated Robert's proposed instruction but added:

> However, a person signing a note, without indicating in the note that he is signing in a representative capacity, is not personally or individually liable on the note if the person in whose favor the note is drawn has knowledge that the signer has signed in a representative capacity, or the person in whose favor the note is drawn has required or requested the person to sign in a representative capacity.

We agree with Robert that the trial court erred in giving its Instruction 6 and rejecting Robert's Proposed Instruction 1. Where the instrument does not name the principal or indicate the representative capacity, the signature of an agent personally obligates the agent and parol evidence is inadmissible to disestablish his obligation. Mid–America Real Estate & Inv. Corp. v. Lund, 353 N.W.2d 286 (N.D.1984). In another similar case, the signer of a note was held personally liable on a promissory note where his signature alone was on the note and where there was no indication on the note that the signer had signed the note in a representative capacity, even though he contended the note was actually an obligation of his corporation. Farmers & Merch. Nat. Bank of Hatton v. Lee, 333 N.W.2d 792 (N.D.1983).

The objectionable part of Instruction 6 states, in effect, that Schramm would not be personally liable to the RFCU on the note drawn to RFCU if RFCU had knowledge that he signed in a representative capacity or if RFCU had required or requested him to sign in a representative capacity. We grant that there is some authority that, *in an action between the original parties to the note*, the intention to bind the principal instead of the agent may be relevant. In this case, however, the action is brought by a subsequent holder, not by an original party. We, therefore, do not reach that specific issue at this time. It is our holding that under the circumstances of this case and the provisions of § 3–403(2) that, as between Schramm and the Coop, Schramm was personally liable and the latter part of the trial court's instruction was erroneous.

Robert next claims error predicated on the admission of parol evidence relating to Schramm's signature on the note. While it is erroneous to admit parol evidence solely for the purpose of showing Schramm's representative capacity, such evidence is admissible to show Schramm's accommodation character in the transaction by virtue of the provisions of § 3–415(3). That statute provides:

> (3) As against a holder in due course and without notice of the accommodation oral proof of the accommodation is not admissible to give the accommodation party the benefit of discharges dependent on his character as such. *In other cases the accommodation character may be shown by oral proof.*

(Emphasis added.) It will be noted that before an accommodation party may show his accommodation character by parol evidence, the holder of the note must be shown not to be a holder in due course. Robert does not qualify as a holder in due course as defined in § 3–302(1). The face of the note reflected a maturity date long prior to the assignment date and Robert had notice that the note was overdue. Furthermore, the trial court found, as a matter of law, that Robert was not a holder in due course and Robert raises no issue on appeal concerning the trial court's ruling in that respect. Therefore, under the above statute, Schramm is entitled to introduce parol evidence to establish the accommodation character of his signature as opposed to establishing his representative character.

A showing of Schramm's accommodation status is essential to his defense of unjustifiable impairment of collateral. The trial court instructed the jury that to the extent that RFCU, without Schramm's consent, unjustifiably impaired any collateral, Schramm would be discharged. This appears to be an adequate statement of § 3–606(1) which states, in pertinent part:

> (1) The holder discharges any party to the instrument to the extent that without such party's consent the holder

(b) Unjustifiably impairs any collateral for the instrument given by or on behalf of the party or any person against whom he has a right of recourse.

There was evidence adduced by Schramm to support the giving of the instruction, including dissipation of escrowed funds and missing assets unaccounted for. Robert had no objection to the court's Instruction 11 on the issue of unjustifiable impairment in the form in which it was given to the jury.

* * *

We reverse and remand for a new trial.

NOTES

1. What would the result in this case be if revised § 3–402(b) applied and Robert was a holder in due course? Was not a holder in due course? Comment 2 to § 3–402. 2 White & Summers, Uniform Commercial Code § 16–5 (4th prac.ed.1995).

2. How would you advise your clients to meet the requirement of § 3–402(b)(1) for an unambiguous signature?

PROBLEM

Agee was authorized to sign notes on behalf of Amalgamated, Inc. In order to evidence a loan obligation incurred by Amalgamated to Bank, Agee signed on the front of the note: "Amalgamated, Inc. by Arthur Agee, Vice President." On the back of the instrument, Agee signed "Arthur Agee." When Amalgamated went into bankruptcy, Bank sued Agee as indorser of the note. Since there seems no reason for Agee to sign as an individual on the back of the note other than to guarantee payment of it, are there any facts that could be admitted into evidence to save Agee from personal liability in such a case? Comment 2 to § 3–402.

2.   LIABILITY OF AGENTS ON CHECKS

Serna v. Milanese, Inc.

District Court of Appeal of Florida, Third District, 1994.
643 So.2d 36.

■ NESBITT, JUDGE.

Jose Serna appeals a final summary judgment in an action filed by Milanese, Inc. (Milanese) to collect on dishonored checks. We affirm.

Milanese sold clothing to Jemaros Investments, Inc., d/b/a Natalia Boutique (Jemaros). Jose Serna, president of Jemaros, paid for the goods by check. Serna signed the checks, which were imprinted with the corporate name, but did not indicate his representative capacity. Following Jemaros' payment for certain merchandise by checks later dishonored, Milanese filed a multi-count action against Jemaros and Serna.[1] The count against Serna sought recovery for the dishonored checks tendered to Milanese. There is no contention that Serna was not authorized to sign the checks.

Milanese sought summary judgment restating the complaint's dishonored check allegations against Jemaros and Serna. In support of its motion, Milanese filed an affidavit of its president stating that Jemaros and Serna issued the dishonored checks. The trial court granted Milanese's motion and pursuant to section 68.065, Florida Statutes (1991)[2] ordered Serna to pay treble the face amount of the checks.

Section 3–403, Florida Statutes (1991), which was in effect when Serna signed the dishonored checks, provides:

> (2) An authorized representative who signs his own name to an instrument:
>
> (a) is personally obligated if the instrument neither names the person represented nor shows that the representative signed in a representative capacity;
>
> (b) Except as otherwise established between the immediate parties, is personally obligated if the instrument names the person represented but does not show that the representative signed in a representative capacity, or if the instrument does not name the person represented but does show that the representative signed in a representative capacity.

During the pendency of the suit this statute was repealed and replaced by the legislature with § 3–402, Florida Statutes (1993), effective January 1, 1993. Section 3–402 provides in part:

> (c) If a representative signs the name of the representative as drawer of a check without indication of the representative status and the check is payable from an account of the represented person who is identified on the check, the signer is not liable on the check if the signature is an authorized signature of the represented person.

---

1. Serna, as part of the credit application to Milanese, executed an individual guaranty "for any indebtedness incurred by virtue of any and all credit extended" to Jemaros by Milanese. Milanese did not seek recovery for the dishonored checks pursuant to Serna's personal guaranty. The trial court, on a separate count, awarded Milanese damages against Serna, under Serna's personal guarantee, for merchandise for which Jemaros did not remit payment. We affirm that portion of the judgment.

2. Section 68.065 provides, in pertinent part: (1) In any civil action brought for the purpose of collecting a check ... the payment of which was refused by the drawee because of the lack of funds, and where the maker or drawer fails to pay the amount owing, in cash, to the payee within 30 days following a written demand ... the maker or drawer shall be liable to the payee, in addition to the amount owing upon such check ... for damages of triple the amount so owing.

Serna argues that the newly created statute operates retrospectively[3] to relieve him of personal liability for treble damages under section 68.065. We disagree.

Statutes that create new rights or take away existing rights, as opposed to furthering existing rights, are substantive in nature and may not be applied retroactively. * * * It is well established in Florida that statutory changes which are substantive in nature are presumed to operate prospectively unless the legislature expressly manifests a contrary intention. Meek v. Layne–Western Co., 624 So.2d 345, 347 (Fla. 1st DCA 1993).

In *Meek*, the court rejected retroactive application of an amended statute that reduced a claimant's wage loss benefits when applied to a wage loss claim that occurred before the amendment. The *Meek* court reasoned that when substantive legislation changes the amount of relief available under the statute, or creates a new quantum of relief, application of such legislation to an injury that occurred before the amendment will be viewed as retroactive, and thus forbidden.

Section 3–402 is not merely a procedural section that changes the method by which a payee can enforce his or her rights. Rather, the section substantively alters rights available to the payee, and should be prospectively applied only, absent an express legislative pronouncement that it should be retroactively applied. The legislature did not provide this express intention for § 3–402 in Chapter 92–82, section 62, at 819, Laws of Florida.

Serna signed the dishonored checks in July and August of 1992. Milanese's substantive right to collect treble damages on the worthless checks under § 3–403(2) arose in September, 1992, when it brought suit to enforce its right. The legislature created § 3–402, effective January 1, 1993. The final judgment granting treble damages in favor of Milanese was rendered one month later, on February 3, 1993. If the statute were retrospectively applied, all the benefits to which Milanese was entitled under § 3–403 in 1992 would be effectively eradicated mid-litigation in 1993, dramatically reducing Milanese's options for recovering its undisputed damages.

We therefore find § 3–402 confers substantive rights and thus cannot be retrospectively applied to this case. Retrospective application of § 3–402(c) would eliminate the substantive right and remedy available to Milanese under section 68.065 and § 3–403(2).

Accordingly, the order under review is affirmed.

■ GERSTEN, J., concurs.

■ BASKIN, JUDGE (dissenting).

---

3. Some courts and commentators differentiate between "retroactive" and "retrospective" applications. The former refers to the application of a new law or case to matured rights, that is, to a case that has gone to final judgment. The latter term refers to application of a new law or case to pending controversies. See Joyner v. Monier Roof Tile, Inc., 784 F.Supp. 872, 874 n. 3 (S.D.Fla. 1992). We use the term "retrospective" in this opinion to refer to those non-final controversies concerning pre-amendment conduct.

I am unable to agree with the majority opinion for two reasons. First, I disagree with the majority's conclusion that § 3–403(2), Florida Statutes (1991), governs this case rather than § 3–402(c), Florida Statutes (Supp. 1992). Second, I find the majority fails to address the issue concerning whether the record reflects unresolved genuine issues of material fact regarding Jose Serna's signing capacity, even under § 3–403. I conclude that genuine issues of material fact remain unresolved and would reverse the summary judgment and remand for further proceedings.

Reviewing § 3–403(2) and § 3–402(c), I find that the latter statute governs. Section 3–402(c) does not diminish the substantive rights and remedies of Milanese, Inc., to collect treble damages on the dishonored checks. Milanese may still pursue a claim against Serna, individually, to recover on the checks. The new statute has merely eliminated the statutory presumption that Serna is liable individually. The elimination of the presumption where, as here, a person signs a corporate check without indicating a representative status does not take away a vested right: Milanese does not have a vested right in a method of procedure.

In Alamo Rent–A–Car, Inc. v. Mancusi, 632 So.2d 1352 (Fla.1994), the court discussed the substantive and procedural or remedial nature of legislation, stating:

A substantive statute is presumed to operate prospectively rather than retrospectively unless the Legislature clearly expresses its intent that the statute is to operate retrospectively. This is especially true when retrospective operation of a law would impair or destroy existing rights. Procedural or remedial statutes, on the other hand, are to be applied retrospectively and are to be applied to pending cases.

As we stated in Benyard v. Wainwright, 322 So.2d 473, 475 (Fla.1975), substantive law prescribes duties and rights and procedural law concerns the means and methods to apply and enforce those duties and rights.

Mancusi, 632 So.2d at 1358 (citations omitted). Consequently, I would hold that § 3–402(c) is procedural or remedial in nature as it merely changes the means employed in redressing an injury and thus may be applied retrospectively.

Under § 3–402(c), Serna is not personally liable on the checks if the statutory criteria are met, absent evidence of an agreement to the contrary. Section 1–102(3), Fla.Stat. (1993). On the other hand, under § 3–403(2), Florida Statutes (1991), Serna is personally liable on the checks, unless the immediate parties establish evidence to the contrary, and the transaction meets the statutory requirements. The statute does not abrogate Milanese's substantive right to collect on the checks or to receive treble damages under section 68.065; it reallocates the burden of proof by shifting the presumption in favor of the agent. "Burden of proof requirements are procedural in nature. The procedural rights granted by the act could be abrogated retroactively because 'no one has a vested right in any given mode of procedure.' " Walker & LaBerge, Inc. v. Halligan, 344 So.2d 239,

243 (Fla.1977) (citations omitted) (quoting Ex Parte Collett, 337 U.S. 55, 71, 69 S.Ct. 944, 953, 93 L.Ed. 1207, 1217 (1949)); * * *. "[T]he statute does not operate to impair rights vested before enactment, create new obligations for the parties in a pre-existing legal relationship or impose new penalties on conduct which occurred before enactment." Oakbrooke Assocs., Ltd. v. Insurance Comm'r of State of Cal., 581 So.2d 943, 946 (Fla. 5th DCA 1991) (citing City of Lakeland v. Catinella, 129 So.2d 133 (Fla.1961)). Thus, § 3–402(c) should be applied to the case before this court.[1]

As to whether the trial court properly granted summary judgment in favor of Milanese under § 3–403(2), I find that Milanese failed to carry its burden of proving that no material fact issues remain unresolved.

[T]he burden of proving the absence of a genuine issue of material fact is upon the moving party. Until it is determined that the movant has successfully met this burden, the opposing party is under no obligation to show that issues do remain to be tried.

This means that before it becomes necessary to determine the legal sufficiency of the affidavits or other evidence submitted by the party moved against, it must first be determined that the movant has successfully met his burden of proving a negative, i.e., the non-existence of a genuine issue of material fact. He must prove this negative conclusively. The proof must be such as to overcome all reasonable inferences which may be drawn in favor of the opposing party.

Holl v. Talcott, 191 So.2d 40, 43 (Fla.1966) (citations omitted). Here, Milanese's affidavit and other evidence failed to establish the absence of factual issues. Pursuant to § 3–403(2)(b), Serna is personally obligated "[e]xcept as otherwise established between the immediate parties. . . ." Milanese's affidavit asserts that Jemaros Investments, Inc., and Serna signed the checks. That assertion confirms the existence of a material fact issue rather than establishing the absence of such issue. Furthermore, the record contains an individual guaranty signed by Serna in which he agreed to pay individually for goods upon Jemaros' failure to remit payment. There would be no need for an individual guaranty promising payment if Serna signed the checks and remitted payment in an individual capacity. The adoption of Milanese's contention that Serna signed the checks individually would render the individual guaranty meaningless. Cf. Tampa Bay

---

1. The statute is remedial in nature in that it "give[s] effect to the acts and contracts of individuals according to their expressed intention." Oakbrooke Assocs., 581 So.2d at 945 (quoting In re Aloma Square, Inc., 116 B.R. 827 (M.D.Fla.1990)). The statute was designed to remedy cases in which the representative was held responsible on a corporate check based on some evidence that the person receiving the check was not aware of the signatory's representative status. The

Uniform Commercial Code Comment following § 3–402 states, in part, that "[v]irtually all checks used today are in personalized form which identify the person on whose account the check is drawn. In this case, nobody is deceived into thinking that the person signing the check is meant to be liable. This subsection is meant to overrule cases decided under former Article 3 such as Griffin v. Ellinger, 538 S.W.2d 97 (Texas 1976)."

Economic Dev. Corp. v. Edman, 598 So.2d 172, 174 (Fla. 2d DCA 1992) ("For a corporation to guarantee its own debt would add nothing to its existing obligation and would be meaningless."); Central Nat'l Bank of Miami v. Muskat Corp. of Am., Inc., 430 So.2d 957 (Fla. 3d DCA 1983) (same). Instead of demonstrating the nonexistence of triable issues, the individual guaranty signed by Serna creates a material fact issue as to whether Serna signed the checks in his individual capacity. I conclude that Milanese did not carry its burden of proving the nonexistence of genuine triable issues of material facts.

For these reasons, I would reverse and remand for further proceedings.

NOTES

1.   The policy for having a separate rule for checks with respect to the liability of agents is set out in Comment 3 to § 3–402. Examine the next check you receive from a law firm. Did the person who signed disclose agency?

2.   The Florida statute set out in footnote 3 of *Serna*, subjecting drawers to damages equal to triple the amount of an NSF check, has been adopted in a number of states. Its enactment has been sponsored by merchant groups alarmed by the prevalence of NSF checks tendered by drawers who do so probably without any true criminal intent (and thus of no interest to criminal prosecutors) but who are careless about the state of their bank balances in a check collection regime in which the float on checks has been reduced to only a day or so in many cases.

3.   The UCC is being redrafted, article by article, and by the end of the century the process will be complete. This raises transition issues like the one that the *Serna* court wrestles with. The arguments raised by the majority and dissenting opinions are illustrative of the difficulties courts are having with the transition issue. When Articles 3 and 4 were promulgated in 1990, no transition provisions were included. Transition provisions applying to all the new articles have now been included, apparently in tentative form, in a new Article 11 as a guide to enacting states. Most of these provisions apply to Article 9 issues but a few are of general application, e.g., §§ 11–102, 11–103 and 11–108. The latter provision reads: "Unless a change in law has clearly been made, the provisions of [new U.C.C.] shall be deemed declaratory of the meaning of the [old U.C.C.]." If Article 11 had been in effect at the time of the litigation in *Serna*, would the result have been different? Some states have enacted their own version of transition provisions. For instance, in 1994 California enacted California Commercial Code §§ 16101–16104. The latter section provides: "Unless a change in law, as contrasted with a clarification, has clearly been made, this code, as it existed on [the date new Articles 3 and 4 became effective] shall be deemed declaratory of the meaning of this code as it existed prior to [that date]."

G. ACCORD AND SATISFACTION

County Fire Door Corp. v. C.F. Wooding Co.

Supreme Court of Connecticut, 1987.
202 Conn. 277, 520 A.2d 1028.

■ PETERS, CHIEF JUSTICE.

The principal issue in this appeal is whether the Uniform Commercial Code modifies the common law of accord and satisfaction so that a creditor can now effectively reserve his rights against a debtor while cashing a check that the debtor has explicitly tendered in full satisfaction of an unliquidated debt. * * *

The trial court's articulation and the exhibits at trial establish the following facts. On November 17, 1981, the defendant ordered a number of metal doors and door frames from the plaintiff. The plaintiff undertook responsibility for delivery of the goods to the worksite. Alleging that the plaintiff's delay in delivery of the doors and frames had caused additional installation expenses, the defendant back charged the plaintiff an amount of $2180. The defendant informed the plaintiff that, on the basis of this back charge, and other payments and credits not at issue, the remaining balance due the plaintiff was $416.88. The plaintiff responded by denying the validity of this back charge. According to the plaintiff, the balance due on its account was $2618.88. The defendant immediately replied, in writing, that it would stand by its position on the validity of the back charge and the accuracy of its calculation of the amount owed to the plaintiff.

The defendant thereafter, on January 10, 1983, sent the plaintiff the check that is at the heart of the present controversy. The check was in the amount of $416.88. It bore two legends. On its face was the notation:

> "Final payment
> Upjohn Project
> Purchase Order # 3302 dated 11/17/81."

On the reverse side, the check stated: "By its endorsement, the payee accepts this check in full satisfaction of all claims against the C.F. Wooding Co. arising out of or relating to the Upjohn Project under Purchase Order # 3302, dated 11/17/81." The plaintiff did not advise the defendant directly that it planned to cash this check under protest. Instead, the plaintiff crossed out the conditional language on the reverse side of the check and added the following: "This check is accepted under protest and with full reservation of rights to collect the unpaid balance for which this check is offered in settlement." The plaintiff then indorsed and deposited the check in its account.

The defendant made no further payments to the plaintiff and the plaintiff brought the present action to recover the remaining amount to which it claimed it was entitled. The trial court rendered judgment for the plaintiff on two grounds. The court agreed with the plaintiff that the enactment of § 1–207 had deprived debtors generally of the power unilaterally to enforce the terms of a conditional tender of a check to their creditors. Furthermore, in the specific circumstances of this case, the court concluded that the plaintiff could rightfully treat the defendant's offer of an accord as if it had been a payment on account, because the amount of the tender had been no more than the amount the defendant itself had calculated to be due and owing to the plaintiff. For these reasons, the court awarded the plaintiff $2100 as the unpaid balance of the account.

The defendant's appeal does not contest the monetary calculation used by the court in arriving at the amount of the judgment against the defendant, but maintains instead that the trial court erred because the plaintiff's cause of action was foreclosed as a matter of law. The defendant maintains that, when the plaintiff knowingly cashed a check explicitly tendered in full satisfaction of an unliquidated debt, the plaintiff became bound by the terms of settlement that the check contained. The defendant's argument takes issue with both aspects of the contrary ruling of the trial court. First, the defendant claims that the plaintiff's action of cashing this check constituted an acceptance of its offer, including its terms of settlement, despite the plaintiff's reliance on § 1–207 for authority to substitute words of protest for words of satisfaction. Second, the defendant claims that the amount that it tendered the plaintiff constituted a valid offer of an accord and satisfaction because the underlying debt was unliquidated in amount. We agree with both of the defendant's claims. We will, however, take them up in reverse order, because we would not reach the statutory issue if the defendant had failed to establish its common law defense to the plaintiff's cause of action.

I

When there is a good faith dispute about the existence of a debt or about the amount that is owed, the common law authorizes the debtor and the creditor to negotiate a contract of accord to settle the outstanding claim. Such a contract is often initiated by the debtor, who offers an accord by tendering a check as "payment in full" or "in full satisfaction." If the creditor knowingly cashes such a check, or otherwise exercises full dominion over it, the creditor is deemed to have assented to the offer of accord. Upon acceptance of the offer of accord, the creditor's receipt of the promised payment discharges the underlying debt and bars any further claim relating thereto, if the contract of accord is supported by consideration. * * *

A contract of accord and satisfaction is sufficiently supported by consideration if it settles a monetary claim that is unliquidated in amount. This court has had numerous occasions to decide whether, in the context of accord and satisfaction, a claim is unliquidated when the debtor tenders payment in an amount that does not exceed that to which the creditor is concededly entitled. "Where it is admitted that one of two specific sums is due, but there is a dispute as to which is the proper amount, the demand is regarded as unliquidated, within the meaning of that term as applied to the subject of accord and satisfaction * * *. Where the claim is unliquidated any sum, given and received in settlement of the dispute, is a sufficient consideration." Hanley Co. v. American Cement Co., 108 Conn. 469, 473, 143 A. 566 (1928); * * *.

Application of these settled principles to the facts of this case establishes, as the defendant maintains, that the parties entered into a valid contract of accord and satisfaction. The defendant offered in good faith to settle an unliquidated debt by tendering, in full satisfaction, the payment of an amount less than that demanded by the plaintiff. Under the common law, the plaintiff could not simultaneously cash such a check and disown the condition on which it had been tendered. * * * Having received the promised payment, the plaintiff discharged the defendant from any further obligation on this account, unless the enactment of § 1–207 of the Uniform Commercial Code has changed this result.

II

The principal dispute between the parties is what meaning to ascribe to § 1–207 when it states that "[a] party who with explicit reservation of rights * * * assents to performance in a manner * * * offered by the other party does not thereby prejudice the rights reserved. Such words as 'without prejudice,' 'under protest' or the like are sufficient." The plaintiff contends, as the trial court concluded, that this section gave the plaintiff the authority to cash the defendant's check "under protest" while reserving the right to pursue the remainder of its underlying claim against the defendant at a later time. The defendant maintains that the statutory reference to "performance" contemplates something other than the part payment of an unliquidated debt. We noted in Kelly v. Kowalsky, 186 Conn. at 622 and n. 3, 442 A.2d 1355, that there was considerable disagreement in the cases and the scholarly commentaries about the scope of the transactions governed by § 1–207, but did not then undertake to resolve this disagreement. We now decide that § 1–207 does not displace the common law of accord and satisfaction and that the trial court erred in so concluding.

Because § 1–207 is part of the Uniform Commercial Code, it is important to reconcile its provisions with those found in other articles of the code. * * *

Two likely candidates for such a reconciliation are the provisions of article 3, dealing generally with the law of negotiable instruments, including checks * * * and the provisions of article 2, dealing generally with contracts for the sale of goods. * * *

Article 3 provides little support for reading § 1–207 to permit a creditor unilaterally to change the terms of a check tendered in full satisfaction of an unliquidated debt. As the parties have noted, § 3–112(1)(f) preserves the negotiability of a check that includes "a term * * * providing that the payee by indorsing or cashing it acknowledges full satisfaction of an obligation of the drawer." There is no such validation, anywhere in article 3, for a term on a check that negates a condition that a drawer has incorporated in a negotiable instrument. On the contrary, § 3–407 takes a dim view of the unauthorized alteration of an instrument. Under § 3–407(1) "[a]ny alteration of an instrument is material which changes the contract of *any* party thereto in *any* respect * * *." (Emphasis added.) The effect of the material alteration of a completed instrument is either to discharge the liability, on the instrument, of "any party whose contract is thereby changed," or to continue the enforceability of the instrument "according to its original tenor." § 3–407(2) and (3). According to this section, the plaintiff's conduct in substituting words of protest for words of satisfaction would have put the plaintiff at risk of discharging the defendant entirely, if such conduct were deemed to have been fraudulent. § 3–407(2)(a). Even without a finding of fraud, however, the most for which the plaintiff could hope, under article 3, was to enforce the instrument "in full satisfaction," because that was "its original tenor." This result is supported by § 3–802(1)(b), which provides that, presumptively, the taking of a negotiable instrument suspends the underlying obligation "until the instrument is due," and that "discharge of the underlying obligor on the instrument also discharges him on the obligation." Under § 3–603(1), a drawer is discharged from liability on an instrument "to the extent of his payment or satisfaction."

The impact of these various article 3 rules is clear. Because the check tendered by the defendant was only enforceable "according to its original tenor," the plaintiff, by receiving "payment or satisfaction," discharged the defendant not only on the instrument but also on the underlying obligation. See J. White & R. Summers, Uniform Commercial Code (2d Ed.1980) pp. 603–604 n. 57. To read § 1–207 to validate the plaintiff's conduct in this case would, therefore, fly in the face of the relevant provisions of article 3, which signal the continued vitality of the common law principles of accord and satisfaction.

Although § 1–207 does not fit easily within the principles of article 3 that govern checks, the section has a close and harmonious connection with article 2. Article 2 regulates ongoing conduct relating to performance of contracts for the sale of goods. That article recurrently draws inferences from acquiescence in, or objection to, the performance tendered by one of the contracting parties. A course of performance "accepted or acquiesced in without objection" is relevant to a determination of the meaning of a contract of sale. § 2–208(1). Between merchants, proposals for additional terms will be added to a contract of sale unless there is a timely "notification of objection." § 2–207(2)(c). A buyer who is confronted by a defective tender of goods must make a seasonable objection or lose his right of rejection. §§ 2–602(1), 2–605, 2–606(1), 2–607(2); * * * In an instalment sale, a party aggrieved by nonconformity or default that substantially impairs the value of the contract as a whole will nonetheless have reinstated the contract "if he accepts a nonconforming instalment without seasonably notifying of cancellation * * *." § 2–612(3). A contract whose performance has become impracticable requires the buyer, after notification by the seller, to offer reasonable alternatives for the modification or the termination of the affected contract; the buyer's failure to respond, within a reasonable period of time, causes the sales contract to lapse. § 2–616(1) and (2). In these and other related circumstances, article 2 urges the contracting parties to engage in a continuing dialogue about what will constitute acceptable performance of their sales contract. See generally J. White & R. Summers, supra, §§ 3–1 through 3–9. It is entirely consistent with this article 2 policy to provide, as does § 1–207, a statutory methodology for the effective communication of objections. See J. McDonnell, "Purposive Interpretation of the Uniform Commercial Code: Some Implications for Jurisprudence," 126 U.Pa.L.Rev. 795, 828 (1978).

From the vantage point of article 2, it is apparent that § 1–207 contemplates a reservation of rights about some aspect of a possibly nonconforming tender of goods or services or payment in a situation where the aggrieved party may prefer not to terminate the underlying contract as a whole. * * * A. Rosenthal, "Discord and Satisfaction: Section 1–207 of the Uniform Commercial Code," 78 Colum.L.Rev. 48, 63 (1978). Indeed, the Official Comment to § 1–207 itself explains that the section supports ongoing contractual relations by providing "machinery for the continuation of performance along the lines contemplated by the contract despite a pending dispute." See W.D. Hawkland, "The Effect of U.C.C. § 1–207 on the Doctrine of Accord and Satisfaction by Conditional Check," 74 Com.L.J. 329, 331 (1969). It is significant, furthermore, that the text of § 1–207 recurrently refers to "performance," for "performance" is a central aspect of the sales transactions governed by article 2. By contrast, article 3 instruments, which promise or order the payment of money, are not characteristically described as being performed by anyone. The contracts encapsulated in various forms of negotiable instruments instead envisage conduct of negotiation or transfer, indorsement or guaranty, payment or acceptance, and honor or dishonor. See, e.g., §§ 3–201, 3–413, 3–414, 3–416, 3–418; see generally J. White & R. Summers, supra, §§ 13–6 through 13–10, 13–12. We conclude, therefore, that, in circumstances like the present, when performance of a sales contract has come to an end, § 1–207 was not intended to empower a seller, as payee of a negotiable instrument, to alter that instrument by adding words of protest to a check tendered by a buyer on condition that it be accepted in full satisfaction of an unliquidated debt.

Our conclusion is supported by the emerging majority of cases in other jurisdictions. While the case law was divided five years ago, when we postponed resolution of the controversy about the meaning of § 1–207; Kelly v. Kowalsky, supra, 186 Conn. at 621–22, 442 A.2d 1355; it is now the view of the substantial majority of courts that have addressed the issue that § 1–207 does not overrule the common law of accord and satisfaction. * * * The majority finds support as well in much of the recent scholarly commentary. See 2 Restatement (Second), Contracts (1981) § 281, comment d; R. Anderson, Uniform Commercial Code (1984) § 3–408–56; W. Grosse & E. Goggin, supra, 546; W.D. Hawkland, supra, 331; J. McDonnell, supra, 824–28; A. Rosenthal, supra, 61; contra, J. Calamari & J. Perillo, Contracts (2d Ed.1977) § 5–16; J. White & R. Summers, supra, § 13–21.

Both under prevailing common law principles, and under the Uniform Commercial Code, the parties in this case negotiated a contract of accord whose satisfaction discharged the defendant from any further monetary obligation to the plaintiff. The plaintiff might have avoided this result by returning the defendant's check uncashed, but could not simultaneously disregard the condition on which the check was tendered and deposit its proceeds in the plaintiff's bank account.

There is error, the judgment is set aside and the case is remanded with direction to render judgment for the defendant.

NOTES

1. Revised Article 3 deals with accord and satisfaction in § 3–311. At the time revised Article 3 was promulgated, § 1–207 was also amended by adding a new subsection (2) as follows:

(2) Subsection (1) does not apply to accord and satisfaction.

A new Comment 3 to § 1–207 was also added.

2. Effectuating an accord and satisfaction of a disputed claim by a "full satisfaction" legend on a check is a cheap and fast way in which to settle a claim. Section 3–311(a) and (b) provide that, as a general rule, if the legend on the check is conspicuous and the claim is subject to a bona fide dispute, the claimant cannot obtain payment of the check without agreeing to the accord and satisfaction. If the claimant wishes to avoid settlement for the amount of the check, it must not cash the check. As Comment 1 to § 3–311 points out, accord and satisfaction by use of notations on checks is useful to consumers in disputes about the quality of goods or services purchased, but it is also commonly employed by insurance companies to settle claims of insured parties. Section 3–311(c)(1) addresses a problem encountered by organizations like large retailers and other high volume recipients of checks who find it burdensome and wasteful to conduct a visual search of tens of thousands of checks to see if a handful contain a proposed accord and satisfaction legend. This provision allows such an organization to notify its customers to send any communications concerning disputed debts, including checks containing full satisfaction legends, to a specified address at which these checks and other communications can be examined and decisions made with respect to whether to accept them as settlement of claims. This allows the retailer to rapidly process other checks without examination to detect accord and satisfaction language. Section 3–311(c)(2) is an alternative to § 3–311(c)(1) which is also designed to prevent an inadvertent accord and satisfaction. It is explained in Comment 6 to § 3–311.

CHAPTER 3

PAYMENT SYSTEMS

A. CHECK COLLECTION

According to Fred R. Bleakley, Electronic Payments Now Supplant Checks at More Large Firms, Wall St.J., April 13, 1994, p.A1, the following scene, reminiscent of Apocalypse Now, occurs nightly in Burbank, California:. Helicopters swirl into the Burbank Airport, landing in rapid succession, carrying hundreds of pounds of bundled checks. Workers race around, hurling the bundles into carts which are run out to Flight 401, a Learjet, in order to meet its 10:30 p.m. flight time. The jet carries $600 million in corporate checks that must be delivered to banks in 46 out-of-state cities to meet an 8 a.m. deadline. Missing the deadline will delay payment of the checks a day, depriving the owners of the checks the use of $600 million for that period. The jet arrived on schedule (5:10 a.m.) at an Ohio airport used by U.S. Check Inc., the largest check courier, as the central clearing point. Waiting there were 18 jets and six propeller plains loaded with 25,000 pounds of checks totaling $20 billion which had come in on other flights. This fleet promptly took off, split up and headed for 46 cities, where they were met by courier trucks which delivered them to 150 banks by the 8 a.m. deadline. Whew!

This article estimates that the printing, mailing and clearing of the 60 billion or so checks written each year in the U.S. costs more than $50 billion. Tons of checks are lugged around by trucks, helicopters and airplanes all over the nation. Some checks are stolen; others are lost. A courier plane carrying Bank of America deposits went down in the Pacific and some of the checks dredged up from the ocean had to be restored by hair dryers. In the age of computers, why can't this enormous cost be greatly reduced by communicating the information on checks electronically or, better still, by getting rid of checks altogether and allowing computers to talk to computers? The so-called checkless society has been talked about for several decades, but, as we shall see later in this chapter, there is now reason to believe that it is finally going to happen.

Since checks are still very much in use, we will go through the process of check collection before discussing alternative systems.

1. TIME CHECK IS PAID BY PAYOR BANK

a. THE MIDNIGHT DEADLINE

Article 4 governs the rights and obligations of banks and their customers with respect to the collection of checks by the banking system, but the

131

Federal Reserve Board has always played a very important role in check collection. This role has been expanded by Regulation CC, 12 C.F.R. § 229, issued pursuant to the Expedited Funds Availability Act of 1987, 12 U.S.C. § 4001 et seq. We discuss the impact of Regulation CC later in this chapter.

The next case in this book discusses the issue of when, under Article 4, the bank on which a check is drawn is deemed to have paid the check. This issue is presented in its most simple form if the payee of a check takes it to the drawee bank and asks for payment in cash over the counter. The check is paid when the bank gives cash equal to the amount of the check to the payee. § 4–215(a)(1). But that case is not at all typical. Very few checks are paid in cash. Almost all checks are deposited to a bank account of the holder of the check.

To understand how Article 4 applies to checks deposited in a bank it is necessary to understand the concept of settlement in Article 4. § 4–104(a)(11) and § 4–213. Typically, in the check-collection process, each bank that takes a check pays for it at, or shortly after, the time that the check is taken. Article 4 uses the terms "settlement" and "settle" to refer to this act of paying for the check. But to say that a bank has settled or paid for a check is not the same as saying that the bank has paid the check. The bank on which a check is drawn is referred to in Article 4 as the payor bank. § 4–105(3). The payor bank can pay the check, but any other bank giving value for the check may be buying the check but is not paying it. And even in the case of the payor bank there is a distinction between the bank's settling for the check and paying the check. For example, suppose the payee of a check deposits it to the payee's account in Bank A. The drawer of the check also has an account in Bank A and the check is drawn on that account. In this case, Bank A is both the depositary bank with respect to the check and the payor bank. § 4–105(2) and (3). Bankers refer to this kind of check as an "on us" item. At or shortly after the time Bank A receives the check from the payee, Bank A will credit the account of the payee for the amount of the check. By making that credit Bank A settles for the check. § 4–104(a)(11) and § 4–213(a)(2)(iii). This settlement, however, is provisional in nature because Bank A has the right to revoke it under certain circumstances.

At the time Bank A settles with the payee for the check, it usually does not know whether, as the payor bank, it should pay the check. For example, suppose the balance in the drawer's account in Bank A is not sufficient to cover the amount of the check. Bank A has no obligation to the payee of the check to pay the check (§ 3–408) and, if Bank A is not assured of reimbursement from the drawer of the check, Bank A normally would refuse to pay the check. Under Article 4, Bank A is given a time-limited right to revoke or recover the payment that it made to the payee when the payee's account was credited. § 4–301(a). The prescribed technique for accomplishing this result is to return the check to the payee and to debit ("charge-back") the payee's account in the amount of the check. As payor bank, Bank A "pays the check" if and when it has not exercised its right to recover a provisional payment that it has made and the right of recovery no longer exists. § 4–215(a)(3) and § 4–301(a). This practice of pay-first-take-back-later is in effect because it is operationally efficient. Since payor banks have reason to refuse payment with respect to only a tiny percentage of the vast number of checks that are processed each day for payment, it is sensible to pay for all checks as they are received ("settlement") and to deal later with the small number of checks that turn out to be bad by revoking the settlement and returning the checks. Although in Montana only one in every 192 checks is returned, in Los Angeles, where guilt is less oppressive, one in every 34 bounces. Roger Lowenstein, Behind the Teller Windows, Wall St.J., Dec. 30, 1996, p. A10.

A similar analysis applies with respect to the more common case in which the depositary bank is not also the payor bank. In that case the depositary bank is a collecting bank that acts as agent of the holder to obtain payment of the check. § 4–105(5). The depositary bank will either present the check directly to the payor bank or it will negotiate the check to an intermediary bank which acts as a collecting bank to obtain payment of the check. § 4–105(4) and (5). The intermediary bank is likely to be a Federal Reserve bank and often there is more than one intermediary bank. Each collecting bank will give provisional settlement to the bank from which the check is received. The last collecting bank will present the check for payment to the payor bank which will give provisional settlement to the presenting bank.

In transactions between banks, settlement is normally made by a credit to the Federal Reserve account of the bank receiving the settlement. The payor bank may refuse payment of the check by returning it to the presenting bank and recovering the amount of the check from that bank. § 4–301(a). In turn the presenting bank and each collecting bank may return the check to the bank from which it received the check and recover the provisional payment. § 4–214(a). As we will see, Regulation CC requires payor and collecting banks to expedite the return of checks and authorizes them to return checks directly to the depositary bank or to any bank that has agreed to handle the checks for expeditious return to the depositary bank. Any bank returning the check may obtain the amount of the check from the bank to which the check is transferred. When the depositary bank receives the returned check it may recover the provisional payment given to the holder from whom it took the check for collection. § 4–214(a).

Blake, which follows, describes in more detail the time-limited right that Article 4 gives to a payor bank to return a check and recover any provisional settlement given for the check or to avoid liability to pay the check under § 4–302.

Blake v. Woodford Bank & Trust Co.

Court of Appeals of Kentucky, 1977.
555 S.W.2d 589.

■ PARK, JUDGE.

This case involves the liability of * * * Woodford Bank and Trust Company on two checks drawn on the Woodford Bank and Trust Company and payable to the order of * * * Wayne Blake. Following a trial without a jury, the Woodford Circuit Court found that the bank was excused from meeting its "midnight deadline" with respect to the two checks. Blake appeals from the judgment of the circuit court dismissing his complaint. The bank cross-appeals from that portion of the circuit court's opinion relating to the extent of the bank's liability on the two checks if it should be determined that the bank was not excused from meeting its midnight deadline.

BASIC FACTS

The basic facts are not in dispute. On December 6, 1973, Blake deposited a check in the amount of $16,449.84 to his account at the Morristown Bank, of Morristown, Ohio. This check was payable to Blake's order and was drawn on the K & K Farm Account at the Woodford Bank and Trust Company. The check was dated December 3, 1973.

On December 19, 1973, Blake deposited a second check in the amount of $11,200.00 to his account in the Morristown Bank. The second check was also drawn on the K & K Farm Account at the Woodford Bank and Trust Company and made payable to Blake's order. The second check was dated December 17, 1973.

When Blake deposited the second check on December 19, he was informed by the Morristown Bank that the first check had been dishonored and returned because of insufficient funds. Blake instructed the Morristown Bank to re-present the first check along with the second check. Blake was a cattle trader, and the two checks represented the purchase price for cattle sold by Blake to James Knight who maintained the K & K Farm Account. Blake testified that he had been doing business with Knight for several years. On other occasions, checks had been returned for insufficient funds but had been paid when re-presented.

The two checks were forwarded for collection through the Cincinnati Branch of the Federal Reserve Bank of Cleveland. From the Federal Reserve Bank, the two checks were delivered to the Woodford Bank and Trust Company by means of the Purolator Courier Corp. The checks arrived at the Woodford Bank and Trust Company on Monday, December 24, 1973, shortly before the opening of the bank for business. The next day, Christmas, was not a banking day. The two checks were returned by the Woodford Bank and Trust Company to the Cincinnati Branch of the Federal Reserve Bank by means of Purolator on Thursday, December 27, 1973.

The two checks were received by the bank on Monday, December 24. The next banking day was Wednesday, December 26. Thus, the bank's "midnight deadline" was midnight on Wednesday, December 26. § 4–104(1)(h) [Revised § 4–104(a)(10)]. As the bank retained the two checks beyond its midnight deadline, Blake asserts that the bank is "accountable" for the amount of the two checks under § 4–302(1)(a) [Revised § 4–302(a)(1)].

HISTORY OF PAYOR BANK'S LIABILITY FOR RETAINING CHECK

Under the Uniform Negotiable Instruments Law a payor bank was not liable to the holder of a check drawn on the bank until the bank had accepted or certified the check. * * * Because of the payor bank's basic nonliability on a check, it was essential that some time limit be placed upon the right of the payor bank to dishonor a check when presented for payment. If a payor bank could hold a check indefinitely without incurring liability, the entire process of collection and payment of checks would be intolerably slow. To avoid this problem, a majority of courts construing § 136 and § 137 of the Uniform Negotiable Instruments Law held that a payor bank was deemed to have accepted a check if it held the check for 24 hours after the check was presented for payment. * * * Thus, in a majority of jurisdictions, the payor bank had only 24 hours to determine whether to pay a check or return it. However, in Kentucky and a few other jurisdictions, the courts held that § 136 and § 137 of the Uniform Negotiable Instruments Law applied only to checks which were presented for acceptance. * * * Consequently, the payor bank would be liable on the check only if it held the check "for an unreasonable length of time" and could thus be deemed to have converted the check.

In order to bring uniformity to the check collection process, the Bank Collection Code was proposed by the American Bankers' Association. The Bank Collection Code was adopted by Kentucky in 1930. Under § 3 of the Bank Collection Code, a payor bank could give provisional credit when a check was received, and the credit could be revoked at any time before the end of that business day. The payor bank became liable on the check if it retained the item beyond the end of the business day received. * * *

Banks had only a few hours to determine whether a check should be returned because of insufficient funds. Banks were required to "dribble post checks" by sorting and sending the checks to the appropriate bookkeepers as the checks were received. This led to an uneven workload during the course of a business day. At times, the bookkeeping personnel might have nothing to do while at other times they would be required to process a very large number of checks in a very short time. * * * Because of the increasingly large number of checks processed each day and the shortage of qualified bank personnel during World War II, it became impossible for banks to determine whether a check was "good" in only 24 hours. The banks were forced to resort to the procedure of "paying" for a check on the day it was presented without posting it to the customer's account until the following day. See First National Bank of Elwood v. Universal C.I.T. Credit Corporation, 132 Ind.App. 353, 170 N.E.2d 238, at 244 (1960). To meet this situation, the American Banking Association proposed a Model Deferred Posting Statute. * * *

Under the Model Deferred Posting Statute, a payor bank could give provisional credit for a check on the business day it was received, and the credit could be revoked at any time before midnight of the bank's next business day following receipt. A provisional credit was revoked "by returning the item, or if the item is held for protest or at the time is lost or is not in the possession of the bank, by giving written notice of dishonor,, nonpayment, or revocation; provided that such item or notice is dispatched in the mails or by other expeditious means not later than midnight of the bank's next business day after the item was received." * * * If the payor bank failed to take advantage of the provisions of the deferred posting statute by revoking the provisional credit and returning the check within the time and in the manner provided by the act, the payor bank was deemed to have paid the check and was liable thereon to the holder. * * *

The Model Deferred Posting Statute was the basis for the provisions of the Uniform Commercial Code. Under § 4–301(1) [Revised § 4–301(a)] of the Uniform Commercial Code (UCC), a payor bank may revoke a provisional "settlement" if it does so before its "midnight deadline" which is midnight of the next banking day following the banking day on which it received the check. Under the Model Deferred Posting Statute, the payor bank's liability for failing to meet its midnight deadline was to be inferred rather than being spelled out in the statute. Under UCC § 4–302, the payor bank's liability for missing its midnight deadline is explicit. If the payor bank misses its midnight deadline, the bank is "accountable" for the face amount of the check. * * *

Like the Model Deferred Posting Statute, the Uniform Commercial Code seeks to decrease, rather than increase, the risk of liability to payor banks. By permitting deferred posting, the Uniform Commercial Code extends the time within which a payor bank must determine whether it will pay a check drawn on the bank. Unlike the Bank Collection Code or the Uniform Negotiable Instruments Law as construed by most courts, the Uniform Commercial Code does not require the payor bank to act on the day of receipt or within 24 hours of receipt of a check. The payor bank is granted until midnight of the next business day following the business day on which it received the check.

EXCUSE FOR FAILING TO MEET MIDNIGHT DEADLINE

UCC § 4–108(2) [Revised § 4–109(b)] provides:

"Delay by a * * * payor bank beyond time limits prescribed or permitted by this Act * * * is excused if caused by interruption of communications facilities, suspension of payments by another bank, war, emergency conditions or other circumstances beyond the control of the bank provided it exercises such diligence as the circumstances require."

The circuit court found that the bank's failure to return the two checks by its midnight deadline was excused under the provisions of UCC § 4–108.

The circuit court dictated its findings of fact into the record:

"From all of the evidence that was presented in this case, it would appear that there was no intentional action on the part of the bank to hold these checks beyond the normal course of business as an accommodation to its customer. In fact, the uncontroverted testimony of the bank officers was to the contrary. To say that the bank failed, through certain procedures, to return the checks by the midnight deadline does not, in the mind of this Court, imply or establish an intentional act on the part of the bank.

"In this instance we have the Christmas Holiday, which caused in the bank, as in all businesses, certain emergency and overloaded situations. This is not unique to the banking industry; but is true of virtually every business in a christian society, in which the holiday of Christmas is observed as the major holiday of the year. Special considerations are always given to employees as well as customers of these banking institutions.

" * * * On the Christmas Holiday, two machines were broken down for periods of time during this critical day in question. There was an absence of a regular bookkeeper."

Under CR 52.01, these findings of fact cannot be set aside by this court unless they are clearly erroneous. The foregoing findings are supported by the record, and are not questioned by Blake on the appeal.

After making findings of fact, the circuit court dictated the following conclusions into the record:

" * * * The entire cumulative effect of what happened would constitute diligence on the part of the bank, as circumstances required.

"It is the opinion of the Court and it is the Finding of the Court that the circumstances described by the banking officers, the standards of banking care, as described by expert witnesses, would bring the bank within 4–108(2), and the Court therefore, finds as a fact that there were circumstances here beyond the control of the bank, and that it exercised such diligence as those circumstances required."

When the circuit court concluded "that there were circumstances here beyond the control of the bank, and that it exercised such diligence as those circumstances required," the circuit court was doing no more than repeating the words of the statute. This court must determine whether the circuit court's findings of fact support these conclusions.

Before turning to the facts presented in this case, it is appropriate to discuss the only two cases involving the application of UCC § 4–108 to a payor bank's midnight deadline. In Sun River Cattle Co. v. Miners Bank of Montana, 164 Mont. 237, 521 P.2d 679 (1974), the payor bank utilized a computer in the adjacent town of Great Falls to process its checks. The checks were picked up at the Miners Bank by an armored car between 5:00 p.m. and 6:00 p.m. on the date of receipt. The checks would normally reach the computer center at Great Falls around 10:30 p.m. Ordinarily the checks would have been processed by 11:30 p.m., returned to the Miners Bank by 8:00 a.m. the next morning. The checks in question were received by the Miners Bank on May 11. On that day, the armored car broke down, and the checks did not reach the computer center at Great Falls until 1:30 a.m. the next morning, May 12. On that morning, the computer malfunctioned and the checks were not returned to the Miners Bank until 2:30 p.m. on May 12. There was no testimony as to what actually happened to the checks after they were received by the Miners Bank on the afternoon of May 12, but the Miners Bank failed to return the checks by midnight of May 12. The trial court held that the failure of the Miners Bank to meet its midnight deadline was excused by the provisions of UCC § 4–108(2). The Montana Supreme Court reversed, holding that the Miners Bank had failed to show the degree of diligence required under the circumstances. The Montana court pointed out that the Miners Bank had more than the normal interest in the activities in the account upon which the checks were drawn, and that due diligence could not be shown merely by following ordinary operating procedures.

In Port City State Bank v. American National Bank, 486 F.2d 196 (10th Cir.1973), the payor bank, American National, was changing from machine posting to computer processing of its checks commencing Monday, December 1, 1969. Two checks were in dispute. The first check arrived at American National on Friday, November 28, 1969. As Monday was the next banking day, the midnight deadline for the first check was December 1. The second check arrived on Tuesday, December 2, 1969, and the midnight deadline for that check was Wednesday, December 3. American National's new computer developed a "memory error" which rendered it unusable at 10:00 a.m. on December 1, the first day of computer operations. The computer manufacturer assured the bank that repairs would not take "too long." Unfortunately repairs and testing were not completed until the early hours of Tuesday, December 2. In the meantime, American National attempted to utilize an identical computer in a bank some two and a half hours away. Processing commenced at the other bank at 11:30 p.m. on December 1, and continued through the night. Although work proceeded to the point of "capturing" all of the items on discs, the backup computer was required by its owner, and the American National personnel returned to the bank to complete the printing of the trial balances. Another memory error developed in the new computer which again rendered the computer unusable. No further use could be made of American National's computer until a new memory module was installed on Thursday, December 4. The trial court held that the computer breakdown constituted a condition beyond the control of American National and that the bank had exercised due diligence. On appeal, the United States Court of Appeals affirmed, holding that the findings of the district court were not clearly erroneous.

* * *

The basic facts found by the circuit court can be summarized as follows: a) the bank had no intention of holding the checks beyond the midnight deadline in order to accommodate its customer; b) there was an increased volume of checks to be handled by reason of the Christmas Holiday; c) two posting machines were broken down for a period of time on December 26; d) one regular bookkeeper was absent because of illness. Standing alone, the bank's intention not to favor its customer by retaining an item beyond the midnight deadline would not justify the application of

§ 4–108(2). The application of the exemption statute necessarily will turn upon the findings relating to heavy volume, machine breakdown, and absence of a bookkeeper.

The bank's president testified that 4,200 to 4,600 checks were processed on a normal day. Because the bank was closed for Christmas on Tuesday, the bank was required to process 6,995 checks on December 26. The bank had four posting machines. On the morning of December 26, two of the machines were temporarily inoperable. One of the machines required two and one half hours to repair. The second machine was repaired in one and one half hours. As the bank had four bookkeepers, the machine breakdown required the bookkeepers to take turns using the posting machines for a time in the morning. One of the four bookkeepers who regularly operated the posting machines was absent because of illness on December 26. This bookkeeper was replaced by the head bookkeeper who had experience on the posting machines, although he was not as proficient as a regular posting machine operator.

Because of the cumulative effect of the heavy volume, machine breakdown and absence of a regular bookkeeper, the bank claims it was unable to process the two checks in time to deliver them to the courier from Purolator for return to the Federal Reserve Bank on December 26. As the bank's president testified:

> "Because we couldn't get them ready for the Purolator carrier to pick them up by 4:00 and we tried to get all our work down there to him by 4:00, for him to pick up and these two checks were still being processed in our bookkeeping department and it was impossible for those to get into returns for that day."

* * *

The increased volume of items to be processed the day after Christmas was clearly foreseeable. The breakdown of the posting machines was not an unusual occurrence, although it was unusual to have two machines broken down at the same time. In any event, it should have been foreseeable to the responsible officers of the bank that the bookkeepers would be delayed in completing posting of the checks on December 26. Nevertheless, the undisputed evidence establishes that no arrangements of any kind were made for return of "bad" items which might be discovered by the bookkeepers after the departure of the Purolator courier. The two checks in question were in fact determined by Mrs. Stratton to be "bad" on December 26. The checks were not returned because the regular employee responsible for handling "bad" checks had left for the day, and Mrs. Stratton had no instructions to cover the situation.

Even though the bank missed returning the two checks by the Purolator courier, it was still possible for the bank to have returned the checks by its midnight deadline. Under UCC § 4–301(4)(b) [Revised § 4–301(d)(2)]an item is returned when it is "sent" to the bank's transferor, in this case the Federal Reserve Bank. Under UCC § 1–201(38) an item is "sent" when it is deposited in the mail. 1 R. Anderson, Uniform Commercial Code § 1–201 pp. 118–119 (2d ed. 1970). Thus, the bank could have returned the two checks before the midnight deadline by the simple procedure of depositing the two checks in the mail, properly addressed to the Cincinnati branch of the Federal Reserve Bank.

This court concludes that circumstances beyond the control of the bank did not prevent it from returning the two checks in question before its midnight deadline on December 26. The circumstances causing delay in the bookkeeping department were foreseeable. On December 26, the bank actually discovered that the checks were "bad," but the responsible employees and officers had left the bank without leaving any instructions to the bookkeepers. The circuit court erred in holding that the bank was excused under § 4–108 from meeting its midnight deadline. The facts found by the circuit court do not support its conclusion that the circumstances in the case were beyond the control of the bank.

RE–PRESENTMENT OF CHECK PREVIOUSLY DISHONORED BY NONPAYMENT

On its cross-appeal, the bank argues that the circuit court erred in holding that there was no difference in the status of the two checks. The bank makes the argument that it is not liable on the first check which had previously been dishonored by nonpayment. Blake received notice of dishonor when the first check was returned because of insufficient funds. The bank claims that it was under no further duty to meet the midnight deadline when the check was re-presented for payment.

The bank relies upon the decision of the Kansas Supreme Court in Leaderbrand v. Central State Bank, 202 Kan. 450, 450 P.2d 1 (1969). A check drawn on the Central State Bank was presented for payment on two occasions over the counter. On both occasions, the holder of the check was advised orally that there were not sufficient funds in the account to honor the check. Later, the holder deposited the check in his own account at the First State Bank. The First State Bank did not send the check through regular bank collection channels, but rather mailed the check directly to the Central State Bank for purposes of collection. The check arrived at the Central State Bank on March 21 or March 22, and the check was not returned by the Central State Bank to the First State Bank until April 5. The Kansas Supreme Court held that there was no liability under § 4–302 of UCC for a check which had previously been dishonored when presented for payment.

Relying on the provisions of UCC § 3–511(4), the Kansas Supreme Court held that "any notice of dishonor" was excused when a check had been "dishonored by nonacceptance" and was later re-presented for payment. The Kansas Supreme Court specifically held that § 3–511(4) [See Revised § 3–502(f)]applied to a check which was dishonored when presented for payment, stating:

"While the language of 84–3–511(4), supra—'Where a draft has been dishonored by nonacceptance'—does not refer to a dishonor by nonpayment, we think reference to the dishonor of a 'draft' 'by nonacceptance' would, a fortiori, include the dishonor of a check by nonpayment."

The Kansas Supreme Court concluded that a payor bank was excused from giving any further notice of dishonor when a previously dishonored check was re-presented for payment and there were still insufficient funds in the drawer's account to cover the check.

* * *

The decision of the Kansas Supreme Court in the *Leaderbrand* case has been criticized. As UCC § 3–511(4) applies by its terms to a "draft" which has been "dishonored by nonacceptance," most of the criticism has been directed to the Kansas court's application of § 3–511(4) to a check which had been dishonored by nonpayment. As stated in B. Clark and A. Squillante, The Law of Bank Deposits, Collections and Credit Cards at 71–72 (1970):

> "Use of this section to excuse retention under § 4–302 seems questionable, since the draftsmen are saying nothing more than dishonor by nonacceptance excuses notice of dishonor by nonpayment. If a time draft is not accepted, it is a useless act to present it for payment. On the other hand, sending a check through a second or third time often yields results, since the depositor may have had time to make a deposit to his account. It is presumably for this reason that the Code draftsmen limited the excuse rule of § 3–511(4) to 'nonacceptance' of 'drafts' and did not by express language indicate 'nonpayment' of 'checks.' "

See also Note, Uniform Commercial Code—Nonapplicability of Payor Banks "Midnight Deadline" to Re–Presented Checks, 18 Kan.L.Rev. 679 (1970).

Two courts have refused to follow the *Leaderbrand* decision. In Wiley, Tate and Irby v. Peoples Bank and Trust Company, 438 F.2d 513 (5th Cir.1971), the United States Court of Appeals for the Fifth Circuit held:

> "We disagree with *Leaderbrand* and hold § 3–511(4) inapplicable here. Acceptance applies only to time items. It has nothing to do with demand items."

In Sun River Cattle Co. v. Miners Bank of Montana, supra, the Montana Supreme Court rejected the *Leaderbrand* decision and followed the decision of the United States Court of Appeals in the *Wiley, Tate and Irby* case. The Montana Supreme Court held that § 3–511(4) of the UCC was inapplicable to checks payable on demand.

* * *

A practical reason also exists for rejecting the *Leaderbrand* decision. In 1972, approximately 25 billion checks passed through the bank collection process. The Federal Reserve Banks handled 8 billion checks that year. * * * An earlier study indicated that only one half of one percent of all checks were dishonored when first presented for payment. Of those initially dishonored, approximately one half were paid upon re-presentment. F.

Leary, Check Handling Under Article Four of the Uniform Commercial Code, 49 Marq.L.Rev. 331, 333, n. 7 (1965). A significant number of previously dishonored checks are paid upon re-presentment in the regular course of the check collection process. Such checks are often presented through intermediate collecting banks, such as the Federal Reserve Bank in this case. Each collecting bank will have made a provisional settlement with its transferor, and, in turn, received a provisional settlement from the bank to which it forwarded the check. In this way, a series of provisional settlements are made as the check proceeds through the bank collection process.

Under UCC § 4–213(2) [Revised § 4–215(c)], final payment of a check "firms up" all of the provisional settlements made in the collection process. Under subsection (1)(d) of UCC § 4–213 [Revised § 4–215(a)(3)], a payor bank makes final payment of a check when it fails to revoke a provisional settlement "in the time and manner permitted by statute, clearing house rule or agreement." As to items not presented over the counter or by local clearing house, this means that a payor bank is deemed to have made final payment of a check when it fails to revoke a provisional settlement by its midnight deadline. See UCC § 4–213, Official Code Comment 6 [Comment 7 to Revised § 4–215]. In his article on check handling, Leary has described § 4–213 as the "zinger" section: "when provisional credit given by the payor bank becomes firm then—'zing'—all prior provisional credits are instantaneously made firm." Leary, op.cit., at 361. If a payor bank was not required to meet its midnight deadline with respect to previously dishonored items, then none of the other banks involved in the collection process could safely assume that the check had been paid. Consider the problems of the depository bank. It must permit its customer to withdraw the amount of the credit given for the check when provisional settlements have become final by payment and the bank has had "a reasonable time" to learn that the settlement is final. See UCC § 4–213(4)(a) [Revised § 4–215(e)(1)]. The depository bank will rarely receive notice that an item has been paid. In actual practice, the depository bank will utilize availability schedules to compute when it should receive the check if it is to be returned unpaid. Leary, op.cit., at 345–346. If a payor bank is not bound by its midnight deadline as to previously dishonored items, then there is no way for the depository bank to know whether a previously dishonored item has been paid upon re-presentment except by direct communication with the payor bank. Such a procedure would impose an unnecessary burden upon the check collection process.

This court concludes that the circuit court was correct in holding that there was no difference in the status of the two checks.

* * *

NOTES

1. Taken together §§ 4–301(a) and 4–302(a) provide that if a check arrives on Day 1, Payor Bank may avoid being held accountable for,

meaning liable for, the amount of the check by returning it before its "midnight deadline" (midnight of Day 2, § 4–104(a)(10)), only if it had settled for the check before midnight of Day 1. We discussed settlement briefly in the text preceding *Blake*. In Hanna v. First National Bank of Rochester, 87 N.Y.2d 107, 637 N.Y.S.2d 953, 661 N.E.2d 683 (N.Y. 1995), checks arrived at Payor Bank on November 12 and were returned on November 13, but Payor Bank was held accountable on the checks because it offered no proof that it had settled for the checks on November 12. Payor Bank objected to this result on the ground that it should not be liable for the full amount of the checks, $44,503, when Depositary Bank's loss was minimal. The court stated:

> Some commentators have questioned the wisdom of imposing liability under UCC 4–302(a) for a payor bank's failure to settle for the item on the day it is received when the bank has dishonored or returned the item within the midnight deadline because if the item has been dishonored before payment of it has become final, the only apparent harm that results is that the depositary bank has been deprived of one day's interest on the amount of the item. They maintain that holding the payor bank accountable for the face value of the item in the light of such minimum damages is an unduly harsh penalty (see 6 Hawkland, Leary & Alderman, UCC Series, § 4–302:01). * * * We do not similarly view the matter.

661 N.E.2d at 688.

The unusual aspect of *Hanna* is how the issue of failure to settle on Day 1 ever arose. *Hanna* is the first case we have seen in which there was no settlement on the date of delivery. A large percentage of checks are presented by Federal Reserve banks, and, as to these checks, there is always settlement on the day of presentment. This is true because the Fed will not present a check to a payor bank unless that bank or its correspondent bank has an account in the Fed; this account will be promptly debited by the Fed. With respect to checks not presented by the Fed, settlement may be made by the payor bank's sending a Fedwire credit to the presenting bank's Fed account before the close of Fedwire (6:30 p.m. ET) on the day of delivery. If, as in *Hanna*, a check is presented through a clearing house, the banks that are members of the clearing house usually have agreements (§ 4–213(a)) providing that as each member exchanges checks at the clearing with each other member, the amounts are netted out with debit balances to be paid that day by wire transfers to the account of the creditor bank in the Fed by an agreed time or by entries in accounts each of the members holds in the others. In short, in clearing house transactions, payor banks must settle for checks on the day the checks are delivered to it. The court has little to say about why this result didn't follow in *Hanna*, other than to observe, laconically, that the payor bank had presented no admissible evidence of settlement on November 12.

2. In the reference to the Wall Street Journal article at the beginning of this chapter describing the hectic pace of check collection, the deadline the courier service was trying to meet was to get the checks to the payor banks by 8 a.m. You don't find anything in the UCC about such a deadline because it is imposed by Federal Reserve regulations (12 CFR §§ 229.34(c), 229.39(d)) which take precedence over Article 4 requirements. § 4–103(b). Section 4–213(a) expressly states that the medium and time of settlement may be prescribed by Federal Reserve regulations. Cash management people view the rule of § 4–301 that settlement may be made at any time before midnight of the day of presentment as terribly lax. They want the balance of their accounts known earlier in the day so that they can invest unneeded funds in overnight money markets. In 1994 the Fed imposed "same-day settlement" (SDS) rules for checks not clearing through the Fed which give certain benefits (e.g., freedom from having to pay presentment fees to payor banks) to checks delivered to payor banks or their check processing facility by 8 a.m. For checks qualifying as SDS checks, settlement must be made by a credit to the presenting bank's Federal Reserve bank account, unless the presenting bank otherwise agrees, and must be made by the close of Fedwire. Failure to meet this deadline will make the payor bank accountable under § 4–302. This rule does not apply to checks cleared through the Fed because payor banks are prohibited from charging the Fed presentment fees, and settlement is made intra-day by the Fed's debiting the payor bank's account in the Fed. In other words, the Fed does not need the same-day settlement rule to protect it. This settlement rule is discussed in Clark & Clark, The Law of Bank Deposits, Collections and Credit Cards ¶ 5.10 (Rev.ed.1995) and Robert D. Mulford, New Federal Reserve Actions Modifying the UCC: Intraday Posting, Same–Day Settlement, and MICR Encoding Warranties, 26 UCC L.J. 99 (1993).

3. The court deals with the question of whether the first check, which was re-presented on December 24, should be treated differently from the second check which was presented for the first time on that date. Woodford Bank argued that because that check had been properly returned the first time that it was presented, it had no duty to return it in a timely manner a second time. A previous case, *Leaderbrand*, discussed in the opinion, supported this argument. The court in *Leaderbrand* relied on old § 3–511(4). That provision was intended to apply to time drafts. It states the principle that if the draft is dishonored when presented for acceptance, it is not necessary to present it again for payment to charge secondary parties. Despite the clear language of former § 3–511(4) restricting the provision to dishonor by nonacceptance, the court in *Leaderbrand* applied it to a check dishonored when presented for payment. Revised Article 3 dropped former § 3–511(4) and replaced it with § 3–502(f) which does not contain the language relied on in *Leaderbrand*. *Leaderbrand* has been widely criticized and the court in *Blake* declined to follow it.

Re-presentment of checks is common, and about one half are paid when presented the second time. The typical case is that of a customer who writes a check to be covered by a check contemporaneously deposited in the customer's account or which will be deposited in the very near future. If the customer's check is presented for payment before the deposited check is collected, the customer's check may be dishonored because of a temporary insufficiency of funds in the account. If the check is re-presented, it must be treated like a check presented for the first time because, if the midnight deadline does not apply to such checks, the depositary bank would have no basis for making a judgment whether the check was paid. The depositary bank receives notice that a check has been dishonored either by return of the check or by a separate notice of dishonor. But it is not told that a check has been paid. The bank normally determines that a check has been paid by the fact that it didn't receive notice of dishonor within the normal time for receiving that notice.

b.   CHECK KITING

The prevalence of check kiting scams in recent years has placed pressure on the strict accountability rule of § 4–302(a). If a depositary bank, knowing that a kite is taking place, presents checks to a payor bank that doesn't know about the kite, is it fair to impose strict accountability on the payor bank that misses its midnight deadline on these checks? The depositary bank is trying to get paid before the kite crashes, while the payor bank ends up liable for the face amount of these "large item" checks which are drawn on uncollected, in fact, uncollectible, funds in the kiter's account. The following case is a good analysis of the problem under revised Article 4. Check kiting is discussed in Clark & Clark, The Law of Bank Deposits, Collections and Credit Cards, Chapter 9 (Rev.ed.1995), and White & Summers, Uniform Commercial Code § 17–3 (4th ed.1995). In the 1990 revision of Article 4, after much discussion, a new defense to the accountability rule was added by § 4–302(b): "The liability of a payor bank to pay an item pursuant to subsection (a) is subject to defenses based on * * * proof that the person seeking enforcement of the liability presented or transferred the item for the purpose of defrauding the payor bank." Comment 3 says: "A payor bank that makes a late return should not be liable to a defrauder operating a check kiting scheme." Why didn't the court in the following case refer to § 4–302(b) and the quoted Comment?

First National Bank in Harvey v. Colonial Bank

United States District Court, N.D. Illinois, 1995.
898 F.Supp. 1220.

■ GRADY, DISTRICT JUDGE.

Before the court are the parties' cross-motions for summary judgment. For the reasons explained, plaintiff First National Bank in Harvey's motion is granted in part and denied in part. Defendant Colonial Bank's motion is granted in part and denied in part. Defendant Federal Reserve Bank of Chicago's motion is granted.

BACKGROUND

Check kiting is a form of bank fraud.[1] The kiter opens accounts at two (or more) banks, writes checks on insufficient funds on one account, then

---

1. 18 U.S.C. § 1344; United States v. LeDonne, 21 F.3d 1418, 1426 (7th Cir.), cert. denied, ___ U.S. ___, 115 S.Ct. 584, 130 L.Ed.2d 498 (1994).

covers the overdraft by depositing a check drawn on insufficient funds from the other account.

To illustrate the operation, suppose that the defrauder opens two accounts with a deposit of $500 each at the First National Bank and a distant Second National Bank. (A really successful defrauder will have numerous accounts in fictitious names at banks in widely separated states.) The defrauder then issues for goods or cash checks totalling $3000 against the First National Bank. But before they clear and overdraw the account, he covers the overdrafts with a check for $4,000 drawn on the Second National Bank. The Second National account will be overdrawn when the $4,000 check is presented; before that happens, however, the defrauder covers it with a check on the First National Bank. The process is repeated innumerable times until there is a constant float of worthless checks between the accounts and the defrauder has bilked the banks of a substantial sum of money.

John D. O'Malley, "Common Check Frauds and the Uniform Commercial Code," 23 Rutgers L.Rev. 189, 194 n. 35 (1968–69). By timing the scheme correctly and repeating it over a period of time, the kiter can use the funds essentially as an interest-free loan. Williams v. United States, 458 U.S. 279, 281 n. 1, 102 S.Ct. 3088, 3090 n. 1, 73 L.Ed.2d 767 (1982) (quoting Brief for the United States).

Check kiting is possible because of a combination of two rules found in Article 4 of the Uniform Commercial Code. Under § 4–208(a)(1), a depositary bank may allow a customer to draw on uncollected funds, that is, checks that have been deposited but not yet paid.[3] Second, under §§ 4–301 and 4–302, a payor bank must either pay or dishonor a check drawn on it by midnight of the second banking day following presentment. Barkley Clark, The Law of Bank Deposits, Collections and Credit Cards P 5.03[5] (3d ed. 1990). Thus when a kite is operating, the depositary bank allows the kiter to draw on uncollected funds based on a deposit of a check. The depositary bank presents that check to the payor bank, which must decide whether to pay or return the check before the midnight deadline. The check may appear to be covered by uncollected funds at the payor bank, and so the payor bank may decide to pay the check by allowing the midnight deadline to pass.

A kite crashes when one of the banks dishonors checks drawn on it and returns them to the other banks involved in the kite. Clark, supra. Usually, such a dishonor occurs when one bank suspects a kite. Id. However, an

---

3. Regulation CC, issued by the Board of Governors of the Federal Reserve System, governs the availability of funds and the collection of checks. 12 C.F.R. pt. 229. Under Regulation CC, a depositary bank must make funds drawn on a local check available two days following the deposit. 12 C.F.R. § 229.12(b)(1). During this two-day period, the funds are "uncollected." The depositary bank may either return checks drawn on those funds or choose to pay the checks. After two days, the depositary bank's records show the check "collected" for Regulation CC purposes, although the check is not actually collected until it is paid by the payor bank.

individual bank may have trouble detecting a check kiting scheme. "Until one has devoted a substantial amount of time examining not only one's own account, but accounts at other banks, it may be impossible to know whether the customer is engaged in a legitimate movement of funds or illegitimate kiting." James J. White & Robert S. Summers, Uniform Commercial Code § 17–1 (3d ed. 1988 & Supp.1994). But each bank is usually able to monitor only its own account, and "[t]here is no certain test that distinguishes one who writes many checks on low balances from a check kiter." White & Summers, supra, § 17–2. Even if a bank suspects a kite, it might decide not to take any action for a number of reasons. First, it may be liable to its customer for wrongfully dishonoring checks. § 4–202. Second, if it reports that a kite is operating and turns out to be wrong, it could find itself defending a defamation suit. White & Summers, supra, § 17–1 (Supp.1994). Finally, if it errs in returning checks or reporting a kite, it may risk angering a large customer. Id.

FACTS

This case involves the fallout of a collapsed check kite. Two of the banks involved, First National Bank in Harvey ("First National") and Colonial Bank ("Colonial") are the parties to this litigation. The Federal Reserve Bank of Chicago (the "Reserve Bank"), through whose clearinghouse the relevant checks were processed, is also a party.

Shelly International Marketing ("Shelly") opened a checking account at First National in December 1989. The principals of Shelly also opened accounts at the Family Bank (a nonparty) in the names of Shelly Brokerage and Crete Trading around December 1990. On December 31, 1991, the principals of Shelly opened a checking account at Colonial Bank in the name of World Commodities, Inc. Shelly and World Commodities were related companies, with the same or similar shareholders, officers, and directors. The principals of Shelly and World Commodities began operating a check kiting scheme among the accounts at the three banks in early 1991.

The main events at issue in this case took place in February 1992. The checks that form the basis of this suit are thirteen checks totalling $1,523,892.49 for which First National was the depositary bank and Colonial was the payor bank (the "Colonial checks"). Also relevant are seventeen checks totalling $1,518,642.86 for which Colonial was the depositary bank and First National was the payor bank (the "First National checks").

On Monday, February 10, Shelly deposited the thirteen Colonial checks to its First National account. First National then sent those checks through the check clearing system. That same day, World Commodities deposited the seventeen First National checks to its Colonial account.

The next day, Tuesday, February 11, the Colonial checks were presented to Colonial for payment, and the First National checks were presented to First National for payment. That day, David Spiewak, an officer with First National's holding company, Pinnacle, reviewed the bank's records to determine why there were large balance fluctuations in Shelly's First National account. Spiewak began to suspect that a kite might be operating.

He did not know whether Colonial had enough funds to cover the Colonial checks that had been deposited on Monday, February 10, and forwarded to Colonial for payment. Later that day, First National froze the Shelly account to prevent any further activity in it.

On the morning of Wednesday, February 12, Spiewak met with First National president Dennis Irvin and Pinnacle's chief lending officer Mike Braun to discuss the Shelly account. Spiewak informed the others of what he knew, and the three agreed that there was a possible kite. They concluded that further investigation was needed. The First National officers decided to return the First National checks to Colonial. First National says that the decision was made at this meeting, but Colonial says the decision was actually made the day before.

On Wednesday, First National returned the First National checks to Colonial. Under Regulation CC, a bank that is returning checks in excess of $2,500.00 must provide notice to the depositary bank either by telephone, actual return of the check, or Fed Wire before 4:00 p.m. on the second business day following presentment. First National notified Colonial by Fed Wire that it was returning the seventeen First National checks. Initially, the large item return form indicated that the reason for the return was "uncollected funds," but Spiewak changed that reason to "refer to maker."

Colonial received the Fed Wire notices at approximately 2:45 p.m. on Wednesday and routed them to its cashier, Joanne Topham. Randall Soderman, a Colonial loan officer, was informed of the large return, and immediately began an investigation. He realized that if the Colonial checks were not returned by midnight that same day, Colonial would be out the money. Returning the Colonial checks before midnight would protect Colonial from liability, but it would risk disappointing the customer. Anthony Schiller, the loan officer in charge of the World Commodities account, called World Commodities comptroller Charles Patterson and its attorney Jay Goldstein. Both assured Schiller that the First National checks were good and should be redeposited. Ultimately, Richard Vucich, Colonial's president, and Joanne Topham, Colonial's cashier, decided not to return the Colonial checks on Wednesday. They decided instead to meet on Thursday morning with Schiller to discuss the matter.

Schiller, Topham, and Vucich met on the morning of Thursday, February 13. At the conclusion of the meeting, they decided to return the thirteen Colonial checks to First National. At about 10:45 a.m., Colonial telephoned First National to say that it intended to return the Colonial checks. Colonial sent the Colonial checks back through the Reserve Bank as a return in a return cash letter. The Reserve Bank debited First National's Reserve Bank account in the amount of the Colonial checks. First National received the returned Colonial checks on Friday, February 14.

First National then resorted to the Fed's "challenge procedure" to contest the return of the Colonial checks after the midnight deadline. First National prepared and submitted to the Reserve Bank a "Sender's Claim of Late Return" form for each of the Colonial checks. The Reserve Bank processed the claim forms and credited the Reserve Bank account of First

National $1,523,892.49 and debited the Reserve Bank account of Colonial in the same amount. On February 24, Colonial prepared and filed a "Paying Bank's Response to Claim of Late Return" form for each of the thirteen Colonial checks. As a consequence of the processing of the response forms, the Reserve Bank reversed the credit given to First National and the debit made to Colonial.

First National then filed this suit against Colonial and the Reserve Bank, alleging that Colonial wrongfully returned the Colonial checks after the midnight deadline and the Reserve Bank wrongfully accepted the late return. * * * Count V against Colonial alleges breach of UCC § 4–302 for Colonial's failure to return the checks by the midnight deadline. * * *

First National moved for partial summary judgment as to Count V. On August 27, 1993, this court denied the plaintiff's motion. First Nat'l Bank in Harvey v. Colonial Bank, 831 F.Supp. 637 (N.D.Ill.1993). The parties now have each moved for summary judgment on all counts. Along with deciding the remaining counts, today's opinion reconsiders portions of our earlier ruling on Count V. * * *

DISCUSSION

* * *

I.   *Count V: Breach of UCC § 4–302 Against Colonial*

A.   Accountability

Article 4 of the Uniform Commercial Code adopts a policy of "final payment"; that is, a check is considered to be finally paid at some specific and identifiable point in time. § 4–215 Comment 1. Final payment is the "end of the line" in the check collection process. Section 4–301 sets up the "midnight deadline" in the process: a payor bank which intends to return a check presented to it must do so before midnight of the next banking day following receipt of the check. §§ 4–301(a), 4–104(a)(10). If a payor bank fails to return a check before the midnight deadline, final payment occurs. * * *

Section 4–302 spells out the payor bank's liability for its late return of an item, that is, return after the midnight deadline:

> (a) If an item is presented to and received by a payor bank, the bank is *accountable* for the amount of:
>
> > (1) a demand item, other than a documentary draft, whether properly payable or not, if the bank ... does not pay or return the item or send notice of dishonor until after its midnight deadline....

§ 4–302 (emphasis added). The operative word in this section is "accountable." Courts interpreting this section have nearly unanimously concluded that § 4–302 imposes strict liability on a payor bank for failing to adhere to the midnight deadline, and makes the measure of damages the face amount of the check. In an early decision, the Illinois Supreme Court held that "accountable" means "liable" for the amount of the item. Rock Island Auction Sales, Inc. v. Empire Packing Co., 32 Ill.2d 269, 204 N.E.2d 721, 723 (Ill.1965). The *Rock Island* court contrasted the "accountability" language in § 4–302 with the language used to specify the measure of damages in what is now § 4–103(e).[7] Section 4–103(e) makes a bank liable for failing to exercise ordinary care in the handling of a check in "the amount of the item reduced by an amount that could not have been realized by the exercise of ordinary care." § 4–103(e). The Official Comment to this section explains: "When it is established that some part or all of the item could not have been collected even by the use of ordinary care the recovery is reduced by the amount that would have been in any event uncollectible." In other words, § 4–103(e) imposes liability in the amount of the loss caused by the negligence, while § 4–302(a) imposes strict liability in the face amount of the check.

The *Rock Island* court reasoned that the special role of the payor bank in the check collection system justifies the imposition of liability regardless of negligence. The midnight deadline requires the payor bank—the bank in the best position to know whether there are funds available to cover the check—to decide whether to pay or return the check:

> The role of a payor bank in the collection process ... is crucial. It knows whether or not the drawer has funds available to pay the item. The legislature could have considered that the failure of such a bank to meet its deadline is likely to be due to factors other than negligence, and that the relationship between a payor bank and its customer may so influence its conduct as to cause a conscious disregard of its statutory duty.

Rock Island, 204 N.E.2d at 723.

The overwhelming majority of courts that have considered the meaning of § 4–302(a) have followed the *Rock Island* court in concluding that the liability of a payor bank that fails to return a check by the midnight deadline is strict and is in the face amount of the check. * * *

Even where the damage suffered by the payee is not caused by the lateness of the return, the midnight deadline still has been strictly enforced. For example, in Chicago Title Ins. Co. v. California Canadian Bank, 1 Cal.App.4th 798, 2 Cal.Rptr.2d 422, 424 (Ct.App.1991), the payor bank decided to return twenty-eight checks involved in a massive check fraud scheme. The checks left the bank before the midnight deadline, but did not arrive at the clearinghouse until the next day—after the midnight deadline had passed. The court held that the bank's return was late. It held the bank strictly accountable for the face amount of the checks, reasoning that the bank "'may be held strictly liable for its failure to return the checks by

---

7. Section 4–103(e) provides:

The measure of damages for failure to exercise ordinary care in handling an item is the amount of the item reduced by an amount that could not have been realized by the exercise of ordinary care. If there is also bad faith it includes any other damages the party suffered as a proximate consequence.

the applicable deadlines, regardless whether [the other party] demonstrated it suffered actual damage solely as a result of [the Bank's] omission.' "Id. at 426–29 (quoting Los Angeles Nat'l Bank v. Bank of Canton, 229 Cal.App.3d 1267, 280 Cal.Rptr. 831, 838 (Ct.App.1991)); see also American Title Ins. Co. v. Burke & Herbert Bank & Trust Co., 813 F.Supp. 423, 426 (E.D.Va.1993) ("[L]iability for the face amount of the check is imposed without regard to whether any damages have been sustained as a result of the payor bank's failure to make a timely return."), aff'd, 25 F.3d 1038 (4th Cir.1994).

* * *

But is it appropriate to enforce the accountability provision of § 4–302 where a check kiting scheme is involved? The Minnesota Supreme Court did in Town & Country State Bank v. First State Bank, 358 N.W.2d 387, 393–95 (Minn.1984). There, the court held that two payor banks that held kited checks beyond the midnight deadline made "final payment" on the checks and were therefore accountable for the amounts of those checks. * * *

* * *

This court's prior opinion held that First National could not recover under the accountability provision of § 4–302 if it would be unjustly enriched by the recovery. § 1–103; 831 F.Supp. at 641. On the undisputed evidence presented by First National on the present motion, however, we now see that it did suffer a loss. At some point during the check kiting scheme, funds were siphoned out of the banking system, causing a deficit in First National's assets. The important point is that First National will not be unjustly enriched by recovering from Colonial. It has suffered a loss at some point, and will not experience a windfall if it recovers from Colonial.

Therefore, we conclude that Colonial is absolutely liable in the face amount of the Colonial checks for missing the midnight deadline. This does not end the analysis, however, because Colonial raises the defenses of good faith and mistaken payment to defeat strict accountability.

B.   Good Faith

The general provisions of the Uniform Commercial Code state: "Every contract or duty within this Act imposes an obligation of good faith in its performance or enforcement." § 1–203. The Code defines "good faith" as "honesty in fact in the conduct or transaction concerned." § 1–201(19). Colonial argues that First National's lack of good faith defeats its § 4–302 claim of accountability, contending that First National orchestrated the events of the week of February 10 in order to cause Colonial to miss the midnight deadline for returning the Colonial checks.

The first question is whether we should even consider bad faith in this check kiting case. First National urges us to refrain from injecting notions of bad faith to reallocate the loss here. It contends that introducing the concept of bad faith will muddy the concepts of certainty and finality, which are central to the treatment of kites by Article 4. However, the UCC itself, in § 1–103, injects notions of good faith into every transaction covered by it, and we cannot simply ignore the statute.

Colonial charges that First National returned the seventeen First National checks to Colonial on Wednesday, February 12, under circumstances amounting to bad faith. Colonial argues that First National deliberately caused confusion in returning the First National checks, which caused Colonial to miss the midnight deadline for the Colonial checks.

Colonial offers the following facts to show First National's bad faith. On Tuesday, February 11, Spiewak thought that a kite was taking place and together with other First National officers decided that the First National checks would be dishonored and returned to Colonial. First National returned the checks the next day, Wednesday, a day on which it is closed for business. It also notified Colonial of the return late in the day (2:45 p.m.) by Fed Wire rather than by telephone, a practice that is rarely used and less desirable than telephone notice because a wire notice may not be picked up by an employee for some time, while telephonic notice is received directly by a bank employee who can take immediate action. Finally, First National changed the reason for the return from "uncollected funds" to "refer to maker." When Colonial received the wire transmittal, it attempted to contact First National to determine why First National returned the checks "refer to maker." No one at Colonial was able to talk to anyone at First National, however, because a recorded message informed Colonial employees that First National was closed on Wednesdays. First National's endorsement stamp contains only its general telephone number, not any other telephone number that would allow telephone calls to be made even when the switchboard is closed, as is the practice at most Chicago area banks.

In short, Colonial argues that First National's failure to advise Colonial of the kite, its delay in giving notice of the return, its use of Fed Wire to give notice of the return, its return of the checks marked "refer to maker," and its return of the checks on a day when it was closed for business caused Colonial to miss the midnight deadline for the Colonial checks. These facts amount to bad faith, Colonial contends; consequently First National may not recover any losses it suffered in the kite. And, in any event, whether First National's acts constitute bad faith is an issue of fact that precludes summary judgment in favor of First National.

Colonial's argument raises specific questions about whether First National's conduct amounts to bad faith. But it also raises more general questions about banks' conduct in check kiting schemes: Does a depositary bank that suspects a kite have a good faith duty to disclose its suspicions to the payor bank? Furthermore, does a bank act in bad faith if it discovers or suspects a kite and attempts to shift the loss to the other bank by returning checks drawn on it while at the same time forwarding checks that have been deposited with it for payment?

Courts that have dealt with these issues usually take the latter two questions together, and most have concluded that a bank has no good faith obligation to disclose a suspected kite or to refrain from attempting to shift the kite loss. These were the conclusions of the Mississippi Supreme Court in the leading case of Citizens Nat'l Bank v. First Nat'l Bank, 347 So.2d 964 (Miss.1977). In *Citizens*, a check kite was operating through accounts at Citizens National Bank and at First National Bank. First National discovered the kite, and returned all checks drawn on its account that Citizens had presented. At the same time, First National presented checks to Citizens that the kiter had drawn on Citizens and deposited with First National. First National also accepted deposits by the kiter and payments by Citizens. After the kite crashed, Citizens sued First National, charging that First National converted funds belonging to Citizens.

The Mississippi Supreme Court upheld the dismissal of the complaint, agreeing with the chancellor's opinion which stated, "I cannot find where FNB has been charged with doing anything other than acting as a prudent and careful bank should act." Id. at 967, 969. In holding that there was no duty on the part of First National to notify Citizens of its conviction that their mutual customer was kiting checks, the court reasoned:

> [T]hese two banks were competitors in the banking field and ordinarily banks deal with each other at arm's length. The bill does not allege any circumstances or facts that tend to show that a confidential or fiduciary relationship existed between these two banks, neither does it show that there is any requirement in the banking field that one bank notify another of its discovery of a customer kiting checks. In the absence of a fiduciary or confidential relationship, or some other legal duty, First National Bank had no duty to inform Citizens National Bank that Duran was kiting checks. This being true, we are of the opinion that First National Bank had the legal right to continue to accept for deposit checks drawn by Duran on accounts at Citizens National Bank and present those checks for payment. At the same time, First National Bank had the legal right to refuse to pay checks drawn by Duran on accounts in First National Bank and deposited in Citizens National Bank.

Id. at 967.

In a more recent case, the district court in Connecticut similarly concluded that a bank's failure to tell another bank about a suspected kite, while returning checks drawn on it and accepting checks drawn on the other bank, is not bad faith. Cumis Ins. Society, Inc. v. Windsor Bank & Trust Co., 736 F.Supp. 1226, 1231–34 (D.Conn.1990). In *Cumis*, the insurer of a credit union that sustained a kite loss sued the winning bank. The facts are similar: the bank suspected a kite and began to dishonor checks drawn against it while continuing to collect on checks drawn on the credit union and deposited with the bank. The bank had even instituted an expedited check clearing procedure specifically to handle drafts drawn on the credit union. Id. at 1230. The court refused to impose a good faith duty to disclose the kite:

> There is thus no duty between competing institutions to inform one another of the existence of a check kiting scheme because these

institutions deal at arms length, have their own means of detecting check kiting, and, realistically, need no protection from other institutions.

Id. at 1233. The court identified several exceptions to this general rule: (1) where a fiduciary or confidential relationship exists; (2) where a contractual relationship exists; (3) where there is a duty created by law; and (4) where there was fraud or misrepresentation by the defendant bank. * * *

* * *

The facts here amount to, at most, an attempt by First National to shift the kite loss to Colonial. First, as First National points out, wire notice is a legally permissible method of notifying another bank of a large return. 12 C.F.R. § 229.33(a). In addition, First National has presented evidence that notifying other banks of large returns by wire rather than by telephone was its usual practice.

Although Colonial makes much of the fact that First National returned the First National checks marked "refer to maker" rather than "uncollected funds," the parties agree that "refer to maker" is a legally permissible reason for returning a check. And Colonial had contacted the maker, World Commodities, and its counsel, receiving assurances that the checks were good. As to First National's delay in informing Colonial of the return, it is undisputed that First National notified a Colonial employee at 9:30 a.m. on Wednesday, February 12, that it would be returning certain checks, although it notified the wrong employee and did not specify the number or dollar amounts of those checks. But First National sent the wire notice later the same day stating that seventeen checks totalling $1,518,642.86 were being returned "refer to maker." Even if, as Colonial contends, First National officers decided to return the checks on Tuesday rather than Wednesday, Colonial had notice more than twelve hours before the midnight deadline that checks drawn on the Shelly account were being returned. And even though Colonial was not able to contact First National on Wednesday, Colonial knew on that day that the First National checks were being returned and that the midnight deadline for the Colonial checks was rapidly approaching.

All of First National's conduct regarding the First National checks was proper under the applicable laws. First National had the right to present the Colonial checks for payment and the right to return the First National checks. At most, First National took advantage of these laws and regulations to attempt to shift the kite loss onto Colonial. But even if this is what happened, such conduct does not constitute bad faith.

First National and Colonial were faced with the same dilemma at the same time: a number of checks totalling a goodly sum of money drawn on the account of a customer with low collected funds balances. First National chose to return the checks unpaid, but Colonial chose to trust its customer to cover the checks. By the time Colonial realized that its decision was wrong, it was too late—the midnight deadline had passed and the checks were paid. Each bank made a business decision; First National's turned out to be the correct one.

C. Mistake and Restitution

The revised UCC § 3–418 sets out rules governing restitution in the event a bank mistakenly pays a negotiable instrument. Colonial argues that the provisions of § 3–418 apply to it and override § 4–302 accountability. Section 3–418 provides:

> (a) Except as provided in subsection (c), if the drawee of a draft pays or accepts the draft and the drawee acted on the mistaken belief that (i) payment of the draft had not been stopped under Section 4–403 or (ii) the signature of the drawer of the draft was authorized, the drawee may recover the amount of the draft from the person to whom or for whose benefit payment was made or, in the case of acceptance, may revoke the acceptance. Rights of the drawee under this subsection are not affected by failure of the drawee to exercise ordinary care in paying or accepting the draft.
>
> (b) Except as provided in subsection (c), if an instrument has been paid or accepted by mistake and the case is not covered by subsection (a), the person paying or accepting may, to the extent permitted by law governing mistake and restitution, (i) recover the payment from the person to whom or for whose benefit payment was made or (ii) in the case of acceptance, may revoke the acceptance.
>
> (c) The remedies provided in subsection (a) or (b) may not be asserted against a person who took the instrument in good faith and for value or who in good faith changed position in reliance on the payment or acceptance.

§ 3–418. There was some doubt before the revision to Article 3 whether this restitution provision overrode the accountability provisions of Article 4, that is, whether a payor bank could recover for a mistaken payment even after passage of the midnight deadline. Compare National Sav. & Trust Co. v. Park Corp., 722 F.2d 1303 (6th Cir.1983) (holding that restitution for mistaken payment is available to bank that holds checks beyond midnight deadline), cert. denied, 466 U.S. 939, 104 S.Ct. 1916, 80 L.Ed.2d 464 (1984), with Northwestern Nat'l Ins. Co. v. Midland Nat'l Bank, 96 Wis.2d 155, 292 N.W.2d 591 (Wis.1980) (holding that restitution for mistaken payment is not available to bank that holds check beyond the midnight deadline); State & Sav. Bank v. Meeker, 469 N.E.2d 55 (Ind.Ct.App.1984) (same). Official Comment 4 to the revised § 3–418 makes it clear that the right of a drawee to recover a mistaken payment is not affected by the Article 4 rules that determine when an item is finally paid. § 3–418 Official Comment 4. Therefore, Colonial's retention of the Colonial checks beyond the midnight deadline is no bar to its ability to recover a mistaken payment.

Subsection (c) of § 3–418 provides that a drawee cannot seek restitution against a person who took the check in good faith and for value or who in good faith relied on payment. In a check kiting scheme, does a depositary bank that suspects a kite take payment of checks in good faith and for value? The drafters of the revised § 3–418 take no position on this question:

> In some cases, however, it may not be clear whether a drawee bank should have a right of restitution. For example, a check-kiting scheme may involve a large number of checks drawn on a number of different banks in which the drawer's credit balances are based on uncollected funds represented by fraudulently drawn checks. No attempt is made in Section 3–418 to state rules for determining the conflicting claims of the various banks that may be victimized by such a scheme. Rather, such cases are better resolved on the basis of general principles of law and the particular facts presented in the litigation.

§ 3–418 Official Comment 3.

In order for Colonial to seek refuge under the restitution principles of the revised § 3–418, two questions must be answered. First, was Colonial's payment of the Colonial checks a payment by mistake under subsection (a) or (b)? Second, if payment was by mistake, did First National take the Colonial checks in good faith and for value, or rely on payment, so as to defeat Colonial's restitution claim as provided in subsection (c)?

Subsection (a) only applies to mistaken payments on forged checks and checks on which the drawer has stopped payment, so it has no application here. Subsection (b) is a catchall, allowing restitution where "an instrument has been paid or accepted by mistake and the case is not covered by subsection (a)." § 3–418(b). Was Colonial's retention of the Colonial checks beyond the midnight deadline payment by mistake?

Several commentators take the position that a losing bank in a check kite has made a conscious extension of unsecured credit to its customer, and has not made a "mistaken payment" under § 3–418. "The decision to allow a customer to draw against uncollected funds is basically a credit decision." Clark, supra, P 5.03[5]. Professors White and Summers agree:[15]

> In these cases, one bank ends the kite by dishonoring a large number of checks. After the dust has settled one bank may sue the other in restitution on the other checks previously paid. It will argue, of course, that it made payment in the mistaken belief that there were or would be sufficient funds.
>
> Is this a case in which one should allow restitution? We think not. In a typical kite it is difficult to maintain that one of the banks is more at fault than another. Moreover, the fact that one bank has decided not to honor checks drawn against uncollected funds is not proof of its knowledge that the other bank's payment is "mistaken." It is hard to

---

15. There is no mistake when a bank chooses to pay an instrument against uncollected funds or against an overdrawn account. Here the bank makes a conscious judgment to make a loan to its customer in the belief the customer is good for it. If the bank is mistaken about its customer's creditworthiness, that is not a payment by mistake, but rather a credit mistake and the bank has no right to restitution. 1B James J. White & Robert S. Summers, Uniform Commercial Code § 17–2 (3d ed. 1993).

see how society is benefitted by spending a good deal of money on lawyers' fees at the conclusion of the kite, even in a fruitful attempt to shift the loss from one bank to another. All are culpable.

White & Summers, supra, P 17–2.

Colonial does not explain why its retention of the Colonial checks beyond the midnight deadline was a payment by mistake that would put its actions within the ambit of § 4–318(b). It is undisputed that after Colonial received notice of the return of the First National checks at 2:45 p.m. on Wednesday, Colonial officers immediately began investigating the Colonial account. Randall Soderman, a Colonial loan officer, realized that Colonial had to return the Colonial checks by midnight the same day or risk losing the money. He knew that returning the Colonial checks before midnight would protect Colonial, but would risk disappointing its customer, World Commodities. Anthony Schiller, the loan officer in charge of the World Commodities account, had called World Commodities comptroller Charles Patterson and its attorney Alan Jay Goldstein. Both assured Schiller that the First National checks were good and should be redeposited. The Colonial officers decided not to return the Colonial checks on Wednesday but rather to meet on Thursday morning to discuss the matter.

It is not surprising that Colonial does not argue that these facts constitute a payment by mistake. Colonial was well aware that the midnight deadline for the Colonial checks was approaching, but deferred the decision of whether to return them until the next day. It contacted its customer and received assurances that the returned First National checks were good. Under these facts, Colonial cannot be said to have paid the Colonial checks by mistake so as to allow it to rely on the mistaken payment rules of § 4–318.

Rather than showing that it paid the checks by mistake, Colonial skips ahead to the inquiry under subsection (c), namely, whether First National took in good faith and for value or changed its position in reliance on payment. Colonial cites several cases for the proposition that a depositary bank with suspicion or knowledge of a kite that forwards checks for payment is not a holder in due course of those checks. Farmers & Merchants State Bank v. Western Bank, 841 F.2d 1433 (9th Cir.1987); Community Bank v. Ell, 278 Or. 417, 564 P.2d 685 (1977). (Colonial's argument is based upon cases decided under the former § 3–418, where the only question was whether the plaintiff was a holder in due course or a good faith relier on payment. But the revision to § 3–418(c) omits the "holder in due course" language in favor of "a person who in good faith took the instrument for value.") But it is unnecessary to inquire whether First National took in good faith and for value under subsection (c), because Colonial has not shown that it made a mistaken payment under subsection (b).

* * *

CONCLUSION

For the reasons explained, plaintiff First National's motion for summary judgment is granted as to Count V of the first amended complaint * * *. Colonial's motion for summary judgment is * * * denied as to Count V.

* * *

NOTES

1. The case above states the prevailing rule, but Oregon courts have taken the view that a depositary bank may be in bad faith if it presents checks knowing of a check kite while dishonoring checks drawn on it. Farmers & Merchants State Bank v. Western Bank, 841 F.2d 1433 (9th Cir.1987), applies Oregon law and reviews the state court authorities. Clark & Clark, The Law of Bank Deposits, Check Collections and Credit Cards ¶ 9.03 (Rev.ed.1995).

2. In the text before the principal case we asked why the court didn't refer to § 4–302(b) and the reference in Comment 3 to check kiting. What is your answer? Is the reference to check kiting in Comment 3 to § 4–302(b) consistent with the reference to check kiting in Comment 3 to § 3–418? White & Summers, Uniform Commercial Code § 17–3 (4th ed.1995).

c.   PROCESS OF POSTING CHECKS BY PAYOR BANK

Merrill Lynch, which follows, describes the process followed by a payor bank in deciding whether to pay a check presented to it for payment. The result in the case turned on an analysis of § 4–109 and § 4–213(1)(c) of the pre–1990 Article 4. Both of these provisions were eliminated in revised Article 4. Section 4–213(1)(c) provided that a payor bank paid a check when the bank completed the process of posting the check to the account of the drawer of the check. Section 4–109 defined "process of posting." Why were these sections deleted? Revised § 4–215 is the successor to the pre–1990 § 4–213. A different result would have been reached in *Merrill Lynch* if revised Article 4 had been in effect at the time.

Merrill Lynch, Pierce, Fenner & Smith, Inc. v. Devon Bank

United States Court of Appeals, Seventh Circuit, 1987.
832 F.2d 1005.

■ EASTERBROOK, CIRCUIT JUDGE.

Manus, Inc., gave the Los Angeles office of Merrill Lynch, Pierce, Fenner & Smith, Inc., a check for $647,250 payable to Merrill Lynch's order. The check was drawn on Devon Bank in Chicago. Merrill Lynch immediately deposited the check with Crocker National Bank in Los Angeles; a clearing house presented the check to Devon for payment at 9:30

a.m. on Wednesday, August 1, 1979. The clearing house and Devon provisionally settled for the check immediately. Under § 4–301(1) [Revised § 4–301(a)]of the Uniform Commercial Code, Devon had to decide no later than midnight of the next banking day whether to make final payment. Devon gave notice of dishonor at 4:22 p.m. on August 3. If this is too late, Devon is liable on the check even though Manus cannot cover the instrument. The district court thought the dishonor timely, 654 F.Supp. 506 (N.D.Ill.1987), and granted summary judgment to Devon in this diversity litigation.

I

The initial question is whether Devon gave notice of dishonor before the deadline on midnight of the "banking day" after it received the instrument. Under § 4–104(1)(c) [Revised § 4–104(a)(3)]of the UCC, a "'banking day' means that part of any day on which a bank is open to the public for carrying on substantially all of its banking functions". On Wednesday, August 1, 1979, Devon's lobby was closed to the public. It offered services, essentially limited to deposits and withdrawals, at a walk-up window. No one could open an account or arrange for a loan; so far as the record reveals, no one could draw down a line of credit previously arranged. Merrill Lynch observes that on Wednesdays Devon processed checks and made inter-bank loans, but neither these nor related activities made it "open to the public" for "substantially all of its banking functions".

Devon is an Illinois bank, and a "bank" in Illinois is "any person doing a banking business whether subject to the laws of this or any other jurisdiction." Ill.Rev.Stat. ch. 17 ¶ 302 (1986). So a person doing a "banking business" but not subject to anyone's laws is not a "bank", but the statute does not illuminate on "banking business". Perhaps the statute uses a circular definition because the elements of banking are not particularly obscure. Making loans is a necessary part of "banking"; consider the definition of a "bank" in the Bank Holding Company Act, the only federal statute defining the term: "an institution * * * which both (i) accepts demand deposits or deposits that the depositor may withdraw by check or similar means for payment to third parties or others; and (ii) is engaged in the business of making commercial loans." 12 U.S.C. § 1841(c)(1)(B) (1987) * * * Banks are financial intermediaries, facilitating transactions between those who want to lend and those who want to borrow. * * * Devon, which was open to the public for only the deposit side of the banking business on August 1, 1979, was not open for "substantially all" of the services of a bank. Its services on August 1 were less extensive than those offered by a "nonbank bank" for purposes of the Bank Holding Company Act. Devon's walk-up window may have been a "branch bank", for both state and federal law define branches as places where deposits are received *or* money lent. 12 U.S.C. § 36(f); Ill.Rev.Stat. ch. 17 ¶ 302 (1986). One of these is not "substantially all" of the *bank's* functions, however. The district court properly resolved this question by summary judgment. It would unacceptably disrupt commercial relations to put to a jury, case-by-case, the question whether a given day was a "banking day". Billions of dollars in transactions must be processed by every midnight deadline, and everyone has an interest in having this time defined with precision. The record supplies enough information to make decision possible. Devon's midnight deadline was 11:59 p.m. on Friday, August 3, 1979.

II

The midnight deadline is only the outside limit, however. Section 4–301(1) allows a bank to return an item if it acts "before it has made final payment (subsection (1) of Section 4–213) *and* before its midnight deadline" (emphasis added). Section 4–213(1) says that a settlement becomes final "when the bank has done any of the following, whichever happens first". The only subsection we need consider is § 4–213(1)(c), which provides that payment becomes final when the bank has "completed the process of posting the item to the indicated account of the drawer, maker, or other person to be charged therewith". Section 4–109 defines the process of posting, to which we return after stating some undisputed facts.

Manus, the maker of the check, had a subsidiary, Cash Reserve Management, Inc. Cash Management maintained an account in Boston. Manus gave its check to Merrill Lynch on July 26; on July 27 Manus deposited in Devon a check for an identical sum of which Cash Management was the maker. Devon promptly submitted that check for payment. Devon places a "hold" of three or four business days on uncollected funds. The Manus check was presented for payment on August 1, the fourth business day (the fifth if Devon counted Saturday, July 28).

When Devon receives a bundle of checks from its clearing house, its computers tally the checks to ensure that the clearing house has debited Devon the correct amount. During the evening, reader/sorter machines read the account code on each check and compute the balance in each active account; a computer compares the balance and activity information with information the bank maintains to facilitate the decision whether to pay checks. The computer prepares, by the morning of the next business day, several reports for the bank's staff. One report lists checks that have caused overdrafts in the account; another report lists checks that are subject to stop payment orders; a third report lists accounts in which uncollected funds are essential to cover the latest checks; there are more. The morning of the second business day, Devon returns most of the checks that appear on these lists—though its staff may elect to pay some of them. The bookkeeping department stamps checks "paid" and photographs them. Devon then examines the signatures on substantial checks. If the signature appears genuine (or if the bank elects not to examine the signature), Devon places the check in the customer's file. This process usually is completed in the afternoon.

Manus's check was processed in the ordinary course. The account contained about $1.2 million, more than enough to cover the check. About $650,000 of this represented the Cash Management check deposited on July 27. Devon's computer treated these as "collected" funds because the check had been deposited four or more business days ago. The uncollected funds reports of August 1 and 2 do not flag the Manus check. Devon verified the signature and placed the Manus check in the file during the afternoon of August 2. There it remained until 4:10 p.m. on August 3, when Continental Illinois National Bank told Devon by telephone that Cash Management's bank in Boston had dishonored the check of July 27. At 4:22 p.m. Devon gave telephonic notice of dishonor of the Manus check. Crocker Bank resubmitted the Manus check, which was dishonored a second time; Manus was placed in receivership on August 28.

Merrill Lynch, which prefers collecting from a solvent Devon Bank to standing in line as one of Manus's creditors, maintains that Devon "completed the process of posting the item" within the meaning of § 4–213(1)(c) during the afternoon of August 2, when it placed the check in the file. Devon had carried out all the steps in its ordinary process and planned to do nothing further. The process was free from operational error; no steps had been omitted, no judgmental blunders made along the way. Devon replies that it does not intentionally pay checks written against uncollected funds, to which Merrill Lynch responds that Devon made a business judgment to pay checks written against instruments that had been on deposit for four business days. Devon applied that rule to Manus's check, and the belated return of the item may show that four days was too short but does not undermine the conclusion that "the process of posting" had come to an end.

The district court sided with Devon, 654 F.Supp. at 509–10, relying on § 4–109, which provides:

> The "process of posting" means the usual procedure followed by a payor bank in determining to pay an item and in recording the payment including one or more of the following or other steps as determined by the bank:
>
> (a) verification of any signature;
>
> (b) ascertaining that sufficient funds are available;
>
> (c) affixing a "paid" or other stamp;
>
> (d) entering a charge or entry to a customer's account;
>
> (e) correcting or reversing an entry or erroneous action with respect to the item.

Devon completed its ordinary steps, including each of (a) through (d), but the court concluded that § 4–109(e) gives a bank the privilege to dishonor a check until the midnight deadline. To return the item is to "reverse" the entry. As the court put it, "Devon's returning the check * * * demonstrated that the posting process was not completed" (654 F.Supp. at 510).

This reading of § 4–109(e) rips § 4–213(1)(c) out of the Uniform Commercial Code. Section 4–301(1) sets the midnight deadline as the last instant at which a check may be returned; § 4–213(1) lists four events that terminate the return privilege sooner. If the return of an item establishes that the "process of posting" was not completed, then § 4–213(1)(c) is meaningless. It is not beyond belief that statutes contain meaningless provisions, but a court should treat statutory words as dross only when there is no alternative. The Uniform Commercial Code is an uncommonly well drafted statute, with links among its provisions. Section 4–213(1) is there for a reason—to expedite the final settlement on checks, so that banks such as Devon Bank may make funds available to customers faster. The "midnight deadline", and "deferred posting" in general, is a concession to the flux of paper with which any bank must contend. See Official Comment 1 to § 4–301. Section 4–213(1)(c) provides that final payment should not take any longer than the bank actually requires to process each item. That function would be defeated if the bank could reverse any posting under § 4–109(e) until the midnight deadline.

Perhaps § 4–213(1)(c) causes more trouble than it is worth. It potentially calls for a case-by-case inquiry into the details of posting; a bank may defeat its function by dragging out its normal processes so that they consume the entire period allotted by § 4–301(1); the drawee's bank cannot rely on § 4–213(1)(c) to credit a customer's account, because it does not know how long the drawer's bank takes to post any given item. Considerations of this sort led the UCC's Permanent Editorial Board, now at work on a Uniform New Payments Code, to propose the repeal of § 4–213(1)(c). * * * Until the Board makes a final revision in the model UCC and states delete § 4–213(1)(c)—if that should occur—our job is to enforce the statute.

That § 4–213(1)(c) has meaning is reinforced by Official Example 3 to § 4–109:

A payor bank receives in the mail on Monday an item drawn upon it. The item is sorted and otherwise processed on Monday and during Monday night is provisionally recorded on tape by an electronic computer as charged to the customer's account. On Tuesday a clerk examines the signature of the item and makes other checks to determine finally whether the item should be paid. If the clerk determines the signature is valid and makes a decision to pay and all processing of this item is complete, e.g., at 12 noon on Tuesday, the "process of posting" is completed at that time. If, however, the clerk determines that the signature is not valid or that the item should not be paid for some other reason, the item is returned to the presenting bank and in the regular Tuesday night run of the computer the debit to the customer's account for the item is reversed or an offsetting credit entry is made. In this case * * * there has been no determination to pay the item, no completion of the process of posting and no payment of the item.

This puts the "payment" of the check at the completion of the bank's ordinary process, whatever that process may be. The check that passes the bank's internal controls and is posted to the account is "paid". None of the official comments suggests that a check that has been accurately handled in accordance with the bank's ordinary procedure nonetheless may be dishonored any time before the midnight deadline.

Doubtless we must give § 4–109(e) meaning, just as we must leave some function for § 4–213(1)(c). The Supreme Court of Wisconsin thought the language of § 4–109(e) so "plain" that it overrode § 4–213(1)(c). West Side Bank v. Marine National Exchange Bank, 37 Wis.2d 661, 669–72, 155 N.W.2d 587 (1968). That court read the language with this emphasis: "correcting or *reversing an entry* or erroneous action with respect to the item." The "reversing an entry" language, the court thought, allowed the bank to dishonor a check at any time before the midnight deadline, whether or not the processing had been completed without error. This reading is inconsistent with the official comments to § 4–109 and any plausible reason for making payment final on posting. As a result, the courts that have addressed the problem since 1968 have rejected West Side. Nelson v. Platte Valley State Bank & Trust Co., 805 F.2d 332 (8th Cir.1986); North Carolina National Bank v. South Carolina National Bank, 449 F.Supp. 616, 620 (D.S.C.1976); H. Schultz & Sons, Inc. v. Bank of Suffolk County, 439 F.Supp. 1137 (E.D.N.Y.1977); R. Hoag v. Valley National Bank, 147 Ariz. 137, 708 P.2d 1328 (1985). Students of the subject likewise disagree with the reading of § 4–109(e) proposed by *West Side,* although they are not entirely in accord on the meaning the section should take. * * * We think it likely that the Supreme Court of Illinois would follow *Nelson* and *Schultz* rather than *West Side.*

Section 4–109(e) does not simply say that a bank may reverse an entry; the full text of the section says that it may correct or reverse an entry or erroneous action. It is not possible to divorce the "reversing an entry" language from the words immediately before and after. If we group the words this way—"(correcting or reversing) an (entry or erroneous action)"—the statute makes sense. The bank may correct (alter) or reverse (set aside completely) an entry that should not have been made or an "erroneous action" that does not involve an "entry". This reading leaves a role for both § 4–109(e) and § 4–213(1)(c), and it also makes sense of the official comment to § 4–109, which states that when the bank's ordinary process is completed before the midnight deadline, the check has been paid.

Nelson, Schultz, and the commentators on the payments process have stressed that the decision to pay a check has both mechanical and judgmental components. The examination of the signature and the determination that an account has sufficient funds are mechanical; the decision whether to permit an overdraft in the account is judgmental. Section 4–109 allows a bank to follow its *ordinary* processes for dealing with both of these. There is nothing magical about putting the instrument in the customer's file. Suppose, for example, the bank mechanically puts all checks in customers' files and then makes random spot checks to verify signatures; that an item with a forged signature had to be pulled from the file to be returned would not prevent its dishonor. Or suppose the bank verifies signatures and puts the checks (stamped "paid") in customers' files before examining the computer printouts for stop payment orders. Again it would not be important that the bank had to remove the stopped check from the customer's file. The alternative—holding all checks in stasis until each of the bank's steps had been completed—would delay "final payment" for the checks as a group even longer, contrary to the purpose of § 4–213(1)(c). *West Side* may have been a case of this sort; if it was, we do not question its result even though its language was unduly broad. But none of this assists Devon. Its process—as Devon defines its process—had been completed by the afternoon of August 2. All of the check-specific steps, mechanical and judgmental, had been finished to the Bank's satisfaction. The system functioned as it was supposed to. True, Devon may wish that it had told its computer to assume that checks take five rather than four business days to clear, but regret over a managerial judgment in the design of the check processing system is not a reason to dishonor a check after it has been posted to the account and finally paid.

* * *

III

Devon makes one last argument. Merrill Lynch sued Crocker Bank, claiming that it dallied in informing Merrill Lynch of the dishonor of the Manus check. The complaint in that suit states that had Merrill Lynch received timely notice of the dishonor, it could have obtained good funds from Manus to cover the check before Manus entered bankruptcy. Devon says that this is an "admission" that Devon's actions did not injure Merrill Lynch. Nonsense. Merrill Lynch had to mitigate any damages it suffered, and its pleading in the California case says that had it known of the problem, it could have mitigated. But it did not know, and therefore could not take the necessary steps. Whatever rights Devon may have against Crocker Bank, this pleading is hardly a reason why Merrill Lynch should lose.

Reversed.

2. RIGHT OF COLLECTING BANK TO REVOKE SETTLEMENT ON DISHONORED CHECK

We saw in the preceding section that a payor bank may inadvertently pay a check by failing to return the check within its midnight deadline. A collecting bank, including a depositary bank, is also subject to a midnight deadline in the case of return of a dishonored check to the bank. If a check forwarded to the payor bank is not paid, the depositary bank may revoke the provisional credit that it gave to its customer with respect to the check. § 4–214(a). But the depositary bank is required either to return the check to its customer or to give notice of dishonor to the customer before the bank's midnight deadline. The case below discusses the revised Article 4 provisions on notice of dishonor and the consequences of the failure of the depositary bank to act within its deadline.

Essex Construction Corporation v. Industrial Bank of Washington, Inc.

United States District Court, D. Maryland, 1995.
913 F.Supp. 416.

■ MOTZ, CHIEF JUDGE.

Plaintiff Essex Construction Corporation (Essex) claims violations of the * * * District of Columbia banking laws. Essex alleges that Defendant Industrial Bank of Washington, Inc. (Industrial) * * * failed to provide timely notice that the check had been dishonored. Plaintiff seeks the amount of the check as damages. Defendant moves to dismiss or for summary judgment, and plaintiff cross-moves for default or summary judgment.

I.

The relevant facts are not in dispute. On March 31, 1995, plaintiff deposited into its account at Industrial a check in the amount of $120,-710.70 from East Side Manor Cooperative Association (East Side). East Side's check was drawn against its account at Signet Bank (Signet). At the time of the deposit, Industrial provisionally credited Essex's account but provided written notice that all but $100 of the funds would not be available for withdrawal until April 6, 1995.

On April 6, Signet notified Industrial that East Side had stopped payment on the check. Industrial placed a permanent hold on the $120,-710.70 deposit, effectively revoking the provisional credit to Essex's account. On April 7, Industrial mailed written notice (including the returned check itself) to Essex.

On April 7, Essex wrote two checks in the amount of $21,224 and $18,084.60 against the funds it thought were available in its account at Industrial. Essex received Industrial's written notice of dishonor on April 11.

* * *

III.

* * * [A] depository bank's right to revoke or charge back an uncollectible deposit * * * must comply with applicable state law. The District of Columbia has adopted the Uniform Commercial Code's system for regulating check processing transactions. The U.C.C. observes a fundamental distinction between "payor" and "collecting" banks. A payor bank is the bank maintaining the account against which a check is drawn, in this case Signet. See § 4–105(3). A collecting bank is a bank handling a check for collection from the payor, in this case Industrial. See § 4–105(5).

Payor and collecting banks have distinct obligations. A payor bank must decide whether to reject a check by midnight on the day it receives a check for collection. Failure to respond by midnight constitutes "final payment," making the payor bank strictly liable for the amount of the check. See First Nat'l Bank in Harvey v. Colonial Bank, 898 F.Supp. 1220, 1226 (N.D.Ill.1995) (discussing U.C.C.'s "final payment" system and role of payor banks); see also § 4–302(a). A collecting bank, in contrast, retains the right to revoke or charge back funds that are provisionally credited to a customer until the collecting bank's settlement with the payor bank becomes final. See § 4–214(a). It is at the moment of "final payment" by the payor bank that the respective liabilities for a check become fixed: the payor bank is strictly liable to the collecting bank for the amount of the check, see § 4–302(a), and the collecting bank loses the ability to revoke a provisional settlement or charge back withdrawn funds. See §§ 4–215(d), 4–214(a).

A.

Essex argues that on April 6 Industrial's provisional credit to its account became a final and irrevocable payment under § 4–215(a). This contention misunderstands the difference between payor and collecting banks. As discussed, a final payment occurs when a payor bank accepts or fails to promptly reject a check presented for collection by a collecting bank. Industrial was the collecting bank in this transaction. Essex's reliance on § 4–215(a) therefore is misplaced. See § 4–215(a) ("An item is finally paid by a *payor* bank when the bank has first done any of the following.... ") (emphasis added). Essex's right to the provisionally credited funds became irrevocable only upon "final payment" by Signet to Industrial, a condition that Essex does not allege occurred.

B.

Essex also argues that Industrial's mailing of the returned check via first class mail on April 7 did not constitute timely notice of dishonor under D.C. law. § 4–214 provides in relevant part:

> § 4–214 Right of charge-back or refund; liability of collecting bank; return of item. (a) If a collecting bank has made a provisional settlement with its customer for an item and fails by reason of dishonor ... to receive settlement for the item which is or becomes final, the bank may revoke the settlement given by it, charge back the amount of any credit given for the item to its customer's account, or obtain refund from its customer ... if by its midnight deadline or within a longer reasonable time after it learns the facts it returns the item or sends notification of the facts....

. . .

There is no dispute that Industrial failed by reason of dishonor to receive a final payment from Signet, the payor bank. Section 4–214(a) therefore provides that Industrial could revoke the provisional credit "if by its midnight deadline or within a longer reasonable time after it learn[ed] the facts it return[ed] the item or sen[t] notification of the facts." A bank's "midnight deadline" is defined as "midnight on its next banking day following the banking day on which it receives the relevant item or notice." § 4–104(a)(10); see also § 3–503(c)(i) ("[W]ith respect to an instrument taken for collection by a collecting bank, notice of dishonor must be given by the bank before midnight of the next banking day following the banking day on which the bank receives notice of dishonor of the instrument.").

The parties do not dispute that Industrial received notice of dishonor from Signet on April 6, that Industrial mailed the returned check to Essex before midnight on April 7 via first class mail, but that Essex did not receive it until April 11.

Essex argues that merely mailing the notice of dishonor before midnight on April 7 was insufficient. Industrial attempts to rely on § 3–508(4) for the proposition that "[w]ritten notice is given when sent although it is not received." However, the District of Columbia Council repealed § 3–508 effective March 27, 1995. See An Act to revise Articles 3 and 4 of the Uniform Commercial Code, 1994 D.C.Laws 10–249. Industrial's position finds alternative support, however, in § 4–214. Section 4–214(a) requires a bank to "*send* notification of the facts" or "*return*" the dishonored item. (emphasis added). Section 4–214(b) defines an item as "returned" "when it is *sent* or delivered to the bank's customer." In addition, § 3–503(b) provides that notice of dishonor may be given by "any commercially reasonable means, including an oral, written, or electronic communication." Industrial did not unduly delay notifying Essex, but instead took the reasonable step of promptly mailing the returned check. Although immediately telephoning Essex may have constituted better customer service, Industrial complied with D.C. notice requirements by mailing the returned check to Essex on April 7.

Moreover, even were I to find that Industrial's method of notice was not sufficient, Essex would not be entitled to the damages it seeks. In a case involving directly analogous provisions of the U.C.C. as enacted in Illinois, the Seventh Circuit has held that a depositor is entitled only to the damages actually resulting from a bank's failure to provide timely notice of dishonor. See Appliance Buyers Credit Corp. v. Prospect Nat'l Bank, 708 F.2d 290, 292–95 (7th Cir.1983). Furthermore, although the Appliance Buyers court reached this well-reasoned conclusion by interpreting an Illinois statute that was silent as to damages,[4] here the D.C. provision contains additional language which expressly so limits a depositor's remedies: a bank that fails to provide timely notice retains its right to charge back dishonored deposits "but is liable for any loss *resulting from the delay*." § 4–214(a) (emphasis added).[5] Plaintiff therefore may have been able to assert a claim for the bank charges associated with the two checks

---

4. In Appliance Buyers, the Seventh Circuit noted that because the charge-back provision at issue in that case did not expressly address damages—in contrast to other U.C.C. provisions that expressly do hold banks "accountable" for the amount of the check—the drafters could not have intended "that banks should be held strictly liable for the face value of dishonored checks." 708 F.2d at 293. Instead, the Appliance Buyers court turned to Illinois' general damages provision, which provided only for actual damages and which was identical to D.C.'s current provision. Compare § 4–103(e) with 708 F.2d at 293 (quoting Ill.Rev.Stat. ch. 26 § 4–103(5)).

5. In fact, prior to revisions that became effective on March 27, 1995, the predecessor to § 4–214(a) was largely identical to the Illinois statute at issue in Appliance Buyers. In 1995, however, the D.C. Council revised its U.C.C. provisions to add, among other changes, the above-quoted language that expressly limits recovery to actual loss. See 1994 D.C.Laws 10–249.

written on April 7, or for other foreseeable damages.[6] Essex, however, has made no showing of damages actually suffered.

IV.

A separate order granting defendant's summary judgment motion and entering judgment on its behalf is being entered herewith.

PROBLEM

Customer was the payee of a $5,000 check drawn on Payor Bank. On April 1, Customer deposited the check in Depositary Bank. When it received the check, Depositary Bank credited $5,000 to Customer's account but neglected to immediately forward the check to Payor Bank for payment. Depositary Bank's teller who received the check inadvertently dropped the check into a desk drawer where it remained until it was discovered about two months later. At the time Depositary Bank received the check on April 1 and for a period of 45 days thereafter there was more than $5,000 in the account of the drawer of the check in Payor Bank. When the check was discovered by Depositary Bank, it was forwarded for payment to Payor Bank, but it was returned to Depositary Bank because there were insufficient funds in the drawer's account to cover the amount of the check. On the same day that Depositary Bank learned of the dishonor, it informed Customer of the dishonor and made a debit of $5,000 to Customer's account. Was Depositary Bank entitled to make the debit to Customer's account? § 4–214(a) and (d)(2). Comment 5 to § 4–214. Does Customer have any cause of action against Depositary Bank? § 4–202(a) and (b); § 4–104(a)(10); § 4–103(a) and (e).

3.   ENCODING OF CHECKS

The conservatism of the banking profession is snickered at by the following oft-told anecdote: When a retiring banker was asked what the single biggest change in banking had been during his long career, he replied: "air conditioning." So far, in the 20th century, the biggest change in check collection to have gained wide-spread acceptance has been an elementary 1950s technology known as Magnetic Ink Character Recognition (MICR) encoding. In order to permit electronic processing of checks for presentment for payment, almost all checks in use today are preprinted with a row of numerals and symbols along the bottom of the check (the "MICR line") that can be read by machines that process the checks for payment. The preprinted MICR encoding identifies the payor bank, the

---

6. To recover the $120,710.70 from Industrial, therefore, Essex would have had to show that, absent the delay from April 7 to April 11, it would have been able to take action to collect from East Side. See Alioto v. United States, 593 F.Supp. 1402, 1416–17 (N.D.Cal.1984) (discussing cases). The record indicates, however, that East Side stopped payment on the check because of its ongoing dispute with Essex, not that East Side lacked funds on April 11 (or any time thereafter) that it had on April 7. In addition, defendant points out that in a separate proceeding East Side has alleged that it directly informed Essex of the stop payment order on April 6, the same day Signet notified Industrial.

Federal Reserve district in which the bank is located, the Federal Reserve Bank or branch that serves the payor bank, the number of the check, and the number of the account at the payor bank on which the check is drawn. When the check is deposited, either the depositary bank or the next collecting bank that has encoding equipment will add to the MICR line numerals that indicate the amount of the check. In some cases the encoding of the amount of the check will be done by the payee of the check before the check is deposited in the depositary bank. This can occur if the payee is a person receiving a very large volume of checks that are processed in processing centers operated by the payee. Examples of such payees are public utilities, insurance companies, and large retailers.

Most checks that have been encoded with the amount of the check will be processed by automated equipment by the payor bank and by collecting banks on the basis of the encoded information without any examination of the check by a human being. What happens if a check is payable in the amount of $123.45 but the person encoding the amount of the check erroneously encodes the amount as $12,345? The misencoding does not change the amount of the check. There has been no alteration of the check. But if the check is read by machines on the basis of the encoded amount, the bank that processes the check will treat it as a check in the amount of $12,345. If the payor bank pays the check, it has paid out the encoded amount to the presenting bank but will be entitled to debit the account of the drawer of the check only for the actual amount of the check. Or, the payor bank might wrongfully dishonor the check because the balance in the drawer's account, although large enough to cover the actual amount of the check, is not enough to cover the encoded amount. Before the 1990 revision, Article 4 did not address the problem of misencoding because MICR encoding did not exist when Article 4 was drafted. The case that follows discusses how losses caused by misencoding were allocated under the pre–1990 Article 4. Consider how that case would have been decided if revised § 4–209 had been in effect.

First National Bank of Boston v. Fidelity Bank

United States District Court, E.D. Pennsylvania, 1989.
724 F.Supp. 1168, aff'd without opinion, 908 F.2d 962 (3d Cir.1990).

■ FULLAM, CHIEF JUDGE.

This dispute between two banks over a mis-handled check transaction requires the court to explore some of the consequences which automation has visited upon the respective legal liabilities of banks under Article 4 of the Uniform Commercial Code, which was enacted before the advent of computerized check-processing.

* * *

The parties have stipulated the facts pertinent to their dispute. Plaintiff is the First National Bank of Boston (hereinafter "Boston"). The defendant is Fidelity Bank, National Association, successor to Industrial

Valley Bank (hereinafter "Fidelity"). On or about September 22, 1986, one of defendant's customers, New York City Shoes ("NYC") issued a check in the amount of $100,000, to the Maxwell Shoe Company ("Maxwell"). The check was drawn on one of NYC's accounts at Fidelity in Philadelphia. Maxwell, a New England concern, deposited the check in its account at Boston, which credited Maxwell's account with the face amount of the check, and then proceeded to process the check through the Federal Reserve system. The check was properly encoded by Boston, and duly presented to Fidelity for payment. But NYC's account did not contain sufficient funds to cover the check, and Fidelity therefore returned the check to Boston for "non-sufficient funds".

Boston did not charge Maxwell's account because of the uncollectability of the check, but instead, at Maxwell's request, undertook to re-present the check to Fidelity. In order to re-process the check, Boston attached a "tape skirt" to the bottom of the check, and thereon re-encoded the check so that it could be processed through the Federal Reserve system. Unfortunately, however, Boston's encoder made an error, and encoded the amount of the check as $10,000, rather than $100,000. The computers which processed the check were, of course, unaware of the error and unable to appreciate it. When the check arrived at Fidelity, it was charged against NYC's account in the amount of $10,000, and that sum was duly forwarded to Boston. At that point, the error surfaced.

Boston made demand on Fidelity for the $90,000 difference between the face amount of the check and the amount which Fidelity had paid. * * * At no time between September 22, 1986 and November 21, 1986, when NYC's account was closed, did NYC's account contain sufficient collected funds to cover Maxwell's $100,000 check, or the balance remaining after the initial payment of $10,000.

Because of the unusual nature of several transactions in NYC's account—a large number of checks drawn against uncollected funds, and a large number of deposits which later proved to be uncollectible—the account had come to the attention of Fidelity's Security Division in July of 1986. As a result of the investigation, Mr. Donald Ebner, vice-president in charge of security at Fidelity, decided to end Fidelity's banking relationship with NYC. By agreement, all of NYC's accounts at Fidelity were closed, as of the end of business on November 21, 1986.

At the start of business the next banking day, November 24, 1986, Mr. Ebner had in his possession, ready for delivery to NYC, a check representing the combined balances of all of NYC's accounts which had just been closed—a total of $101,383.61. That same morning, Mr. Ebner received from Fidelity's Adjustment Department the adjustment request which had been resubmitted by Boston, seeking the $90,000 balance on the Maxwell check. NYC, however, refused to permit Fidelity to use funds from any of its other accounts to make good the Maxwell check; and, since the account on which the check had originally been drawn was insufficient to cover it, Mr. Ebner rejected the adjustment request, and delivered to NYC the $101,383.61 check closing out its various accounts.

After this final rejection of Boston's adjustment request, Boston attempted to collect the $90,000 from NYC. An agreement was reached for NYC to pay off the balance in installments. NYC paid a total of $40,000 on account, but then defaulted and, on July 7, 1987, filed for bankruptcy.

* * *

As the foregoing recital demonstrates, the court is presented with two separate but related sets of questions. The first is the liability of Fidelity as payor bank, for having paid only $10,000 when the check was in the amount of $100,000, and the effect of Boston's encoding error on that liability. The second area of inquiry centers upon Fidelity's handling of the adjustment request, and its payout to NYC notwithstanding its awareness of Fidelity's adjustment request.

I.

* * *

Section 4–213(1) of the UCC provides:

" * * * An item is finally paid by a payor bank when the bank has done any of the following, whichever happens first:

"(c) Completed the process of posting the item to the indicated account of the drawer, maker or other person to be charged therewith * * *

"Upon final payment under subparagraphs (b), (c) or (d), the payor bank shall be accountable for the amount of the item."

Boston's argument is straightforward: Fidelity did post the check against NYC's account on October 3, 1986, and is therefore, under the plain language of the statute, accountable to Boston "for the amount of the item". The fact that Fidelity listed the item in the wrong amount is irrelevant, since it is undisputed that Fidelity "completed the process of posting the item to the indicated account of the drawer" on October 3, 1986.

The defendant, on the other hand, argues that, for purposes of § 4–213(1) the "amount of the item" for which the payor bank must account should be the encoded amount of the check, rather than its actual face amount. Alternatively, the defendant contends that equitable principles mandate rejection of plaintiff's claims.

Both parties find support for their respective positions in Georgia R.R. Bank & Trust Co. v. First National Bank & Trust Co. of Augusta, 139 Ga.App. 683, 229 S.E.2d 482 (1976), aff'd per curiam, 238 Ga. 693, 235 S.E.2d 1 (1977). The facts of that case are strikingly similar to the present case: plaintiff bank erroneously encoded a $25,000 check as a $2500 check. The defendant, the payor bank, charged the drawer's account in the lesser amount, and remitted that sum to plaintiff. The error was not discovered for several weeks, by which time the cancelled check had already been returned to the maker. When plaintiff made demand upon the defendant, the defendant brought the error to the maker's attention, but the latter refused to allow the defendant to charge his account with the additional $22,500. The Georgia court held, without extended discussion, that the defendant was liable to the plaintiff for the face amount of the check, pursuant to UCC § 4–213(1), and also pursuant to the "midnight deadline" provisions of § 4–302. The court reasoned that the defendant had made "final payment" by charging the maker's account, albeit in the wrong amount, and that it was therefore liable as payor for the full amount of the check; and that, alternatively, it had retained the check beyond the midnight deadline without "completely settling for it".

Although the actual holding of the *Georgia R.R. Bank & Trust Co.* case plainly supports plaintiff's arguments, one part of the court's explanation for its decision suggests that the true rationale for the decision is one which vindicates defendant's position in the present case: the court made much of the fact that, at all times, the maker's account contained more than sufficient funds to honor the check in its full amount. The court stated:

"We are not here concerned with a situation wherein the drawee cannot recover from the drawer the amount of the deficiency. In such a situation, there would possibly exist a defense or counterclaim in favor of the drawee bank against the collecting bank which had underencoded the check. See J. Clarke, *Mechanized Check Collection,* supra at 1004. The record in the present case shows that the drawer's account contained sufficient funds, as of the date payment was demanded by plaintiff, to cover the deficiency. 229 S.E.2d at p. 484.

It thus appears that, to the extent liability is sought to be imposed under the "final payment" rule of § 4–213(1), the Georgia court might well sustain an equitable defense where plaintiff's encoding error caused the payor bank to suffer a loss which it could not avoid by charging its customer's account. Recognition of such equitable defenses is more problematical when liability is sought to be imposed under the "midnight deadline" provisions of § 4–302. With due deference to the views of the Georgia courts, however, I am not persuaded that § 4–302 has any application in these circumstances. The whole purpose of the "midnight deadline" rule is to promptly remove uncertainties concerning the collectability of a check, and to enable depositary and collecting banks to rely upon the payor's silence as an unconditional assurance of collectability. If the payor bank acts before the deadline, it seems to me, § 4–302 is no longer implicated.

Like the Georgia court, however, I reject the argument that the "amount of the item" for § 4–213(1) purposes is the encoded amount, rather than the face amount, of the check. Stated that broadly, the argument is manifestly unacceptable, for if the encoded amount were greater than the face amount of the check, the error would produce a windfall for the collecting bank, and patently unjustifiable increases in the potential liability of the payor bank, the maker, or both. Any such rule would have chaotic repercussions, and would be totally inconsistent with the scheme of the UCC.

A more narrowly stated rule—that the "amount of the item" for purposes of § 4–213(1) is the face amount of the check or the encoded amount, whichever is less—is merely another way of stating what I conceive to be the true thrust of defendant's argument in this case, namely, that as between the encoding bank and all other banks in the collecting process, including the payor bank, the encoder is estopped from claiming more than the encoded amount of the check. Framing the argument in terms of estoppel is, I believe, preferable, in that it avoids the problems inherent in trying to ascribe different meanings to the same words in various parts of the UCC.

Section 1–103 of the UCC preserves equitable principles and common-law tort law, except where inconsistent with specific UCC provisions. Most of the decided cases have arisen under the "midnight deadline" provisions of § 4–302, which mandates automatic liability for missing the acceptance deadline "in the absence of a valid defense such as breach of a presentment warranty, settlement effected, or the like." In Bank Leumi Trust Co. v. Bank of Mid–Jersey, 499 F.Supp. 1022 (D.N.J.), aff'd without opinion, 659 F.2d 1065 (3d Cir.1981), it was held that the quoted language precludes assertion of an equitable defense based upon mis-encoding, where the payor bank failed to act before the deadline. In Chrysler Credit Corp. v. First National Bank & Trust Co., 746 F.2d 200 (3d Cir.1984), however, the Court of Appeals expressly declined to consider whether the defense of equitable estoppel could be asserted in a "midnight deadline" case, because the evidence in that case did not adequately support the asserted defense. The court made clear that, at the very least, the facts giving rise to the claimed estoppel would have to be such as to have been a cause of the payor's failure to meet the "midnight deadline".

Whether or not equitable defenses are available in "midnight deadline" cases, I am satisfied that such defenses are not precluded under § 4–302. That appears to be the view of most commentators. * * * The proposed ALI/NCCUSL revisions to Article 4 (specifically, revised § 4–209) would explicitly provide that an encoding bank warrants the accuracy of encoded amounts, and is liable for any resulting loss; this on the theory that the encoding bank is the party best able to avoid the loss. * * *

In my view, most, if not all, of the reported decisions can readily be harmonized with the existence of the right of the payor bank to hold the encoding bank liable for any under-encoding error, if this equitable right is considered in conjunction with the obligation to mitigate damages. That is, the payor bank has the corollary obligation of attempting to avoid loss altogether, by recourse to the account of the maker of the check. If the maker's account, when the check is correctly presented, is insufficient to cover the item, the payor bank has a claim against the encoding bank, which it can offset against any claim made by the encoding bank under § 4–213(1).

I therefore conclude that Fidelity may not be held liable to plaintiff under § 4–213(1) of the UCC, the "final payment" rule.

II.

Plaintiff's alternative claim that the defendant is liable * * * for permitting NYC to close out its accounts without honoring the check in question, is readily disposed of. At no time during the entire period did the account on which the check was drawn contain sufficient collected funds to cover the correct amount of the check (or, more particularly, the $90,000 balance due on that check). * * *

It is true that, by the time Fidelity released $101,383.61 to NYC on November 24, 1986, it was fully aware of plaintiff's adjustment request and the circumstances which occasioned it. But when NYC insisted upon receiving the entire balance from all of its accounts, Fidelity was obliged to comply. The underlying check, and plaintiff's adjustment request, established no basis for a charge against any account but the one upon which the check was drawn; and that account was insufficient. In the circumstances, Fidelity had no legal right to freeze NYC's other accounts, and certainly had no obligation to do so.

For all of the foregoing reasons, judgment will be entered in favor of the defendant.

NOTE

How would the case be decided under § 4–209 if the $100,000 check had been misencoded for $110,000 and Payor Bank had paid the check for that amount? Assume that Depositary Bank had misencoded the check but Collecting Bank had presented it to Payor Bank for payment. Comment 2 to § 4–209.

4.   ELECTRONIC PRESENTMENT

With respect to collection of checks by a depositary bank, the present system depends upon transportation of the check through the banking system from the depositary bank to the payor bank. More than one billion checks a week are processed by the banking system; the transportation of this volume of paper to the payor bank is very expensive and delays payment. In the 1994 Wall Street Journal article cited at the beginning of this chapter, the cost of transporting and processing checks was estimated at more than $50 billion per year.

It is not surprising that the banking system, which has been aggressively seeking methods of cutting costs, has considered alternatives to flying and trucking mountains of checks across the nation each day. One method discussed is often referred to by bankers as "truncation," but this is a confusing term because it is used to describe two quite different transactions. One use of the term describes the practice of payor banks of retaining checks after payment rather than returning them to the drawers who wrote them. Some banks are attempting to persuade their customers though differential pricing to agree to this practice. We will discuss this matter later.

It is the second use of the term, sometimes described as "radical truncation," that we are concerned with at this point. In order to avoid confusing it with the other meaning of truncation, revised Articles 3 and 4 refer to this process as "electronic presentment." Under this process most checks would be retained by the depositary bank for destruction after a relatively short period of time. Presentment for payment of a check would be made to the payor bank by electronic transmittal of essential information describing the check rather than by delivery of the check. After the check is destroyed, an image of the check would be stored electronically so that a copy of the check could be produced if needed at some later time.

Although, under the present system, the check itself is normally transported to the payor bank, most checks are not examined by anybody in the payor bank's process of payment. In these cases the check serves only as the carrier of the electronic encoding on the MICR line which is read by the automated machinery of the payor bank. Use of the check itself to convey the information contained on the MICR line is both inefficient and unnecessary. It is technologically feasible to provide this information to the payor bank by electronic transmission. Since a system of electronic presentment was believed to be a possible solution to the banking industry's difficulties with the present check payment system, much discussion during the drafting of revised Articles 3 and 4 centered around how the revision should deal with electronic presentment. The agreement reached was that it was not the role of the UCC to mandate business practices in the banking industry. Electronic presentment, if found economically feasible, should come by inter-bank agreements or through the Federal Reserve pursuant to its broad regulatory authority. Articles 3 and 4 should be revised to remove any legal barriers to a regime of electronic presentment. The assumptions under which the Drafting Committee proceeded are set out in Comments 2 and 3 to § 4–110. The changes made in Articles 3 and 4 to accommodate electronic presentment are explained in the following paragraphs.

With respect to collection of checks, presentment is simply a demand made to the drawee to pay the check. § 3–501(a). The demand may be made by an electronic communication. § 3–501(b)(1). But revised Article 3 follows the pre–1990 law in preserving the right of the drawee to demand exhibition of the check and its surrender as a condition to payment. § 3–501(b)(2). This right of the drawee to require exhibition and surrender of the check is subject, however, to rules stated in Article 4 and may be waived by the drawee by agreement. Section 4–110 permits electronic presentment by means of a "presentment notice" which is defined as "transmission of an image of an item or information describing the item." The presentment notice is in lieu of delivery of the check itself. Presentment under § 4–110 requires an "agreement for electronic presentment" which provides for the presentment notice. The quoted term includes not only an agreement between the drawee and the presenting bank, but also a clearing-house rule or Federal Reserve regulation or operating circular providing for electronic presentment.

Electronic presentment raises a number of problems. The payor bank will not be able to examine the signature of the drawer to detect a possible forgery, but this problem exists under current practice as well, because most checks are not examined for forgery. Under the current practice, payor banks look at the drawer's signature only on some checks such as those in large dollar amounts. This practice could continue under a regime of electronic presentment by a requirement that large checks be excluded from electronic presentment. Or, presentment of some checks might be made by transmitting an image of the check rather than information describing the check to allow examination of the drawer's signature. Current imaging technology would allow depository banks to send to payor banks miniature digitized images of checks. The process, encouraged by § 4–110(a), is described in Clark & Clark, The Law of Bank Deposits, Check Collections and Credit Cards ¶ 16.02[1] (Rev.ed.1995).

The agreement for electronic presentment would also have to provide for retention and destruction of the check in order to protect the drawer of the check against further negotiation of the check. Under present practice many payor banks return all cancelled checks to the drawer after the checks are paid. This will not be possible with respect to checks paid pursuant to electronic presentment. But this practice of returning checks to the drawer has become less prevalent in recent years. Many banks have induced customers to opt for checking-account plans in which cancelled checks are not returned and instead the customer is given a statement describing the checks paid. Under electronic presentment the payor bank would be able to obtain, at the request of a customer, a copy of any check paid for the customer's account for which the customer may have a particular need. The agreement for electronic presentment would provide for electronic storage of copies of checks presented electronically and would impose a duty on the storing bank to provide a copy of a check on request of the payor bank. § 4–406(a) and (b).

The future of electronic presentment is not clear. In the late 1980s its prospects seemed bright. The Expedited Funds Availability Act, discussed in the next section, mandated that the Fed "shall consider * * * requiring by regulation, that * * * the Federal Reserve banks and depositary institutions provide for check truncation." 12 U.S.C. § 4008(b). If the Fed decides to require electronic presentment, it needs no further authorization from Congress because 12 U.S.C. § 4008(c) gives the Fed the power to regulate any aspect of the payment system with respect to checks in order to carry out expedited funds availability. But so far the Fed has declined to act. It summarized its views as follows:

> The Federal Reserve studied the feasibility of mandatory and voluntary electronic presentment in the Electronic Clearinghouse Study, submitted to Congress in August 1988. Although electronic presentment is feasible given current technology, the study concluded that the benefits of mandatory electronic presentment would be outweighed by the potential risks borne by the paying banks. Paying banks may wish to participate in voluntary electronic presentment

arrangements with Reserve banks or other presenting banks. Absent such an arrangement, the Board believes it is appropriate to require settlement only after physical presentment so that the paying bank will have the opportunity to verify receipt of the cash letter.

57 Fed. Reg. 46,952 (1992).

There is some question whether the Fed has sufficient incentive to reduce the level of check collection activity. Although in most countries the central bank leaves the check collection function to the private sector, the majority of the Fed's 25,000 employees, its $2 billion budget, and, presumably, its fleet of 47 Learjets, is devoted to processing and collecting checks. John R. Wilke, Fed's Huge Empire, Set Up Years Ago, Is Costly and Inefficient, Wall St.J., Sept. 12, 1996, p.A1. However, in 1996 the New York Clearing House adopted a form of electronic presentment for all checks presented through the Clearing House at night, when most local checks move. Each member bank must send an electronic file giving the account number and amount of all checks it expects to collect from the other member banks the next day. The payor bank must notify the collecting bank the next day whether the check will be paid. Martin Mayer, The Fed Wants More Free Use of Your Money, Wall St.J., Jan. 3, 1997, p. A 8. This article quotes Fed chairman Alan Greenspan as stating that he does not wish to push the banking system into making the capital expenditures necessary to increase payment systems efficiency until the return justifies the expenditure. As we shall see, both businesses and consumers are finding alternatives to payment by check. Wilke, supra.

5. FUNDS AVAILABILITY AND REGULATION CC

Suppose Father living in Sacramento, California, mails a check for $1,000, drawn on First Bank in Sacramento, to Daughter, attending school in College Town, New York, 80 miles from New York City. The check arrives on Monday morning. Daughter takes it to Second Bank's College Town branch and deposits it in her account. On Monday night the check is driven by a courier to Second Bank's central check processing center in New York City and is run through a reader-sorter machine. On Tuesday morning it is taken to the New York Fed where it goes through another reader-sorter and is sent by air courier on Tuesday night to the San Francisco Fed where it arrives early Wednesday morning. There it goes through a reader-sorter machine, and on Wednesday afternoon is driven by a courier to First Bank in Sacramento. By early Thursday morning the check has been posted by automation to Father's account which was then debited. When Daughter deposited the check in Second Bank she asked when she could withdraw her money; she was told it would be available for her in two weeks. She needed the money earlier and called Father to describe her plight. He was irritated to learn that although the banking system had withdrawn the amount of the check from his account on Thursday morning, Daughter would not be able to withdraw the funds until eleven days later.

Second Bank's action in placing a two week "hold" period on Daughter's check was thought necessary to protect itself from the possibility that the check would not be paid by First Bank, owing to insufficient funds in the account, entry of a stop-payment order or other reasons. Relatively long hold periods were necessary because of the slow and inefficient system banks use for returning checks that have been dishonored. Second Bank may not learn whether the check has been dishonored until the unpaid check is physically returned to it. The forward collection of the check in this case from College Town to Sacramento was fairly prompt because the MICR line enabled the collecting banks to utilize an automated system for sorting checks and directing them to the banks on which they are drawn. But there is no automated system for the return of checks. Each must be processed manually by clerks who must attempt to return the check to the proper bank by deciphering the sometimes unintelligible indorsements on the back of the check. Moreover, before institution of the reforms discussed below, the system of provisional credits made it desirable to send the check back through the same chain of banks as in the forward collection of the check. Thus, had First Bank dishonored the check which arrived there after that bank's 2:00 p.m. cutoff hour on Wednesday, it could have waited until its Friday night midnight deadline to send the check back to the San Francisco Fed. That bank would probably need a second banking day after the banking day of receipt for the manual processing of the check. The same is true for the New York Fed. Although the check would probably be returned by truck and air courier services, returning banks could slow the process down even more by mailing the returns back. One study found that although the forward collection process for checks averaged 1.6 days, the return averaged 5.2 days. Barkley Clark & Barbara Clark, Regulation CC Funds Availability and Check Collection 1–4 (1988).

Banks met the growing chorus of customer complaints about what seemed to be excessive hold periods by justifying their actions as necessary to protect them from bad check losses. But in the 1980s several states passed laws limiting hold periods, and in 1987 Congress enacted the Expedited Funds Availability Act of 1987, 12 U.S.C. § 4001 et seq. The Board of Governors of the Federal Reserve System implemented this statute by promulgating Regulation CC in 1988, 12 C.F.R. 229. Subpart B of Regulation CC prescribes mandatory availability schedules. Next day availability is required for "low risk" deposits for which a hold period is not needed to protect the depositary bank from risk. Examples are cashier's checks, certified checks, teller's checks, electronic payments (wire transfers and ACH credits), "on us" items, Treasury and state and local government checks. § 229.10. For local checks the funds must be made available to the depositor not later than the second day after the banking day of deposit. § 229.12(b). For nonlocal checks funds must be made available not later than the fifth business day following the banking day of deposit. § 229.12(c). But a depositor is allowed to withdraw up to $100 on the next banking day after deposit of either local or nonlocal checks. § 229.10(c). Section 229.13 sets out exceptions to these mandatory availability schedules with respect to new accounts, large deposits, redeposited checks, repeated overdrafts, and cases in which there is reasonable cause to doubt collectibility.

Clark & Clark, The Law of Bank Deposits, Check Collections and Credit Cards ¶ 10.01[6][b] (Cum.Supp.1995), reports that a 1994 American Bankers Association study has shown that banks are generally making funds available to depositors earlier than Regulation CC requires. For local checks drawn on consumer demand accounts, over 90% of the banks surveyed reported that they are making funds available on either the day of deposit or the next day. And over 50% of the banks are following the same practice for nonlocal checks on these accounts. With respect to business demand accounts, most banks are also exceeding the availability standards mandated by Regulation CC. The reasons for the banks' early availability policy are not entirely clear. Customer relations must play a big part, but the operational difficulties of dealing with the multiple availability schedules of Regulation CC may be another factor. Moreover, as indicated in the preceding paragraph, in cases in which a bank has reason to question the collectibility of a check it can protect itself by withholding payment.

To allow the banking system to meet the funds availability standards set by Regulation CC without exposing depositary banks to excessive bad check losses, it was necessary to expedite the return system. Subpart C of Regulation CC sets out a sweeping revision of the law of check collection and return in order to speed the return of dishonored checks, thereby preempting portions of Article 4. As two commentors put it:

> In biblical terms, the genesis of Regulation CC might be stated as follows: The slow check return process begat risks perceived as unacceptable by depositary banks in allowing customers to draw on uncollected funds. This perception of risk begat extended blanket holds. Extended blanket holds begat consumer agitation. Consumer agitation begat state legislative initiatives focusing on mandatory expedited availability. State legislative initiatives begat congressional response in the form of the EFAA. The EFAA begat Regulation CC. Regulation CC begat an entirely new check collection code to speed the return process. And all of this is certain to beget confusion and litigation.

Clark & Clark, supra, 1–10.

In the early stages of the revision of Article 4, before the EFAA had been passed, the drafters had proposed several provisions designed to speed the return of dishonored checks. These provisions included: facilitating direct return of dishonored checks to depositary banks; reducing the number of returned checks by extending the payor bank's midnight deadline for checks under $100 (thus giving the drawer time to put enough money in the account to pay the check); requiring compliance with uniform indorsement standards governing the content and placement of bank indorsements; commencing the running of the midnight deadline for return from the time of delivery of checks to central bank processing centers; and imposing on payor banks the duty to give prompt notice of the nonpayment of items of $2,500 or more. Regulation CC preempted all these provisions except the extension of the midnight deadline for small checks which was not included in Regulation CC and dropped from Article 4 because of the belief that it would slow the collection of checks; hence, all these provisions were deleted from Article 4.

But Regulation CC went far beyond these modest steps. In sections 229.30 and 229.31, it authorizes a payor or returning bank to return a check directly to the depositary bank or to any returning bank agreeing to handle the returned check for expeditious return to the depositary bank, regardless of whether the returning bank had handled the check for forward collection. The contemplation was that the banks most likely to agree to handle a returning check expeditiously were the regional Federal Reserve banks. The consequences of allowing a check presented by one bank to be returned by the payor bank to a different bank undermined the usual methods of interbank settlements. Under these methods, the payor bank gives the presenting bank a provisional settlement which it revokes when it returns the dishonored check to that bank. If the payor bank returns the check to a bank that was not the presenting bank, the payor bank cannot obtain settlement for the returned check by revoking the settlement with the presenting bank. Rather, it must recover settlement from the bank to which it returned the check. But in order to give banks incentive to make expeditious returns, even if the payor bank does return the dishonored check to the presenting bank, section 229.31(c) forbids a payor bank to obtain settlement for the check by charging back against a credit it had previously given the presenting bank. The payor bank cannot recover settlement from a bank to which it has returned a check until the check has reached the returning bank, as though in forward collection. In harmony with these two provisions, section 229.36(d) provides that all settlements between banks for the forward collection of checks are final when made.

The interbank settlement provisions of Article 4 are stated in terms of provisional settlements. § 4–201(1). Bank credit given by a settling payor or collecting bank is provisional in the sense that it can be revoked upon return of the item. The Fed's decision in Regulation CC to make all settlements final meant that now the conceptual approach of Article 4 to interbank settlements differed from that of Regulation CC, though, at least with respect to the issues addressed by Article 4, there is little functional difference between the two laws. The fact that under Regulation CC any credit given for a check is final rather than provisional was not intended by the drafters of Regulation CC to limit the right of a payor or collecting bank to return a check and recover the amount of the check from the bank to which it was returned. After stating that settlement under Regulation CC is final rather than provisional, the commentary to section 229.36(d) of Regulation CC explains: "Settlement by a paying bank is not considered to be final payment for the purposes of U.C.C. [§ 4–215(a)], because a paying bank has the right to recover settlement from a returning or depositary bank to which it returns a check under this subpart." Appendix Commentary, 53 Fed.Reg. 19,486 (1988). The check collection aspects of Regulation CC are discussed in Clark & Clark, Bank Deposits, Chapter 8 (Rev.ed. 1995).

Today the law of check collection and return is found in Regulation CC as well as in Article 4, to the extent that its provisions are not preempted by Regulation CC. Consideration in the revision of Article 4 was given to redrafting Article 4 in order to make it compatible with Regulation CC. This approach was rejected because of the likelihood that Regulation CC will continue to evolve, leaving inconsistencies between Article 4 and Regulation CC.

B. ELECTRONIC FUNDS TRANSFERS

1. THE BASIC TRANSACTION COVERED BY ARTICLE 4A

Article 4A was promulgated by ALI and National Conference in 1989; by 1996 it had been enacted in all 50 states. Representatives of the Federal Reserve Board and of the New York Federal Reserve Bank were very active in the four-year drafting process of Article 4A, and, after Article 4A was completed, Regulation J, which governs Fedwire (described below), was revised by the Federal Reserve Board to bring it into conformity with Article 4A. 12 C.F.R. § 210.25 et seq. The Fed's stated policy in doing so was to provide a "level playing field" in which the rights and obligations of the parties in all funds transfers would be governed by essentially the same set of rules. Ernest T. Patrikis, Thomas C. Baxter, Jr. and Raj K. Bhala, Wire Transfers 140 (1993) (hereafter Patrikis, et al., Wire Transfers). At the time their book was published, Patrikis was Executive Vice President and General Counsel of the New York Federal Reserve Bank; Baxter was an officer of the bank and Counsel in the its legal department; and Bhala was an attorney in the legal department. Patrikis and Baxter participated in the drafting of Article 4A and the revision of Regulation J.

Article 4A does not apply to the consumer electronic funds transfers governed by the Electronic Fund Transfer Act, 15 U.S.C. § 1693 et seq. § 4A–108. Typical transactions covered by the EFTA are: point-of-sale transactions in which retail customers pay for purchases by use of an access or debit card inserted in a terminal at a retail store that allows the bank account of the customer to be instantly debited; automated teller machine transactions; direct deposit of pay checks in consumer accounts and preauthorized withdrawals from consumer accounts to pay consumer obligations like insurance premiums. 15 U.S.C. § 1993a(6). "Small dollar" wire transfers by Western Union and its competitors are not covered by Article 4A because payment orders are defined in § 4A–103 as orders to banks and Western Union and its competitors are not banks.

The typical funds transfer transaction covered by Article 4A is a large payment of money from one business or financial organization to another made through the banking system by electronic means. The average size of a wire transfer is measured in the millions of dollars. Vastly more money is transferred through wire transfers than by checks. A common transaction might be: Los Angeles Seller is selling $100 million in property to a New York Buyer. The closing is in Buyer's counsel's office in New York. When negotiations are concluded and the deal is made, Buyer calls its office and requests that an instruction be given to its bank, New York Bank (NYB), to transfer $100 million to Seller's account in Seller's bank, Los Angeles Bank (LAB). Within an hour and a half, Seller receives a call from its office stating that it has been notified by LAB that the funds are now in Seller's account in LAB and are available for withdrawal by Seller. The deal is done. The parties shake hands and leave.

What went on behind the scenes to move $100 million from New York to Los Angeles in a couple of hours? Some of the alternative methods follow. These are described in detail in Patrikis, et al., Wire Transfers, Chapter 2.

(a) *Two bank transfer.* Buyer, the "originator" (§ 4A–104(c)), instructs NYB, the "originator's bank" (§ 4A–104(d)), to send $100 million to LAB, the "beneficiary's bank" (§ 4A–103(a)(3)), for the account of the Seller, the "beneficiary" (§ 4A–103(a)(2)). The instruction is a "payment order" (§ 4A–103(a)(1)) and it may be transmitted "orally [e.g., by telephone], electronically, or in writing." NYB "accepts" (§ 4A–209(a)) the payment order when it "executes" (§ 4A–301(a)) that order by sending a payment order to LAB intended to carry out the payment order it received from Buyer. LAB accepts the payment order of NYB by crediting the Seller's account and notifying Seller of this fact. § 4A–209(b)(1). When LAB accepted the payment order, the "funds transfer" (§ 4A–104(a)) was completed. Since Seller has received payment, Buyer's obligation to pay Seller for the property is discharged. § 4A–406.

This transaction involved two payment orders: the first, from Buyer to NYB and the second, from NYB to LAB. With respect to the first, Buyer is the "sender" (§ 4A–103(a)(5)), and NYB is the "receiving bank" (§ 4A–103(a)(4)). With respect to the second, NYB is the sender and LAB is the receiving bank. In crediting Seller's account, LAB was not sending a payment order.

It is important to understand that Article 4A prescribes the liability of the parties to a funds transfer. It does not mandate a mode of settlement. That is, when NYB accepted Buyer's payment order, Buyer, as sender, became liable to pay the amount of that payment order to NYB, the receiving bank. § 4A–402(c). When LAB, the beneficiary's bank, accepted NYB's payment order, NYB became liable to pay the amount of the order to LAB. § 4A–402(b). When LAB credited Seller's account and gave notice to Seller, LAB paid Seller and Seller can withdraw the funds.

How these debts are settled, that is, how the money changes hands, is not covered by Article 4A which merely provides for a series of bank credits, usually ending in a credit in the beneficiary's account in the beneficiary bank. NYB became a creditor of Buyer when it accepted Buyer's payment order by sending its own order to LAB. Buyer will pay its debt to NYB either by having enough money in its account in NYB which NYB can debit to cover the payment or by depositing enough money into the account, usually by the end of the banking day, to cover the payment made on Buyer's behalf. If no satisfactory agreement has been reached between

Buyer and NYB to fund the payment order, NYB will probably not accept the order.

LAB became a creditor of NYB when it accepted NYB's payment order by crediting Seller's account. Unless NYB and LAB have some agreement on how NYB will pay this debt, LAB probably would not accept the payment order. Usually in two-bank cases, settlement will be accomplished either through "cross accounts" or a "common account." In a cross-account situation, each bank will have an account in the other. When NYB accepts Buyer's payment order, it will debit Buyer's account and credit LAB's account. When LAB accepts NYB's payment order, it will debit NYB's account and credit Seller's account. Common-account settlement is possible when both NYB and LAB have accounts in a common correspondent bank. The correspondent bank will debit NYB's account and credit that of LAB.

(b) *CHIPS.* If both NYB and LAB are participants in the Clearing House Interbank Payments System (CHIPS) of the New York Clearing House Association, they can utilize the CHIPS facilities for both transmission of the payment order and settlement of the ensuing obligations. CHIPS is one of the two major wire transfer systems in the nation; it handles a large volume of international transfers and a number of its participants are foreign banks. Under CHIPS, NYB will send its payment order to LAB through the central CHIPS clearing system. At the end of the day, CHIPS computers will net out the difference between the total value of payments orders NYB has sent to LAB on that day, and vice versa, and the net balance debtor will pay through Fedwire the amount of the debit balance to the CHIPS Settlement Account at the New York Federal Reserve Bank; the net balance creditor will receive the amount of the credit balance from this account through Fedwire sent by the FRBNY at the end of the day. Patrikis, et al., Wire Transfers Chapter 17.

(c) *Fedwire.* This system is owned and operated by the 12 Federal Reserve banks and is the other major wire transfer system. It can be used only by banks in privity with Reserve banks. These banks must have accounts in the Fed. However, other banks can use Fedwire through correspondent banks that are in privity with the Fed. If both LAB and NYB have access to Fedwire, the transaction would go like this: Buyer instructs NYB to send the funds to LAB for credit to Seller's account. NYB instructs the New York Fed to send the funds to LAB, for Seller. The NY Fed will instruct the San Francisco Fed to send funds to LAB for Seller's account. The SF Fed will instruct LAB to credit Seller's account. LAB will notify Seller that the money is available for withdrawal. In this case four payment orders have been sent: from Buyer to NYB, from NYB to NY Fed, from NY Fed to SF Fed, and from SF Fed to LAB.

Fedwire is not only a communication system that receives and sends payment orders, but, like CHIPS, it is also a settlement system. However, there is a difference. As soon as the NY Fed sends the instruction to the SF Fed, it debits NYB's Federal Reserve account and credits the Federal Reserve account of the SF Fed. As soon as the SF Fed sends the instruction to LAB, it debits the NY Fed's Federal Reserve account and credits the Federal Reserve account of LAB. As they say in the business, with Fedwire "the message is the money." By the time LAB receives the payment order, all prior payment orders are settled. No end of day settlement, as in CHIPS, is necessary. Each senders's payment order is settled for at the time of acceptance by the receiving bank by debiting the Federal Reserve account of the sender and crediting the Federal Reserve account of the receiving bank.

At the time Article 4A was being written, the United Nations Commission on International Trade Law (UNCITRAL) was drafting the Model Law on International Credit Transfers which is intended to be a model for any nation that wishes to have legislation on the subject. Advisers who had been active in the Article 4A project served as members of the U.S. delegation to the Working Group which constituted the drafting committee for the Model Law. Article 4A and the Model Law bear many similarities but there are differences as well. As yet no nation has adopted the Model Law and it is exceedingly unlikely the U.S. will do so. The Model Law is discussed extensively in Patrikis, et al., Wire Transfers, Chapters 19–23.

2.   RECEIVER FINALITY

In Chapter 10 we discussed why obligees might not choose to take payment in uncertified checks or even in cashier's checks. At that point we suggested that they might demand to be paid by wire transfer in order to provide maximum safety. In the following case we see why this is so.

Aleo International, Ltd. v. Citibank

Supreme Court, New York County, 1994.
160 Misc.2d 950, 612 N.Y.S.2d 540.

■ HERMAN CAHN, JUSTICE:

Defendant Citibank, N.A. ("Citibank") moves for an order, pursuant to CPLR 3212, granting it summary judgment dismissing the complaint.

Plaintiff Aleo International, Ltd. ("Aleo") is a domestic corporation. On October 13, 1992, one of Aleo's vice-presidents, Vera Eyzerovich ("Ms. Eyzerovich"), entered her local Citibank branch and instructed Citibank to make an electronic transfer of $284,563 US dollars to the Dresdner Bank in Berlin, Germany, to the account of an individual named Behzad Hermatjou ("Hermatjou"). The documentary evidence submitted shows that at 5:27 p.m. on October 13, 1992, Citibank sent the payment order to the Dresdner Bank by electronic message. Dresdner Bank later sent Citibank an electronic message: "Regarding your payment for USD 284.563,00 DD 13.10.92 [indecipherable] f/o Behzad Hermatjou, Pls be advised that we have credited A.M. beneficiary DD 14.10.92 val 16.10.92 with the net amount of USD 284.136,16." This information was confirmed by the Dresdner Bank by fax to Citibank on July 29, 1993: "Please be advised that on 14.10.92 at 09:59 o'clock Berlin time Dresdner Bank credited the account of Behzad Hermatjou with USD 284.136,16 (USD 284.563,00 less our charges)." It is undisputed that Berlin time is six hours ahead of New York time, and that 9:59 a.m. Berlin time would be 3:59 a.m. New York time. At approximately 9 a.m. on October 14, 1992, Ms. Eyzerovich instructed Citibank to stop the transfer. When Citibank did not, this action ensued.

Article 4A of the Uniform Commercial Code ("UCC") governs electronic "funds transfers." The Official Comment to UCC § 4A–102 states that the provisions of Article 4A

> "are intended to be the exclusive means of determining the rights, duties and liabilities of the affected parties in any situation covered by particular provisions of the Article. Consequently, resort to principles of law or equity outside of Article 4A is not appropriate to create rights, duties and liabilities inconsistent with those stated in this Article."

Article 4A does not include any provision for a cause of action in negligence. Thus, unless Citibank's failure to cancel Ms. Eyzerovich's transfer order was not in conformity with Article 4A, plaintiff Aleo has failed to state a cause of action, and this action must be dismissed.

UCC 4A–211(2), which governs the cancellation and amendment of payment orders, provides that

> "A communication by the sender cancelling or amending a payment order is effective to cancel or amend the order if notice of the communication is received at a time and in a manner affording the receiving bank a reasonable opportunity to act on the communication before the bank accepts the payment order."

"Acceptance of Payment Order" is defined by UCC 4A–209 (2), which provides that:

> "a beneficiary's bank accepts a payment order at the earliest of the following times: (a) when the bank (i) pays the beneficiary ... or (ii) notifies the beneficiary of receipt of the order or that the account of the beneficiary has been credited with respect to the order ..."

The documentary evidence shows that Hermatjou's account was credited on October 14, 1992 at 9:59 a.m. Berlin time. Thus, as of 3:59 a.m. New York time, the Dresdner Bank "paid the beneficiary" and thereby accepted the payment order. Because this payment and acceptance occurred prior to Ms. Eyzerovich's stop transfer order at 9 a.m. on that day, according to UCC 4A–211(2), Ms. Eyzerovich's attempt to cancel the payment order was ineffective, and Citibank may not be held liable for failing to honor it.

"Summary judgment is designed to expedite all civil cases by eliminating from the Trial Calendar claims which can properly be resolved as a matter of law.... [W]hen there is no genuine issue to be resolved at trial, the case should be summarily decided." Andre v. Pomeroy, 35 N.Y.2d 361, 364, 362 N.Y.S.2d 131, 320 N.E.2d 853.

Accordingly, defendant's motion is granted and this action is dismissed.

NOTES

1. The attractions of the wholesale wire transfer system, as regulated by Article 4A, are that it is cheap, fast and final. After LAB accepted the payment order in the hypothetical case above by crediting Seller's account and notifying Seller of this fact, Buyer could not stop payment by canceling the payment order unless LAB agreed to do so, and then only in the four cases set out in § 4A–211(c)(2). These are that the payment order was (i) unauthorized; (ii) a duplicate; (iii) made to the wrong beneficiary; or (iv) in an excessive amount. "Buyer's remorse" is not listed. Since LAB will have little incentive to antagonize its customer, Seller, by agreeing to the cancellation of the payment order and may not be sure whether any of the four events has actually occurred, it is unlikely that many beneficiary banks will agree to cancel.

2. A concern often expressed by banks during the process of drafting Article 4A was that a beneficiary bank might need protection against the insolvency of prior banks in the chain. If the payment order is sent through Fedwire, the beneficiary's bank is fully protected because "the message is the money," and the beneficiary's bank is paid as soon as it receives the Fedwire payment order. §§ 4A–209(b)(2) and 4A–403(a)(1). But in most other cases, the beneficiary's bank has not received settlement on the payment order until after it has received the order. If it turns the money over to the beneficiary as soon as it receives the payment order, it faces the risk that a prior bank in the chain may suspend payments before it settles with the beneficiary bank. Some banks wanted to solve this problem by being allowed to make provisional payments to their customers which would allow the beneficiary's bank to grab back the money paid out to the beneficiary if a prior bank failed before settlement. Strong arguments were made against this view by both users of the wire transfer system and the Fed; they contended that once the beneficiary's bank had made the money available to the beneficiary, it should be able to keep it. Receiver finality should be the goal of Article 4A. The users won this argument. Section 4A–405(c) invalidates provisional payments to beneficiaries, except in case of ACH transfers (§ 4A–405(d), Comment 3) or, with respect to CHIPS transfers, in case of a meltdown of the entire American banking system (§ 4A–405(e)), an event that Comment 4 cheerfully assures us "should never occur."

3. If a beneficiary bank cannot protect itself against up-stream insolvencies by making provisional payments to its customers, what can it do to guard against this risk? Patrikis, et al., Wire Transfers, Chapter 10. First, it can reject the payment order if it doubts the solvency of the sending bank. § 4A–210. Second, it can notify the beneficiary that it will not be allowed to withdraw the funds until the bank receives settlement from the sender of the order. § 4A–209(b)(1). Third, it can withhold the funds until an hour after the opening of business on the day after receipt, by which time, if it has not already received settlement, it must reject to avoid acceptance. § 4A–209(b)(3). But the competitive pressure on beneficiary banks to afford their customers prompt payment upon receipt of payment orders is great. This is particularly true with respect to CHIPS banks, which are in direct competition with the Fedwire system which offers beneficiaries of Fedwire payments immediate access to the incoming funds. By adoption of new rules after the completion of Article 4A, CHIPS has created a loss-sharing system that requires CHIPS banks to contribute funds to allow the system to settle for payment orders sent over the system during a given day in the event that one or more banks are unable to meet their settlement obligations. Patrikis, et al., Wire Transfers, Chapter 18. The level playing field between CHIPS and Fedwire has been achieved with respect to the early release of funds to beneficiaries.

3.   ERRONEOUS EXECUTION OF PAYMENT ORDERS

A fertile field of litigation with respect to wire transfers is the case in which the receiving bank executes the sender's payment order by sending an erroneous payment order. In such cases the general principle adhered to by Article 4A is that the sender is liable for its own errors. The subject is discussed in Richard F. Dole, Jr., Receiving Bank Liability for Errors in Wholesale Wire Transfers, 69 Tulane L.Rev. 877 (1995).

For illustration, assume these facts. Originator (O) instructs its bank, Originator's Bank (OB), to send $100,000 to the account of Beneficiary (B) in Beneficiary's Bank (BB). OB executed O's payment order by instructing its correspondent bank, Intermediary Bank (IB) (§ 4A–104(b)), to pay BB as indicated in the cases below. With respect to the payment order, O, OB and IB are senders and OB, IB and BB are receiving banks, and BB is also the beneficiary's bank. Thus the funds transfer looks like this:

O———OB———IB———BB———B

Work through these elementary problems:

Case #1. OB executed the payment order by instructing IB to pay BB $100,000 for the account of B. IB mistakenly instructed BB to pay $100,000 for the account of X.

    a.   Did IB execute the payment order of OB? § 4A–301(a).

    b.   Is OB entitled to payment from O? § 4A–402(c).

    c.   Is IB entitled to payment from OB? § 4A–402(c).

    d.   Is BB entitled to payment from IB? § 4A–402(b).

    e.   Is IB entitled to recover from X? § 4A–303(c).

Comment 2 to § 4A–402 discusses the "money-back guarantee" provided by § 4A–402.

Case #2. OB mistakenly instructed IB to pay BB $200,000 for B's account. IB executed OB's payment order by sending the same payment order to BB. BB deposited the funds in B's account and B withdrew the money. What are OB's rights against O and B under § 4A–303(a)?

Banque Worms v. BankAmerica International

New York Court of Appeals, 1991.
77 N.Y.2d 362, 568 N.Y.S.2d 541, 570 N.E.2d 189.

■ ALEXANDER, JUDGE.

On April 10, 1989, Security Pacific International Bank (Security Pacific), a Federally chartered banking corporation with offices in New York City, mistakenly wired $1,974,267.97 on behalf of Spedley Securities (Spedley), an Australian corporation, into the account of Banque Worms, a French Bank, maintained with BankAmerica International (BankAmerica), another Federally chartered bank with New York offices. Initially intending to make payment on its debt to Banque Worms under a revolving credit agreement, Spedley instructed Security Pacific, which routinely effected wire transfers for Spedley, to electronically transfer funds from Security Pacific to Banque Worms' account at BankAmerica.

A few hours after directing this wire transfer, Spedley, by a second telex, directed Security Pacific to stop payment to Banque Worms and to make payment instead to National Westminster Bank USA (Natwest USA) for the same amount. At the time Security Pacific received the telexes, Spedley had a credit balance of only $84,500 in its account at Security Pacific, but later that morning, Security Pacific received additional funds sufficient to cover the transaction and then began to execute the transaction. However, in mistaken disregard of Spedley's second telex canceling the wire transfer to Banque Worms, Security Pacific transferred the funds into Banque Worms' account at BankAmerica. The funds were credited to the account after Banque Worms was notified through the Clearing House Interbank Payment System (CHIPS) that the funds had been received. That afternoon, Security Pacific executed Spedley's second payment order and transferred $1,974,267.97 to Natwest USA. Spedley's account at Security Pacific was debited twice to record both wire transfers thus producing an overdraft.

Meanwhile, at Security Pacific's request made prior to the transfer to Natwest USA, BankAmerica agreed to return the funds mistakenly transferred, provided Security Pacific furnished a United States Council on International Banking, Inc. (CIB) indemnity. The indemnity was furnished and the funds returned to Security Pacific on the following day. Banque Worms, however, refused BankAmerica's request that it consent to its account being debited to reflect the return of the funds. Consequently BankAmerica called upon Security Pacific to perform pursuant to the CIB indemnity and return the funds. Security Pacific's attempt to obtain funds from Spedley to cover this indemnity was unavailing because by that time, Spedley had entered into involuntary liquidation.

Banque Worms brought suit against BankAmerica in the United States District Court for the Southern District of New York seeking to compel BankAmerica to recredit $1,974,267.97 to Banque Worms' account. BankAmerica instituted a third-party action against Security Pacific for return of the funds, and Security Pacific counterclaimed against Banque Worms seeking a declaration that neither Banque Worms nor BankAmerica were entitled to the $1,974,267.97. Eventually, for reasons not here pertinent, Security Pacific returned the funds to BankAmerica, BankAmerica recredited Banque Worms' account and was voluntarily dismissed from the case leaving only Banque Worms and Security Pacific as the sole contestants seeking entitlement to the $1,974,267.97.

On their respective motion and cross motion for summary judgment, the District Court, applying the "discharge for value" rule, granted judgment for Banque Worms. Security Pacific appealed to the United States Court of Appeals for the Second Circuit, arguing that New York neither recognized nor applied the "discharge for value" rule in situations such as this; that the controlling rule under New York law was the "mistake of fact" rule pursuant to which, in order to be entitled to retain the mistakenly transferred funds, Banque Worms was required to demonstrate detrimental reliance. The case is before us upon a certified question from the Second Circuit * * * inquiring "[w]hether in this case, where a concededly mistaken wire transfer by [Security Pacific] was made to [Banque Worms], a creditor of Spedley, New York would apply the 'Discharge for Value' rule as set forth at section 14 of the Restatement of Restitution or, in the alternative, whether in this case New York would apply the rule that holds that money paid under a mistake may be recovered, unless the payment has caused such a change in the position of the receiving party that it would be unjust to require the party to refund."

For the reasons that follow, we conclude that, under the circumstances of this case, the "discharge for value" rule should be applied, thus entitling Banque Worms to retain the funds mistakenly transferred without the necessity of demonstrating detrimental reliance.

I

A

In the area of restitution, New York has long recognized the rule that "if A pays money to B upon the erroneous assumption of the former that he is indebted to the latter, an action may be maintained for its recovery. The reason for the rule is obvious. Since A was mistaken in the assumption that he was indebted to B, the latter is not entitled to retain the money acquired by the mistake of the former, even though the mistake is the result of negligence." (Ball v. Shepard, 202 N.Y. 247, 253, 95 N.E. 719.) This rule has been applied where the cause of action has been denominated as one for money had and received * * * for unjust enrichment or restitution * * * or upon a theory of quasi contract * * *. Where, however, the receiving party has changed its position to its detriment in reliance upon the mistake so that requiring that it refund the money paid would be "unfair," recovery has been denied * * *.

This rule has evolved into the "mistake of fact" doctrine, in which detrimental reliance is a requisite factor, and which provides that "money paid under a mistake of fact may be recovered back, however negligent the party paying may have been in making the mistake, unless the payment has caused such a change in the position of the other party that it would be unjust to require him to refund." (National Bank v. National Mechanics' Banking Assn., 55 N.Y. 211, 213; see also, Hathaway v. County of Delaware, 185 N.Y. 368, 78 N.E. 153; Mayer v. Mayor of City of N.Y., 63 N.Y. 455, 457 ["general rule that money paid under a mistake of material fact may be recovered back * * * is subject to the qualification that the payment cannot be recalled when the position of the party receiving it has been changed in consequence of the payment, and it would be inequitable to allow a recovery."].)

The Restatement of Restitution, on the other hand, has established the "discharge for value" rule which provides that "[a] creditor of another or one having a lien on another's property who has received from a third person any benefit in discharge of the debt or lien, is under no duty to make restitution therefor, although the discharge was given by mistake of the transferor as to his interests or duties, if the transferee made no misrepresentation and did not have notice of the transferor's mistake" (Restatement of Restitution § 14[1]).

The question as to which of these divergent rules New York will apply to electronic fund transfers divides the parties and prompts the certified question from the Second Circuit. Security Pacific argues that New York has rejected the "discharge for value" rule and has required that detrimental reliance under the "mistake of fact" rule be demonstrated in all cases other than where the mistake was induced by fraud. Banque Worms, on the other hand, invokes the "discharge for value" rule, arguing that because it is a creditor of Spedley and had no knowledge that the wire transfer was erroneous, it is entitled to keep the funds. It points out, as indicated by the official comment to section 14(1) of the Restatement of Restitution, that the "discharge for value" rule is simply a "specific application of the underlying principle of bona fide purchase" set forth in section 13 of the Restatement (Restatement of Restitution § 14, *comment a*).

* * *

Indeed one may find, as does Banque Worms, language in a myriad of cases that arguably lends support to the proposition that New York, long ago, embraced the "discharge for value" rule * * *.

On the other hand, cases can also be cited where the language employed supports the contrary view—that New York not only eschews the "discharge for value" rule, as Security Pacific argues, but also embraces exclusively the detrimental reliance rule-mistake of fact doctrine * * *. These cases for the most part, however, present issues involving more traditional aspects of mistake and restitution, and do not satisfactorily address the unique problems presented by electronic funds transfer technology.

While courts have attempted in wire transfer cases to employ, by analogy, the rules of the more traditional areas of law, such as contract law, the law of negotiable instruments and the special relations between banks, these areas are governed by principles codified in articles 3 and 4 of the

Uniform Commercial Code. Various commentators found these efforts ineffective and inadequate to deal with the problems presented (see, Official Comment to UCC 4A–102 * * *). As pointed out by the Official Comment to article 4A, "attempts to define rights and obligations in funds transfers by general principles or by analogy to rights and obligations in negotiable instruments law or the law of check collection have not been satisfactory" * * *. Consequently, it was concluded, as the Prefatory Note to the new article 4A of the UCC approved by the National Conference of Commissioners on Uniform State Law and the American Law Institute observes, that a new article was needed because "[t]here is no comprehensive body of law that defines the rights and obligations that arise from wire transfers." * * *

B

Electronic funds transfers have become the preferred method utilized by businesses and financial institutions to effect payments and transfers of a substantial volume of funds. These transfers, commonly referred to as wholesale wire transfers, differ from other payment methods in a number of significant respects, a fact which accounts in large measure for their popularity. Funds are moved faster and more efficiently than by traditional payment instruments, such as checks. The transfers are completed at a relatively low cost, which does not vary widely depending on the amount of the transfer, because the price charged reflects primarily the cost of the mechanical aspects of the funds transfer (Prefatory Note to UCC art. 4A). Most transfers are completed within one day and can cost as little as $10 to carry out a multimillion dollar transaction * * *. The popularity of wholesale wire transfers is evidenced by the fact that nearly $1 trillion in transactions occur each day, averaging $5 million per transfer and on peak days, this figure often approaches $2 trillion * * *.

Wholesale wire transfers are generally made over the two principal wire payment systems: the Federal Reserve Wire Transfer Network (Fedwire) and the CHIPS.[2] The CHIPS network handles 95% of the international transfers made in dollars, transferring an average of $750 billion per day * * *. These funds are transferred through participating banks located in New York because all of the banks belonging to the CHIPS network must maintain a regulated presence in New York. As a result, this State is considered the national and international center for wholesale wire transfers.

The low cost of electronic funds transfers is an important factor in the system's popularity and this is so even though banks executing wire transfers often risk significant liability as a result of losses occasioned by mistakes and errors, the most common of which involve the payment of funds to the wrong beneficiary or in an incorrect amount * * *. Thus, a major policy issue facing the drafters of UCC article 4A was determining

2. CHIPS is owned and operated by the New York Clearing House Association and the Federal Reserve Bank owns and operates Fedwire, the largest American wire transfer network.

how the risk of loss might best be allocated, while preserving a unique price structure. In order to prevent or minimize losses, the industry had adopted and employed various security procedures designed to prevent losses[3] such as the use of codes, identifying words or numbers, call-back procedures and limits on payment amounts or beneficiaries that may be paid.

As indicated above, it was the consensus among various commentators that existing rules of law did not adequately address the problems presented by these wholesale electronic funds transfers. Thus, the National Conference of Commissioners on Uniform State Laws (NCCUSL) and the American Law Institute (ALI) undertook to develop a body of unique principles of law that would address every aspect of the electronic funds transfer process and define the rights and liabilities of all parties involved in such transfers (Prefatory Note to UCC art. 4A, *op. cit.*). After extensive investigation and debate and through a number of drafts, in 1989, both the NCCUSL and the ALI approved a new article 4A of the Uniform Commercial Code * * *. In 1990, the New York State Legislature adopted the new article 4A and incorporated it into the New York Uniform Commercial Code (N.Y. UCC art. 4–A).[4] Although the new statute, which became effective January 1, 1991, may not be applied retroactively to resolve the issues presented by this litigation, the statute's legislative history and the history of article 4A of the Uniform Commercial Code from which it is derived and the policy considerations addressed by this legislation, can appropriately inform our decision and serve as persuasive authority in aid of the resolution of the issue presented in this case * * *.

II

Both the NCCUSL and ALI drafters of article 4A and the New York Legislature sought to achieve a number of important policy goals through enactment of this article. National uniformity in the treatment of electronic funds transfers is an important goal, as are speed, efficiency, certainty (i.e., to enable participants in fund transfers to have better understanding of their rights and liabilities), and finality. Establishing finality in electronic fund wire transactions was considered a singularly important policy goal * * *. Payments made by electronic funds transfers in compliance with the provisions of article 4A are to be the equivalent of cash payments, irrevoca-

---

3. The Official Comment to UCC 4A–201 as drafted by the American Law Institute and National Conference of Commissioners on Uniform State Laws states that "it is standard practice to use security procedures that are designed to assure the authenticity of the message * * * [and] to detect error in the content of messages. * * * The question of whether loss that may result from the transmission of a spurious or erroneous payment order will be borne by the receiving bank or the sender or purported sender is affected by whether a security procedure was or was not in effect and whether there was or was not compliance with the procedure." * * *

4. The new article 4A will regulate funds transfers other than consumer transactions governed by the Federal Electronic Fund Transfer Act of 1978 (15 USC § 1693 et seq.). It will not apply to consumer transactions such as check payments or credit card payments for the Federal EFTA will continue to govern these transactions. If any part of a fund transfer is covered by the EFTA, the entire funds transfer will be excluded from article 4A.

ble except to the extent provided for in article 4A (see, Assn of Bar of City of NY, Committee on Banking Law, Report on proposed New York UCC art. 4–A; see also, Delbrueck & Co. v. Manufacturers Hanover Trust Co., 609 F.2d 1047, 1049–1051 [2d Cir.] [once an electronic fund transfer is completed and the funds released, the transaction is final and irrevocable under the CHIPS system]).

This concern for finality in business transactions has long been a significant policy consideration in this State. In a different but pertinent context, we observed in Hatch v. Fourth Natl. Bank, 147 N.Y. 184, 192, 41 N.E. 403 that "to permit in every case of the payment of a debt an inquiry as to the source from which the debtor derived the money, and a recovery if shown to have been dishonestly acquired, would disorganize all business operations and entail an amount of risk and uncertainty which no enterprise could bear".

A consequence of this concern has been the adoption of a rule which precludes recovery from a third person, who as the result of the mistake of one or both of the parties to an original transaction receives payment by one of them in good faith in the ordinary course of business and for a valuable consideration (see, Ball v. Shepard, 202 N.Y. 247, 95 N.E. 719, supra). This rule is grounded in "considerations of public policy and convenience for the protection and encouragement of trade and commerce by guarding the security and certainty of business transactions, since to hold otherwise would obviously introduce confusion and danger into all commercial dealings" (44 N.Y.Jur., Payment, § 107; see also, Southwick v. First Natl. Bank, 84 N.Y. 420). We have previously held that from these considerations, "[t]he law wisely * * * adjudges that the possession of money vests the title in the holder as to third persons dealing with him and receiving it in due course of business and in good faith upon a valid consideration." (Stephens v. Board of Educ., 79 N.Y. 183, 187–188.)

The "discharge for value" rule is consistent with and furthers the policy goal of finality in business transactions and may appropriately be applied in respect to electronic funds transfers. When a beneficiary receives money to which it is entitled and has no knowledge that the money was erroneously wired, the beneficiary should not have to wonder whether it may retain the funds; rather, such a beneficiary should be able to consider the transfer of funds as a final and complete transaction, not subject to revocation.

We believe such an application accords with the legislative intent and furthers the policy considerations underlying article 4–A of the New York Uniform Commercial Code. Although no provision of article 4–A calls, in express terms, for the application of the "discharge for value" rule, the statutory scheme and the language of various pertinent sections, as amplified by the Official Comments to the UCC, support our conclusion that the "discharge for value" rule should be applied in the circumstances here presented.

Subject to certain exceptions not here relevant, § 4A–209(b)(1) provides that a beneficiary's bank accepts a payment order when the bank pays the beneficiary by crediting the beneficiary's account and notifying the beneficiary of the right to withdraw the credit. When a payment order has been accepted by the beneficiary's bank, cancellation or amendment of that payment order is not effective unless, for example, the order was issued because of a mistake of the sender resulting in a duplicate payment order or an order that directs payment to a beneficiary not entitled to receive the funds. § 4A–211(c)(2)(i) and (ii). Where a duplicate payment order is erroneously executed or the payment order is issued to a beneficiary different from the beneficiary intended by the sender, the receiving bank in either case is entitled to recover the erroneously paid amount from the beneficiary "to the extent allowed by the law governing mistake and restitution". § 4A–303(a) and (c).

More specifically, § 4A–303(c) instructs that "[i]f a receiving bank executes the payment order of the sender by issuing a payment order to a beneficiary different from the beneficiary of the sender's order and the funds transfer is completed on the basis of that error, the sender * * * [is] not obliged to pay the payment order[ ]. The issuer of the erroneous order is entitled to recover from the beneficiary * * * to the extent allowed by the law governing mistake and restitution." Official Comment 1 to § 4A–303 from which the identical New York statute is derived, explains that although section 4A–402(c) obligates the sender to pay the [payment] order to the beneficiary's bank if that bank has accepted the payment order, section 4A–303 takes precedence and "states the liability of the sender and the rights of the receiving bank in various cases of erroneous execution".

Thus, as in the example discussed in comment 2 [to § 4A–303], where the originator's bank mistakenly directs payment of $2,000,000 to the beneficiary's bank but payment of only $1,000,000 was directed by the originator, the originator's bank is obligated to pay the $2,000,000 if the beneficiary's bank has accepted the payment, although the originator need only pay its bank the $1,000,000 ordered. The originator's bank ordinarily would be entitled to recover the excess payment from the beneficiary. The comment points out, however, that "if Originator owed $2,000,000 to Beneficiary and Beneficiary received the extra $1,000,000 in good faith in discharge of the debt, Beneficiary may be allowed to keep it. In this case Originator's Bank has paid an obligation of Originator and under the law of restitution * * * Originator's Bank would be subrogated to Beneficiary's rights against Originator on the obligation paid by Originator's Bank".

A further example discussed in comment 3 of the Official Comment is of a duplicate payment order erroneously made, which transfers a second $1,000,000 payment to beneficiary's bank and beneficiary's bank accepts the payment. Although the originator's bank is only entitled to receive $1,000,000 from the originator, it must pay $2,000,000 to beneficiary's bank and would be relegated to a remedy the same as "that of a receiving bank that executes by issuing an order in an amount greater than the sender's order. It may recover the overpayment from Beneficiary to the extent allowed by the law governing mistake and restitution and in a proper case * * * may have subrogation rights if it is not entitled to recover from Beneficiary''.

* * *

Application of the "discharge for value" rule to the circumstances presented here is particularly appropriate. The undisputed facts demonstrate that Security Pacific executed Spedley's initial order directing payment to Banque Worms notwithstanding having already received a cancellation of that order. The District Court also found that the second transfer to Natwest USA was executed despite the fact that Spedley's account did not have sufficient funds to cover this second transfer. Moreover, it appears that, as a creditor of Spedley, Banque Worms was a beneficiary entitled to the funds who made no "misrepresentation and did not have notice of the transferor's mistake."

Accordingly, we conclude, in answer to the certified question, that the "discharge for value" rule as set forth at section 14 of the Restatement of Restitution, should be applied in the circumstances in this case.

* * *

NOTE

In General Electric Capital Corp. v. Central Bank, 49 F.3d 280 (7th Cir.1995), the court, purportedly applying Wisconsin law, adopted the discharge-for-value rule in a wire payment case even though the state courts had never passed on the rule. The court justified its decision by citing the need for uniformity in the treatment of funds transfers. New York, the center of the wire transfer world, adopted the rule in *Banque Worms*, and the Restatement of Restitution § 14(1) (1937) does so as well. Hence, the court believed that Wisconsin should go along both in the interest of finality of payments, a prime Article 4A objective, as well as uniformity. In Bank of America N.T. & S.A. v. Sanati, 11 Cal.App.4th 1079, 14 Cal.Rptr.2d 615 (Cal.App.1992), a pre-Article 4A case, the court applied the discharge-for-value rule and stated that it should be applied only if the recipients in good faith believed that the funds were sent to them in satisfaction of or in discharge of a valid preexisting debt or lien.

4. FAILURE OF RECEIVING BANK TO EXECUTE PAYMENT ORDER

In *Evra,* the case that follows, Hyman–Michaels issued a payment order to Continental (Chicago) to pay a sum of money to an account in Banque de Paris in Geneva. Continental (Chicago) executed the order by issuing a payment order to Continental (London) and debited the account of Hyman–Michaels in the amount of the order. Continental (London) executed that payment order of Continental (Chicago) by issuing a payment order to Swiss Bank in Geneva. Swiss Bank was supposed to issue a payment order to Banque de Paris to complete the funds transfer, but failed to do so. As a result of the failure to complete the wire transfer,

Hyman–Michaels suffered a loss. *Evra,* which was decided before Article 4A was drafted, discusses the issue of whether, under general commonlaw principles, Hyman–Michaels was entitled to any recovery from either Continental (Chicago) or Swiss Bank.

Consider how *Evra* would have been decided if Article 4A had been in effect. Under Article 4A Hyman–Michaels is the originator of the funds transfer, Continental (Chicago) is the originator's bank, and Continental (London) and Swiss Bank are both "intermediary banks" (§ 4A–104(b)). Each of the three banks is also a receiving bank with respect to the payment order it received. The duty of a receiving bank with respect to a payment order that it receives is stated in § 4A–212. The duty of a receiving bank in executing a payment order is stated in § 4A–302. The extent of liability of a receiving bank for late or improper execution or for failure to execute a payment order is stated in § 4A–305. The right of the originator or other sender of a payment order to refund of amounts paid by them if the funds transfer is not completed is stated in § 4A–402(c) and (d).

Evra Corp. v. Swiss Bank Corp.

United States Court of Appeals, Seventh Circuit, 1982.
673 F.2d 951.

■ POSNER, CIRCUIT JUDGE.

The question—one of first impression—in this diversity case is the extent of a bank's liability for failure to make a transfer of funds when requested by wire to do so. The essential facts are undisputed. In 1972 Hyman–Michaels Company, a large Chicago dealer in scrap metal, entered into a two-year contract to supply steel scrap to a Brazilian corporation. Hyman–Michaels chartered a ship, the *Pandora,* to carry the scrap to Brazil. The charter was for one year, with an option to extend the charter for a second year; specified a fixed daily rate of pay for the hire of the ship during both the initial and the option period, payable semi-monthly "in advance"; and provided that if payment was not made on time the *Pandora*'s owner could cancel the charter. Payment was to be made by deposit to the owner's account in the Banque de Paris et des Pays–Bas (Suisse) in Geneva, Switzerland.

The usual method by which Hyman–Michaels, in Chicago, got the payments to the Banque de Paris in Geneva was to request the Continental Illinois National Bank and Trust Company of Chicago, where it had an account, to make a wire transfer of funds. Continental would debit Hyman–Michaels' account by the amount of the payment and then send a telex to its London office for retransmission to its correspondent bank in Geneva—Swiss Bank Corporation—asking Swiss Bank to deposit this amount in the Banque de Paris account of the *Pandora*'s owner. The transaction was completed by the crediting of Swiss Bank's account at Continental by the same amount.

When Hyman–Michaels chartered the *Pandora* in June 1972, market charter rates were very low, and it was these rates that were fixed in the charter for its entire term—two years if Hyman–Michaels exercised its option. Shortly after the agreement was signed, however, charter rates began to climb and by October 1972 they were much higher than they had been in June. The *Pandora*'s owners were eager to get out of the charter if they could. At the end of October they thought they had found a way, for the payment that was due in the Banque de Paris on October 26 had not arrived by October 30, and on that day the *Pandora*'s owner notified Hyman–Michaels that it was canceling the charter because of the breach of the payment term. Hyman–Michaels had mailed a check for the October 26 installment to the Banque de Paris rather than use the wire-transfer method of payment. It had done this in order to have the use of its money for the period that it would take the check to clear, about two weeks. But the check had not been mailed in Chicago until October 25 and of course did not reach Geneva on the twenty-sixth.

When Hyman–Michaels received notification that the charter was being canceled it immediately wired payment to the Banque de Paris, but the *Pandora*'s owner refused to accept it and insisted that the charter was indeed canceled. The matter was referred to arbitration in accordance with the charter. On December 5, 1972, the arbitration panel ruled in favor of Hyman–Michaels. The panel noted that previous arbitration panels had "shown varying degrees of latitude to Charterers"; "In all cases, a pattern of obligation on Owners' part to protest, complain, or warn of intended withdrawal was expressed as an essential prerequisite to withdrawal, in spite of the clear wording of the operative clause. No such advance notice was given by Owners of M/V Pandora." One of the three members of the panel dissented; he thought the *Pandora*'s owner was entitled to cancel.

Hyman–Michaels went back to making the charter payments by wire transfer. On the morning of April 25, 1973, it telephoned Continental Bank and requested it to transfer $27,000 to the Banque de Paris account of the *Pandora*'s owner in payment for the charter hire period from April 27 to May 11, 1973. Since the charter provided for payment "in advance," this payment arguably was due by the close of business on April 26. The requested telex went out to Continental's London office on the afternoon of April 25, which was nighttime in England. Early the next morning a telex operator in Continental's London office dialed, as Continental's Chicago office had instructed him to do, Swiss Bank's general telex number, which rings in the bank's cable department. But that number was busy, and after trying unsuccessfully for an hour to engage it the Continental telex operator dialed another number, that of a machine in Swiss Bank's foreign exchange department which he had used in the past when the general number was engaged. We know this machine received the telexed message because it signaled the sending machine at both the beginning and end of the transmission that the telex was being received. Yet Swiss Bank failed to comply with the payment order, and no transfer of funds was made to the account of the *Pandora*'s owner in the Banque de Paris.

No one knows exactly what went wrong. One possibility is that the receiving telex machine had simply run out of paper, in which event it would not print the message although it had received it. Another is that whoever took the message out of the machine after it was printed failed to deliver it to the banking department. Unlike the machine in the cable department that the Continental telex operator had originally tried to reach, the machines in the foreign exchange department were operated by junior foreign exchange dealers rather than by professional telex operators, although Swiss Bank knew that messages intended for other departments were sometimes diverted to the telex machines in the foreign exchange department.

At 8:30 a.m. the next day, April 27, Hyman–Michaels in Chicago received a telex from the *Pandora*'s owner stating that the charter was canceled because payment for the April 27–May 11 charter period had not been made. Hyman–Michaels called over to Continental and told them to keep trying to effect payment through Swiss Bank even if the *Pandora*'s owner rejected it. This instruction was confirmed in a letter to Continental dated April 28, in which Hyman–Michaels stated: "please instruct your London branch to advise their correspondents to persist in attempting to make this payment. This should be done even in the face of a rejection on the part of Banque de Paris to receive this payment. It is paramount that in order to strengthen our position in an arbitration that these funds continue to be readily available." Hyman–Michaels did not attempt to wire the money directly to the Banque de Paris as it had done on the occasion of its previous default. Days passed while the missing telex message was hunted unsuccessfully. Finally Swiss Bank suggested to Continental that it retransmit the telex message to the machine in the cable department and this was done on May 1. The next day Swiss Bank attempted to deposit the $27,000 in the account of the *Pandora*'s owner at the Banque de Paris but the payment was refused.

Again the arbitrators were convened and rendered a decision. In it they ruled that Hyman–Michaels had been "blameless" up until the morning of April 27, when it first learned that the Banque de Paris had not received payment on April 26, but that "being faced with this situation," Hyman–Michaels had "failed to do everything in [its] power to remedy it. The action taken was immediate but did not prove to be adequate, in that [Continental] Bank and its correspondent required some 5 or 6 days to trace and effect the lost instruction to remit. [Hyman–Michaels] could have ordered an immediate duplicate payment—or even sent a Banker's check by hand or special messengers, so that the funds could have reached owner's Bank, not later than April 28th." By failing to do any of these things Hyman–Michaels had "created the opening" that the *Pandora*'s owner was seeking in order to be able to cancel the charter. It had "acted imprudently." The arbitration panel concluded, reluctantly but unanimously, that this time the *Pandora*'s owner was entitled to cancel the agreement. The arbitration decision was confirmed by a federal district court in New York.

Hyman–Michaels then brought this diversity action against Swiss Bank, seeking to recover its expenses in the second arbitration proceeding plus the profits that it lost because of the cancellation of the charter. The contract by which Hyman–Michaels had agreed to ship scrap steel to Brazil had been terminated by the buyer in March 1973 and Hyman–Michaels had promptly subchartered the *Pandora* at market rates, which by April 1973 were double the rates fixed in the charter. Its lost profits are based on the difference between the charter and subcharter rates.

Swiss Bank impleaded Continental Bank as a third-party defendant, asking that if it should be ordered to pay Hyman–Michaels, then Continental should be ordered to indemnify it. Continental filed a cross-claim against Hyman–Michaels seeking to shift back to Hyman–Michaels the cost of any judgment that Swiss Bank might obtain against it, on the ground that any errors by Continental were caused by Hyman–Michaels' negligence. Hyman–Michaels in turn counterclaimed against Continental, alleging that Continental had both been negligent and broken its contract with Hyman–Michaels in failing to effect payment on April 26, and was therefore liable to Hyman–Michaels along with Swiss Bank.

The case was tried to a district judge without a jury. In his decision, 522 F.Supp. 820 (N.D.Ill.1981), he first ruled that the substantive law applicable to Hyman–Michaels' claim against Swiss Bank was that of Illinois, rather than Switzerland as urged by Swiss Bank, and that Swiss Bank had been negligent and under Illinois law was liable to Hyman–Michaels for $2.1 million in damages. This figure was made up of about $16,000 in arbitration expenses and the rest in lost profits on the subcharter of the *Pandora*. The judge also ruled that Swiss Bank was not entitled to indemnification from Continental Bank, which made Continental's cross-claim moot; and lastly he dismissed Hyman–Michaels' counterclaim against Continental on the ground that Continental had not breached any duty to Hyman–Michaels. The case comes to us on Swiss Bank's appeal from the judgment in favor of Hyman–Michaels and from the dismissal of Swiss Bank's claim against Continental Bank, and on Hyman–Michaels' appeal from the dismissal of its counterclaim against Continental Bank.

Logically the first question we should address is choice of law. The parties seem agreed that if Swiss law applies, Hyman–Michaels has no claim against Swiss Bank, because under Swiss law a bank cannot be held liable to someone with whom it is not in privity of contract and there was no contract between Swiss Bank and Hyman–Michaels. Illinois does not have such a privity requirement. But this creates a conflict of laws only if Hyman–Michaels has a good claim against Swiss Bank under Illinois law; if it does not, then our result must be the same regardless of which law applies. Because we are more certain that Hyman–Michaels cannot recover against Swiss Bank under Illinois law than we are that Swiss rather than Illinois law applies to this case under Illinois choice-of-law principles (which we must apply in a diversity suit tried in Illinois, see Klaxon Co. v. Stentor Elec. Mfg. Co., 313 U.S. 487, 496–97, 61 S.Ct. 1020, 1021–22, 85 L.Ed. 1477 (1941)), we shall avoid the choice-of-law question and discuss Swiss Bank's liability to Hyman–Michaels under Illinois law without deciding—for, to repeat, it would make no difference to the outcome—whether it really is Illinois law or Swiss law that governs.

When a bank fails to make a requested transfer of funds, this can cause two kinds of loss. First, the funds themselves or interest on them may be lost, and of course the fee paid for the transfer, having bought nothing, becomes a loss item. These are "direct" (sometimes called "general") damages. Hyman–Michaels is not seeking any direct damages in this case and apparently sustained none. It did not lose any part of the $27,000; although its account with Continental Bank was debited by this amount prematurely, it was not an interest-bearing account so Hyman–Michaels lost no interest; and Hyman–Michaels paid no fee either to Continental or to Swiss Bank for the aborted transfer. A second type of loss, which either the payor or the payee may suffer, is a dislocation in one's business triggered by the failure to pay. Swiss Bank's failure to transfer funds to the Banque de Paris when requested to do so by Continental Bank set off a chain reaction which resulted in an arbitration proceeding that was costly to Hyman–Michaels and in the cancellation of a highly profitable contract. It is those costs and lost profits—"consequential" or, as they are sometimes called, "special" damages—that Hyman–Michaels seeks in this lawsuit, and recovered below. It is conceded that if Hyman–Michaels was entitled to consequential damages, the district court measured them correctly. The only issue is whether it was entitled to consequential damages.

If a bank loses a check, its liability is governed by Article 4 of the Uniform Commercial Code, which precludes consequential damages unless the bank is acting in bad faith. See Ill.Rev.Stat. ch. 26, § 4–103(5). If Article 4 applies to this transaction, Hyman–Michaels cannot recover the damages that it seeks, because Swiss Bank was not acting in bad faith. Maybe the language of Article 4 could be stretched to include electronic fund transfers, see section 4–102(2), but they were not in the contemplation of the draftsmen. For purposes of this case we shall assume, as the Second Circuit held in Delbrueck & Co. v. Manufacturers Hanover Trust Co., 609 F.2d 1047, 1051 (2d Cir.1979), that Article 4 is inapplicable, and apply common law principles instead.

Hadley v. Baxendale, 9 Ex. 341, 156 Eng.Rep. 145 (1854), is the leading common law case on liability for consequential damages caused by failure or delay in carrying out a commercial undertaking. The engine shaft in plaintiffs' corn mill had broken and they hired the defendants, a common carrier, to transport the shaft to the manufacturer, who was to make a new one using the broken shaft as a model. The carrier failed to deliver the shaft within the time promised. With the engine shaft out of service the mill was shut down. The plaintiffs sued the defendants for the lost profits of the mill during the additional period that it was shut down because of the defendants' breach of their promise. The court held that the lost profits were not a proper item of damages, because "in the great multitude of cases of millers sending off broken shafts to third persons by a carrier under ordinary circumstances, such consequences [the stoppage of the mill and resulting loss of profits] would not, in all probability, have occurred; and these special circumstances were here never communicated by the plaintiffs to the defendants." 9 Ex. at 356, 156 Eng.Rep. at 151.

The rule of Hadley v. Baxendale—that consequential damages will not be awarded unless the defendant was put on notice of the special circumstances giving rise to them—has been applied in many Illinois cases, and *Hadley* cited approvingly. See, e.g., Underground Constr. Co. v. Sanitary Dist. of Chicago, 367 Ill. 360, 369, 11 N.E.2d 361, 365 (1937); Western Union Tel. Co. v. Martin, 9 Ill.App. 587, 591–93 (1882); Siegel v. Western Union Tel. Co., 312 Ill.App. 86, 92–93, 37 N.E.2d 868, 871 (1941); Spangler v. Holthusen, 61 Ill.App.3d 74, 80–82, 18 Ill.Dec. 840, 378 N.E.2d 304, 309–10 (1978). In *Siegel,* the plaintiff had delivered $200 to Western Union with instructions to transmit it to a friend of the plaintiff's. The money was to be bet (legally) on a horse, but this was not disclosed in the instructions. Western Union misdirected the money order and it did not reach the friend until several hours after the race had taken place. The horse that the plaintiff had intended to bet on won and would have paid $1650 on the plaintiff's $200 bet if the bet had been placed. He sued Western Union for his $1450 lost profit, but the court held that under the rule of Hadley v. Baxendale Western Union was not liable, because it "had no notice or knowledge of the purpose for which the money was being transmitted." 312 Ill.App. at 93, 37 N.E.2d at 871.

The present case is similar, though Swiss Bank knew more than Western Union knew in *Siegel*; it knew or should have known, from Continental Bank's previous telexes, that Hyman–Michaels was paying the Pandora Shipping Company for the hire of a motor vessel named *Pandora*. But it did not know when payment was due, what the terms of the charter were, or that they had turned out to be extremely favorable to Hyman–Michaels. And it did not know that Hyman–Michaels knew the *Pandora*'s owner would try to cancel the charter, and probably would succeed, if Hyman–Michaels was ever again late in making payment, or that despite this peril Hyman–Michaels would not try to pay until the last possible moment and in the event of a delay in transmission would not do everything in its power to minimize the consequences of the delay. Electronic funds transfers are not so unusual as to automatically place a bank on notice of extraordinary consequences if such a transfer goes awry. Swiss Bank did not have enough information to infer that if it lost a $27,000 payment order it would face a liability in excess of $2 million. * * *

It is true that in both *Hadley* and *Siegel* there was a contract between the parties and here there was none. We cannot be certain that the Illinois courts would apply the principles of those cases outside of the contract area. * * *The district judge found that Swiss Bank had been negligent in losing Continental Bank's telex message and it can be argued that Swiss Bank should therefore be liable for a broader set of consequences than if it had only broken a contract. But *Siegel* implicitly rejects this distinction. Western Union had not merely broken its contract to deliver the plaintiff's money order; it had "negligently misdirected" the money order. "The company's negligence is conceded." 312 Ill.App. at 88, 91, 37 N.E.2d at 869, 871. Yet it was not liable for the consequences.

Siegel, we conclude, is authority for holding that Swiss Bank is not liable for the consequences of negligently failing to transfer Hyman–Michaels' funds to Banque de Paris; reason for such a holding is found in the animating principle of Hadley v. Baxendale, which is that the costs of the untoward consequence of a course of dealings should be borne by that party who was able to avert the consequence at least cost and failed to do so. In *Hadley* the untoward consequence was the shutting down of the mill. The carrier could have avoided it by delivering the engine shaft on time. But the mill owners, as the court noted, could have avoided it simply by having a spare shaft. 9 Ex. at 355–56, 156 Eng.Rep. at 151. Prudence required that they have a spare shaft anyway, since a replacement could not be obtained at once even if there was no undue delay in carting the broken shaft to and the replacement shaft from the manufacturer. The court refused to imply a duty on the part of the carrier to guarantee the mill owners against the consequences of their own lack of prudence, though of course if the parties had stipulated for such a guarantee the court would have enforced it. The notice requirement of Hadley v. Baxendale is designed to assure that such an improbable guarantee really is intended.

This case is much the same, though it arises in a tort rather than a contract setting. Hyman–Michaels showed a lack of prudence throughout. It was imprudent for it to mail in Chicago a letter that unless received the next day in Geneva would put Hyman–Michaels in breach of a contract that was very profitable to it and that the other party to the contract had every interest in canceling. It was imprudent thereafter for Hyman–Michaels, having narrowly avoided cancellation and having (in the words of its appeal brief in this court) been "put ... on notice that the payment provision of the Charter would be strictly enforced thereafter," to wait till arguably the last day before payment was due to instruct its bank to transfer the necessary funds overseas. And it was imprudent in the last degree for Hyman–Michaels, when it received notice of cancellation on the last possible day payment was due, to fail to pull out all the stops to get payment to the Banque de Paris on that day, and instead to dither while Continental and Swiss Bank wasted five days looking for the lost telex message. Judging from the obvious reluctance with which the arbitration panel finally decided to allow the *Pandora*'s owner to cancel the charter, it might have made all the difference if Hyman–Michaels had gotten payment to the Banque de Paris by April 27 or even by Monday, April 30, rather than allowed things to slide until May 2.

This is not to condone the sloppy handling of incoming telex messages in Swiss Bank's foreign department. But Hyman–Michaels is a sophisticated business enterprise. It knew or should have known that even the Swiss are not infallible; that messages sometimes get lost or delayed in transit among three banks, two of them located 5000 miles apart, even when all the banks are using reasonable care; and that therefore it should take its own precautions against the consequences—best known to itself—of a mishap that might not be due to anyone's negligence.

We are not the first to remark the affinity between the rule of Hadley v. Baxendale and the doctrine, which is one of tort as well as contract law and is a settled part of the common law of Illinois, of avoidable consequences. See Dobbs, Handbook on the Law of Remedies 831 (1973); cf. Benton v. J.A. Fay & Co., 64 Ill. 417 (1872). If you are hurt in an automobile accident and unreasonably fail to seek medical treatment, the injurer, even if negligent, will not be held liable for the aggravation of the injury due to your own unreasonable behavior after the accident. See, e.g., Slater v. Chicago Transit Auth., 5 Ill.App.2d 181, 185, 125 N.E.2d 289, 291 (1955). If in addition you failed to fasten your seat belt, you may be barred from collecting the tort damages that would have been prevented if you had done so. See, e.g., Mount v. McClellan, 91 Ill.App.2d 1, 5, 234 N.E.2d 329, 331 (1968). Hyman–Michaels' behavior in steering close to the wind prior to April 27 was like not fastening one's seat belt; its failure on April 27 to wire a duplicate payment immediately after disaster struck was like refusing to seek medical attention after a serious accident. The seat-belt cases show that the doctrine of avoidable consequences applies whether the tort victim acts imprudently before or after the tort is committed. See Prosser, Handbook of the Law of Torts 424 (4th ed. 1971). Hyman–Michaels did both.

The rule of Hadley v. Baxendale links up with tort concepts in another way. The rule is sometimes stated in the form that only foreseeable damages are recoverable in a breach of contract action. E.g., Restatement (Second) of Contracts § 351 (1979). So expressed, it corresponds to the tort principle that limits liability to the foreseeable consequence of the defendant's carelessness. * * * The amount of care that a person ought to take is a function of the probability and magnitude of the harm that may occur if he does not take care. * * * If he does not know what that probability and magnitude are, he cannot determine how much care to take. That would be Swiss Bank's dilemma if it were liable for consequential damages from failing to carry out payment orders in timely fashion. To estimate the extent of its probable liability in order to know how many and how elaborate fail-safe features to install in its telex rooms or how much insurance to buy against the inevitable failures, Swiss Bank would have to collect reams of information about firms that are not even its regular customers. It had no banking relationship with Hyman–Michaels. It did not know or have reason to know how at once precious and fragile Hyman–Michaels' contract with the *Pandora*'s owner was. These were circumstances too remote from Swiss Bank's practical range of knowledge to have affected its decisions as to who should man the telex machines in the foreign department or whether it should have more intelligent machines or should install more machines in the cable department, any more than the falling of a platform scale because a conductor jostled a passenger who was carrying fireworks was a prospect that could have influenced the amount of care taken by the Long Island Railroad. See Palsgraf v. Long Island R.R.,

248 N.Y. 339, 162 N.E. 99 (1928); cf. Ney v. Yellow Cab Co., 2 Ill.2d 74, 80–84, 117 N.E.2d 74, 78–80 (1954).

In short, Swiss Bank was not required in the absence of a contractual undertaking to take precautions or insure against a harm that it could not measure but that was known with precision to Hyman–Michaels, which could by the exercise of common prudence have averted it completely. As Chief Judge Cardozo (the author of *Palsgraf*) remarked in discussing the application of Hadley v. Baxendale to the liability of telegraph companies for errors in transmission, "The sender can protect himself by insurance in one form or another if the risk of nondelivery or error appears to be too great. * * * The company, if it takes out insurance for itself, can do no more than guess at the loss to be avoided." Kerr S.S. Co. v. Radio Corp. of America, 245 N.Y. 284, 291–92, 157 N.E. 140, 142 (1927).

* * *

The legal principles that we have said are applicable to this case were not applied below. Although the district judge's opinion is not entirely clear, he apparently thought the rule of Hadley v. Baxendale inapplicable and the imprudence of Hyman–Michaels irrelevant. See 522 F.Supp. at 833. He did state that the damages to Hyman–Michaels were foreseeable because "a major international bank" should know that a failure to act promptly on a telexed request to transfer funds could cause substantial damage; but *Siegel*—and for that matter [other cases discussed in omitted portion of opinion]—make clear that that kind of general foreseeability, which is present in virtually every case, does not justify an award of consequential damages.

We could remand for new findings based on the proper legal standard, but it is unnecessary to do so. The undisputed facts, recited in this opinion, show as a matter of law that Hyman–Michaels is not entitled to recover consequential damages from Swiss Bank.

Since Hyman–Michaels' complaint against Swiss Bank must be dismissed, Swiss Bank's third-party complaint against Continental Bank and Continental Bank's cross-claim against Hyman–Michaels are moot. That leaves only Hyman–Michaels' counterclaim against Continental Bank still to be considered.

* * *

On the merits, we agree with the district judge that Hyman–Michaels did not prove its case. Continental did not break any contract with Hyman–Michaels. All it undertook to do on April 25 was to transmit a telex message to Swiss Bank, and it did so. All it undertook to do on April 27, by the evidence of Hyman–Michaels' own confirming letter, was to advise its correspondent—that is, Swiss Bank—to "persist in attempting to make * * * payment," and it did so advise its correspondent. Nor was Continental negligent on either occasion. Its telex operator had used the machine in Swiss Bank's foreign department before, for the same purpose and without incident; he had no reason to expect a mishap. And Continental used due care in assisting Swiss Bank in the latter's vain hunt for the missing telex. The district court's findings on these issues were skimpy but the facts are clear and a remand is unnecessary.

No other issues need be decided. The judgment in favor of Hyman–Michaels against Swiss Bank is reversed with directions to enter judgment for Swiss Bank. The judgment in favor of Continental Bank on Swiss Bank's third-party complaint is vacated with instructions to dismiss that complaint as moot. The judgment dismissing Continental's cross-claim against Hyman–Michaels as moot, and the judgment in favor of Continental on Hyman–Michaels' counterclaim, are affirmed. The costs of the appeals shall be borne by Hyman–Michaels (Evra Corporation).

5.   FRAUDULENT PAYMENT ORDERS

A wire transfer is a very efficient method of payment. Large amounts can be transferred in a short time at low cost. But this great efficiency also provides a highly efficient method for the theft of money. The thief might steal funds in a bank account by fraudulently inducing either the bank or the owner of the account to make a wire transfer of the funds to an account controlled by the thief in some other bank. For example, the thief might electronically transmit to the bank a payment order purporting to be that of the owner of the account. If the bank is unaware that its customer did not send the order, the fraud can succeed. If the bank executes the fraudulent payment order, it has transferred funds on behalf of the customer without authority of the customer to do so. Who takes the loss? Has the thief stolen funds of the customer or funds of the bank? Under Article 4A a receiving bank that executes a payment order is not acting as the agent of the sender. § 4A–212. But if the bank executes an order that it believes to be the order of its customer but which in fact was issued by a person not authorized to act for its customer, should the law of agency determine whether the customer is bound by the unauthorized payment order issued in its name? If agency law applies, the customer is not bound by the unauthorized order, the bank has no authority to debit the customer's account and the bank takes the loss.

But the law of agency is not very useful in determining whether the risk of loss with respect to an unauthorized payment order transmitted electronically should fall upon the receiving bank's customer, the purported sender of the fraudulent payment order, or the receiving bank that accepted it. The agency doctrines of actual, implied, and apparent authority grew out of cases in which the person purporting to be the agent and the third party acting in reliance on the acts of the purported agent have some personal contact with each other. These doctrines do not work well in cases in which a commercial transaction normally is carried out in the name of a principal by a person who is anonymous and who has no direct contact with the third person. In the case of electronic transmission of a payment order, the receiving bank is acting on the basis of a message that appears on a computer screen. There is no way of determining the identity or authority of the person who caused the message to be sent. The receiving bank is not relying on the authority of any particular person to act for its customer. Instead, the receiving bank relies on a security procedure pursuant to which the authenticity of the message can be "tested" by various devices such as identification codes or other security information in the control of the customer designed to provide certainty that the message is that of the customer identified in the payment order as its sender.

In the wire transfer business, the concept of "authorized" is different from the concept found in agency law. A payment order is treated as the order of the person in whose name it is issued if it is properly tested pursuant to a security procedure and the order passes the test. Risk of loss rules regarding unauthorized payment orders with respect to which verification pursuant to a security procedure is in effect are stated in § 4A–202 and § 4A–203. The general rule is that a payment order is effective as the order of the customer, whether or not authorized, if the security procedure is commercially reasonable and the receiving bank proves that it accepted the order in good faith after verifying the order in compliance with the security procedure. There are certain exceptions and qualifications to this rule that are explained in the Comment to § 4A–203. The general rule is based on the assumption that losses due to unauthorized payment orders can best be avoided by the use of commercially reasonable security procedures, and that the use of such procedures should be encouraged. If a commercially reasonable security procedure is not in effect or if the bank fails to comply with a commercially reasonable procedure, ordinary rules of agency apply with the effect that, if the payment order was not authorized by the customer, the receiving bank acts at its peril in accepting the order.

The Article 4A rules are designed to protect both the customer and the receiving bank. A receiving bank needs to be able to rely on objective criteria to determine whether it can safely act on a payment order. Employees of that bank can be trained to "test" a payment order according to the various steps specified in the security procedure. The bank is responsible for the acts of these employees. The interests of the customer are protected by providing an incentive to a receiving bank to make available to the customer a security procedure that is commercially reasonable. Prudent banking practice may require that security procedures be utilized with respect to virtually all payment orders, except for those in which personal contact between the customer and the bank eliminates the possibility of an unauthorized order. The burden of making available commercially reasonable security procedures is imposed on receiving banks because generally they determine what security procedures can be used and are in the best position to evaluate the efficacy of procedures offered to customers to combat fraud. The burden on the customer is to supervise its employees to assure compliance with the security procedure, to safeguard confidential security information, and to restrict access to transmitting facilities so that the security procedure cannot be breached.

Sections 4A–202 and 4A–203 were among the most contentious provisions in the drafting of Article 4A. Customers strongly believed that they should not be liable for unauthorized funds transfers; the banks control the security procedures and if a fraudulent payment order penetrates the security controls the bank should bear the loss. Bank representatives were just as firm in their belief that they could not transfer trillions of dollars a day all over the world at great speed in a highly automated process if they had to be concerned about whether the customer had actually authorized the payment order; if the payment order "tests," that is, meets their security procedures, they should be able to send the order without fear of liability. Sections 4A–202 and 4A–203 represent a compromise solution which satisfied neither side. Each time the authorization issue was discussed, customer representatives brought up the possibility that a brilliant hacker might crack even the most sophisticated security procedure and pull off the world's biggest bank robbery at the expense of the customer. Bankers said that it was tried every day and just couldn't be done. Maybe they were wrong.

PROBLEM

Under the heading "Cyber Caper," the Wall Street Journal reported that a 28–year-old Russian biochemistry grad student, "Vova," who worked for a trading company in St. Petersburg, broke into Citicorp's computers on Wall Street and, over a period of months, transferred about $12 million from customer's accounts to banks in Finland, Israel, Netherlands, San Francisco and Switzerland, where his confederates attempted to withdraw the funds. They succeeded in getting $400,000 out before the accounts were traced and frozen. Since, according to the Journal article, Citicorp moves about $500 billion a day in funds transfers, Vova seemed almost restrained in his thievery. Customers of Citicorp in Buenos Aires and Jakarta were shocked to see that unauthorized transfers were being made from their accounts before their very eyes. In order to get into Citicorp's computers, Vova had to penetrate a security system so sophisticated that industry experts said what he did was "almost impossible." William M. Carley and Timothy L. O'Brien, How Citicorp System Was Raided and Funds Moved Around the World, Wall St.J., September 12, 1995, p.A1. As between the customers whose accounts were charged and Citicorp, where would §§ 4A–202 and 4A–203 throw the loss in the Cyber Caper case?

In the Problem that we have just examined, the dispute was between a bank customer, the purported originator of a funds transfer, and the originator's bank that executed the unauthorized order. *Bradford Trust,* the case that follows, raises a different issue and a more complex type of fraud. Bradford, as transfer agent for a mutual fund, sent a payment order to State Street, which in turn sent a payment order to Texas American, the beneficiary's bank. Bradford issued its payment order to carry out instructions given by an impostor who impersonated Rochefort, a customer of the mutual fund, who owned the funds that Bradford's payment order was intended to transfer. Bradford conceded that it was not entitled to reimbursement from either the mutual fund or Rochefort. Rather, Bradford was attempting to shift the loss to Texas American, the beneficiary's bank. The fraud in *Bradford Trust* was made possible because the identity of the beneficiary of the fraudulent payment order was disguised. The beneficiary was described in the payment order by a name which identified one person, Rochefort, and a bank account number that identified another person, Colonial. The beneficiary's bank paid Colonial rather than Rochefort. *Bradford Trust* was decided before Article 4A was drafted and the court used principles of fault based on negligence to allocate the loss. Article 4A follows a different approach. If the case had arisen under Article 4A, § 4A–207(b)(1), (c), and (d) would have governed. Under Article 4A, would Bradford have been entitled to recover the payment from either Texas American or Colonial? Comment 2 to § 4A–207.

Bradford Trust Co. v. Texas American Bank

United States Court of Appeals, Fifth Circuit, 1986.
790 F.2d 407.

■ W. EUGENE DAVIS, CIRCUIT JUDGE:

This diversity case presents the question of who should bear the loss flowing from a fraudulently induced $800,000 wire transfer. We must choose between the institution that honored the forged order of its customer to wire funds and the bank to whom the funds were wired which did not credit the account as directed. On cross-motions for summary judgment the district court applied the Texas comparative negligence statute * * * and apportioned the loss equally between the two parties. Both parties appeal and argue that the other party should bear the entire loss. We decline to apply comparative negligence principles and reverse the judgment of the district court. We conclude that the initial bank that honored the forged order must bear the entire loss.

I.

In an ingenious scheme, two con artists, using aliases of Hank and Dave Friedman, arranged to buy rare coins and gold bullion from Colonial Coins, Inc. (Colonial) in Houston for $800,000. The impostors informed Colonial that they would wire funds from their bank in Boston to Colonial's account at Texas American Bank—Houston N.A. (Texas American) to pay for the coins. Colonial agreed and gave the Friedmans its account number at Texas American.

The impostors next sent a forged letter and stock power to Bradford Trust Company (Bradford), the agent for a mutual fund, directing the liquidation of $800,000 from the mutual fund account of Frank Rochefort. The forged order also instructed Bradford to wire the $800,000 from this account to Colonial's account in Texas American in Houston. Bradford, without following internal procedures recently instituted because of a similar scam,[3] ordered its correspondent bank, State Street Bank of Boston (State Street) to wire the funds to Texas American. The text of the transfer included the number of Colonial's account at Texas American, but stated that it was for the account of Frank S. Rochefort.[4] When the funds were received, Texas American notified Colonial that the funds had been deposited into Colonial's account. With this assurance, Colonial released the coins to the impostors.

Bradford became aware of the scam when an astonished Rochefort received notice of the withdrawal and informed Bradford that he had not authorized it. Bradford reinstated Rochefort's account and demanded that Texas American and Colonial reimburse it. Texas American and Colonial refused and this lawsuit followed. Bradford compromised its claim against Colonial, which was dismissed from the litigation. The district court, on summary judgment, applied the Texas comparative negligence statute and divided the loss equally between Bradford and Texas American. Bradford appeals, contending that Texas American should bear the entire loss because its negligence in failing to follow Bradford's order to deposit the funds in Rochefort's account was the primary cause of the loss. Texas American cross-appeals, arguing that Bradford should suffer the entire loss because Bradford dealt with the impostor, honored the forged order to pay and hence was in the best position to prevent the loss.

II.

* * *

B.

Having decided that the Texas comparative negligence statute does not apply to this case, we widen our search for Texas law that does apply. Unfortunately, we have found no direct authority that resolves the question. * * * Other courts faced with resolving controversies relating to wire transfers have applied the UCC by analogy. * * * Because of the close analogy between allocation of fraud losses in negotiable instruments and wire transfers we look to both Texas court decisions before Texas adopted the UCC and the UCC for guidance. Two factors emerge from these sources that are helpful in analyzing the question of who should bear the loss in this case: 1) which party was in the best position to avoid the loss; and 2) which solution promotes the policy of finality in commercial transactions?

The first factor, which party is in the best position to avoid the loss, is a principal reason underlying a number of loss allocation calls in the UCC.

3. In April of 1980, Bradford was the victim of a similar fraudulent scheme. As a result, new security procedures were instituted. For transactions over $100,000, the new procedures required thorough review of the documents, shareholder confirmation when the shareholder instructed Bradford to wire the money to a person or to an address other than that on record, and approval by senior management.

4. The wire transfer stated: "State Street Bos/Michealpiemont MCMT 5207 X 6386 Southern Hou/A/O/Frank S. Rochnefort, Jr. Acct. * 057 141." (Note that Rochefort was misspelled.)

For example, it provides the essential reason for requiring the drawee bank to bear the loss if it pays on the drawer's forged signature. * * * This is because the bank, which can verify its customer's signature, is in the best position to discover the forgery and avoid the loss. Similarly, if an endorsement on an instrument is forged, the loss is ordinarily placed on the party in the collection chain who accepted the instrument from the forger. * * * Again, the UCC recognizes that the party dealing directly with the forger has an opportunity to verify the endorser's identity and is in the best position to avoid the loss. Indeed, the common thread running through the impostor cases is to "throw the loss resulting from dealing with an impostor on the person who dealt with the impostor, and presumably, had the best opportunity to take precautions that would have detected the fraud, rather than on a subsequent holder, who had no similar opportunity." Fair Park National Bank v. Southwestern Investment Co., 541 S.W.2d 266, 269–70 (Tex.Civ.App.1976).

Bradford dealt directly with the impostor. It received the forged order directing the liquidation of Rochefort's account. If Bradford had followed procedures it had in place that called for verification of the customer's order, the loss would not have occurred. Instead of following those procedures and verifying Rochefort's order, Bradford set the fraudulent scheme into motion by liquidating Rochefort's account and wiring the funds to Texas American. Although Texas American should have recognized the discrepancy between the account number and the name of the owner of the account to whom the wire directed the funds be credited, we are persuaded that Texas American's fault was secondary to that of Bradford's. It is far from certain that the loss would have been prevented even if Texas American had noticed the discrepancy between the account number and the holder of the account and had called this discrepancy to Bradford's attention. To conclude that this action by Texas American would have avoided the loss requires us to assume that such a call to Bradford would have caused Bradford to contact Rochefort and verify his order. On the other hand, it is certain that if Bradford had called Rochefort to verify his purported order to transfer funds to Colonial this scheme would have been discovered and no loss would have been suffered.

* * *

For the reasons set forth above, we are persuaded that Bradford, by honoring the forged order to transmit Rochefort's funds after dealing directly with the impostor, was in the best position to avoid the loss.

* * *

C.

Bradford urges us to find that Texas American's failure to follow Bradford's instructions in the wire transfer was the primary, overriding cause of the loss. Bradford argues that its earlier negligence in accepting the forged order of Rochefort to pay would have been inconsequential had Texas American handled the transfer with due care and in accordance with ordinary standards and practices of the banking industry. We agree with Bradford that Texas American was negligent in failing to notice the discrepancy between the account number and the name of the owner of the account to which the funds were to be credited. Even if allocation of the loss depended entirely upon a determination of which party was more at fault, however, this would not alter our decision to lay the loss at Bradford's feet. We are persuaded that Bradford's act in honoring the forged authorization without following its own internal procedures to verify the genuineness of the request was the primary cause of the loss. The fault of Texas American failing to note the discrepancy between the account number and the name of the owner of the account to whom the money was to be credited was less grave than that of Bradford.

* * * For the reasons stated above, despite the negligence of Texas American, we conclude that Bradford must bear the loss. Accordingly, the judgment of the district court is reversed and the action is remanded to the district court for entry of judgment in favor of Texas American and against Bradford.

6. AUTOMATED CLEARING HOUSE (ACH)

a. CONSUMER TRANSFERS

A lower cost, somewhat slower manner of making electronic payments is through an automated clearing house (ACH), a method widely used used to transfer money to or from consumer bank accounts. These transfers may be either credit or debit transfers. The difference between the two is discussed in Comment 4 to § 4A–104. In a credit transfer the instruction to pay is given by the person making the payment, as is the case in Article 4a transfers. In a debit transfer the instruction to pay is made by the person receiving payment. An example of a credit transfer is one in which an employer pays its employees by direct deposit to their bank accounts. Suppose its employees have accounts in ten banks in the area. In such a case, the employer will prepare a magnetic tape or or other electronic device with information concerning the bank accounts of each employee in which a deposit is to be made. This tape will go to the employer's bank which electronically forwards the information on the tape to an ACH facility in the area. The ACH performs its clearing house function by repackaging this information on a tape for each bank in which the employees have accounts which it forwards electronically to these banks. ACH allows the party initiating the transfer to time the dates when the payments will be credited to the employees' accounts by their banks and when the debits will be made to the originator's account in its bank. After the ACH has determined the net balances between the employer's bank and the employees' banks, these banks will settle through the Federal Reserve System. Numerous government payments, like social security and other benefits and pensions are made in this manner.

Equally common is the debit transaction. An example is one in which the debtor authorizes its creditor to draw each month on its bank account to make its monthly mortgage payments. The mortgage company (mortgagee) will prepare a tape or other electronic device giving information on all mortgagors whose payments are due on a given date and give this tape to its bank. The bank will forward the tape electronically to an ACH that will prepare new tapes for each bank in which mortgagors have accounts. The ACH will forward the new tapes electronically to each of these banks which will debit the mortgagors' accounts on the prescribed date. The mortgagee's bank will credit the mortgagee's account on that date and settlement between the banks will be made through the Federal Reserve System. Insurance premiums, and other recurring payments, are frequently made in this manner.

The operational details of the ACH system are discussed in Donald I. Baker & Roland E. Brandel, The Law of Electronic Fund Transfer Systems, Chapter 3 (1988, Cum.Supp.1995); James V. Vergari & Virginia V. Shue, Fundamentals of Computer High Technology Law 463–472 (1991), and Clark & Clark, The Law of Bank Deposits, Check Collections and Credit Cards ¶ 2.03.[1] and ¶ 6.04 (Rev.ed.1995). There are some 40 ACHs in the nation, most of which are operated by the Fed, and these have over 14,000 financial institutions as members. These ACHs are used by over 20,000 participating financial institutions. Clark & Clark, supra. In 1993 the ACH system processed over $9 trillion in transfers, including direct deposits of payrolls, pensions and annuities, as well as preauthorized bill payments and corporation-to-corporation payments. Scott E. Knudson, Jack K Walton, Jr., and Florence M. Young, Business-to-Business Payments and the Role of Financial Electronic Data Interchange, 80 Federal Reserve Bulletin 269 (1994). The ACH trade association is the National Automated Clearinghouse Association (NACHA) which prescribes operating rules for ACH transfers. White & Summers, Uniform Commercial Code § 22–2 (4th prac.ed.1995), discusses the intricacies of what law governs ACH payments and concludes that for all practical purposes the NACHA rules effectively do so. Clark & Clark, supra, concurs.

b.   COMMERCIAL PAYMENTS

At the beginning of this Chapter we referred to an article by Fred R. Bleakley, Electronic Payments Now Supplant Checks at More Large Firms, April 13, 1994, p.A1, to show how burdensome it is for banks to manage the vast bulk of checks that must be cleared each day. The point of this article was that major corporations are moving to electronic payments to avoid having to use checks. The usual method employed by these corporations to pay their bills electronically to suppliers and governmental units is by ACH payments. One executive is quoted as saying: "We want computers talking to computers." Since ACH is a value-dated system, cash managers can plan the exact date payments will be credited to their payees' accounts and debited to their own accounts, and this knowledge allows them to utilize their funds more efficiently.

The use of ACH to pay bills is similar in concept to Fedwire and Chips payments in that, for the most part, these business-to-business payments are credit transfers. But there are important differences. Fedwire and Chips are "big dollar" wholesale wire transfers that can often give same-day service. In 1993, $262.2 trillion was sent over Chips and $207.6 trillion was sent over Fedwire. Knudsen, et al., supra, 271. By 1996, the Wall Street Journal reported that Fedwire was transferring $1.5 trillion each day. John R. Wilke, Fed's Huge Empire, Set Up Years Ago, Is Costly and Inefficient, Wall St.J., September 12, 1996, p.A1. Although many more transfers are made by ACH, the amount of money sent, as indicated above, is much less. Credit transfers over ACH between businesses are nominally covered by Article 4A, but § 4A–501(b) effectively cedes governance to the NACHA rules.

Not only do businesses wish to send payments electronically, they also seek means of transmitting the documents relating to the transaction for which payment is made (invoices, and the like) by electronic means. Services outside the banking system which operate electronic data interchange (EDI) systems are meeting this need by use of uniform formats for various documents that can be transmitted electronically. ACH has made progress toward being able to send through the banking system both the payment instructions and the related documents to the suppliers or other parties who receive payment. Baker & Brandel, supra, ¶ 3.02[2][a][iv] (Cum.Supp.1995). This is sometimes referred to as "financial EDI." What we have now is two systems for sending payments and related documents. The more common is for the documents and the payments to go over separate systems, EDI and ACH. The other is for both documents and payments to go through ACH. These methods are explained in Knudsen, et al., supra, 271–275. Some giant corporations like GM are pressuring their suppliers to make the investment that is necessary to be able to receive electronic payments and documents. Observers predict rapid growth in this area.

C. CREDIT AND DEBIT CARDS

1. INTRODUCTION

a. CREDIT CARDS

Credit cards fall into two broad categories. In the first category are credit cards issued by a merchant as a means of identifying customers who have charge accounts with the merchant. They are particularly convenient for merchants who have numerous retail outlets located over a large geographical area. These cards originally could be used to make purchases only from the merchant that issued the card, but in some cases use of the card to purchase from a limited number of other merchants is also permitted. Included in this first category are cards issued by oil companies for use at affiliated or independently owned service stations that sell products of the company that issued the card. The most important characteristic of this category of credit card is that the primary purpose of the issuer is to facilitate sales of goods or services of the issuer.

A second category comprises credit cards issued by financial institutions that provide short-term credit, usually unsecured, to cardholders to allow them to make purchases from a multitude of merchants and other sellers of goods and services who are not related to the issuer of the card. Prominent examples of the second category are the Visa card, MasterCard, Discover card and the American Express card. This category of credit card has emerged as an important substitute for cash or a personal check in paying for goods or services. A merchant who accepts this type of credit card as the payment mechanism is party to a preexisting arrangement either directly with the issuer of the card or with an interbank system to which the issuer belongs, such as Visa or MasterCard. Pursuant to this arrangement the merchant can obtain payment from the issuer for purchases made by use of the card. In a face-to-face purchase, the cardholder signs a credit card slip indicating the amount of the purchase and containing the card number and other information taken from the card.

The merchant is faced with several risks in honoring a credit card. First, the person using the card may not be a person authorized to use the card. Second, the card may have been revoked by the issuer. One common reason for revocation is a report to the issuer that the card has been lost or stolen. Third, the amount of credit given by the issuer to the cardholder may not be sufficient to cover the amount of the purchase. The merchant can normally avoid the last two risks. At the time a purchase is to be made, the merchant can determine, through telephonic or electronic access to a computer center having a record of the card, whether the card is valid and whether the charge is within the cardholder's line of credit. Through this process the merchant obtains approval of the charge before the purchase is made and has assurance of receiving payment in accordance with the arrangement to which the issuer and merchant are parties. Normally the merchant receives the amount of the charge less a discount to compensate the issuer for financing the purchase. The issuer obtains this compensation by obtaining payment of the full amount of the charge from the cardholder. Thus, the credit risk of nonpayment by the cardholder is taken by the issuer. The issuer normally sends a monthly statement of charges to the cardholder. Under most plans, the cardholder has the option of paying the full amount by a specified date without an interest charge or of making payment in installments with an interest charge. Estimates are that the average American household carries a monthly balance of $4,000 in credit card debt, totalling $367 billion. Laurie Hays, Banks' Marketing Blitz Yields Rash of Defaults, Wall St.J., Sept. 25, 1996, p. B1.

The growth of credit cards issued by financial institutions has been phenomenal. The Bank of America first issued its BankAmericard in the 1950s. A consortium of banks formed an association to issue a competing card, MasterCharge, in 1960. The BankAmericard was later taken over by an association of banks and renamed the Visa card. MasterCharge became MasterCard. Today most American banks issue both cards. By 1995, of the $1.157 trillion charged on credit cards world-wide, $588.7 billion, was charged on Visa cards, giving it nearly 51% of the market. After Visa came MasterCard with 31%, American Express with 14%, and Discover with 6%.

Laurie Hays, No.1 Standing of Visa Could Be Impediment in the Debit Market, Wall St.J., June 6, 1996, p.B1.

Visa and MasterCard do not issue credit cards. They set up the network of participating banks and handle the clearing and settlement of credit card debts. The usual procedure is that a merchant, authorized to honor Visa cards or MasterCards, will present to a "merchant bank," a member of the Visa or MasterCard network, the credit card slips signed by cardholders at the time of purchase and receive immediate credit for the amount of the slips, less discount, in its account with the merchant bank. The merchant bank then sends the slips through the Visa or MasterCard clearing system to the various "issuing banks," which issued the credit cards to the cardholders. The issuing banks then transfer funds for the slips to the merchant bank through the credit card settlement process of Visa or MasterCard and bill the cardholders for their purchases. If the cardholder returns goods, the issuing bank credits the cardholder's account and charges back this amount against the merchant bank.

At first credit cards were restricted to middle or upper income groups, but over the years aggressive competition for market share led issuers to lower their credit standards with sometimes disastrous results. Direct mail solicitation with low six-month "teaser" rates of less that 6%, followed by much higher regular rates, became common, as did "preapproved" card offers. In 1995 banks mailed out an astonishing 2.7 billion preapproved credit card solicitations, 17 for each American in the 18–64 age bracket. Hays, Banks' Marketing Blitz Yields Rash of Defaults, supra. Horror stories emerged of bankrupts with ten or twelve credit cards, all hopelessly delinquent. The average household has about nine credit cards, three of which are all-purpose bank cards. Kathy M. Kristof, Banks Strongly Pushing 'Secured' Credit Cards, Los Angeles Times, August 21, 1994, p.D4. E.S. Browning, Bank Stocks Fall on Fears About Cards, Wall St.J., June 21, 1996, p.C1, reported that in the first quarter of 1996, a time of relatively high prosperity, banks that were big credit card issuers reported greatly increased percentages of credit card write-offs. In mid–1996 banks were writing off bad card loans at a 4.48% annual rate, the highest since the 1992 recession. John R. Wilke, Banks' Loan Write–Offs Rise Sharply With Bad Card Debts Playing Major Role, Wall St.J., September 12, 1996, p.A2. In dealing with these unacceptable losses, banks generally raised their credit standards and restricted direct mail advertising.

With respect to less creditworthy customers who cannot qualify for a regular credit card (bankrupts, people with bad payment records, and people with no credit history like young people, divorcees, widows and immigrants), an increasing number of banks offer secured credit cards. Kristof, supra. This practice usually requires these customers to maintain a balance in their account in the issuing bank and to limit the amount they can charge on the credit card to this balance. Clark & Clark, The Law of Bank Deposits, Check Collections and Credit Cards ¶ 15.13 (Rev.ed.1995). Some consumers use a successful experience with a secured credit card as a means of rehabilitating or establishing their credit rating, leading to ultimate issuance of an unsecured credit card. Citibank reports that 70% of its secured card customers "graduate" to an unsecured card. Kristof, supra.

b.   DEBIT CARDS

A working definition of the difference between a debit and a credit transfer is found in Comment 4 to § 4A–104: "In a credit transfer the instruction to pay is given by the person making the payment. In a debit transfer the instruction to pay is given by the person receiving the payment." Thus a debit transfer may be an order from a creditor, pursuant to authority from a debtor, to the debtor's bank to pay the creditor. Article 4A does not cover debit wire transfers. § 4A–103(a)(1) ("payment order"). But several kinds of consumer debit transfers are covered by the Electronic Fund Transfer Act, 15 U.S.C. § 1693 et seq. Regulation E, which implements the EFTA, defines "electronic fund transfer" as including "all transfers resulting from debit card transactions, including those that do not involve an electronic terminal at the time of the transaction." 12 CFR § 205.2(g).

A common use of the debit card is in the point-of-sale (POS) transaction. The buyer pays for goods or services by using a plastic coded card, called an access or debit card, inserted into an electronic terminal on the merchant's premises which is linked to the merchant's bank and to the buyer's bank, usually by means of an interbank network. The debit card contains a machine readable identification of the buyer's bank account. When the card is inserted into the terminal, the amount of the transaction and the buyer's personal identification number (PIN) are also entered. The result is that the buyer's account is debited and the merchant's account is credited in that amount at the same time. For a variety of reasons, POS systems were slow in obtaining widespread acceptance after they were first introduced, but in recent years they have become increasingly popular and are emerging as an important alternative to checks and credit cards as a means of payment for goods and services. They are convenient for consumers and allow merchants to obtain immediate and irrevocable payment at the time of the sale. As the quoted language from Regulation E indicates, debit cards may also be used in transactions with merchants who do not maintain electronic terminals. The card authorizes the merchant to draw on the buyer's account in the issuing bank for the amount of the sale price. If the card used is a Visa card or MasterCard, the merchant sends the credit card slip through the interbank network to the issuing bank which immediately debits the cardholder's account, instead of billing the cardholder as is done for credit cards.

The most popular use of debit or access cards is with respect to the ubiquitous automated teller machine (ATM) system. These terminals are located in all manner of places convenient to customers: street corners, supermarkets, and, for safety, even in police stations. Their utility to customers is greatly enhanced by the fact that they are usually available for use around the clock. The customer can use the card and a PIN to make deposits and withdrawals from the customer's account in a bank or other financial institution. The cost of human teller-handled deposits and withdrawals is far more than the cost of deposits and withdrawals made by ATM.

In 1995, $46.84 billion in debit card purchases were made. It is no surprise that the leaders in the field are Visa and MasterCard, with their extensive bank networks. American Express, which does not enjoy such a bank network, is struggling to gain market share. Hays, supra, Wall St.J., June 6, 1996, B1.

2. FRAUDULENT USE OF LOST OR STOLEN CREDIT CARDS

a. ALLOCATION OF LOSS UNDER COMMON LAW

In *Sears,* the case that follows, the court discusses common law principles for allocation of loss when a lost credit card is fraudulently used to charge purchases of goods to the cardholder's account. *Sears* is one of the most favorable decisions to the issuer of the credit card, but many other courts, on one theory or another, imposed the loss on the issuer of the card. After the *Sears* case was decided liability of the cardholder for unauthorized use of the card was limited by Federal statute.

Sears, Roebuck & Co. v. Duke

Supreme Court of Texas, 1969.
441 S.W.2d 521.

■ REAVLEY, JUSTICE. Sears, Roebuck and Co. sued Waldo Duke for the price of merchandise sold to an impostor using the Sears credit card issued to Duke. The purchases were made within two weeks following Duke's loss of the card, and two weeks before either he or Sears had knowledge of its loss. After the jury absolved both parties of negligence, the trial court entered judgment for Sears. The Court of Civil Appeals ordered a new trial on the ground that Sears failed to offer sufficient proof of the exercise of care, on the occasion of each sale, to ascertain the identity of the credit card user. 433 S.W.2d 919. We hold that the Court of Civil Appeals imposed an incorrect duty on Sears, that Sears was entitled to rely upon the card alone as identification unless circumstances presented cause for further inquiry; and we remand the case to that court for reconsideration of points before it.

Duke and his wife lived in Lubbock, Texas and did business with the Sears store located there. In 1960 he signed a "Sears Revolving Charge Account Agreement" which began as follows:

"In consideration of your selling merchandise to me on Sears revolving Charge Account, I agree to the following regarding all purchases made by me or on my Sears revolving Charge Account identification * * * ".

Two credit cards were issued with the account number and the name, Waldo N. Duke, on the front of the cards. There is no question raised at any point in this record but that the credit cards were the Sears "identification" to which the credit agreement refers. No additional terms of agreement appear on the back of the card, but there is a statement saying that the card is the property of Sears and its loss or theft should be reported. Mrs. Duke signed as "authorized purchaser" and used one of the cards. The second card, unsigned, was carried by Duke with a number of other credit cards.

Duke was in New York on a business trip during the week of December 12, 1965, and he left his credit cards in a suitcase in his hotel room. Apparently the thief took the Sears card and a Sinclair Refining Company card, made a note of Duke's home address and signed "Waldo N. Duke" in his own handwriting on the Sears card. Presumably the card was taken December 13, and over $1,200 in merchandise was purchased in various Sears stores in the New York area within the following two weeks. On January 12, 1966, the credit department of the Sears store in Lubbock received notice of the unusual number of charges on the Duke account, and an inquiry was made to Mr. and Mrs. Duke. It was then that all of the parties first realized that the card was missing.

Duke has taken the position that he is not liable for the unauthorized use of his credit card, or for sales made by Sears to a stranger. There is no basis here for tort liability against Duke. The evidence clearly supports the findings of the jury to the effect that Duke was not negligent in the loss of his card or in the failure to report the loss to Sears. The jury has found that Duke was not negligent in failing to sign his card, and no point in that connection is presented to us. The question then is his contractual obligation, and this turns upon the construction of the words of the credit agreement set forth above. By that agreement Duke did more than promise to pay for merchandise he purchased. He promised to pay for "all purchases made on my Sears revolving Charge Account identification." The meaning we give to these words is that Duke will pay for *all* sales made by Sears to a purchaser identifying himself by the use of the credit card, which was issued by Sears upon receipt of the executed credit agreement.

Duke says that his obligation does not cover the sale to a person who is not in fact authorized to use the card or to make a purchase on Duke's credit. But this is precisely the purpose of this card: to satisfy the question of identity and of authorization. It is the reason why Duke was called upon to sign an agreement to pay not only for his purchases from Sears but for those made on the issued identification as well.

Duke further argues that if Sears wanted the agreement to have so drastic an effect as to bind him to pay for unauthorized purchases, Sears should have expressly so stated on either the agreement or the credit cards. We believe this to be the meaning of the agreement, and we do not regard this result to be so surprising in this credit card age. When Duke himself made a purchase and presented his credit card, he would not expect to be questioned. He should not expect the disguised thief to be.

The convenience of the credit card to both issuer and holder presents both with attendant risks. In general, and subject to contrary agreement by the parties, the one who can best control the risk should assume it. Thus, the issuer who puts a card into the mail without prior agreement with its intended holder should assume the larger part of the risk of improper use. After a holder accepts the card or agrees to pay for purchases made through its use, the risk of misuse is his unless and until he notifies the issuer otherwise. The holder can destroy his card if he feels that this is too great a burden. But if he is to carry it about, he must guard it as he does his currency if he is to avoid the expense of use by an impostor. If it is lost or stolen, by notifying the issuer, the holder shifts the risk of misuse back to the one who created the device. Texaco, Inc. v. Goldstein, 34 Misc.2d 751, 229 N.Y.S.2d 51 (N.Y.Mun.Ct.) aff'd 39 Misc.2d 552, 241 N.Y.S.2d 495 (App.Div., 1962).

The issuer of the card, or the seller of the goods, cannot ignore suspicious circumstances when selling to an impostor. The holder's liability has its limitations whether it be said that the issuer cannot avoid liability for his own negligence, or that the promise of the holder should be construed as being conditional upon the merchant's fulfillment of his obligation. See Comment: The Tripartite Credit Card Transaction: The Legal Infant, 48 Calif.L.R. 459, 483 (1960). In Gulf Refining Co. v. Williams Roofing Co., 208 Ark. 362, 186 S.W.2d 790, 158 A.L.R. 754 (1945), the holder of the card had printed "GOOD FOR TRUCK ONLY" on the face of the credit card. It was held that the seller was required to observe the limitation. In an often cited Oregon case, the address on the credit card of the holder was shown to be in Oregon, while Idaho license plates were on the car used by the impostor when the purchases were made. This was held to raise a fact question as to the seller's care. Union Oil Co. of California v. Lull, 220 Or. 412, 349 P.2d 243 (1960).

The cases differ as to the nature of the issuer-seller's duty of care, and as to the burden of proof. We hold that the seller need not demand more identification than the credit card as a matter of normal procedure. This is the function of the credit card, and it should be considered satisfactory evidence of identity of the holder or authorized user, unless the appearances or circumstances would raise a question in the mind of a reasonable seller. Proof that the seller did fail to use ordinary care in this respect is a defense to the liability of the holder of the card, and the burden of proof should be placed upon him.

The Court of Civil Appeals has ruled that the jury finding in favor of Sears, as to its care in ascertaining the identity and authority of the persons using the credit card, was not supported by sufficient evidence. However, that court has incorrectly placed the burden of proof upon Sears and has further enlarged the burden on Sears by holding that it could not discharge its duty of care by accepting the credit card as the only proof of identity. The judgment must therefore be reversed. We are unable to render judgment here in favor of Sears by holding, as Sears urges, that there was no evidence of its lack of care. Many purchases were made in the same stores, and one New York area store inquired of the Lubbock store as to Duke's credit standing in connection with one large purchase without any question being raised about the irregularity. The case must be remanded to the Court of Civil Appeals for reconsideration of the points of factual insufficiency to support the jury finding, which is a matter solely within that court's jurisdiction.

The judgment is reversed and the cause is remanded to the Court of Civil Appeals for further proceedings consistent with this opinion.

b. LIMITATION OF LIABILITY OF CARDHOLDER FOR UNAUTHORIZED USE

In 1970 Congress enacted legislation banning the practice of some issuers of acquiring cardholders by issuing credit cards to people who did not request them. Consumer Credit Protection Act ("CCPA") § 132, 15 U.S.C. § 1642. At the same time Congress severely limited the amount of liability of a cardholder for unauthorized use of a credit card. That legislation, in amended form, is CCPA § 133, 15 U.S.C. § 1643. This limitation applies to any credit card whether used for consumer or business purposes. CCPA § 135, 15 U.S.C. § 1645. What policy justifies limiting cardholder liability on lost or stolen credit cards to only $50, an amount that has not been increased since this provision was enacted? What incentive does a cardholder have to report the loss or theft of a credit card?

Walker Bank & Trust Co. v. Jones

Supreme Court of Utah, 1983.
672 P.2d 73.

■ HALL, CHIEF JUSTICE:

At issue in these consolidated cases is the liability of defendants to plaintiff Walker Bank for expenses allegedly incurred by defendants' separated spouses upon credit card accounts established by the plaintiff bank in the names of the defendants. Defendants appeal from adverse summary judgment orders on the grounds that their rights under the Federal Truth in Lending Act[1] were violated.

A. Defendant Betty Jones

In 1977, Defendant Jones established VISA and Master Charge accounts with plaintiff Walker Bank (hereinafter "Bank"). Upon her request, credit cards were issued on those accounts to herself and her husband in each of their names.

On or about November 11, 1977, defendant Jones informed the Bank, by two separate letters, that she would no longer honor charges made by her husband on the two accounts, whereupon the Bank immediately revoked both accounts and requested the return of the credit cards.[2] Despite numerous notices of revocation and requests for surrender of the cards, both defendant Jones and her husband retained their cards and continued to make charges against the accounts.

---

1. 15 U.S.C. §§ 1601, et seq.

2. By the terms of the credit card account agreement, an account can be closed by returning to the Bank all outstanding credit cards.

It was not until March 9, 1978, that defendant Jones finally relinquished her credit cards to the Bank, and then only after a persuasive visit to her place of employment by a Bank employee. At the time she surrendered her cards, the balance owing on the combined accounts (VISA and Master Charge) was $2,685.70. Her refusal to pay this balance prompted the Bank's institution of this suit to recover the same.

B.   Defendant Gloria Harlan

In July, 1979, defendant Harlan, who was prior to that time a VISA cardholder at plaintiff Bank, requested that her husband, John Harlan, be added to the account as an authorized user. The Bank honored this request and issued a card to Mr. Harlan. Shortly thereafter, at some point between July and the end of 1979, the Harlans separated and defendant (Mrs.) Harlan informed the Bank by letter that she either wanted the account closed or wanted the Bank to deny further extensions of credit to her husband.

Notwithstanding the explicit requirement in the account agreement that all outstanding credit cards be returned to the Bank in order to close the account, defendant Harlan did not tender either her card or her husband's at the time she made the aforementioned request. As to her card, she informed the Bank that she could not return it because it had been destroyed in the Bank's automated teller. Notwithstanding, however, she returned the card to the Bank some three months later (March, 1980).

In the interim period, i.e., after defendant's correspondence with the Bank regarding the exclusion of her husband from her account and prior to the relinquishment of her card, several charges were made (purportedly by Mr. Harlan) on the account for which the Bank now seeks recovery. The Bank has sued only Mrs. Harlan, as owner of the account.

Defendants' sole contention on appeal is that the Federal Truth in Lending Act (hereinafter "TILA") limits their liability, for the unauthorized use of the credit cards by their husbands, to a maximum of $50. The specific section of the Act upon which this contention rests is 15 U.S.C. § 1643. In pertinent part, it reads thus:

> (a) A cardholder shall be liable for the unauthorized use of a credit card only if the card is an accepted credit card, the liability is not in excess of $50.00 * * * and the unauthorized use occurs before the cardholder has notified the issuer that an unauthorized use of the credit card has occurred or may occur as the result of loss, theft, or otherwise.

* * *

> (d) Except as provided in this section, a cardholder incurs no liability from the unauthorized use of a credit card.

The Bank's rejoinder is that § 1643 does not apply, inasmuch as defendants' husbands' use of the credit cards was at no time "unauthorized use" within the meaning of the statute. Whether such use was "unauthorized," as that term is contemplated by the statute, is the pivotal question in this case.

The term "unauthorized use" is defined in 15 U.S.C. § 1602(*o*) (1974) as:

> [U]se of a credit card by a person other than the cardholder who does not have actual, implied, or apparent authority for such use and from which the cardholder receives no benefit.

A "cardholder" is described in 15 U.S.C. § 1602(m) as:

> [A]ny person to whom a credit card is issued or any person who has agreed with the card-issuer to pay obligations arising from the issuance of a credit card to another person.

Defendants contend that they alone occupied the status of "cardholder," by reason of their request to the bank that credit cards be issued to their husbands and their assumption of liability therefor. Accordingly, they maintain that their husbands were no more than authorized users of defendants' accounts.

Defendants further aver that the effect of their notification to the Bank stating that they would no longer be responsible for charges made against their accounts by their husbands was to render any subsequent use (by their husbands) of the cards unauthorized. This notification, defendants maintain, was all that was necessary to revoke the authority they had once created in their husbands and thereby invoke the § 1643 limitations on cardholder liability.

The Bank's position is that unauthorized use within the meaning of § 1643 is precisely what the statutory definition (§ 1602(*o*) supra) says it is, to wit: "[U]se * * * by a person * * * who does not have actual, implied, or apparent authority * * *," and that notification to the card issuer has no bearing whatsoever on whether the use is unauthorized, so as to entitle a cardholder to the statutory limitation of liability. We agree with this position.

Where § 1643 governs, the liability of the cardholder for unauthorized charges is limited to $50 regardless of any notification to the card issuer. Notification, if given prior to the unauthorized charges, serves only to eliminate the $50 liability and not, as defendants argue, to render a use unauthorized. Unless and until the unauthorized nature of the use has been established, the notification provision, as well as the statute itself, is irrelevant and ineffectual.

The language of the statute defining unauthorized use (§ 1602(*o*) supra) is clear and unambiguous. It excludes from the category of unauthorized users, any person who has "actual, implied, or apparent authority."

The Bank maintains that defendants' husbands clearly had "apparent" authority to use the cards, inasmuch as their signatures were the same as the signatures on the cards, and their names, the same as those imprinted upon the cards. Accordingly, it contends that no unauthorized use was made of the cards, and that defendants therefore cannot invoke the limitations on liability provided by the TILA.

Again, we find the Bank's position to be meritorious. Apparent authority exists:

> [W]here a person has created such an appearance of things that it causes a third party reasonably and prudently to believe that a second party has the power to act on behalf of the first person * * *.[5]

> As previously pointed out, at defendants' request their husbands were issued cards bearing the husbands' own names and signatures. These cards were, therefore, a representation to the merchants (third parties) to whom they were presented that defendants' husbands (second parties—card-bearers) were authorized to make charges upon the defendants' (first parties—cardholders) accounts. This apparent authority conferred upon defendants' husbands by reason of the credit cards thus precluded the application of the TILA.

In view of our determination that the TILA has no application to the present case, we hold that liability for defendants' husbands' use of the cards is governed by their contracts with the Bank. The contractual agreements between defendants and the Bank provided clearly and unequivocally that *all* cards issued upon the accounts be returned to the Bank in order to terminate defendants' liability. Accordingly, defendants' refusal to relinquish either their cards or their husbands', at the time they notified the Bank that they no longer accepted liability for their husbands' charges, justified the Bank's disregard of that notification and refusal to terminate defendants' liability at that time.

The dissent expresses concern that the decision of the Court imposes an unreasonable burden on the cardholder. We disagree because in our opinion justice is better served by placing the responsibility for the credit escapades of an errant spouse (or son, daughter, mother, father, etc.) on the cardholder rather than the Bank. The cardholder is not left powerless to protect against misuse of the card. He or she need only surrender the cards and close the account, just as the defendants in the instant case were requested by the Bank to do.

Affirmed. No costs awarded.

■ Oaks, J., and J. Robert Bullock, District Judge, concur.

■ Durham, Justice (dissenting):

I dissent from the majority opinion because I believe that the federal statute and the specific cardholder agreements in question relieve the defendants of liability for the unauthorized use of their credit cards by their spouses.

The pertinent portions of § 1643 of the Federal Truth in Lending Act (hereafter "TILA") are set forth in the majority opinion. See 15 U.S.C.A. § 1643 (1982). Section 1643(a) of the TILA limits a cardholder's liability to

---

5. Wynn v. McMahon Ford Co., Mo. App., 414 S.W.2d 330, 336 (1967).

a maximum of $50 for any unauthorized use of a credit card which occurs *before* the cardholder has notified the card issuer of the possibility of any unauthorized use. More importantly, however, § 1643(d) relieves a cardholder of "all" liability for any unauthorized use which occurs *after* the cardholder has notified the card issuer of the possibility of an unauthorized use. The cardholder agreements in the present case contain provisions which implement, and are virtually identical to, § 1643:

> Unauthorized Use. Cardholder is responsible for all authorized transactions made and credit extended by use of Cardholder's [credit card], regardless of credit limits and the party using them. Cardholder may be liable for the unauthorized use of the cards where the cards are used by a person other than the Cardholder who does not have actual, implied or apparent authority for such use and from which the Cardholder receives no benefit. However, *Cardholder will not be liable for the unauthorized use of a [credit card] which occurs after written or oral notice of the loss, theft or possible unauthorized use is given* either verbally at any office of Bank or in writing * * *. Liability for unauthorized use shall in no event exceed $50.00 on each account established. (Emphasis added.)

Thus, as recognized by the majority opinion, the resolution of this case focuses on whether the defendants' husbands' use of the defendants' credit cards constitutes an "unauthorized use" within the meaning of the statute and the cardholder agreements.

The term "unauthorized use" is defined as follows:

> "[U]nauthorized use" * * * means use of a credit card by a person * * * who does not have actual, implied, or apparent authority for such use and from which the cardholder receives no benefit.

15 U.S.C.A. § 1602(*o*) (1982). Thus, the pivotal issue in this case is whether the defendants' notification to the Bank was sufficient to revoke the defendants' husbands' "actual, implied, or apparent authority" to use the credit cards, thereby rendering the husbands' use unauthorized. The majority opinion responds in the negative by contending that the defendants' husbands were clothed with apparent authority because they carried credit cards imprinted with the husbands' names and bearing the husbands' signatures. The majority opinion holds that, despite notification to the Bank by the defendants that all authority has been expressly revoked, this apparent authority continues to exist until the defendants obtain the cards from their estranged husbands and return them to the Bank. I disagree with that holding for three reasons.

First, the result of the majority opinion runs counter to the purpose of § 1643 of the TILA, which has been described as follows:

> The federal credit card statute reflects a policy decision that it is preferable for the issuer to bear fraud losses arising from credit card use.
>
> * * * [I]ssuers are in a better position to control the occurrence of these losses. They not only select the merchants who may accept the

card and the holders who may use it, but also design the security systems for card distribution, user identification, and loss notification. Hence, *the statutory choice of issuer liability assures that the problem of credit card loss is the responsibility of the party most likely to take efficient steps in its resolution.*

Weistart, Consumer Protection in the Credit Card Industry: Federal Legislative Controls, 70 Mich.L.Rev. 1475, 1509–10 (1972) (citations omitted) (emphasis added). Cf. First National Bank of Mobile v. Roddenberry, 701 F.2d 927 (11th Cir.1983) (stating that, by issuing a credit card, a bank assumes the risk of nonpayment and that only the bank can decide when and if credit will be revoked). Under the present circumstances, I acknowledge that the burden or risk of liability should initially fall on the cardholder because use of the credit card by a spouse is, and remains, authorized until notice is given to the card issuer that the authority to use the credit card is revoked. However, once the cardholder notifies the card issuer of the revocation of that authority, it is clear that the card issuer is in the best position to protect itself, the cardholder and third parties. The card issuer can protect both itself and the cardholder by refusing to pay any charges on the account, and it can protect third parties by listing the credit card in the regional warning bulletins. See Weistart, supra; Standard Oil Co. v. State Neon Co., 120 Ga.App. 660, 171 S.E.2d 777 (1969). The issuer need only terminate the existing account, transfer all existing charges to a new number, and issue a new card to the cardholder.

In circumstances similar to the present case, the Supreme Court of New York stated:

> It is interesting to note, parenthetically, that under the provisions above quoted, defendant [cardholder] would not be liable for purchases made after notice of loss or theft of the card and if he was in fact unable to obtain the card from his estranged wife, the result was not greatly different. Indeed the plaintiff's [card issuer's] situation was no worse than in the case of a loss of theft but probably considerably better since it knew the whereabouts of the card and of the holder.

Socony Mobil Oil Co. v. Greif, 10 A.D.2d 119, 197 N.Y.S.2d 522, 523–24 (1960) (decided prior to the enactment of § 1643 of the TILA and based on the language of the particular cardholder agreement). Thus, in conformance with the purpose of § 1643 of the TILA, the better holding in this case, as a policy matter, is that, after notification to the card issuer, the cardholder should be relieved of all liability for the unauthorized use of the credit card by an estranged spouse.

Second, the language of § 1643 and the law of agency require that the defendants be relieved of liability. As the majority opinion recognizes, state law determines the question of whether the defendants' husbands are clothed with "apparent authority." See, e.g., FRB Letter of July 23, 1974, No. 822, by J. Kluckman, Chief, Truth-in-Lending Section (excerpted in Consumer Credit Guide (CCH) ¶ 31,144 (October 8, 1974)). Under Utah law, a husband or wife may terminate an agency created in the spouse in the same manner as any other agency. See U.C.A., 1953, § 30–2–8. The majority opinion holds that the defendants' husbands' use was authorized because the husbands had "apparent authority." This is apparently a reference to the relationship between the husband and third-party merchants who rely on the husband's possession of a credit card with his name and matching signature on it. It cannot refer to the existence of apparent authority vis-a-vis the Bank, because the Bank has been *expressly notified* of the revocation of all authority. I fail to see why the existence of "apparent authority" as to third-party merchants should govern the liability of a cardholder whose spouse "steals" a card in the context of marital difficulties, any more than it would govern in the case of a cardholder whose card is stolen before delivery and bears a "matching signature" forged thereon by a thief.

It is well recognized that apparent authority exists only to the extent that the *principal* represents to a third person that another is one's agent. See, e.g., Restatement (Second) of Agency § 8 & comments (1958). In the present case, with respect to the Bank, the husbands' authority, actual, implied and apparent, was specifically terminated by the defendants (the principals) when the Bank was notified that the husbands' authority to use the defendants' credit cards was revoked. See, e.g., id. §§ 124A, 125 & 130. Thus, after notification, the husbands' use was unauthorized and both § 1643 and the provisions of the cardholder agreements relieved the defendants of all liability for charges incurred by their husbands subsequent to that notification. See, e.g., In re Shell Oil Co., 95 F.T.C. 357 (1980); Socony Mobil Oil Co. v. Greif, supra. Accord Neiman–Marcus Co. v. Viser, La., 140 So.2d 762 (1962).

In the *Shell Oil* case, supra, several cardholders petitioned the Federal Trade Commission (hereafter "FTC"), which is vested with authority to enforce both the Federal Trade Commission Act and the TILA, for relief from certain practices of the Shell Oil Co. which were allegedly in violation of those Acts. Shell Oil Co. issued credit cards to cardholders to enable them to purchase goods and services at Shell's service stations. Some cardholders authorized third persons to use their credit cards. In certain instances, several cardholders notified Shell Oil Co. that such previously authorized users were no longer authorized. Shell Oil Co. responded by informing the cardholders that they would remain liable for charges incurred by the third persons until the credit cards used by the third persons were returned. The FTC ordered Shell Oil Co. to forthwith cease and desist from:

> 1. *Failing to limit the liability of a cardholder* for use of a credit card by a third person, in those cases where such third person has been given authorization by the cardholder to use such credit card, *to the amount* of money, property, labor, or services *obtained by use prior to notification* * * * by the cardholder that such use is no longer authorized * * * [and]

> 2. Informing a cardholder that [the card issuer] considers the cardholder liable for use of a credit card by a third person which occurs

after the cardholder notifies [the card issuer] that such use is no longer authorized.

In re Shell Oil Co., supra, at 359–60 (emphasis added). Thus, under § 1643 as interpreted by the FTC in the *Shell Oil* case, the defendants' liability in the present case is limited to the charges incurred by their husbands prior to notification.

The majority opinion sanctions the Bank's refusal to terminate the defendants' liability based on the majority opinion's interpretation that the cardholder agreements require "clearly and unequivocally that *all* cards issued upon the accounts be returned to the Bank in order to terminate defendants' liability." To the contrary, the cardholder agreements do not mandate the return of the credit cards as a condition precedent to termination of *liability*. The cardholder agreements provide that "Cardholder may terminate this *Agreement* at any time by returning the cards issued under this Agreement to the Bank." (Emphasis added.) This provision deals with termination of the "account," not termination of liability for unauthorized use. In fact, like § 1643, the relevant portions of the cardholder agreements, quoted above, provide specifically that the cardholder is not liable for charges incurred *after* notice of the possible unauthorized use is given to the Bank. Contrary to the majority opinion's suggestion, there are no provisions in the cardholder agreements that require the return of the credit cards to the Bank as a prerequisite to relieving the defendants of "liability" for the unauthorized use of their credit cards.

Finally, the majority opinion ignores the impracticality of imposing the burden on a cardholder of obtaining a credit card from an estranged spouse in order to return it to the Bank. It is unrealistic to think that estranged spouses will be cooperative. Moreover, it is extremely unwise to arm one spouse with a weapon which permits virtually unlimited spending at the expense of the other. As is illustrated by the facts of these cases, where the whereabouts of the unauthorized spouse are unknown, the cardholder may be powerless to acquire possession of his or her card and return it to the Bank, which, according to the majority opinion, is the only way to limit liability. One result of the majority opinion will surely be to encourage the "theft" by divorcing spouses of credit cards they were authorized to use during the marriage and the liberal use of those cards at the other spouse's expense.

In conclusion, I dissent from the majority opinion because (1) it runs counter to the language and purpose of § 1643 of the TILA and the language of the cardholder agreements, (2) it violates principles of the law of agency, and (3) it imposes an unreasonable burden on cardholder spouses and sets the stage for abusive use of credit cards by estranged spouses. I believe that § 1643 of the TILA and the provisions of the cardholder agreements relieve the defendants from liability for the unauthorized charges incurred by their husbands subsequent to the notification given to the Bank.

■ Howe, J., concurs in the dissenting opinion of Durham, J.

NOTE

The meaning of the term "unauthorized use" in CCPA § 103(*o*), 15 U.S.C. § 1602, was also at issue in Martin v. American Express, Inc., 361 So.2d 597 (Ala.Civ.App.1978). In that case Martin, the cardholder, authorized a business associate, McBride, to use the credit card but McBride was not authorized to make charges in excess of $500. McBride made charges of over $5,000 and Martin refused to pay. Martin argued that all charges by McBride beyond $500 constituted "unauthorized use" within the meaning of the Federal statute and that Martin's liability with respect to the unauthorized use was limited to $50. Under the statute, use is unauthorized if the use is "by a person who does not have actual, implied or apparent authority for such use." It seems clear that mere possession by McBride of a credit card bearing the name of Martin did not give McBride apparent authority to make any charge on the card. Although McBride may not have had any apparent authority to use the card, he had actual authority to use the card to make charges up to $500 but no actual authority, express or implied, to use it above that amount. Is it reasonable that Congress intended this type of unauthorized use to be subject to the $50 limitation? The definition of "unauthorized use" is not very helpful. The court in *Martin* refused to apply the $50 limitation and held Martin liable for the entire amount charged by McBride. This result seems right as a matter of policy and is probably what Congress intended, but the court's rationale seems shaky: "McBride was actually authorized by Martin to use the latter's card. Martin admitted this fact. And the authority to use it, if not actual, remained apparent even after McBride ignored Martin's directions by charging over $500 to Martin's credit card account." 361 So.2d at 600.

3.   ASSERTION AGAINST ISSUER BY CARDHOLDER OF DEFENSES ARISING FROM TRANSACTION IN WHICH CREDIT CARD USED

In Chapter 9, with respect to a promissory note issued by a consumer to obtain goods or services, we saw that various doctrines of case law or provisions of statutory or administrative law have been used to allow the consumer to assert against a financial institution that holds the note defenses that the consumer has against the seller of the goods or services. If a consumer uses a bank credit card to buy goods and the goods are either never delivered or are defective, should the cardholder be allowed to refuse to pay the issuer of the credit card to the extent that the cardholder would have been excused from paying the seller of the goods if the sale had been a credit sale by the seller? This question was hotly debated at the state level in the late 1960s. Financial institutions that were issuers of credit cards argued that they had only the most tenuous relationship with retailers honoring their cards, and should not be subjected to claims and defenses arising out of sales made pursuant to their cards. The card issuer, it was contended, should be no more involved in the sale transaction financed by a credit card than should a drawee bank in a sale paid for by a check drawn on the bank. Moreover, would not subjecting card issuers to sales defenses ultimately restrict the acceptability of credit cards by retailers? The concern of the retailer was that the card issuer would insist on a right to charge back against the retailer debts as to which the cardholder raised claims or defenses. Would a retailer in Maine feel secure in honoring a credit card presented by a cardholder who lives in California knowing that if the cardholder claims the goods are defective the retailer may end up with an unsecured claim against the debtor three thousand miles away?

In 1974 Congress enacted an amendment to the Consumer Credit Protection Act stating rights and obligations of the cardholder and the issuer of the credit card with respect to the correction of a billing error that the cardholder believes has been made in the billing statement received from the issuer. The statement of these rights and obligations now appears, in amended form, in CCPA § 161, 15 U.S.C. § 1666. "Billing error" is defined in CCPA § 161(b) and includes reflection on the statement of an extension of credit not made by the cardholder and reflection on the statement of goods or services not accepted by the cardholder or not delivered to the cardholder in accordance with the agreement made at the time of the sales transaction. The 1974 legislation covered a number of other aspects of the issuer-cardholder relationship in CCPA §§ 162–170, 15 U.S.C. §§ 1666a–1666i. CCPA § 170, 15 U.S.C. § 1666i, addressed the issue of the extent to which the cardholder can assert, as a defense to the obligation to pay the issuer, claims and defenses of the cardholder arising from the transaction in which the credit card was used. That section is discussed in the case that follows.

Izraelewitz v. Manufacturers Hanover Trust Co.

Civil Court, City of New York, Kings County, 1983.
120 Misc.2d 125, 465 N.Y.S.2d 486.

■ IRA B. HARKAVY, JUDGE.

As the texture of the American economy evolves from paper to plastic, the disgruntled customer is spewing its wrath upon the purveyor of the plastic rather than upon the merchant.

Plaintiff George Izraelewitz commenced this action to compel the Defendant bank Manufacturers Hanover Trust Company to credit his Mastercharge account in the amount of $290.00 plus finance charges. The disputed charge, posted to Plaintiff's account on July 16, 1981, is for electronic diagrams purchased by Plaintiff via telephone from Don Britton Enterprises, a Hawaii-based mail order business.

On September 9, 1981 Plaintiff advised Defendant bank, Manufacturers Hanover Trust Company (Trust Company), that the diagrams had been unsuitable for his needs and provided Defendant with a UPS receipt indicating that the purchased merchandise had been returned to Don Britton. Defendant's Customer Service Department credited Plaintiff's account and waived finance charges on the item. Trust Company subsequently proceeded to charge back the item to the merchant. The merchant refused the charge back through The 1st Hawaii Bank, and advised Defendant bank of their strict "No Refund" policy. Don Britton also indicated that Plaintiff, during the course of conversation, had admitted that he was aware of this policy. On April 1, 1982 Defendant advised Plaintiff that his account would be redebited for the full amount. At two later dates, Plaintiff advised Trust Company of said dispute, denied knowledge of the "No Refund" policy and stated that the goods had been returned. The Trust Company once again credited Plaintiff's account and attempted to collect from Don Britton. The charge back was again refused and Plaintiff's account was subsequently redebited.

Bank credit agreements generally provide that a cardholder is obligated to pay the bank regardless of any dispute which may exist respecting the merchandise. An exception to this rule arises under a provision in the Truth in Lending Law which allows claimants whose transactions exceed $50.00 and who have made a good faith attempt to obtain satisfactory resolution of the problem, to assert claims and defenses arising out of the credit card transaction, if the place of the initial transaction is in the same state or within 100 miles of the cardholder. Consumer Credit Protection Act, 15 U.S.C.A. § 1666i.

It would appear that Plaintiff is precluded from asserting any claims or defenses since Britton's location exceeds the geographical limitation. This assumption is deceiving. Under Truth in Lending the question of where the transaction occurred (e.g. as in mail order cases) is to be determined under state or other applicable law. Truth in Lending, 12 CFR, § 226.12(c). Furthermore, any state law permitting customers to assert claims and defenses against the card issuer would not be preempted, regardless of whether the place of the transaction was at issue. In effect, these federal laws are viewed as bare minimal standards.

In Lincoln First Bank, N.A. v. Carlson, 103 Misc.2d 467, 426 N.Y.S.2d 433 (1980), the court found that:

> "(T)he statement that a card issuer is subject to all defenses if a transaction occurred less than 100 miles from the cardholder's address, does not automatically presume a cardholder to give up all his defenses should the transaction take place at a distance of greater than 100 miles from the mailing address." Id. at 436.

The facts at bar do not warrant a similar finding. Whereas in *Lincoln,* supra, the cardholder's defense arose due to an alleged failure of the card issuer itself to comply with statutory rules, the Defendant herein is blameless. The geographical limitation serves to protect banks from consumers who may expose them to unlimited liability through dealings with merchants in faraway states where it is difficult to monitor a merchant's behavior. These circumstances do not lend the persuasion needed to cast-off this benefit.

Considering, arguendo, that under the Truth in Lending Act, Plaintiff was able to assert claims and defenses from the original transaction, any claims or defenses he chose to assert would only be as good as and no better than his claim against the merchant. Accordingly, Plaintiff's claim against the merchant must be scrutinized to ascertain whether it is of good faith and substantial merit. A consumer cannot assert every miniscule dispute he may have with a merchant as an excuse not to pay an issuer who has already paid the merchant.

The crux of Plaintiff's claim, apparently, is that he returned the diagrams purportedly unaware of merchant's "No Refund" policy. The merchant contends that Plaintiff admitted that he knew of the policy and nonetheless used deceptive means to return the plans; in that they were sent without a name so they would be accepted; were not delivered to an employee of the company; were not in the original box; and showed evidence of having been xeroxed.

"No Refund" policies, per se, are not unconscionable or offensive to public policy in any manner. Truth in Lending Law "(n)either requires refunds for returns nor does it prohibit refunds in kind." Truth in Lending Regulations, 12 CFR, § 226.12(e). Bank-merchant agreements, however, usually do contain a requirement that the merchant establish a fair policy for exchange and return of merchandise.

To establish the fairness in Don Britton's policy, the strength of the reasons behind the policy and the measures taken to inform the consumer of it must necessarily be considered. Don Britton's rationale for its policy is compelling. It contends that printing is a very small part of its business, which is selling original designs, and "once a customer has seen the designs he possesses what we have to sell." Britton's policy is clearly written in its catalog directly on the page which explains how to order merchandise. To compensate for not having a refund policy, which would be impractical considering the nature of the product, Britton offers well-advertised backup plans with free engineering assistance and an exchange procedure, as well, if original plans are beyond the customer's capabilities. The Plaintiff could have availed himself of any of these alternatives which are all presumably still open to him.

On the instant facts, as between Plaintiff and the Defendant bank, Plaintiff remains liable for the disputed debt, as he has not shown adequate cause to hold otherwise.

Judgment for Defendant dismissing the complaint.

D. EMERGING TRENDS IN FUNDS TRANSFERS

1. "SMART" CARDS

Long used in Europe, particularly in France, the "smart" or "stored value" cards are being introduced in the United States. Douglas Lavin, French Smart Card Proves Bright Idea, Wall. St.J. April 22, 1996, p.A10. The plastic cards that we call credit or debit cards are merely bearers of information, encoded in machine readable form on a magnetic stripe on the back of the card. The smart or stored value cards contain a microchip that can hold much more information than a magnetic stripe. The uses of a "chip card" are unlimited. They meet needs as disparate as serving as a health insurance card, containing the patient's medical records, or as being electronic "dog tags" for soldiers. In short, in an information age they can store great quantities of any information we wish to impart. "Smart cards" are extensively treated in Donald I. Baker & Roland E. Brandel, The Law of Electronic Fund Transfer Systems, Chapter 9 (1988, Cum.Supp.1995).

Our interest in them concerns their function as cash substitutes. The most simple application is a card "loaded" with a sum of money, say $500, that the cardholder can use to purchase goods or services from participating merchants, telephone companies, transit systems or the like. The cardholder obtains the card either by buying it from a bank teller or by using a bank dispenser by inserting money or an ATM or credit card. The card is off-line and self-contained, in that a record of value transferred by the card is carried only in the card itself and not in a central account. It is disposable; when it is used up, it is worthless and may be thrown away. If the cardholder makes a purchase from a merchant, no identification need be sought by the merchant; the card has its own verification code and passwords. The merchant deducts the price of the sale by running the card through a terminal that transfers the amount paid on the card to the merchant. The amount left on the card is ascertainable by balance checker machines. The merchant aggregates balances daily or more frequently and transmits them to its bank to receive credit. At least with respect to participating sellers, the card is a complete substitute for cash. Its proponents see as one of its major functions its use in the enormous small-cash purchase market in which the amounts involved are sometimes too small for credit card use. Fast food stores, gas stations, video stores, even parking meters are some of the target markets. These cards have been used for years in France for telephone calls. By honoring smart cards, convenience stores open all night can avoid having cash be stolen by robbers.

More sophisticated cards may be "reloadable" by accessing the cardholder's bank account through an ATM machine. They may be on-line through the use of ATM's or POS terminals, and, like debit cards, the debtor's bank account is debited upon use. However, until reloaded, these cards can transfer value only to the extent of the amount stored on the card. The three major credit card companies, Visa, MasterCard and American Express, are each developing technologies that will allow consumers to download dollar amounts directly from their bank accounts onto cards. Stephen E. Frank, MasterCard Buys 51% Stake in Mondex, Wall St.J., Nov. 19, 1996, p. B11.

The question facing the American banking system is whether the potential for smart cards justifies the costs of converting from the present magnetic stripe technology to the one that will accommodate smart cards. If sufficiently high volume can be obtained, banks may profit handsomely from smart cards by the "float," that is, having the cardholder's money until the card is used up, by charging fees from participating merchants and by keeping the few cents left on the card when the holder discards it.

As is true with the introduction of any new operational technology, the chicken-and-egg dilemma arises: banks would prefer not to convert to smart cards until there are enough customers to promise ultimate profitability; customers would like not to go to the trouble of obtaining smart cards until enough providers of goods and services are prepared to accept them. Leslie Helm, Plans for Electronic Currency, Los Angeles Times, September 6, 1995, p.D4. Banks made a major promotional effort to popularize smart cards in connection with the 1996 Olympic Games in Atlanta. They signed up merchants with some 1500 retail outlets, mostly fast food outlets and gas stations, and the Atlanta transit system. The results were encouraging but hardly a gold medal performance. Other pilot programs are planned in New York City and elsewhere. Nikhil Deogun, The Smart Money is on 'Smart Cards,' But Electronic Cash Seems Dumb to Some, Wall St.J., August 5, 1996, p. B1. Widespread acceptance of smart cards is thought to be several years away. Potential legal and regulatory problems arising with respect to smart cards are discussed in 5 Clarks' Bank Deposits and Payments Monthly 1–6 (1996).

The Task Force on Stored Value Cards of the American Bar Association has prepared an extensive report that will be published in Volume 52 of the Business Lawyer. The Task Force, of which R. David Whitaker was Reporter, describes this report an "An Analysis of Commercial Law Issues Associated With Stored Value Cards and Electronic Money." It describes the current electronic money systems, comments on how they work, and speculates on the legal problems they raise.

2. INTERNET PAYMENTS

In the future, sales may be made on the Internet. A rush is on among banks, credit card companies and other interested parties to develop a system that would allow consumers to shop that vast global computer network and to pay for goods or information purchased through the use of smart cards. These would be inserted in the user's computer to obtain an electronic check which would be sent to a merchant, who would, in turn, forward the "check" to its bank which would clear it over the present banking network. Internet is good on communication but bad on safety, and security is a major problem to be resolved in any such payments system. Jared Sandberg, Electronic Check–Payment Plan for the Internet to Be Developed, Wall St.J., August 23, 1995, p.B8. The Future of Money, Business Week, June 12, 1995, p.66.

Alternative systems, like the DigiCash system, currently licensed for use in this country by Mark Twain Bank, of St.Louis, dispense with the need for the smart card. This system produces Ecash, DigiCash's name for its digital money. Craig Winchester, Electronic Commerce on the Internet: The Rise of Anonymous Digital Coin Transfer (1996) (unpublished manuscript in possession of the Editors). Mr. Winchester's description of the Ecash system follows. The footnotes are omitted.

In October of 1995, Mark Twain Bank (MTB) was the first entity to issue DigiCash's® electronic money called Ecash®, a blinded electronic coin protocol. Located in Amsterdam, DigiCash has pioneered development of electronic payment mechanisms for open, closed and network systems which provide security and privacy. DigiCash's technology is based on patented advances in public key cryptography developed by the Company's founder and Managing Director, Dr. David Chaum. Ecash is DigiCash's trademark name for its digital money. DigiCash is licensing the technology to various entities throughout the world. In order to understand how such a system works and the impact it will have on consumers, it is best to divide its analysis up into four parts; (1) bank account (2) Ecash Mint®, (3) Ecash software and (4) electronic coins.

In order to use DigiCash's electronic dollars one must open up a WorldCurrency Access® (WCA) account with MTB. The purpose of this deposit account is to serve as some tangible backing for the electronic currency that is in turn backed by the U.S. government. Next, a customer must install software licensed by DigiCash on his/her personal computer. Installing software for the first time will establish a personal Ecash Mint account. The purpose of the Ecash Mint is to collect and issue "electronic coins" that will be transmitted to or from a customer's personal computer. It also authenticates electronic coins paid to a merchant or individual and provides a convenient means for MTB to charge a customer. MTB can collect a fee by taxing transfers between the Mint and the WCA account in addition to accumulating float on the money not bearing any interest (for the consumer) in the Mint. It also may limit MTB's liability to its customers. The purpose of DigiCash's software residing on a personal computer is to enable the consumer to withdraw and deposit money from the Ecash Mint in addition to making and receiving payments to other Ecash users. The software also keeps a record of all transactions. This is important due to the anonymous nature of Ecash. Unlike the transactions between the Ecash Mint and the consumer's PC (which MTB would keep a parallel record on file), any purchases the consumer makes with his digital coins will only be stored by the software in a file on the user's hard drive. Finally, the electronic coins are the monetary units transferred between two Ecash users. Once they are deposited on a consumer's PC they can be used like cash to make anonymous purchases from merchants who accept Ecash payments on the Internet. The coins spent can not be traced back to any particular user. Neither the bank nor the merchant can collude to determine the identity of the payor. This privacy is one-sided, i.e., only the payor is anonymous, the recipient of the money has no anonymity at all. In this particular system, the digital coins can only be spent once, hence all money that the payee receives must be given to the bank. This is designed to limit any money laundering or tax evasion schemes while at the same time maximizing personal privacy.

3.   HOME BANKING

We have seen that checks are being replaced by a number of devices. Businesses are paying more of their bills through ACH credit transfers, and consumer bank accounts are being accessed through ACH debit transfers to meet recurring obligations like mortgage payments and insurance premiums. Credit cards are being used by consumers to buy goods and services at a level undreamed of when bank cards were developed less than four decades ago. Debit cards are beginning to be used more often as more point-of-sale terminals are being installed. Bank customers are accessing their bank accounts for cash more through ATMs than by cashing their personal checks at banks.

Another method by which consumers are replacing checks is by what is commonly known as home banking. A detailed treatment of home banking and telephone bill paying is found in Donald I. Baker & Roland E. Brandel, The Law of Electronic Fund Transfer Systems, Chapter 10 (1988, Cum. Supp.1995). For a number of years customers have used telephones to carry on home banking activities. By use of the keypad on their telephone, they can learn the amount of their account balances, which checks have cleared, which checks have been deposited, transfer funds from one account to another, apply for credit cards or loans and pay bills. An attraction of this service is that it is usually available every day at all hours. There is no means of withdrawing money or making deposits; users must still use ATMs or bank offices for these important functions. Telephone banking has become quite popular.

In more recent years banks and computer software companies are offering personal finance programs to make possible home banking by computer. Some computer companies are joining with banks to offer online banking, e.g., IBM's Integrion Financial Network includes major banks like the Bank of America, Mellon Bank and Nationsbank. Lawrence J. Magid, Checks and Balances Made Easy, Los Angeles Times, September 16, 1996, p. D4. Thus far only about 1% of the population uses banking by computer. Nikhil Deogun, A Tough Bank Boss Takes on Computers With Real Trepidation, Wall St.J., July 25, 1996, p.A1. But with the onslaught of the Nintendo generation there are predictions that computer banking will soon become the norm. Timothy L. O'Brien, Will Home Banking That Uses Computers Take Off This Time? Wall St.J., June 8, 1995, B1. The American Bankers Association predicts that market penetration will grow to 6% by 1998, but others dispute whether consumers really want full-scale electronic home banking and whether banks will find it profitable. Patrick Lee, So Far, Online Banking Is Mostly Wishful Thinking, L.A. Times, Sept. 30, 1996, p. D1. These programs usually enable customers to do everything that can be done through telephone banking, with the added benefit of being able to see the information on the computer screen and download it. Thus customers can use computer banking to, in effect, balance their checkbooks. Withdrawals and deposits still cannot be done by computer banking programs now in use. Walter S. Mossberg, Banking By PC Doesn't Do Enough to Ease a Grim Task, Wall St.J., December 7, 1995, p.B1.

Banks and other companies offering computer banking are making an effort to make bill paying by computer a major function of computer banking. "No checks to write, stamps to lick or envelopes to mail!" say the ads. In theory a customers can use a computer to make payments to anyone having a bank account, and the payments can be scheduled a year in advance. Thus a customer can schedule at the beginning of the year all recurring payments to be made during the year; can keep his or her money in interest bearing savings accounts until the time of payment when the money can be transferred into a checking account; and can get a confirmation on the screen for every transaction. A problem is that a transfer can be made electronically only to payees whose bank and account number is known either to the customer or the payor bank. To meet this problem, banks have signed up large numbers of businesses which are prepared to accept electronic payments to their accounts. Thus in the usual case of a payment to a business, all the customer has to be sure about is the name and address of the business, for the bank will know its account number. In cases in which the databank does not contain the payee's account number and the payee has not provided that number to the customer, the payment may be made by the customer's bank's sending that person a check drawn on the customer's account. Banks advertise that "virtually all" payments can be made electronically.

CHAPTER 4

FRAUD, FORGERY, AND ALTERATION

A. FORGERY

1. ALLOCATION OF LOSS BETWEEN CUSTOMER AND PAYOR BANK WITH RESPECT TO CHECKS BEARING FORGERY

a. INTRODUCTION

Suppose Customer has a checking account in Payor Bank. Thief steals Customer's checkbook, writes a check payable to Payee, and signs Customer's name to the check as drawer. Because Thief was not authorized to sign Customer's name to the check, the signature is ineffective as the signature of Customer unless some provision of Article 3 or Article 4 makes it effective. § 3–403(a). Since Customer did not sign the check and did not authorize Thief to sign the check, Customer is not liable on the check. § 3–401(a). The check, however, is not a nullity. Although it is not Customer's check, Article 3 treats it as Thief's check even though Thief signed it by using Customer's name. § 3–403(a) and § 3–401(b). Checks like the check in this example, i.e. a check bearing a forged drawer's signature, are known as "forged checks." Such checks sometimes are transferred for value and paid by the drawee bank. Rights of a holder with respect to such checks can be acquired by persons who take them.

A more common type of forgery can be illustrated by the following example. Customer writes a check to the order of Payee, signs it as drawer, and mails it to Payee. Thief steals the check from Payee, indorses the check by signing Payee's name on the back of the check, and obtains payment of the check from Payor Bank. The check in this example is not a forged check because Customer's signature was not forged. Rather, the infirmity of the check is that it bears a "forged indorsement." Under § 3–403(a) and § 3–401 the signature by Thief is ineffective as the indorsement of Payee. Since Payee did not indorse the check, Thief cannot negotiate the check and nobody can obtain rights as a holder unless some provision of Article 3 otherwise provides. § 3–201(b) and § 3–109(b).

What are the rights of Customer and Payor Bank toward each other if Payor Bank pays the forged check in the first example or the check bearing the forged indorsement in the second example? Under § 4–401(a) a payor bank "may charge against the account of a customer an item that is properly payable from the account" and, to be properly payable, the check must be "authorized by the customer." Thus, in the case of the forged check, the normal rule is that Payor Bank may not debit Customer's account and is not entitled to reimbursement from Customer. The risk of loss falls on Payor Bank even though it may not have had any way of discovering the forgery.

The result is the same in the case of the check bearing the forged indorsement. By the terms of the check Payor Bank was ordered by Customer to pay the check to the order of Payee. Since Payee did not receive payment and did not order payment to anybody else, Payor Bank did not comply with the terms of the check. Since Payor Bank did not pay a holder or other person entitled to receive payment, it has no right to reimbursement from Customer.

The normal rule protecting Customer from loss from forgery is changed in some cases by other provisions of Article 3 or Article 4. Two of the most important provisions that may allow Payor Bank to shift the forgery loss to Customer are § 3–406(a), discussed in *Thompson Maple Products,* and § 4–406, discussed in *Story Road Flea Market.*

b. NEGLIGENCE OF CUSTOMER CONTRIBUTING TO FORGERY

With respect to payment by a payor bank of a forged check or a check bearing a forged indorsement, if the bank can prove a failure by the customer to exercise ordinary care that substantially contributed to the making of the forged signature, the customer is precluded from asserting the forgery. § 3–406(a). "Ordinary care" is defined in § 3–103(a)(7). The leading case on the meaning of the words "substantially contributes to * * * the making of a forged signature" in § 3–406(a) is *Thompson Maple Products,* the case that follows. Comment 2 to § 3–406 discusses the meaning of the quoted words. In the absence of proof of negligence by the bank contributing to the loss, the effect of the preclusion is to give to the bank a right to reimbursement from the customer for the amount paid on the check. Under the original § 3–406, discussed in *Thompson Maple Products,* the preclusion against the customer did not occur if the bank was negligent in paying the check. This result is changed by revised § 3–406. Negligence by the bank does not prevent the preclusion from arising but, under subsection (b), the loss from the forgery can be apportioned between the negligent customer and the negligent bank.

Thompson Maple Products, Inc. v. Citizens National Bank

Superior Court of Pennsylvania, 1967.
211 Pa.Super. 42, 234 A.2d 32.

■ HOFFMAN, JUDGE:

* * *

The plaintiff [Thompson Maple Products] is a small, closely-held corporation, principally engaged in the manufacture of bowling pin "blanks" from maple logs. Some knowledge of its operations from 1959 to 1962 is essential to an understanding of this litigation.

The plaintiff purchased logs from timber owners in the vicinity of its mill. Since these timber owners rarely had facilities for hauling logs, such transportation was furnished by a few local truckers, including Emery Albers.

At the mill site, newly delivered logs were "scaled" by mill personnel, to determine their quantity and grade. The employee on duty noted this information, together with the name of the owner of the logs, as furnished by the hauler, on duplicate "scaling slips."

In theory, the copy of the scaling slip was to be given to the hauler, and the original was to be retained by the mill employee until transmitted by him directly to the company's bookkeeper. This ideal procedure, however, was rarely followed. Instead, in a great many instances, the mill employee simply gave both slips to the hauler for delivery to the company office. Office personnel then prepared checks in payment for the logs, naming as payee the owner indicated on the scaling slips. Blank sets of slips were readily accessible on the company premises.

Sometime prior to February, 1959, Emery Albers conceived the scheme which led to the forgeries at issue here. Albers was an independent log hauler who for many years had transported logs to the company mill. For a brief period in 1952, he had been employed by the plaintiff, and he was a trusted friend of the Thompson family. After procuring blank sets of scaling slips, Albers filled them in to show substantial, wholly fictitious deliveries of logs, together with the names of local timber owners as suppliers. He then delivered the slips to the company bookkeeper, who prepared checks payable to the purported owners. Finally, he volunteered to deliver the checks to the owners. The bookkeeper customarily entrusted the checks to him for that purpose.

Albers then forged the payee's signature and either cashed the checks or deposited them to his account at the defendant bank, where he was well known. * * *

In 1963, when the forgeries were uncovered, Albers confessed and was imprisoned. The plaintiff then instituted this suit against the drawee bank, asserting that the bank had breached its contract of deposit by paying the checks over forged endorsements. * * *

The trial court determined that the plaintiff's own negligent activities had materially contributed to the unauthorized endorsements, and it therefore dismissed the substantial part of plaintiff's claim. We affirm the action of the trial court.

Both parties agree that, as between the payor bank and its customer, ordinarily the bank must bear the loss occasioned by the forgery of a payee's endorsement.

* * *

The trial court concluded, however, that the plaintiff-drawer, by virtue of its conduct, could not avail itself of that rule, citing § 3–406 of the Code: "Any person who by his negligence substantially contributes to * * * the making of an unauthorized signature is precluded from asserting the * * * lack of authority against * * * a drawee or other payor who pays the instrument in good faith and in accordance with the reasonable commercial standards of the drawee's or payor's business." * * *

Before this Court, the plaintiff Company argues strenuously that this language is a mere restatement of pre-Code law in Pennsylvania. Under those earlier cases, it is argued, the term "precluded" is equivalent to "estopped," and negligence which will work an estoppel is only such as "directly and proximately affects the conduct of the bank in passing the forgery * * *." See, e.g., Coffin v. Fidelity–Philadelphia Trust Company, 374 Pa. 378, 393, 97 A.2d 857, 39 A.L.R.2d 625 (1953); Land Title Bank and Trust Company v. Cheltenham National Bank, 362 Pa. 30, 66 A.2d 768 (1949). The plaintiff further asserts that those decisions hold that "negligence in the conduct of the drawer's business," such as appears on this record, cannot serve to work an estoppel.

Even if that was the law in this Commonwealth prior to the passage of the Commercial Code, it is not the law today. The language of the new Act is determinative in all cases arising after its passage. This controversy must be decided, therefore, by construction of the statute and application of the negligence doctrine as it appears in § 3–406 of the Code. * * *

Had the legislature intended simply to continue the strict estoppel doctrine of the pre-Code cases, it could have employed the term "precluded," without qualification, as in § 23 of the old Negotiable Instruments Law, 56 P.S. § 28 (repealed). However, it chose to modify that doctrine in § 3–406, by specifying that negligence which *substantially contributes to * * * the making of an unauthorized signature * * *.*" will preclude the drawer from asserting a forgery. [emphasis supplied]. The Code has thus abandoned the language of the older cases (negligence which "directly and proximately affects the conduct of the bank in passing the forgery") and shortened the chain of causation which the defendant bank must establish. "[N]o attempt is made," according to the Official Comment to § 3–406, "to specify what is negligence, and the question is one for the court or jury on the facts of the particular case."

In the instant case, the trial court could readily have concluded that plaintiff's business affairs were conducted in so negligent a fashion as to have "substantially contributed" to the Albers forgeries, within the meaning of § 3–406.

Thus, the record shows that pads of plaintiff's blank logging slips were left in areas near the mill which were readily accessible to any of the haulers. Moreover, on at least two occasions, Albers was given whole pads of these blank logging slips to use as he chose. Mrs. Vinora Curtis, an employee of the plaintiff, testified:

"Q. Did you ever give any of these logging slips to Mr. Albers or any pads of these slips to Mr. Albers?

"A. Yes.

"Q. What was the reason for giving [a pad of the slips] to him, Mrs. Curtis?

"A. Well, he came up and said he needed it for [scaling] the logs, so I gave it to him."

Mrs. Amy Thompson, who also served as a bookkeeper for the plaintiff, testified:

"Q. As a matter of fact, you gave Mr. Albers the pack of your logging slips, did you not?

"A. Yes, I did once.

"Q. Do you remember what you gave them to him for?

"A. I don't right offhand, but it seems to me he said he was going out to look for some logs or timber or something and he needed them to mark some figures on * * *.

"Q. Well, if he was going to use them for scratch pads, why didn't you give him a scratch pad that you had in the office?

"A. That's what I should have done."

In addition, the plaintiff's printed scaling slips were not consecutively numbered. Unauthorized use of the slips, therefore, could easily go undetected. Thus, Mr. Nelson Thompson testified:

"Q. Mr. Thompson, were your slips you gave these haulers numbered?

"A. No, they were not.

"Q. They are now, aren't they?

"A. Yes.

"Q. Had you used numbered logging slips, this would have prevented anybody getting logging slips out of the ordinary channel of business and using it to defraud you?

"A. Yes.

Moreover, in 1960, when the company became concerned about the possible unauthorized use of its scaling slips, it required its own personnel to initial the slips when a new shipment of logs was scaled. However, this protective measure was largely ignored in practice. Mrs. Amy Thompson testified:

"Q. And later on in the course of your business, if you remember Mr. Thompson said he wanted the logging slips initialed by one of the so-called authorized people?

"A. Yes.

"Q. [D]idn't you really not pay too much attention to them at all?

"A. Well, I know we didn't send them back to be sure they were initialed. We might have noticed it but we didn't send them back to the mill.

"Q. In other words, if they came to you uninitialed, you might have noticed it but didn't do anything about it.

"A. Didn't do anything about it."

The principal default of the plaintiff, however, was its failure to use reasonable diligence in insuring honesty from its log haulers including Emery Albers. For many years, the haulers were permitted to deliver both the original and the duplicate of the scaling slip to the company office, and the company tolerated this practice. These slips supplied the bookkeeper with the payees' names for the checks she was to draw in payment for log deliveries. Only by having the company at all times retain possession of the original slip could the plaintiff have assured that no disbursements were made except for logs received, and that the proper amounts were paid to the proper persons. The practice tolerated by the plaintiff effectively removed the only immediate safeguard in the entire procedure against dishonesty on the part of the haulers.

Finally, of course, the company regularly entrusted the completed checks to the haulers for delivery to the named payees, without any explicit authorization from the latter to do so.

While none of these practices, in isolation, might be sufficient to charge the plaintiff with negligence within the meaning of § 3–406, the company's course of conduct, viewed in its entirety, is surely sufficient to support the trial judge's determination that it substantially contributed to the making of the unauthorized signatures.[6] In his words, that conduct was "no different than had the plaintiff simply given Albers a series of checks signed in blank for his unlimited, unrestricted use."

* * *

Judgment affirmed.

■ WATKINS, J., dissents.

c.   FAILURE OF CUSTOMER TO REPORT FORGERY

In a large percentage of cases involving forged checks, the malefactor forges a series of checks on the same account over a considerable period of time. Forgery with respect to a single check is much more likely to involve a forged indorsement rather than a forgery of the drawer's signature. Typically, repeated forged check cases involve a dishonest employee of the person whose signature is forged. Usually the employee has access to the employer's checkbook and often has duties related to bookkeeping. In the case of repeated forgeries the later forgeries could have been easily prevented if the person whose signature was forged had detected the earlier forgeries. Such detection is relatively easy because in most cases the payor bank, after paying a check, returns the cancelled check to the customer on

---

6. In this connection, the trial court also noted that the plaintiff at all times prior to the commencement of this litigation failed to keep an accurate inventory account. It could not therefore verify, at any given point in time, that it actually possessed the logs which it had paid for.

whose account the check was drawn. The customer should be able to determine whether a check written on the customer's account is a forgery. On the other hand it is very difficult for the payor bank to detect forgery. Since it is easy for the customer to detect a forgery, § 4–406 imposes a duty on the customer to report forged checks to the bank. Failure of the customer to comply with this duty can, in some cases, result in a shifting of the loss from the bank to the customer. Although § 3–406 applies to checks bearing a forged indorsement as well as forged checks, § 4–406 does not apply to forged indorsements. Both sections also apply to altered checks which are discussed later in this chapter.

Given the rule that a payor bank bears the loss on a check it pays over a forged drawer's signature, banks had traditionally engaged in the labor intensive activity of sight review of all checks drawn on the bank. Bank employees compared the signature on each check with that on the signature card on file. For a large bank, a typical setting was a big room, crammed with desks, with soft music, free softdrinks and aspirin, and other amenities designed to keep these unfortunate workers from losing their minds. As the volume of checks grew and automation became the norm, banks abandoned sight review except for checks that met certain criteria, the principal one being the amount of the check. These criteria are discussed in *Story Road*, which follows.

Now that forgers utilize desktop printers, sight review has become obsolete for the large volume of corporate and government checks on which signatures are printed. Even on personal checks in which a signature is written in ink, a sight reviewer, who can normally spend only a few seconds on each check, is no match for a skillful forger. Thus banks came to the conclusion that sight review was not cost effective. Some banks purported to find no greater forgery losses without sight review than with it, and others contended that whatever losses they might suffer on the payment of forged checks of relatively small amounts did not justify the heavy labor costs involved. As we shall see, payor banks have better ways of fighting forgeries than sight review.

The legal problems raised by the abandonment of sight review occupied the courts for years. Julianna J. Zekan, Comparative Negligence Under the Code: Protecting Negligent Banks Against Negligent Customers, 26 U. Mich. J.L. Ref. 125, 166–178 (1992). Under both old and new § 4–406, the customer is obliged to examine its cancelled checks for forgeries and to notify the payor bank if any are found. If it fails to do so in a timely manner, the customer is precluded from raising the forgery *unless the bank fails to exercise ordinary care*. Before the 1990 revision of Articles 3 and 4 became effective, the case law was sharply divided on the issue whether a bank that did not conduct sight review of the checks in question was exercising ordinary care. In Medford Irrigation District v. Western Bank, 66 Or.App. 589, 676 P.2d 329 (Or.App.1984), the bank's automated system was programmed to pay all checks of $5,000 or less unless there was a hold or stop order on the check; checks for amounts in excess of that sum were "kicked out" by the check sorting machine and individually reviewed. The court held that the bank was precluded from raising the customer's negligence on the ground that in order to exercise ordinary care a bank's system must be reasonably related to the detection of forged signatures. Since in this case the bank had no procedure for detecting forgeries in checks under $5,000 the bank was negligent *as a matter of law.*

The *Medford* view has been rejected in a number of cases. The Illinois Supreme Court held in Wilder Binding Co. v. Oak Park Trust & Savings Bank, 135 Ill.2d 121, 142 Ill.Dec. 192, 552 N.E.2d 783 (Ill.1990), that whether a bank exercised ordinary care in paying a check is a question of fact. In Rhode Island Hospital Trust National Bank v. Zapata Corp., 848 F.2d 291 (1st Cir.1988) (Breyer,J.), the court approved the cost-benefit analysis rejected in *Medford.* Judge Breyer opined that there was no evidence that any increased forgery loss from the bank's automated system was unreasonable in light of the costs that the new practices would save. He relied on Learned Hand's view that duty should be defined by calculating the probability of injury times the gravity of harm to determine the burden of precaution that is warranted. United States v. Carroll Towing Co., 159 F.2d 169 (2d Cir.1947).

In the revision of Articles 3 and 4 the Drafting Committee was mindful of the need to make sure that revised Article 4 would accommodate a system of electronic presentment, discussed in the preceding chapter, if such a system were developed. This tipped the scale in favor of adopting the line of authority rejecting *Medford.* This was implemented in the definition of "ordinary care" in § 3–103(7), discussed in Comment 5 to § 3–104 and Comment 4 to § 4–406. The following pre-revision case discusses § 3–103(7).

Story Road Flea Market, Inc. v. Wells Fargo Bank, N.A.

Court of Appeal, Sixth District, 1996.
42 Cal.App.4th 1733, 50 Cal.Rptr.2d 524.

■ MIHARA, ASSOCIATE JUSTICE.

Defendant Wells Fargo honored more than a hundred forged checks against plaintiff's account. Plaintiff did not discover the forgeries until more than a year after defendant began honoring these checks. Defendant refused to credit plaintiff's account for any of these unauthorized checks, and plaintiff filed suit against defendant. Plaintiff alleged causes of action for negligence, breach of contract and common counts and asserted a cause of action for money damages for defendant's alleged violation of Commercial Code section 4406. Defendant's demurrer to plaintiff's negligence, breach of contract and common counts causes of action was sustained without leave to amend on the theory that Commercial Code section 4406 displaced all other actions based on these forged checks. Defendant's motion for summary judgment on the Commercial Code section 4406 cause of action was granted after defendant established that its system for reviewing checks was consistent with general banking usage and that it had utilized that system with respect to these checks. On appeal, plaintiff claims that summary judgment was improper because there was a triable issue of fact and the demurrer should not have been sustained since Commercial Code section 4406 does not displace all other causes of action. We affirm the judgment.

BACKGROUND

In 1981 plaintiff established a checking account with defendant. The written agreement between plaintiff and defendant provided that defendant would honor only checks signed by authorized signatories. The authorized signatories on the account were Glen Norris and Suzanne Norris. Plaintiff's then-attorney, Kenneth Fehl, was responsible for plaintiff's accounts payable. He delegated this task to Helen Shino, whom he employed as a bookkeeper. Between August 1990 and May 1992, Shino stole more than 100 of plaintiff's checks. Beginning in September 1990, Shino forged the signature of one of the authorized signatories on these checks and used the checks to obtain funds for her own purposes. In all, Shino managed to drain $255,761.60 from plaintiff's checking account without its knowledge. Shino intercepted the bank statements sent to plaintiff by defendant, destroyed them and posted false entries in plaintiff's books to conceal her scheme. Plaintiff discovered Shino's scheme on June 6, 1992, and immediately filed this action. Plaintiff also demanded that defendant credit plaintiff's account for the unauthorized checks defendant had honored. Defendant refused to do so. Plaintiff alleged that defendant's conduct in paying these unauthorized checks was due to "a lack of ordinary care."

Plaintiff's complaint alleged causes of action for negligence, breach of contract and "common counts" and it purported to allege a cause of action based on defendant's breach of its obligations under Commercial Code section 4406. Defendant demurred to the complaint by asserting that the negligence, breach of contract and "common counts" causes of action were barred because section 4406 defined plaintiff's exclusive remedy against defendant under these circumstances. The demurrer was sustained without leave to amend. Defendant then brought a motion for summary judgment on the remaining cause of action. Defendant asserted that plaintiff could not succeed on this cause of action because plaintiff had failed to discover and notify defendant of the forgeries promptly after receipt of the bank statement which contained the initial forgeries. The declarations in support of defendant's summary judgment motion established that it had exercised "ordinary care" in honoring the unauthorized checks by processing the checks in accordance with its own check processing procedures, which procedures were "in accord with reasonable commercial standards ... [and] with general banking practice" in the area.

Plaintiff did not dispute defendant's evidence, and defendant's motion for summary judgment was granted. However, the order granting defendant's motion gave plaintiff 60 days in which to seek reconsideration if it obtained evidence that defendant had failed to exercise "ordinary care" in paying the unauthorized checks. Plaintiff thereafter sought reconsideration and submitted declarations which it claimed established a material dispute of fact regarding whether defendant had exercised "ordinary care." The court found that plaintiff had failed to raise a material triable issue of fact by submitting any proof that defendant had failed to exercise "ordinary care." Plaintiff's motion for reconsideration was denied, and judgment was entered in favor of defendant. Plaintiff filed a timely notice of appeal.

ANALYSIS

The critical statute at issue in this case is former Commercial Code section 4406. This statute provided as follows.

"(1) When a bank sends to its customer a statement of account accompanied by items paid in good faith ..., the customer must exercise reasonable care and promptness to examine the statement and items to discover his unauthorized signature or any alteration on an item and must notify the bank promptly after the discovery thereof.

(2) If the bank establishes that the customer failed with respect to an item to comply with the duties imposed on the customer by subdivision (1) the customer *is precluded from asserting against the bank*

(a) His unauthorized signature or any alteration on the item if the bank also establishes that it suffered a loss by reason of such failure; and

(b) An unauthorized signature or alteration by the same wrongdoer on any other item paid in good faith by the bank after the first item and statement was available to the customer for a reasonable period not exceeding 14 calendar days and before the bank receives notification from the customer of any such unauthorized signature or alteration.

(3) The preclusion under subdivision (2) does not apply if the customer establishes *lack of ordinary care* on the part of the bank in paying the item(s)." (Former Comm.Code, § 4406, emphasis added.)

* * *

B.   PRECLUSION APPLIED

* * *

2.   DEFENDANT PROVED THAT IT HAD USED "ORDINARY CARE"

Plaintiff alleged that defendant's conduct in paying these unauthorized checks was due to "a lack of ordinary care." In order to establish its defense, defendant had to prove that it had used ordinary care in honoring the forged checks. Defendant submitted evidence which showed that the unauthorized checks had been processed by defendant's "automated check processing procedure." This process involved an initial procedure in which certain checks were selected for "individual sight review" based on a set of criteria. None of the unauthorized checks on plaintiff's account were selected for sight review. Nevertheless, defendant established that it had processed the forged checks "in accordance with its own check processing procedures," and that these procedures were "in accord with reasonable commercial standards ... [and] with general banking practice" in the area.

Whether defendant's declarations are sufficient to establish that defendant used "ordinary care" in honoring the forged checks depends on what former section 4406 meant by "ordinary care." Section 4406 did not and does not define "ordinary care," but the Commercial Code did and does elsewhere specify the meaning of this term. The Commercial Code was revised in 1992. Prior to these revisions, the Commercial Code defined how a "prima facie" showing of "ordinary care" could be made by a bank. "[A]ction or nonaction *consistent ... with a general banking usage ...* prima facie constitutes the exercise of ordinary care." (Former Comm.Code, § 4103, subd. (3), emphasis added.) "The term 'general banking usage' is not defined [by statute] but should be taken to mean a general usage common to banks in the area concerned." (Uniform Commercial Code Comment to Former Comm.Code, § 4103.) By defining a bank's standard of "ordinary care" in terms of "general banking usage," former section 4103 reflected the Legislature's decision to subject some conduct of banks to a "professional negligence" standard of care which looks at the procedures utilized in the banking industry rather than what a "reasonable person" might have done under the circumstances. * * * The Legislature's decision to utilize a professional standard of care with respect to the conduct of banks was rational because banking is a complicated process which requires special training and skill, and the nature of this process is not a matter of common knowledge. This standard of care seems even more appropriate when it is noted that, even prior to the enactment of the Commercial Code, courts faced with the issue of the propriety of a bank's procedures for detecting unauthorized signatures considered whether the bank's process comported with "the accepted modern practice" of banks in the area. * * *

Noting that former section 4103 explained the meaning of "ordinary care" in terms of "general banking usage" prior to the 1992 revision of the Commercial Code, defendant asserts that the Legislature's 1992 addition of a more detailed definition of "ordinary care" to Commercial Code section 3103 was not a "change in law" and therefore governs this case. Plaintiff asserts that the Legislature's 1992 addition of a new definition of "ordinary care" changed the law, and therefore it is not applicable to this case because the checks herein at issue were honored prior to the effective date of this statutory change. "Unless a change in law, as contrasted with a clarification, has clearly been made, this code, as it existed on January 1, 1993, shall be deemed declaratory of the meaning of this code as it existed prior to January 1, 1993." (Comm.Code, § 16104.) "'Ordinary care' [means] ... [i]n the case of a bank that takes an instrument for processing for collection or payment by automated means, reasonable commercial standards do not require the bank to examine the instrument if the failure to examine does not violate the bank's prescribed procedures and the bank's procedures do not vary unreasonably from general banking usage not disapproved by this division or Division 4 (commencing with Section 4101)." (Comm.Code, §§ 3103, 4104, subd. (c).)

We agree with defendant that this definition of ordinary care did not "change" the law but merely clarified it, and therefore the definition of "ordinary care" in Commercial Code section 3103 is "declaratory" of the meaning of "ordinary care" in former Commercial Code section 4406. Prior to the 1992 changes, "ordinary care" could be established by a bank by showing that the bank's practices comported with "general banking usage" in the area. (Former Comm.Code, § 4103, subd. (3); see § 3103, subd. (a)(7), emphasis added.) The 1992 addition of a more precise definition of ordinary care clarified this standard by detailing that "reasonable commercial standards do not require the bank to *examine the instrument* if the failure to examine does not violate the bank's prescribed procedures *and the bank's procedures do not vary unreasonably from general banking usage....* " (Comm.Code, § 4104, subd. (c), emphasis added.) The 1993 definition of "ordinary care" does not vary demonstrably from the pre–1993 definition. Both definitions require a bank to show that its practices comported with general banking usage. The revised definition simply notes that "ordinary care" can be established notwithstanding the bank's failure to "examine the instrument" so long as the bank's processing of the instrument was in accordance with *both* the bank's practices *and general banking usage.* This qualification means that a bank cannot establish "ordinary care" unless it can show that its practices comported with "general banking usage." The fact that the pre–1993 definition of "ordinary care" did not expressly mention a duty to "examine the instrument" implies that a bank could then establish "ordinary care" even if the bank had failed to examine the instrument so long as the bank was able to establish that its practices comported with general banking usage.

We can see no "change" in the law in regard to the definition of "ordinary care" in this context. Before the 1992 revision of the Commercial Code, a bank could establish that it had processed an instrument in accordance with practices which comported with general banking usage and thereby establish a prima facie case of "ordinary care." The provisions of the Commercial Code prior to the 1992 revisions did not prohibit the bank from making such a showing even if it had failed to examine the instrument. The revised provisions of the Commercial Code continue to provide that a bank can show that it used "ordinary care" by establishing that it processed an instrument using procedures that were consistent with general banking usage. Consistent with these requirements, defendant made an adequate showing that the procedures it utilized in dealing with the forged checks comported with "general banking practice" in the area. This showing was sufficient to establish, in the absence of evidence to the contrary, that defendant had used "ordinary care" in processing the checks in question.

3.   PLAINTIFF'S EVIDENCE FAILED TO RAISE A TRIABLE IS-SUE

Once defendant established that it had used "ordinary care," the burden shifted to plaintiff to raise a triable issue of fact as to either whether defendant had followed its own procedures or whether defendant had utilized procedures which were consistent with "general banking practice" in the area. Plaintiff submitted evidence that the signatures on the unauthorized checks "did not bear any reasonable resemblance" to the authorized signatures. It also submitted evidence that the unauthorized checks were "out-of-sequence with respect to the other accounts payable checks. . . . " Plaintiff also submitted evidence which purported to establish that *there is no industry standard* for check processing systems because they are proprietary and each bank keeps its system secret. Because the evidence established that none of the unauthorized checks on plaintiff's account had been sight reviewed and that defendant's check processing system ordinarily detected unauthorized signatures on sight reviewed checks, plaintiff sought to establish that defendant's system for deciding which checks to "out-sort" for sight review was inadequate. Plaintiff's evidence established that (1) there was no specific dollar limit below which the system ignores a particular check, but all checks over $50,000 are sight reviewed, (2) the system is not able to detect unsigned checks, (3) the criteria used by the system for determining whether a check should be "out-sorted" included "location information," the dollar amount of the check and whether the check is "out-of-sequence," (4) a check that is "in-sequence" and under $10,000 will not ordinarily be sight reviewed, (5) a business check payable to an individual which is deposited at a non-Wells Fargo branch and is out-of-sequence will not be sight reviewed unless it exceeds $10,000 and (6) checks that are out-of-sequence or over $10,000 may be out-sorted if they meet other criteria. Plaintiff attempted to show that the unauthorized checks at issue herein were "out-of-sequence," but this showing is immaterial because plaintiff's evidence indicated that even an out-of-sequence check which was deposited at a non-Wells Fargo branch and was for less than $10,000 would not be sight reviewed. All of the checks at issue here were deposited at non-Wells Fargo branches, were for less than $10,000 and were not sight reviewed. It is irrelevant whether these checks were "out-of-sequence."

Defendant established its entitlement to judgment by showing that the preclusion set forth in former section 4406 applied. None of plaintiff's evidence established any material triable issue of fact with regard to defendant's showing that its check processing system comported with general banking usage in the area. Instead, plaintiff's showing was merely an attempt to show that defendant's system was inadequate because it did not result in sight review of checks like those herein in question. Plaintiff's expert opined that defendant's check processing system was "commercially unreasonable" because it resulted in sight review of only 1% of the checks processed and it did not require sight review of all out-of-sequence checks. However, plaintiff's expert did not provide any evidence that defendant's check processing system was inconsistent with the general practice in the banking industry in the area. Plaintiff's evidence failed to controvert defendant's showing.

Plaintiff nevertheless claims that summary judgment was precluded because it was entitled to proceed on its theory that "the procedures followed by a bank are unreasonable, arbitrary or unfair." Plaintiff derives this language from a comment to section 3103, subdivision (a)(7). "The second sentence of subsection (a)(7) is a particular rule limited to the duty of a bank to examine an instrument taken by a bank for processing for collection or payment by automated means. This particular rule applies primarily to Section 4–406 and it is discussed in Comment 4 to that section. Nothing in Section 3–103(a)(7) is intended to prevent a customer from proving that the procedures followed by a bank are unreasonable, arbitrary or unfair." (Uniform Commercial Code Comment to Comm.Code, § 3103.) Plaintiff apparently believes that this comment *obviates the preclusion* stated in former section 4406 when there is evidence that a bank has used "unreasonable" procedures. We find no such meaning in this comment.

Neither section 4406 nor section 3103 provides that the preclusion set forth in section 4406 is obviated if bank procedures which are consistent with general banking usage are nevertheless shown to be unfair, unreasonable or arbitrary. The import of the comment to section 3103, subdivision (a)(7) is that, *in an action where the fairness of bank procedures is relevant,* a customer may prove that certain bank practices were unreasonable, unfair or arbitrary, even though those practices were consistent with general banking usage. For instance, a bank customer might bring an action for negligence against a bank which was based on something other than unauthorized signatures on checks. * * * Such an action could be supported by proof that the bank's procedures were unfair even though they were consistent with general banking usage. The language in question indicates that the professional standard of care, imported into section 4406 by its use of the term "ordinary care," is applicable to bank procedures for processing checks in an action based on unauthorized signatures, but may not be applicable in actions based on independent wrongs by the bank. This comment does not obviate the clear and unambiguous preclusion set forth in section 4406.

Defendant proved that it had a complete defense to all of plaintiff's causes of action. Plaintiff failed to dispute defendant's showing by raising any triable issue of fact. The trial court's judgment must be upheld.

CONCLUSION

The judgment is affirmed.

■ PREMO, ACTING P.J., and ELIA, J., CONCUR.

NOTES

1. If the customer and payor bank enter into the increasingly common agreement that allows the bank to retain the cancelled checks and to send the customer a periodic statement of account, does the customer have enough information to detect forged checks drawn on its account? § 4–406(a) and (b). Comment 1.

2. There has been some disagreement in the courts on the question of what constitutes reasonable promptness by the customer in discovering an unauthorized signature and in notifying the bank when the wrongdoer is the person designated by the customer to check the monthly statement. Under § 1–201(27) the customer would seem to be bound by the information supplied by the bank when that information reaches the customer's employee who is authorized to receive it and act on it. Under the law of agency, if that employee fails to notify the bank of the forgery the customer should be bound by the employee's conduct regardless of whether the employee's failure to notify is due to negligence or is the deliberate act of the employee to cover up the employee's wrongdoing. The issue should not be whether the customer was negligent in the procedure chosen for reviewing the bank statements if the employee receiving and acting on the statements was the designated agent of the customer for that purpose. See Warren Seavey, Notice Through An Agent, 65 U. of Pa.L.Rev. 1, 7–8 (1916).

3. In Pine Bluff National Bank v. Kesterson, 257 Ark. 813, 520 S.W.2d 253 (1975), the bank paid checks of a trust bearing the signatures of two trustees. There were three trustees of the trust and the agreement with the bank required the signatures of all three on checks. The court held that the authorized signature of the trust was comprised of the signature of all three trustees; therefore, the bank paid checks bearing an unauthorized signature of the trust and § 4–406 applied. Wolfe v. University National Bank, 270 Md. 70, 310 A.2d 558 (1973), represents a contrary view. In that case the customer, a partnership, agreed with its bank that all checks drawn on the partnership account had to be signed by two of the three partners. The bank paid out on 37 checks signed by only one partner. Customer brought suit nearly two years after the last check in issue was written, and the bank claimed the one-year limitation in former § 4–406(4) (now § 4–406(f)) barred the action. The court disagreed stating: "UCC § 4–406 is inapplicable here because it is only concerned with unauthorized signatures and alterations. An 'unauthorized signature' 'means one made without actual, implied or apparent authority and includes a forgery,' UCC § 1–201(43) * * * The signatures of the * * * [the partners who signed] were not forged, not made without authority, nor did they constitute an alteration of any kind." 310 A.2d at 560. The court saw the infirmity not as the presence of an unauthorized signature but the absence of a second authorized signature.

This split of authority has been resolved by revised Article 3 in favor of the view stated in *Pine Bluff*. § 3–403(b) and § 4–104(c) ("unauthorized signature").

PROBLEM

Corporation has a checking account in Bank. The agreement with respect to the account states that Bank may pay a check drawn on Corporation's account only if the check is signed by both the president and the treasurer of Corporation. The treasurer fraudulently wrote three checks on Corporation's account payable to the order of the treasurer. Each check bore two signatures on behalf of Corporation. One was that of the treasurer. The other purported to be that of the president of Corporation, but in fact it was a forgery made by the treasurer.

1. The first check, in the amount of $1,000, was paid by Bank on January 2 by automated equipment without any human examination of the check. The cancelled check was returned to Corporation on January 4.

2. The second check, in the amount of $2,000, was paid by Bank on February 20 by automated equipment without any human examination of the check. The cancelled check was returned to Corporation on March 3.

3. The third check, in the amount of $5,000, was paid by Bank on February 28. Before the check was paid an employee of Bank examined the check but failed to detect the forgery of the president's signature. The cancelled check was returned to Corporation on March 3.

Under the established procedures of Bank, checks presented for payment in amounts less than $2,500 were not examined by anybody before payment. All checks paid by Bank were returned to Corporation each month along with Corporation's monthly statement of account.

The fraud by the treasurer was discovered by Corporation in June. The treasurer, who is insolvent, used the proceeds of the three checks to pay gambling debts. Corporation notified Bank of the forged checks on June 7, promptly after discovery of the fraud. Corporation demanded that Bank restore to Corporation's account the $8,000 debited to the account as a result of payment of the checks.

With respect to each of the checks, state your opinion whether, under § 4–406, Corporation is entitled to recover from Bank.

NOTE: FRAUD PREVENTION MEASURES

According to Clark & Clark, The Law of Bank Deposits, Collections and Credit Cards ¶ 10.01[6][a] (Cum.Supp.1995), the American Bankers Association estimated losses from check fraud at $815 million in 1993, stemming from 1,267,000 cases. A substantial number of these forgeries was believed done by "professionals," particularly at larger banks. Banks have attempted to reduce these losses by adopting fraud prevention measures. These are described in Clark & Clark, supra, ¶ 10.01[5] (Rev.ed. 1995) and ¶ 10.01[6] (Cum.Supp.1995). Traditional methods involving sight review, random examination, and special paper for printing checks are not very effective against professionals who have available desktop computers and color printers.

Large banks offer a service under which business customers notify the bank each day of the checks drawn by the customer. When checks drawn by that customer are presented for payment, the bank compares these checks with the list given by the customer. If the checks don't match, they are returned to the presenting bank. When the checks reach the depositary bank, it will erase the provisional credit given its depositor. If the depositary bank has already allowed the depositor to withdraw the funds, it has the burden of pursuing this person to get the money back. Since, as we indicated in the preceding chapter, banks under Reg CC are making funds available for most checks either on the day of deposit or the next day, it is likely that the money has been withdrawn in cases in which the forger is the depositor. After Reg CC one of the favorite handiworks of skilled forgers has been cashier's checks, which must be available for withdrawal by the depositor the day after deposit.

Software companies have developed programs which allow banks to scan accounts for possible forgeries without the assistance of customers. The software allows a bank to review the past activity of customers' accounts in order to construct an archive for each account that shows a profile of the customer's usage. Checks presented for payment on these accounts will be reviewed for aberrations from this profile that may point to suspect checks. Fraud detection factors may include whether the check is larger in amount than checks drawn on this account in the past, whether the check number duplicates other checks already paid, whether the check number is out of sequence with other checks the customer is currently drawing, whether the check lacks any check number, and whether the volume of activity in the customer's account exceeds past levels.

2.   RIGHT OF PAYOR BANK TO RECOVER MISTAKEN PAYMENT OF CHECK

a.   FORGED CHECKS

The law of mistake and restitution recognizes the general principle that a person who confers a benefit upon another person because of a mistake is entitled to restitution from the person receiving the benefit. For example, a shopkeeper receives a $10 bill from a customer in payment of goods purchased by the customer for a price of $8. The shopkeeper, who has an obligation to give the customer $2 change, gives the customer $12 because of a mistaken belief that the customer had paid with a $20 bill. The shopkeeper is entitled to get back the $10 paid by mistake. Restatement of Restitution § 19 (1937).

Mistake can also occur when money is paid for a negotiable instrument either by a person who buys the instrument or by a person such as a payor bank who pays the instrument. The law of mistake and restitution applies to negotiable instrument cases, but special rules apply in some cases. The mistake cases fall into various categories and most of the cases involve payment or acceptance of a check or other draft by the drawee. The principal categories involve forged checks, checks bearing a forged indorsement, altered checks, checks on which the drawer has stopped payment, and checks drawn on an account with insufficient funds to cover the check.

The seminal case in this area is Price v. Neal, 3 Burr. 1354, 97 Eng.Rep. 871 (1762), which involved two forged bills of exchange drawn on Price and indorsed to Neal, a bona fide purchaser for value. Price paid Neal on the first bill and then accepted the second bill which was subsequently purchased by Neal. After Price paid the second bill he learned that the signature of the drawer of the bills had been forged. Price sued Neal to get his money back. Lord Mansfield, in deciding in favor of the defendant, stated:

It is an action upon the case, for money had and received to the plaintiff's use. In which action, the plaintiff can not recover the money, unless it be against conscience in the defendant, to retain it: and great liberality is always allowed, in this sort of action.

But it can never be thought unconscientious in the defendant, to retain this money, when he has once received it upon a bill of exchange indorsed to him for a fair and valuable consideration, which he had bona fide paid, without the least priority or suspicion of any forgery.

Here was no fraud: no wrong. It was incumbent upon the plaintiff, to be satisfied "that the bill drawn upon him was the drawer's hand," before he accepted or paid it: but it was not incumbent upon the defendant, to inquire into it. Here was notice given by the defendant to the plaintiff of a bill drawn upon him: and he sends his servant to pay it and take it up. The other bill he actually accepts; after which acceptance, the defendant innocently and bona fide discounts it. The plaintiff lies by, for a considerable time after he has paid these bills; and then found out "that they were forged:" and the forger comes to be hanged. He made no objection to them, at the time of paying them. Whatever neglect there was, was on his side. The defendant had actual encouragement from the plaintiff himself, for negotiating the second bill, from the plaintiff's having without any scruple or hesitation paid the first: and he paid the whole value, bona fide. It is a misfortune which has happened without the defendant's fault or neglect. If there was no neglect in the plaintiff, yet there is no reason to throw off the loss from one innocent man upon another innocent man: but, in this case, if there was any fault or negligence in any one, it certainly was in the plaintiff, and not in the defendant.

Payment or acceptance by the drawee of a forged check or other draft is addressed in § 3–418(a) and (c) and § 3–417(a)(3). Under these provisions the rule of Price v. Neal is preserved. Section 4–208(a)(3) is identical in effect to § 3–417(a)(3) and applies specifically to warranties made in the bank-collection process to a payor bank with respect to an Article 4 "draft" (§ 4–104(a)(7)) which includes a check.

PROBLEMS

1. Nieman introduced himself to Altman, a diamond merchant, as a buyer for J.W. Mays, a corporation. Nieman then selected some diamonds to be purchased by J.W. Mays. Altman put the diamonds into a sealed envelope and set them aside for Nieman. Altman retained possession of the envelope containing the diamonds. A few days later Altman received a letter from Nieman confirming the purchase by J.W. Mays of the diamonds. Enclosed was a check for $22,000 to the order of Altman. The check was drawn on the account of J.W. Mays in City Bank in full payment of the diamonds. Altman deposited the check in Altman's account in Trade Bank and Trade Bank presented the check to City Bank for payment. A few days later Nieman appeared to pick up the diamonds. Altman called Trade Bank

and asked whether the $22,000 check had been paid. When Altman was told that the check had been paid by City Bank, Altman delivered the diamonds to Nieman. Later, City Bank learned that the signature of J.W. Mays on the check was forged and demanded that Altman repay the $22,000 received in payment of the check. Altman refused to repay.

What warranty did Altman make to City Bank when the $22,000 check was presented for payment? § 3–417(a)(3). Did Altman breach that warranty? Did Altman take the check in good faith and for value? Did Altman in good faith change position in reliance on the payment by City Bank? Is City Bank entitled to recover the $22,000 payment from Altman? § 3–418(a) and (c). Would your answers to the last two questions be different if Altman had not called Trade Bank to verify that the check had been paid before he released the diamonds to Nieman?

This problem is based on the facts of First National City Bank v. Altman, 3 UCC Rep.Serv. 815, 1966 WL 8964 (N.Y.Sup.Ct., N.Y.Co.1966).

2. Buyer drew a check on the account of Dupont in Payor Bank and forged Dupont's signature as drawer of the check. The check was payable to the order of Buyer. Buyer bought an automobile from Dealer and offered to negotiate the check to Dealer as a down payment of the price of the automobile. Dealer refused to take the check unless it was certified by Payor Bank. Buyer took the check to Payor Bank and obtained certification of the check. Buyer then negotiated the check to Dealer and received delivery of the automobile. The next day, while still in possession of the check, Dealer learned from a credit reporting agency that Buyer had a criminal record that included arrests for forgery. Dealer then took the check to Payor Bank and demanded payment without disclosing the information about Buyer's criminal record. Payor Bank paid Dealer the amount of the check. Ten days later Payor Bank discovered the forgery and demanded that Dealer repay the money received in payment of the check. Dealer refused to repay.

What warranty did Dealer make to Payor Bank when the check was presented for payment? Does § 3–417(a) apply? Does § 3–417(d) apply? Was there any breach of warranty by Dealer? Is Payor Bank entitled to recover from Dealer the amount paid on the check? § 3–418(a) and (c). Does Payor Bank have any cause of action against Buyer? § 3–417(a)(3) and Comment 4 to § 3–417.

Suppose Dealer, at the time the check was presented for payment, told Payor Bank about Buyer's criminal record. Payor Bank called Dupont and was informed that the check was a forgery. Payor Bank refused to pay Dealer. Is Dealer entitled to payment? § 3–413(a).

b. **FORGED INDORSEMENT**

PROBLEM

Drawer drew a check to the order of Payee. The check was stolen from Payee by Thief who signed Payee's name to the check as a blank indorsement. Thief then delivered the check to Jennifer, who purchased for value, in good faith and without notice that the indorsement was forged. Jennifer deposited the check with Depositary Bank which presented the check and received payment from Payor Bank. Depositary Bank credited Jennifer's account and the credit was withdrawn. Payee then notified Drawer of the theft. Drawer notified Payor Bank but was told that the check had already been paid. Is Payor Bank entitled to recover the amount of the check from either Depositary Bank or Jennifer? § 3–417(a)(1), § 4–208(a)(1), and Comments 2 and 3 to § 3–417. If Depositary Bank has to pay, is Depositary Bank entitled to recover from Jennifer? § 3–416(a)(1) and (2). Is the result in this case consistent with Price v. Neal?

NOTE

The preceding Problem is discussed by Judge Goldberg in Perini Corp. v. First National Bank of Habersham County, 553 F.2d 398, 403–406 (5th Cir.1977):

A.   The Code Framework

Perpetuating a distinction introduced into the legal annals by Lord Mansfield in the eighteenth century, the Code accords separate treatment to forged drawer signatures (hereinafter "forged checks") and forged indorsements. In general, the drawee bank is strictly liable to its customer drawer for payment of either a forged check or a check containing a forged indorsement. In the case of a forged indorsement, the drawee generally may pass liability back through the collection chain to the party who took from the forger and, of course, to the forger himself if available. In the case of a forged check, however, liability generally rests with the drawee. The patchwork of provisions from which this general allocation of liability emerges merits more detailed description.

1.   Forged Indorsements

A check bearing a forged indorsement, included in the § 1–201(43) definition of unauthorized signatures,[6] is not "properly payable." J. White and R. Summers, Uniform Commercial Code 559 (1972).[7] Re-

---

6.   Section 1–201(43) provides:

"Unauthorized" signature or indorsement means one made without actual, implied or apparent authority and includes a forgery.

7.   A check drawn to the order of the payee, i.e., an order instrument, may not be negotiated without the payee's indorsement. * * * The unauthorized indorsement by the forger does not operate as the true payee's signature. See § 3–404(1), which provides that "any unauthorized signature is wholly inoperative as that of the person whose name

is signed unless he ratifies it or is precluded from denying it." A forged indorsement check therefore lacks the payee's indorsement and, without that necessary indorsement, may not be negotiated. * * * Negotiation is necessary to confer holder status on a check's transferee. Id. Accordingly, the transferee of a forged indorsement check does not become a holder. Only a holder or the holder's agent may properly present the check for payment. * * * Thus the UCC reaffirms the general pre-Code rule that a drawee may not charge its drawer customer's accounts for

gardless of the care exercised, a drawee bank is with few exceptions liable to its drawer customer for payment of such a check. * * *

Upon recrediting the drawer's account after payment over a forged indorsement, the drawee will seek redress against prior parties in the collection chain through an action for breach of the statutory warranty of good title. Each person who obtains payment of a check from the drawee and each prior transferor warrants to the party who in good faith pays the check that he has good title to the instrument. * * * A forged indorsement is ineffective to pass title * * *. The drawee may therefore bring a breach of warranty action against a person who presented a check bearing a forged indorsement. These· warranty actions will continue up the collection chain to the party who took from the forger or to the forger himself.

Additionally, payment of a check bearing a forged indorsement constitutes conversion * * *. This conversion action at least provides the check's "true owner," the payee or indorsee from whom it was stolen and whose name was falsely indorsed, direct relief from the drawee. * * * Without the conversion action the true owner would have to seek payment from the drawer, who might be overcautious and unaware of his right to force the drawee to recredit his account for any payment over a forged indorsement.

The danger created by forged indorsements is that the party designated by the instrument as entitled to its proceeds will appear with a claim to those proceeds after payment has been made to the malefactor. The statutory actions for improper payment, conversion, and breach of warranty of good title combine, however, inartfully, to safeguard the drawer against double liability and to assure the payee of payment. The loss falls on the party who took the check from the forger, or on the forger himself.

2.   Forged Checks

As opposed to diverting an intended payment to someone other than the intended recipient, forged checks present the problem of depleting the ostensible drawer's funds when he had intended no payment. The Code's treatment of forged checks, however, begins in the same place as its treatment of forged indorsements. The forgery does not operate as the ostensible drawer's signature. * * * Payment consequently is not to the ostensible drawer's order and violates the drawee bank's strict duty to charge its customer's account only for properly payable items. * * *

payment of an order instrument bearing a forged indorsement. * * *

It may be assumed for purposes of this introductory sketch that the analysis described for forged indorsement checks equally applies to checks drawn to a principal and indorsed by an ostensible agent with no showing of representative capacity. Considerations unique to the representative capacity problem are developed more fully in Part III infra.

The Code's analysis of forged check liability not only begins with the drawee, however; it also generally ends there. The drawee's payment of a forged check is final in favor of a holder in due course or one who has relied on the payment in good faith. § 3–418. This final payment rule codifies and attempts to clarify the rule of Price v. Neal, 3 Burr. 1354 (K.B.1762), "under which a drawee who accepts or pays an instrument on which the signature of the drawer is forged is bound on his acceptance and cannot recover back his payment." * * * Prior parties in the collection chain who meet the prerequisites set out in § 3–418 will be immunized by its final payment rule from any liability for negligence in dealing with the forged check.

The above scheme allocating forgery losses among the various parties to the check collection process operates without regard to fault. The drawee's duty to charge its customer's account only for "properly payable" items and the warranty of title given by prior parties in the chain of transfer impose standards of strict liability.

Fault does occupy a secondary role in the UCC treatment of forgery losses. One whose negligence substantially contributes to the making of an unauthorized signature cannot assert the invalidity of that signature against a holder in due course or a drawee who without negligence pays the check. § 3–406. Thus the drawee can pass the loss back to a drawer or forward to a prior party in the collection chain whose negligence substantially contributed to a forgery. The complaining party's negligence will not, however, bar otherwise available recovery against a party, including a drawee, who is also negligent. Id. Additionally, while nothing in the Code precludes a bank and its customer from modifying the forgery loss rules by contract, the bank cannot enforce an agreement permitting it to act in violation of reasonable commercial standards. § 4–103(1).

B.   The Code Policy: Incompletely Greasing the Commercial Wheels

In sum, the Code, while allowing for some modification on the basis of fault or agreement, sets up a system of strict liability rules allocating loss according to the type of forgery. The system uneasily rests on two policy bases. First, it incorporates an at least partially outmoded notion of the relative positions of drawee banks and prior parties in the collection chain with respect to detecting different types of forgeries. Second, it incompletely serves the notion that commerce will be facilitated by bringing to the swiftest practicable conclusion the processing of a check transaction.

As mentioned, the separate treatment given forged checks and forged indorsements harkens back to the eighteenth century decision of the King's Bench in Price v. Neal. That decision left forged check liability on the drawee on the view that, as against other parties in the line of transfer, the drawee stood in the best position to recognize the signature of the drawer, its customer. The corollary principle for forged indorsements is that the person who takes the check from the forger—

frequently, as here, the depositary bank—is in the best position to detect the bogus indorsement.

Reaffirming Price v. Neal in the final payment rule of § 3–418, the Code drafters recognized that the case's appraisal of relative opportunity to scrutinize drawer signatures was somewhat unrealistic in a nation where banks may handle some 60 million checks daily.[9] The contemporary pace of commerce has eroded the five senses used by bankers in the face-to-face era of Price versus Neal; little remains save the sensory activity of punching keys. While the drafters thus concluded that Price v. Neal had been drained of all its personality, they nevertheless insisted that its conclusion survives. The drafters noted that modern groundwork for the final payment rule could be found in the

> less fictional rationalization * * * that it is highly desirable to end the transaction on an instrument when it is paid rather than reopen and upset a series of commercial transactions at a later date when the forgery is discovered.

§ 3–418, Comment 1. In recognition of the frenetic commerce of our time, the thrust of the UCC here and elsewhere is for speed and facility at some expense to exact checks and balances.

Leaving forged check liability on the drawee may serve well this finality policy. That policy, however, does not itself justify separate treatment for forged checks and indorsements. The concern that commercial transactions be swiftly brought to rest applies with equal force to both varieties of wrongdoing. See White and Summers, supra, at 522–23; Comment, Allocation of Losses From Check Forgeries Under the Law of Negotiable Instruments and the Uniform Commercial Code, 62 Yale L.J. 417, 459–60 (1953).

While finality viewed alone calls for equal treatment of forged checks and forged indorsements, one might still maintain that forged indorsements merit separate rules. The modern demands of commerce have as the drafters recognized, deprived drawees of any superior opportunity to detect forged drawer's signatures. Only a concern for finality therefore justifies placing forged check losses on drawee banks.

---

9. For a discussion of the volume of checks processed and the resultant interplay between the law of forgery losses and bankers' perceptions of the forgery problem, see Murray, Price v. Neal in the Electronic Age: An Empirical Survey, 87 Banking L.J. 686 (1970). We note the commentator's interesting observation that many banks do not record separately losses from forged checks and forged indorsements, contrary to the implicit assumption in the final payment rule that the two types of losses represent security breakdowns in different functions of a bank—accepting checks for deposit to its customers accounts and paying checks drawn by its customers—which might call for different protective measures.

On the other hand, the author does suggest specific measures for protecting banks against forged check losses. The possibility remains that the separate allocation of strict liability for forged check and forged indorsement losses may act as some incentive for the development of those precautionary measures that consistent with the press of business will most effectively reduce the risk of loss from either type of forgery.

Such simple expedients as requiring identification, however, may still permit transferees of checks to provide a significant protection against forged indorsements that drawees cannot. To insure such protective measures are taken, it may be sensible to override the finality policy and to place forged indorsement losses on the depositary bank or other party who takes from the forger. * * *

c. OVERDRAFTS

If a payor bank pays a check that is forged or which bears a forged indorsement, it is clear that the bank paid the check by mistake. No bank would knowingly pay such a check because the check is not properly payable and the payor bank is not entitled to charge the account of the drawer. The payment of a check drawn on an account in which there are insufficient funds to cover the check is different. Under § 4–401(a) such a check is properly payable and the drawer's account can be charged. Thus, it may not be clear at the time of payment whether the payor bank paid by mistake or intended to grant credit to the drawer. Intentional payment of checks that create overdrafts is very common. There is some authority denying a payor bank any right of restitution in overdraft cases, but most courts follow Restatement of Restitution § 29 (1937) which recognizes a limited right of restitution in such cases. In revised Article 3, overdraft cases are governed by § 3–418(b) which gives to the payor bank a right to recover "to the extent permitted by the law governing mistake and restitution." But § 3–418(b) is subject to § 3–418(c). No right of restitution may be asserted against a person who took the check in good faith and for value or who in good faith changed position in reliance on payment of the check.

National Savings, which follows, discusses the issue under common law and § 3–418 of the original Article 3.

National Savings & Trust Co. v. Park Corp.

United States Court of Appeals, Sixth Circuit, 1983.
722 F.2d 1303, cert. denied, 466 U.S. 939, 104 S.Ct. 1916, 80 L.Ed.2d 464 (1984).

■ BOYCE F. MARTIN, JR., CIRCUIT JUDGE.

In this diversity action, National Savings and Trust challenges the summary denial of its claim for restitution of $74,737.25 it mistakenly paid to Park Corporation on a bad check.

On January 8, 1980, Park Corporation contracted to sell some used mining equipment to DAI International Investment Corporation. The sales agent for the transaction was Garland Caribbean Corporation. As part of its down payment, DAI gave Garland a check for $75,000 drawn on its account with the plaintiff, National Savings and Trust Company. On January 16, Garland called National Savings to determine if DAI had sufficient funds in its account to cover this check. The bank said DAI did not. That same day, Garland endorsed the check over to Park Corporation. Park Corporation then sent the check to National Savings "for collection."

On January 22, Garland once again called the bank to determine if DAI had sufficient funds in its account to cover the check. Once again, the bank said DAI did not.[1] Moreover, on this occasion, the banking employee who received the inquiry went to the bank's "platform officer" and notified him not to accept any DAI checks drawn on insufficient funds. Unfortunately for the bank, the platform officer only saw checks arriving through normal banking channels and not those coming in "for collection."

DAI's check arrived at the bank that same day. However, the employee who normally processed "for collection" checks was scheduled to work in another department that day. Prior to her departure, she did manage to open the incoming mail, including the DAI check. Her supervisor then volunteered to help out by taking the DAI check to the wire room for payment. Neither employee followed the bank's standard procedure and checked DAI's account to ensure that it held sufficient funds to cover the check. Each assumed that the other had done so. As a result, the check was paid even though DAI had only $263.75 in its account.

On January 28, 1980, after discovering its mistake, National Savings asked Park Corporation to return the $75,000. Park refused and National Savings subsequently brought this lawsuit. On motion for summary judgment by the defendant, the court found for Park on the grounds that National Savings had made an improvident extension of credit and that the bank was in a better position to know the true facts and to guard against mistakes. We disagree.

The basic law of restitution in Ohio, the state whose law controls, is summarized in Firestone Tire & Rubber Co. v. Central Nat'l Bank of Cleveland, 159 Ohio St. 423, 112 N.E.2d 636 (1953). The *Firestone* case held that money paid to another by mistake is recoverable unless the other person has changed his position in reliance on the payment. This rule applies even if the mistake was the result of negligence.

Park Corporation attempts to circumvent the holding in *Firestone* by arguing that banks are not protected by normal restitutionary principles when they pay an insufficient funds (NSF) check. There is some support for this position. See, e.g., Spokane & Eastern Trust Co. v. Huff, 63 Wash. 225, 115 P. 80 (1911); 7 Zollman, *The Law of Banks and Banking* § 5062 (1936). Nonetheless, this rule has not been universally applied, see, e.g., Manufacturers Trust Co. v. Diamond, 17 Misc.2d 909, 186 N.Y.S.2d 917, 919 (1959), and Park has not cited, nor have we been able to find, any Ohio cases adopting this rule. Moreover, it is questionable whether such a doctrine, if ever in existence, would survive the subsequent enactment of the Uniform Commercial Code in Ohio and the particular provisions applicable to the facts of the present case.

Park Corporation next argues that *Firestone* does not control because National Savings' payment was not a mistake but rather a knowing

---

1. There is no evidence Park was ever aware of Garland's phone conversations with   the bank.

extension of credit. Park relies heavily on the New Jersey case of Demos v. Lyons, 151 N.J.Super. 489, 376 A.2d 1352 (Law Div.1977). The factual circumstances of *Demos,* however, are quite distinct from the present case. In *Demos,* the bank actually examined the customer's account, realized the customer had insufficient funds to cover the check, yet paid the check anyway. The bank did not want to embarrass its customer and it hoped that he had made a late deposit to cover the check which would appear on the next day's balance sheet. No such deposit was ever made. In our case, National Savings never intended to make good on an NSF check. The platform officer had been notified not to pay out on DAI's check. The "for collection" employees were operating under standing orders to check balances before paying a check and never to pay on an NSF check. Despite all these precautions, the check was paid. At no time, however, did the employees making the payment decision know that DAI's account had insufficient funds to cover the check.

[Omitted is the part of the opinion in which the court holds that the case is governed by § 3–418.]

Park Corporation next contends that, even if section 3–418 controls, it is both a holder in due course and one who has changed its position in reliance on National Saving's payment and therefore should be allowed to retain the $75,000. We find no support in the record for either proposition. On the holder in due course issue, Park does not qualify because it did not give value for the check. It was still in possession of the machinery it had contracted to sell to DAI. Although it had promised to deliver the equipment to DAI, such an executory promise does not constitute value. U.C.C. § 3–303, Comment 3. Park Corporation is, of course, no longer required to carry out its promise because DAI has breached its agreement to pay.

As for detrimental reliance, Park contends that it paid $37,500 as a commission to Garland Corporation on the assumption that DAI's check was good. However, Park did not pay Garland until February 13, 1980, two weeks after National Savings had informed Park that it had paid the DAI check by mistake and that it wanted Park to return the money. Section 3–418 only makes payment by the bank final in favor of someone who has "*in good faith* changed his position in reliance on the payment." Once aware of the insufficiency in funds, Park could not have "in good faith" paid Garland $37,500 in reliance on that check. Park also alleges it paid rent for storing the equipment and painted the equipment in reliance on the payment. There is no evidence to support these allegations.

Accordingly, the decision of the district court is reversed.

3. CONVERSION ACTIONS REGARDING CHECKS BEARING FORGED INDORSEMENT

a. ACTION BY PAYEE

(i) Introduction

In a common type of forged-indorsement case the check is stolen by an employee of the payee. The check is an ordinary check mailed to the payee by the drawer in payment of an obligation owed to the payee. The check is received by the payee when the mail delivery is made and the payee becomes a holder of the check at that time. Suppose the check is stolen by an employee of the payee who works as a clerk in the payee's mailroom. The employee forges the payee's name as an indorsement of the check, and obtains payment from the drawee bank. How does the theft of the check and its collection affect the payee's rights with respect to the check and the obligation of the drawer to the payee that the check was intended to pay? Under § 3–310(b) the obligation for which the check was received becomes "suspended" at the time the payee receives the check. In the hands of the payee the check represents a right to receive money which is a property right of the payee. This property right is provisionally substituted for the right of the payee to enforce the obligation for which the check was received. If the payee receives payment of the check, the obligation for which the check was received is discharged to the extent of the payment. § 3–310(b)(1). If the payee presents the check for payment and the check is dishonored, the payee has a cause of action against the drawer of the check either on the check (§ 3–414(b)) or on the obligation for which the check was received. § 3–310(b)(3).

What rights does the payee have if the check is stolen from the payee and the thief obtains payment from the drawee? Under § 3–310(b)(1) "payment * * * of the check" results in discharge of the obligation for which a check was taken, but under § 3–602(a), the check is not paid unless payment is made to a person entitled to enforce the check. Payment to the thief or a transferee of the thief does not result in payment of the check and the obligation of the drawer on the check is not discharged. The payee of the check remains the owner of the check and the person entitled to enforce it. § 3–301 and § 3–309. The drawee's payment to a person not entitled to enforce the check does not affect the payee's rights in the check. The payee, however, does not have a right to enforce the obligation for which the check was received. That obligation remains suspended under § 3–310(b) because neither dishonor nor payment of the check has occurred. Under the last sentence of § 3–310(b)(4), the payee of a stolen check who is not in possession of the check, has rights against the drawer only on the check. § 3–309, § 3–414, and Comment 4 to § 3–310. Thus, the payee has the burden of asserting rights with respect to the stolen check, and there are several possible courses of action available to the payee against third parties as well as the drawer.

Although the payee from whom a check has been stolen has no right to obtain a substitute check from the drawer, sometimes the drawer will issue such a check. In the case in which payment with respect to the stolen check has not yet been made by the drawee, the drawee can be informed of the theft and payment to the thief may be avoided. If payment by the drawee has already been made, the drawer can insist that the drawee recredit the drawer's account because payment to the thief did not entitle the drawee to debit the drawer's account. § 4–401. If the drawer refuses to issue a replacement check, the payee has a remedy against the drawer on the check, but that remedy may not be convenient. § 3–309. Often a forged indorsement case involves thefts of many checks from one payee by the same thief. Actions against the various drawers of the stolen checks may not be feasible. An action against the person who took the checks from the thief is usually a better remedy.

In the hands of the payee, a check is property and, if that property is stolen, the rules of conversion applying to personal property also apply to the check. Thus, the payee of the stolen check has an action in conversion against the thief for the amount of the check. But the law of conversion also allows an action to be brought against "innocent converters," i.e. persons who exercise dominion over stolen property without knowledge that it was stolen. Thus, if a thief sells stolen goods to a good faith purchaser for value, the owner has an action against the BFP as well. A stolen check bearing the forged indorsement of the payee can be turned into money by selling it to a depositary bank or other purchaser for cash, by depositing it to the thief's bank account for bank credit that can subsequently be withdrawn, or by presenting the check for payment to the drawee bank. Each of these takers of the check is a potential defendant. The common law was clear that a conversion action could be brought by the payee against the person who bought the check. The common law cases were divided on the issue of whether the drawee bank was liable in conversion if it paid a stolen check bearing a forged indorsement, but most courts held that a conversion action was available and that view was adopted by original Article 3. Revised Article 3 states the current rules regarding conversion in § 3–420.

(ii) Possession of Check by Payee

Barclays Bank, which follows, discusses the conversion remedy of the payee of a stolen check and the necessity of possession by the payee. The issue which is the focus of this case is now specifically addressed in § 3–420(a).

State of New York v. Barclays Bank of New York

Court of Appeals of New York, 1990.
76 N.Y.2d 533, 561 N.Y.S.2d 697, 563 N.E.2d 11.

■ HANCOCK, JUDGE.

In the absence of actual or constructive possession of a check, does the named payee have a right of action against the depositary bank which has paid out the proceeds over a forged indorsement? This is the question presented in plaintiff's appeal from a dismissal of its action to recover the amounts of several checks drawn by taxpayers to the order of various State taxing authorities. The checks were never delivered to plaintiff; the taxpayers' dishonest accountant misappropriated them, and deposited them in his own account at Banker's Trust Company of Hudson Valley, N.A.[1] For

---

1. Defendant Barclays Bank of New York, N.A. is a successor to Bankers Trust Company. Henceforth, "defendant" will refer to Barclays and Bankers Trust as one entity.

reasons stated hereafter, we hold that plaintiff has no right of action and accordingly affirm the order granting summary judgment to defendant.

The case stems from the activities of Richard Caliendo, an accountant. Caliendo prepared tax returns for various clients. To satisfy their tax liability, the clients issued checks payable to various State taxing entities, and gave them to Caliendo. Between 1977 and 1979, he forged indorsements on these checks, deposited them in his own account with defendant, and subsequently withdrew the proceeds. In November 1980—shortly after the scheme was uncovered—Caliendo died when the plane he was piloting crashed. The State never received the checks. In 1983, after learning of these events, the State commenced this action seeking to recover the aggregate face amount of the checks.

Supreme Court denied defendant's motion to dismiss the complaint and its subsequent motion for summary judgment, concluding that the payee's possession of the checks was not essential to its action against the depositary bank. On appeal, the Appellate Division reversed and dismissed the complaint. It held that requiring "delivery, either actual or constructive, [as] an indispensable prerequisite for" a conversion action under UCC 3–419(1)(c) is consistent with the view of most authorities and supported by practical considerations (State of New York v. Barclays Bank, 151 A.D.2d 19, 21–24, 546 N.Y.S.2d 479). We agree.[2]

II

It has long been held that a check has no valid inception until delivery * * *. Further, a payee must have actual or constructive possession of a negotiable instrument in order to attain the status of a holder (see, UCC 1–201[20])and to have an interest in it. These are established principles of negotiable instruments law * * *.

Permitting a payee who has never had possession to maintain an action against the depositary bank would be inconsistent with these principles. It would have the effect of enforcing rights that do not exist. For this reason, most courts and commentators have concluded that either actual or constructive delivery to the payee is a necessary prerequisite to a conversion action * * *.

Significant practical considerations support this conclusion. Where a payee has never possessed the check, it is more likely that the forged

---

2. Plaintiff's complaint is framed as one for money had and received. Supreme Court in denying defendant's dismissal motion under CPLR 3211(a)(7), however, treated the action as one in contract, alone, or in both contract and conversion. Although, in its brief, plaintiff now appears to view the action primarily as one for money had and received or quasi contract, it cites cases and authorities pertaining to a conversion action under UCC 3–419(1)(c), and the Appellate Division apparently viewed it as such. For purposes of resolving the legal question before us—the effect of lack of delivery of the checks—it makes no difference whether plaintiff's action is under UCC 3–419(1)(c) or under some common-law theory. The result is the same (see, part III, infra). We accordingly discuss the authorities as being applicable to both the statutory and common-law theories.

indorsement resulted from the drawer's negligence, an issue which could not be readily contested in an action between the payee and the depositary bank * * *. Moreover, as noted by the Appellate Division, the payee is not left without a remedy, inasmuch as it can sue on the underlying obligation * * *.

Henderson v. Lincoln Rochester Trust Co., 303 N.Y. 27, 100 N.E.2d 117, on which plaintiff relies, does not support its argument in this respect. There, in concluding that the payee could maintain an action either in contract or conversion, the court did not reach the issue of nondelivery of the check. Other cases cited by plaintiff are readily distinguished. They involve situations where the plaintiff, unlike the State here, had received constructive possession of the check through delivery to the payee's agent, to a copayee, or to a coindorsee (see, e.g., Lund's, Inc. v. Chemical Bank, 870 F.2d 840 [2d Cir.] [delivery to coindorsees];[3] United States v. Bankers Trust Co., 17 UCC Rep.Serv. 136 [E.D.N.Y.1975] [delivery to copayee]; Burks Drywall v. Washington Bank & Trust Co., 110 Ill.App.3d 569, 66 Ill.Dec. 222, 442 N.E.2d 648 [1982] [delivery to copayee or agent]; Thornton & Co. v. Gwinnett Bank & Trust Co., 151 Ga.App. 641, 260 S.E.2d 765 [1979] [delivery to agent]).

Plaintiff maintains, however, citing language in *Burks Drywall,* 66 Ill.Dec. at 226, 442 N.E.2d, supra, at 652 and *Thornton,* 260 S.E.2d, supra, at 767, that, based solely on its status as named payee and intended beneficiary of the checks, it has a sufficient interest to bring a conversion action under UCC 3–419(1)(c) or a common-law action for money had and received. We believe such a rule would be contrary to the underlying theory of the UCC and, to the extent that the cases cited by plaintiff suggest it, we decline to follow them.

* * *

Nor are we persuaded by plaintiff's suggestion that permitting a suit * * * by a payee not-in-possession would promote judicial economy and avoid circuity of action. On the contrary, relegating such a payee to a suit against the drawer on the underlying obligation would give full effect to the UCC's loss allocation scheme by furthering the aim of placing ultimate responsibility on the party at fault through an orderly process in which each defendant in the transactional chain may interpose the defenses available to it * * *. And requiring a payee-not-in-possession to sue the drawer on the underlying claim would actually avoid circuity of action in some instances—for example, where the drawer's suit against the drawee bank is barred by valid defenses (see, UCC 3–406, 4–406) or where the drawer has an effective defense against the payee's claim. This concern has particular pertinence here where—as the Appellate Division observed (151

---

3. *Lund's* involved three checks, two of which were indorsed and delivered to coindorsees of plaintiff, thus, giving plaintiff sufficient possession to maintain a conversion action with respect to those checks under UCC 3–419(1)(c). A third check indorsed sole- ly to Lund's Inc. was determined on remand not to have been constructively delivered to plaintiff Lund. As to that check, the action was dismissed in reliance upon the Appellate Division's decision in this case (see, Lund v. Chemical Bank, 1990 WL 17711 [S.D.N.Y.]).

A.D.2d, at 20, 546 N.Y.S.2d 479)—it is contended that some of the checks were for inflated or nonexistent tax liabilities for which the drawers-taxpayers would have valid defenses against the State. In such cases, permitting a payee-not-in-possession to sue the depositary bank at the other end of the transactional chain would only produce unnecessary litigation. Accordingly, we agree with the Appellate Division that the rule requiring actual or constructive possession by a payee as a prerequisite for a suit against the depositary bank is preferable * * * and we adopt it.

III

Plaintiff contends, nevertheless, that even if possession is a prerequisite to a cause of action by a named payee against a depositary bank, it should prevail because the drawers' delivery of the checks to Caliendo constituted constructive delivery to the State. It is a general rule that putting a check in the hands of the drawer's own agent for purpose of delivery to the payee does not constitute delivery to the payee * * *; this is so because the drawer has control of the agent and the check is revocable and ineffective until the agent delivers it * * *. Here, of course, Caliendo had no agency or other relationship with the State which might have imputed his possession of the checks to it. Indeed, the State does not contend that it knew of Caliendo's dealings with the drawers or even of the checks' existence. Thus, applying these general rules, the State's claim must fail.

Wolfin v. Security Bank, (170 App.Div. 519, 156 N.Y.S. 474, affd. 218 N.Y. 709, 113 N.E. 1068), relied on by plaintiff, is not to the contrary. There, the drawer of the check gave it to the named payee with instructions that it be indorsed and delivered to plaintiff. Unlike the case at bar—where the checks were never delivered to the payee but remained in the hands of the drawers' accountant and agent—in *Wolfin* the drawer retained no control after the check was delivered to the named payee as a fully negotiable instrument * * *.

Finally, contrary to plaintiff's contentions, it cannot recover under a theory of unjust enrichment or quasi contract. It is true that, in creating a statutory right to bring a conversion action for payment over a forged indorsement * * * at the time of the Uniform Commercial Code's enactment, the Legislature did not intend to abrogate the payee's pre-Code common-law rights to sue in assumpsit, for money had and received or unjust enrichment * * *. This does not help plaintiff, however.

The theory of an action in quasi contract "rests upon the equitable principle that a person shall not be *allowed to enrich himself unjustly at the expense of another.* * * * It is an obligation which the law creates, in the absence of any agreement, when and because the acts of the parties or others have placed in the possession of one person money, or its equivalent, under such circumstances that in equity and good conscience he ought not to retain it" (Miller v. Schloss, 218 N.Y. 400, 407, 113 N.E. 337 [emphasis added]; *see,* Restatement of Restitution § 1, at 12–15). The general rule is that "the plaintiff *must have suffered a loss* and an action not based upon loss is not restitutionary." (Restatement of Restitution § 128, comment f, at 531 [emphasis added]). On this point, plaintiff's action in quasi contract, like its action for conversion * * *, must fail. The checks were never actually or constructively delivered to plaintiff. It, therefore, never acquired a property interest in them and cannot be said to have suffered a loss.

The order of the Appellate Division should, accordingly, be affirmed, with costs.

(iii) Liability of Depositary Bank as Agent for Collection

When a check is transferred to a depositary bank by its customer, the bank sometimes purchases the check from the customer by giving cash for it or by giving the customer a credit to the customer's account immediately available for withdrawal as of right. More commonly the depositary bank doesn't buy the check. Rather, it takes the check as agent of the customer to obtain payment of the check from the payor bank and pays the proceeds of the check to the customer after the check is paid. This distinction can have some importance in Article 3 because the status of the depositary bank as a holder in due course may depend upon whether it had given value for the check at the time the check was presented for payment. But in Article 4 the depositary bank is normally treated as an agent for collection whether or not the bank gave value to the customer for the check. § 4–201(a).

Under original Article 3 the law was clear that a person that cashed a check stolen from the payee could be held liable in conversion to the payee. But the question of whether a depositary bank that took a stolen check as an agent for collection was also liable was made unclear by a highly controversial provision of that statute, § 3–419(3). That issue is discussed in *Denn,* the case that follows. The result in *Denn* is reversed in revised Article 3 by § 3–420(c).

Denn v. First State Bank

Supreme Court of Minnesota, 1982.
316 N.W.2d 532.

■ WAHL, JUSTICE.

This appeal raises the issue of whether a depositary bank[1] which collected and paid out on two checks bearing forged indorsements is absolved from liability to the payee of the checks under UCC § 3–419(3)

---

1. The Uniform Commercial Code provides these definitions: "(a) 'Depositary bank' means the first bank to which an item is transferred for collection even though it is also the payor bank; * * * (d) 'collecting bank' means any bank handling the item for collection except the payor bank." UCC § 4– 105. Under the facts of this case, the First State Bank of Spring Lake Park is both a depositary bank and a collecting bank. Northfield National Bank, the drawee (or payor) bank, is neither a collecting nor a depositary bank.

when it acted in good faith and in accordance with reasonable commercial standards. We hold that it is.

The facts are straightforward. Plaintiff Edward Denn, the sole shareholder of Advance Foam of Minnesota, brought an action against the First State Bank of Spring Lake Park (Spring Lake) and Northfield National Bank (Northfield) for conversion of two checks paid over a forged indorsement. Both checks were drawn on Northfield by Blesener Roofing and Insulation and were issued to Advance Foam. The first check, dated July 7, 1978, was in the amount of $5,004.67. The second check, dated August 5, 1978, was in the amount of $2,468.38.

Dennis Carlson, a former employee of Advance Foam, deposited the checks to an account which he had opened at Spring Lake on March 29, 1978. He and his wife were joint owners of that account, which was titled "Dennis Carlson/Advanced Foam Account." Carlson indorsed the checks "Advanced Foam/Dennis Carlson" before depositing them.

Spring Lake gave Carlson provisional credit and then presented the checks to drawee Northfield, which paid them. Once Northfield had paid the checks, Spring Lake allowed Carlson to withdraw the money from the account. On September 5, 1978, Denn executed an Affidavit of Forgery in which he stated that he had not received the proceeds of the checks in question, but the affidavit reached Northfield too late to prevent payment.

After Denn brought his conversion action against the two banks, Spring Lake cross-claimed against Northfield on the ground of failure to comply with proper banking procedures and initiated a third-party complaint against Carlson. Plaintiff then also asserted a claim against Carlson, and Northfield cross-claimed against Spring Lake, alleging that Spring Lake had breached the presentment warranties imposed on a collecting bank by § 4–207(1)(a) [now § 4–208(a)(1)]. The trial court granted Northfield's motion for summary judgment on its cross-claim against Spring Lake, after which Denn dismissed without prejudice his cause of action against Northfield.

The court submitted the remaining issues to a jury which found that (1) Spring Lake had acted in accordance with reasonable commercial standards in accepting for deposit the two checks in question, (2) Denn and Carlson were not business partners, (3) Carlson did not have the authority to indorse and deposit the two checks, (4) the check proceeds were not used in furtherance of the Denn business, (5) Denn had been negligent in the use of his corporate name, and (6) Denn's negligence did not contribute to the making of the indorsement at issue.

The court found Carlson liable to Denn in the amount of the forged checks and denied Denn's claim against Spring Lake. The court held, in effect, that UCC § 3–419(3) absolves from liability in conversion a depositary bank which acts in good faith and in accordance with reasonable commercial standards. Since the depositary bank is ultimately liable on the presentment warranties of § 4–207(1)(a), the effect of the trial court's decision is to require the rightful payee of a check to bring his conversion action against the drawee bank, which will then proceed against the depositary bank. Denn appeals from the trial court's decision in this regard and argues that he should be allowed to collect directly from Spring Lake, the depositary bank.

Appellant's position would be unassailable at common law. A payee was allowed to bring his conversion suit directly against the depositary bank. Moler v. State Bank of Bigelow, 176 Minn. 449, 223 N.W. 780 (1929). The depositary bank was liable to the true owner of the check because the first party to take from a forger was ultimately liable on his indorsement. F. Kessler, Forged Instruments, 47 Yale L.J. 863 (1938). In Minnesota, this result obtained prior to the adoption of the U.C.C. whether the bank cashed the check or gave the forger provisional credit. Rosacker v. Commercial State Bank, 191 Minn. 553, 254 N.W. 824 (1934).

The Minnesota legislature adopted the Uniform Commercial Code (U.C.C.) in 1965. Although the Code contemplates actions in conversion, there is no provision which expressly governs suits by a payee against a depositary bank. Spring Lake does not claim that the U.C.C. prohibits Denn from bringing this action. It does claim, however, to be absolved from liability to Denn by UCC § 3–419(3), which provides:

> Subject to the provisions of this Act concerning restrictive indorsements a representative, including a depositary or collecting bank, who has in good faith and in accordance with the reasonable commercial standards applicable to the business of such representative dealt with an instrument or its proceeds on behalf of one who was not the true owner is not liable in conversion or otherwise to the true owner beyond the amount of any proceeds remaining in his hands.

Spring Lake claims it is free of liability to Denn because it (1) was acting in a representative capacity, (2) was acting in good faith and in accordance with reasonable commercial standards, and (3) did not retain any "proceeds" of the forged instruments.

There is considerable controversy among the courts and legal commentators over the question of when a bank is acting in a representative capacity. The Code itself defines a representative simply as "an agent, an officer of a corporation or association, and a trustee, executor or administrator of an estate, or any other person empowered to act for another." UCC § 1–201(35). At common law such an agent is "liable in conversion when he disposes of goods for his principal, even though the agent has acted in good faith and no longer exercises control over the converted goods." Cooper v. Union Bank: California Protects the True Owner Against a Forged Indorsement Despite Uniform Commercial Code Section 3–419(3), 25 Hastings L.J. 715, 719 (1974) (hereinafter *California Protects*). There was a common-law exemption from such liability, however, for a broker who dealt with stolen negotiable bonds on behalf of his principal. Id.; First National Bank v. Goldberg, 340 Pa. 337, 17 A.2d 377 (1941).

Did the Code drafters intend merely to codify the existing exemption for brokers, or did they intend also to exempt from liability depositary and collecting banks dealing with order instruments in the normal check collection process? To resolve this question we turn to the history of U.C.C. § 3–419(3) and its comments.

The "representative exception" was first included in the May 1949 draft, which stated that "A representative who in good faith has dealt with an instrument or its proceeds is not liable for conversion even though his principal was not the owner of the instrument." Payee v. Depositary Bank: What is the UCC Defense to Handling Checks Bearing Forged Indorsements? 45 U.Colo.L.Rev. 281, 308 (1974) (quoting ALI & National Conference of Commissioners on Uniform State Laws, Uniform Commercial Code § 3–427 (May 1949 Draft)). Under "Purposes of Section," the drafters went on to state that the intent of the section is "to adopt the rule of decisions which have held that a *broker* who *sells* a negotiable instrument for his principal * * * is not liable for conversion of the instrument." Id. at 309 (citing Official Comment) (emphasis added). It is quite likely that the drafters of the 1949 version of the Code meant to exempt from liability only those brokers who had been exempt at common law.

However, in 1951 the drafters added to section 3–419(3) the phrase "including a depositary or collecting bank." Id. The fact that this crucial phrase was added to the Code and was not part of the original version supports the idea that the 1951 drafters intended specifically to exempt depositary and collecting banks from liability. In 1952, the drafters added Comment 5, which also included a reference to depositary banks. Id. Comment 5 states:

> Subsection (3), which is new, is intended to adopt the rule of decisions which has held that a representative such as a broker or depositary bank, who deals with a negotiable instrument for his principal in good faith is not liable to the true owner for conversion of the instrument or otherwise, except that he may be compelled to turn over to the true owner the instrument itself or any proceeds of the instrument remaining in his hands.

UCC § 3–419. The fact that the phrase "such as a broker or *depositary bank*" is used to describe representative strongly suggests that the drafters intended to expand the scope of the common-law exception for brokers.[4]

Comment 6 to section 3–419(3) further supports the idea that the drafters intended to offer defenses to a depositary bank which took from a forger. Comment 6 states:

> The provisions of this section are not intended to eliminate any liability on warranties of presentment and transfer (Section 3–417).

---

4. At least one commentator believes that the bankers, who presumably urged the addition of the phrase "including a depositary or collecting bank," intended to relieve such banks from liability only when they were acting in the capacity of a broker:

> Unfortunately, the drafters of the Code did not leave this provision in a separate action where it belongs. When it was incorporated as a subsection under Section 3–419, its meaning was inevitably intermingled with the notion of handling checks bearing forged indorsements. It is probable that the drafters never foresaw the way in which its meaning would get expanded.

Payee v. Depositary Bank: What is the UCC Defense to Handling Checks Bearing Forged Indorsements?, 45 U.Colo.L.Rev. 281, 311 (1974).

Thus a collecting bank might be liable to a drawee bank which had been subject to liability under this section, even though the collecting bank might not be liable directly to the owner of the instrument.

Id. Since, at common law, a collecting bank which took from a forger would have been liable to the true payee, the suggestion here that such a bank "might not be liable" implies that the bank now has some defenses by which it may absolve itself from its common-law liability.

Several courts have interpreted "representative" not to include a depositary or collecting bank. The Pennsylvania Court of Common Pleas, in Ervin v. Dauphin Deposit Trust Co., 84 Dauph. 280, 38 Pa.D. & C.2d 473, 3 U.C.C.Rep. 311 (1965), reasoned that the legislature could not have intended to exempt collecting and depositary banks from their common-law liability to the true payee because such an exception would lead to an unreasonable result. Id. at 287, 38 Pa.D. & C.2d at 483, 3 U.C.C.Rep. at 318–19. It would seem to limit the liability of the collecting bank "in the face of other sections of the code which place the ultimate liability on the check cashing bank when the payee's name is forged * * * because of the check cashing bank's warranties on the indorsements." Id. at 287, 38 Pa.D. & C.2d at 483, 3 U.C.C.Rep. at 319.

The California Supreme Court has reached the same results primarily because of the absence of Code comment on such a major change from the common law: "Had such substantial and controversial deviation from prior law been intended, moreover, it could be expected that the official commentary to section 3419 would have so stated and would have included extensive explanation of the reasons for the change." Cooper v. Union Bank, 9 Cal.3d 371, 382, 107 Cal.Rptr. 1, 9–10, 507 P.2d 609, 617 (1973). Similarly, the District Court of the Northern District of Texas has concluded simply that section 3–419(3) does not contemplate the normal check collection process. Tubin v. Rabin, 389 F.Supp. 787 (N.D.Tex.1974).

The arguments of the *Ervin* and *Cooper* courts are persuasive, but we are compelled to reach an opposite conclusion. We can ignore neither the plain language of the statute which expressly includes depositary and collecting banks in its description of representatives nor the comments which appear to exclude such banks from liability.

Professor Stanley V. Kinyon, in his comment to the Minnesota version of the Code, noted that UCC § 3–419(3) applies to collecting banks and went on to distinguish *Moler* from *Rosacker*. The *Moler* decision "is *not* within the rule of this subsection and will not be changed" because the bank acted as a purchaser in cashing the check and not as a representative or collecting bank. UCC § 3–419(3) (1966), p. 468 (emphasis in original). However, the *Rosacker* decision would be changed by the U.C.C. because the bank, acting in a representative capacity, credited the forger's account and permitted withdrawals from it. Id. at 469. Appellant offers us no authority for ignoring this comment, which the legislature has left in its original form since its adoption.

Professor Allan Farnsworth's analysis parallels that of Kinyon: "The depositary bank would be liable under the Code if it cashed checks, but it would not be liable if it took them for collection and gave a provisional credit. If it cashed them, then it is not a representative, but is purchasing the checks." Farnsworth & Leary, U.C.C. Brief No. 10: Forgery and Alteration of Checks, 14 Prac.Law, No. 3, 75, 79 (1968).

The facts of this case are similar to those of *Rosacker.* In allowing Carlson to deposit the Advance Foam checks in his account and then presenting the checks to Northfield for payment, Spring Lake was acting as Carlson's representative. Spring Lake is, therefore, absolved of liability to Denn unless it has failed to act in good faith and in accordance with reasonable commercial standards or has retained any proceeds of the checks.

The trial court found on the jury's special verdict that Spring Lake had acted in good faith and in accordance with reasonable commercial standards. Denn did not contest testimony to this effect at trial. Rather, he urges this court, as a matter of law, to find, as did the Court of Appeals of Washington, that a bank is not acting in accordance with reasonable commercial standards when it accepts for deposit to a personal account checks which are payable to a corporation. Von Gohren v. Pacific National Bank, 8 Wash.App. 245, 505 P.2d 467 (1973). This we decline to do absent proof that the bank would know either that these checks were payable to a corporation or that Carlson was depositing them in an individual account. Denn has failed to show that the facts of this case fall within the *Von Gohren* rule.

The California Supreme Court rested its decision in the *Cooper* case on the theory that, even though the depositary bank had paid over money to the forger, it had not turned over the "proceeds" of the checks. With reference to the law of constructive trusts, which allows a claimant to trace funds which are rightfully his, the court concludes that "the banks retain the proceeds of the instruments even though amounts set forth in the instruments, in the banks' own money, were remitted to [the forger]." 9 Cal.3d at 379, 107 Cal.Rptr. at 7, 507 P.2d at 615.

The Florida Court of Appeals, faced with this "proceeds" rationale in Jackson Vitrified China Co. v. People's American National Bank, 388 So.2d 1059 (Fla.Dist.Ct.App.1980), could find no evidence that the drafters of the Code intended such a strained construction. Nor can we. "To the extent that a distinction is drawn regarding the time of payment vis à vis the time of collection, such a distinction is artificial; to the extent that no distinction is made, the provision is rendered nugatory." Id. at 1061.

Furthermore, it is the law of this state that, when the depositary bank had disbursed the amount it had received from the drawee bank, it had "paid out the entire proceeds of the check." Soderlin v. Marquette National Bank, 214 Minn. 408, 412, 8 N.W.2d 331, 332 (1943). Minnesota thus favors the less mechanistic "balance sheet" view of proceeds, with the result in this case that, because Spring Lake has paid out the total amount to the forger, it no longer holds proceeds of the checks and is not liable to Denn.

There are strong policy arguments in Denn's favor. It is judicially efficient to allow the true payee to proceed directly against a collecting bank. The collecting bank will bear the ultimate loss in most cases. If the payee must sue the drawee bank, the drawee bank will sue the collecting bank on the warranties of UCC § 4–207 as Northfield did in this case. Therefore, "a suit by the owner-payee against the depositary bank avoids an additional suit and thus resolves the entire dispute in a more economical manner." J. White & R. Summers, Uniform Commercial Code 590 (2d ed.1980). Collecting banks are also more convenient defendants. While the forged checks may be drawn on several different banks, the forger often cashes or deposits them all at the same bank, or at banks in the same geographical area. Both the payee and the judicial system suffer when the payee is required to sue the drawee banks in a number of jurisdictions to recover on a forged indorsement. The Michigan Court of Appeals relied on this policy consideration when it held that "3–419(3) provides no defense for the collecting bank in a suit by the true owner of the instrument in this type of fact situation." Sherriff–Goslin Co. v. Cawood, 91 Mich.App. 204, 210, 283 N.W.2d 691, 694 (1979). The court was concerned about the number of suits that would result if it did not allow a payee's direct action against a depositary bank.

We reluctantly conclude, however, that to deny a collecting bank the defenses of UCC § 3–419(3) in Denn's case is to ignore the clear intent of our legislature. As the Florida Court of Appeals so well stated, where the choice is "between following what appears to be bad law, or 'adapting' that law to what we perceive to be commercial reality, * * * [o]ur role commands adherence to lawful legislative decree." Jackson, 388 So.2d at 1063. The authority for changing the plain meaning of [UCC §] 3–419(3) lies with the Minnesota legislature. Although the people of Minnesota would benefit by a change which would hold a depositary bank directly liable to the true payee of a check which it has paid over a forged indorsement, we hold that UCC § 3–419(3), as it was passed by the legislature in 1965, provides defenses which absolve the depositary bank of such liability.

Affirmed.

PROBLEM

Drawer's check was payable to

Bay Village Inc. Michael
Bijlani & Assoc.

The check was deposited in Depositary Bank (DB) without the indorsement of Michael Bijlani. Payor Bank paid the check and the proceeds were withdrawn from DB. Bijlani sued DB for conversion and contended that the check was payable to Bay Village and Michael Bijlani. Under § 3–403(b) if the signature of more than one person is required, the signature is unauthorized if one of the required signatures is lacking. Is the signature unauthorized under § 3–110(d)? The facts are based on Bijlani v. Nationsbank of Florida, N.A., 25 UCC Rep.Serv.2d 1165, 1995 WL 264180 (Fla.Cir. Ct.1995). What if there had been a slash or virgule (/) between "Inc." and "Michael"? Purina Mills, Inc. v. Security Bank & Trust, 215 Mich.App. 549, 547 N.W.2d 336 (Mich.App.1996).

(iv) Forgery by Entrusted Employee of Payee

The following scenario is a summary of some of the facts, somewhat modified, of Cooper v. Union Bank, 9 Cal.3d 371, 107 Cal.Rptr. 1, 507 P.2d 609 (1973):

> Stell, a lawyer, was retained by Ruff to represent her in connection with her insolvency and litigation brought against her by several creditors. She informed Stell that her financial difficulties were primarily due to gambling losses she had sustained. A short time later Stell hired Ruff as a secretary and bookkeeper. Ruff's duties included posting the amounts of checks received by Stell to the proper accounts in Stell's accounting records and to reconcile the monthly bank statement of deposits and withdrawals with respect to Stell's checking account with Stell's accounting records. Over a period of a year and a half Ruff stole 29 checks payable to Stell that were received in the mail and she forged Stell's indorsement to these checks. Most of these checks were cashed over the counter at Depositary Bank at which both Stell and Ruff had checking accounts. A few of the checks were deposited to Ruff's account in Depositary Bank. Stell was well known to the tellers at the bank as a customer of the bank and Ruff was well known as Stell's secretary. It was the policy of Depositary Bank to allow checks payable to known customers to be cashed over the counter by the customer or the customer's secretary. The forgeries by Ruff were so well done that only a handwriting expert could have detected them.

> Stell exercised practically no supervision over Ruff, never reviewed the books that she kept, and never checked the bank reconciliation of deposits to Stell's checking account.

> Stell brought an action in conversion against Depositary Bank with respect to the 29 checks that were transferred by Ruff to that bank. Assume that revised Article 3 governs the case.

Under the second sentence of § 3–420(a), Depositary Bank is liable to Stell as a converter of the 29 checks that Ruff transferred to it if (1) Depositary Bank did not become the holder of the checks as a result of the transfer, i.e. the transfer was not a negotiation, and (2) Ruff was not a person entitled to enforce the checks when she transferred them to Depositary Bank, i.e. she was not a holder at the time of the transfer. Both of these elements depend upon whether the forgery by Ruff of Stell's signature was effective as Stell's indorsement in spite of the fact that it was a forgery. Section 3–405 addresses this issue.

Section 3–405 applies to this case if a "fraudulent indorsement" (§ 3–405(a)(2)) was made by Ruff, and Ruff was entrusted by Stell, her employer, with "responsibility" (§ 3–405(a)(3)) with respect to the checks that she transferred to Depositary Bank. Under the first sentence of § 3–405(b), is the indorsement by Ruff effective as the indorsement of Stell? The first and last paragraphs of Comment 1 to § 3–405 address this issue. The Ruff–Stell scenario should be compared with Case #1, Case #3, and Case #4 of

Comment 3 to § 3–405. If Stell is not entitled to recover from Depository Bank as a converter of the 29 checks because of the first sentence of § 3–405(b), is Stell entitled to any recovery against Depository Bank based on the last sentence of § 3–405(b)? Under that sentence is there any difference in result with respect to the checks cashed over the counter and the checks deposited to Ruff's account?

b.   ACTION BY DRAWER

Forged indorsement cases usually involve a theft of the check from the payee, but sometimes the theft of the check occurs before the check is received by the payee. *Barclays Bank,* supra, is such a case. In *Stone & Webster,* which follows, an employee of the drawer of several checks stole the checks from the drawer before the checks could be mailed to the payee. The stolen checks were intended to pay debts of the drawer to the payee. We saw in *Barclays Bank* that in such a case the payee has no legal claim with respect to the checks because the payee never received them. How does the act of the thief affect the payee? The theft of the check and payment by the drawee to the thief do not change payee's rights with respect to the debt for which the check was written. The payee never became the owner of the check and the drawer's debt to the payee remains unpaid. § 3–310 does not apply. The drawer of the stolen check has a continuing obligation to pay the debt for which the check was issued and thus is obliged to issue a replacement check to the payee. The drawer normally will not suffer any loss with respect to a check bearing a forged indorsement if the drawer is free of negligence contributing to the theft and forgery. § 3–406. The payor bank's payment with respect to the stolen check does not give it a right to debit the drawer's account. The drawer is entitled to have the account credited for the amount of the payment. This remedy of the drawer is clear and convenient since in most cases the drawer's account will be in a local bank. Nevertheless, there have been a number of cases in which the drawer, instead of suing the payor bank, sued the depositary bank. Such a suit might be brought in the uncommon case in which the depositary bank is a local bank and the payor bank is out of state, or the drawer may simply be reluctant to sue the payor bank with which the drawer has a favorable business relationship.

The issue in these cases is whether the drawer of a check stolen from the drawer has a property right in the check that can be asserted in a conversion action. The authority on the issue was divided under original Article 3. The view expressed in *Stone & Webster* was adopted by revised Article 3 in § 3–420(a).

Stone & Webster Engineering Corp. v. First National Bank & Trust Co.

Supreme Judicial Court of Massachusetts, 1962.
345 Mass. 1, 184 N.E.2d 358.

■ WILKINS, CHIEF JUSTICE. In this action of contract or tort in four counts for the same cause of action a demurrer to the declaration was sustained, and the plaintiff, described in the writ as having a usual place of business in Boston, appealed. G.L. (Ter.Ed.) c. 231, § 96. The questions argued concern the rights of the drawer against a collecting bank which "cashed" checks for an individual who had forged the payee's indorsement on the checks, which were never delivered to the payee.

In the first count, which is in contract, the plaintiff alleges that between January 1, 1960, and May 15, 1960, it was indebted at various times to Westinghouse Electric Corporation (Westinghouse) for goods and services furnished to it by Westinghouse; that in order to pay the indebtedness the plaintiff drew three checks within that period on its checking account in The First National Bank of Boston (First National) payable to Westinghouse in the total amount of $64,755.44; that before delivery of the checks to Westinghouse an employee of the plaintiff in possession of the checks forged the indorsement of Westinghouse and presented the checks to the defendant; that the defendant "cashed" the checks and delivered the proceeds to the plaintiff's employee who devoted the proceeds to his own use; that the defendant forwarded the checks to First National and received from First National the full amounts thereof; and that First National charged the account of the plaintiff with the full amounts of the checks and has refused to recredit the plaintiff's checking account; wherefore the defendant owes the plaintiff $64,755.44 with interest.

Count 2, also in contract, is on an account annexed for money owed, namely $64,755.44, the proceeds of checks of the plaintiff "cashed" by the defendant on forged indorsements between January 1, 1960, and May 15, 1960.

Counts 3 and 4 in tort are respectively for conversion of the checks and for negligence in "cashing" the checks with forged indorsements.

By order, copies of the three checks were filed in court. The checks are respectively dated at Rowe in this Commonwealth on January 5, March 8, and May 9, 1960. Their respective amounts are $36,982.86, $10,416.58 and $17,355. They are payable to the order of "Westinghouse Electric Corporation, 10 High Street, Boston." The first two checks are indorsed in typewriting, "For Deposit Only: Westinghouse Electric Corporation By: Mr. O. D. Costine, Treasury Representative" followed by an ink signature "O. D. Costine." The Third check is indorsed in typewriting, "Westinghouse Electric Corporation By: [Sgd.] O. D. Costine Treasury Representative." All three checks also bear the indorsement by rubber stamp, "Pay to the order of any bank, banker or trust co. prior indorsements guaranteed * * * [date][1] The First National Bank & Trust Co. Greenfield, Mass."

The demurrer, in so far as it has been argued, is to each count for failure to state a cause of action.

* * *

[1] The respective dates are January 13, March 9, and May 11, 1960. Each check bears the stamped indorsement of the Federal Reserve Bank of Boston and on its face the paid stamp of The First National Bank of Boston.

1.   Count 1, the plaintiff contends, is for money had and received. We shall so regard it. "An action for money had and received lies to recover money which should not in justice be retained by the defendant, and which in equity and good conscience should be paid to the plaintiff." Cobb v. Library Bureau, 268 Mass. 311, 316, 167 N.E. 765, 767; Adams v. First Nat. Bank, 321 Mass. 693, 694, 75 N.E.2d 502; Trafton v. Custeau, 338 Mass. 305, 308, 155 N.E.2d 159.

The defendant has no money in its hands which belongs to the plaintiff. The latter had no right in the proceeds of its own check payable to Westinghouse. Not being a holder or an agent for a holder, it could not have presented the check to the drawee for payment. * * * See Uniform Commercial Code § 3–419, comment 2: "A negotiable instrument is the property of the holder." See also Restatement 2d: Torts, Tent. draft no. 3, 1958, § 241A. The plaintiff contends that "First National paid or credited the proceeds of the checks to the defendant and charged the account of the plaintiff, and consequently, the plaintiff was deprived of a credit, and the defendant received funds or a credit which 'in equity and good conscience' belonged to the plaintiff."

In our opinion this argument is a non sequitur. The plaintiff as a depositor in First National was merely in a contractual relationship of creditor and debtor. * * * The amounts the defendant received from First National to cover the checks "cashed" were the bank's funds and not the plaintiff's. The Uniform Commercial Code does not purport to change the relationship. * * * Section 3–409(1) provides: "A check or other draft does not of itself operate as an assignment of any funds in the hands of the drawee available for its payment, and the drawee is not liable on the instrument until he accepts it." * * * Whether the plaintiff was rightfully deprived of a credit is a matter between it and the drawee, First National.

If we treat the first count as seeking to base a cause of action for money had and received upon a waiver of the tort of conversion—a matter which it is not clear is argued—the result will be the same. In this aspect the question presented is whether a drawer has a right of action for conversion against a collecting bank which handles its checks in the bank collection process. Unless there be such a right, there is no tort which can be waived.

The plaintiff relies upon the Uniform Commercial Code § 3–419, which provides, "(1) An instrument is converted when * * * (c) it is paid on a forged indorsement." This, however, could not apply to the defendant, which is not a "payor bank," defined in the Code, § 4–105(b), as "a bank by which an item is payable as drawn or accepted." * * *

A conversion provision of the Uniform Commercial Code which might have some bearing on this case is § 3–419(3).[3] This section implicitly

---

3. "Subject to the provisions of this chapter concerning restrictive indorsements a representative, including a depositary or collecting bank, who has in good faith and in accordance with the reasonable commercial standards applicable to the business of such representative dealt with an instrument or its proceeds on behalf of one who was not the

recognizes that, subject to defences, including the one stated in it, a collecting bank, defined in the Code, § 4–105(d), may be liable in conversion. In the case at bar the forged indorsements were "wholly inoperative" as the signatures of the payee, Code §§ 3–404(1), 1–201(43), and equally so both as to the restrictive indorsements for deposits, see § 3–205(c), and as to the indorsement in blank, see § 3–204(2). When the forger transferred the checks to the collecting bank, no negotiation under § 3–202(1) occurred, because there was lacking the necessary indorsement of the payee. For the same reason, the collecting bank could not become a "holder" as defined in § 1–201(20), and so could not become a holder in due course under § 3–302(1). Accordingly, we assume that the collecting bank may be liable in conversion to a proper party, subject to defences, including that in § 3–419(3). See A. Blum, Jr.'s, Sons v. Whipple, 194 Mass. 253, 255, 80 N.E. 501, 13 L.R.A.,N.S., 211. But there is no explicit provision in the Code purporting to determine to whom the collecting bank may be liable, and consequently, the drawer's right to enforce such a liability must be found elsewhere. Therefore, we conclude that the case must be decided on our own law, which, on the issue we are discussing, has been left untouched by the Uniform Commercial Code in any specific section.

In this Commonwealth there are two cases (decided in 1913 and 1914) the results in which embrace a ruling that there was a conversion, but in neither was the question discussed and, for aught that appears, in each the ruling seems to have been assumed without conscious appreciation of the issue here considered. Franklin Sav. Bank v. International Trust Co., 215 Mass. 231, 102 N.E. 363; Quincy Mut. Fire Ins. Co. v. International Trust Co., 217 Mass. 370, 140 N.E. 845, L.R.A.1915B, 725. * * *

The authorities are hopelessly divided. We think that the preferable view is that there is no right of action. * * *

We state what appears to us to be the proper analysis. Had the checks been delivered to the payee Westinghouse, the defendant might have been liable for conversion to the payee. The checks, if delivered, in the hands of the payee would have been valuable property which could have been transferred for value or presented for payment; and, had a check been dishonored, the payee would have had a right of recourse against the drawer on the instrument under § 3–413(2). Here the plaintiff drawer of the checks, which were never delivered to the payee * * *, had no valuable rights in them. Since, as we have seen, it did not have the right of a payee or subsequent holder to present them to the drawee for payment, the value of its rights was limited to the physical paper on which they were written, and was not measured by their payable amounts. * * *

The enactment of the Uniform Commercial Code opens the road for the adoption of what seems the preferable view. An action by the drawer against the collecting bank might have some theoretical appeal as avoiding circuity of action. * * * It would have been in the interest of speedy and

true owner is not liable in conversion or otherwise to the true owner beyond the amount of any proceeds remaining in his hands." See Code §§ 1–201(35); 4–201(1).

complete justice had the case been tried with the action by the drawer against the drawee and with an action by the drawee against the collecting bank. * * * So one might ask: If the drawee is liable to the drawer and the collecting bank is liable to the drawee, why not let the drawer sue the collecting bank direct? We believe that the answer lies in the applicable defences set up in the Code.[4]

The drawer can insist that the drawee recredit his account with the amount of any unauthorized payment. Such was our common law. * * * This is, in effect, retained by the Code §§ 4–401(1),[5] 4–406(4). But the drawee has defences based upon the drawer's substantial negligence, if "contributing," or upon his duty to discover and report unauthorized signatures and alterations. §§ 3–406, 4–406. As to unauthorized indorsements, see § 4–406(4).[6] Then, if the drawee has a valid defence which it waives or fails upon request to assert, the drawee may not assert against the collecting bank or other prior party presenting or transferring the check a claim which is based on the forged indorsement. § 4–406(5).[7] * * * If the drawee recredits the drawer's account and is not precluded by § 4–406(5), it may claim against the presenting bank on the relevant warranties in §§ 3–417 and 4–207, and each transferee has rights against his transferor under those sections.

If the drawer's rights are limited to requiring the drawee to recredit his account, the drawee will have the defences noted above and perhaps others; and the collecting bank or banks will have the defences in § 4–207(4)[8] and § 4–406(5), and perhaps others. If the drawer is allowed in the present case to sue the collecting bank, the assertion of the defences, for all practical purposes, would be difficult. The possibilities of such a result would tend to compel resort to litigation in every case involving a forgery of commercial paper. It is a result to be avoided.

[The court sustained demurrers to all plaintiff's counts.]

4. Cases where a payee has acquired rights in an instrument may stand on a different footing.

5. "As against its customer, a bank may charge against his account any item which is otherwise properly payable from that account * * * ."

6. "Without regard to care or lack of care of either the customer or the bank a customer who does not within one year from the time the statement and items are made available to the customer (subsection [1])discover and report his unauthorized signature or any alteration on the face or back of the item or does not within three years from that time discover and report any unauthorized indorsement is precluded from asserting against the bank such unauthorized signature or indorsement or such alteration."

7. "If under this section a payor bank has a valid defense against a claim of a customer upon or resulting from payment of an item and waives or fails upon request to assert the defense the [drawee] may not assert against * * * [a] collecting bank or other prior party presenting or transferring the item a claim based upon the unauthorized signature or alteration giving rise to the customer's claim." [Eds. See revised § 4–208(c) and Comment 5 to § 4–406.]

8. "Unless a claim for breach of warranty under this section is made within a reasonable time after the person claiming learns of the breach, the person liable is discharged to the extent of any loss caused by the delay in making claim."

4. IMPOSTORS AND FICTITIOUS PAYEES

a. INTENT OF ISSUER

In some cases in which a forged indorsement is alleged, it may not be clear whether there is a forged indorsement because it is not clear to whom the instrument is payable. In identifying the person to whom the instrument is payable, the starting point is § 3–110.

Suppose Jane Doe writes a check to the order of Richard Roe. Under § 3–110(a) the intent of Doe determines to whom the check is payable. There may be many people in the world named Richard Roe, but only the Richard Roe intended by Doe is the payee of the check. If the check gets into the hands of a different Richard Roe, an indorsement by that Richard Roe is ineffective as an indorsement of the payee of the check.

Change the facts. Suppose Doe made a mistake in writing the check. Intending to issue a check to a person that she thinks is Richard Roe, she writes that name as the payee of the check. In fact the name of the person to whom she intended to issue the check is Peter Poe and Poe has never used the name Richard Roe. If Doe delivers the check to Poe, Poe becomes the holder of the check even though the check states that it is payable to Richard Roe. An indorsement by Poe is effective because Poe is the payee of the check. Poe may indorse by signing either the name on the check or Poe's name. § 3–110(a) and § 3–204(d).

The rules stated in § 3–110(a) apply to the issuer of a negotiable instrument in determining to whom the instrument is initially payable and the same rules apply in determining to whom an instrument is subsequently made payable by a holder making a special indorsement. § 3–205(a). Thus, if Jane Doe is the payee of the check rather than the drawer and she indorses the check with the indorsement "Pay to Richard Roe," the person to whom the check becomes payable is determined by Doe's intent according to the rules in § 3–110.

Section 3–110 is also important with respect to forged checks. Suppose Thief steals Jane Doe's checkbook and forges her name to a check on her bank account. The check is made payable to Richard Roe. Although Thief's act of signing Doe's name to the check is ineffective as the signature of Doe, the signature is effective as Thief's signature. § 3–403(a). Under § 3–110(a), it is the intention of Thief, the drawer of the check, that determines to whom the check is payable.

An organization such as a corporation must act through human agents in the drawing of checks and the organization normally identifies officers who are authorized to sign checks in behalf of the organization. Often, the organization requires that its checks be signed by more than one authorized officer. Under § 3–110(a) the intent of the authorized officer or officers signing in behalf of the organization determines to whom the check is payable. But in many cases, checks of organizations do not bear any manually-made signature in behalf of the organization. Rather, the check is produced by a check-writing machine and the signature of the drawer is a printed or facsimile signature. The terms of the check, including the name of the payee, are determined by information entered into the computer that controls the check-writing machine. The person providing the information usually is an authorized employee acting in good faith in behalf of the organization, but sometimes the person providing the information is acting fraudulently and might be either an employee authorized to operate the machine or a wholly unauthorized person. In all of these cases the intention of the person supplying the information determines to whom the check is payable. § 3–110(b).

People engaged in fraud usually try to mask the fraud. For example, an employee authorized to operate a corporation's check-writing machine wants to steal money by obtaining payment of checks produced by the machine. Instead of causing the machine to produce checks payable to the employee, the employee causes the machine to produce checks payable to a different payee. The payee named on the check may be an imaginary person, a so-called "fictitious payee," or the check may name as payee a real person who is not intended to have any interest in the check. In either case, the intent of the dishonest employee is to produce a check for the employee's benefit that the employee can turn into cash after indorsing it by signing the name of the payee indicated on the check. In either case, to whom is the check payable? Is the indorsement by the employee an effective indorsement or a forgery? These cases are governed by § 3–404(b) which validates the indorsement and allows the check to be negotiated by the employee.

b.   IMPOSTORS

Although § 3–110(a) states that the intent of the person writing the check determines to whom the check is payable, in some cases it is not possible to clearly identify the payee that way. These cases involve issuance of checks to impostors. For example, if Rogers by impersonating Jacobs induces Drawer to issue to him an instrument payable to Jacobs, Drawer might well have dual intent: to make the check payable to the person to whom he issued the instrument (Rogers) and to the person he thought Rogers was (Jacobs). In this case the statute resolves the case by providing that if Rogers induced Drawer to issue the instrument to him by impersonating Jacobs, Roger's indorsement of Jacobs' name on the instrument is effective. § 3–404(a). Since business organizations must operate through the acts of their agents, cases involving malefactors who impersonate agents are common. Unlike its predecessor, § 3–404(a) applies to such impersonations. The following case compares the former and the present impostor provisions with respect to agency impersonations.

Title Insurance Company of Minnesota v. Comerica Bank–California

Court of Appeal, Sixth District, 1994.
27 Cal.App.4th 800, 32 Cal.Rptr.2d 735.

■ MIHARA, ASSOCIATE JUSTICE.

At issue in this appeal is the applicability and scope of the "impostor rule," which makes an indorsed check effective if the drawer was induced to issue the check by an impersonator of the payee. (Com.Code, § 3404, subd. (a); former Com.Code, § 3405, subd. (1)(a).) Plaintiff Title Insurance Company of Minnesota contends the trial court erroneously applied this rule in sustaining the demurrer of the drawee bank, respondent Comerica Bank–California ("Bank"), to plaintiff's complaint for negligence. We agree that the impostor rule is not applicable under the circumstances presented, and accordingly reverse the judgment of dismissal.

Allegations of the Complaint

* * *

Plaintiff is the assignee of the interests of First National Mortgage Company ("FNMC"), who made two equity loans to Helen Nastor ("Helen"), secured by deeds of trust. Plaintiff issued a policy of land title insurance for each of these loans.

On September 22, 1988, FNMC issued a check payable to Helen in the amount of $58,659.29, the proceeds of the first loan. FNMC gave the check to Helen's son, Rudy Nastor ("Rudy"), for delivery to Helen. That day, someone impersonating Helen indorsed the check and presented it to Bank, where FNMC held an account. Bank paid the impersonator the full amount of the check.

On December 29, 1988, FNMC made a second loan to Helen in the amount of $108,300. Part of the proceeds of this loan were used to pay off the first loan. The remainder was issued to Rudy in the form of a check made payable to him.

When FNMC failed to receive payment on the $108,300 loan, it initiated nonjudicial foreclosure proceedings against Helen's property. On October 17, 1989, Helen's attorney informed FNMC that its deed of trust on the property was invalid because it had been executed by Rudy using a forged power of attorney. Helen thereafter testified by deposition that she had not executed the power of attorney, nor had she indorsed or presented the check to Bank for payment.

FNMC made a claim for payment under the second title insurance policy, and plaintiff paid FNMC $108,300. Plaintiff, acting as subrogee and assignee with respect to FNMC's claim, then sued Bank for negligence, seeking recovery of the $108,000. According to the first amended complaint, Bank had a duty "to establish and practice such procedures and business practices as are or may be reasonably necessary and effective to avoid a breach of any of the duties of care owed by BANK . . . to the depositors and customers of BANK . . . including therein a duty to immediately inform customers such as FNMC when impostors and/or forgers attempt to cash a check drawn on such customers' accounts with BANK." Bank breached this duty, plaintiff alleged, by failing to ensure "that only properly endorsed and presented checks of its depositors [were] paid." Had Bank "caught" the impostor trying to cash the check payable to Helen, it would have informed FNMC of the attempt, and FNMC would have discovered the forged power of attorney before it made the second loan.

Applicability of the Impostor Rule

Bank's demurrer is based entirely on the asserted applicability of the impostor rule, which, according to Bank, interposes an "absolute defense" against plaintiff's allegations of negligence. Bank relies on the current provisions of section 3404, subdivision (a) (hereafter, "section 3404(a)"), which makes an indorsement by any person effective if an impostor had induced the issuance of the instrument to either the impostor or "a person acting in concert with the impostor."[1] In this case, argues Bank, Rudy was acting in concert with the impostor (the impersonator of Helen), who presented the check to Bank for payment.

Plaintiff responds that section 3404(a) is not applicable, because it was not enacted until 1992, after the events alleged in the complaint. Instead, plaintiff maintains, this case is controlled by former section 3405, subdivision (1)(a) (hereafter, "former section 3405(1)(a)"). The expression of the rule in the latter statute is substantially the same as that of the current provisions, but excluded from its reach are false representations of agency. Because Rudy obtained the check from FNMC by falsely representing that he was authorized to act as Helen's agent, plaintiff argues the transaction at issue is outside the scope of the impostor rule.

We agree with plaintiff that former section 3405(1)(a) governs the disposition of this case, since the events at issue took place in 1988, while that statute was still in effect. Former section 3405(1)(a) provided: "An indorsement by any person in the name of a named payee is effective if (a) An impostor by use of the mails or otherwise has induced the maker or drawer to issue the instrument to him or his confederate in the name of the payee. . . . "

This section does not protect Bank from liability under the circumstances presented. As one California court explained prior to the enactment of former section 3405, the impostor rule is applicable only when the issuance of the check has been accomplished through *impersonation* of the payee: "[W]here a check is delivered to an impostor as payee and the drawer believes that the impostor is the person upon whose endorsement it will be paid, the endorsement by such impostor in the name which he is using to impersonate another is not a forgery. . . . The soundness of the rule obtains in the fact that the money has actually been paid to the person for whom it was really intended. Because another person might bear the very name assumed by the impostor and might have some contractual relationships with the impostor does not subject to a loss the drawee bank

---

1. Section 3404(a) states: "If an impostor, by use of the mails or otherwise, induces the issuer of an instrument to issue the instrument to the impostor, or to a person acting in concert with the impostor, by impersonating the payee of the instrument or a person authorized to act for the payee, an indorsement of the instrument by any person in the name of the payee is effective as the indorsement of the payee in favor of a person who, in good faith, pays the instrument or takes it for value or for collection."

when it has paid the check to the person intended as the payee." (Schweitzer v. Bank of America (1941) 42 Cal.App.2d 536, 540, 109 P.2d 441.) * * *

The reasoning of the *Schweitzer* court directs our analysis in the present case. If FNMC (the drawer) had been induced *by an impostor* of Helen to issue the check either to Rudy or to the impostor, then the indorsement would be considered effective as to FNMC under the impostor rule. The rationale for this result is that Bank has paid the person whom FNMC intended to receive the money. When viewed under principles of negligence or estoppel, the outcome of this scenario would be the same: the risk of loss would be shifted to the drawer of the instrument (FNMC), who was in a better position to detect the fraud. (See Fireman's Fund Ins. Co. v. Security Pacific Nat. Bank (1978) 85 Cal.App.3d 797, 830, 149 Cal.Rptr. 883 [burden of loss on party who deals with the forger]; Intelogic v. Merchants Nat. Bank (Ind.App. 2 Dist.1993) 626 N.E.2d 839, 842 [under UCC, loss resulting from forged indorsement should fall upon party best able to prevent it]; East Gadsden Bank v. First City Nat. Bank of Gadsden (1973) 50 Ala.App. 576, 281 So.2d 431, 433 [intended payee theory distinguished from negligence or estoppel theory].)

This case presents different facts, however. Here, FNMC made the check payable to the true Helen, not to an impostor representing herself as Helen. FNMC intended that Helen herself—not a person it believed to be Helen—indorse the check and receive the proceeds. There is no question that FNMC intended to deal solely with Helen. The rationale underlying the protection of the impostor rule thus does not apply here. * * *

A person's false representation that he or she is an agent of the payee is not sufficient. Uniform Commercial Code Comment 2 to former section 3405 notes: "'Impostor' refers to impersonation, and does not extend to a false representation that the party is the authorized agent of the payee. The maker or drawer who takes the precaution of making the instrument payable to the principal is entitled to have his indorsement." (See Uniform Com.Code com., 23B to § 3405.) Here, Rudy obtained issuance of the check to Helen not by impersonating her, but by falsely representing that he was authorized to act on her behalf. Although clearly fraudulent, this conduct does not constitute impersonation and thus cannot be considered an inducement to issue the instrument within the meaning of former section 3405(1)(a). * * *

Bank's emphasis on the asserted fact that Rudy was acting in concert with Helen's impostor is of no consequence. To invoke the protection of former section 3405(1)(a) Bank would have to point to facts showing that *by impersonation* the impostor induced FNMC to issue the check either to her or to Rudy, her confederate. The complaint alleges no such facts, however. The only impersonation that took place was in the presentation of the check to Bank.

* * *

The result is no different even under section 3404(a), the current version of the rule. The only significant change in this section is its recognition that the impostor may pretend to be either the payee or the payee's agent. As the Uniform Commercial Code Comment to the revised law notes, "Under former Section 3–405(1)(a), if Impostor impersonated Smith and induced the drawer to draw a check to the order of Smith, Impostor could negotiate the check. If Impostor impersonated Smith, the president of Smith Corporation, and the check was payable to the order of Smith Corporation, the section did not apply.... Section 3–404(a) gives Impostor the power to negotiate the check in both cases." (See Uniform Com.Code com., 23B to § 3404.) This comment makes it clear that impersonation is still required to invoke the impostor rule, whether the perpetrator of the deception pretends to be the principal or the agent. Misrepresentation of the perpetrator's agency status does not suffice. * * *

We must conclude, therefore, that the impostor rule is inapplicable under these circumstances. By correctly identifying himself as Rudy but falsely representing himself to be Helen's agent Rudy did not engage in the impersonation required by the impostor rule, as expressed both in former section 3405, which was applicable at the time of the transactions at issue, and in its contemporary form, section 3404(a). The impersonation by Helen's impostor cannot be said to have induced FNMC to issue the check, since it took place only afterward, when the impostor presented the check to Bank.

Bank does not challenge the legal sufficiency of the complaint in any respect other than the asserted bar of the impostor rule. Accordingly, we hold that the trial court incorrectly sustained Bank's demurrer based on the application of the impostor rule.

* * *

The judgment of dismissal is reversed. The trial court shall enter a new order overruling the demurrer to the first amended complaint and directing Bank to answer. Plaintiff is entitled to costs on appeal.

■ PREMO, ACTING P.J., and WUNDERLICH, J., concur.

NOTE

Contrast these two cases: Case #1. Rudy induced Drawer to issue a check to Helen Corporation by falsely representing that he was the treasurer of that organization. Case #2. Rudy induced Drawer to issue a check to Helen Corporation by representing that he was Barnes, who actually was the treasurer of Helen Corporation. How would § 3–404(a) apply to these cases? Which of these cases most resembles *Title Insurance Company*?

c. FICTITIOUS PAYEES

In the following problem we have two questionable signatures: that of Dowager, which is forged, and that of Priscilla Prim, who does not exist. How does Article 3 allocate loss in a "double forgery" case? § 3–404(b). Clark & Clark, The Law of Bank Deposits, Collections and Credit Cards

¶¶ 10.09, 12.07[3] (Rev.ed.1995); White & Summers, Uniform Commercial Code §§ 15–6, 16–4 e (4th ed.1995).

PROBLEM

Dowager is a wealthy widow who frequently makes large gifts to charitable institutions. She has a checking account in Centerville Bank. Faith has been employed by Dowager for many years as a housekeeper and companion. Faith has a younger brother who is a ne'r do well with an addiction to illegal betting on the outcome of sports events. He told Faith that he had been making bets on credit with a bookie reputed to be a violent criminal and owed him $21,000 which had to be paid within 30 days. He told Faith that he had no money and feared for his life if the debt was not paid. Faith earns very little and had no available funds, but she agreed to help.

Faith travelled to Metropolis, a large city several hundred miles from Centerville, and called upon the manager of a branch of Metropolis Bank. She introduced herself as Priscilla Prim, the owner of Prim Academy, a school for girls located in a city in an adjoining state. There is such a school but Faith had no connection with it. She explained to the bank manager that she planned to open a second campus of Prim Academy in Metropolis and needed a checking account in a local bank. An account was then opened in Metropolis Bank in the name of Prim Academy and Priscilla Prim was designated as the person authorized to act with respect to the account. Faith gave the bank manager an unindorsed check for $25,000 payable to the order of Prim Academy and asked that it be deposited to the Prim Academy account. The bank manager followed Faith's instructions. The check was drawn on the account of Dowager in Centerville Bank. Faith had written the check and forged Dowager's signature after taking a blank check from Dowager's checkbook which Faith found in a drawer in Dowager's desk. A few days later Metropolis Bank presented the check for payment and received $25,000 from Centerville Bank. Before the payment was made an employee of Centerville Bank examined the check and approved it for payment. Faith's forgery of Dowager's signature was not detected because it was skillfully done and appeared to be genuine.

Two weeks later Faith returned to Metropolis Bank. She identified herself to a teller as Priscilla Prim and requested that the bank issue a cashier's check for $21,000 to the order of Prim Academy. The check was issued and delivered to Faith. As payment for issuance of the cashier's check, Metropolis Bank debited $21,000 to the Prim Academy account in that bank. No checks on the Prim Academy account were ever written.

Faith indorsed the cashier's check "Prim Academy by Priscilla Prim" and gave the check to her brother. He delivered it to the bookie. A few days later Metropolis Bank paid the cashier's check.

When Dowager received her monthly statement of account from Centerville Bank she found the forged check among the checks paid by the bank that month. She immediately informed Centerville Bank of the forgery and demanded that the bank restore $25,000 to her account. The bank complied with her demand and then brought an action against Metropolis Bank.

1. Is Centerville Bank entitled to recover from Metropolis Bank on the basis that Faith forged Dowager's signature on the check? § 3–418 and § 3–417(a)(3).

2. Is Centerville Bank entitled to recover from Metropolis Bank on the basis that the signature of Prim Academy as an indorsement of the check was not authorized? § 3–417(a)(1), § 3–110, § 3–404, Case #5 of Comment 2 to § 3–404, and Comment 3 to § 3–404.

5. PAYROLL PADDING

We have seen examples of employee fraud that involve forgery of the employer's signature either as an indorsement of checks payable to the employer or as drawer of a check drawn on the employer's bank account. Another common type of employee fraud does not involve forgery of the employer's signature. This type of fraud is sometimes referred to as "payroll padding" and it can be illustrated by the following cases.

Case #1. Corporation pays its employees by check. Treasurer is authorized to sign checks on behalf of Corporation, but a signature by one other officer of Corporation is also necessary. Treasurer signed checks to pay employees on the April payroll. Intending to defraud Corporation, Treasurer included in the checks for that month three checks payable either to fictitious people or real people who sometimes work for Corporation but who did not work in April and therefore were not entitled to any pay. At the request of Treasurer, Vice President also signed the checks. Vice President did not know who was entitled to payment and did not raise any question about the checks. The checks were returned to Treasurer after they were signed. Treasurer took the three fraudulent checks and indorsed each of them by signing the name of the payee. She then deposited each of the checks in a bank in which Treasurer had an account. The checks were paid and Treasurer withdrew the proceeds of the checks. Assume Treasurer is judgment proof. If the indorsements by Treasurer are effective as indorsements of the payees of the three checks, Corporation takes the loss. If the indorsements are treated as forged indorsements, the depositary banks that collected the checks will take the loss. § 3–417(a)(1). The analysis of this case is similar to that in the Prim Academy problem above with respect to the liability of Metropolis Bank for breach of warranty under § 3–417(a)(1). In this case the intent of Treasurer determines the person to whom each of the three checks is payable. § 3–110(a) (last sentence). Under § 3–404(b), Treasurer became the holder of each check and her indorsement in the name of the stated payee was effective as the indorsement of the payee of the check. Thus, Corporation takes the loss.

Case #2. Same as Case #1 except that Corporation's checks are produced by a check-writing machine. Treasurer had access to the computer that operates the machine. She made entries in the computer that caused the machine to issue the three fraudulent checks. She obtained possession of the checks and then proceeded as in Case #1. Under § 3–

110(b) the intent of Treasurer determines the person to whom each of the three checks is payable. The analysis of Case #2 is identical to that of Case #1.

Case #3. Treasurer signs checks on behalf of Corporation to pay employees, but Clerk prepares the April payroll which tells Treasurer to whom to issue the checks and in what amount. This time the culprit is Clerk. Intending to defraud Corporation, Clerk includes in the payroll the names of three people who work part time for Corporation, but who performed no work during April. Clerk prepared checks of Corporation in accordance with the payroll and gave them to Treasurer for signature. Treasurer signed the checks and returned them to Clerk. Clerk took the three fraudulent checks, indorsed each in the name of the payee named in the check, and deals with the checks as Treasurer did in Case #1. This case is more complex. Assume Treasurer knew each of the three employees named in the three fraudulent checks, but she did not know that they did not work in April. Treasurer intended each check to be payable to the payee named in the check and, under § 3–110(a), Treasurer's intent controls; hence § 3–404(b) doesn't apply. Thus, Clerk's indorsements are forged indorsements and the normal result is that the loss is taken by the depositary bank that collected the check. In Case #1 and Case #2, Corporation took the loss because it was held responsible for the conduct of Treasurer, its faithless employee. In Case #3 the faithless employee is Clerk. Is there any good reason why Corporation should not also be responsible for the conduct of Clerk? In each case the faithless employee had duties with respect to the issuance of checks. The three cases are essentially similar. In Case #3, Treasurer performed the same function as Vice President did in Case #1 and the check writing machine did in Case #2. By preparing the payroll, Clerk as a practical matter determined to whom Corporation's checks were to be made payable. However, the result in Case #3 is not determined solely by § 3–110(a) because § 3–405 also applies. We previously examined cases covered by § 3–405(a)(2)(i). This time the relevant provision is § 3–405(a)(2)(ii).

Merrill Lynch, which follows, is an example of the kind of case to which § 3–405(a)(2)(ii) relates. *Merrill Lynch* was decided under § 3–405(1)(c) of original Article 3. Although § 3–405(a)(2)(ii) and (3), read in conjunction with § 3–405(b), applies to all of the cases covered by § 3–405(1)(c) of original Article 3, the revised Article 3 provisions are broader in scope and will, in some cases, produce results different from those under original Article 3. See the second paragraph of Comment 1 and Comment 2 to § 3–405. The scope of § 3–405 is illustrated by the hypothetical cases discussed in Comment 3 to § 3–405.

Merrill Lynch, Pierce, Fenner & Smith v. Chemical Bank

Court of Appeals of New York, 1982.
57 N.Y.2d 439, 456 N.Y.S.2d 742, 442 N.E.2d 1253.

■ FUCHSBERG, JUDGE.

This appeal requires us to explore the extent to which, if at all, immunity from liability accorded a drawee bank by section 3–405 (subd. [1], par. [c]) of the Uniform Commercial Code may be limited by the drawee's negligence in paying checks over forged indorsements.

The section at issue, commonly referred to in commercial circles as either the "fictitious payee" or "padded payroll" rule, provides: "An indorsement by any person in the name of a named payee is effective if * * * an agent or employee of the maker or drawer has supplied him with the name of the payee intending the latter to have no such interest".

The factual context in which the case is here is undisputed. The defendant, Chemical Bank, unaware that the indorsements of the payees' names were forged, routinely paid 13 checks drawn by the plaintiff, Merrill Lynch, on its Chemical account in the aggregate sum of $115,180. The forgeries were occasioned by chicanery of a Merrill Lynch accounts payable employee who, by presenting his employer's New York check issuing department with false invoices which ostensibly represented obligations due its suppliers, caused checks to be issued to the order of these supposed creditors. The malefactor or accomplices then indorsed the names of the payees and, in face of the fact that New York addresses appeared below the payees' names, caused the checks to be deposited in California and Ohio bank accounts in names other than those to whose order they had been drawn. Seven of the checks were presented to Chemical by the Federal Reserve Bank (FRB) as collecting bank and the remainder by the depositary banks themselves. In due course, Chemical charged its Merrill Lynch account.

This suit, instituted by Merrill Lynch to recover the amount so debited, was brought on three theories. As set out in its complaint, the first was that "Chemical acted negligently and contrary to normal and accepted banking practices, breached its duty of good faith and failed to exercise ordinary care". Particularizing, it added that Chemical should have been alerted to the irregular nature of the checks because "the purported indorsements of the corporate payees were handwritten, and in many instances illegible", were indorsed "in blank, rather than for deposit only" and bore "second indorsements of unrelated persons or entities." Reiterating the allegations of the first count, the second sounded in breach of contract and the third in conversion. In its answer, Chemical relied, among other affirmative defenses, on what, in the circumstances of this case, it took to be the exculpatory effect of section 3–405.

At the same time, Chemical, by way of a third-party summons and complaint, impleaded FRB essentially on the rationale that, if Merrill Lynch recovered, Chemical, in turn, should be made whole by FRB, which, as a collecting bank, would then have to be found in breach of its warranty of good title (Uniform Commercial Code, § 4–207). FRB countered with a motion for summary judgment, premised on the position that, under section 3–405, "endorsement of the checks in the name of the payee thereof was sufficient and effective to transfer title to the instrument". On the same ground, Chemical thereupon cross-moved for partial summary judgment dismissing Merrill Lynch's complaint * * *. Special Term denied both motions.

On appeal, the Appellate Division unanimously modified Special Term's order, on the law, by granting the motion directed to Chemical's third-party case against FRB. In so deciding, the court agreed that, under section 3–405 of the Uniform Commercial Code, the forged indorsements were effective to transfer title to the checks. However, as to Chemical's cross motion against Merrill Lynch, the court, by a vote of 3 to 2, found that section 3–405 was "not available to defendant to avoid liability for its own negligence" (82 A.D.2d 772, 773, 440 N.Y.S.2d 643); on this view, it affirmed, thus relegating the issue of Chemical's negligence to trial.

On the present appeal, which brings up for review Chemical's motion against Merrill Lynch only, the appellant in the main presses the point that its alleged negligence in disregarding irregularities in the indorsements may not deprive it of the benefits of section 3–405 of the Uniform Commercial Code and, in the alternative, that, in any event, it was not negligent because it was under no obligation to inspect the indorsements, a duty which, it insists, was the responsibility of FRB and the depositary banks alone. Echoing the dissent of Presiding Justice Murphy and Justice Silverman at the Appellate Division, Chemical also advances the pragmatic argument that a contrary reading of the statute would impose what, at least for large commercial banks, would constitute an unrealistically onerous and expensive burden of inspecting an "immense volume of checks", all the more so since these checks must be "processed and paid or alternatively, returned or dishonored by midnight of the following business day" (see David Graubart, Inc. v. Bank Leumi Trust Co. of N.Y., 48 N.Y.2d 554, 557–558, 423 N.Y.S.2d 899, 399 N.E.2d 930). Merrill Lynch, on the other hand, choosing to interpret our decision in Underpinning & Foundation Constructors v. Chase Manhattan Bank, N.A., 46 N.Y.2d 459, 414 N.Y.S.2d 298, 386 N.E.2d 1319 as supportive of its stance, continues to contend that section 3–405 of the Uniform Commercial Code will not absolve a banking institution, be it a depositary, drawee or collecting bank, from liability for its own negligence.

For the ensuing reasons, we believe that, under the circumstances of this case, Chemical's motion for partial summary judgment should have been granted.

Our analysis may well begin with the observation that section 3–405 (subd. [1], par. [c]) bespeaks an exception to the general rule governing the responsibility of a bank to its customers. For it is basic that ordinarily a drawee bank may not debit its customer's account when it pays a check over a forged indorsement. This is because the underlying relationship between a bank and its depositor is the contractual one of debtor and creditor * * * implicit in which is the understanding that the bank will pay out its customer's funds only in accordance with the latter's instructions * * *. Thus, absent contrary instruction or legislative exception, when a drawer issues a check in the name of a particular payee, the drawee bank is to apply funds from the drawer's account to its payment only upon receiving the payee's authorized indorsement. In this perspective, a forged indorsement, since it is an unauthorized signature (Uniform Commercial Code, § 1–201, subd. [43]), in and by itself would be "wholly inoperative" (Uniform Commercial Code, § 3–404, subd. [1]).

It follows that, in the typical case in which payment is made on a check that is not properly payable (see Uniform Commercial Code, § 4–401, subd. [1]), the payment is deemed to have been made solely from the funds of the drawee bank rather than from those of its depositor. But, when the conditions which section 3–405 contemplates prevail, the indorsement, though forged, is still effective, and the instrument then must be treated as "both a valuable instrument and a valid instruction to the drawee to honor the check and debit the drawer's account accordingly" (Underpinning & Foundation Constructors v. Chase Manhattan Bank, N.A., supra, at p. 465, 414 N.Y.S.2d 298, 386 N.E.2d 1319).

This departure from the general rule is explained by section 3–405's Official Comment 4, which advises, "The principle followed is that the loss should fall upon the employer as a risk of his business enterprise rather than upon the subsequent holder or drawee. The reasons are that the employer is normally in a better position to prevent such forgeries by reasonable care in the selection or supervision of his employees, or, if he is not, is at least in a better position to cover the loss by fidelity insurance; and that the cost of such insurance is properly an expense of his business rather than of the business of the holder or drawee".

Since the assumptions instinct in this rationalization are hardly indisputable, it is no surprise that the rule it supports represents a conscious choice between the traditional one, which, as we have seen, was more protective of the bank's customer, and the one in the code, which, as some commentators have bluntly acknowledged, was "a banker's provision intended to narrow the liability of banks and broaden the responsibility of their customers" (White & Summers, Uniform Commercial Code, § 16–8, p. 639). Thus, whatever, in the abstract, may have been the equities of the respective contentions of the competing commercial camps, there can be little doubt but that the outcome, so far as the adoption of section 3–405 of the Uniform Commercial Code is concerned, was calculated to shift the balance in favor of the bank "in situations in which the drawer's own employee has perpetrated the fraud or committed the crime giving rise to the loss" (1 Hawkland, A Transactional Guide to the Uniform Commercial Code, pp. 391–394).

That this represents contemporary legislative thinking is clear from the way in which the statutory scheme evolved. Long before section 3–405 of the Uniform Commercial Code came into being, subdivision 3 of section 28 of the former Negotiable Instruments Law already provided that a check is "payable to bearer * * * [w]hen it is payable to the order of a fictitious or non-existing person, and such fact was known to the person making it so payable". Carrying this language to its logical limits, one then might have thought that, because an instrument forged by an employee was to be treated as bearer paper, the fact of forgery had been rendered irrelevant to its negotiability.

Nevertheless, most courts, reluctant to read the statute this broadly, applied it only when the faithless employee made or drew the check himself, but not, as in the case before us now, when he had merely furnished the payee's name to the employer, for then the falsity presumably would not be "known to the person making it so payable" (Hawkland, op. cit.). This narrow interpretation apparently fell short of the drafters' intention because the reaction, first, in 1960, was to amend section 28 of the Negotiable Instruments Law to make it explicit that knowledge to the malefactor who furnished the name was sufficient (Britton, Handbook of the Law of Bills and Notes, § 149, pp. 433–437). And, secondly, by the adoption of section 3–405 of the Uniform Commercial Code, the bearer fiction device was replaced by the more forthright effective indorsement concept (see Official Comment 1 to § 3–405 * * *).

The special scrutiny this legislative course demanded also highlights the fact that section 3–405's failure to delineate a standard of care, to which a bank itself must adhere if it is to advantage itself of this section, was no oversight. In contrast are sections 3–406 and 4–406 of the Uniform Commercial Code, which, along with section 3–405's "padded payroll" provision, deal with defenses which may be available to a drawee bank in forged indorsement cases.

For instance, subdivision (2) of section 4–406, which otherwise precludes a customer from asserting a claim which might have been averted but for its neglect in examining "the [bank] statement and items to discover his unauthorized signature or any alteration on an item" (subd. [1]), makes preclusion inapropos when "the customer establishes lack of ordinary care on the part of the bank in paying the item" (subd. [3]). And, similarly, section 3–406, which puts the onus for a forgery on a customer who "substantially contributes to a material alteration of the instrument or to the making of an unauthorized signature", still requires the bank to have paid the instrument "in good faith and in accordance with the reasonable commercial standards of the drawee's or payor's business".

It is fair to conclude, therefore, that, unlike cases which fall within the foregoing sections, a drawee bank's mere failure to use ordinary care in the handling of a check whose forgery has brought it within the embrace of section 3–405 (subd. [1], par. [c])will not subject it to liability (White & Summers, Uniform Commercial Code, § 16–8, p. 639).[3]

---

3. Because of the manifest advantages of uniformity in the law of bills and notes, we observe that other courts which have considered the matter have arrived at the same conclusion (see, e.g., Prudential Ins. Co. of Amer. v. Marine Nat. Exch. Bank of Milwaukee, 371 F.Supp. 1002; Kraftsman Container Corp. v. United Counties Trust Co., 169 N.J.Super. 488, 404 A.2d 1288; Fair Park Nat. Bank v. Southwestern Inv. Co., 541 S.W.2d 266 [Tex.]; General Acc. Fire & Life Assur. Corp. v. Citizens Fid. Bank & Trust Co., 519 S.W.2d 817 [Ky.]; Western Cas. & Sur. Co. v. Citizens Bank of Las Cruces, 33 UCC Rep. 1018).

This is not to say that, if a check is "tainted in *some other way* which would put the drawee on notice, and which would make its payment unauthorized" (Underpinning & Foundation Constructors v. Chase Manhattan Bank, N.A., 46 N.Y.2d 459, 466, 414 N.Y.S.2d 298, 386 N.E.2d 1319, *supra;* emphasis supplied), a drawee bank may yet not be liable. For instance, a drawee bank surely is not immunized by section 3–405 when it acts dishonestly. In short, "a basis for liability *independent* of any liability which might be created by payment over a forged instrument alone" may very well survive (Underpinning & Foundation Constructors v. Chase Manhattan Bank, N.A., supra, at p. 469, 414 N.Y.S.2d 298, 386 N.E.2d 1319; emphasis supplied).

In contrast, without more, in the present case, it is at once clear that the irregularities on which Merrill Lynch here focuses were part and parcel of the forgeries themselves and, as the dissenters at the Appellate Division observed, "could not possibly have alerted the bank to the fact that the checks were tainted, indeed it would have been most remarkable if the drawee bank had even noticed them". (82 A.D.2d 772, 774, 440 N.Y.S.2d 643, supra.)

* * *

Accordingly, the order of the Appellate Division, insofar as appealed from, should be reversed, with costs, and defendant Chemical's motion for partial summary judgment granted. The certified question should be answered in the negative.

■ COOKE, CHIEF JUDGE (concurring).

To permit a drawee bank to avoid liability for paying a check on a forged indorsement by asserting the "fictitious payee" rule, when the bank itself may have acted negligently in paying the check, is a harsh result. Inasmuch as section 3–405 of the Uniform Commercial Code does not include any requirement that a bank act with ordinary care, however, I am constrained to concur in the majority's result.

* * *

The absence of a standard of care in section 3–405 must be deemed an intentional omission by the Legislature in light of its ability to include such language when it desires, as manifested by sections 3–406 and 4–406. This court should not require ordinary care by the drawee when the Legislature has declined to do so * * *. Instead, section 3–405 should be amended to preclude its invocation by a drawee or other transferee who has failed to exercise due care * * *.

■ JASEN, GABRIELLI, JONES and MEYER, JJ., concur with FUCHSBERG, J.

■ COOKE, C.J., concurs in a separate opinion in which WACHTLER, J., concurs.

NOTE

The court in *Merrill Lynch* took the view that the absence of any reference to negligence on the part of the drawee bank under old § 3–405 meant that its negligence was not to be considered. Most, but not all, courts agreed. Clark & Clark, The Law of Bank Deposits, Collections and Credit Cards ¶ 12.07[5] (Rev.ed.1995). The drafters of revised Article 3 responded to Chief Justice Cooke's exhortation to remedy this deficiency by including §§ 3–404(d) and 3–405(b) (last sentence), both of which adopt a comparative negligence approach.

B. ALTERATION

1. COMPLETE INSTRUMENTS

"Alteration," defined in § 3–407(a), refers to a change that purports to modify the obligation of a party to an instrument if the change is unauthorized. Thus, if the payee raises the amount of a check without the consent of the drawer the check has been altered. But if the payee's act is authorized by the drawer before any other person becomes obligated on the check, the check has not been altered; the change is treated as a change made by the drawer.

The definition of alteration is very broad. It includes fraudulent changes as well as changes made in good faith. For example, the holder of a note changes the due date of the note because the holder believes in good faith that the original due date was erroneous. Even if the holder was mistaken, the alteration is not fraudulent. Under the second sentence of § 3–407(b) the non-fraudulent alteration is ineffective to modify the obligation of the maker and the note is enforceable according to its original terms. Non-fraudulent alteration is described in the first paragraph of Comment 1 to § 3–407.

The concept of alteration can apply to incomplete instruments described in § 3–115 as well as complete instruments, but the effect of alteration is not the same in each case. A discussion of alteration of incomplete instruments follows the next section.

Fraudulent alteration is the principal focus of § 3–407 and can be illustrated by the following hypothetical case:

> An authorized employee of Drawer, a large corporation, signed and delivered a typewritten check for $10 payable to the order of Payee. Without Drawer's consent Payee raised the amount of the check to $10,000 by adding a comma and three zeroes after the figure "10" and the word "thousand" after the word "ten." Payee deposited the check in Payee's account with Depositary Bank and the bank obtained $10,000 from Drawee in payment of the check. Drawee then debited Drawer's account in the same amount. Payee withdrew the $10,000 that had been credited to Payee's account in Depositary Bank with respect to the check. When Drawer learned that Drawee had debited $10,000 to Drawer's account with respect to the check, Drawer notified Drawee of the alteration.

Who takes the loss in the hypothetical case? The liability of the drawer with respect to a check is based on the terms of the order to pay made by the person against whom the drawer's liability is asserted. Liability on an altered check can be compared to liability on a forged check. In the absence of fault, the person whose signature as drawer is forged has no liability on the check because the order to pay on which liability is asserted was not made by that person. In the case of the check in the hypothetical case, Drawer can reasonably be held liable with respect to the order to pay $10 because that order was made by Drawer, but in the absence of fault by Drawer it is not reasonable to hold Drawer liable with respect to the raised amount because Drawer did not order payment of that amount.

How is this analysis reflected in § 3–407? In the hypothetical case, to what extent is Drawee entitled to debit Drawer's account with respect to the check? § 3–407(c). If Drawee had dishonored the check, to what extent would Depositary Bank have had a right to recover from Drawer? § 3–414(b) and § 3–407(c). What is the significance of the first sentence of § 3–407(b) which states that "a party whose obligation is affected by the alteration" is discharged? Comment 1 (second paragraph) to § 3–407. If Drawee pays the check but is not entitled to full reimbursement from Drawer, what remedy does it have against Depositary Bank? § 3–417(a)(2) and (b). If Depositary Bank is liable to Drawee, what recourse does Depositary Bank have against Payee? § 3–416(a)(3) and (b).

Suppose, in the hypothetical case, that the employee who wrote the check in behalf of Drawer left blank spaces in the amount lines on the check allowing Payee to raise the amount of the check without leaving any easily detectable evidence that the check had been altered. How does this additional fact affect your answers to the questions asked in the preceding paragraph? § 3–406.

2. CERTIFIED CHECKS

The liability of a bank that certifies an altered check has long troubled the courts. The common law view that a bank which certified an altered check was liable on the check only as originally drawn was justified in Marine National Bank v. National City Bank, 59 N.Y. 67, 17 Am.Rep. 305 (1874) as follows:

That an acceptor of a bill of exchange by acceptance only admits the genuineness of the signature of the drawer, and does not admit the genuineness of the indorsements, whether of the drawee of the same bill, or of any other person whose name appears upon it, or any other part of the bill, is elementary and sustained by an unbroken current of authority. (Story on Bills, §§ 262, 263, and cases cited in notes.) Judge Story says the reason usually assigned is, that when the bill is presented for acceptance the acceptor looks to the handwriting of the drawer with which he is presumed to be acquainted, and he affirms its genuineness by giving credit to the bill, by his acceptance in favor of the legal holder thereof. But the acceptor cannot be presumed to have any such knowledge of the other facts upon which the rights of the holder may depend. In analogy to this, courts have held that the certificate only holds the bank for the truth of the facts presumed to be within its own knowledge, viz., the genuineness of the signature of the drawer and the state of his account. Moneys paid upon checks and drafts which have been forgeries, either in the body of the instrument or in the indorsements, or in any respect, except the name of the drawer, have uniformly been held recoverable as for money paid by mistake, and expressly upon the ground that payment, as an admission of the genuineness of the instrument, was the same as an acceptance, and only operated as an admission of the signature of the drawer. 59 N.Y. at 76–77.

However, two leading cases, National City Bank v. National Bank of the Republic, 300 Ill. 103, 132 N.E. 832 (1921), and Wells Fargo Bank & Union Trust Co. v. Bank of Italy, 214 Cal. 156, 4 P.2d 781 (1931), interpreted the NIL as changing the common law rule and as binding a certifying bank to the terms of the instrument at the time of certification. After the California and Illinois decisions banks adopted the practice of qualifying their certifications: "payable as originally drawn." Under the UCC, what is the liability of a bank that certifies an altered check? Does it make any difference whether the bank qualifies the certification as stated in the quoted language? § 3–413(a).

PROBLEM

Payee receives a check in the amount of $10 drawn on Payor Bank. Payee raises the amount of the check to $10,000 and obtains certification of the check from Payor Bank. Is there a breach of warranty by Payee when certification is obtained? § 3–417(a)(2).

Payee negotiates the certified check to Holder who takes as a holder in due course. Holder presents the certified check to Payor Bank and is paid $10,000. Is there a breach of warranty by Holder when payment is obtained? Does § 3–417(a)(2) apply? Does § 3–417(d) apply? Is Payor Bank entitled to recover from Payee for breach of warranty? § 3–417(a)(2) and (b); Comment 4 to § 3–417.

Suppose that Payor Bank refused to pay Holder when the certified check was presented for payment. Is Payor Bank obliged to pay? § 3–413(a). What is the effect of the penultimate sentence of § 3–417(b)? Is Holder subject to the defense? § 3–305(b) and the first paragraph to Comment 2 to § 3–305.

Brower v. Franklin National Bank

United States District Court, S.D. New York, 1970.
311 F.Supp. 675.

■ WYATT, DISTRICT JUDGE. This is a motion by defendant Franklin National Bank, a successor in interest to the Federation Bank & Trust Company (the Bank) for summary judgment in its favor (Fed.R.Civ.P. 56(b)). For reasons to be given, the motion must be denied.

* * *

The complaint, filed May 27, 1968, avers that in July 1967 one Anthony Ricci maintained a checking account at the Bank's branch on Williamsbridge Road in the Bronx; that on July 12, 1967 Anthony drew two checks on the Bank in the amounts of $8 and $10 payable to the plaintiff Frederick J. Brower (Frederick) and procured the Bank's certification of those checks; that Anthony subsequently raised the checks from $8 to $28,600 and from $10 to $10,000 and delivered them to Frederick in payment for real property in New Jersey; that the Bank refused to honor the checks because they had been "raised"; that the Bank was negligent in certifying the checks, among other things, because when certified they contained blank spaces and could easily be raised. Frederick claims damages of $75,000.

It may be noted that the complaint purports to plead a claim based on negligence of the Bank in certifying the checks under circumstances which made it easy to raise them thereafter and thus to cause them to be passed off to plaintiff in their altered form. The claim ought to be treated, however, as in legal theory based on the Bank's certifications but governed by New York Uniform Commercial Code § 3–406: "Any person who by his negligence substantially contributes to a material alteration of the instrument * * * is precluded from asserting the alteration * * * against a holder in due course * * * ." It may be noted that plaintiff does not sue simply for the amounts of the two checks as raised, $38,600, but rather for $75,000 averring other damages, such as dishonor of his own checks, impairment of "credit standing", etc.

* * *

Apart from damages, there is no dispute as to any material fact. The facts are as follows:

On July 12, 1967, Anthony presented two checks, numbered 139 and 140, to the Bank for certification. "Every item" (apparently the date, payee's name, drawer's name and the amount) in both checks was filled out. Number 139 was in the amount of $10; number 140 in the amount of $8. Both were payable to "Mr. F. Brower." The checks were certified by the Assistant Manager of the Bank. The certification stamp does not show the amount for which the checks were certified.

Check number 139 was raised after certification apparently by Anthony from $10 to $10,000 and deposited by Frederick in the Plainfield Trust State National Bank, Plainfield, New Jersey. Check number 140 was likewise raised after certification from $8 to $28,600 and deposited in the National Bank of New Jersey, bearing the endorsements of "Mr. F. Brower" and "Edward A. Ryan." Both checks were presented to the Bank on July 19, 1967 and were returned unpaid, because the checks had been altered as to amount. Neither check has been paid and this action was commenced to secure payment.

Before adoption of the Uniform Commercial Code (U.C.C.) effective in 1964, the law of New York appears to have been clear that a bank certifying a check was not liable on its certification for an altered amount of the check, whether alteration took place after or before certification. * * *

Under the U.C.C. this rule is changed and the certifying bank is liable on its certification where the alteration was *before* certification. The engagement in certifying is now to pay the check "according to its tenor at the time of his engagement". U.C.C. § 3–413(1). If alteration (raising) occurs *after* certification, the certifying bank is not bound by its certification to pay the instrument as raised.

As to *negligence,* at common law it was believed, on the authority of Young v. Grote, 4 Bing. 253 (1827), that a *drawer* who negligently drew a check in such a way as to make it easy to raise the check was responsible to a drawee who paid the raised check in good faith.

It was sought in a leading English case to extend this rule to the acceptor. Just as here, a check was drawn for 500[4] with spaces left so that it could be raised to 3,500[4]. As originally drawn, it was presented and certified (accepted); thereafter it was raised to 3,500[4] as planned and negotiated to a holder in due course. It was said as against the acceptor that the acceptance was negligent because the check was in such form that alteration (raising) was made easy and was a likely result. The House of Lords refused to sanction an action against an acceptor for negligence because there is no duty on an acceptor to take precautions against a possible alteration. Scholfield v. Earl of Londesborough, (1896) A.C. 514.

The plain words of the Uniform Commercial Code § 3–406 seem clearly to change the old rule and to authorize this action. "Any person who by his negligence substantially contributes to a material alteration of the instrument * * * is precluded from asserting the alteration * * * against a holder in due course * * * ." U.C.C. § 3–406.

The certifying bank would certainly seem to be included in the words "any person." Under the averments of the complaint, plaintiff should be given an opportunity to show at trial that he is "a holder in due course."

Plaintiff therefore is entitled to a trial of the issues (a) whether or not he is "a holder in due course", and if he is such a holder, (b) whether defendant was or was not guilty of negligence when it certified these checks and if it was negligent (c) whether or not such negligence substantially contributed to the raising of the checks.

There are lower court decisions in New York which reach a contrary result. Sam Goody, Inc. v. Franklin Nat. Bank, 57 Misc.2d 193, 291 N.Y.S.2d 429 (Sup.Ct.Nassau Cty.1968); Wallach Sons, Inc. v. Bankers Trust Co., 307 N.Y.S.2d 297 (Civ.Ct.New York Cty.1970). After carefully reading the opinions in these two cases and with great deference to the two distinguished judges who wrote them, I cannot accept their result and feel that the Court of Appeals of New York would not reach their result.

It is, of course, true that the plaintiff is here in form suing in tort whereas his claim is more properly on the certification. The effect of negligence and its substantial contribution to the raising, if proved, is not to give rise to a tort claim but to preclude the Bank "from asserting the alteration." The Bank would not appear to be liable in any event for more than the amount of the checks as altered. See Official Comment 5, McKinney's U.C.C. § 3–406, page 263. However, the form of pleading adopted by plaintiff would not justify dismissing his action.

The motion is denied.

NOTE

How would *Brower* be decided under revised Article 3? § 3–413(b).

PROBLEMS

1.   Thief stole a check payable to Payee and had it certified. Thief then wrote Payee's name on the back as an indorsement and transferred the check to Depositary Bank that paid value in good faith without notice of the forged indorsement. Depositary Bank obtained payment of the check from Drawee Bank. Drawee Bank then discovered the forged indorsement. What are the rights of Drawee Bank against Depositary Bank? § 3–417(d) and § 3–301.

2.   John Smithson stole a check payable to John Smith and altered the check by adding "son" to the end of "Smith." Smithson then obtained certification of the check and indorsed it to Depositary Bank that paid value in good faith without notice of the alteration. Depositary Bank obtained payment of the check from Drawee Bank. Drawee Bank then discovered the alteration. What are the rights of Drawee Bank against Depositary Bank? § 3–413(a)(i). Was there a breach of warranty by Depositary Bank when it obtained payment of the check? § 3–417(d). Who was the payee of the check when Smithson obtained certification?

3.   INCOMPLETE INSTRUMENTS

Assume that A is indebted to B but is not sure of the precise amount of the debt. In payment of the debt A sends to B a check payable to B, leaving the amount of the check blank. A instructs B to complete the check by filling in the amount of the debt. If the amount of the debt is $10 and B fills in the check for that amount there is no difficulty in enforcing the check against A. The intent of A has been carried out by B's completion of the check. The result is the same as if A had personally completed the check. When the check was received by B the check was an "incomplete instrument" defined in § 3–115(a). Because the amount of the check was not stated, the check was not a negotiable instrument under § 3–104 and the last sentence of § 3–115(b) applies. If B completes the check by writing in $10 as its amount, the check becomes an instrument under § 3–104 and the last sentence of § 3–115(b) states that the check can be enforced as completed. There is no alteration.

But if B fills in $10,000 rather than $10, the act of B is not authorized by A. Under § 3–115(c) there is an alteration of the incomplete instrument and § 3–407 applies. The case is analogous to the hypothetical case on p. 768 in which a check payable in the amount of $10 was altered by changing the amount to $10,000. In each case the drawer intended a check in the amount of $10 and in each case the payee raised the intended amount to $10,000.

Suppose B deposited the altered check to B's account in Depositary Bank and the bank obtained $10,000 from Drawee Bank in payment of the check. Drawee Bank then debited A's account in the same amount. B withdrew the $10,000 that had been credited to B's account in Depositary Bank with respect to the check. When A learned that Drawee Bank had debited $10,000 to A's account with respect to the check, A notified Drawee Bank of the alteration. Who takes the loss in this case? To what extent is Drawee Bank entitled to debit A's account with respect to the check? § 3–407(c). If Drawee Bank had dishonored the check, to what extent would Depositary Bank have had a right to recover from A? § 3–414(b) and § 3–407(c).

Compare the results in this case with the results in the hypothetical case in the section on Complete Instruments, supra. Why are the results different? Is there any relationship between § 3–406 and § 3–407(c) as it applies to fraudulent completion of incomplete instruments?

C. FRAUDULENT MISENCODING OF CHECKS

In Chapter 11 there is a description of the way in which checks are encoded with preprinted machine-readable numerals and symbols which allow presentment of the checks for payment by automated processing. We examined the consequences of mistake by the depositary bank when it encodes the check by adding to the preprinted MICR line numerals and symbols that indicate the amount of the check. Such mistakes are inevitable. Unfortunately it is also inevitable that somebody will find in the MICR line an opportunity to steal money.

USF & G, the case that follows, involved the preprinted part of the MICR line that identifies the payor bank, the Federal Reserve district in which the bank is located, and the Federal Reserve Bank or branch that serves the payor bank. On the basis of this encoded information, sorting machines of the depositary bank and other collecting banks will determine the route that the check will take to get to the payor bank. Since the routing of the check is determined by the MICR encoding, there is an opportunity to commit fraud by depositing a counterfeit check, drawn on a nonexistent account, that is reprinted with MICR encoding designed to cause confusion and delay in the presentment of the check for payment.

United States Fidelity & Guaranty Co. v. Federal Reserve Bank of New York

United States District Court, Southern District of New York, 1985.
620 F.Supp. 361, *aff'd,* 786 F.2d 77 (2d Cir.1986).

■ HAIGHT, DISTRICT JUDGE:

Plaintiff Union Trust Company of Maryland ("Union Trust") and its insurer, United States Fidelity and Guaranty Company, brought this action to recover damages caused by a clever check fraud perpetrated upon Union Trust by a nonparty. Following denial of its motion to dismiss, in an opinion reported at 590 F.Supp. 486 (hereafter cited as *"USF & G I"*), defendant Federal Reserve Bank of New York ("New York Fed") impleaded third-party defendants State Bank of Albany ("Albany State"), Philadelphia National Bank ("PNB"), and First Pennsylvania Bank ("First Penn"). Soon after filing of the third-party complaint, plaintiffs amended their complaint to assert claims against Albany State. It was unnecessary for them to assert claims against the remaining third-party defendants because the Court accepted for transfer and consolidation a suit which plaintiffs had previously filed against those two Pennsylvania banks in the Eastern District of Pennsylvania, United States Fidelity and Guaranty Co. v. Philadelphia National Bank, No. 83–1304 (E.D.Pa.).

* * *

I.

As described more fully in *USF & G I,* 590 F.Supp. at 489–91, Union Trust was fraudulently induced to permit a depositor to withdraw funds against a worthless check. In April 1980, a man who called himself Marvin Goldstein established a checking account with Union Trust. Soon after, he deposited a check for over $880,000 in the account. The account upon which the check purported to be drawn did not exist, but a clever manipulation of the numerals on the face of the check caused it to be routed among a number of New York and Pennsylvania banks before being returned to Union Trust as uncollectible. In the meantime, Union Trust had permitted Goldstein to withdraw a substantial amount of cash from his account, having assumed from the lapse of time that the check had been paid.[2] The foregoing information was pleaded in the original complaint, and discovery has confirmed its accuracy. The interesting details unearthed in discovery primarily concern not the behavior of the defendant banks in

---

2. As explained in *USF & G I,* 590 F.Supp. at 489, familiarity with which is assumed throughout this decision, this would ordinarily have been an entirely legitimate assumption; indeed, it is an assumption made thousands of times daily by every bank in the nation without adverse consequences.

routing the bogus check but that of Union Trust's employees in accepting it and releasing funds against it. A summary of that new information follows.

On April 16, 1980, Goldstein walked into a Baltimore branch of Union Trust. He told the branch manager, John Gemmill, that he and his father were precious metals dealers and that he planned to establish a Baltimore office of his father's New York business, Goldstein Precious Metals and Stones. In preparation, he sought to open a checking account with Union Trust in the name of the business. In opening the account, Goldstein produced one piece of personal identification, a New Jersey driver's license, and a New York certificate of business proprietorship, and supplied a New York bank reference. Gemmill recorded this and other information on a "New Account Information Form." Goldstein opened the new account with a cash deposit of $15,000.

Gemmill then turned the new account form over to assistant branch manager John Clement with instructions to prepare two signature cards. Clement did so, but he unaccountably neglected to transcribe the bank reference from the new account form to the signature cards. The form and one card were then sent to central Union Trust files, while one card was retained at the local branch.

One week later, Goldstein returned to the branch and withdrew $14,000 from his account, reducing his balance to $1,000. Little was heard from him until May 6, when he deposited a check for $880,000 at a second Union Trust branch located a few blocks from the branch with which he had opened the account. Deposit of such a large check ordinarily triggers self-protective internal alerts at a bank, and Union Trust was no exception. Tellers who received for deposit checks over $100,000 were supposed to notify the branch manager, according to written Union Trust procedural guidelines. The manager was then to decide whether a "hold" should be placed on the check—that is, whether the depositor should be denied access to the deposited funds for an extended period of time in order to permit the bank to confirm the collectibility of the check. In the absence of such a hold, funds ordinarily become available to the depositor within one to two days of deposit of the check. The teller who accepted Goldstein's check, however, neither notified bank officers of the large deposit nor placed a hold on it.

The teller, however, was merely the bank's first line of defense against fraud. During the next few days, Gemmill, the branch manager, was reviewing a document known as a "balance fluctuation report," designed to alert bank officers to unusually large balance changes in the accounts under their supervision. The leap in the Goldstein Precious Metals account balance from one thousand to nearly a million dollars naturally caught his attention, and he decided to investigate. Gemmill first requested, or had Clement request, credit reports on the Goldstein business from two national credit reporting services. Both services reported that they had no record of Goldstein Precious Metals and Stones. Upon receiving this information, Gemmill had Clement retrieve the Goldstein signature card in order to pursue the credit references which would ordinarily be listed on it. Because

Clement had neglected to transfer the reference from the account form, however, the signature card was no help, and neither bank employee pursued this further.[3]

Wisely, Gemmill instructed Clement to look into the $880,000 check. The check was drawn on an account at First Penn of a company called Metropolitan Investment Corporation. On instructions from Clement, an employee of Union Trust's credit department called officials at First Penn and was told that no such account existed. First Penn had no banking relationship with Metropolitan Investment Corporation. This information was relayed to Clement, who told Gemmill. All of the foregoing occurred on or before Friday, May 9, within four days of the check's May 6 deposit.

According to his deposition testimony, Gemmill, who was leaving for vacation on May 9, told Clement to report to senior bank officers any activity in the Goldstein account, perhaps recognizing that the First Penn report made it unlikely that the Goldstein check would be honored. Clement remembers no such instructions. Either way, no other action was taken at that time to prevent Goldstein from withdrawing funds against the check.

On Monday, May 12, Gemmill was temporarily replaced by another bank officer. The next day, Goldstein telephoned Clement to ask instructions for making a "wire transfer" of funds, that is, for arranging the automatic transfer of funds from his account to an account in another bank. When Goldstein arrived at the branch to arrange for the transfer, he presented Clement with a bottle of expensive champagne. They discussed arrangements for the transfer, and Clement told him that the bank could only wire "collected" balances, that is, could only wire funds from the check after a sufficient time had passed to permit the bank to conclude that the check had been paid.[4] Apparently Goldstein was willing to wait. No further action was taken on Tuesday.

Two days later, on Thursday, May 15, seven business days after deposit of the check, Goldstein returned and sought both to effect a wire transfer of $660,000 and to withdraw $95,000 in cash. The wire transfer was to be made to the account of a Maryland coin dealer. Apparently concluding that sufficient time had passed, Clement undertook to make the wire transfer. His first step was to check the Union Trust computer to find out whether sufficient funds were available in Goldstein's account to satisfy the transfer request. Because this act was crucial to the success of the fraud, it must be examined in some detail.

3. According to an affidavit filed by New York Fed, the New York bank reference, if contacted, would have reported no history of dealings with the Goldstein company.

4. As explained in *USF & G I,* 590 F.Supp. at 489, banks are never actually notified when a check which has been deposited with them is paid by, or "clears," the payor bank. Instead, they are only told if it fails to clear. Therefore, before releasing funds against a suspect check, banks commonly hold the check for the number of days which experience has taught them will be required for the check to reach the payor bank and for that bank to inform them if the check is uncollectable. If no word arrives in this time, it is assumed that the check has been paid.

As explained in note 4, supra, banks are never notified when checks deposited with them are paid by the payor bank. The large volume of checks in the banking system would make any such notification system expensive and unwieldy. If payment is refused, however, the payor bank must notify the depositary bank of the refusal within roughly twenty-four hours of its receipt of the check. See N.Y.U.C.C. § 4–302. In order to protect themselves against uncollectible checks, banks commonly guess at the amount of time the check is likely to spend in the collection system before reaching the payor bank and place a hold on the deposited check for at least that amount of time. Union Trust's computer was charged with keeping track of such holds.

The Union Trust computer apparently registered two types of holds. When a check was deposited into a checking account such as Goldstein's, the Union Trust computer automatically placed a one-or two-day hold on the deposited check. These holds were keyed to the Federal Reserve clearing system. Member banks of the Federal Reserve system keep accounts with their local Federal Reserve bank. See *USF & G I*, 590 F.Supp. at 490 n. 7. One of the functions of these accounts is to permit the Reserve bank to credit and debit member banks for checks cleared through the Reserve bank. Banks are ordinarily not given immediate credit for or access to the funds represented by checks such as that deposited with Union Trust by Goldstein. In other words, regardless of whether a depository bank gives its depositor immediate access to the funds represented by a deposited check, the Federal Reserve will not, in most instances, give the bank immediate credit for the check in the account which the bank maintains with the Reserve bank. Instead, the Reserve bank credits the check to a one-or two-day deferred account, equivalent to placing a hold on the check, with the length of the deferral depending primarily upon the distance the check must travel to reach the payor bank. Once the deferral period elapses, the Reserve bank grants the depositary bank a provisional credit for the amount of the check.

In reality, however, checks frequently do not clear in the one-or two-day time period allotted for this purpose by the Federal Reserve. The provisional status of the credit given by the Reserve bank signifies that although a credit has been given to the account of the depositary bank, no corresponding debit has been made in the account of the payor bank. Once the payor bank receives the check, it must notify the Reserve bank within twenty-four hours whether it will honor the check. If the Reserve bank is notified that the check has been honored, it debits the account of the payor bank and removes the provisional status of the credit given the depositary bank.

The Union Trust computer automatically placed the equivalent of a hold on all deposited checks corresponding to the length of the deferral imposed by the Federal Reserve. The duration of Reserve system deferrals were never intended, however, to estimate or correspond precisely to the actual clearing time of a check. On the contrary, they intentionally underestimate this time. For that reason, as suggested above, banks frequently place their own extended hold on checks which are not likely to clear within one or two days. This prevents the depositor from withdrawing funds until the bank has satisfied itself that no word of dishonor has arrived or, in theory, will arrive. Such holds could also be recorded on the Union Trust computer, but they were not imposed automatically.

As noted above, no such hold was placed on the Goldstein check. The only hold in the Union Trust computer was a two-day Federal Reserve hold, which expired several days before May 15. Therefore, when Clement checked, he found no hold on the Goldstein funds. This, of course, did not indicate that the Goldstein check had been paid. It simply indicated that whatever precautions Union Trust had taken against premature withdrawal had expired, and the check had not been returned. Clement called the bookkeeping department of the bank, which confirmed that no hold was in effect—in other words, that, according to the bank's computer, the funds from the check were available for withdrawal.

Apparently misunderstanding the nature of the information supplied by the computer, Clement, according to his deposition testimony, concluded from his computerized inquiry not only that all holds had expired but that the check had actually cleared. Although he was aware of the First Penn report that no account existed against which the check could possibly have been drawn, he concluded that the report must have been incorrect. Without checking once again with First Penn, he authorized the wire transfer and the cash withdrawal.

Goldstein picked up the cash in person on May 15. The wire transfer was made to the bank of the Maryland coin dealer the same day. The dealer, however, had insufficient coins on hand to satisfy Goldstein's order. The dealer gave Goldstein the coins available on May 15; the remainder were delivered to him in mid-afternoon the following day. Goldstein thereafter disappeared with the cash and coins.

At about the same time Goldstein was receiving his coins on May 16, a Union Trust Vice President was informed that First Penn was returning the $880,000 check. Only later was it discovered that the Goldstein check was a fraud. The numbers printed in magnetic ink at the bottom of the check and the routing number, printed in ordinary ink in the top right hand corner, did not match, a circumstance which caused the check to be routed to several banks over several days before arriving at First Penn. It is now possible to describe the circumstances surrounding the routing of the check in more detail.

Union Trust's central check processing facility attempted to computer-process the check on May 6, the day of deposit. This machine rejected the check because the magnetic ink character recognition number ("MICR number") was not printed in magnetic ink and was the wrong size, necessitating hand processing.[8] At that time all of Union Trust's non-local checks which required hand processing were sent to PNB for processing

8. It is interesting to note that Goldstein's technique of printing an improper MICR number has been used in other types of fraud. According to published reports, the scheme which resulted in the well-publicized May, 1985, conviction for fraud of the broker-

and collection. The Goldstein check was accordingly dispatched to PNB in the early morning of May 7; because of its great value, it was sent by courier.

Based on the check's routing number, it was sent by PNB to a New York Fed processing center in Utica, New York, for forwarding to Albany State. Albany State received the check on the morning of May 9 and returned it to the Utica center of New York Fed, stamped "Sent in Error," on May 12. The next day the Utica center sent the check to New York Fed's New York City office.

Despite irregularities in the check described as "glaring" by a New York Fed chief of operations, that office failed to detect the fraudulent nature of the check. Instead, on May 14, New York Fed sent the check to the Federal Reserve Bank of Philadelphia. A document accompanying the check indicated that New York Fed intended the check to be presented for collection to First Penn rather than returned to PNB as an unpaid item.[10] The Philadelphia Reserve bank presented the check to First Penn at 9:00 a.m. on the same day it received it, May 14. At this time, it must be remembered, Goldstein had not yet been permitted to withdraw any funds against the check by Union Trust.

If First Penn was going to dishonor the Goldstein check, it was required by the U.C.C. to notify PNB of this fact by midnight of May 15. It did not. Instead, processing of the check was not completed until 9:45 a.m. on the morning of May 16, when First Penn finally notified PNB of the dishonor. At this point it was still not too late to recover the fraudulently gained funds, for the second shipment of gold coins had not yet been made to Goldstein. Quick action might have caught him. Quick action, however, was not forthcoming. PNB did not pass word of the dishonor to Union Trust until mid-afternoon of May 16, too late to prevent Goldstein from slipping away. He has never been located.

II.

Albany State and the three defendant banks all move for summary judgment on plaintiffs' claims. Each is in a somewhat different factual

---

age firm of E.F. Hutton & Co. also used improperly printed checks. Hutton had checks printed with incorrect MICR numbers to foil its banks' computer-aided check-processing machines, thereby lengthening the time needed for processing the checks and increasing Hutton's "float," or amount of funds on deposit by checks which have not yet been collected from the payor bank. Hutton deposited the flawed checks drawn on its own accounts at various banks in its accounts at other banks. Until the checks were paid by the former banks, Hutton received payment for use of the funds by both banks at once. The longer the time required to process the check, the greater the "double" payments

Hutton received. This was where the incorrect MICR numbers came in handy. See Bleakley, How Hutton Scheme Worked, N.Y. Times, May 17, 1985, at D4, cols. 2–4.

10. Because both PNB, to which the check would have been returned, and First Penn, to which it was sent for collection, are in the same Federal Reserve district, it was impossible to determine on the facts pleaded in the complaint whether New York Fed had returned the check or sent it for collection. See *USF & G I*, 590 F.Supp. at 497. It now seems clear, based on discovered materials, that New York Fed did not return the item but sent it for collection.

posture, and each accordingly raises somewhat different legal issues. Over-hanging all of the arguments, however, is the issue of the effect of Union Trust's behavior in its dealings with Goldstein. It cannot be contended that Union Trust's behavior was anything but reckless. Gemmill opened an account with a man who presented only one form of personal identification, an out-of-state driver's license. Whether or not this alone was poor com-mercial practice, it placed particular importance on the bank reference which he provided, for the reference was Union Trust's only independent means of confirming Goldstein's identity. Yet Clement left the reference off the signature card, and neither man made an effort to track it down when it was needed. In addition, the teller who accepted the check for deposit did so without presenting it to a branch manager, in breach of bank regula-tions.[12] This failure was particularly serious, for it deprived the banking system of its one opportunity for the check to be examined by an experi-enced professional who was unhurried by time pressures and simultaneous-ly had access to information about the depositor. The most astounding act of carelessness, however, was the bank's release of funds against a check which it had been told was drawn on a non-existent account. Such an act was more than mere negligence, for it entailed acting in the face of a known and obvious risk. Viewed in its entirety, Union Trust's conduct was breathtakingly foolhardy; nay, commercially suicidal.[13]

New York Fed argues, with backing from Albany State, that such almost incomprehensible conduct should act as a bar to any recovery based on the dramatically lesser negligence of other banks in the check's chain of collection.

A.

In understanding this claim, it is helpful to review the basis of New York Fed's alleged liability. Section 4–202(1) of the U.C.C. imposes upon all banks which handle checks sent for collection a duty of ordinary care both in forwarding checks for collection and in returning checks deemed uncol-lectible. Care must be exercised both in the promptness of action and in the choice of action. Timing is handled by the "midnight deadline" rule; banks exercise care in the timing of an action by responding, generally, before midnight of the business day following the day on which the check is received. N.Y.U.C.C. §§ 4–104 and 4–202(2). The proper choice of action

---

12. In retrospect, the teller's failure to place a hold on the check, while poor prac-tice, was of less consequence. Union Trust's standard, and apparently proper, hold for a check drawn on a Pennsylvania bank was five to six days. Since Goldstein withdrew funds on the seventh day, the hold would not have prevented execution of his scheme.

13. This is not the whole of the bank's carelessness. First, discovery revealed that after being rejected by the automatic sorting machinery the check was examined by a Un-ion Trust supervisor, but this supervisor failed to detect the "glaring" facial irregulari-ties in the check and instead forwarded it to PNB. Second, Clement's wire transfer of $660,000 exceeded the amount of money he was authorized by bank regulations to trans-fer. Third, several of Goldstein's actions known to Clement labelled him as "shady," including his transparent attempt at a bribe and his request that the money be wired to a coin dealer, who presumably would convert the funds into highly liquid assets.

cannot be so easily codified and is governed by a general rule of reasonableness borrowed from tort law. *USF & G I*, 590 F.Supp. at 491–92. This is the duty New York Fed is accused of failing to satisfy.

At the time of *USF & G I*, the lack of discovery made it impossible to define precisely New York Fed's alleged breach of care, since its exact actions were then unknown. It now appears that plaintiffs' claim is twofold: that New York Fed should have, in the exercise of ordinary care, either 1) recognized the risk of fraud inherent in the check and sent it for return to PNB rather than collection from First Penn or 2) recognized that the routing of the check to Albany State caused a significant risk that Union Trust would release funds before the check cleared and sent wire notice to Union Trust or PNB that the check had taken the long route to First Penn. See *USF & G I*, 590 F.Supp. at 494–99. Union Trust argues that these actions would have permitted it either to prevent the fraud or to catch Goldstein before he absconded with the cash and coins.

It is by no means a foregone conclusion that New York Fed's failure to take these actions, given the realities of modern check processing, was negligent. *USF & G I*, 590 F.Supp. at 499. On the other hand, as discussed above, Union Trust's recklessness was gross and obvious. New York Fed argues, on several grounds, that the tenuous nature of its alleged negligence should not serve as a basis for recovery in the face of Union Trust's conduct.

The primary difficulty with defendant's theory is that it is not expressly sanctioned by the UCC. Plaintiffs' suit is for violation of a duty imposed in the first instance by the UCC, and it is to that body of law which resort must first be had to determine the rights and liabilities of the parties. Although the UCC in some specific circumstances apportions liability on the basis of relative fault—most notably in the law of forged signatures and endorsements, see, generally, Five Towns College v. Citibank, N.A., 108 A.D.2d 420, 489 N.Y.S.2d 338, 342–43 (1985), it incorporates no general rule of comparative or contributory negligence. In the area with which we are concerned, check collection, the Code imposes upon collecting banks a duty of due care and subjects them to "but for" liability for violations of the duty. N.Y.U.C.C. §§ 4–103(5) and 4–202(1); Northpark National Bank v. Bankers Trust Co., 572 F.Supp. 524, 531 (S.D.N.Y.1983) (hereafter "*Northpark* "). There is no express requirement that the plaintiff demonstrate its own due care as a prerequisite to recovery, nor is there any mention of comparative negligence.[14] There is simply no mention of the effect, if any, of a plaintiff's negligence on its recovery under § 4–202(1).

The question cannot be permitted to end there, however. Article 4 of the Code, governing check collection, was developed in the 1950s, prior to the advent of large scale fraud upon the check collection system. See

14. The latter is not surprising. The UCC predated the widespread acceptance of comparative negligence of the 1970s. More important, the concept of comparative negligence is anathema to a code which had as a primary aim the fostering of swift resolution of disputes through the clear delineation of commercial liabilities. See Perini Corp. v. First National Bank of Habersham County, 553 F.2d 398, 405 (5th Cir.1977).

Northpark, 572 F.Supp. at 533. The rules of liability which govern the allocation of losses arising from check transit were not—could not have been—designed with such fraud in mind. In these circumstances, to adhere blindly to the limitations imposed by those rules, if to do so would violate the policies which the UCC otherwise seeks to promote, would be unwise and unjust. Nor does the Code demand such adherence. As Judge Knapp noted in his seminal *Northpark* decision, "the history of the UCC makes it abundantly clear that, especially in the context of those provisions which impose a duty of care, the Code's watchword is 'flexibility.' "572 F.Supp. at 533. I do not, therefore, find the lack of a rule of contributory or comparative negligence in Article 4 to be an insuperable barrier to defendants' claim that such a rule should be imposed. Rather, the decision turns upon whether to do so would, on the one hand, be consistent with the aims of § 4–202(1) and Article 4 as a whole and, on the other, would promote the policies which animate the rules of liability found elsewhere in the Code.

B.

In making its claim, New York Fed argues primarily by analogy to tort law. Because, the argument goes, the ordinary care standard of § 4–202(1) is borrowed from tort law, tort principles of comparative or contributory negligence should apply. As plaintiffs point out, however, this is not a tort case. The standard of care, though reliant on a concept borrowed from tort law, is imposed by the UCC. In allegedly violating § 4–202(1), defendants did not breach a duty imposed by tort law; they breached a duty imposed by statute, the UCC. It is the policies served by the UCC, therefore, rather than those served by tort law, which must determine whether plaintiff's negligence should affect its recovery under § 4–202(1). Because, as discussed below, the aims of tort law are not identical with those of the UCC, I decline to borrow the tort rule.

Tort law is designed primarily to apportion loss. Because it is typically imposed upon lay parties with little or no appreciation of its finer points, only secondarily can it hope to guide behavior so as to minimize harm. Rather, it most often becomes relevant only after the fact; the courts are asked to decide who must bear or respond for a loss previously incurred, and to what degree. As such, its guiding principle is fairness. In tort law courts have equated fairness with fault. The rule of comparative negligence is a perfect expression of this principle.

The UCC, however, was designed to facilitate commerce primarily by guiding and making predictable the consequences of behavior. It is imposed primarily upon a comparatively sophisticated group, businessmen and bankers, who look to its provisions to direct their business transactions. This is not to overlook its loss allocation function. Rules designed to guide behavior are inevitably turned against those who fail to follow them, and even the most carefully planned transactions may end in dispute. This function, however, is secondary to the creation of a system of rules to bring order and predictability to commercial transactions.

Interestingly, this fact is forcefully demonstrated by a series of provisions in the Code which were designed, unlike the bulk of the Code, to distribute loss. Several provisions of Article 3 determine which party must bear loss which results from the use of a forged signature or endorsement on a negotiable instrument. Tort law would ordinarily distribute such a loss on the basis of fault: that party or parties whose carelessness resulted in the forgery would bear the consequences of it. The UCC, however, for the most part does not look at actual fault.[15] Instead, it places responsibility on the party which ordinarily would be in the best position to prevent the loss.[16] See *Northpark, supra,* 572 F.Supp. at 535 and n. 26; Underpinning & Foundation Constructors, Inc. v. Chase Manhattan Bank, N.A., 46 N.Y.2d 459, 468, 414 N.Y.S.2d 298, 302, 386 N.E.2d 1319 (1979). Such a result accomplishes two purposes: first, it increases the efficiency and fraud-resistance of the banking system by placing upon those best able to guard against it the responsibility for preventing fraud,[17] and, second, it speeds the resolution of disputes by establishing clear rules of liability which do not depend heavily upon the specific facts of individual instances of fraud. See Perini Corp. v. First National Bank, 553 F.2d 398, 405–06 (5th Cir.1977) (describing this policy as promoting "finality"). Therefore, while the purpose of these rules is, as with tort law, to apportion loss, they are guided not by the policy which guides tort loss apportionment—fairness in the circumstances—but by the policies which shape the UCC—the promotion of efficient and predictable commerce.

Because tort law and the UCC are designed to serve different ends, I find it inappropriate to borrow a rule of comparative or contributory negligence from tort law for use in the UCC. Nevertheless, the question remains open whether such a rule should be implied from within the UCC itself.

C.

The policies which underlie the UCC were explored above. As relevant here, they were usefully summed up by Judge Knapp in *Northpark:* "[i]f there is a policy implicit in the UCC's rules for the allocation of losses due to fraud, it is surely that the loss be placed on the party in the best position to prevent it." 572 F.Supp. at 535. See similarly, Leigh Co. v. Bank of New

15. The exception, discussed infra, is UCC § 3–406.

16. In most cases, loss falls on the forger's immediate transferee. N.Y.U.C.C. §§ 3–417(2)(a), 4–207(2)(a), 3–414(1), and 4–212(1). However, when a check is paid over a forged signature, loss is placed upon the drawee bank, which in theory could have checked its client's signature. N.Y.U.C.C. § 3–417, comment 3. See generally, *Northpark, supra,* 572 F.Supp. at 535 n. 26.

17. Because such parties are generally commercial banks, they are presumed to be aware of the UCC's rules of liability and to take precautions to guard against forgeries. The rule of absolute liability regardless of fault would, one would think, tend to increase their efforts at protecting against forgeries, since to avoid liability they would be forced to guard against not only their own carelessness but the carelessness and deviousness of others. In theory, by placing this burden upon the shoulders of those best able to guard against fraud the UCC achieves such fraud resistance in the most efficient manner.

York, 617 F.Supp. 147 (S.D.N.Y.1985), at 151. These rules are most elaborately developed in connection with the law of forged endorsements and signatures. Liabilities for forgeries are assigned in the first instance without regard to fault. Instead, as noted above, the drafters placed liability upon the party which they determined would typically be best situated to prevent a particular type of forgery.

Creation of this type of rule is essentially a legislative task, outside the scope of the proper exercise of judicial power. Even assuming that courts are competent to determine which party most commonly can prevent a particular type of forgery, the decision whether to assign liability to that party in all circumstances, without regard to fault, is best left to the legislature. This is particularly true where, as here, the legislature has already undertaken to create a complex network of laws in the area. For that reason, I rejected in *USF & G I* New York Fed's request that I create such a rule, on grounds of public policy, assigning strict liability for MICR fraud to depositary banks. 590 F.Supp. at 500 and n. 23.

Nor is it particularly clear that depositary banks are best situated in all, or even most, cases to detect MICR fraud. If such fraud is carried out with more sophistication than demonstrated by Goldstein, the deposit and collection of funds may escape the notice of even a careful bank. In such cases, the bank best situated to detect the fraud might be the first bank to refuse payment, Albany State in this case. That bank would be the first with concrete knowledge that the check is flawed.[18] On the other hand, the fraud could not be confirmed until the check has been examined by the purported payor. Which of these banks should be assigned liability under all circumstances, if any of them should, is a choice I declined and decline to make.

If such legislative assignments of strict liability comprised the whole of the UCC's system for distributing loss due to forgeries, it might properly be concluded that the concept of contributory or comparative negligence had no role to play within the UCC. However, all rules governing liability for forged signatures are subject to the following provision, which incorporate what is, in effect, a rule of contributory negligence:

18. It appears that the first banks in the collection chain, Union Trust, PNB, and New York Fed here, would not automatically be suspicious of a check bearing a routing number inconsistent with its listed name of the payor bank. According to the deposition testimony of a Union Trust employee, such checks may be intentionally and properly circulated. They are used, when one bank maintains an account at a second bank. Union Trust, in fact, participated in such an arrangement. On these checks, Union Trust's routing number appeared in the upper right corner of the checks, and the checks were drawn on an account held by Union Trust, but the name of a second bank, Union Trust's customer bank which maintained the account at Union Trust, appeared where one would otherwise have expected Union Trust's name. The employee called such checks "due-from" checks.

The Goldstein check, of course, had other irregularities which might have attracted attention: the MICR numbers were neither in magnetic ink nor of the proper size and style, and they were nonsensical. The discrepancy between the Albany State and First Penn designations alone, however, would not automatically have suggested fraud to a collecting bank.

Any person who by his negligence substantially contributes to a material alteration of the instrument or to the making of an unauthorized signature is precluded from asserting the alteration or lack of authority against a holder in due course or against a drawee or other payor who pays the instrument in good faith and in accordance with the reasonable commercial standards of the drawee's or payor's business.

N.Y.U.C.C. § 3-406.[19]

Section 3-406 is consistent with the remainder of the Code. It places a burden of due care on a person well situated to prevent a forgery: the drawer of the check. Drawers are forced to draw their checks so as to prevent alterations and to safeguard their blank checks so as to prevent their falling into unauthorized hands.[20]

While § 3-406 does not directly apply to the case at bar, I am persuaded that it is appropriate to apply its spirit by analogy to apportionment of loss due to MICR fraud. The depositary bank, like the drawer of the check, is well situated to protect the system against MICR fraud. The depositary bank has an opportunity to examine the check free of the time pressures which prevent collecting banks from giving checks more than a cursory glance. Perhaps more important, the depositary bank is in the unique position of being able to examine both the depositor and the check. No other bank in the collecting chain can examine the depositor, a crucial disadvantage given the seeming difficulty of detecting this type of fraud.

In many cases examination of the depositor and check might well reveal nothing unusual or alarming,[21] in which event the collecting banks will be obliged, to avoid liability, to demonstrate their compliance with § 4-202. As this case proves, however, a careful examination of either depositor or check, or both, might well reveal the fraud and protect the banking system. Because the depositary bank is uniquely situated to perform such an examination, it is entirely consistent with the policies served by the UCC to place upon it the duty to do so. Conversely, to refuse to imply such a duty would be equally inconsistent with those policies. It would permit the individual or entity in the best position, at least in those circumstances, to prevent the fraud to evade any duty to do so. Not only would such an approach be inefficient, it could well be, as this case demonstrates, entirely unjust.

Moreover, because only the depositary bank possesses this ability to examine both the depositor and the check, it is appropriate to place upon it the initial burden of care. In the banking system, the depositary bank is the

---

19. A more complex and specific provision, N.Y.U.C.C. § 4-406, establishes non-exclusive circumstances which constitute *per se* negligence by checking account customers who are victims of forged signatures.

20. According to the Code, "[t]he most obvious case is that of the drawer who makes use of a signature stamp or other automatic signing device and is negligent in looking after it." N.Y.U.C.C. § 3-406, comment 7. Again, this shows the commercial orientation of the Code; businessmen are warned to watch those with access to signing machines.

21. See note 18, supra.

first line of defense against MICR fraud, and the most efficient point at which to take precautions against it. It may properly be prevented from holding other banks liable if it has not adequately fulfilled this role.[22]

I hold that a depositary bank which is a victim of MICR fraud may be precluded from recovering damages from collecting banks under UCC § 4–202(1) if those banks can demonstrate that the negligence of the depositary bank played a substantial role in the success of the fraud.[23] I have no hesitation in holding that, for the reasons stated previously, it has been demonstrated as a matter of law that the recklessness of Union Trust played a substantial—nay, indispensable—role in the success of this fraud. I grant summary judgment in favor of defendants Albany State, New York Fed, and PNB.

III.

First Penn stands on a somewhat different footing, since it is alleged to be liable not under § 4–202(1) but § 4–302. Section 4–302 makes a payor bank which fails to return a dishonored check within its midnight deadline liable for resulting damages. It has been repeatedly recognized, however, that § 4–302 does not shift the burden of loss to a payor bank which misses its deadline if the payee was already aware when presenting the check that it would not be accepted or paid except by mistake. See N.Y.U.C.C. § 3–511(2)(b); Bank Leumi Trust Co. v. Bally's Park Place, 528 F.Supp. 349 (S.D.N.Y.1981); Leaderbrand v. Central State Bank of Wichita, 202 Kan. 450, 450 P.2d 1, 9 (1969); cf. Continental National Bank v. Sanders, 581 S.W.2d 293, 296 (Tex.Civ.App.1979). Although Union Trust did not know

---

22. To this extent, this imposed rule differs from § 3–406, which requires an otherwise liable bank seeking to evade liability to demonstrate not only the drawer's lack of due care but its own exercise of due care. The rules of liability of which § 3–406 is a part are quite different, however, from § 4–202. "Otherwise liable" banks are not liable, as is the case with banks liable under § 4–202, because of their negligence. They are strictly liable. It is arguably appropriate to require them to demonstrate their own exercise of care before evading the severe standard of strict liability. Further, drawers, who may be made liable under § 3–406, stand on a much different footing than the banks which would be liable. They are generally individuals and corporations, and the forgeries are presumably carried out without their awareness. Because of this, they do not possess the tools to protect against fraud—for example, the chance to ask a customer for identification or to check a signature card—which the strictly liable banks do. Indeed, it is these tools to protect against forgery which the UCC uses to justify holding those particular banks lia-

ble. See *Northpark,* supra, 572 F.Supp. at n. 26.

By contrast, depositary banks under § 4–202(1) differ from the collecting banks in their ability not only to examine the check but the depositor. They thus have advantage over the collecting banks. It is therefore appropriate to place liability on their shoulders should they fail to exercise due care, even if the collecting banks have also failed to do so.

23. It might be contended that application of comparative negligence would be more fair. The UCC, however, contains no provision for comparative negligence. See *Northpark,* supra, 572 F.Supp. at n. 28. Even in New York the legislature has left the UCC's all-or-nothing rules alone while statutorily adopting comparative negligence in other areas. See N.Y.Civ.P.L.R. § 1411. Contributory negligence serves the UCC's aims of efficiency and finality by definitively assigning liability. See note 14, infra. It would be improper to impose the more tort-oriented comparative negligence in the absence of legislative approval of such a step.

that the Goldstein check would not be paid when it forwarded the check for collection, it learned long before releasing funds to Goldstein that First Penn had no account from which to pay the check. The same policy reasons which preclude recovery under § 4–302 by those who forward checks which they have reason to know are uncollectible also argue in favor of precluding Union Trust from recovering. It had reason to know of the uncollectibility of Goldstein's check. Therefore, it can and should be estopped from claiming that at the time it suffered the loss it was not aware that First Penn would refuse the check.

To hold otherwise would be inequitable to First Penn. First Penn informed Union Trust that it had no account relationship with the purported drawer of the check. It should not now be held liable because Union Trust chose to ignore that information and subsequently release funds against the check.

Also relevant is National Savings and Trust Co. v. Park Corp., 722 F.2d 1303, 1304 (6th Cir.1983), cert. denied, 466 U.S. 939, 104 S.Ct. 1916, 80 L.Ed.2d 464 (1984), in which it was held that a bank may recover funds paid by mistake on a bad check unless the plaintiff has changed its position in reliance on the payment. Because Union Trust had been informed before allowing Goldstein to withdraw funds that First Penn would not pay the check, Union Trust may be estopped from claiming that it permitted withdrawal in reliance on First Penn's deemed payment at the expiration of its midnight deadline. Under both lines of authority, First Penn is entitled to summary judgment on plaintiffs' claims.

IV.

For the reasons stated above, all defendants are entitled to summary judgment on plaintiffs' claims. The third-party claims are therefore moot. The Clerk is directed to dismiss both complaints with prejudice.

NOTE

In *USF & G* the fraud was crudely done and the conduct of the depositary bank was ludicrously deficient. However, as Judge Haight pointed out, "If such fraud is carried out with more sophistication than demonstrated by Goldstein the deposit and collection of funds may escape the notice of even a careful bank." Which bank would be liable in a case in which the depositary bank is not negligent? The MICR fraud cases are exhaustively discussed in Fairfax Leary & Patricia B. Fry, MICR Fraud: A Systems Approach to Foiling the Felon's Fun, 40 U. of Miami L.Rev. 737 (1986). The authors conclude: "By a proper interpretation of U.C.C. section 4–202(1)(e), liability would be placed on the bank diverting the return from the normal route back to the depositary bank. The diverting bank, by its own actions, will have actual knowledge that the transit from depositary bank to one bank, thought to be a payor bank, and back has been delayed by transit to the second bank for payment and back. This places the burden for giving notice of delay on the first bank to have actual knowledge of the delay." Id. at 765. How would this test be applied in *USF & G* had the depositary bank not been negligent?

D.   RESTRICTIVE INDORSEMENTS

Indorsement of an instrument may serve several purposes, but most commonly an indorsement is made in order to negotiate the instrument. § 3–204(a). The form of the indorsement can affect rights with respect to the instrument if it is stolen and collected or transferred to a third party. If a check indorsed in blank by the holder is stolen, the thief may negotiate the check to a transferee who may obtain rights as a holder in due course. If the stolen check was payable to an identified person and the payee made a special indorsement or did not indorse the check at all, the thief cannot negotiate the check and nobody taking through the thief can become a person entitled to enforce the check. Thus, the rights of a person taking a stolen check may depend upon whether an indorsement by the holder was made and whether the indorsement was special or in blank. The rights of the taker, however, can also depend upon whether the holder made a "restrictive indorsement" governed by § 3–206.

The purpose of a restrictive indorsement is to restrict payment of the instrument. That restriction can be expressed as part of a special indorsement or an indorsement in blank. For example, an indorsement of a check consisting solely of the signature of the holder under the words "for deposit only" is a blank indorsement because it does not identify a person to whom it makes the check payable, and is a restrictive indorsement because it indicates that the check is to be deposited to an account. This restrictive indorsement is governed by § 3–206(c). Comment 3 to § 3–206. An indorsement "Pay to John Doe in trust for Jane Doe" is a special indorsement because it identifies John Doe as the person to whom the check is payable, and is a restrictive indorsement because it indicates that the proceeds of the check are to be paid for the benefit of Jane Doe. This restrictive indorsement is governed by § 3–206(d). Comment 4 to § 3–206.

Some attempts to restrict payment of an instrument by an indorser are nullified by § 3–206. An indorsement "Pay to John Doe only" is ineffective to prohibit payment to any other holder. In spite of the indorsement John Doe may indorse the instrument to another person and that person may become entitled to enforce the instrument. § 3–206(a). An indorsement that attempts to prohibit payment unless a stated condition is satisfied is also ineffective to restrict payment. § 3–206(b). Invalid restrictions are discussed in Comment 2 to § 3–206.

PROBLEMS

1.   Banking by mail is a common practice. This problem considers the degree of protection the payee of a check gains by using a restrictive indorsement under § 3–206. Peter, the payee of a check for $10,000 drawn on Payor Bank, indorsed and mailed the check to Bank # 1 where he had an account. Before the check arrived at Bank # 1, Thief stole the check and wrote Thief's name under Peter's indorsement. Thief then deposited the check to Thief's account in Bank # 2. Bank # 2 presented the check to Payor Bank and Payor Bank paid the check. Thief then withdrew the $10,000 that had been credited to Thief's account in Bank # 2 with respect to the check.

What are Peter's rights against Bank # 2 and Payor Bank if Peter's indorsement had been as follows:

Case # 1

   For deposit only

   Peter

Case # 2

   Pay to Bank # 1 for Account No. 1234321

   Peter

Case # 3

   Peter

   For deposit only

With respect to Case #3, see State of Qatar v. First American Bank, 885 F.Supp. 849 (E.D.Va.1995).

2.   Peter, the payee of a check for $10,000 drawn on Payor Bank, gave the check to Faith, the legal guardian of Ward, her elderly father who had become legally incompetent. Peter told Faith that the check was a contribution to defray Ward's nursing home expenses. Before giving the check to Faith, Peter indorsed the check as follows:

Pay to Faith as Guardian for Ward

Peter

Faith indorsed the check by signing her name under Peter's indorsement and deposited the check to her personal account in Depositary Bank. Faith also had a fiduciary account as guardian for Ward in the same bank. Pursuant to her instructions, Depositary Bank credited Faith's personal account $10,000 and obtained payment of the check from Payor Bank. Faith subsequently withdrew the $10,000 that had been credited to her personal account by writing checks on the account for her personal expenses.

Suit on behalf of Ward has been brought against Faith for breach of trust and against Depositary Bank and Payor Bank. Faith is insolvent and has no funds. What is the liability of Depositary Bank and Payor Bank? § 3–206.

CHAPTER 5

THE BANK–CUSTOMER RELATIONSHIP

A. INTRODUCTION

A customer with a deposit account in a bank has a contractual relationship with the bank that is governed by Part 4 of Article 4. If the bank pays a check written on the customer's account, § 4–401(a) allows the bank to charge the customer's account only if the check is "properly payable," that is if the customer has authorized the payment and it violates no agreement between the customer and the bank. Thus a bank cannot charge a customer's account if the customer's signature is forged, but may charge the account even though the charge creates an overdraft. Of course, the bank does not have to pay an overdraft unless it has agreed to do so. § 4–402(a). Agreements by banks to pay overdrafts up to specified limits are common. If a bank fails to pay a check that is properly payable and covered by funds in the customer's account, the bank has wrongfully dishonored the check under § 4–402(a) and may be liable in damages under § 4–402(b). A customer has the right for any reason or no reason to order a bank to stop payment of checks on the customer's account or to close the account, and if the bank fails to do so it may be liable for the loss caused by its failure. § 4–403. However, a bank is not liable for dishonoring a "stale" check, one presented more than six months after its date. § 4–404.

The provisions of Article 4 are only one source of rules on the bank-customer relationship. Federal statutes and Federal Reserve regulations are another source. The Truth-in-Savings Act, discussed later, became effective in 1992; it requires disclosure of the terms of consumer deposit accounts. The Expedited Funds Availability Act and Regulation CC expressly override the UCC. Regulation J does so as well. Still another source is provided by § 4–103(a) under which the "effect of the provisions" of Article 4 may be varied by bank-customer agreements; it is customary for banks to have some form of deposit agreement with their customers. Thus § 4–103(a) restates and even enlarges upon the "freedom of contract" principle embodied in § 1–102. Comment 1 to § 4–103 says, "This section, therefore, permits within wide limits variation of the effect of provisions of the Article by agreement." Since deposit agreements have aspects of contracts of adhesion, a continuing matter of dispute between banks and their customers is what are the "wide limits" the comment speaks of. We discuss this issue later.

B. STOP PAYMENT ORDERS

Section 4–403(a) affords the customer an unrestricted right to stop payment on checks drawn on the customer's account or to close the account. Comment 1 is a ringing affirmation of this cherished right of bank customers, and Comment 7 adds that a payment in violation of a stop order is an improper payment even though made by inadvertence or mistake. But § 4–403(c) imposes the burden of establishing any loss resulting from a bank's violation of a stop order on the customer. What justification is there for this provision? If the bank is the wrongdoer, shouldn't the burden of proving absence of loss be on the bank?

Suppose Customer wrote a check payable to a real estate agent for advance rental on a vacation cottage in Florida. When Customer arrived at the cottage she found that it was not as advertised and stopped payment on the check in ample time for her Bank, located in New York, to act on the stop order. When Customer received her cancelled checks at the end of the month, she found to her surprise that Bank had mistakenly paid the check. She immediately demanded that Bank recredit her account for the amount of the check. Bank declined to recredit the account on the ground that Customer 'had not established her loss by merely showing that Bank had violated the stop order and had refused to recredit her account. The real estate agent was located in Florida and Bank had no way of knowing about the transaction between Customer and the agent. For all Bank knew, Customer may have owed the money to the agent, thus Bank's payment might have paid a legitimate debt of Customer. Since only Customer knew these facts, Bank argued that she should have the burden of convincing Bank before it returned the money to her.

Minority view. These facts are based on Hughes v. Marine Midland Bank, 127 Misc.2d 209, 484 N.Y.S.2d 1000 (City Ct.Rochester 1985). Customer sued Bank for the amount of the check. Her proof of loss was her showing that Bank had paid the check over her valid stop order and had refused to recredit her account. A summary judgment for Customer was entered. The court held that Bank should have recredited Customer's account immediately and sought its remedy under § 4–407. Under that provision, if Bank can show that its payment was made either to a holder in due course (§ 4–407(1)) or to a holder of the check who was entitled to payment from Customer (§ 4–407(2)), in order to prevent unjust enrichment, Bank is subrogated to the right of the holder to recover the amount of the check from Customer. If Bank finds that it has paid a holder who was not entitled to payment from Customer (e.g., this would be true if the agent had defrauded Customer), in order to prevent unjust enrichment, Bank is subrogated to Customer's right to get the money back from the holder (§ 4–407(3)).

Majority view. Most courts believe that holdings like *Hughes* do not give adequate weight to the requirement of § 4–403(3) that the customer must establish the loss. The classic statement of this view is found in the following quotation from Siegel v. New England Merchants National Bank, 386 Mass. 672, 437 N.E.2d 218, 222–223 (1982):

> The rule of § 4–403(3), that a depositor must prove his loss, may at first seem at odds with our earlier conclusion that § 4–401(1) provides the depositor with a claim against the bank in the amount of the check, leaving the bank with recourse through subrogation under § 4–407. * * * We believe, however, that § 4–403(3) was intended to operate within the process of credit and subrogation established by §§ 4–401(1) and 4–407. See § 4–403, comment 8. When a bank pays an item improperly, the depositor loses his ability to exercise any right he had to withhold payment of the check. His "loss," in other words, is equivalent to his rights and defenses against the parties to whose rights the bank is subrogated—the other party to the initial transaction and other holders of the instrument. Section 4–403(3) simply protects the bank against the need to prove events familiar to the depositor, and far removed from the bank, before it can realize its subrogation rights. The depositor, who participated in the initial transaction, knows whether the payee was entitled to eventual payment and whether any defenses arose. Therefore, § 4–403(3) requires that he, rather than the bank, prove these matters. * * *

This view of the three relevant sections of the code suggests a fair allocation of the burden of proof. The bank, which has departed from authorized bookkeeping, must acknowledge a credit to the depositor's account. It must then assert its subrogation rights, and in doing so must identify the status of the parties in whose place it claims. If the bank's subrogation claims are based on the check, this would entail proof that the third party subrogor was a holder, or perhaps a holder in due course. This responsibility falls reasonably upon the bank, because it has received the check from the most recent holder and is in at least as good a position as the depositor to trace its history.

The depositor must then prove any facts that might demonstrate a loss. He must establish defenses good against a holder or holder in due course, as the case may be. See UCC §§ 3–305, 3–306. If the initial transaction is at issue, he must prove either that he did not incur a liability to the other party, or that he has a defense to liability. Thus the bank, if it asserts rights based on the transaction, need not make out a claim on the part of its subrogor against the depositor. Responsibility in this area rests entirely with the depositor, who participated in the transaction and is aware of its details. Further, the depositor must establish any consequential loss.

A case applying the majority rule to interesting facts follows. Which has the better of the argument, the majority or the dissent?

Dunnigan v. First Bank

Supreme Court of Connecticut, 1991.
217 Conn. 205, 585 A.2d 659.

■ BORDEN, ASSOCIATE JUSTICE.

In this appeal, we are called upon to define the meaning and scope of § 4–403(3)[1] of the Uniform Commercial Code (Code) as applied to the facts of this case. The defendant bank appeals, after a court trial, from the judgment of the trial court in favor of the plaintiff, the trustee in bankruptcy of Cohn Precious Metals, Inc. (Cohn), a customer of the bank. We transferred the appeal to this court pursuant to Practice Book § 4023, and we now reverse the trial court's judgment.

The plaintiff brought this action against the bank for wrongfully paying a check issued by Cohn over Cohn's valid stop payment order. The trial court determined that the plaintiff had established a loss within the meaning of § 4–403(3) as a result of the bank's payment of the check, and that the subrogation provisions of General Statutes § 4–407[2] did not defeat the rights of Cohn. The court accordingly rendered judgment for the amount of the check. This appeal followed.

The bank claims that judgment was improperly rendered for the plaintiff because (1) as a matter of law, Cohn did not suffer a loss within the meaning of § 4–403(3), and (2) the bank was subrogated to the rights of the payee of the check and of the collecting banks, pursuant to § 4–407. We agree with the bank's first claim and therefore need not reach its second claim. Furthermore, it is not necessary to define the relationship between §§ 4–403(3) and 4–407.

The parties stipulated to the following facts. On November 8, 1978, pursuant to purchase order 1142, Lamphere Coin, Inc. (Lamphere), a trader in coins and precious metals, delivered to Cohn certain silver dollars with a unit price of $1.71 and with a total value of $27,492.07. Cohn's bookkeeper incorrectly recorded the unit price of those coins, however, as $17.10, resulting in an erroneous total value of $47,098.93. On November 9, 1978, Cohn paid Lamphere $47,098.93 by wire transfer to Lamphere's bank

---

1. Section 4–403 provides as follows: "Customer's Right To Stop Payment; Burden Of Proof Of Loss. (1) A customer may by order to his bank stop payment of any item payable for his account but the order must be received at such time and in such manner as to afford the bank a reasonable opportunity to act on it prior to any action by the bank with respect to the item described in section 4–303.

"(2) An oral order is binding upon the bank only for fourteen calendar days unless confirmed in writing within that period. A written order is effective for only six months unless renewed in writing.

"(3) The burden of establishing the fact and amount of loss resulting from the payment of an item contrary to a binding stop payment order is on the customer."

2. Section 4–407 provides as follows: "Payor Bank's Right To Subrogation On Im-

proper Payment. If a payor bank has paid an item over the stop payment order of the drawer or maker or otherwise under circumstances giving a basis for objection by the drawer or maker, to prevent unjust enrichment and only to the extent necessary to prevent loss to the bank by reason of its payment of the item, the payor bank shall be subrogated to the rights

(a) of any holder in due course on the item against the drawer or maker; and

(b) of the payee or any other holder of the item against the drawer or maker either on the item or under the transaction out of which the item arose; and

(c) of the drawer or maker against the payee or any other holder of the item with respect to the transaction out of which the item arose."

account, resulting in an overpayment to Lamphere by Cohn of $19,606.86. On November 10, 1978, Lamphere delivered three and one-half bags of silver dollars to Cohn pursuant to Cohn's purchase order 1145. The value of the silver dollars was $21,175. On the same day, Cohn issued two checks drawn on its account at the bank to Lamphere, one in the amount of $12,175 and one in the amount of $9000, totaling $21,175.

Between November 10 and November 15, Cohn discovered its bookkeeper's error and, on November 14, 1978, directed the bank to stop payment on the two checks totaling $21,175 that had been issued on November 10, 1978. The bank stopped payment on the $9000 check, but on or about November 20, 1978, the bank inadvertently honored the $12,175 check over the valid stop payment order. Cohn retained the three and one-half bags of silver dollars, but never recovered its overpayment from Lamphere. As of November 20, 1978, the date of the improper payment of the check by the bank, and at all times thereafter Lamphere owed Cohn in excess of $13,000 as a result of these transactions.

The merits of this controversy revolve around the meaning of § 4-403(3), which provides that "[t]he burden of establishing the fact and amount of loss resulting from the payment of an item contrary to a binding stop order is on the customer." The bank argues that where there is good consideration for a particular check, or where the check was given as payment on a binding contract, the bank that paid the check over a valid stop payment order is not liable to its customer, because there was no "loss resulting from [its] payment. . . . " Thus, in the bank's view a customer cannot establish a loss under this provision of the code by relying on the loss of credits due the customer from prior unrelated transactions between the customer and the payee of the check. The plaintiff argues, as the trial court concluded, that whether a customer has incurred a "loss" within the meaning of § 4-403(3) cannot be determined solely by focusing on the transaction underlying the particular check involved, but must be determined by focusing on the entire relationship between the customer and the payee of the check. The plaintiff contends that it is unreasonable to disregard the relative positions of the parties, especially where they have demonstrated a continuing course of business dealings, where there are likely to be such credits. Under such circumstances, the plaintiff claims that focusing on a single transaction is contrary to the intent of the Code. Thus, in the plaintiff's view, Cohn would have had a good "defense" to a claim by Lamphere on the check because of the overpayment, and by paying the check the bank caused Cohn a loss within the meaning of § 4-403(3).

The issue, therefore, is whether, on the facts of this case, the bank customer who sought to establish "the fact and amount of loss resulting from the payment of an item contrary to a binding stop payment order" pursuant to § 4-403(3) was entitled to do so by resorting to credits from prior transactions unrelated to that for which the check was issued, or whether the customer was limited to the facts of the particular transaction for which the check was issued. We conclude that the customer was limited to the facts of the particular transaction for which the check was issued, and that § 4–403(3) does not contemplate taking into account a loss by the customer of credits that arose from prior unrelated transactions.

* * *

Under § 4–403(1), a bank customer has the right to order his bank to stop payment on a check, so long as he does so in a timely and reasonable manner, and, under § 4–403(2), an oral stop payment order is binding on the bank for a limited period of time. See footnote 1, supra. The fact that the bank has paid the check over the customer's valid stop payment order does not mean, however, that the customer is automatically entitled to repayment of the amount of the check. Under § 4–403(3), the customer must also establish "the fact and amount of loss resulting from" the bank's improper payment.

The case law makes clear that "[t]he loss ... must be more than the mere debiting of his account." * * * Siegel v. New England Merchants National Bank, 386 Mass. 672, 437 N.E.2d 218 (1982) * * *. The commentators agree. See W. Hillman, Basic UCC Skills 1989, Article 3 and Article 4, p. 302; E. Peters, A Negotiable Instruments Primer (1974) p. 79; 1 J. White & R. Summers, Uniform Commercial Code (3d Ed.1988) § 18–6, pp. 909–10. Otherwise, § 4–403(3) would be superfluous. Furthermore, whether the customer has suffered such a loss is in the first instance a question of fact. * * *

The cases and commentators also agree that where the check in question was supported by good consideration, or where the payee has enforceable rights against the maker based on the transaction underlying the check, the customer has suffered no loss within the meaning of § 4–403(3). Siegel v. New England Merchants National Bank, supra 386 Mass. at 678–79, 437 N.E.2d 218; * * * W. Hillman, supra, 302; E. Peters, supra; J. White & R. Summers, supra. As then Professor Peters explained, it "is implicit in § 4–403(3) that if a check was issued for good consideration ... failure to observe a stop payment order does no more than to accelerate the drawer's inevitable liability, and is therefore a defense to the payor bank." E. Peters, supra.

Applying these principles to the facts of this case, we conclude that as a matter of law Cohn suffered no "loss" within the meaning of § 4–403(3). The check was supported by good consideration because it was issued in payment for the silver coins that Lamphere delivered to Cohn. Furthermore, on the basis of that underlying transaction Lamphere had enforceable rights to payment by Cohn for those coins.

The plaintiff argues, however, that, although the particular check was supported by valid consideration and although there were no defenses available to it arising out of that particular transaction, the previous transaction between Cohn and Lamphere had supplied Cohn with a defense to payment of the check based on Cohn's overpayment to Lamphere. We disagree.

First, the language of § 4–403(3) suggests a narrower reading than would be required by the plaintiff's position. Section 4–403(3) places on the bank's customer the "burden of establishing the *fact and amount of loss resulting from the payment* of an item contrary to a binding stop payment order. . . . " (Emphasis added.) By contrast, § 4–402, which deals with a bank's liability to its customer for a wrongful *dishonor*, as opposed to a wrongful payment, provides as follows: "A payor bank is liable to its customer for *damages proximately caused by the wrongful dishonor* of an item. When the dishonor occurs through mistake liability is limited to actual damages proved. If so proximately caused and proved damages may include damages for an arrest or prosecution of the customer or other consequential damages. Whether any consequential damages are proximately caused by the wrongful dishonor is a question of fact to be determined in each case." (Emphasis added.) Thus, pursuant to § 4–402 the wrongfully dishonoring bank may be liable for all consequential damages proximately caused by its wrongful conduct, including damages resulting from arrest or prosecution of the customer, whereas there is a conspicuous absence from § 4–403(3) of language indicating such a broad scope of liability for wrongful payment.

This difference in the scope of the language used in § 4–403(3), as compared to that used in § 4–402, is consistent with the notion that § 4–403(3) is intended to impose a limited, rather than broad, form of liability on banks. "The trade-off for requiring banks to accept stop orders under § 4–403(1) was the limitation of their liability under §§ 4–403(3) and 4–407." E. Peters, supra.

The case law and commentary support this more restrictive view of the scope of § 4–403(3). In determining whether a customer has established a "loss" under this section of the code, they focus on the check itself and on the transaction underlying it, and not on whether there were other prior, unrelated transactions between the maker and payee of the check. "In order to prove a loss under [§ 4–403(3) of] the Code, a customer must prove he was not liable to the payee *on the check*. White & Summers, Uniform Commercial Code 560 (2d ed. 1980); Brady, Brady on Bank Checks § 20.20 p. 20–45 (5th ed. 1979); 6 Reitman & Weisblatt, Banking Law § 133.–07(2) (Bender's Banking Law Service 1981)." (Emphasis added.) Bryan v. Citizens National Bank In Abilene, 628 S.W.2d 761, 763 (Tex. 1982) * * *. Although Cohn had an offset or counterclaim available to it with respect to Lamphere, it did not have a defense to payment of the check itself.

Finally, we find guidance in Siegel v. New England Merchants National Bank, supra. In that case, the court held that § 4–403(3) must be read together with the subrogation provisions of § 4–407. Id., 386 Mass. at 678, 437 N.E.2d 218. Although we need not go that far because on the facts of this case § 4–403(3) can be read independently of § 4–407, we are persuaded by the holding of *Siegel* that in order to establish a § 4–403(3) "loss" the customer must show that he had defenses to payment of the check that were good against a holder or holder in due course under §§ 3–305 and 3–

306, as the case may be, or that he had a good defense to liability on the underlying transaction. Id. at 679, 437 N.E.2d 218. None of these defenses arise from facts outside the confines of the particular check in question or the transaction underlying it.

In this case, the plaintiff seeks more than to establish a loss caused by the bank's failure to honor Cohn's stop payment order. That "loss" occurred in fact on November 9, 1978, when Cohn overpaid for the coins it had received. Rather, the plaintiff seeks to recoup a loss resulting from a prior transaction separate from and independent of the stopped check. Thus, the plaintiff's position would permit the customer to establish a "loss" based on offsets or counterclaims against the payee based on prior unrelated transactions, no matter how remote from the check in question or from the transaction underlying it. We do not believe that the intent of § 4–403(3) ranges that far.

The dissent reads the commentary of Peters and of White & Summers too broadly. Although both refer to the situation, unlike the case at bar, where a customer seeks to establish a loss resulting from the dishonor of subsequent checks, neither commentator states with any confidence that the customer would prevail under § 4–403(3). Peters discusses the hypothetical without coming to any conclusion other than "[w]hatever the inferences that may appropriately be drawn ... it can hardly alter the conviction that § 4–403(3) accomplishes its purpose of severely limiting a drawer's power to stop payment." E. Peters, supra, 80. White & Summers do venture that they would find the bank liable, but "confess uncertainty about this conclusion, for it leaves little substance to § 4–403(3)." J. White & R. Summers, supra, 912. In any event, that is a case where the purported "loss" *follows* the wrongful payment and thus could arguably be said to be the result thereof, and not, as in this case, where it *precedes* that payment. Furthermore, the dissent's equation of § 4–403(3) to the law of causation in negligence ignores the difference in statutory language between § 4–402, where that concept is incorporated, and § 4–403(3), where such language is absent.

A factual finding must be reversed as clearly erroneous if it was based on an incorrect rule of law. Hydro–Hercules Corporation v. Gary Excavating, Inc., 166 Conn. 647, 654, 353 A.2d 714 (1974). The trial court's finding in this case that the plaintiff had established a loss within the meaning of § 4–403(3) was so based.

The judgment is reversed, and the case is remanded with direction to render judgment for the defendant.

In this opinion CALLAHAN and HULL, JJ., concurred.

■ SHEA, ASSOCIATE JUSTICE, with whom GLASS, ASSOCIATE JUSTICE, joins, dissenting.

In this case it is undisputed that the drawer, Cohn Precious Metals, Inc. (Cohn), complied fully with General Statutes § 4–403(1) in stopping payment on the checks it had delivered to Lamphere Coin, Inc. (Lamphere), on November 10, 1978, while unaware of the overpayment of $19,606.86 on

November 9, 1978. It is also clear that, but for the negligence of the bank in paying the $12,175 check contrary to the stop payment order, Cohn could have offset its overpayment of the previous day against the value of the coins received from Lamphere on November 10, 1978. Thus, as the trial court concluded, the plaintiff trustee, on behalf of Cohn, sustained his "burden of establishing the fact and amount of loss resulting from payment of an item contrary to a binding stop payment order" by the defendant bank, as § 4–403(3) requires.[1]

The majority opinion does not challenge, as unsupported by the evidence, the trial court's factual finding that Cohn suffered a loss resulting from the bank's negligent payment of the $12,175 check to Lamphere, but rejects this straightforward "but for" causation analysis in favor of a narrower view of the "resulting from payment" provision of § 4–403(3). The majority would restrict a bank's liability for paying a check contrary to a stop order to losses arising from the transaction in which the check was issued, such as a failure of consideration. I disagree, because there is nothing in the text of § 4–403(3) or its history to support such an unjustifiable curtailment of the right of the drawer recognized by § 4–403(3) to stop payment on a check for any reason, so long as the order is given to the bank in a timely and reasonable manner, as in this case. The right, of course, would be illusory without recourse against the negligent bank.

"The right to stop payment is an established right that was recognized prior to the Code. The right is absolute." J. Reitman et al., 6 Banking Law § 133.02. "If the drawer has a good defense on a check against a payee or holder, then the drawer suffers a loss when the bank wrongfully pays the check over a stop payment order." Id. The plaintiff trustee had the burden of proving that Cohn's loss resulted from noncompliance with the stop payment order, just as any negligence victim must prove causation. Even if the standard of causation applicable to breaches of contract should govern, reasonable foreseeability of the damages at the time the drawer and bank enter into this relationship; Neiditz v. Morton S. Fine & Associates, Inc., 199 Conn. 683, 689 n. 3, 508 A.2d 438 (1986); 3 Restatement (Second), Contracts § 351(1); it is evident that a bank must be deemed to foresee that its payment of a check over a valid stop payment order is likely to cause a loss to the drawer in the amount of the payment. There is nothing in § 4–403(3) that warrants a narrower approach to the issue of causation than that applicable to breaches of contract. In order to prevail against a

---

1. On the basis of the facts before us, the trial court's award of $12,175 damages may have been excessive. The amount of the overpayment of November 9, 1978, was $19,606.86. The value of the silver dollars received by Cohn on November 10, 1978 was $21,175. Before the two checks totaling $21,175 were issued for this purchase, Cohn owed Lamphere $1568.14. That debt was discharged by the bank's erroneous payment of the $12,175 check. Thus Cohn received good consideration of $1568.14 as a result of the bank's payment and its loss is limited to the balance of the amount paid on the $12,175 check, $10,606.86.

The defendant bank has not challenged the amount of the award and, since it has fully prevailed on appeal, it is unnecessary to consider the issue further.

bank that has ignored a stop payment order, "[t]he customer must show that (i) the account was debited, (ii) some other loss was suffered, if applicable, and (iii) bank's noncompliance with the stop order was the 'but for' cause." W. Hillman, Basic UCC Skills 1989, Article 3 and Article 4, p. 319. As the trial court found, those criteria were satisfied by the plaintiff trustee in this case.

In adopting its constricted view of the "loss resulting from the payment of an item contrary to a binding stop payment order" provision of § 4–403(3), the majority cites a plethora of authorities, none of which address the issue of whether a bank is excused from liability for failing to obey a stop payment order simply because the drawer had no defense arising out of the transaction in which the check was issued but only a right of set-off from another transaction. Most of the cases cited involve the principle that, when a bank has paid a check on which payment has been stopped, it becomes subrogated to the rights of the payee on the check. The quotation relied upon from E. Peters, A Negotiable Instruments Primer (1974) p. 79, it "is implicit in § 4–403(3) that if a check was issued for good consideration . . . failure to observe a stop payment order does no more than to accelerate the drawer's inevitable liability," is also based on the right of the bank to assert the rights of the payee on the check as a defense to an action by the drawer. Such a defense would not have been effective in this case, however, because the drawer, Cohn, had no such "inevitable liability," given its right to set off the previous overpayment to Lamphere against the bank's claim as subrogee of Lamphere's rights on the check.

Two of the commentators relied upon by the majority refer to the situation in which a bank has wrongfully debited a customer's account after a stop payment order and this action has resulted in dishonoring for insufficient funds subsequent checks issued by the drawer with the consequence of impairing his credit. E. Peters, supra; 1 J. White & R. Summers, Uniform Commercial Code (3d Ed.1988) p. 912. Although they disagree as to how this problem should be resolved under § 4–403(3), they implicitly recognize that the bank's liability for failing to obey a stop payment order may well subject it to liability with respect to other transactions resulting in damages to a drawer that have been caused by the bank's oversight. The narrow concept of causation adopted by the majority cannot be reconciled with the views of these commentators.

The majority stresses the difference between the "resulting from" causation language of § 4–403(3) and the more elaborate provision of § 4–402 that expressly makes the bank liable for consequential damages for wrongfully dishonoring a check, including such damages as may result from the arrest or prosecution of the customer. Such a provision in § 4–402 is probably necessary if liability for such damages is to be imposed because of the contract law limitation of damages to those that are reasonably foreseeable at the time of the contract. 3 Restatement (Second), Contracts § 351(1). Such a provision in § 4–403(3) is unnecessary to make a bank liable for the amount of a check it has paid after a stop payment order, however, because it is obvious that such a loss to the drawer from the bank's oversight is readily foreseeable.

As the majority acknowledges in a footnote, the official commentary in § 4–403 takes the position "that stopping payment is a service which depositors expect and are entitled to receive from banks notwithstanding its difficulty, inconvenience and expense" and that "[t]he inevitable occasional losses through failure to stop should be borne by the banks as a cost of the business of banking." The view of the majority that a drawer should be made to bear a loss that would have been avoided but for the bank's neglect, because it did not arise from the transaction in which the check was issued, places a substantial restriction on the right to stop payment that § 4–403(1) purports to give.

With respect to § 4–407 and the defendant's claim to be a holder in due course, there is nothing in the record to indicate that the collecting bank ever allowed the payee to draw on the check after it was deposited. Since there is no proof that the collecting bank gave value, the defendant's claim to be subrogated to the status of a holder in due course is without foundation.

Accordingly, I dissent.

NOTE

Section 4–403(c) has long been a bone of contention between customers and banks. In violating a customer's stop payment order, even if the payment is made to a holder on a valid debt of the customer, the bank has deprived the customer of the tactical advantage of forcing the holder to proceed against the customer for payment. Had the stop order in *Hughes* been honored by the bank, the agent might well have been unwilling to undertake the expense of suing the customer for the amount of the check, and might have given up on the transaction. But there is no basis in §§ 4–403 or 4–407 for compensating a customer for this kind of loss.

A major difference between the majority and minority views is that under the majority view the bank keeps the money while the parties litigate; under the minority view the bank must recredit the customer's account upon learning that it has paid over a valid stop payment order and must then proceed under § 4–407 to get its money back from either the holder or the customer. The banks seek to shore up the policy of the majority view by claiming that many stop payment orders are the result of "buyer's remorse" rather than valid defenses on the part of the customer; moreover, they strongly object to getting tied up in messy contract disputes between obligors and obligees. Customers find unfairness in a system that allows a bank that has wrongfully paid out over a stop payment order to sit back and force the customer to proceed against it to get its money back.

A number of attempts were made to redraft § 4–403 during the revision of Article 4, but no solution found consensus. The only substantive change made was the addition of the last sentence in § 4–403(c) which clarified an issue on which there was some dispute in the case law. If a customer's checks presented subsequent to the violation of the stop order are dishonored because the check that should not have been paid depleted the customer's account balance, the customer can proceed against the bank under § 4–402 to recover damages for wrongful dishonor. Since it costs money to attract customers and banks are reluctant to lose them, anecdotal evidence indicates that banks have worked out informal procedures to satisfy meritorious customer demands for a recredit after the bank violates a stop order. Under one plan, discussed as a possible model for the redraft of Article 4, if the bank believes the customer's representations that it had paid out money the customer did not owe, it would require the customer (1) to sign an affidavit stating facts indicating that the payment was made on a debt for which the customer was not liable, and (2) to enter into an agreement that it would cooperate in any litigation the bank might have to bring against the person who received the mistaken payment. Once this was done the bank would recredit the customer's account and initiate proceedings against the person who received payment.

PROBLEMS

1. Customers ordered Bank to stop payment on check number 292 drawn on their account number 315–726 for $1000. The stop order was communicated to Bank in plenty of time to act on it. However, since the correct number of the check in question was 280 and not 292, Bank's computer, which was directed to identify only checks on a customer's account which bore the correct check number, did not identify the check and it was paid. Bank denied liability for violating the stop order because under § 4–403(a) banks must stop payment on a check only if the check is described by the customer "with reasonable certainty." Bank conceded that its computer could have been directed to stop payment by (1) check number alone, (2) by check number and amount of check, or (3) by amount of check alone. Did Customers identify the check with reasonable certainty?

2. Would the decision in Problem 1 be affected by a clause in the bank's deposit agreement stating: "In order to stop payment on a check, you must inform the bank of the exact amount of the item, the number of the check, and your account number; otherwise our computer may not catch the stop order. Unless this is done the bank will not be responsible for any loss resulting from its failure to stop payment"? Clark & Clark, The Law of Bank Deposits, Collections and Credit Cards ¶ 3.06[1][b] and [d] (Rev.ed.1995). Is this clause valid under § 4–103(a) as determining "the standards by which the bank's responsibility is to be measured" or is it invalid as an attempt to disclaim the bank's responsibility for its "failure to use ordinary care"? Comment 1 to § 4–403.

3. Suppose Bank induces its customer to sign a stop payment form containing the following clause: "In requesting you to stop payment of this or any other item, the undersigned agrees to hold you harmless for all expenses and costs incurred by you on account of refusing payment of said item, and further agrees not to hold you liable on account of payment contrary to this request if same occurs through inadvertence, accident or oversight, or if by reason of such payment other items drawn by the undersigned are returned insufficient.'' Is this clause, or any part of it, enforceable? § 4–103(a) and § 4–403. Opinion of Attorney General of Connecticut, 25 UCC Rep.Serv. 238, 1978 WL 23495 (1978).

4. In view of the fact that the customer has an absolute right to stop payment by complying with § 4–403, is the drawee bank entitled to impose a charge for processing a stop payment order? Opinion of Attorney General of Michigan, 30 UCC Rep.Serv. 1626, 1981 WL 137970 (1981); 33 UCC Rep.Serv. 1445, 1981 WL 138014 (1981). Clark & Clark, supra, ¶ 3.06[1][b]. If a typical charge for a stop order is $10, could a bank legally impose a $100 charge for a stop order?

NOTE: POSTDATED CHECKS

A luxury that manual processing of checks allowed customers was the postdated check. The customer could hold off an impatient creditor by writing a check for the debt and could control the time of payment by postdating the check. The customer could be confident that the check would not be paid before its date because a bank clerk would examine the check for date before payment by the bank. Under original Article 3 and pre–1990 Article 4 the check was not properly payable until the date of the check, and the bank could not charge the customer's account until that time. But when automated processing of checks became universal in the 1960s, there was no visual examination of the vast majority of checks. Checks were paid or dishonored on the basis of the balance in the account and the machine-readable information on the MICR line. Since there is no space on that line for the date of the check, the usual result is that the check is paid or dishonored without regard to its date. A bank prematurely paying a postdated check that depleted the customer's account balance could be liable for wrongfully dishonoring subsequent checks that would have been paid had the postdated check not been paid. A bank might seek protection against this liability by a clause in the bank-customer agreement allowing payment of any check at the time of presentment regardless of the date of the check. To the extent such a clause was enforceable, it deprived the customer of the ability to rely on postdating.

Section 4–401(c) offers a compromise that allows customers to utilize postdating while protecting banks from potential liability for failure to examine each check for its date. Under this provision the bank can pay all checks at the time of presentment unless it has received a notice of postdating from the customer. This allows the bank time to order its computer to identify the described check when it is presented so that its date may be examined before a decision to pay is made. Banks charge a fee for processing notices of postdating just as they charge for stop payment orders.

C. SECTION 4–303 AND THE "FOUR LEGALS"

1. CLAIMS AFFECTING THE CUSTOMER'S ACCOUNT

In Chapter 11 we considered when a check is paid in order to determine how long a payor bank has to decide whether to dishonor. A related issue concerns the priority of parties who assert rights that affect the customer's bank account as against a check that is presented for payment from that account. Whether a payor bank will pay a check depends on whether the balance in the customer's account is large enough to cover the check. A number of events may occur after a check has been presented for payment that give rise to claims that affect the size of the customer's balance. The priority between these claims, often referred to as the "four legals," and the right of the holder of the check to be paid is governed by Section 4–303. These events, enumerated in § 4–303(a), are (1) knowledge or notice by the bank of the customer's death, incompetency or bankruptcy; (2) a customer's order received by the bank to stop payment; (3) legal process (e.g., garnishment) served on the bank by a creditor of the customer; and (4) setoff against the customer's account exercised by the payor bank. The "four legals" are discussed in Clark & Clark, The Law of Bank Deposits, Collections and Credit Cards ¶ 6.03 (Rev.ed.1995); 2 White & Summers, Uniform Commercial Code § 21–7 (4th prac.ed.1995).

We have seen in the previous section that a customer has an absolute right to stop payment on a check under § 4–403(a), and the payor bank must honor a stop order received at a time that gives the bank "a reasonable opportunity" to act on it. Just as a bank's authority to pay a check of a customer may be revoked by the express direction of the customer, as in the case of a stop payment order, it may also be revoked by operation of law as in the case of the death, adjudication of incompetency or bankruptcy of the customer. The risk to the bank in making unauthorized payment in these cases is similar to that involved in the case of stop payment orders. Section 4–405(a) deals specifically with the bank's authority in the case of death or incapacity and § 4–405(b) gives to the bank additional authority in the case of death. On the latter point see Comments 2 and 3 to § 4–405.

The authority of the bank to act in the case of the bankruptcy of the customer is not dealt with by the UCC because the question is governed by federal rather than state law. Under Bankruptcy Code § 541(a) the property of the bankrupt (including bank accounts) passes to the estate in bankruptcy when the bankruptcy case is commenced. Thus, after bankruptcy any payment by the bank would be a payment of funds owned by the bankruptcy estate rather than by the bankrupt customer. Authority to dispose of property of the bankruptcy estate rests with the trustee in bankruptcy, and in the case of a Chapter 7 bankruptcy, this means that the bankrupt has no right to dispose of assets of the estate. But, under Bankruptcy Code § 542(c) a bank, until it has "actual notice or actual knowledge" of the bankruptcy of its customer, may continue to pay checks of the customer. The latter provision codifies the result of Bank of Marin v. England, 385 U.S. 99, 87 S.Ct. 274, 17 L.Ed.2d 197 (1966), which recognized the same right of the bank under the previous statute, the Bankruptcy Act of 1898.

Attaching and judgment creditors of the customer are given the right under conditions set out in state statutes to reach the customer's bank accounts by legal process. The asset reached is the debt the payor bank owes the customer for the amount of the account. The process used is generally described as garnishment under which a writ is served on the payor bank notifying it to pay over to a judicial officer for the benefit of the creditor the amount in the account up to the unpaid balance of the claim.

If the payor bank itself is a creditor of the customer, the bank may collect its debt extrajudicially by exercise of its traditional right of setoff. The bank may offset debts the customer owes the bank (loans the bank has made to the customer) against the debt the bank owes the customer (the balance of the customer's bank account). No legal process is involved in the bank's exercise of its right of setoff; bookkeeping entries indicating that the money has been withdrawn from the account suffice to effectuate the setoff.

2. PRIORITY RULES OF SECTION 4–303

The problem that must be solved is at what point a given check has reached the stage in the payor bank's payment process that the amount of that check can no longer be considered part of the customer's account balance and subject to the "legals." Section 4–303(a) addresses this issue. Under § 4–303(a)(1), when a bank certifies a check, the amount of that check is no longer considered to be in the customer's account for purpose of the legals. The same is true under § 4–303(a)(2) when the check is "cashed" over the counter at the payor bank. Under § 4–303(a)(3) and (4), if the check has been effectively paid by expiration of the midnight deadline, any subsequent claim under one of the legals comes too late to be prior to the check.

A special rule is set out in § 4–303(a)(5) for checks which will apply to the great bulk of checks that are presented to payor banks through banking channels. This provides that if a check is presented to a payor bank on Day 1, the amount of that check is no longer considered to be included in the customer's account for purposes of the legals after the close of business on Day 2. However, the bank can shorten that period by setting a cutoff hour on Day 2 no earlier than one hour after the opening of business. This means that if a garnishment order is served on the payor bank after that cutoff hour, the balance of the account subject to the garnishment does not include the amount of the check in question and the bank is protected if it pays the check. By the same token the balance of the account subject to the payor's bank's right of setoff is similarly reduced after this point. Nor can a customer stop payment on the check after the cutoff hour.

D. WRONGFUL DISHONOR

Most business lawyers at some time receive a call from an irate client whose check has been bounced by a bank. Sometimes the bank has not been sufficiently contrite about its error, and your client wants to "teach that bank a lesson." What can you do for this client? As we will see, the answer to this in most cases is not much, other than to awaken the bank to the fact that it has a very unhappy customer so that it can get a customer relations person on the case to initiate the usual low cost, customer-soothing nostrums that banks employ in these cases, e.g., a letter to the payee of the check confessing the bank's error. Nonetheless, the lawyer would do well to ask the client some detailed questions about the facts surrounding the wrongful dishonor, for, under certain circumstances, § 4–402(b) not only offers the wronged customer direct damages but it is one of the few provisions in the UCC that offers consequential damages.

Section 4–402(b) is only the latest step in a long series of judicial and legislative efforts to strike a balance between the erring bank and the wronged customer. In nineteenth century rural America, in which everyone knew everyone else's business, wrongful dishonor of checks was treated as slander against the character of a business person ("trader"). Clark & Clark, The Law of Bank Deposits, Collections and Credit Cards ¶ 3.05[9][c] (Rev.ed.1995). Being a "no account" was a serious accusation. The so-called "trader rule" was stated in 2 Morse, Banks and Banking 1007–1008 (6th ed., Voorhees, 1928): "[T]he better authority seems to be, that, even if * * * actual loss or injury is not shown, yet more than nominal damages shall be given. It can hardly be possible that a customer's check can be wrongfully refused payment without some impeachment of his credit, which must in fact be an actual injury, though he cannot from the nature of the case furnish independent distinct proof thereof. It is as in cases of libel and slander, which description of suit, indeed, it closely resembles, inasmuch as it is a practical slur upon the plaintiff's credit and repute in the business world. Special damage may be shown, if the plaintiff be able; but, if he be not able, the jury may nevertheless give such [temperate] damages as they conceive to be a reasonable compensation for that indefinite mischief which such an act must be assumed to have inflicted, according to the ordinary course of human events."

This was a plaintiff's lawyer's dream. Apparently if a bank wrongfully dishonored the check of a business customer, the customer got to the jury without showing any actual damage, and juries weren't any more fond of banks then than now. The banks fought back in the legislatures. At the behest of the American Bankers Association a number of states enacted a version of the following: "No bank shall be liable to a depositor because of the nonpayment through mistake or error, and without malice, of a check which should have been paid unless the depositor shall allege and prove actual damage by reason of such nonpayment and in such event the liability shall not exceed the amount of damage so proved." Cal.Civ.Code § 3320 (repealed).

The original version of what is now § 4–402(b) read: "A payor bank is liable to its customer for damages proximately caused by the wrongful dishonor of an item. When the dishonor occurs through mistake liability is limited to actual damages proved. If so proximately caused and proved damages may include damages for an arrest or prosecution of the customer or other consequential damages. Whether any consequential damages are proximately caused by the wrongful dishonor is a question of fact to be determined in each case." Comment 1 to § 4–402 contains a critique of this language and discusses the changes made in the revision.

Loucks v. Albuquerque National Bank

Supreme Court of New Mexico, 1966.
76 N.M. 735, 418 P.2d 191.

■ LA FEL E. OMAN, JUDGE, COURT OF APPEALS.

The plaintiffs-appellants, Richard A. Loucks and Del Martinez, hereinafter referred to as plaintiffs, Mr. Loucks and Mr. Martinez, respectively, were partners engaged in a business at Albuquerque, New Mexico, under the partnership name of L & M Paint and Body Shop.

By their complaint they sought both compensatory and punitive damages on behalf of the partnership, on behalf of Mr. Loucks, and on behalf of Mr. Martinez against the defendants-appellees, Albuquerque National Bank and W. J. Kopp, hereinafter referred to as defendants, the bank, and Mr. Kopp, respectively.

Prior to March 15, 1962 Mr. Martinez had operated a business at Albuquerque, New Mexico, under the name of Del's Paint and Body Shop. He did his banking with defendant bank and he dealt with Mr. Kopp, a vice-president of the bank.

On February 8, 1962 Mr. Martinez borrowed $500 from the bank, which he deposited with the bank in the account of Del's Paint and Body Shop. He executed an installment note payable to the bank evidencing this indebtedness.

On March 15, 1962 the plaintiffs formed a partnership in the name of L & M Paint and Body Shop. On that date they opened a checking account with the bank in the name of L & M Paint and Body Shop and deposited $620 therein. The signatures of both Mr. Loucks and Mr. Martinez were required to draw money from this account. The balance in the account of Del's Paint and Body Shop as of this time was $2.67. This was drawn from this account by a cashier's check and deposited in the account of L & M Paint & Body Shop on April 18, 1962.

Two payments of $50.00 each were made on Mr. Martinez' note of February 8, 1962, or on notes given as a renewal thereof. These payments were made by checks drawn by plaintiffs on the account of L & M Paint and Body Shop. The checks were payable to the order of the bank and were dated June 29, 1962 and August 28, 1962. A subsequent installment note was executed by Mr. Martinez on October 17, 1962 in the principal amount of $462 payable to the order of the bank. This was given as a replacement or renewal of the prior notes which started with the note of February 8, 1962.

Mr. Martinez became delinquent in his payments on this note of October 17, 1962 and the bank sued him in a Justice of the Peace court to recover the delinquency.

As of March 14, 1963 Mr. Martinez was still indebted to the bank on this note in the amount of $402, and on that date, Mr. Kopp, on behalf of the bank, wrote L & M Paint and Body Shop advising that its account had been charged with $402 representing the balance due "on Del Martinez installment note," and the indebtedness was referred to in the letter as the "indebtedness of Mr. Del Martinez."

The charge of $402 against the account of L & M Paint and Body Shop was actually made on March 15, 1963, which was a Friday.

Although Mr. Martinez at one time testified he telephoned Mr. Kopp on either Friday or the following Monday about this charge, when he was questioned more closely he admitted he discussed the matter with Mr. Kopp by telephone on Friday. Mr. Loucks testified that as he recalled, it was on Monday. Both plaintiffs went to the bank on Monday, March 18, and talked with Mr. Kopp. They both told Mr. Kopp that the indebtedness represented by the note was the personal indebtedness of Mr. Martinez and was not a partnership obligation. Mr. Loucks explained that they had some outstanding checks against the partnership account. Mr. Kopp refused to return the money to the partnership account. There was evidence of some unpleasantness in the conversation. The partnership account, in which there was then a balance of only $3.66, was thereupon closed by the plaintiffs.

The bank refused to honor nine, and possibly ten, checks drawn on the account and dated between the dates of March 8 and 16, inclusive.

The checks dated prior to March 15 total $89.14, and those dated March 15 and 16 total $121.68. These figures do not include the tenth check to which some reference was made, but which was not offered into evidence and the amount of which does not appear in the record.

The case came on for trial before the court and a jury. The court submitted the case to the jury upon the question of whether or not the defendants wrongfully made the charge in the amount of $402 against the account of L & M Paint and Body Shop. The allegations of the complaint concerning punitive damages and compensatory damages, other than the amount of $402 allegedly wrongfully charged by the defendants against the partnership account, were dismissed by the court before the case was submitted to the jury. The jury returned a verdict for the plaintiffs in the amount of $402.

The plaintiffs have appealed and assert error on the part of the trial court in taking from the jury the questions of (1) punitive damages, (2) damages to business reputation and credit, (3) damages for personal injuries allegedly sustained by Mr. Loucks, and (4) in disallowing certain costs claimed by plaintiffs.

* * *

The plaintiffs, as partners, sought recovery on behalf of the partnership of $402 allegedly wrongfully charged against the partnership account. This question was submitted to the jury, was decided in favor of the partnership, and against the defendants, and no appeal has been taken from the judgment entered on the verdict. They also sought recovery on behalf of the partnership of $5,000 for alleged damages to its credit, good reputation, and business standing in the community, $1,800 for its alleged loss of income, and $14,404 as punitive damages.

Each partner also sought recovery of $5,000 for alleged damages to his personal credit, good reputation and business standing. Mr. Martinez sought punitive damages individually in the amount of $10,000, and Mr. Loucks sought punitive damages individually in the amount of $60,000. Mr. Loucks also sought $25,000 by way of damages he allegedly sustained by reason of an ulcer which resulted from the wrongful acts of the defendants.

The parties have argued the case in their respective briefs and in their oral arguments upon the theory that the questions here involved, except for Point IV, which deals with the disallowance by the trial court of some claimed costs, are questions of the damages which can properly be claimed as a result of a wrongful dishonor by a bank of checks drawn by a customer or depositor on the bank, and of the sufficiency of the evidence offered by plaintiffs to support their claims for damages.

Both sides quote UCC § 4–402. * * *

It would appear that the first question to be resolved is that of the person, or persons, to whom a bank must respond in damages for a wrongful dishonor. Here, the account was a partnership account, and if there was in fact a wrongful dishonor of any checks, such were partnership checks.

We have adopted the Uniform Commercial Code in New Mexico. In UCC § 4–402 it is clearly stated that a bank "is liable to its customer." In UCC § 4–104(1)(e), entitled "Definitions and index of definitions" it is stated that:

"(1) In this article unless the context otherwise requires

"(e) 'Customer' means any person having an account with a bank or for whom a bank has agreed to collect items and includes a bank carrying an account with another bank; * * * "

This requires us to determine who is a "person" within the contemplation of this definition. Under part II, article I of the Uniform Commercial Code, entitled "General Definitions and Principles of Interpretation," we find the term "person" defined in § 1–201(30) as follows: "'Person' includes an individual or an organization * * * ."

Subsection (28) of the same section expressly includes a "partnership" as one of the legal or commercial entities embraced by the term "organization."

It would seem that logically the "customer" in this case to whom the bank was required to respond in damages for any wrongful dishonor was the partnership. The Uniform Commercial Code expressly regards a partnership as a legal entity. This is consistent with the ordinary mercantile conception of a partnership. * * *

The Uniform Partnership Act, which has been adopted in New Mexico and appears as chapter 66, article I, N.M.S.A.1953, recognizes that a partnership has a separate legal entity for at least some purposes. * * *

Suits may be brought in New Mexico by or against the partnership as such. * * * A partnership is a distinct legal entity to the extent that it may sue or be sued in the partnership name. National Surety Co. v. George E. Breece Lumber Co., 60 F.2d 847 (10th Cir. 1932).

* * *

The relationship, in connection with which the wrongful conduct of the bank arose, was the relationship between the bank and the partnership. The partnership was the customer, and any damages arising from the dishonor belonged to the partnership and not to the partners individually.

The damages claimed by Mr. Loucks as a result of the ulcer, which allegedly resulted from the wrongful acts of the defendants, are not consequential damages proximately caused by the wrongful dishonor as contemplated by § 4–402. In support of his right to recover for such claimed damages he relies upon the cases of Jones v. Citizens Bank of Clovis, 58 N.M. 48, 265 P.2d 366 and Weaver v. Bank of America Nat. Trust & Sav. Ass'n., 59 Cal.2d 428, 30 Cal.Rptr. 4, 380 P.2d 644. The California and New Mexico courts construed identical statutes in these cases. The New Mexico statute appeared as § 48–10–5, N.M.S.A.1953. This statute was repealed when the Uniform Commercial Code was adopted in 1961.

Assuming we were to hold that the decisions in those cases have not been affected by the repeal of the particular statutory provisions involved and the adoption of the Uniform Commercial Code, we are still compelled by our reasoning to reach the same result, because the plaintiffs in those cases were the depositor in the California case and the administratrix of the estate of the deceased depositor in the New Mexico case. In the present case, Mr. Loucks was not a depositor, as provided in the prior statute, nor a customer, as provided in our present statute. No duty was owed to him personally by reason of the debtor-creditor relationship between the bank and the partnership.

It is fundamental that compensatory damages are not recoverable unless they proximately result from some violation of a legally-recognized right of the person seeking the damages, whether such be a right in contract or tort. * * *

Insofar as the damage questions are concerned, we must still consider the claims for damages to the partnership. As above stated, the claim on behalf of the partnership for the recovery of the $402 was concluded by judgment for plaintiffs in this amount. This leaves (1) the claim of $5,000 for alleged damage to credit, reputation and business standing, (2) the claim of $1,800 for alleged loss of income, and (3) the claim of $14,404 as punitive damages.

The question with which we are first confronted is that of whether or not the customer, whose checks are wrongfully dishonored, may recover damages merely because of the wrongful dishonor. We understand the provisions of UCC § 4–402 to limit the damages to those proximately caused by the wrongful dishonor, and such includes any consequential damages so proximately caused. If the dishonor occurs through mistake, the damages are limited to actual damages proved.

It is pointed out in the comments to this section of the Uniform Commercial Code that:

" * * *

"This section rejects decisions which have held that where the dishonored item has been drawn by a merchant, trader or fiduciary he is defamed in his business, trade or profession by a reflection on his credit and hence that substantial damages may be awarded on the basis of defamation 'per se' without proof that damage has occurred. * * * " Uniform Commercial Code, § 4–402, Comment 3.

If we can say as a matter of law that the dishonor here occurred through mistake, then the damages would be limited to the "actual damages proved." Even if we are able to agree, as contended by defendants in their answer brief, that the defendants acted under a mistake of fact in "* * * that Mr. Kopp acting on behalf of the bank thought that the money was invested in the partnership and could be traced directly from Mr. Martinez to the L & M Paint and Body Shop," still defendants cannot rely on such mistake after both Mr. Martinez and Mr. Loucks informed them on March 15 and 18 that this was a personal obligation of Mr. Martinez and that the partnership had outstanding checks. At least it then became a question for the jury to decide whether or not defendants had wrongfully dishonored the checks through mistake.

The problem then resolves itself into whether or not the evidence offered and received, together with any evidence properly offered and improperly excluded, was sufficient to establish a question as to whether the partnership credit and reputation were proximately damaged by the wrongful dishonors. There was evidence that ten checks were dishonored, that one parts dealer thereafter refused to accept a partnership check and Mr. Loucks was required to go to the bank, cash the check, and then take the cash to the parts dealer in order to get the parts; that some persons who had previously accepted the partnership checks now refused to accept them; that other places of business denied the partnership credit after the dishonors; and that a salesman, who had sold the partnership a map and for which he was paid by one of the dishonored checks, came to the partnership's place of business, and ripped the map off the wall because he had been given "a bad check for it."

This evidence was sufficient to raise a question of fact to be determined by the jury as to whether or not the partnership's credit had been damaged as a proximate result of the dishonors. This question should have been submitted to the jury.

Damages recoverable for injuries to credit as a result of a wrongful dishonor are more than mere nominal damages and are referred to as "* * * compensatory, general, substantial, moderate, or temperate, damages as would be fair and reasonable compensation for the injury which he [the depositor] must have sustained, but not harsh or inordinate damages. * * *" 5A Michie, Banks and Banking, § 243 at 576.

What are reasonable and temperate damages varies according to the circumstances of each case and the general extent to which it may be presumed the credit of the depositor would be injured. * * * The amount of such damages is to be determined by the sound discretion and dispassionate judgment of the jury. * * *

The next item of damages claimed on behalf of the partnership, which was taken from the jury, was the claim for loss of income in the amount of $1,800 allegedly sustained by the partnership as a result of the illness and disability of Mr. Loucks by reason of his ulcer. We are of the opinion that the trial court properly dismissed this claim for the announced reason that no substantial evidence was offered to support the claim, and for the further reason that the partnership had no legally-enforceable right to recover for personal injuries inflicted upon a partner.

Even if we were to assume that a tortious act had been committed by defendants which proximately resulted in the ulcer and the consequent personal injuries and disabilities of Mr. Loucks, the right to recover for such would be in him. An action for damages resulting from a tort can only be sustained by the person directly injured thereby, and not by one claiming to have suffered collateral or resulting injuries. * * *

As was stated by Mr. Justice Holmes in Robins Dry Dock & Repair Co. v. Flint, 275 U.S. 303, 48 S.Ct. 134, 72 L.Ed. 290:

> " * * * no authority need be cited to show that, as a general rule, at least, a tort to the person or property of one man does not make the tort-feasor liable to another merely because the injured person was under a contract with that other, unknown to the doer of the wrong. * * * The law does not spread its protection so far."

The last question of damages concerns the claim for punitive damages. The trial court dismissed this claim for the reason that he was convinced there was no evidence of willful or wanton conduct on the part of defendants. Punitive or exemplary damages may be awarded only when the conduct of the wrongdoer may be said to be maliciously intentional, fraudulent, oppressive, or committed recklessly or with a wanton disregard of the plaintiffs' rights. * * *

Malice as a basis for punitive damages means the intentional doing of a wrongful act without just cause or excuse. This means that the defendant not only intended to do the act which is ascertained to be wrongful, but that he knew it was wrong when he did it. * * *

Although, as expressed above, we are of the opinion that there was a jury question as to whether defendants acted under a mistake of fact in dishonoring the checks, we do not feel that the unpleasant or intemperate remark or two claimed to have been made by Mr. Kopp, and his conduct, described by Mr. Martinez as having "run us out of the bank more or less," are sufficient upon which an award of punitive damages could properly have been made. Thus, the trial court was correct in taking this claim from the jury.

* * *

It follows from what has been said that this cause must be reversed and remanded for a new trial solely upon the questions of whether or not the partnership credit was damaged as a proximate result of the dishonors, and, if so, the amount of such damages.

NOTES

1. *"Liable to its customer."* Since *Loucks*, interesting developments have taken place on the issue of who can recover for damages incurred from a wrongful dishonor of the check of a corporate customer. Obviously a corporation cannot suffer emotional distress or acquire ulcers resulting from the bank's mistake, much less the personal embarrassment and social ostracism stemming from being jailed for writing a check that was wrongfully dishonored. But in a closely held corporation these damages may well be sustained by the individuals who own and operate the business. In an era in which plaintiffs are successfully seeking more adequate awards for their injuries, it comes as no surprise that courts are finding ways of reading the term "customer" more flexibly or finding alternative bases for liability. In Kendall Yacht Corp. v. United California Bank, 50 Cal.App.3d 949, 123 Cal.Rptr. 848 (1975), Corporation was the depositor and Laurence and Linda Kendall were officers and prospective shareholders who personally guaranteed Corporation's debts to Bank. Corporation never issued stock and "it was, in effect, nothing but a transparent shell, having no viability as a separate and distinct legal entity." 123 Cal.Rptr. at 853. The court held that the Kendalls were "customers" within the meaning of § 4-402. "Thus it was entirely foreseeable that the dishonoring of the Corporation's check would reflect directly on the personal credit and reputation of the Kendalls and that they would suffer the adverse personal consequences which resulted when the Bank reneged on its commitments." 123 Cal.Rptr. at 853. The court allowed recovery by the Kendalls of damages for emotional distress under § 4-402.

Parrett v. Platte Valley State Bank & Trust Co., 236 Neb. 139, 459 N.W.2d 371 (1990), goes beyond *Kendall Yacht*. Parrett was the principal shareholder and president of the corporate customer. He personally participated in the business relationship between the corporate customer and the bank and entered into a personal guaranty for the corporation's obligations to the bank. When the bank wrongfully dishonored the corporate customer's check, Parrett was charged with felony theft and went to trial on the charge; at trial the charge was dismissed. Parrett sued for wrongful dishonor under § 4–402. The lower court sustained the bank's demurrer on the ground that Parrett was not the customer. The Supreme Court of Nebraska, relying on *Kendall Yacht,* reversed and said:

> As reflected by Parrett's petition, the parties' business relationship, which included Parrett's personal guaranty for P & P Machinery's obligations to the bank, was such that it was foreseeable that dishonoring the corporation's check would reflect directly on Parrett. This is borne out by the fact that a criminal charge based on the dishonored check was brought against Parrett, but was dismissed during Parrett's trial. Since the consequences of the wrongful dishonor fell upon Parrett, it would elevate form over substance to say that he was not the bank's "customer" within the meaning of § 4–402. This is not to say that in every case a corporate officer has a wrongful dishonor action against the depository bank on which the corporation's check has been drawn and later dishonored. However, in view of the facts of this case alleged in Parrett's petition, Parrett has a cause of action against the bank.

459 N.W.2d at 378. Although the majority opinion in *Parrett* purported to rely on *Kendall Yacht,* the dissent pointed out that the key factor in that case was that the corporation was not a separate legal entity; the decision was based on veil-piercing. But in *Parrett* the corporate customer was clearly a separate legal entity and had always been treated as such by the bank.

Another line of decisions has held fast to the view expressed in *Loucks* that only the corporate customer can proceed under § 4–402. See, e.g., Farmers Bank v. Sinwellan Corp., 367 A.2d 180 (Del.1976) (president of corporate customer denied right to sue under § 4–402 for damages resulting from a criminal action brought against him because of the dishonor). An approach to allowing insiders to recover in cases in which corporate checks have been dishonored even in jurisdictions taking the *Sinwellan* point of view is to contend that § 4–402 does not displace any cause of action that such an insider may have had against the bank at common law. § 1–103 and Comment 5 to § 4–402.

2. *Damages.* Section 4–402(b) provides very broadly that a bank is liable for any damages proximately caused by a wrongful dishonor. Comment 1 to § 4–402 vaguely describes a customer's right to sue as a "statutory cause of action." In most cases no damages can be proved, but if economic loss can be shown consequential damages will be awarded. Skov v. Chase Manhattan Bank, 407 F.2d 1318 (3d Cir.1969). The principal damages issue has been whether aggrieved customers can recover for emotional distress. Certainly a wrongful dishonor can proximately cause emotional distress and this type of damage is within the limitation in the second sentence of § 4–402(b) that the damages must be "actual." Although courts show their concern about the potential for abuse present in allowing damages for emotional distress, a number of courts have awarded customers damages for emotional distress in wrongful dishonor cases. The precedents are collected and discussed in Buckley v. Trenton Saving Fund Society, 111 N.J. 355, 544 A.2d 857 (1988). In that case the court held that the facts did not justify recovery for mental anguish and said:

> To some extent, slight emotional distress arising from the occasional dishonor of a check is one of the regrettable aggravations of living in today's society. See Restatement, [(Second) of Torts], § 436A comment b. Accordingly, we are reluctant to allow compensation for the intentional infliction of emotional distress when a bank wrongfully dishonors a check unless the bank's conduct is intentional, as well as reckless or outrageous, and the distress is severe or results in bodily injury. See Hume, 178 N.J.Super. 310, 428 A.2d 966; Restatement, [(Second) of Torts], § 46. When those conditions are met, a customer should be compensated for the emotional distress that is caused by the wrongful dishonor of a check.

544 A.2d at 864. Comment 1 to § 4–402 points out in its last sentence that whether punitive damages are appropriate depends, under § 1–106, on non–UCC state law. The matter is discussed in Buckley.

E.   THE BANK-CUSTOMER AGREEMENT

1.   DISCLOSURE: THE TRUTH-IN-SAVINGS ACT

Among the demands that consumer groups have made of deposit-holding institutions in recent years, one of the most persistent has been the call for improved disclosure of the terms of deposit accounts so that consumers may better understand the agreements they are entering into with banks. The drive for improved disclosure has been at the core of the consumer movement in the second half of the century. At the earliest stage of this movement, Senator Paul Douglas of Illinois, a former economics professor, noted that financial institutions quoted their finance charges to consumers in several different ways: annual percentage rate, monthly percentage rate, annual dollar amount, and so forth. These practices made it difficult for consumers to do effective credit shopping because they could not be sure which creditor was offering the lowest rates. He proposed what sounded like a modest solution: require all creditors to state their finance charges as an annual percentage rate or "simple annual interest," as he liked to put it. Creditors, seeing the head of the federal camel under the tent, tried to head off the legislation by asserting that the variety and complexity of consumer credit transactions were so great that such a law would be operationally impossible for creditors to comply with. After many years of heated discussions about the subject, Congress passed the Truth-in-Lending Act in 1968, which required disclosure of finance charges in terms of an annual percentage rate. 15 U.S.C. § 1601 et seq. Congress passed on to a reluctant Federal Reserve Board the task of solving by regulations the innumerable operational problems encountered. Regulation Z, 12 C.F.R. Part 226. There now is a considerable body of legislative, administrative and case law on the subject of the disclosure of consumer finance charges. The Truth-in-Lending Act served as a model for the deposit account disclosure legislation that came along more than two decades later.

Consumers had the same problems in attempting to compare the terms offered by banks and other depository institutions with respect to deposit accounts. These terms are usually contained either in the bank-customer agreement or in a separate brochure and are selectively publicized in advertisements designed to attract more depositors. Consumers complained that although most deposit institutions disclosed the interest rates they were paying on deposit accounts as an annual percentage rate based on the full amount of the principal in the account, others used methods that made it appear that the interest rate offered was higher than it actually was. As was the case with Truth in Lending, negotiations leading to Truth in Savings went on for decades in Congress before the Act was finally passed in 1991 as part of the Federal Deposit Insurance Act, 12 U.S.C. § 4301 et seq. Again Congress fobbed off on the Fed the task of making the law workable, and Regulation DD, 12 C.F.R. Part 230, was completed in 1992 for this purpose. The Act and the Regulation are extensively discussed in Clark & Clark, The Law of Bank Deposits, Collections and Credit Cards, Chapter 19 (Rev.ed.1995).

(1) *Initial disclosure.* In brief, the Truth-in-Savings Act (TISA) requires federal and state deposit-holding institutions, e.g., banks, savings and loan associations, and credit unions, to disclose in a uniform manner the terms of their consumer deposit accounts at the time of entering into the deposit relationship with the customer. This initial disclosure must include interest rate information, the amounts of any service charges or other fees that may be imposed in connection with the account, and other salient features of the deposit account like minimum balance requirements, time account features (e.g., the effect of early withdrawal), and transaction limitations (e.g., limitations on the number of withdrawals or deposits). Reg DD § 230.4. Although TISA applies to credit union accounts, Regulation DD does not; credit unions have parallel regulations. Reg DD § 230.1(c).

The key items disclosed are the interest rate and the "annual percentage yield" (APY), which is the yield the interest rate produces with compounding. Reg DD § 230.2(c). It is this figure that should be most useful to consumers in interest rate shopping. The model clause suggested by the Appendix to Regulation DD is:

The interest rate on your account is _____% with an annual percentage yield of _____%.

(2) *Periodic statement disclosures.* Additional disclosures must be made in the periodic, often monthly, statements that depository institutions send to their customers. Reg DD § 230.6. These disclosures must include the "annual percentage yield earned" during the statement period, the dollar amount of the interest earned during that period, the dollar amounts and kinds of fees imposed and the number of days in the statement period or the beginning and ending dates of the period.

(3) *Advertising.* The third level of disclosure regulation relates to advertising. As is true with any law attempting to regulate advertising, Reg DD § 230.8 is very complex. In an attempt to force the depository institution to be fair in its advertising, Reg DD calls for so much explanatory language that it will probably result in either less advertising or an information overload in the ads that are published. If the ad states a rate of return, it must state the rate as an APY, but if it does so it must include a host of additional disclosures if they relate to the kind of deposit being advertised, e.g., explanations concerning variable rates, the period of time the APY is offered, any minimum balance required to obtain the APY advertised, any minimum opening balance, a statement that the fees charged could reduce the earnings, a number of features of time accounts, and on and on. However, if the advertising is being done on radio, TV or billboards, the disclosure requirements are much reduced.

(4) *Changes in the terms of the deposit account.* Advance notice, usually 30 days, is required for changes "if the change may reduce the annual percentage yield or adversely affect the consumer." Reg DD § 230.5. Normally the bank-customer agreement will give the bank the right to change unilaterally certain terms of the account so long as some prior notice is given. Among the most common changes made are those in the service charges and fee amounts. Despite the specific reference in the quotation above to changes in annual percentage yield, Clark & Clark, supra, ¶ 19.02[2][t] and ¶ 19.07[1][f], points out that the broad definition of "variable-rate account," Reg DD § 230.2(v), as "an account in which the interest rate may change after the account is opened," means that most interest rate changes need not be disclosed in a change-in-terms notice unless the bank specifically commits to give advance notice of rate decreases. This result flows from Reg DD § 230.5(a)(2)(i) which provides that no notice of change need be given for changes in interest rates in variable rate accounts. Since all deposit accounts in which the bank has the power to change rates are arbitrarily considered to be variable rate accounts under the broad definition of the term in Reg DD § 230.2(v), which bears no relation to the common meaning of the term, the most important information that a customer needs to know, that the bank is lowering its interest rate, need be disclosed to the customer only if the bank has specifically agreed to make the disclosure. This result seems absurd.

2.   "FREEDOM OF CONTRACT" UNDER SECTION 4–103(1)

The UCC adopts the principle of freedom of contract in § 1–102(3) which provides that "The effect of provisions of this Act may be varied by agreement * * *." How far can the parties go in contracting away the provisions of the Code? Comment 2 to § 1–102 cautions that it is only the "effect" of the provisions of the UCC that may be varied by agreement, but "The meaning of the statute itself must be found in its text, including its definitions, and in appropriate extrinsic aids; it cannot be varied by agreement."

Section 4–103(a) reiterates the freedom-of-contract principle for Article 4: "The effect of the provisions of this Article may be varied by agreement * * *." But Comment 1 to § 4–103(a) seems to say that, because of the constant technological change affecting banking operations, the parties must be given greater latitude to make changes by agreement than is the true with respect to § 1–102(3). This comment asserts that it would be unwise to interpret Article 4 as freezing the law in this dynamic area by mandatory rules. The comment concludes, "This section, therefore, permits within wide limits variation of the effect of provisions of the Article by agreement." This comment impliedly recognizes two short-comings of the UCC. First, amending the provisions of the Code is a cumbersome procedure that usually takes a minimum of ten years before the changes are adopted in all states; thus the Code is not good at keeping up with technological change. Second, there is no state administrative agency devoted to keeping the Code up to date by issuance of regulations. To an extent the Federal Reserve Board serves as such an administrative agency. Section 4–103(b) recognizes the Fed's power to make regulations varying the provisions of Article 4, and the Fed has frequently acted to modernize the law of bank collections. But the Fed is not particularly interested in bank-customer relations; its focus is on interbank relations.

Hence, the drafters of Article 4 look to private agreement making as one of the means of keeping the Code relevant to the needs of modern bank collection operations. Is this a realistic solution to the problem? Surely there must be some limits on the degree to which banks can use the deposit agreements that they require their customers to enter into to vary or contradict the provisions of Article 4. These agreements have all the earmarks of contracts of adhesion, and, if the customer doesn't like the terms offered by the bank, its only choice is to go to another bank. However, with the rapid movement toward bank consolidations that has characterized the 1990s, there are fewer and fewer banks available.

The only limitations stated in § 4–103(a) are that "the parties to the agreement cannot disclaim a bank's responsibility for its lack of good faith or failure to exercise ordinary care or limit the measure of damages for the lack or failure. However, the parties may determine by agreement the standards by which the bank's responsibility is to be measured if those standards are not manifestly unreasonable." How should a court apply § 4–103(a) to the following Problems? The issues raised by these Problems are discussed in detail in Clark & Clark, The Law of Bank Deposits, Collections and Credit Cards § 3.01[3] (Rev.ed.1995), and White & Summers, Uniform Commercial Code § 18–2 (4th ed.1995).

PROBLEMS

1. Husband (H) and Wife (W) have a joint checking account in Bank. Their deposit agreement with Bank provides among other matters: (1) that either party may write checks on the account, may stop payment of any check drawn on the account, or may close the account, and (2) that Bank may pay an overdraft drawn by either party, the account may be debited for the overdraft, and either party is liable for the amount of the overdraft without respect to whether that party signed the check or benefited from the overdraft. H wrote a check which Bank paid that overdrew the account. W did not know of the overdraft and she did not benefit in any way from the proceeds of the overdraft. H is insolvent and Bank seeks to hold W liable for the amount of the overdraft. May it do so? § 4–401(b).

2. Corporate depositor (D) opens a demand deposit account in Bank from which D intends to pay its bills. The deposit agreement that D entered into with Bank contains the following clause: "You (D) may authorize the use of a facsimile signature device by a corporate resolution communicated to Bank. If you have authorized the use of a facsimile signature device, Bank may honor any check that bears or appears to bear your facsimile signature even if it was made by an unauthorized person or with a counterfeit facsimile device." Use of a facsimile device was duly authorized. Burglar breaks into D's premises and uses the facsimile machine to write a check to himself which Bank pays on presentment. May Bank debit D's account? Is the quoted clause enforceable in the face of § 3–403(a), which provides that an unauthorized signature is ineffective, and § 4–401(a), which provides that a bank may charge a customer's account only for checks that are properly payable? Comment 1 to § 4–401 states "An item containing a forged drawer's signature * * * is not properly payable." Clark & Clark, supra, ¶ 3.01[3][c][iii], cites cases on both sides of the question, and, like White & Summers, supra, § 18–2 a, favors upholding the exculpatory clause. The quoted clause is based on one that appears in a model deposit account set out in Clark & Clark, supra, ¶ 3.13[1].

3. Corporate depositor (D) opens a demand deposit account in Bank from which D intends to pay its bills. The deposit agreement that D entered into with Bank contains the following clause: "Unless you (D) shall notify Bank within fifteen calendar days of the delivery or mailing to you of any statement of account and cancelled checks of any objection to any check or item on the account, all objections for any cause or reason whatsoever, whether known or unknown, shall be absolutely barred and waived." A forged check was returned by Bank to D on June 1; D's reconciliation process did not turn up the forgery until July 15, at which time D gave Bank prompt notice of the forgery. Bank claimed that because D had failed to give the notice within the 15–day period prescribed in the agreement, D had no right to challenge its payment of the check. D noted that under § 4–406(f), it had a year in which to object. Is Bank protected by the quoted clause? Clark & Clark, supra, ¶ 3.01[3][c][ii], cites some cases tending to uphold similar clauses. E.g., J. Sussman, Inc. v. Manufacturers Hanover Trust Co., 140 A.D.2d 668, 529 N.Y.S.2d 327 (N.Y.Sup.Ct.1988).

White & Summers, Uniform Commercial Code § 18–2 (4th ed.1995), questions whether a clause with a 15–day cutoff date should be upheld. Herzog, Engstrom & Koplovitz P.C. v. Union National Bank, 226 A.D.2d 1004, 640 N.Y.S.2d 703 (N.Y.1996) (refused to enforce a 14–day cutoff period).

3. SERVICE CHARGES AND FEES

Most banks impose charges on depositors for services performed by the bank in processing stop payment orders, NSF checks and overdrafts. The level of these fees has been a battlefield for class action litigation between customers and banks. Before we look at some of the leading cases in this area, we should note that according to a 1994 report of the Federal Reserve Board the approximate average fees charged at the time of the survey were: $13 for stop orders; $15 for NSF checks; and $15 for overdrafts. The report showed that about 65% of banks impose charges for items deposited in the customer's account that have to be returned because they were not paid by the bank on which they were drawn. Here the average fee was about $6. The Fed report is discussed in Clark & Clark, supra, ¶ 3.01[4][d][v] (Cum.Supp.1995). Bear in mind that since 1992, TISA has required that the bank make an initial disclosure of the types and amounts of these fees, Reg DD § 230.4(b)(4); that periodic statements must disclose the types and amounts of fees imposed during the statement period, Reg DD § 230.6(a)(3); and that a 30–day advance notice must be given of any new fees or any increase in the amounts of fees, Reg DD § 230.5(a).

Perdue v. Crocker National Bank

Supreme Court of California, 1985.
38 Cal.3d 913, 216 Cal.Rptr. 345, 702 P.2d 503.

■ BROUSSARD, JUSTICE.

Plaintiff filed this class action to challenge the validity of charges imposed by defendant Crocker National Bank for the processing of checks drawn on accounts without sufficient funds. (The parties refer to such checks as NSF checks and to the handling charge as an NSF charge.) He appeals from a judgment of the trial court entered after that court sustained defendant's general demurrer without leave to amend.

On July 3, 1978, plaintiff filed suit on behalf of all persons with checking accounts at defendant bank and a subclass of customers who have paid NSF charges to the bank. The complaint first alleges a contract under which the bank furnishes checking service in return for a maintenance charge. It then asserts that "It is the practice of defendants to impose and collect a unilaterally set charge for processing checks presented against plaintiffs' accounts when such accounts do not contain sufficient funds to cover the amount of the check." "Defendants have at various times unilaterally increased the NSF charge to an amount the defendants deemed appropriate, without reference to any criteria, and defendants imposed and collected the said increased amount without any explanation or justification by defendants to plaintiffs." At the time of filing of the suit, the charge was $6 for each NSF check, whether the check was honored or returned unpaid, even though "the actual cost incurred by the defendants in processing an NSF check is approximately $0.30."

The bank requires each depositor to sign a signature card which it uses "to determine and verify the authenticity of endorsements on checks". In extremely small (6 point) type, the signature card states that the undersigned depositors "agree with Crocker National Bank and with each other that * * * this account and all deposits therein shall be * * * subject to all applicable laws, to the Bank's present and future rules, regulations, practices and charges, and to its right of setoff for the obligations of any of us." The card does not identify the amount of the charge for NSF checks, and the bank does not furnish the depositor with a copy of the applicable bank rules and regulations.

On the basis of these allegations, plaintiff asserts * * * causes of action: (1) for a judicial declaration that the bank's signature card is not a contract authorizing NSF charges [and] (2) for a judicial declaration that such charges are oppressive and unconscionable * * *.

I. *Plaintiff's first cause of action: whether the signature card is a contract authorizing NSF charges.*

The complaint alleges that "The signature card prepared by the defendants does not identify the amount of any charge to be paid by the plaintiffs for processing NSF checks and is not an agreement for such payment. The card does not constitute mutual assent to NSF charges in any particular sum or at all and accordingly is not a contract conferring authority to do the acts complained of herein." "Based upon the language of the signature card, the plaintiffs believed and expected that the signature card was intended as a handwriting example for purposes of identification and verification only." Plaintiff therefore seeks a judicial declaration "as to whether the signature card is a valid or enforceable contract and * * * a lawful basis for the imposition of the NSF charge."

The cases unanimously agree that a signature card such as the Crocker Bank card at issue here is a contract. "The bank is authorized to honor withdrawals from an account on the signatures authorized by the signature card, which serves as a contract between the depositor and the bank for the handling of the account."

* * *

Plaintiff does not seriously dispute this proposition. His complaint alleges that the depositors "agreed to pay [the bank's] maintenance charge * * * "in return for checking privileges, and one could infer that they agreed to do so by affixing their signatures to the card. Complaints filed by plaintiff in an earlier action stated expressly that the signature card was a contract.

Plaintiff argues, however, that even if a signature card is a contract to establish a checking account, it is not a contract authorizing NSF charges.

He contends that the contract is illusory because it permits the bank to set and change the NSF charges at its discretion, and without assent from the customer except such as may be inferred from the fact that the customer does not cancel his account after the bank posts notice of its rates.[6]

Plaintiff relies on the rule that "[a]n agreement that provides that the price to be paid, or other performance to be rendered, shall be left to the will and discretion of one of the parties is not enforceable." (Automatic Vending Co. v. Wisdom (1960) 182 Cal.App.2d 354, 357, 6 Cal.Rptr. 31.) That rule, however, applies only if the total discretion granted one party renders the contract lacking in consideration. (See ibid.) If there are reciprocal promises, as in the present case, the fact that the contract permits one party to set or change the price charged for goods or services does not render the contract illusory. Thus in Cal. Lettuce Growers v. Union Sugar Co. (1955) 45 Cal.2d 474, 289 P.2d 785, the court upheld a contract permitting the buyer of sugar beets to set the price to be paid. The buyer did not have arbitrary power, the court explained, because "where a contract confers on one party a discretionary power affecting the rights of the other, a duty is imposed to exercise that discretion in good faith and in accordance with fair dealing." * * * Likewise, "a contracting party's discretionary power to vary the price or other performance does not render the agreement illusory if the party's *actual* exercise of that power is reasonable."

* * *

We conclude that plaintiff here is not entitled to a judicial declaration that the bank's signature card is not a contract authorizing NSF charges. To the contrary, we hold as a matter of law that the card is a contract authorizing the bank to impose such charges, subject to the bank's duty of good faith and fair dealing in setting or varying such charges. Plaintiff may, upon remand of this case, amend his complaint to seek a judicial declaration determining whether the charges actually set by the bank are consonant with that duty.

II. *Plaintiff's second cause of action: whether the bank's NSF charges are oppressive, unreasonable, or unconscionable.*

Plaintiff's second cause of action alleges that the signature card is drafted by defendant bank which enjoys a superior bargaining position by reason of its greater economic power, knowledge, experience and resources. Depositors have no alternative but to acquiesce in the relationship as offered by defendant or to accept a similar arrangement with another bank. The complaint alleges that the card is vague and uncertain, that it is unclear whether it is intended as an identification card or a contract, that it imposes no obligation upon the bank, and permits the bank to alter or terminate the relationship at any time.[8] It then asserts that "The disparity

6. Financial Code section 865.4, subdivision (b)(1) requires a bank to give customers 15 days' notice of any change in charges imposed on bank accounts.

8. The depositor also has the right to terminate the relationship at any time, but lacks the right asserted by the bank to alter the relationship without terminating it.

between the actual cost to defendants and the amount charged by defendants for processing an NSF check unreasonably and oppressively imposes excessive and unfair liability upon plaintiffs." Plaintiff seeks a declaratory judgment to determine the rights and duties of the parties.

Plaintiff's allegations point to the conclusion that the signature card, if it is a contract, is one of adhesion. The term contract of adhesion "signifies a standardized contract, which, imposed and drafted by the party of superior bargaining strength, relegates to the subscribing party only the opportunity to adhere to the contract or reject it." (Neal v. State Farm Ins. Co. (1961) 188 Cal.App.2d 690, 694, 10 Cal.Rptr. 781 * * * The signature card, drafted by the bank and offered to the customer without negotiation, is a classic example of a contract of adhesion; the bank concedes as much.

In Graham v. Scissor–Tail, Inc., 28 Cal.3d 807, 171 Cal.Rptr. 604, 623 P.2d 165, we observed that "To describe a contract as adhesive in character is not to indicate its legal effect * * *. [A] contract of adhesion is fully enforceable according to its terms [citations] unless certain other factors are present which, under established legal rules—legislative or judicial—operate to render it otherwise." (Pp. 819–820, 171 Cal.Rptr. 604, 623 P.2d 165, fn. omitted.) "Generally speaking," we explained, "there are two judicially imposed limitations on the enforcement of adhesion contracts or provisions thereof. The first is that such a contract or provision which does not fall within the reasonable expectations of the weaker or 'adhering' party will not be enforced against him. [Citations.] The second—a principle of equity applicable to all contracts generally—is that a contract or provision, even if consistent with the reasonable expectations of the parties, will be denied enforcement if, considered in its context, it is unduly oppressive or 'unconscionable.' "(P. 820, 171 Cal.Rptr. 604, 623 P.2d 165, fns. omitted.)

In 1979, the Legislature enacted Civil Code section 1670.5, which codified the established doctrine that a court can refuse to enforce an unconscionable provision in a contract. Section 1670.5 reads as follows: "(a) If the court as a matter of law finds the contract or any clause of the contract to have been unconscionable at the time it was made the court may refuse to enforce the contract, or it may enforce the remainder of the contract without the unconscionable clause, or it may so limit the application of any unconscionable clause as to avoid any unconscionable result. [¶] (b) When it is claimed or appears to the court that the contract or any clause thereof may be unconscionable the parties shall be afforded a reasonable opportunity to present evidence as to its commercial setting, purpose, and effect to aid the court in making the determination."

In construing this section, we cannot go so far as plaintiff, who contends that even a conclusory allegation of unconscionability requires an evidentiary hearing. We do view the section, however, as legislative recognition that a claim of unconscionability often cannot be determined merely by examining the face of the contract, but will require inquiry into its setting, purpose, and effect.

Plaintiff bases his claim of unconscionability on the alleged 2,000 percent differential between the NSF charge of $6 and the alleged cost to the bank of $0.30.[11] The parties have cited numerous cases on whether the price of an item can be so excessive as to be unconscionable. The cited cases are from other jurisdictions, often from trial courts or intermediate appellate courts, and none is truly authoritative on the issue. Taken together, however, they provide a useful guide to analysis of the claim that a price is so excessive as to be unconscionable.

To begin with, it is clear that the price term, like any other term in a contract, may be unconscionable. * * * Allegations that the price exceeds cost or fair value, standing alone, do not state a cause of action. * * * Instead, plaintiff's case will turn upon further allegations and proof setting forth the circumstances of the transaction.

The courts look to the basis and justification for the price (cf. A & M Produce Co. v. FMC Corp., supra, 135 Cal.App.3d 473, 487, 186 Cal.Rptr. 114), including "the price actually being paid by * * * other similarly situated consumers in a similar transaction." (Bennett v. Behring Corp., supra, 466 F.Supp. 689, 697, italics omitted.) The cases, however, do not support defendant's contention that a price equal to the market price cannot be held unconscionable. While it is unlikely that a court would find a price set by a freely competitive market to be unconscionable (see Bradford v. Plains Cotton Cooperative Assn. (10th Cir.1976) 539 F.2d 1249, 1255 [cotton futures]), the market price set by an oligopoly should not be immune from scrutiny. Thus courts consider not only the market price, but also the cost of the goods or services to the seller (Frostifresh Corporation v. Reynoso (N.Y.Dist.Ct.1966) 52 Misc.2d 26, 274 N.Y.S.2d 757; Toker v. Westerman (1970) 113 N.J.Super. 452, 274 A.2d 78), the inconvenience imposed on the seller (see Merrel v. Research & Data, Inc., supra, 589 P.2d 120, 123), and the true value of the product or service (American Home Improvements, Inc. v. MacIver (1964) 105 N.H. 435, 201 A.2d 886, 889).

In addition to the price justification, decisions examine what Justice Weiner in *A & M Produce* called the "procedural aspects" of unconscionability. (See *A & M Produce Co.,* supra, 135 Cal.App.3d at p. 489, 186 Cal.Rptr. 114.) Cases may turn on the absence of meaningful choice (Patterson v. Walker–Thomas Furniture Co., supra, 277 A.2d 111, 113 and cases there cited), the lack of sophistication of the buyer (compare Geldermann & Co., Inc. v. Lane Processing, Inc. (8th Cir.1975) 527 F.2d 571, 576

11. The bank's briefs claim the alleged $0.30 cost is too low and plaintiff's briefs admit that a higher figure, but still $1 or less, might be more accurate. We do not, however, find in plaintiff's briefs a sufficiently clear concession to enable us to depart from the general principle that, in reviewing a judgment after the sustaining of a general demurrer without leave to amend, we must assume the truth of all material factual allegations in the complaint. (Alcorn v. Anbro Engineering, Inc., supra, 2 Cal.3d 493, 496, 86 Cal.Rptr. 88, 468 P.2d 216.)

[relief denied to sophisticated investor] with Frostifresh Corporation v. Reynoso, supra, 274 N.Y.S.2d 757 [relief granted to unsophisticated buyers])and the presence of deceptive practices by the seller (ibid.; Vom Lehn v. Astor Art Galleries, Ltd., supra, 380 N.Y.S.2d 532).

Applying this analysis to our review of the complaint at hand, we cannot endorse defendant's argument that the $6 charge is so obviously reasonable that no inquiry into its basis or justification is necessary.[12] In 1978 $6 for processing NSF checks may not seem exorbitant,[13] but price alone is not a reliable guide. Small charges applied to a large volume of transactions may yield a sizeable sum. The complaint asserts that the cost of processing NSF checks is only $0.30 per check, which means that a $6 charge would produce a 2,000 percent profit; even at the higher cost estimate of $1 a check mentioned in plaintiff's petition for hearing, the profit is 600 percent.[14] Such profit percentages may not be automatically unconscionable, but they indicate the need for further inquiry.[15]

Other aspects of the transaction confirm plaintiff's right to a factual hearing. Defendant presents the depositor with a document which serves at least in part as a handwriting exemplar, and whose contractual character is not obvious. The contractual language appears in print so small that many could not read it. State law may impose obligations on the bank (e.g., the duty to honor a check when the account has sufficient funds (Allen v. Bank of America, supra, 58 Cal.App.2d 124, 127, 136 P.2d 345)), but so far as the signature card drafted by the bank is concerned, the bank has all the rights and the depositor all the duties. The signature card provides that the

12. In Jacobs v. Citibank, N.A. (1984) 61 N.Y.2d 869, 474 N.Y.S.2d 464, 462 N.E.2d 1182, the New York Court of Appeals upheld a summary judgment for defendant bank in a suit attacking NSF check charges. In rejecting the claim that such charges were unconscionable, the court said that "[p]laintiffs have failed to show that they were deprived of a meaningful choice of banks with which they could do business and that the terms of these agreements with defendant were unreasonably favorable to the bank." (P. 872, 474 N.Y.S.2d 464, 462 N.E.2d 1182.)

While the New York court ruled on a motion for summary judgment, we rule upon a demurrer, and look only to plaintiff's allegations, not to the proof he had advanced to support those allegations. Plaintiff here has alleged that the charges imposed by defendant bank were excessive, and that similar arrangements would be imposed by other banks. Such allegations, which we must assume to be true, distinguish the New York decision.

13. Defendant cites Merrel v. Research & Data, Inc., supra, 589 P.2d 120, which held a $5 fee imposed by merchants for NSF checks was a "modest" amount (p. 123) and not unconscionable. NSF checks pose a substantial inconvenience to a seller, who has been deceived into an involuntary extension of credit to a customer whose credit standing may not be very good. A bank, however, is not deceived. It checks the balance of the account, and may reject any overdraft. A fee reasonable to compensate the merchant for the cost, inconvenience, and risk of an NSF check may be excessive if exacted by a bank.

14. The complaint does not state the market price for the service of processing NSF checks, although one might infer it is similar to defendant's price since plaintiff alleges that if he did not contract with defendant, he would be "forced to accept a similar arrangement with other banks." The complaint does not set a figure for the "fair" or "true" value or worth of the service.

15. We observe that the bank charges the same fee whether it honors or rejects an NSF check. The fee, consequently, cannot be intended as compensation for the credit risk arising from paying such a check, or for the interest on the amount loaned.

depositor will be bound by the bank's rules, regulations, practices and charges, but the bank does not furnish the depositor with a copy of the relevant documents. The bank reserves the power to change its practices and fees at any time, subject only to the notice requirements of state law.

In short, the bank structured a totally one-sided transaction. The absence of equality of bargaining power, open negotiation, full disclosure, and a contract which fairly sets out the rights and duties of each party demonstrates that the transaction lacks those checks and balances which would inhibit the charging of unconscionable fees. In such a setting, plaintiff's charge that the bank's NSF fee is exorbitant, yielding a profit far in excess of cost, cannot be dismissed on demurrer. Under Civil Code section 1670.5, the parties should be afforded a reasonable opportunity to present evidence as to the commercial setting, purpose, and effect of the signature card and the NSF charge in order to determine whether that charge is unconscionable.

* * *

NOTES

1. The court reached the decision in *Perdue* in the face of a regulation promulgated by the Comptroller of the Currency stating:

"(b) Establishment of deposit account service charges, and the amounts thereof, is a business decision to be made by each bank according to sound banking judgment and federal standards of safety and soundness. In establishing deposit account service charges, the bank may consider, but is not limited to considering: [¶] (1) Costs incurred by the bank, plus a profit margin, in providing the service; [¶] (2) The deterrence of misuse by customers of banking services; [¶] (3) The enhancement of the competitive position of the bank in accord with the bank's marketing strategy; [¶] (4) Maintenance of the safety and soundness of the institution.

"(c) A national bank may establish any deposit account service charge pursuant to paragraphs (a) and (b) of this section notwithstanding any state laws which prohibit the charge assessed or limit or restrict the amount of that charge. Such state laws are preempted by the comprehensive federal statutory scheme governing the deposit-taking function of national banks."

216 Cal.Rptr. at 360. The court stated:

We conclude that the Comptroller's assertion that state laws regulating service charges are preempted by a "comprehensive federal statutory scheme governing the deposit-taking function of national banks" (12 C.F.R. § 7.8000) is not a reasonable interpretation of the controlling statutes. It is not an attempt to interpret the language of the statute, fill in the gaps in the statutory coverage, or to explain how the Comptroller will exercise his discretion. Instead, the regulation, insofar as it claims federal preemption, represents legislation of far-reaching character and effect, of a type never considered by Congress, which would radically alter the respective roles of the states and the Comptroller in the regulation of bank-depositor contracts. Such legislation cannot be enacted in the guise of statutory interpretation.

216 Cal.Rptr. at 365.

2. The Supreme Court of the United States has taken a different view of the weight to be accorded to regulations of the Comptroller of the Currency in Smiley v. Citibank (South Dakota), N.A., ___ U.S. ___, 116 S.Ct. 1730, 135 L.Ed.2d 25 (1996). In this case, plaintiff, a resident of California was the holder of a credit card issued by defendant, a national bank located in South Dakota. She objected that late payment charges imposed by the defendant bank, though legal under South Dakota law, violated California law. Defendant contended that the controlling law was that of South Dakota because of a provision of the National Bank Act of 1864 that allows national banks to charge its borrowers "interest" at the rate allowed by the laws of the state where the bank is located. However, plaintiff argued that late charges were not interest charges, and the federal preemption law should not apply to them. *After the California Supreme Court upheld the dismissal of the plaintiff's complaint but before the United States Supreme Court heard the case,* the Comptroller of the Currency, who had participated in this litigation as *amicus curiae* on the side of the bank, issued a regulation interpreting interest to include late payment fees. 12 C.F.R. § 7.4001(a).

A unanimous Court held for the bank. It said that it accorded deference to the regulation because "of a presumption that Congress, when it left ambiguity in a statute meant for implementation by an agency, understood that the ambiguity would be resolved, first and foremost, by the agency, and desired the agency (rather than the courts) to possess whatever degree of discretion the ambiguity allows. * * * Nor does it matter that the regulation was prompted by litigation, including this very suit. * * * That it was litigation which disclosed the need for the regulation is irrelevant." ___ U.S. ___, 116 S.Ct. at 1733. *Smiley* was but one of many cases on this issue that had been brought around the country.

Tolbert v. First National Bank of Oregon

Supreme Court of Oregon, 1991.
312 Or. 485, 823 P.2d 965.

■ Carson, Chief Justice.

This class action involves the obligation of good faith in the performance of contracts. The primary issue is the nature of the good faith obligation owed by defendant First National Bank of Oregon (Bank) to its non-business checking account customers (depositors) in setting and revising, from time to time, the fees it charged to depositors who wrote checks when there were not sufficient funds in their accounts (NSF fees).

The trial court granted Bank's motion for summary judgment on the issue of whether it had failed to act in good faith regarding the NSF fees. The Court of Appeals reversed the judgment of the trial court and remanded the case. Tolbert v. First National Bank, 96 Or.App. 398, 772 P.2d 1373 (1989). Bank and plaintiffs each sought review by this court. We allowed both plaintiffs' and Bank's petitions for review, and we now reverse in part and affirm in part the decision of the Court of Appeals.

This case began as a companion case to Best v. U.S. National Bank, 303 Or. 557, 739 P.2d 554 (1987), and a review of our opinion in that case is essential to an understanding of this case. Accordingly, we begin with an examination of Best.

In *Best*, the plaintiff depositors brought a class action alleging, among other things, that the bank "had an obligation to set its NSF fees in good faith and that it breached this obligation by setting its fees at amounts greatly in excess of the costs incurred by it in processing NSF checks." 303 Or. at 561, 739 P.2d 554. In addressing this issue, the *Best* court began by stating the general rule that there is an obligation of good faith in the performance and enforcement of every contract. Id. The bank in that case argued that it had no obligation of good faith, because the depositors agreed to the NSF fees, as manifested by their choice not to close their accounts.

The *Best* court rejected this argument, pointing out that it was not the bank's practice to inform depositors of the initial NSF fees or of changes in the amount of such fees: "It would be improper under this evidence to conclude on a motion for summary judgment that the depositors agreed to the charges through failing to close their accounts." Id. at 562, 739 P.2d 554. Having concluded that there was no agreement regarding the NSF fees, the court went on to determine whether there was a genuine issue of material fact whether the bank set (and revised) its NSF fees in good faith.

After reviewing cases from this court and examining the Restatement (Second) of Contracts, the court explained the role of the parties' expectations in the framework of the good faith obligation:

"It is therefore not necessarily sufficient * * * that the Bank acted honestly in setting its NSF fees or that its fees were similar to those of other banks. Undoubtedly, parties to a contract always expect that the other party will perform the contract honestly and, where the performance of a commercial enterprise is at issue, ordinarily expect that it will do so in a commercially reasonable manner. But the reasonable expectations of the parties need not be so limited.

" * * * In general, * * * whether a specified price violates the obligation of good faith should be decided by the reasonable contractual expectations of the parties." 303 Or. at 564–65, 739 P.2d 554.

The court continued the "reasonable expectations" analysis, applying the general rules of law set forth above to the *Best* facts:

"Because NSF fees were incidental to the Bank's principal checking account fees and were denominated 'service charges,' a trier of fact could infer that the depositors reasonably expected that NSF fees would be special fees to cover the costs of extraordinary services. This inference could reasonably lead to the further inference that the depositors reasonably expected that the Bank's NSF fees would be priced similarly to those checking account fees of which the depositors were aware—the Bank's monthly checking account service fees and per check fees, if any. By 'priced similarly,' we mean priced to cover the Bank's NSF check processing costs plus an allowance for overhead costs plus the Bank's ordinary profit margin on checking account services." Id. at 565–66, 739 P.2d 554.

Because there were genuine issues of material fact regarding the depositors' expectations and regarding whether the bank had, in fact, set the NSF fees in accordance with those expectations, the court concluded that summary judgment was inappropriate on the good faith claim. Id. at 566, 739 P.2d 554.

The holdings of the *Best* case relevant to the case before us may be summarized as follows:

● It is improper to decide on summary judgment whether depositors have agreed to a bank's NSF fees when neither the initial fees nor changes in the fees are disclosed to the depositors before assessment of the charges.

● In determining whether a bank has acted in good faith in setting its NSF fees, the reasonable expectations of its depositors are relevant. A depositor may reasonably expect that NSF fees are set using the same mechanism as other checking account service charges of which the depositor is aware—a "cost-plus" basis in that case.

The parties to this case agree that there are two important factual differences between this case and *Best*; the dispute is over the legal significance of those differences. The first difference is that, unlike the bank in *Best*, Bank followed the practice of informing depositors of its current NSF fees at the time they opened their accounts. Depositors signed an account agreement, which included an agreement that all deposits to the account would be governed by, among other things, "the rules, regulations, and customs of this Bank including, but not limited to, those which relate to interest and *service charges* on active and dormant accounts." (Emphasis added.)

At the time depositors opened their accounts, they received a Service Charge Guide or similar document listing the charges assessed by Bank for various services. The guide listed a fee for "Non-sufficient Funds Checks Paid or Returned." The guide also included the following statement:

"These charges are subject to change at the discretion of First National. If you have questions or need additional information regarding our services, procedures, or charges, please contact any First National branch for assistance."

Further, the evidence before the trial court was that Bank employees routinely explained Bank's service charges to new depositors at the time an account was opened. If a depositor did not agree to the terms of the account agreement, Bank would refuse to open an account.

The second difference between this case and *Best* is that, here, depositors were informed of changes in the service charges by mail at or near the time the changes were made. Bank produced evidence that it periodically sent notices to each depositor, with depositor bank statements, stating current prices for all bank service charges related to checking accounts (including NSF fees).

Plaintiffs take the position that our holding in Best v. United States National Bank, supra, dictates the result in this case and that the factual distinctions between the two cases have no legal significance. They assert:

> "[T]he Bank's Service Charge Guides made two separate representations to its depositors at contract formation: (1) a representation concerning the amount of the NSF charge then in existence and (2) a representation that this charge was a service charge. * * * [T]he latter representation creates an expectation of the mechanism used in setting the amount of the disclosed charge and to be used in setting future charges. Consequently, when the Bank, in the performance of the contract, exercised its unilateral discretion to assess a charge priced dissimilarly from other service charges and not reasonably related to costs, it violated the expectations reasonably created by this contract, even if that charge equalled in dollar amount the charge initially disclosed."

In contrast, Bank argues that the reasonable expectations of the parties are irrelevant when depositors first are apprised of the amount of the fees and then agree to open accounts: "Plaintiffs cannot agree to pay certain fees and then attack those fees as made in bad faith." Bank further argues that the Court of Appeals is correct in its statement that "the depositors' reasonable expectations about pricing are irrelevant to charges that were in effect when a depositor opened an account and of which [the depositor] was apprised at that time." Tolbert v. First National Bank, supra, 96 Or.App. at 403, 772 P.2d 1373.

Although portions of the *Best* opinion may be read to support plaintiffs' position, we agree with Bank: The expectations of depositors are irrelevant if they have agreed to the NSF fees charged by the bank. As discussed above, the *Best* court analyzed the reasonable expectations of the parties only after determining that it could not assume the existence of an agreement. Although "[e]very contract imposes upon each party a duty of good faith and fair dealing in its performance and its enforcement," Restatement (Second) of Contracts § 205 (1981), that duty does not extend to the formation of the contract. See id. at 100, comment c (section 205 of the Restatement "does not deal with good faith in the formation of a contract"); 1 Farnsworth, Contracts 312, § 3.26a (1990) (no duty of good faith in precontractual negotiation). Cf. Sheets v. Knight, 308 Or. 220, 232–33, 779 P.2d 1000 (1989) (recognizing that duty of good faith is imposed in the performance of every contract).

In *Best*, this court held that depositors were entitled to assume that the bank would price unknown NSF fees in the same manner as they priced other known service charges, and that, because the bank established the known charges by cost-plus pricing, it would use cost-plus pricing to set the unknown charges. Best v. U.S. National Bank, supra, 303 Or. at 565, 739 P.2d 554. As the portion of the *Best* opinion quoted above suggests, *Best* goes through a series of inferences to arrive at that conclusion. Yet, the "reasonable expectations" analysis in *Best* was necessary only because the NSF fees were not agreed to by the depositors.

In this case, there is uncontroverted evidence that the depositors did agree to the specific NSF fees charged by Bank. As noted above, if a potential depositor did not agree to the terms offered by Bank, no account was opened. In the context of contract formation, when there is an agreement after full disclosure, the depositors' expectations are irrelevant. Agreement after full disclosure is the critical difference between this case and *Best*.[5]

The Court of Appeals distinguished between the terms agreed to by the parties at the time accounts were opened and the later changes in Bank's NSF fees:

"We do not agree with [Bank] that its revised charges are also beyond the reach of *Best*. Although [Bank] provided customers with periodic information about the revisions, we understand *Best* to mean that the obligation of good faith arises in connection with the unilateral fixing of charges after the parties have reached an original agreement. That obligation is not eliminated by the facts that [Bank] notified its depositors about increases in the charges and that the depositors had the ability to terminate their accounts after receiving the notification. Good faith is required in the performance of the contract and the exercise of discretion under it, and it is immaterial that a party could terminate the contract if it were dissatisfied with the way in which the other exercises its discretion. We also agree with plaintiffs, for essentially the same reasons as those stated in *Best*, that there are genuine issues of material fact about whether defendant acted in good faith in setting the revised charges." Tolbert v. First National Bank, supra, 96 Or.App. at 403, 772 P.2d 1373.

The Court of Appeals' statement of the law is correct—good faith is required in the performance of the contract and the exercise of discretion under it. See generally U.S. National Bank v. Boge, 311 Or. 550, 556–68, 814 P.2d 1082 (1991) (discussing obligation of good faith and citing cases). However, as discussed below, there is no genuine issue of material fact regarding whether Bank acted in good faith, in the circumstances of this case.

The contract in this case is not unusual in that it explicitly granted one party the right to exercise its discretion regarding one aspect of the

5. Although the Court of Appeals' holding suggests that disclosure of the NSF fees are sufficient to make the parties' expectations irrelevant, it is disclosure together with agreement to the contract terms that takes this case out of the *Best* holding.

performance and enforcement of the contract. In changing the amount of the NSF fees, Bank enforced a right specifically granted to it under the contract. Because the exercise of that right was pursuant to Bank's unilateral discretion, the good faith obligation discussed in *Best* applies. Whether any changes in the NSF fees were determined in good faith, therefore, "should be decided by the *reasonable* contractual expectations of the parties." Best v. U.S. National Bank, supra, 303 Or. at 565, 739 P.2d 554. (Emphasis added.)

We emphasize that it is only the objectively reasonable expectations of parties that will be examined in determining whether the obligation of good faith has been met.[6] In the context of this case—when (1) the parties agree to (and their contract provides for) a unilateral exercise of discretion regarding changes in one of the contract terms, and (2) the discretion is exercised after prior notice—we hold as a matter of law that the parties' reasonable expectations have been met.

* * *

Unlike the situation in *Best*, where the depositors were aware of the pricing mechanism for some service charges, and were entitled reasonably to expect that similar charges would be priced accordingly, in this case there is no evidence that depositors were aware of any particular pricing formula. Accordingly, it would be unreasonable for depositors to have any expectation that changes in NSF fees would be pursuant to any particular formula.

Applying the above principles, we are left with the following framework for our decision in this case: If there was no genuine issue of fact before the trial court regarding whether (1) depositors agreed to a unilateral exercise of discretion regarding changes in the amount of the NSF fee, and (2) Bank changed the amount of the NSF fee after notice to depositors, then summary judgment was appropriate.

The uncontroverted evidence before the trial court on summary judgment in this case was that: (1) the depositors initially agreed that Bank could change the amount of the NSF fees in its unilateral discretion; (2) Bank's practice was to inform depositors of future changes to the NSF fees before such changes became effective; and (3) plaintiffs continued to maintain their accounts with Bank and, in some cases, even continued to write NSF checks after Bank informed them of the changes. No inference available to plaintiffs (other than flat disbelief, which is not an inference that plaintiffs may invoke on summary judgment) creates an issue of fact as to these pivotal circumstances. Based on this record, any reasonable

---

6. We note that it is the common law "objective" good faith standard which is applicable in this case. The Uniform Commercial Code's "subjective" good faith standard is not at issue here. See U.S. National Bank v. Boge, 311 Or. 550, 558, 814 P.2d 1082 (1991) (In the context of ORS chapter 79 (UCC Article 9), the UCC "subjective" good faith standard displaces common law "objec- tive" standard, but the "subjective" standard does not necessarily displace the common law "objective" standard in the context of other commercial transactions.). As we observed in *Boge*, the UCC and its definitions do not apply to the fee contract between a bank and its customer. Id. ("Nothing in ORS chapter 74 [UCC Article 4] addresses the limitations on a bank's discretion to set NSF fees.").

expectations held by the depositors were met by Bank's procedures. As a matter of law, Bank acted in good faith in its treatment of the NSF fees; there was no issue regarding any material fact, and Bank was entitled to a judgment as a matter of law. The trial court correctly granted summary judgment in favor of Bank.

The decision of the Court of Appeals is affirmed in part and reversed in part. The judgment of the circuit court is affirmed.

NOTE

In 1996 the Comptroller of the Currency adopted a series of interpretive rules on operations of national banks. Among these is the following provision concerning bank charges which is found in 12 C.F.R. § 7.4002. This provision replaces the one set out in Note 1 following *Perdue*.

(a) *Customer charges and fees*. A national bank may charge its customers non-interest charges and fees, including deposit account service charges. * * *

(b) *Considerations*. The establishment of non-interest charges and fees, and the amounts thereof, is a business decision to be made by each bank, in its discretion, according to sound banking judgment and safe and sound banking principles. A bank reasonably establishes non-interest charges and fees if the bank considers the following factors, among others:

(1) The cost incurred by the bank, plus a profit margin, in providing the service;

(2) The deterrence of misuse by customers of banking services;

(3) The enhancement of the competitive position of the bank in accordance with the bank's marketing strategy; and

(4) The maintenance of the safety and soundness of the institution.

(c) *Interest*. Charges and fees that are "interest" within the meaning of 12 U.S.C. 85 are governed by § 7.4001 and not by this section.

(d) *State law*. The OCC evaluates on a case-by-case basis whether a national bank may establish non-interest charges or fees pursuant to paragraphs (a) and (b) of this section notwithstanding a contrary state law that purports to limit or prohibit such charges or fees. In issuing an opinion on whether such state laws are preempted, the OCC applies preemption principles derived from the Supremacy Clause of the United States Constitution and applicable judicial precedent.

Criticisms of previous drafts of this rule were that providing a reasonableness standard for bank charges would invite litigation challenging the reasonableness of every charge. Revisions were made in the final rule to allay this concern. The OCC discussion of the new rule says "The final ruling clarifies, in § 7.4002(b), the intent of the proposal that banks have discretion in setting the amount of charges and fees, and that any charge or fee is 'reasonably' established if the bank considered the factors enumerated in the final ruling." 61 Fed.Reg. 4859 (1996).

CHAPTER 6

LETTERS OF CREDIT

A. INTRODUCTION

Until mid-century, letter of credit law dealt largely with transactions involving sales of goods, primarily international transactions, the area in which letters of credit originated. A letter of credit issued as a part of a sale transaction is usually called a "commercial" letter of credit. Today letters of credit are also widely used to provide what is functionally a bank guaranty of obligations arising from a variety of transactions. The term "standby" is used to describe this type of letter of credit. The ubiquity of letters of credit in business transactions today means that no business lawyer can competently advise clients without a working knowledge of the rapidly growing body of letter of credit law.

The original version of Article 5 was drafted in what now must be regarded as the stone age of letters of credit, before standby letters of credit became popular and long before the use of electronic media became common. Ferment has grown for legislative reform. A useful critique of letter of credit law with recommendations for amendments to Article 5 is found in the report of the Task Force on the Study of U.C.C. Article 5, 45 Bus.Law 1521–1646 (1990). The reform movement culminated in a major revision of Article 5, commenced in 1990 and finally promulgated by the National Conference of Commissioners on Uniform State Laws and the American Law Institute in 1995. In this Chapter references to the provisions of Article 5 will distinguish between the former version and the 1995 revision.

Treatises on letter of credit law include: Barkley Clark & Barbara Clark, The Law of Bank Deposits, Collections and Credit Cards, Chapter 10 (Rev.ed.1995) (herein Clark & Clark, Bank Deposits, etc.); John F. Dolan, The Law of Letters of Credit: Commercial and Standby Credits (2d ed.1991) (herein Dolan, Letters of Credit); and 3 James J. White & Robert S. Summers, Uniform Commercial Code, Chapter 26 (4th Prac.ed.1995) (herein White & Summers, Prac.ed.). The Practitioner's Edition of White & Summers contains a detailed analysis of revised Article 5, presumably written by Professor White who was the Reporter for the Article 5 revision. The treatment of letters of credit in White & Summers' one volume edition is much less complete and will not be cited in this Chapter.

Baird, Standby Letters of Credit in Bankruptcy

49 U. of Chi.L.Rev. 130, 133–135 (1982).

I. The Letter-of-Credit Transaction

A. Background

As recently as twenty years ago, letters of credit were used principally in international sales. No seller willingly sends its goods across national borders unless it is confident it will be paid, because no seller welcomes the prospect of having its goods in the care of unknown parties in a foreign port, where finding a new buyer may be impossible and bringing a legal action extremely difficult. The letter of credit as we now know it arose in the middle of the nineteenth century in response to this problem.

Although letter-of-credit transactions vary, their basic structure can be stated briefly. In a typical letter-of-credit transaction, a seller specifies that payment be made with a letter of credit in its favor. The buyer (known as the "customer" in the letter-of-credit transaction) contracts with the bank to issue the letter. The bank, knowing the creditworthiness of its customer, is willing to issue the letter for a small fee, typically some fraction of one per cent of the price of the goods. The bank sends the letter to the seller, promising to pay the full price of the goods when the seller presents it with a draft and the documents specified in the letter. These documents typically include a negotiable bill of lading.

This arrangement benefits all parties to the transaction. The seller can manufacture goods to the buyer's order, confident it will be paid regardless of what befalls the buyer, because it can rely on the bank's commitment. The buyer that secures the letter of credit is better off than if it had advanced cash to the seller, because it does not become liable for the price until a trustworthy party (the bank) has possession of a negotiable document of title. The bank, in turn, earns a fee for issuing the letter and exposes itself to only a small risk, because it can readily assess the creditworthiness of its customer and, as the holder of a negotiable bill of lading, it has a perfected security interest in the goods involved in the transaction.

The linchpin of the letter-of-credit transaction is the unique legal relationship between the bank and the beneficiary.[16] Unlike a guarantor, the bank is primarily liable whenever the beneficiary presents a draft and documents that conform to the letter. Unlike its counterpart in a third-party beneficiary contract, the bank may not invoke the defenses its customer might have on the underlying contract. Moreover, the status of a

---

16. In their discussion of the legal relationship created by the letter of credit, Professors White and Summers note that a letter of credit is not like other devices creating legal obligations, but rather that

> a letter of credit is a letter of credit. As Bishop Butler once said, "Everything is what it is and not another thing." Thus,

when a beneficiary sues an issuer for refusal to honor drafts drawn pursuant to a letter of credit, his theory is not that of breach of contract, nor does he sue "on a negotiable instrument." Rather, he sues "on a letter of credit."

J. White & R. Summers, supra note 15, § 18–2, at 715 (footnotes omitted).

beneficiary of a letter of credit is radically different from that of a payee of a check, who has no right to compel payment from the drawee bank. In the letter-of-credit transaction, the beneficiary does have the right to compel payment, and once the letter of credit is issued, the customer is powerless to stop payment in the absence of fraud. This difference exists because a letter of credit, unlike a negotiable instrument such as a check, is a binding and irrevocable obligation of the bank itself, not of the customer who procured it. The legal relationship between bank and beneficiary is governed by special principles which, like the law merchant in an earlier era, are nearly uniform throughout the world.

B.   The Standby Letter of Credit

The archetypal letter-of-credit transaction described above is the means by which the parties pay one another if the underlying transaction takes place as planned. Standby letters of credit, in contrast, are never drawn upon if the transaction runs smoothly. For example, a builder might require a developer to have a bank issue a letter of credit in its behalf to ensure payment if the developer defaults. Such a letter of credit might require that the bank honor the builder's draft when accompanied by an architect's certificate that the building was finished and a statement by the builder that it had not been paid. In this kind of transaction, the bank usually will issue the letter only if the developer gives it a security interest in some property to which the bank will have recourse if the letter is drawn upon. If all goes well, the builder never presents its draft because it has been paid on schedule by the developer. If the developer defaults, however, the builder is still assured payment under the letter of credit. The bank then must seek reimbursement from the developer or enforce its security interest.

The parties to this transaction might employ a standby letter of credit in a different way. The developer might want to ensure that any money it advances to the builder is used to build the building. The developer could require the builder to have its bank issue a letter of credit in the developer's favor. Such a letter might provide that the developer's draft, accompanied by its statement that the builder had defaulted on its obligations, would be honored by the bank. Unlike the negotiable document of title specified in the usual commercial letter-of-credit transaction, the documents in the standby letter-of-credit transaction have no intrinsic value. For this reason, the bank is likely to insist that the builder give it a security interest as a condition of the letter's issuance.

Standby letters of credit also are used in transactions involving sales of goods. A supplier of raw materials, for example, might prefer to have a letter of credit in its favor from the buyer's bank rather than a security interest in the goods. Alternatively, a buyer of manufactured goods might want to protect itself when it advances money to finance its seller's purchase of raw materials. Such a buyer risks more in the event of default than one who sells on credit, because the buyer cannot easily acquire a purchase money security interest in the raw materials its seller uses. As the beneficiary of a standby letter of credit issued by the seller's bank, however, the buyer obtains equivalent protection.

A business that wishes to raise money may issue commercial paper backed by a standby letter of credit. This type of transaction involves larger dollar amounts than other uses of letters of credit. The business's bank may be more willing to accept the risk of its customer's insolvency than will the buyers of commercial paper. The buyers, however may be willing to extend cash to the business if they can rely on the bank to ensure repayment. The letter of credit makes it easy for all of the parties to allocate among themselves the risk of the business's failure. The business acquires the cash it needs, the bank lends its credit to the business without having to supply cash, and the buyers of commercial paper enjoy a relatively safe investment. As in the other letter-of-credit transactions, all parties directly involved benefit.

B. SOURCES OF LETTER OF CREDIT LAW

It has long been a cause of confusion in the United States that letter of credit law has two sources, Article 5 of the UCC and the Uniform Customs and Practice for Documentary Credits, of the International Chamber of Commerce (UCP). The latest version of the UCP became effective in 1994. Since its ICC publication number is 500, the new edition is referred to as UCP 500. Letters of credit were first used in international transactions and the need for a uniform international formulation of the legal rules governing letters of credit was great. The ICC met this need with the UCP which has been frequently amended to keep up with developments in the field.

Since the ICC has no authority to make laws binding on U.S. Courts, the UCP applies only if a letter of credit expressly incorporates it "into the text of the Credit." UCP 500, Art. 1. If the letter of credit does incorporate the UCP, to what extent does Article 5 also apply? The official text of the old version of Article 5 made no reference to the UCP, and was inconsistent with the UCP on several important matters. The usual assumption was that to the extent there was conflict between the UCP and Article 5, the UCP would prevail if incorporated by the letter of credit; otherwise Article 5 would control. However, for a large volume of letters of credit, this was not true; the explanation lay in the legislative background of Article 5. Since the UCP was well established by the time Article 5 was drafted, there was controversy in the financial community about the need for Article 5. In the most important jurisdiction for the issuance of letters of credit, New York, banking interests remained unconvinced about the utility of Article 5 and resisted passage of the Code until a nonuniform amendment was added (§ 5–102(4)) which stated that if a letter of credit provided that the credit was subject to the UCP, Article 5 was entirely preempted and had no application to the credit. Since New York banks typically issue letters of credit, both domestic and foreign, which expressly incorporate the UCP, Article 5 had only marginal application in New York and a few other states that have followed its lead.

Former Article 5, although enacted in all states, must be counted something of a legislative failure. It did not bring uniformity to the law of letters of credit in the United States because it had almost no application to the large number of letters of credit issued by New York banks. The new version of Article 5 addresses this problem in two ways. First, revised § 5–116(c) makes clear that if the credit is made subject to the UCP, the UCP displaces Article 5 (1) only to the extent of the conflict and (2) only if the UCP provisions do not conflict with the nonwaiver provisions specified in revised § 5–103(c). Comment 3 to revised § 5–116 states that "This section does not permit what is now authorized by the nonuniform Section 5–102(4) in New York." Second, in order to induce New York to enact revised Article 5 without a crippling amendment like § 5–102(4), the drafters have substantially conformed the provisions of Article 5 to those of UCP 500. The Prefatory Note to Article 5 says "To facilitate its usefulness and competitiveness, it is essential that U.S. law be in harmony with international rules and practices * * *." Thus, a stated goal of the drafting effort was "conforming the Article 5 rules to current customs and practices." In Comment 3 to revised § 5–116, the drafters claim success in this endeavor; they conclude that the revised version of Article 5 "* * * is generally consistent with UCP 500 * * *."

C.   FORMAL REQUIREMENTS

A letter of credit is a unique arrangement. We learned in earlier chapters the difficulties that a secured creditor encounters in realizing on its collateral after default by a debtor. However, if a lender, seller or other obligee is able to contract for a letter of credit, it avoids these difficulties, for, upon complying with the terms of the credit, it is entitled to prompt payment from a bank (virtually all letters of credit are issued by banks), instead of engaging in the expensive, time-consuming and often risky task of repossessing and disposing of used equipment or chasing balky account debtors. Hence, the tactical advantage that a letter of credit offers a creditor in being assured of almost immediate payment in money rather than the tedious task of trying to realize on collateral is great.

But a creditor can assure itself of payment in money and avoid the messy process of dealing with collateral by contracting for a solvent guarantor; if the debtor defaults the creditor can pursue the guarantor. Here the unique feature of the letter of credit becomes most apparent, for while a guarantor can resist payment by raising defenses of the principal debtor, the issuer of a letter of credit, under the independence principle, with only a few limited exceptions, must pay if the beneficiary has complied with the terms of the credit whether or not the beneficiary has performed the underlying contract. Pay now; litigate later.

If the beneficiary of a letter of credit can enjoy these remarkable benefits, what must a writing say to qualify as a letter of credit? Since the guiding principle of letter of credit law is that the credit is independent of the underlying contract, the form of the credit must reflect this fact. Form should follow function. In the following case, Notes and Problems, we inquire what form a letter of credit must take.

Wichita Eagle and Beacon Publishing Company, Inc. v. Pacific National Bank of San Francisco

United States Court of Appeal, Ninth Circuit, 1974.
493 F.2d 1285.

■ Before CHAMBERS and BROWNING, CIRCUIT JUDGES, and KING DISTRICT JUDGE.

■ PER CURIAM:

The facts are summarized in the district court's opinion, 343 F.Supp. 332 (N.D.Cal.1971).

* * *

[Summary by Eds.: Lessors leased a site on which Lessee (Circular Ramp Garages), under the terms of the lease, undertook to build a parking garage. In order to assure Lessors that Lessee would perform, Lessee obtained from Bank (Pacific National Bank) a writing addressed to Lessors in which Bank established its "Letter of Credit No. 17084" in favor of Lessors for payment of $250,000 "available by drafts drawn at sight on the Pacific National Bank providing that all of the following conditions are met at the time said draft is received by the undersigned." The conditions were (1) that Lessee has failed to perform the terms of the lease; (2) that Lessors have given Bank an affidavit stating that it has given notice to Lessee and its contractor specifying how Lessee has failed to perform its lease; and (3) that either Lessee or its contractor has failed to cure defaults under the lease during a period of thirty days after receiving Lessor's notice. Lessee failed to obtain the financing necessary to build the parking garage and defaulted on the lease. Lessors' assignee (Plaintiff) presented to Bank a draft for $250,000 drawn upon Letter of Credit No. 17084, together with the required documents. When Bank refused payment, Plaintiff brought suit against Bank. The district court concluded that "Although the question is not free from doubt, the Instrument denominated 'Letter of Credit No. 17084' should be treated as a letter of credit and be subject to the law respecting letters of credit to the extent applicable and appropriate." 343 F.Supp. at 339.]

We do not agree with the district court that the instrument sued upon is a letter of credit, though it is so labeled. Rather, the instrument is an ordinary guaranty contract, obliging the defendant bank to pay whatever the lessee Circular Ramp Garages, Inc., owed on the underlying lease, up to the face amount of the guaranty. Since the underlying lease clearly contemplated the payment of $250,000 in case of default, and since this provision appears to be a valid liquidated damages clause, the judgment below must be modified to award the plaintiff $250,000 plus interest.

We do not base our holding that the instrument is not a letter of credit on the fact that payment was triggered by default rather than performance or on the fact that the instrument was written in a lease context, for we recognize that the commercial use of letters of credit has expanded far beyond the international sales context in which it originally developed. * * *

The instrument involved here strays too far from the basic purpose of letters of credit, namely, providing a means of assuring payment cheaply by eliminating the need for the issuer to police the underlying contract. * * * The instrument neither evidences an intent that payment be made merely on presentation on a draft nor specifies the documents required for termination or payment. To the contrary, it requires the actual existence in fact of most of the conditions specified: * * * for payment, that the lessee have failed to perform the terms of the lease and have failed to correct that default, in addition to an affidavit of notice.

True, in the text of the instrument itself the instruments is referred to as a 'letter of credit,' and we should, as the district court notes, 'give effect wherever possible to the intent of the contracting parties.' 343 F.Supp. at 338. But the relevant intent is manifested by the terms of the agreement, not by its label. * * * And where, as here, the substantive provisions require the issuer to deal not simply in documents alone, but in facts relating to the performance of a separate contract (the lease, in this case), all distinction between a letter of credit and an ordinary guaranty contract would be obliterated by regarding the instrument as a letter of credit.

It would hamper rather than advance the extension of the letter of credit concept to new situations if an instrument such as this were held to be a letter of credit. The loose terms of this instrument invited the very evil that letters of credit are meant to avoid—protracted, expensive litigation. If the letter of credit concept is to have value in new situations, the instrument must be tightly drawn to strictly and clearly limit the responsibility of the issuer.

* * *

NOTES

1. How would this case be decided under revised Article 5? See revised § 5–102(a)(10) ("letter of credit") and Comment 6 to revised § 5–102. How could the document in *Wichita* be rewritten to remove all doubt about its status as a letter of credit? Does revised § 5–108(g) allow the court in this case to find that the writing is a valid letter of credit by disregarding the two nondocumentary conditions? Comment 9 to revised § 5–108. See Dolan, Letters of Credit ¶ 2.05; White & Summers, Prac. ed. § 26–2.

2. The cardinal principle of letter of credit law, the "independence principle," is codified in revised § 5–103(d). Revised § 5–104 recognizes that the day of an exclusively paper-based system of letter of credit transactions has long since passed. Comment 3 notes: "Many banking transactions, including the issuance of many letters of credit, are now conducted mostly by electronic means. * * * By declining to specify any particular medium in which the letter of credit must be established or communicated, Section 5–104 leaves room for future developments." See the definitions of "document" (revised § 5–102(a)(6)) and "record" (revised § 5–102(a)(14)).

3. The documents to be presented to the issuer of the letter of credit to obtain payment are usually accompanied by a draft drawn by the beneficiary (revised § 5–102(a)(3)) on the issuing bank (revised § 5–102(a)(9)) payable "at sight" (that is on presentment) to the order of the beneficiary. A sight draft is merely a demand for payment that may be negotiable in form, thus conferring upon the beneficiary the power to transfer the draft to a third person who may take the rights of a holder in due course. Comment 11 to revised § 5–102.

PROBLEMS

1. Paysaver Credit Union executed the following writing at the request of Wells and Titan Tool, which owed Transparent Products $33,000 on open account:

Transparent Products Corporation

Bensenville, IL 60101

RE: Thomas Wells

Gentlemen:

We hereby establish our letter of credit at the request of Thomas Wells of 1315 South 3rd Avenue, Maywood up to the aggregate amount of fifty-thousand dollars ($50,000).

Titan wanted to buy more plastics from Transparent and obtained Paysaver's issuance of the writing directed to Transparent to bolster Titan's creditworthiness. Wells is an employee of Titan who was not indebted to Transparent. It was Wells' $50,000 certificate of deposit with Paysaver that apparently persuaded Paysaver to issue this writing. Transparent ultimately declined to extend more credit to Titan and, when the latter filed in bankruptcy, Transparent demanded payment under Paysaver's "letter of credit" to defray the remaining $33,000 debt. Is the quoted writing sufficiently "definite" to be a letter of credit under revised § 5–102(a)(10); Comment 6 to revised § 5–102? If it is not, is it effective as a guaranty? A guarantor undertakes to pay the debt of another and can raise the principal debtor's defenses; the issuer of a letter of credit is primarily liable and cannot set up defenses of the applicant. The facts are based on Transparent Products Corp. v. Paysaver Credit Union, 864 F.2d 60 (7th Cir.1988). Comment 1 to § 5–

104 states: "* * * a letter of credit will typically specify the amount available, the expiration date, the place where presentation should be made, and the documents that must be presented to entitle a person to honor."

2.   What would the result be in Problem 1 if the body of the writing had said: "We hereby establish our letter of credit at the request of Thomas Wells of 1315 South 3d Avenue, Maywood up to the aggregate amount of fifty-thousand dollars ($50,000) on which Transparent Products Corporation may draw at any time within the next year by presentation of a draft payable at sight for any amount up to the credit limit?" See revised § 5–102(a)(6) ("document"), (10) ("letter of credit") and (12) ("presentation").

NOTE: REVOCABILITY OF LETTER OF CREDIT

In June 1975 Pete Beathard, a college football star of some note, signed with the Chicago Winds, of the World Football League, for a $12,000 signing bonus and $70,000 in salary for the season; big money in those days. Beathard and his agent had good reason to view the future of both Winds and the WFL with caution, and insisted that the Winds guarantee the salary payment with either an escrow of the funds or a letter of credit. The Winds chose the latter and obtained from Bank a writing entitled "Domestic Letter of Credit No. 160." It stated its purpose to be to guarantee payment for services rendered and had a December 3, 1975 expiry date, soon after the last scheduled game of the season. It authorized Beathard to draw on Bank by presenting a draft accompanied by an affidavit that the Winds had not paid Beathard. The letter of credit stated that it was subject to the UCP; the 1962 Revision was then in effect. After two games the WFL revoked the Winds' franchise, and Beathard presented his letter of credit to Bank for payment. He must have been astonished to learn that, without his knowledge or consent, the credit had been revoked. The letter of credit was silent on the issue of revocability. When Beathard sued Bank, the court held for Bank on the basis of a provision in the UCP stating that (1) all credits should clearly indicate whether they are revocable or irrevocable, and (2) in the absence of such indication the credit shall be deemed to be revocable even though an expiry date is stipulated. Beathard v. Chicago Football Club, Inc., 419 F.Supp. 1133 (N.D.Ill.1976).

Former § 5–103(1)(a) provided: "A credit may be either revocable or irrevocable." Nothing was said in the statute about what happened in a case like *Beathard* in which the letter of credit was silent on revocability. Comment 1 to former § 5–103 waffled and referred the issue to the courts for decision with only the vague standards of § 1–205 on course of dealing and usage of the trade as guidance. Several cases, citing the illusory aspects of a revocable letter of credit, sensibly read in a presumption of irrevocability in cases covered by Article 5, e.g., Data General Corp., Inc. v. Citizens National Bank, 502 F.Supp. 776 (D.Conn.1980). But the UCP left courts no room for such views.

Not until UCP 500 (1994) was a change finally made. Article 6(c) now provides that if the credit does not clearly indicate whether it is revocable or irrevocable, "the Credit shall be deemed to be irrevocable." Revised § 5–106(a) takes the same view: "A letter of credit is revocable only if it so provides." Revised § 5–106(c) states that if there is no stated expiration date in a letter of credit, it expires one year after issuance, and revised § 5–106(d) provides that if it purports to be perpetual, the credit expires five years after issuance.

D. ISSUER'S DUTY TO HONOR OR DISHONOR

1. THE STRICT COMPLIANCE RULE

So far we have sketched for you a highly efficient payment mechanism in which banks issue undertakings suitably definite and specific to constitute letters of credit and beneficiaries (whatever the state of affairs on the underlying contract) duly present the prescribed documents to issuing banks, promptly receive payment, and acquire the coveted status of a paid obligee. In this section we confront the disturbing reality that beneficiaries are not perfect and that in a very substantial percentage of all letter of credit presentations (estimated by some to run as much as 40 or 50%) some element of the presentation is, arguably at least, at variance with the terms of the credit. White & Summers, Prac.ed. § 26–9, at 165. A second reality is that issuing banks sometimes have incentive to find reasons to dishonor their own letters of credit. Letters of credit are issued for relatively small fees, and an issuing bank that has to pay a standby letter of credit must, as we shall see, look to the applicant for reimbursement to make itself whole. If the prospect of meaningful recovery from the applicant is impaired by the applicant's insolvency or bankruptcy, a prudent issuing bank may look for reasons not to pay.

In this section we examine perhaps the most litigated issue in the law of letters of credit, that is, the duty of the issuer to both the beneficiary and the applicant to honor or dishonor a presentation. The following case is a good example of the way in which the courts attempt to address the problem of a nonconforming presentation under former Article 5 which provides no clear guidance on the issue.

American Coleman Co. v. Intrawest Bank

United States Court of Appeals, Tenth Circuit, 1989.
887 F.2d 1382.

■ BARRETT, SENIOR CIRCUIT JUDGE.

* * *

In this diversity case, the American Coleman Company (American Coleman), plaintiff below, appeals from the district court's order granting summary judgment on behalf of the defendant below, Intrawest Bank of

Southglenn, N.A., the predecessor to the United Bank of Southglenn, N.A. (Bank). The court dismissed, with prejudice, American Coleman's action for damages for an alleged wrongful dishonor of a request for payment pursuant to a letter of credit.

In 1984, American Coleman sold some real property located in Littleton, Colorado, to James E. Gammon (Gammon) and the South Santa Fe Partnership (the Partnership) and took a note secured by a first deed of trust on the property. The note and deed of trust were dated November 16, 1984, but not recorded until November 21, 1984. The terms of the repayment of the note required Gammon and the Partnership to post a letter of credit, of which American Coleman would be the beneficiary. The Bank, on behalf of its customer, Gammon and Associates, established a "Clean, Irrevocable Letter of Credit" in amount of $250,000 in favor of American Coleman. It was dated February 15, 1985, and was to expire on November 15, 1986. In consideration, the Bank received from Gammon a letter of credit fee and a second deed of trust on the Littleton property under a reimbursement contract whereby Gammon was to repay Bank for all payments made by Bank to American Coleman pursuant to the letter of credit. The letter of credit arrangement, once established, is often referred to as a statutory obligation on the part of the issuer (Bank) to honor drafts drawn by the beneficiary (American Coleman) that comply with the terms of the letter of credit. The transaction is separate and independent from the underlying business transaction between the beneficiary (American Coleman) and the Bank's customer (Gammon and Associates) which is contractual in nature. * * * A letter of credit is not an evidence of indebtedness; it is merely a promise by a bank to lend money under certain circumstances. * * *

The Bank was to make funds available to American Coleman pursuant to its sight drafts to be accompanied by the "[o]riginal Letter of Credit and your signed written statement that Jim Gammon and Associates is in default on the Note and Security Agreement dated November 21, 1984, between American Coleman and Jim Gammon and Associates." * * * The above reference to a note and security agreement dated November 21, 1984, was an error, inasmuch as no such documents ever existed. The record does not resolve the dispute relative to the party responsible for the error. However, on November 16, 1984, Gammon and Associates executed and delivered to American Coleman a note in the principal sum of $1,037,500 secured by a first deed of trust on the Littleton property sold which were recorded on November 21, 1984.

Thereafter, on December 31, 1985, and on May 16, 1986, American Coleman requested payments of $75,000, respectively, under the letter of credit. Both of these requests included the original letter of credit and the specific default language previously referred to, i.e., "Jim Gammon and Associates is in default on the Note and Security Agreement dated November 21, 1984, between American Coleman and Jim Gammon and Associates." Thus, a balance of $100,000 remained available to be drawn on under the letter of credit when on November 13, 1986, American Coleman tendered to Bank a sight draft in amount of $100,000 with the following statement appended thereto:

> [T]he American Coleman Company informs you that Jim Gammon and Associates is in default on the Note and Security Agreement dated November 21, 1984, and the Promissory Note dated November 16, 1984, between American Coleman and Jim Gammon and Associates.

Bank formally dishonored the draft on November 17, 1986, two days after the letter of credit expired because (1) the amount requested was in advance of any default, and (2) no default could occur until November 16, 1986. Bank did not give as a reason for dishonor the fact that the wording of American Coleman's request was not in strict compliance with the terms of the letter of credit.

In the district court, both parties moved for summary judgment, agreeing that there was no genuine dispute of material fact relative to Bank's liability for its dishonor of American Coleman's request of November 13, 1986, for the balance of funds under the letter of credit. Bank contended that the fact that the note was not then in default constituted a valid ground for dishonor and, further, that dishonor was proper because American Coleman's request was not in strict compliance with the terms of the letter of credit. American Coleman argued that Bank should be estopped from raising the defense of strict compliance because Bank had not asserted this defense at the time of dishonor. Further, should Bank not be estopped, American Coleman contended that its request for funds was in strict compliance with the terms of the letter of credit. In considering the cross-motions for summary judgment, the district court relied upon the pleadings, the briefs, affidavits and other documentation.

The district court found/concluded that Bank was not estopped from raising the defense of strict compliance and that American Coleman's request of November 13, 1986, was not in strict compliance with the terms of the letter of credit. The court did not reach the issue whether the original reason given by the Bank, i.e., that the note was not yet in default, was a valid ground for dishonor.

On appeal, American Coleman contends that the district court's decision was erroneous, contrary to law, and an abuse of discretion in the court's holdings that: (1) the note was not yet in default, (2) the demand was not in strict compliance, technically or literally, with the terms of the letter of credit, (3) the Bank was not estopped from raising lack of strict compliance as a reason for dishonor, and (4) the beneficiary (American Coleman) was not misled, and could not have cured the defect because Bank was allowed, pursuant to § 5–112(1)(a), to defer payment or dishonor for three banking days.

* * *

I.

American Coleman argues that the district court was clearly erroneous in finding/concluding that the Note of November 16, 1984, was not yet in default when the November 13, 1986, demand for payment was made by American Coleman upon Bank. The record shows, however, that the district court made no such finding.

It is true that after the draft of November 13, 1986, was submitted Bank did inform American Coleman that it would not fund the letter of credit because the Note was not in default and could not be in default until November 16, 1986. Because this was the only ground relied upon by Bank to dishonor the draft, American Coleman argued, unsuccessfully, that Bank should be estopped from raising the defense of strict compliance in the district court action because it failed to assert the issue of nonconformity at the time it dishonored the draft.

The district court plainly did not find/conclude that the Note of December 16, 1984, was in default. In the district court's Memorandum Opinion and Order of December 17, 1987, the court stated:

> Since I conclude that the bank is not estopped from raising the defense of strict compliance, and since I further find that American Coleman's request for funds was not in strict compliance with the terms and conditions of the letter of credit, I need not reach the issue of whether the original reason given by the bank (that the note was not yet in default) was a valid ground for dishonor.

II.

American Coleman contends that the district court erred in holding that the doctrine of strict compliance required American Coleman, as beneficiary of the letter of credit from Bank, as issuer, to literally and technically adhere to the requirements of the letter of credit. The district court found/concluded:

> In the present case, it is clear that American Coleman's request for payment presented November 13, 1986 was not in technical or literal compliance with the terms of the letter of credit. American Coleman's reference to two different notes could easily have caused the bank's documents examiner some confusion. Accordingly, because I conclude that the rule of strict compliance, as it is applied in Colorado, requires literal compliance with the terms and requirements set forth in the letter of credit, and there was no such literal compliance in this case
> * * *.

The district court recognized that many courts refuse to allow an issuing bank to dishonor a demand for payment when the nonconformity between the language contained in the draft or demand and the terms contained in the letter of credit is trivial or technical. The court observed that the Colorado Supreme Court has not as yet ruled on the distinction between traditional strict compliance versus substantial compliance, and particularly so where the deviation is "[a]s minor and technical as in this case." Even so, based upon Colorado National Bank v. Board of County Commissioners, 634 P.2d 32, 40 (Colo.1981) ("To maintain the commercial vitality of the letter of credit device, strict compliance with the terms of the letter of credit is required"); Guilford Pattern Works, Inc. v. United Bank of Boulder, 655 F.Supp. 378, 379–80 (D.Colo.1987) ("Colorado courts have held that in order to maintain the commercial validity of the vehicle of letters of credit, strict compliance with the terms and conditions is necessary."), and other cases and authorities, the district court reasoned that the Colorado Supreme Court "[w]ould shun the non-standard of substantial compliance and would require literal and technical adherence to the requirements of the letter of credit." We agree.

§ 5–114(1) provides:

> An issuer must honor a draft or demand for payment which complies with the terms of the relevant credit, regardless of whether the goods or documents conform to the underlying contract for sale or other contract between the customer and the beneficiary. The issuer is not excused from honor of such a draft or demand by reason of an additional general term that all documents must be satisfactory to the issuer, but an issuer may require that specified documents must be satisfactory to it.

In Raiffeisen–Zentralkasse Tirol v. First National Bank, 671 P.2d 1008 (Colo.App.1983), the court held that the obligation of the issuer of a letter of credit to honor the letter is wholly separate from the beneficiary's compliance with the terms of the underlying contract and is dependent solely on the terms and conditions contained in the letter of credit. This separation is supportive of the rule laid down in Colorado National Bank v. Board of County Commissioners, supra, that strict compliance with the terms of a letter of credit is required to maintain the commercial vitality of the letter of credit device. Failure on the part of Bank to oversee careful compliance with the terms of the letter of credit would have prohibited Bank from collecting the funds paid to the beneficiary (American Coleman) from its customer, the Partnership (Jim Gammon and Associates). * * * The duty of the issuing Bank is ministerial in nature, confined to checking the presented documents carefully against what the letter of credit requires. * * *

The district court found that the language in American Coleman's draft of November 13, 1986, referring to "[T]he Note and Security Agreement dated November 21, 1984, *and the Promissory Note dated November 16, 1984,* between American Coleman and Jim Gammon and Associates" was not in strict compliance because of the extra language that was included. We agree.

It has been observed that most courts apply the "strict compliance" standard which leaves "no room for documents which are almost the same or which will do just as well." A minority of the courts hold that a beneficiary's "reasonable" or "substantial" performance of the letter of credit's requirement will do. However, no matter how one reads the cases, strict compliance endures as the central test. White & Summers, Uniform Commercial Code, Third Edition (1988), Vol. 2, § 19–5, p. 31. The authors state that cases applying the "reasonable" or "substantial" compliance standard "[a]re so few and their notion so inherently fuzzy that they give little or no clue as to what might be 'reasonable' or 'substantial' compliance.''

While it is apparent from the cases that minute discrepancies which could not possibly mislead a document examiner are usually disregarded, this does not constitute a retreat from the strict compliance standard applicable in this case inasmuch as the district court found that "[A]merican Coleman's reference to two different notes could easily have caused the bank's documents examiner some confusion." We agree.

We hold that the district court did not err in applying the strict compliance standard. We reject American Coleman's argument that reference in the November 13, 1986, draft to the second note was mere "surplusage." The apparent existence of two promissory notes supports the district court's finding that Bank could have been misled by American Coleman's November 13, 1986, draft. American Coleman's contention that Bank could not have been misled by the draft because Bank drafted the letter of credit is without support in this record. The deposition testimony of American Coleman representative Joseph E. McElroy demonstrates that American Coleman's attorney assisted in drafting the letter of credit. There is no other evidence in the record on appeal relative thereto.

III.

American Coleman contends that the district court was clearly erroneous in holding that Bank was not estopped from raising the defense of lack of strict compliance as a reason for its dishonor of the November 13, 1986, draft.

The district court recognized that in Colorado the general rule is that "[w]hen an issuer of a letter of credit formally places its refusal to pay upon specified grounds, it is held to have waived all other grounds," quoting from Colorado National Bank v. Board of County Commissioners, 634 P.2d 32, 41 (Colo.1981). However, the district court relied upon that same case for the proposition that the waiver-estoppel rule "[i]s limited to situations where the statements have misled the beneficiary who would have cured the defect but relied on the stated grounds to its injury."

The district court relied on Colorado National Bank v. Board of County Commissioners, supra, for its ruling that Bank was not estopped from raising a ground for dishonor in defense of suit brought by American Coleman even though it failed to state such ground at the time of dishonor.

In Colorado National Bank v. Board of County Commissioners, the letter of credit provided for a 15–day sight draft. However, the beneficiary submitted a demand draft on the day the letter of credit was to expire. Bank gave several reasons for dishonor, but did not rely upon the fact that the beneficiary had presented a demand draft in lieu of the required 15–day sight draft. Even so, the court held that the bank was not estopped from raising this ground in defense of the suit because the non-conforming demand draft was presented on the same day that the letter of credit expired. The court observed that under § 5–112(1)(a) a bank called upon to honor a draft or demand for payment under a letter of credit may defer payment or dishonor until the close of the third banking day following receipt of the documents. Thus, the court reasoned that the beneficiary could not have cured the defect since any subsequent presentment would have been untimely. Accordingly, the beneficiary could not have detrimentally relied on the bank's failure to state the discrepancy as a ground for dishonor.

We agree with the district court's conclusion that the facts of the instant case are quite similar to those in *Colorado National* and that American Coleman cannot be said to have detrimentally relied on Bank's failure to state the strict compliance discrepancy as one ground for dishonor, and that Bank is not estopped from raising the doctrine of strict compliance in its defense. November 13, 1986, was a Thursday. Three banking days thereafter would extend to November 18, 1986, just one day after Bank gave formal notice of dishonor. American Coleman could not have submitted another draft before the note expired. § 5–112(1) provides, in pertinent part:

> A bank to which a documentary draft or demand for payment is presented under a credit may without dishonor of the draft, demand or credit (a) defer honor until the close of the third banking day following receipt of the documents * * *.

American Coleman insists that the letter of credit in this case is clearly denominated a "clean" letter of credit as distinguished from a "documentary" letter of credit and that, accordingly, the three-banking-day rule does not apply. We agree that this statute applies only to a documentary draft or demand for payment. We disagree with American Coleman's contention that simply because the letter of credit here was denominated "Clean Irrevocable Letter of Credit", it was treated by the parties as such.

§ 5–103(1)(b) defines a "documentary draft" or a "documentary demand for payment" as one honor of which is conditioned upon the presentation of a document or documents. "Document" is defined therein as any paper, including invoice, certificate, notice of default, and the like. In the case at bar, American Coleman was required under the terms of the letter of credit to present the original letter of credit (a document) and a notice of default (a document) with each draft. American Coleman's effort to restrict the definition of "documentary draft" to documents of title or shipping invoices must fail.

We AFFIRM.

NOTES

1.   The plight of the issuing bank is described by Albert J. Givray, Letters of Credit, 44 Bus.Law. 1567, 1589 (1989):

> Consider the letter of credit department in a large bank. When the presented documents arrive, they are routed to an examining clerk. He pulls the related letter of credit from the bank's files and lays it next to

the presented documents. He compares these documents against the letter's requirements and decides whether compliance has occurred. This happens daily for many sets of documents. Some are presented against a commercial letter, others against a standby. Yet the routine stays the same. It must move along steadily.

Each time, the examiner has only the letter's words and the face of the presented documents to go by. Much may be going on outside these papers. For example, a presented certificate may swear customer's default even though such default is being honestly disputed. Or a bill of lading may show goods loaded on a ship that later sank in a storm. Or perhaps some practice in customer's or beneficiary's industry shades the meaning of a presented document and none of the papers before the examiner explain such practice. The document examiner is ill-equipped to deal with outside events like these. He has no lawyer by his side. He will probably have little or no command of any industry practice not within banking spheres. Nor can he afford the expense, risk, and delay of any elaborate reasoning as he checks the presented papers against the letter's requirements. For the letter of credit to work quickly as a cheap and sure device, then, the examiner must disregard outside influences like these as he routinely asks, "From what appears on their face, do the presented documents meet all the letter's requirements?"

2. Former Article 5 takes no explicit position on the strict/substantial compliance dispute. As indicated in *American Coleman*, most decisions embrace the strict construction rule, but the extent to which the strict construction rule requires literal compliance is the subject of much dispute. Revised Article 5 expressly adopts the strict compliance rule in revised § 5–108(a) as governing the issuer's obligation to both the beneficiary and the applicant. In determining whether the documents presented meet the requirements of this rule, revised § 5–108(e) states that "An issuer shall observe standard practice of financial institutions that regularly issue letters of credit. Determination of the issuer's observance of the standard practice is a matter of interpretation for the court." Comment 1 explains: "Strict compliance does not mean slavish conformity to the terms of the letter of credit. * * * By adopting standard practice as a way of measuring strict compliance, this article indorses the conclusion of the court in * * *" certain enumerated cases which do not require literal, technical adherence to the requirements of the letter of credit. Article 5's adoption of "standard practice" as determining the level of compliance conforms to UCP 500 Art. 13(a) which relies on "international standard banking practice." Comment 8 to revised § 5–108 discusses the intended meaning of "standard prac-tice." Revised § 5–108(e) makes the question of whether the issuer has observed standard practice one for the court and not a jury. Comment 1 explains, "* * * it is hoped that there will be more consistency in the outcomes and speedier resolution of disputes if the responsibility for determining the nature and scope of standard practice is granted to the court, not to a jury." Does this unconstitutionally deprive the parties of a jury trial? Compare §§ 2–302 and 4A–202(c) which use a similar approach.

The strict compliance rule and related issues are extensively discussed in Clark & Clark, Bank Deposits, etc. ¶ 10.05; Dolan, Letters of Credit Chapter 6; and White & Summers, Prac.ed. § 26–6.

3. Will revised § 5–108(a) and (e) advance the cause of certainty in letter of credit law? Accepting Comment 1's statement that strict compliance does not mean "slavish conformity," how should *American Coleman* be decided under revised § 5–108? In that case the triggering event for the bank's obligation to pay was presentation to the bank of a sight draft accompanied by a written statement by the beneficiary that the "Note and Security Agreement dated November 21, 1984" were in default. Even though there was no such note, the beneficiary's statement contained the required representation. Out of an abundance of caution and because of its unease about representing that the customers were in default on a nonexistent note, the beneficiary added the fatal words "and the Promissory Note dated November 16, 1984," which described the true note on which the customers were actually in default. In one of the cases expressly approved in Comment 1 to revised § 5–108, New Braunfels National Bank v. Odiorne, 780 S.W.2d 313 (Tex.App.1989), the correct letter of credit number was 86–122–S but the request for payment listed it as 86–122–5. The court held that the bank's dishonor was wrongful and observed that strict compliance meant "something less than absolute, perfect compliance." Did the *American Coleman* court demand absolute, perfect compliance?

4. Does the strict compliance rule enhance the reliability of letters of credit as payment mechanisms or does it encourage an issuing bank to find a minor defect in the documents in cases in which the bank doesn't want to pay, such as cases in which the applicant has gone into bankruptcy and reimbursement of the bank's claim against the applicant may be difficult? An "Editors' Note" in 41 UCC Rep.Serv. 921 (1985) quotes the following: "In their article, 'Strict Compliance Seen Deterring Reliability of Letters of Credit' New York Law Journal, Sept. 10, 1985, p.1, Messrs. Franz S. Leichter and Stephen M. Harnik question whether the decisions in [Bank of Cochin Ltd. v. Manufacturers Hanover Trust Co., 41 UCC Rep.Serv. 920, 612 F.Supp. 1533 (S.D.N.Y.1985)] and in Beyene v. Irving Trust Co., 40 UCC Rep. 1811, 762 F.2d 4 (2d Cir.1985) 'enhance the reliability of letters of credit as payment mechanisms—which is the stated purpose of the rule of strict compliance.' In their view, 'when technicalities are used as they were in Beyene and Cochin they permit the opener of the letter of credit to convert it from an irrevocable method of payment into a contract revocable at will.' Technical discrepancies in documentation are unavoidable, they say, and the courts should place greater responsibility on banks to review the terms of the letter of credit for 'commercial sense' in determining whether documents presented meet these terms. P.6." Professor White is notably unmoved by such arguments and states, without remorse, "the issuer may examine the documents microscopically and may assert small discrepancies to excuse its duty to pay." White & Summers, Prac.ed. § 26–5 at 141.

5. Under revised § 5–108(a), an issuing bank must honor a conforming presentation. Must it dishonor a nonconforming presentation? Suppose in the case of questionable documentation like that in *American Coleman*, the bank called the applicant and asked its consent to the bank's payment of the credit. If the applicant gave its consent, (1) may the bank safely pay the credit? (2) may it safely decline to pay the credit? Section 5–108(a) and Comment 7. Does the issuer have a duty to seek a waiver from the applicant in the case of a nonconforming presentation? Comment 2 to § 5–108.

6. Matter of Coral Petroleum, Inc., 878 F.2d 830 (5th Cir.1989), presented the issue of whether impossibility excuses strict compliance with a letter of credit. Seller sold Buyer 31,000 barrels of West Texas Intermediate crude oil for $880,400 and required Buyer to obtain a standby letter of credit in a form acceptable to Seller for the price. Bank issued the letter of credit under Buyer's instructions that the credit would be payable upon receipt of certain documents including (1) a statement by Seller that West Texas Intermediate oil had been delivered to Buyer and (2) a copy of the shipper's transfer order showing transfer to Buyer of 31,000 barrels of "WTNM SO or SR." Buyer's instructions were mistaken. West Texas Intermediate crude is a sweet oil (meaning not containing certain undesirable elements found in sour oil), but WTNM SO or SR refers to sour oil. Thus, the letter of credit required two documents that were contradictory: a shipper's order showing transfer of sour oil to Buyer and a statement that sweet oil had been delivered to Buyer. After Buyer filed in bankruptcy under Chapter 11, Seller demanded payment under the letter of credit. Bank refused to pay because Seller's demand was accompanied by a shipper's order showing transfer of sweet oil to Buyer. Seller had inspected the letter of credit before accepting it and did not ask that the erroneous description be corrected. Seller argued that the terms of the credit were impossible to perform. Seller could not deliver sweet oil to Buyer and procure a shipper's transfer order showing that sour oil had been delivered. Seller also argued that the letter of credit was ambiguous and the ambiguity should be construed against Bank. The court held that the letter of credit was not ambiguous. The fact that it was impossible for Seller to comply did not excuse compliance by Seller. Bank is not required to know the meaning of technical trade terms used in the letter of credit. Moreover, Seller was negligent in accepting a letter of credit with requirements that could not be met. Accord: First State Bank v. Diamond Plastics Corp., 891 P.2d 1262 (Okl.1995). In Albert J. Givray, Letters of Credit, 45 Bus.Law. 2381, 2404 (1990), it is suggested that issuers add a conspicuous legend stating "Please examine this letter of credit at once. If you feel unable to meet any of its requirements, either singly or together, please contact customer immediately to see if the letter of credit can be amended. Otherwise, you risk losing payment under this letter of credit for failure to comply strictly with its terms as written."

2. NOTICE OF DISCREPANCIES, WAIVER AND ESTOPPEL

The opinion in *American Coleman* demonstrates some of the major differences between former Article 5 and the UCP.

Former Article 5. There is no express requirement in former Article 5 that an issuer who dishonors because of discrepancies in the beneficiary's presentation must make timely disclosure of what the discrepancies are. But common law doctrines of waiver and estoppel have been invoked to ameliorate the strict compliance rule in such cases. *American Coleman* is an example of this. There the issuer gave the beneficiary two grounds for its dishonor but later relied on another ground that it had not disclosed. The court conceded that the law of Colorado was that if the issuer had placed its refusal to pay on certain grounds it had waived all other grounds. Courts tend to mix waiver and estoppel together in such cases; the *American Coleman* court refers to the "waiver-estoppel" rule. But if the beneficiary is relying on estoppel it must show detrimental reliance, and in *American Coleman* this could not be shown. Since the issuer had three days in which to decide whether to dishonor under former § 5–112(1), it was within its rights to dishonor on November 17, two days after the credit had expired. The beneficiary could show no detrimental reliance because had the issuer stated the correct discrepancy the beneficiary would not have had time to cure the defect by making a new presentation.

UCP provisions. There are major differences between former Article 5 and the UCP with respect to (1) the time period accorded the issuer in which to decide whether to honor, and (2), in the case of dishonor, the duty of the issuer to specify the discrepancies in the presentation. As stated above, former § 5–112(1) gave an issuer three banking days after receipt of the documents to honor but did not require the issuer to state the reasons for dishonor. Before UCP 500, the UCP contained the provisions set out in *Esso* below which allowed the issuer a reasonable time to examine the documents and decide whether to honor but, in cases of dishonor, required the issuer to specify the reasons for dishonor "without delay." UCP 500 Art. 13(b) allows the issuer a reasonable time, not to exceed seven banking days following the day of receipt of the documents, to examine the documents and determine whether to honor. If the issuer dishonors it must give notice of the discrepancies in the presentation by expeditious means and without delay but no later than the close of the seventh banking day following the day of receipt of the documents. Art. 14(d).

Revised Article 5. The revised version of Article 5 has adopted the UCP approach. Revised § 5–108(b) gives the issuer "a reasonable time after presentation, but not beyond the end of the seventh business day of the issuer after the day of its receipt of the documents" either to honor or, if it dishonors, to give notice to the presenter of discrepancies in the presentation. Failure to act within the time permitted by § 5–108(b) constitutes dishonor by the issuer. Comment 2 to revised § 5–108. The issue of what is a "reasonable time" to decide whether to honor or give notice of discrepancies has been a troublesome one for courts construing the UCP. As *American Coleman* indicates, courts under former Article 5 have usually treated the three-day period prescribed in § 5–112(1) as a safe harbor; notice of dishonor given by the end of the period is effective, even if a decision to dishonor had been made at the beginning of the period. White & Summers, Prac.ed. § 26–9(c). Comment 2 reminds us that the seven-day period prescribed by revised § 5–108(b) is not a safe harbor: the issuer must act within a reasonable period, but no later than the end of the seven-day period. Thus under revised Article 5 the courts will have to wrestle with the same issues concerning the time for giving notice of discrepancies as the courts dealing with the UCP. The following UCP case discusses these matters.

Esso Petroleum Canada v. Security Pacific Bank

United States District Court, D. Oregon, 1989.
710 F.Supp. 275.

■ FRYE, DISTRICT JUDGE:

The matters before the court are the motion for summary judgment (# 45) of defendant, The Oregon Bank (the Bank), on all claims brought by plaintiff, Esso Petroleum Canada (Esso), and Esso's motion for partial summary judgment on its first and third claims for relief (#).

Esso alleges that the Bank wrongfully dishonored its irrevocable stand-by letter of credit by failing to specify the discrepancies which caused the Bank to reject the documents submitted by Esso or to notify Esso of the discrepancies in a timely fashion.

UNDISPUTED FACTS

Esso is a division of Imperial Oil Limited, a company organized and existing under the laws of Canada, with its principal place of business in Toronto, Canada. The Bank, presently known as Security Pacific Bank, is a banking corporation organized and existing under the laws of the State of Oregon.

Prior to October 22, 1987, Esso entered into a contract with Valley Oil Co., Inc. (Valley Oil) to sell to Valley Oil amounts of aviation gasoline for a total purchase price of $1,196,580. As a condition of sale, Esso required Valley Oil to obtain a standby letter of credit naming Esso as the beneficiary. As a condition to issuing the standby letter of credit, the Bank required Valley Oil to obtain a backup letter of credit from Western Pioneer, Inc., dba Delta Western (Delta), Valley Oil's customer. On October 21, 1987, Delta transferred by wire $1,288,140 to the Bank for deposit to Valley Oil's account.

On October 22, 1987, the Bank executed and delivered to Esso an irrevocable standby letter of credit, a copy of which is attached as Exhibit "A." On November 1, 1987, Esso delivered the aviation fuel to Delta.

The letter of credit issued by the Bank to Esso on October 22, 1987 provides that it is subject to the Uniform Customs and Practice for Documentary Credits (1983 Revision) International Chamber of Commerce (Publication 400) (the UCP). Article 48 of the UCP provides that letters of credit expiring on a day on which the issuing bank is not open for business do not expire until the end of the following day on which the bank is open for business. Therefore, since November 15, 1987 fell on a Sunday, the letter of credit did not expire until Monday, November 16, 1987.

At approximately 1:00 p.m. on Friday, November 13, 1987, Esso presented its draft for $1,218,116.90, drawn on the Bank under the letter of credit, and documents fulfilling the terms and conditions of the letter of credit. Esso demanded immediate payment.

At 5:15 p.m. on Friday, November 13, 1987, the Bank informed Esso that it would not honor Esso's draft and demand for payment due to certain discrepancies. In a Memorandum for Credit Files dated November 16, 1987, Fred Hammack, commercial loan officer for the Bank, states that although Fulvio Santin, supervisor for foreign crude oil supply and scheduling for Esso, demanded a list of these discrepancies on November 13, 1987, the Bank did not inform Esso of them at that time. This memorandum reads as follows:

"On 11/13/87 at approximately 5:15 pm, I informed Mr. Santin that the Bank had uncovered discrepancies in the documents and would give to him by 9:00 am on 11/16/87 a written response stating what these discrepancies were.

"Mr. Santin asked me if I could tell him what those discrepancies were. I told Mr. Santin and the other representatives that the discrepancies involved the supporting documents but that I could not give him specifics since it was the obligation of the International Banking Department who is responsible for the review process to give the written response. I further stated that this response per Bank policy must be signed by the Head of the International Banking Department. He would be back in his office by 7:30 on 11/16/87 and would be available to sign the letter in order to meet the 9:00 am delivery time. The Head of the International Banking Department was not in the office today."

In a deposition dated August 30, 1988, Hammack states that on behalf of the Bank he informed Esso's representatives on November 13, 1987 that they would have to wait for a written response by the Bank to discover the discrepancies in the documents they had submitted to the Bank on that date. The relevant portion of this deposition states:

"Q What was their response?

"A They wanted to know what the discrepancies were.

"Q What was your response?

"A I said, I did not know.

"Q What did they say?

"A They implored me again about the discrepancies, and if they could talk, I believe, to someone upstairs.

"Q What was your response?

"A My response was they had to wait for the written response by the bank.

"Q Did that satisfy them?

"A I think the conversation ended, I don't think it satisfied them."

The Bank sent Esso a list of the discrepancies in a letter dated Monday, November 16, 1987. This letter stated that Esso's draft under the letter of credit:

"remains unpaid due to the following discrepancies:

—Invoice does not show beneficiary as stated in Letter of Credit.

—Merchandise description on invoice not per Letter of Credit.

—Applicant name and address on invoice not per Letter of Credit.

—Documentary requirement number 2 as stated in the Letter of Credit not presented."

On November 16, 1987, Esso attempted to correct these discrepancies and again presented its draft for $1,218,116.90 drawn on the Bank under the letter of credit demanding immediate payment. The Bank again refused to honor Esso's draft on the grounds of uncorrected discrepancies.

On January 20, 1988, various creditors of Valley Oil filed a petition in the United States Bankruptcy Court for the District of Oregon, naming Valley Oil as the debtor.

On February 10, 1988, Esso filed this action against the Bank seeking money damages in the amount of $1,218,116.90 plus interest, $935,000 in punitive damages, and costs incurred in this action.

The second amended complaint states several claims for relief in contract, equity and tort. The contract and equity claims are as follows:

(1) that the Bank wrongfully dishonored its irrevocable standby letter of credit;

(2) that the Bank failed to specify the discrepancies which caused it to reject the draft and documents submitted by Esso;

(3) that the Bank failed to notify Esso of the discrepancies in a timely fashion;

(4) that the Bank wrongfully set off amounts owed to it by Valley Oil against funds from the special deposit made by Delta;

(5) that the Bank's conduct in this matter amounted to a waiver of its opportunity to claim that the alleged discrepancies were not in accordance with the letter of credit; and

(6) that the Bank's conduct estops it from asserting the alleged discrepancies as a defense in this action.

Esso also seeks punitive damages on the grounds that the Bank tortiously breached its obligation to deal in good faith by wrongfully, deliberately, or recklessly disregarding Esso's rights under the letter of credit.

* * *

DISCUSSION

I.   Dishonor of Letter of Credit—(Claims for Relief 1, 2, 3, 5, 6 and 7).

Esso alleges that the Bank wrongfully dishonored the Bank's irrevocable standby letter of credit when Esso properly presented Esso's draft drawn on the Bank under the letter of credit for payment. Esso contends that Article 16(e) of the UCP precludes a bank from dishonoring the letter of credit once the Bank failed to timely notify Esso of the specific discrepancies on November 13, 1987.

The Bank responds that it properly dishonored the letter of credit on both November 13, 1987 and on November 16, 1987 because the documents presented by Esso on those dates contained numerous discrepancies. In addition, the Bank contends that the letter of credit is subject to the Oregon Commercial Code, arguing that the Bank gave Esso sufficient and timely notice of the discrepancies under O.R.S. 75.1120, which grants banks three days to determine whether to dishonor letters of credit.

Both parties concede that they are bound by the UCP. Article 16 of the UCP provides, in pertinent part, that:

"c. The issuing bank shall have a reasonable time in which to examine the documents and to determine ... whether to take up or to refuse the documents.

"d. If the issuing bank decides to refuse the documents, it must give notice to that effect without delay by telecommunication or, if that is not possible, by other expeditious means, to the bank from which it received the documents (the remitting bank), or to the beneficiary, if it received the documents directly from him. *Such notice must state the discrepancies in respect of which the issuing bank refuses the documents and must also state whether it is holding the documents at the disposal of, or is returning them to the presentor (remitting bank or the beneficiary, as the case may be).* The issuing bank shall then be entitled to claim from the remitting bank refund of any reimbursement which may have been made to that bank.

"e. If the issuing bank fails to act in accordance with the provisions of paragraphs (c) and (d) of this article and/or fails to hold the documents at the disposal of, or to return them to, the presentor, the issuing bank shall be precluded from claiming that the documents are not in accordance with the terms and conditions of the credit."

UCP Article 16(c)-(e) (emphasis added).

The issue is not whether the Bank had cause to reject the documents presented by Esso, but whether, once the Bank made its decision to reject those documents, it properly notified Esso of its decision by specifying the alleged discrepancies in accordance with Article 16(d).

In Bank of Cochin v. Manufacturers Hanover Trust Co., 808 F.2d 209 (2d Cir.1986), the Second Circuit held that an issuing bank was estopped under the UCP from asserting the confirming bank's noncompliance with the terms of a letter of credit where the issuing bank delayed twelve to thirteen days in notifying the confirming bank of specific defects in the presented documents and of its intent to return those documents. The court stated that "'[w]ithout delay' is defined neither in Article 8 nor in any case law dealing with international letters of credit. However, the phrase is akin to 'immediate (at once), instant, instantaneous, instantly, prompt.' W. Burton, Legal Thesaurus 1053 (1980). All of these synonyms connote a sense of urgent action within the shortest interval of time possible." Id. at 213.

In Datapoint Corp. v. M & I Bank, 665 F.Supp. 722 (W.D.Wis.1987), the United States District Court held that a bank was precluded from claiming that a draft varied from the terms of the letter of credit where it failed to notify the beneficiary of the dishonor by telecommunication or other expeditious means. The court found that "[u]nder the provisions of the Uniform Customs and Practice, incorporated by the Letter of Credit, once defendant decided to refuse the Original Draft, it was obligated to notify plaintiff to that effect without delay by telecommunication or, if that was impossible, by other expeditious means." Id. at 727.

In the present action, Esso presented its draft for $1,218,116.90, drawn on the Bank under the letter of credit, at 1:00 p.m. on November 13, 1987. The Bank notified Esso of its decision to dishonor the letter of credit by 5:15 p.m. that afternoon. Under Article 16(d) of the UCP, the Bank was required to state the discrepancies in respect of which it refused the documents at the time it notified Esso of its refusal to honor the letter of credit. Since the Bank's notice did not state these discrepancies at that time, under UCP Article 16(e), the Bank is now precluded from claiming that the documents were not in accordance with the terms and conditions of credit. Esso is, therefore, entitled to collect funds from the Bank under the terms of the letter of credit.

Esso's motion for partial summary judgment on its first and third claims for relief is granted. Since the court has granted Esso summary judgment under its claim of wrongful dishonor of the letter of credit, it need not address Esso's equitable claim for money had and received.

* * *

NOTE

How would this case be decided under revised § 5–108? Comments 2 and 4 to revised § 5–108. In Rhode Island Hospital Trust Nat. Bank v. Eastern General Contractors, Inc., 674 A.2d 1227 (R.I.1996), a UCP case, the beneficiary made presentation on Thursday, September 26, 1985. On Friday, September 27, the bank did not open for business owing to Hurricane Gloria. Monday, September 30 was the expiry date. On Tuesday, October 1, the bank notified the beneficiary of certain discrepancies and stated that it would hold the documents for beneficiary's disposal. The court concluded that the trial court erred in directing a verdict for the bank. Expert testimony was to the effect that the bank did not act within a reasonable time; if the date of receipt of the presentation to the issuing bank is close to the expiry date of the credit, common banking procedure was to act expeditiously, presumably so that any discrepancy could be cured before expiration of the credit.

PROBLEM

Over the period of a year, Beneficiary presented three drafts for payment to Issuer. Each presentation contained the same discrepancy. The first two times Issuer paid the draft without objection after receiving permission of the Applicant to pay despite the nonconformity. The third time Applicant refused to consent to payment and Issuer dishonored the draft on the ground that the presentation was nonconforming. Has Issuer wrongfully dishonored? Comments 3 and 7 to § 5–108. White & Summers, Prac.ed. § 26–9(a).

3. ISSUER'S RIGHT TO REIMBURSEMENT AND OTHER REMEDIES

a. REIMBURSEMENT

Each letter of credit transaction usually involves three undertakings: the underlying agreement between the applicant and the beneficiary; the issuer's undertaking to honor upon a presentation made pursuant to the letter of credit; and the applicant's agreement to reimburse the issuer if payment is made. Revised § 5–108(i) arms the issuer with a statutory right of reimbursement against the applicant.

The credit risk that an issuer takes with respect to payment of a letter of credit depends on whether the transaction involves a commercial or a standby letter of credit. Commercial letters of credit are payment mechanisms and are meant to be paid in every case, usually upon presentation of the seller-beneficiary's bill of lading covering the goods sold to the buyer-applicant. When the issuer has paid, it receives possession of the bill of lading which the applicant must obtain from the issuer in order to receive the goods from the carrier that issued the bill of lading. Revised § 5–108(i)(2). The issuer can secure its claim for reimbursement by holding the bill of lading until the applicant either pays or arranges for credit.

A standby letter of credit functions as a guaranty and is usually meant to be paid only in case of the applicant's failure to perform the underlying contract. When the issuer pays a standby letter of credit, it receives no bill of lading or like document that can be used to induce the applicant to pay. Functionally, a letter of credit is a conditional loan made to the applicant by the issuer, and issuing banks treat it as such. Since it is a loan that will usually not have to be funded unless the applicant is in financial difficulty, as when the applicant is in bankruptcy, the statutory reimbursement right under revised § 5–108(i) is invariably supplemented with a express reimbursement agreement between the issuer and applicant containing the usual terms of commercial loans with respect to security, interest rates, set-off, and the like.

As we have said before, if obligees are able to obtain standby letters of credit from their obligors, they are in a position far superior to that of secured parties under Article 9. Upon default by their obligor, they can go to the issuing bank and obtain prompt payment of the obligation. They do not need to engage in the expensive and time-consuming exercise of collecting the debt by repossessing and foreclosing on collateral, with all the attendant problems that we raised in the preceding chapters of this book, problems that are exacerbated by the obligor's bankruptcy. If no rational obligee would take a security interest in preference to a standby letter of credit, does this mean the death of security interests? Not at all; it merely changes the identity of the secured party from the obligee to the bank issuing the letter of credit. Unless the applicant is a customer who could borrow money on unsecured credit, banks will usually not issue standby letters of credit without receiving a security interest in the applicant's property. Efficiencies flowing from this tripartite arrangement have con- tributed to the great popularity of standby letters of credit. The credit worthiness of the obligor is determined by the bank, a professional credit grantor, rather than by the obligee who may be a seller of goods, a centerfielder, or others who are not in the business of credit granting. In this respect, the efficiency of the standby letter of credit resembles that present in the consumer bank credit card transaction. Retail stores, hotels, restaurants and others who sell goods and services can rely on a credit card issued by a bank that will guarantee payment on transactions made pursuant to the card; they don't need to maintain credit departments making costly credit evaluations of their customers. Banks will make the determination of the consumer's creditworthiness in deciding whether to issue the credit card.

b.   STANDARD OF COMPLIANCE

Under revised § 5–108(i), an issuer is entitled to reimbursement from the applicant only if it "has honored a presentation as permitted or required by this article." Under revised § 5–108(a) an issuer must dishonor a presentation that does not strictly comply with the terms of the letter of credit. Comment 1 says "The standard of strict compliance governs the issuer's obligation to the beneficiary and to the applicant." The view adopted by revised Article 5 that an issuing bank which pays on a presentation that does not strictly comply with the terms of the letter of credit cannot receive reimbursement from the applicant was rejected by some cases under the old law which applied a "bifurcated" standard of compliance. This approach applied a strict compliance standard for the issuer's liability to the beneficiary for wrongful dishonor but a substantial compliance standard for the issuer's liability to the applicant for wrongful honor. The bifurcation view was thought to be justified by an appreciation of the difficulty an issuing bank experiences in a case in which the applicant is demanding that the bank dishonor while the beneficiary is threatening suit if the bank does not pay.

In rejecting the bifurcated approach, revised Article 5 takes the realistic position that institutions issuing letters of credit, usually commercial banks, are sophisticated parties which are eminently capable of looking out for themselves. Revised § 5–108(a) recognizes that an issuing bank can safely pay on a noncomplying presentation if the applicant will waive the discrepancy and consent to the payment. But what if the bank is uncertain about whether there is a discrepancy in the presentation and the applicant will not waive the potential discrepancy? Revised § 5–103(c) allows the parties to alter the provisions of revised Article 5, with some exceptions, by agreement. Prudent issuers will safeguard themselves against liability for wrongful payment by including exculpatory clauses in the reimbursement agreement designed to allow them to obtain reimbursement even though they pay a letter of credit in a case in which the documents do not strictly comply with the letter of credit. Provisions imposing a standard of only substantial compliance on issuing banks with respect to their duty to dishonor are clearly enforceable. Comment 2 to revised § 5–103. Though, under the last sentence of revised § 5–103(c), terms "generally excusing liability or generally limiting remedies for failure to perform obligations" are not enforceable.

c.   SUBROGATION, RESTITUTION AND BREACH OF WARRANTY

As we have seen, the prudent issuer of a standby letter of credit makes sure that if it has to pay the credit the applicant will be able to reimburse it. This is usually done by requiring that the applicant give security for its reimbursement obligation. However, in some cases the security proves worthless and the applicant is insolvent, hence the issuer is unable to obtain reimbursement from the applicant. In those situations the issuer will explore alternative remedies. If the applicant has given the beneficiary security, the issuer may seek to be subrogated to the beneficiary's rights to the security. If the issuer can claim to have paid because of fraud or mistake, it may demand restitution from the beneficiary. Or the issuer may claim that the beneficiary has breached its presentation warranties to the issuer. In the materials below we will examine the availability of these remedies.

Whether an issuer, having paid the beneficiary of a letter of credit, is entitled to the equitable remedy of subrogation has been much litigated. For reasons discussed in *Tudor*, below, a majority of courts have denied issuers the right to subrogation. In the revision of Article 5, § 5–117(a) recognizes subrogation for issuers: "An issuer that honors a beneficiary's presentation is subrogated to the rights of the beneficiary to the same extent as if the issuer were a secondary obligor of the underlying obligation owed to the beneficiary and of the applicant to the same extent as if the issuer were the secondary obligor of the underlying obligation owed to the applicant." Professor White, the Reporter of revised Article 5, states in White & Summers, Prac. ed. § 26–15 that Judge Becker's dissenting opinion in *Tudor* is the correct analysis of the problem, and Comment 1 to

§ 5–117 indorses the Becker position. Hence, we summarize the holding of the majority in *Tudor* and reproduce only the Becker dissent.

Tudor Development Group, Inc. v. United States Fidelity & Guaranty Company

United States Court of Appeals, Third Circuit, 1992.
968 F.2d 357.

* * *

[Summary by Eds. Associates was the developer of a subdivision construction project. SCC agreed with Associates to construct the buildings on the site. USF & G issued two performance bonds to Associates to guarantee performance of SCC's duties. ECU agreed with Associates to construct roadways, parking areas and storm drainage systems on the project. Wausau issued performance bonds to Associates guaranteeing performance of ECU's duties. Before Associates could commence the project it had to obtain the approval of the local government, Township, by agreeing to complete various other improvements on the site such as roads, driveways, and parking and recreation areas. Township required Associates to provide it with either a bond or a standby letter of credit guaranteeing the completion of the improvements. Associates obtained an irrevocable standby letter of credit from Dauphin Deposit Bank in the amount of $1,088,646, payable upon Township's certification that the required site improvements had not been completed. Dauphin received a fee of $75 plus 1.5% per annum of the face amount of the letter of credit. Associates agreed to reimburse Dauphin if it honored the letter of credit. As security for the reimbursement agreement, Associates assigned to Dauphin its rights in the Wausau performance bonds but not in the USF & G bonds. Dauphin also received a collateral note from Tudor, Associates' general partner in the venture.

SCC defaulted in its contract with Associates and Associates had to default in its obligations to build the site improvements. In consequence, Township drew on the letter of credit against Dauphin for $800,000. Associates submitted a claim to USF & G and settlement was reached by USF & G's agreeing to pay $609,000; of this amount, $594,000 was paid into court to be held pending resolution of the competing claims to the fund of (1) Associates, claiming as the obligee of the bonds, (2) Investors, claiming as a partial assignee of Associate's rights in the fund, and (3) Dauphin, contending that it was equitably subrogated to Associates' interest in the fund by reason of its payment to Township under the letter of credit, for which it has not been reimbursed. Dauphin obtained a judgment against Tudor on its note but has not executed on the judgment; Dauphin has not sought a judgment against Associates.

The majority opinion, written by Judge Cowen, concluded that when Dauphin honored the letter of credit it was satisfying its own primary liability rather than the liability of Associates. Hence, it was not entitled be equitably subrogated to Associates' rights to the USF & G funds. Equitable subrogation is allowed only when a party secondarily liable, like a guarantor, pays the debt of a party primarily liable. A letter of credit is not a guaranty, subjecting the issuer to secondary liability for its customer's failure to perform its contract with the beneficiary. In fact the key feature of a letter of credit is the independence principle which requires the issuer to satisfy its own primary obligation on the letter of credit without reference to the rights of its customer on the underlying transaction. The court noted that although authorities are split on the issue, its view represents the majority rule. Even had Dauphin met the technical requirements of equitable subrogation, the equities do not favor Dauphin in this case. It took as security for Associates' reimbursement obligation an assignment of rights under the Wausau bonds but failed to do so for the USF & G bonds; having made a bad bargain, Dauphin now seeks the rights it failed to bargain for by invoking equitable subrogation. The court should not rewrite the contract to give Dauphin more security than it bargained for.]

■ BECKER, CIRCUIT JUDGE, dissenting.

This appeal presents a close, difficult, and important question that has divided both courts and scholars. The majority concludes that, under Article 5 of the Uniform Commercial Code and the common law, a bank that has issued a standby letter of credit may never qualify for equitable subrogation to the rights of its defaulting customer in the underlying commercial transaction. The majority opinion is a fine piece of advocacy for a respectable position, one that has been adopted by a majority of the courts to face the issue (although rejected by the only federal appellate court that has reached the question). Nevertheless, I believe that the majority has backed the wrong horse. I would hold that an issuer of a standby letter of credit may, in proper circumstances, obtain equitable subrogation to the rights of its customer.

The majority also concludes that, even assuming that equitable subrogation is available in some cases, the equities in this case do not warrant it. Because I believe that genuine issues of material fact remain on this issue, I would not decide it on summary judgment. I would instead remand the case to the district court for further proceedings to determine whether the facts and equities here weigh in favor of or against Dauphin Deposit's claim. I therefore respectfully dissent.

I.   THE GENERAL AVAILABILITY OF SUBROGATION TO AN ISSUER OF A LETTER OF CREDIT

Investors offers three reasons why issuers of standby letters of credit should not be entitled to subrogation. First, Investors argues that an issuer does not qualify for subrogation as a matter of common law because the issuer is primarily liable on its obligation to the beneficiary, not secondarily liable for the debt of another, as the common law requires. Second, Investors contends that the principles undergirding Article 5 of the U.C.C. bar subrogation by issuers of letters of credit. Finally, Investors suggests that an issuer can (and Dauphin Deposit did) protect itself adequately by insisting on security before agreeing to issue a letter of credit. In Investors' view, subrogation should be denied because it would only protect the imprudent issuer. Because each issue is close, difficult, and important, and because Article 5 of the U.C.C. is under study for possible major revision, I will discuss all three.

A. *Common Law Bar: Primariness of the Issuer's Obligation*

The centerpiece of the majority's position is that Dauphin Deposit was primarily liable on its own obligation to the township under the letter of credit. In its view, Dauphin Deposit, as a primary obligor paying its own debt rather than the debt of another, cannot seek subrogation. In my view, the majority takes undue advantage of the ambiguity of the terms "primary" and "secondary" liability.

Certainly, Dauphin Deposit was "primarily" liable in one temporal sense, in that, pursuant to the letter of credit arrangement, it had to pay the township immediately on the township's proper demand, with (unlike a guarantor or surety) no right to assert any defenses that Associates may have had. On the other hand, even the majority concedes that Dauphin Deposit was temporally "secondarily" liable in the sense that its obligation arose only after Associates failed to satisfy its obligation. I agree with the majority that Dauphin Deposit was "primarily" liable in the sense that (like a surety) it was directly liable, under its own contractual agreement, to make a payment to the township. But that is not the relevant meaning of "primary" liability in the subrogation context, for if it were, then no guarantor or surety would ever qualify for equitable subrogation.

In my view, the relevant question is whether Dauphin Deposit was "secondarily" liable in the sense that it paid the debt of another, Associates. Investors, and the majority, have

> failed to distinguish the primary liability of a debtor to its creditor to repay a loan and the primary obligation of the issuer to its beneficiary to honor a letter of credit. When a standby credit supporting a loan is honored, the issuer admittedly is satisfying its obligation as a primary obligor to honor the standby credit, but at the same time it is in fact satisfying a debt for which a person other than the issuer is primarily liable. . . .
>
> [T]he notion that an issuer's obligation to honor the letter of credit is a "primary obligation" should be interpreted to mean that, under the independence principle, the issuer may not avoid its obligation to honor the credit by identifying deficiencies in underlying contracts or by otherwise asserting defenses that are typically available to parties who are generally considered to be "secondarily liable" such as guarantors and sureties. Thus . . . the "primary obligation" language in the

letter of credit context concerns itself with the issuer's ability to avoid honoring its letter of credit, whereas the "primary liability" language in the subrogation context concerns itself with whether the entity, after reducing a claim of a creditor, received the consideration from the creditor.

In re Valley Vue Joint Venture, 123 B.R. 199, 204, 206 (Bankr.E.D.Va. 1991).

In this case, Dauphin Deposit paid the debt of another when it satisfied Associates' obligation. Associates was liable to the township to make site improvements. Dauphin Deposit's letter of credit served as the township's backup in case Associates defaulted. Associates did default, and Dauphin Deposit, pursuant to its obligation under the letter of credit, satisfied Associates' obligation to the township.

As the issuer of a letter of credit, Dauphin Deposit had fewer defenses than would the issuer of a guaranty or performance bond, but the substance of Dauphin Deposit's obligation was nevertheless essentially similar to that of a guarantor or surety. There can be no doubt that all three parties considered Dauphin Deposit as a de facto surety and the letter of credit as a substitute for a performance bond. Paragraph 5 of the subdivision agreement provides:

> As a further condition to approval of said Plan, Subdivider shall furnish a ~~bond~~ * in the amount of One Million Eighty-eight Thousand Six Hundred Forty Six ($1,088,646.00) Dollars to guarantee the proper completion of the improvements required by the Ordinance. * Irrevocable Straight Letter of Credit No: S–10181 from Dauphin Deposit Bank and Trust Company

The parties struck out the word "bond" and replaced it with a reference to the letter of credit. Quite clearly, the parties intended the letter to serve the same economic role as a performance bond would have: "to *guarantee* the proper completion of the improvements required by the Ordinance" (emphasis added).

Guarantors and sureties pay their own legal obligations, yet they are still entitled to seek equitable subrogation as well as contractual subrogation. That is because in meeting their own "primary" obligations, guarantors and sureties are also "secondarily" liable to pay others' debts. So far as the common law is concerned, the same logic should apply to issuers of letters of credit such as Dauphin Deposit.

Thus I conclude that the common law by itself poses no bar to the assertion of subrogation rights by issuers of letters of credit. I next turn to whether the U.C.C.'s statutory provisions on letters of credit require a different result.

B.   *The U.C.C. Statutory Bar*

1.   Prohibition by the Text of Article 5

As just mentioned, Dauphin Deposit's basic theory is that its role was as a quasi-guarantor, and thus, like a guarantor, it is entitled to equitable subrogation. As the majority notes, however, the text of and official commentary to Article 5 of the U.C.C. make clear that a letter of credit is not equivalent to a guaranty.

The "independence principle" is the cornerstone of Article 5 and the law of letters of credit. Under the independence principle, the issuer of a letter of credit (unlike a guarantor) generally may not look to the underlying transaction and assert the defenses of the party whose obligation is guaranteed. Instead, the issuer must look only at the documents presented by the beneficiary and determine if they, on their face, meet the conditions that invoke the issuer's obligation to pay on the letter of credit. See § 5–114(1) and comment 1 thereto. In short, the issuer must pay first and worry about its reimbursement and the merits of the dispute involving its customer later. Id.

Accordingly, the issuer's duty to its customer does not ordinarily include liability for performance of the underlying contract. See § 5–109(1). The commentary explicitly notes that "the issuer receives compensation for a payment service rather than for a guaranty of performance." Id. comment 1. Correlatively, the customer must, upon request, immediately reimburse the issuer if the issuer honored the letter according to its terms, again without regard to the merits of any dispute over the underlying transaction. See § 5–114(3). Moreover, the commentary to Article 5 suggests that the law of letters of credit has been marred by "occasional unfortunate excursions into the law of guaranty." Comment to § 5–101. The U.C.C. undeniably declares its intention "to set an independent theoretical framework for the further development of letters of credit." Id.

From these snippets, Investors argues and the majority apparently concludes that subrogation would be contrary to the spirit, if not the letter, of the Code. I am not persuaded. The drafters' concern about importing the law of guaranty was not about subrogation, but about eroding the independence principle (which, as I shall explain in the next section, is not compromised by allowing subrogation). The drafters of Article 5 took great pains to establish the independence principle in order to promote smooth commercial relations, but it does not follow that they intended to do away with subrogation simply because guarantors are eligible for subrogation. As one court has observed,

> [w]hile a letter of credit may require conformity with certain obligations and formalities which are not required of a guarantee, where there is no contrary policy reason for treating them dissimilarly for other purposes, precluding the assertion of subrogation rights to issuers of standby letters of credit while allowing guarantors to assert them would be no more than an exercise in honoring form over substance.

In re Minnesota Kicks, Inc., 48 B.R. 93, 104–05 (Bankr.D.Minn.1985) (citation omitted).

Indeed, the U.C.C. commentary explicitly anticipates that issuers will have recourse against beneficiaries by way of subrogation to the rights of their customers, at least in appropriate cases:

> The customer will normally have direct recourse against the beneficiary if performance fails, whereas the issuer will have such recourse only by assignment of or in a proper case subrogation to the rights of the customer.

Comment to § 5–109.

This official commentary disproves any suggestion that the drafters of Article 5 considered subrogation antithetical to the law of letters of credit. On the other hand, this comment does not prove that subrogation should apply in this case as a matter of course. First, the comment speaks of subrogation to the customer's right against the beneficiary, and Dauphin Deposit seeks subrogation to Associates' rights against USF & G, not the township. More basically, the question remains what classes of cases are "proper" cases. On that score, there is little legislative history behind Article 5 to turn to, for the case law on subrogation in letter of credit contexts was extremely sparse before the adoption of the Code. See Michael Evan Avidon, Subrogation in the Letter of Credit Context, 56 Brook.L.Rev. 129, 133–34 (1990); Peter R. Jarvis, Standby Letters of Credit—Issuers' Subrogation and Assignment Rights—Part I, 9 U.C.C. L.J. 356, 375–77 (1976).

In sum, the text and commentary of the U.C.C. itself do not rule in or rule out subrogation in the letter of credit context. I therefore look to policy reasons (including policies embedded in the Code, such as the independence principle) to determine what is a "proper" case for subrogation.

2.   Interference with the Independence Principle

The recent American Bar Association/U.S. Council on International Banking Task Force on the Study of U.C.C. Article 5 reached no definitive conclusion on when and whether subrogation is available in the letter of credit context, although it agreed that statutory resolution of the question would be useful. See its report, An Examination of U.C.C. Article 5 (Letters of Credit) 21 (Sept. 29, 1989), reprinted in 45 Bus.Law. 1527 (1990). The task force did agree, however, that "the question of the availability of subrogation is one which must be regarded as being essentially outside of credit law and the letter of credit transaction," and that "the primary factor in determining [subrogation's] availability should be whether it would affect the integrity of principles vital to letter of credit law." Id.

As noted above, the cornerstone of the law of letters of credit is the independence principle, and thus if granting subrogation to issuers of letters of credit would undermine the independence principle, then such subrogation must not be permitted. In my view, allowing the issuer of a letter of credit to subrogate to the rights of its customer would not undermine the independence principle.

The independence principle ensures the beneficiary of prompt payment and basically determines that the beneficiary will have the dollars in its pocket if there is a dispute between it and the customer over the underlying transaction. * * * As discussed above, this distinguishes a letter of credit from an ordinary guaranty: a guaranty is not independent in this sense, and guarantors may generally assert defenses available to the party whose obligation is guaranteed.

Investors suggests that the independence principle must be viewed as a wall between the letter of credit side and the underlying transaction side. Some courts have similarly argued that allowing subrogation would permit an issuer to interfere with the underlying contract. See, for example, In re Economic Enterprises, 44 B.R. 230, 232 (Bankr.D.Conn.1984). But the point of the independence principle is not to set up a wall for the sake of a wall, but to serve certain purposes. The independence principle undoubtedly requires the issuer to pay first, without looking through to the underlying transaction. Subrogation should therefore be unavailable before the issuer has paid the beneficiary. Once the issuer has done so, however, as Dauphin Deposit has here, the purpose of the independence principle has been served: the beneficiary has the money.

Insistence on perpetual separation is thus pointless formalism.[2] On a more pragmatic level, I would agree that if the possibility of subsequent subrogation would discourage issuers from honoring already-issued letters of credit,[3] then subrogation should not be permitted, because that would undercut the purposes of Article 5. But I cannot see why that would be so. If anything, the unavailability of subsequent subrogation might discourage issuers from honoring the letters because they would have one less means of obtaining reimbursement.

In sum, the policies underlying Article 5 of the U.C.C. do not require courts to deny subrogation to all issuers of standby letters of credit. The remaining question is whether other policy considerations commend the per se rule argued by Investors and adopted by the majority.

C. *Other Policy Considerations*

1. The Issuer's Ability to Protect Itself Contractually

In my view, Investors' (and the majority's) best argument is that the issuer of a letter of credit is perfectly able to protect itself contractually. That is, the issuer receives a payment for its services and may also demand assignment rights to collateral in the event that it is forced to pay on the letter. Investors argues that Dauphin Deposit made a deal with Associates and received certain collateral rights, including assignment rights to the other bonds involved in the Green Hill Project (the "Wausau bonds"). It is certainly fair to ask why Dauphin Deposit should receive the additional

2. The majority appears to recognize this, for it concedes that "the vitality of the independence principle is unlikely to be substantially diminished were we to allow subrogation in this situation." Majority op. at 363.

3. I discuss below incentives regarding the issuance of letters of credit in the first place.

right of subrogation, simply because it made a bad gamble or wasn't wary enough when negotiating its reimbursement agreement with Associates. Many courts have voiced similar concerns. See, for example, In re Agrownautics, Inc., 125 B.R. 350, 353 (Bankr.D.Conn.1991); In re Carley Capital Group, 119 B.R. 646, 650 (W.D.Wis.1990).

Nevertheless, this argument, although powerful, proves too much. Generally applied, the same argument would virtually eliminate equitable subrogation altogether, for it would apply to every guaranty or suretyship contract. Moreover, in many cases this may lead to the customer receiving an undeserved windfall. A customer may default on both its obligation on the underlying transaction and its obligation to reimburse the issuer of the letter of credit, yet retain any income deriving from the original transaction. In short, the issuer's ability to protect itself may be a strong equity against it, as is the fact that it receives a fee for its services, but countervailing equities may outweigh these considerations in certain cases. See In re Glade Springs, Inc., 826 F.2d 440, 442 (6th Cir.1987) (reinstating the subrogation remedy that had been ordered by the bankruptcy court, 47 B.R. 780 (Bankr.E.D.Tenn.1985)).

2. Efficiency

At bottom, what concerns me most is how the rule that courts adopt will affect incentives to issue letters of credit in the first place. It is possible that if no equitable subrogation were permitted, fewer banks would issue such letters, which would be commercially undesirable. Given the vagaries of commerce, it may be difficult for the issuer to forecast precisely which security will have value years down the road. If courts allow traditional equitable subrogation, the transaction costs in negotiating letters of credit may be lower than under a rule where the parties must specify subrogation rights contractually.

On the other hand, with the law as unsettled as it now is, prudent would-be issuers may already have reacted by demanding greater fees or security, and the system appears to be functioning well. Parties may even be willing to incorporate the entire body of equity jurisprudence by contractual reference. Perhaps in the long run, the rule that the majority adopts will not make much of a difference, as good lawyers and prudent issuers will react accordingly. I concede too that a bright-line no-subrogation rule would promote legal certainty and thereby reduce litigation costs.

The issue is very close, but on balance I think that the better rule is to retain subrogation on a case-by-case basis and apply it sparingly. When the unexpected happens, as it so often does, it is desirable to leave courts with equitable powers to avoid windfalls and to achieve a result fair to all parties. Certainly that was the solution of the common law, and I have found nothing in the U.C.C. as adopted in Pennsylvania that justifies my predicting that the Pennsylvania Supreme Court would vote to oust the common law in this field. See § 1–103 (supplemental common law principles continue to apply unless explicitly displaced by the U.C.C.).

As noted above, Article 5 of the U.C.C. has been under study by a task force. That study recommended that the question of subrogation rights be resolved statutorily. I agree that that is the best solution. Perhaps further policy study will show that the equitable subrogation game isn't worth the candle, and the U.C.C. will be amended so to provide. Under the law as it stands, however, I cannot agree with the majority that equitable subrogation should be completely unavailable in the letter of credit context.

* * *

NOTE

The most common case in which the subrogation issue is litigated concerns the applicability of Bankruptcy Code § 509(a) which states: "Except as provided in subsection (b) or (c) of this section, an entity that is *liable with the debtor* on, or that has secured, a claim of a creditor against the debtor, and that pays such claim, is subrogated to the rights of such creditor to the extent of such payment." (Emphasis added.) In CCF, Inc. v. First National Bank & Trust, 69 F.3d 468 (10th Cir.1995), the court held that the independence principle (an issuer is not "liable with the debtor") precluded subrogating an issuer to the beneficiary's right to setoff against funds of the applicant that the beneficiary had collected on behalf of the applicant. Although revised § 5–117 was not yet law in the jurisdiction in question, the court was aware of it and said: "Although the revised Article Five provides an issuer with the remedy of subrogation, the UCC does not determine the availability of subrogation in a bankruptcy proceeding. Rather, § 509 of the Bankruptcy Code governs an entity's eligibility for subrogation in a bankruptcy proceeding. Thus, the effect of the revised § 5–117 on § 509 subrogation is presently undecided, and suitable for resolution by a future court." 69 F.3d at 476 n. 7.

NOTE: RESTITUTION AND BREACH OF WARRANTY

Issuers who have honored a draft drawn pursuant to a letter of credit but have been unable to obtain reimbursement from the applicant may attempt to get their money back from the beneficiary under doctrines of restitution or breach of warranty. The common law of restitution in a given state may allow one who has paid out under mistake or who has honored a forged or fraudulent presentation to recover the payment. Former Article 5 was silent on the subject. Or the issuer may invoke former § 5–111(1) which provides broadly that a beneficiary demanding payment on a letter of credit "warrants to all interested parties that the necessary conditions of the credit have been complied with." Case authority under former Article 5 is sparse on these subjects and the meaning of former § 5–111(1) has never been authoritatively determined. Revised Article 5 has addressed both these subjects rather decisively.

Revised § 5–108(i)(4) provides that an issuer who has honored a presentation "(4) except as otherwise provided in Sections 5–110 and 5–

117, is precluded from restitution of money paid or other value given by mistake to the extent the mistake concerns discrepancies in the documents or tender which are apparent on the face of the presentation * * *."

Revised § 5–110 states "(a) If its presentation is honored, the beneficiary warrants: (1) to the issuer, any other person to whom presentation is made, and the applicant that there is no fraud or forgery of the kind described in § 5–109(a); and (2) to the applicant that the drawing does not violate any agreement between the applicant and beneficiary or any other agreement intended by them to be augmented by the letter of credit."

PROBLEMS

In the following Problems assume the following facts: Applicant, a movie producer with limited assets, engaged Beneficiary to appear in a new film, entitled "Legal Nights." In order to induce Beneficiary to agree to perform, Applicant caused Bank to issue a standby letter of credit to her payable on presentation to Bank of the letter of credit, a draft drawn on Bank payable 15 days after the date of presentation, and an affidavit that Beneficiary had satisfactorily completed the film and had not been paid by Applicant. Upon presentation by Beneficiary, Bank honored the draft but was unable to obtain reimbursement from Applicant. Bank proceeded against Beneficiary invoking the remedies of restitution and breach of warranty. What result in the following two cases under revised Article 5? The issues in these Problems are discussed in White & Summers, Prac.ed. § 26–8 (warranties), § 26–9(e) (restitution).

1.   The documents presented by Beneficiary included a draft drawn on Bank "at sight," meaning at the time of presentation. Bank did not notice that the draft did not comply with the documents specified by the letter of credit and paid the draft according to its terms. Had the draft complied with the terms of the credit, Bank might not have paid it at all because during the 15–day period Applicant filed in bankruptcy and Bank's right of reimbursement became virtually worthless.

2.   The documents presented by Beneficiary complied with the requirements of the credit, including the affidavit of completion. After honoring the draft, Bank learned that Beneficiary had not completed the film and had breached her contract with Applicant.

4.   DAMAGES FOR WRONGFUL DISHONOR

As we have seen it is fundamental that the letter of credit undertaking between an issuer and a beneficiary is independent of the underlying contract between the beneficiary and the applicant. Revised § 5–103(d). Does it follow that if the issuer wrongfully dishonors a draft made pursuant to a letter of credit, the beneficiary should be able to recover the full amount of the draw from the issuer, leaving the applicant to litigate with the beneficiary in a separate action over any amount the beneficiary has received in excess of its rights on the underlying contract? The issue is not clear under the former version of Article 5. Under former § 5–115(1), in a sale of goods transaction involving a letter of credit, the seller-beneficiary's recovery for wrongful dishonor is limited by requiring it to deduct from the face amount of the credit any amount realized by it upon disposition of the goods. Hence, that provision required reference to the underlying sales contract to prevent a beneficiary from receiving double recovery. But the statute does not impose a clear duty on the seller-beneficiary to resell the goods, and the cases were divided on what the consequences were if the seller did nothing. White & Summers, Prac.ed. § 26–14(b). Former § 5–115(1) appears to have been drafted with the traditional commercial letter of credit transaction in mind, but the mitigation provision seems also to apply to cases in which a standby letter of credit is involved, so long as the beneficiary is a seller of goods. It was never clear under former Article 5 what the rights of the beneficiary were under a standby letter of credit when the transaction did not involve a sale of goods. The revised version of Article 5 clarifies the remedies of both the beneficiary (§ 5–111(a)) and the applicant (§ 5–111(b)). How would you apply revised § 5–111 to the following Problems? White & Summers, Prac.ed. § 26–14(e) discusses damages under revised Article 5.

PROBLEMS

1. Seller in New York agreed to sell goods to Buyer in Los Angeles by rail shipment with payment to be made pursuant to a commercial letter of credit. Buyer obtained issuance of a letter of credit by Issuer, Buyer's bank. The credit was payable to Seller on presentation to Issuer of a bill of lading, invoice, inspection and insurance certificates, sight draft drawn on Issuer, and the letter of credit. Issuer sent the letter of credit to Seller in New York (this is usually done through an "adviser" bank, § 5–102(a)(1)). Seller shipped the goods and obtained an order bill of lading from the carrier. Seller then assembled the required documents and sent them through banking channels to Issuer for payment. Buyer decided that it had made a bad bargain and urged Issuer to dishonor the credit. Buyer threatened that if Issuer honored the letter of credit, Buyer would take its business elsewhere. Issuer reluctantly dishonored. When the goods arrived in Los Angeles, Seller ordered the carrier to store them in a warehouse. Several months later, Seller sold the goods for only a fraction of their invoice price. Seller sued Issuer for wrongful dishonor and sought the face amount of the draft drawn pursuant to the letter of credit in damages. Issuer contended that Seller should have mitigated damages, and that the goods should have been sold for a much higher price; moreover, at the very least, Seller must offset the amount actually recovered from the resale against its claim on the letter of credit. What result under revised § 5–111(a)? Comment 1 to revised § 5–111. What incentive does an Issuer have not to dishonor wrongfully? Revised § 5–111(e), Comment 6.

2. Applicant planned to develop a recreational community. County approval of Applicant's subdivision was conditional on Applicant's agreement to provide a standby letter of credit payable to the County as beneficiary to ensure that Applicant would complete roads and related improvements in accordance with subdivision design specifications. The required letter of credit was obtained from Issuer. Applicant never commenced construction of the roads or other improvements. Issuer wrongfully dishonored the letter of credit upon presentation. The County sued Issuer for the face amount of the credit plus interest from the date of the demand for payment. Issuer defended on the ground that the County would receive a windfall since it had not expended or committed itself to expend any funds to complete the improvements. The facts are based on Colorado National Bank v. Board of County Commissioners, 634 P.2d 32 (Colo.1981). What result under revised § 5–111? Dolan, Letters of Credit ¶ 9.02[5][6][ii] and White & Summers, Prac.ed. § 26–14(b) at 207 & n.15., discuss the existing law.

3. Sport manufactured running shoes for various retail chains. It made the shoes to the specifications of retailers who sold the shoes under their own brand names. Sport was thinly capitalized and the business was highly competitive. Sport had contracts for large deliveries to Retailer A on March 1, Retailer B on June 1, and Retailer C on September 1. Sport required A to obtain a standby letter of credit for the invoice price of the goods on which Sport could draw if A failed to pay for the goods within 15 days of delivery. When the shoes arrived, A contended that they were defective and ordered Issuer not to honor the letter of credit. Sport made timely presentation to Issuer of the required documents and Issuer wrongfully dishonored. Sport immediately implored Issuer to pay, explaining that without the proceeds of this large sale it would be unable to fulfill its obligations to B and C and would lose the profits that it anticipated making on these contracts. When Issuer continued to refuse payment, Sport sued Issuer for wrongful dishonor and claimed damages measured by the face amount of the credit plus the amount of lost profits on its contracts with B and C. What result under revised § 5–111(a)? Do you believe that this is a desirable result? Comment 4 to revised § 5–111.

E.   FORGERY AND FRAUD

The influential pre-Code case, *Sztejn v. J. Henry Schroder Banking Corp.* 177 Misc. 719, 31 N.Y.S.2d 631 (Sup.Ct.1941), was a concession to the reality that the independence principle, however important, must have limits. The facts of *Sztejn* are summarized in the following case. In short, the contract of sale between the applicant and beneficiary was for the beneficiary to ship bristles to the applicant, and the bill of lading presented to the issuing bank described the goods as bristles, but the applicant had discovered that the beneficiary had actually shipped what the court described as rubbish. The applicant sought to enjoin the issuer from honoring the draft on the ground of fraud. On the pleadings, assuming the applicant was correct about the fraud, the court held for the applicant. Although the documents were in compliance on their face, they were not genuine and, therefore, the issuer did not have to honor.

This case seemed to undermine the independence principle in that it allowed the court to look outside the documents presented to determine whether the issuer must honor. Would this mean that honor could be enjoined if the applicant could make a showing that the goods shipped by the beneficiary were defective in a degree amounting to a breach of warranty of quality? Or if the applicant could show that it had been induced to enter into the underlying sale transaction by misrepresentations by the beneficiary about the goods? Former § 5–114, set out in the case below, was an attempt to codify and delimit *Sztejn*. It allowed the applicant to obtain an injunction against honor even though the documents appear on their face to be in compliance so long as a required document "is forged or fraudulent or there is fraud in the transaction." The breadth of the "fraud in the transaction" test seemed to place the independence principle in peril. The following case is the leading case on how this language has been construed by the courts. After *Intraworld*, we will examine the revised Article 5 treatment of the subject in § 5–109. For an extensive discussion of fraud in the transaction, see Dolan, Letters of Credit ¶ 7.04.

Intraworld Industries, Inc. v. Girard Trust Bank

Supreme Court of Pennsylvania, 1975.
461 Pa. 343, 336 A.2d 316.

■ ROBERTS, JUSTICE.

This appeal requires us to review the trial court's denial of a preliminary injunction to restrain honor of a draft under an international letter of credit. A precise statement of the facts, which are complex, is necessary for a proper understanding.

On February 11, 1972, a lease was executed by Intraworld Industries, Inc., a corporation headquartered in Wilkes–Barre, Pennsylvania, and Paulette Cymbalista, a citizen of Switzerland and resident of Italy. Cymbalista agreed to lease to Intraworld the Hotel Carlton, a luxury hotel located in St. Moritz, Switzerland, for a term of 15 years at an annual rental of 800,000 Swiss francs, payable in semi-annual installments.[2] The lease provided that Intraworld was required to prepay the rent for the initial 18–month period. Intraworld was also obligated to procure, within the first 100 days of the term, a performance bond in the amount of $500,000 "to insure to lessor the payment of the rent."[3]

Intraworld entered into possession of the hotel on May 1, 1972. Shortly thereafter, Intraworld assigned its interest in the lease to its subsidiary,

2. The lease contained a formula for the adjustment of the annual rental with respect to changes in the value of the Swiss franc. At the time of the execution of the lease, the annual rental was approximately equivalent to $200,000.

3. The record does not establish whether Intraworld performed its obligation to procure a performance bond.

The lease also provided: "This agreement shall be governed by the Swiss law. The competent forum shall be in Saint Moritz Court."

Vacanze In Paradiso Hotels, S.A., a Swiss corporation.[4]

At a later time, Intraworld and Cymbalista executed an addendum to the lease (to which the parties have referred by its German title "Nachtrag"). The Nachtrag cancelled Intraworld's obligation to procure a performance bond and substituted a duty to provide letters of credit issued by "the Girard Trust Company of Philadelphia" in order to guarantee rental payments one year in advance. Two letters of credit were specifically required, each in the amount of $100,000, maturing in November, 1973, and May, 1974, to secure the rent due at those times. After each rental payment, Intraworld was to provide a new letter of credit "in order that the lessor remains secured one years [sic] rent in advance." The Nachtrag also provided:

> "In the event the lessee should not fulfill its obligation to pay, so that the letter of credit must be used, * * * then the lessor can terminate the lease immediately without further notice. In this case, the lessor retains the rent paid or guaranteed for the following year as a stipulated penalty for non-performance of the contract from the lessee, in doing so the lessor retains the right to make a claim for additional damages not covered by the stipulated penalty."

On September 1, 1972, Intraworld and the Girard Trust Bank, Philadelphia, entered into an agreement to provide the letters of credit required by the Nachtrag. Girard agreed to

> "issue a letter of credit * * * in the amount of $100,000 under which the Lessor may draw a sight draft on [Girard] for payment of the sum due under said lease (a) on November 10, 1973 and (b) May 10, 1974. Under the terms of such letter of credit, payments will be made if the Lessor presents a draft as provided in such letter of credit. Each such letter of credit will expire * * * on the twentieth day after the payment under said lease is due."[6]

In accordance with the agreement, Girard issued two irrevocable letters of credit on September 5, 1972. Each authorized Cymbalista to draw a draft on Girard in the amount of $100,000.00 if Intraworld failed to pay the rent when due.[7]

---

4. For convenience we will refer to the lessee as Intraworld.

6. The agreement also provided: "This agreement shall be construed in accordance with the law of the State of Pennsylvania and the Acts of Congress of the United States affecting transactions under the provisions hereof."

7. "IRREVOCABLE LETTER OF CREDIT

NO. 35798

Date: September 5, 1972

"Amount: $100,000.00

"Beneficiary: Paulette Cymbalista
                     c/o Carlton Hotel
                     St. Moritz, Switzerland

"For account of: Intraworld Industries, Inc.
                     116 South Main Street
                     Wilkes Barre, PA 18701

"Madam:

"You are hereby authorized to draw on us at sight the sum of One Hundred Thousand and 00/100 Dollars United States Currency ($100,000.00) due on November 10, 1973 under a lease, a copy of which is attached to both Beneficiary's copy and Bank's copy of this letter of

In the summer of 1973, the relationship between Cymbalista and Intraworld began to go awry. Norbert Cymbalista, Paulette's husband, visited the hotel in August and, after discussions with the manager, became very concerned over the hotel's financial condition. He discovered that there were unpaid bills in excess of $100,000, that all telephone and Telex communications had been cut off for nonpayment of bills, and that the filing of mechanics liens against the hotel was imminent. After a trans-Atlantic telephone call, the Cymbalistas travelled to the United States within several days of Norbert's discoveries to attempt to resolve the hotel's difficulties with Intraworld. However, as Norbert testified,

"I tried to reach [the president of Intraworld] innumerable times by telephone and each time his secretary answered that he would call me back and he never did. I stayed a whole month in the United States trying continually to reach him and it was never possible."

On August 20, 1973, apparently while the Cymbalistas were in the United States, their Swiss counsel sent a letter to Intraworld reciting the unpaid bills, erosion of the Carlton's reputation, and internal corporate difficulties (apparently of Intraworld's Swiss subsidiary). It concluded:

"Based upon [Swiss law] and in reference to the provisions of the Lease Contract, we herewith extend to you a final time limit up to September 15, 1973 in order to:

(a) to pay all due debts,

(b) to supply the necessary means to safeguard proper management of the business,

(c) to complete the Board of Directors according to the law.

Within this time limit you must prove to the Hotel Owners that the aforementioned measures have been effectuated. Should you [fail to?] comply with this demand within the time-limit, the Lease Contract will be regarded as void."

credit as Exhibit 1, available by your draft for said amount, accompanied by:

"1. Simple receipt for amount drawn.

"2. A signed statement of the drawer of the draft to the effect that the drawer is the lessor under said lease and that the lessee thereunder has not paid the installment of rent due under said lease on November 10, 1973 within 10 days after said installment was due and payable.

"This credit expires on November 30, 1973.

"Drafts under this credit must contain the clause 'drawn under Credit No. 35798 of Girard Trust Bank, dated September 5, 1972.'

"Girard Trust Bank hereby agrees with the drawers, endorsers and bona fide owners of the bills drawn strictly in compliance with the terms of this credit that the same will be duly honored upon presentation.

"Except so far as otherwise expressly stated, this credit is subject to the uniform customs and practices for documentary credits (1962 revision), International Chamber of Commerce Brochure No. 222."

Credit No. 35799 was identical to 35798, except that it applied to the rent due on May 10, 1974, and expired on May 30, 1974.

Intraworld's Swiss counsel replied to the August 20 letter (but this reply is not in the record). Finding this reply unsatisfactory, Cymbalista's Swiss counsel answered on September 18, 1973:

"As [Intraworld] did not comply with our demand within this time-limit, we regard the leasing contract as terminated effective from 15 September 1973 * * *. From now on, the proprietor will have direct and sole control over the hotel real estate respective to the hotel management."

Further correspondence was exchanged by Swiss counsel, including, apparently, a demand on November 3 for the rent due in November. On November 7, 1973, Intraworld's Swiss counsel wrote to Cymbalista's counsel:

"You state on behalf of the lessor that [Intraworld] has the obligation to pay * * * rent by November 1. My client [Intraworld], who is presently in close contact with their American Bank [Girard], however, have [sic] informed me that the payment of the rent can be made up to November 10 * * * My client informed me further that accordingly these payments shall be legally undertaken by the 'Girard Trust Bank' * * * [M]y client cannot agree with your position according to which the lease contract can be considered as terminated either because of [Swiss law] or because of the terms of the lease agreement * * *."

That letter was followed on November 9, 1973, by another from Intraworld's counsel to Cymbalista's counsel in which he stated:

"If the transfer of the rent from the United States should not be made in timely fashion, your client [Cymbalista] is at liberty to obtain payment by way of the guarantee contracts [i.e., letters of credit]. In any event, there exist the two guarantee contracts, valid until November 30, 1973 and May 30, 1974, respectively, in order to preserve the rights of your client."

The rent due on November 10, 1973, was not paid by Intraworld. Accordingly, on November 21, 1973, Cymbalista's American counsel presented to Girard a draft drawn on Girard for $100,000 under Credit No. 35798. The draft was accompanied, all parties agree, by documentation that conformed to the terms of the credit. In his letter to Girard, Cymbalista's counsel stated:

"Your attention is directed to correspondence dated November 7 and November 9, 1973, copies of which are attached, in which Swiss counsel representing the Lessee invites the Lessor to draw upon the Letters of Credit; our client, as Lessor, takes the position that the lease * * * has terminated for various reasons, including the failure timely to pay the amount due pursuant to the 'Nachtrag' * * *."

Girard informed Intraworld on November 21 that it intended to honor the draft. Intraworld immediately filed an action in equity in the Court of Common Pleas of Philadelphia seeking injunctive relief prohibiting Girard from honoring the draft. Cymbalista filed a petition to intervene, which was granted by the trial court.

The November action was terminated on December 6, 1973, by agreement of all parties. Pursuant to the agreement, Girard placed $100,000 in escrow with a Swiss bank, with entitlement to that fund to be determined by the courts of Switzerland.

The situation remained unchanged for about six months. The rent due on May 10, 1974, was not paid. On May 21, 1974, Cymbalista's American counsel presented to Girard a draft for $100,000 under Credit No. 35799, accompanied by conforming documentation. Girard immediately advised Intraworld that it intended to honor the draft.

On May 24, Intraworld filed this equity action in the Court of Common Pleas of Philadelphia. It sought preliminary and permanent injunctions restraining Girard from honoring Cymbalista's draft under the letter of credit. The court issued a preliminary restraining order and set a date for a hearing. Cymbalista again petitioned for leave to intervene, which the court granted on May 29.

After the filing of additional pleadings, including preliminary objections and an amended complaint, a hearing was held and testimony taken on May 30 and 31, 1974. On July 11, the trial court issued a memorandum and decree in which it denied a preliminary injunction. Intraworld has appealed to this Court. We affirm.

* * *

Girard's obligations to Cymbalista are "subject to" the Uniform Customs and Practice. However, the UCP "is by definition a recording of practice rather than a statement of legal rules," and therefore does not purport to offer rules which govern the issuance of an injunction against honor of a draft. Harfield, Practice Commentary, N.Y.U.C.C., § 5–114 (McKinney's Consol.Laws, c. 38, 1964).

All parties have briefed and argued the case on the assumption that the Pennsylvania Uniform Commercial Code controls, and with this assumption we agree.

The great utility of letters of credit flows from the independence of the issuer-bank's engagement from the underlying contract between beneficiary and customer. Long-standing case law has established that, unless otherwise agreed, the issuer deals only in documents. If the documents presented conform to the requirements of the credit, the issuer may and must honor demands for payment, regardless of whether the goods conform to the underlying contract between beneficiary and customer. Absent its agreement to the contrary, the issuer is, under the general rule, not required or even permitted to go behind the documents to determine if the beneficiary has performed in conformity with the underlying contract.

* * *

This principle of the issuer's right and obligation to honor upon presentation of conforming documents has been codified in § 5–114:

"(1) An issuer must honor a draft or demand for payment which complies with the terms of the relevant credit regardless of whether the goods or documents conform to the underlying contract for sale or other contract between the customer and the beneficiary. * * *

"(2) Unless otherwise agreed when documents appear on their face to comply with the terms of a credit but a required document * * * is forged or fraudulent or there is fraud in the transaction

* * *

"(b) in all other cases as against its customer, an issuer acting in good faith may honor the draft or demand for payment despite notification from the customer of fraud, forgery or other defect not apparent on the face of the documents but a court of appropriate jurisdiction may enjoin such honor."

Intraworld seeks to enjoin honor under § 5–114(2)(b) on the basis that there is "fraud * * * not apparent on the face of the documents." It points to what it believes are two respects in which Cymbalista's demand for payment and supporting documentation are false and fraudulent, although conceding that the documents on their face conform to the credit. First, it contends that Cymbalista's statement (as required by the credit) that "lessee * * * has not paid the installment of rent due under said lease on May 10, 1974," is false and fraudulent because, after Cymbalista purported to terminate the lease in September, 1973, Intraworld was not obligated to pay rent and because the statement failed to disclose the termination of the lease. Second, it argues that the demand is fraudulent because Cymbalista is not seeking rent at all (as, Intraworld contends, she represents in the documents) but rather the "stipulated penalty" pursuant to the Nachtrag.

In light of the basic rule of the independence of the issuer's engagement and the importance of this rule to the effectuation of the purposes of the letter of credit, we think that the circumstances which will justify an injunction against honor must be narrowly limited to situations of fraud in which the wrongdoing of the beneficiary has so vitiated the entire transaction that the legitimate purposes of the independence of the issuer's obligation would no longer be served. A court of equity has the limited duty of

"guaranteeing that [the beneficiary] not be allowed to take unconscientious advantage of the situation and run off with plaintiff's money on a *pro forma* declaration which has *absolutely no basis in fact*."

Dynamics Corp. of America v. Citizens and Southern National Bank, 356 F.Supp. 991, 999 (N.D.Ga.1973) (emphasis supplied).

The leading case on the question of what conduct will justify an injunction against honor is Sztejn v. J. Henry Schroder Banking Corp., 177 Misc. 719, 31 N.Y.S.2d 631 (Sup.Ct.1941). In that case as here, the customer sought an injunction against the issuer of a letter of credit restraining honor of a draft drawn by the beneficiary. The customer had contracted to purchase a quantity of bristles from the beneficiary and arranged to have the issuer issue a letter of credit in favor of the beneficiary. The credit required that the draft be accompanied by an invoice and bill of lading.

The beneficiary placed fifty cases of merchandise on a steamship and obtained a bill of lading describing the material as bristles. The beneficiary then drew a draft and presented it, along with the required documents, through a collecting bank. The customer's complaint alleged that the material shipped was not bristles as described in the documents, but rather "cowhair, other worthless material and rubbish [shipped] with intent to simulate genuine merchandise and defraud the plaintiff * * *."

The collecting bank moved to dismiss the complaint for failure to state a cause of action. The court, assuming the pleaded facts to be true, denied the motion. The court recognized that the issuer's obligation was independent from the underlying contract between customer and beneficiary. That independence is predicated, however, on the genuineness of the documents. The court noted:

"This is not a controversy between the buyer and seller concerning a mere breach of warranty regarding the quality of the merchandise; on the present motion, it must be assumed that the seller has intentionally failed to ship any goods ordered by the buyer."

177 Misc. at 721, 31 N.Y.S.2d at 634. When the beneficiary has intentionally shipped no goods at all, the court held, the documentation was not genuine and therefore the predicate of the independence of the issuer's engagement was removed.

We conclude that, if the documents presented by Cymbalista are genuine in the sense of having some basis in fact, an injunction must be refused. An injunction is proper only if Cymbalista, comparable to the beneficiary in *Sztejn,* has no bona fide claim to payment under the lease. Dynamics Corp. of America v. Citizens and Southern National Bank, 356 F.Supp. 991, 999 (N.D.Ga.1973). Of course, neither the trial court nor this Court may attempt to determine Cymbalista's actual entitlement to payment under the lease. Such is not the proper standard for the grant or denial of an injunction against honor. Moreover, questions of rights and obligations under the lease are required by the lease to be determined under Swiss law in the courts of Switzerland. See Dynamics Corp. of America v. Citizens and Southern National Bank, supra.

On this record, we are unable to conclude that Intraworld established that Cymbalista has no bona fide claim to payment or that the documents presented to Girard have absolutely no basis in fact. Intraworld's argument rests on the basic premise that the lease was terminated in September, 1973. From this premise Intraworld asserts the falsity of Cymbalista's representations that she is the lessor and that the rent was due and unpaid. However, Intraworld did not attempt to prove to the trial court that, under Swiss law, Cymbalista's attempted termination was effective. In fact, Intraworld's Swiss counsel informed Cymbalista's counsel on November 7, 1973, that Intraworld "cannot agree with your position according to which the lease contract can be considered as terminated * * *." Counsel added that Cymbalista was "at liberty to obtain payment by way of" the letters of credit. Thus, Intraworld failed to prove that, under Swiss law, Cymbalista had no bona fide claim to rent under the lease despite Intraworld's repudiation of termination.

Intraworld's argument that Cymbalista fraudulently concealed the purported termination from Girard is unpersuasive. When presenting the draft and documents to Girard in November, 1973, Cymbalista's American counsel candidly admitted that "our client, as Lessor, takes the position that the lease has terminated * * * for various reasons * * *." In addition, Girard was a party to the first equity action and its counsel joined the agreement which terminated that action. Cymbalista could reasonably have assumed in May, 1974, that Girard was fully aware of the positions of both Intraworld and Cymbalista.

Intraworld's further contention that Cymbalista's demand was fraudulent in that she was not seeking "rent" at all but the "stipulated penalty" pursuant to the Nachtrag is more substantial but, under scrutiny, also fails. It argues that payment under the credit was permitted only for "rent," and that Cymbalista (as she concedes) was in fact seeking the "stipulated penalty," which is not "rent." Intraworld concludes that Cymbalista was fraudulently attempting to draw under the credit for satisfaction of an obligation not secured by the credit. There are two flaws in this argument.

First, we are not persuaded that the credit was issued for payment of "rent," narrowly defined, only. The letter of credit (see note 7 supra) authorized Cymbalista to draw "the sum * * * due * * * under [the] lease," without specifying that the "sum due" contemplated was only "rent." The letter required that a draft must be accompanied by Cymbalista's statement that "the lessee * * * has not paid the installment of rent due under said lease." This is not equivalent to a limitation on availability of the credit only for nonpayment of rent; in fact, such nonpayment of rent is precisely the condition which triggers Cymbalista's entitlement to the "stipulated penalty." In short, Intraworld has failed to persuade us that the letter of credit was not available to Cymbalista for satisfaction of the "stipulated penalty."

Second and more important, the Nachtrag does not, in our view, create the sharp distinction between "rent" and "stipulated penalty" that Intraworld hypothesizes. It provides that "[i]n the event the lessee should not fulfill its obligation to pay, so that the letter of credit must be used," then the lessor was entitled to terminate the lease and "retain the *rent* paid or *guaranteed* [by the letters of credit] for the following year as a stipulated penalty for non-performance of the contract * * *." (Emphasis supplied.) Because Intraworld did fail to pay the rent due on November 10, 1973, and May 10, 1974, Cymbalista could reasonably and in good faith have concluded that she had the right to draw on the credit for the "rent * * * guaranteed for the following year."

Whether Intraworld was in fact obligated to pay the rent nonpayment of which triggered Cymbalista's right to retain the "rent guaranteed" by the credit or whether Cymbalista is not entitled to the "stipulated penalty" for some other reason are questions to be decided under Swiss law in the courts of Switzerland. We hold only that Intraworld failed to establish that Cymbalista lacked a bona fide claim to the "rent * * * guaranteed * * * as a stipulated penalty" or that her demand under the credit lacked some basis in fact. Therefore, her documented demand was not shown to be fraudulent because she was seeking satisfaction of the "stipulated penalty."

In summary, we are unable to conclude on this record that Intraworld succeeded in proving that Cymbalista had no bona fide claim for payment under the lease and that her documented demand had absolutely no basis in fact. Accordingly, it is clear that there is an apparently reasonable ground for refusing an injunction.

In addition, Intraworld alleged in its complaint and contends in this Court that Girard's decision to honor Cymbalista's draft was not formed in good faith. Intraworld asserts that Girard's bad faith constituted an additional ground justifying an injunction. It is clear that an issuer of a letter of credit must act in good faith, see §§ 5–114(2)(b), 5–109(1). However, we are not persuaded that issuer bad faith is a circumstance justifying an injunction against honor; in most if not all instances of issuer bad faith, it would seem that a customer would have an adequate remedy at law in a claim against the issuer or a defense against the issuer's claim for reimbursement. In any event, in this case Intraworld has failed to prove the existence of bad faith on the part of Girard. It has proved no more than that Girard failed to resolve the dispute over the rights and obligations of the parties to the lease in Intraworld's favor. This Girard was not obligated to do. Its obligations included a careful scrutiny of the documents, but once it determined that the documents conformed to the requirements of the credit, it bore no responsibility for the performance of the lease obligations or the genuineness of the documents. § 5–109(1)(a) & (2). It would, we think, place an issuer in an intolerable position if the law compelled it to serve at its peril as an arbitrator of contract disputes between customer and beneficiary.

* * *

NOTES

1. Applicants seeking to enjoin honor by issuers have more than the tough *Intraworld* standards to contend with. They must also comply with the law of the jurisdiction on granting injunctions. Revised § 5–109(b)(3). This normally requires a showing of irreparable harm. An equitable suit for an injunction is not appropriate if there is an adequate remedy at law. Since the remedy would usually be an action by the applicant against the beneficiary for a money judgment, an injunction would be inappropriate if the beneficiary were solvent and subject to service of process. Moreover, the applicant must show that it is more likely than not to succeed on the merits of the fraud or forgery issue. Revised § 5–109(b)(4).

2. Professor White concedes that the Drafting Committee was unable to agree on a definition of fraud. White & Summers, Prac. ed. § 26–10 at 185. Revised § 5–109(a) adopts the standard of "material fraud" and Comment 1 embraces the *Intraworld* test: "Material fraud by the beneficiary occurs only when the beneficiary has no colorable right to expect honor and where there is no basis in fact to support such a right to honor." Revised § 5–109(a) also abandons the "fraud in the transaction" formulation which had led scholars and courts to differ on whether the transaction meant was only the credit transaction or whether it extended to the underlying transaction as well. A critique of the differing positions on this issue appears in White & Summers, Prac.ed. § 26–10 at 179–180. With the addition of "or honor of the presentation would facilitate a material fraud by the beneficiary on the issuer or applicant," revised § 5–109(a) expressly applies to fraud in the underlying transaction.

3. In some cases applicants have attempted to forestall payment pursuant to a letter of credit by seeking to enjoin the beneficiary from making presentation to the issuer. An occasional opinion has applied a lesser standard for granting an injunction in such a case than in the usual case of an injunction against the issuer. Dolan, Letters of Credit ¶ 7.04[4][f]. Revised § 5–109(b) makes clear that the same standards must apply to limit injunctions in both cases by the addition of the language: "or grant similar relief against the issuer or other persons." Comment 5.

4. Former § 5–114(2) provided that in fraud or forgery cases the issuer could honor "despite notification from the customer [applicant] of fraud, forgery or other defect not apparent on the face of the documents" unless the applicant were able to obtain an injunction against honor. Revised § 5–109(a)(2) omits the quoted language and merely states that the issuer "acting in good faith" may honor. Is an issuer acting in good faith if it honors after the applicant has given it notice of the fraud or forgery? Issuing banks sometimes resort to interpleader in such cases. Dolan, Letters of Credit ¶ 7.04[4][g]. White & Summers, Prac.ed. § 26–10 at 183 disapproves such a practice.

5. "Good faith" is defined in § 5–102(a)(7) as "honesty in fact," but in some other parts of the UCC the term is defined differently. E.g., § 3–103(4): "'Good faith' means honesty in fact and the observance of reasonable commercial standards of fair dealing." Why is the "fair dealing" language not included in the Article 5 definition? Comment 3 to § 5–102.

PROBLEM

A letter of credit issued by Bank provided for payment by Bank of invoices for goods purchased by Applicant from Beneficiary upon presentment of the invoices and a certificate of Beneficiary that the invoices had not been paid. The letter of credit covered only goods shipped by Beneficiary before September 1. On October 9, Applicant and Beneficiary met and agreed that all unpaid invoices dated before September 11 would be paid by Applicant's wiring the payment to Beneficiary rather than by the Beneficiary's presenting the invoices to Bank. Six days after the meeting Applicant wired enough money to Beneficiary to pay all pre-September 11 invoices. But Beneficiary, in apparent violation of the agreement, allocated the wire payment to invoices dated after September 11, and used the letter of credit to draw on Bank for several pre-September 11 invoices. In doing so Beneficiary submitted its certificate that the invoices had not been paid. When Applicant learned of this, it urged Bank not to pay the letter of credit, contending that Beneficiary was defrauding Bank and Applicant by drawing on invoices that it knew were already paid. Bank dishonored the letter of credit. Beneficiary sued Bank for wrongful dishonor and justified its conduct by stating its understanding of the agreement with Applicant to be that Beneficiary had to apply the wire payment to pre-September 11 invoices only if Applicant had sent the payment on October 10, and Applicant did not do so. If you were Bank's counsel would you have advised Bank to dishonor the letter of credit in this case? Comment 2 to § 5–109. If Applicant had applied to your court for an injunction against payment of the letter of credit by Bank, would you have issued the injunction? The facts are based on Roman Ceramics Corp. v. Peoples National Bank, 714 F.2d 1207 (3d Cir.1983).

F. LETTERS OF CREDIT IN BANKRUPTCY

If a standby letter of credit is to be useful as the functional equivalent of a guaranty, it must pass muster in bankruptcy. So far it has. The initial question is whether the automatic stay of Bankruptcy Code § 362(a) restrains the beneficiary from drawing on the issuer after the applicant's bankruptcy. If it does, the utility of letters of credit is greatly impaired for the beneficiary would be forced to go through the expensive and time-consuming procedure to lift the stay under § 362(d). As we have shown, the usual letter of credit transaction involves three undertakings: the letter of credit between the issuer and the beneficiary; the underlying contract between the applicant and the beneficiary; and the reimbursement contract between the applicant and the issuer. There is no question that the automatic stay precludes any action by the beneficiary against the applicant on the underlying contract as well as any action by the issuer against the applicant on the reimbursement agreement.

That § 362(a) does not stay the beneficiary's draw against the issuer was decided in In re Page, 18 B.R. 713 (D.D.C.1982), and has been widely accepted. In that case the applicant granted security interests in its assets to issuer to secure its obligation to reimburse the issuer if the issuer had to pay the letter of credit. The bankruptcy court held that unless payment of the letter of credit were enjoined, the issuer, after payment, would be able to realize on its security interest in debtor's property, thereby reducing the assets available to the other creditors. The district court reversed on the ground that before the applicant had filed in bankruptcy the issuer already had a perfected security interest in the applicant's assets to secure its contingent claim for reimbursement. In its payment of the letter of credit, the issuer merely liquidated its claim against the applicant for reimbursement, and applicant's other creditors are no worse off because the property of the applicant's bankruptcy estate has not been depleted. The letter of credit was not, of course, property of the applicant's estate. The court demonstrated its respect for the importance of the independence principle of letter of credit law: "Moreover, enjoining the payment of the letter of credit, even temporarily, would frustrate the commercial purposes of letters of credit to the detriment of financial institutions as well as their customers. * * * If payment on a letter of credit could be routinely delayed by the filing of a Chapter 11 petition the intended substitution of a bank for its less credit-worthy customer would be defeated." 18 B.R. at 717.

The more difficult problems concerning letters of credit in bankruptcy have arisen in the area of voidable preferences law as illustrated in the following case.

Matter of Compton Corp.

United States Court of Appeals, Fifth Circuit, 1987.
831 F.2d 586.

■ JERRE S. WILLIAMS, CIRCUIT JUDGE:

This is a bankruptcy preference case in which a bankruptcy trustee seeks to recover a transfer made via a letter of credit for the benefit of one of the debtor's unsecured creditors on the eve of bankruptcy. The bankruptcy court and the district court found there to be no voidable preference. We reverse.

I. *Factual Background*

In March 1982, Blue Quail Energy, Inc., delivered a shipment of oil to debtor Compton Corporation. Payment of $585,443.85 for this shipment of oil was due on or about April 20, 1982. Compton failed to make timely payment. Compton induced Abilene National Bank (now MBank–Abilene) to issue an irrevocable standby letter of credit in Blue Quail's favor on May 6, 1982. Under the terms of the letter of credit, payment of up to $585,443.85 was due Blue Quail if Compton failed to pay Blue Quail this amount by June 22, 1982. Compton paid MBank $1,463.61 to issue the letter of credit. MBank also received a promissory note payable on demand for $585,443.85. MBank did not need a security agreement to cover the letter of credit transaction because a prior 1980 security agreement between the bank and Compton had a future advances provision. This 1980 security agreement had been perfected as to a variety of Compton's assets through the filing of several financing statements. The most recent financing statement had been filed a year before, May 7, 1981. The letter of credit on its face noted that it was for an antecedent debt due Blue Quail.

On May 7, 1982, the day after MBank issued the letter of credit in Blue Quail's favor, several of Compton's creditors filed an involuntary bankruptcy petition against Compton. On June 22, 1982, MBank paid Blue Quail $569,932.03 on the letter of credit after Compton failed to pay Blue Quail.

In the ensuing bankruptcy proceeding, MBank's aggregate secured claims against Compton, including the letter of credit payment to Blue Quail, were paid in full from the liquidation of Compton's assets which served as the bank's collateral. Walter Kellogg, bankruptcy trustee for Compton, did not contest the validity of MBank's secured claim against Compton's assets for the amount drawn under the letter of credit by Blue Quail. Instead, on June 14, 1983, trustee Kellogg filed a complaint in the bankruptcy court against Blue Quail asserting that Blue Quail had received a preferential transfer under § 547 through the letter of credit transaction. The trustee sought to recover $585,443.85 from Blue Quail pursuant to § 550.

Blue Quail answered and filed a third party complaint against MBank. On June 16, 1986, Blue Quail filed a motion for summary judgment asserting that the trustee could not recover any preference from Blue Quail because Blue Quail had been paid from MBank's funds under the letter of credit and therefore had not received any of Compton's property. On August 27, 1986, the bankruptcy court granted Blue Quail's motion, agreeing that the payment under the letter of credit did not constitute a transfer of debtor Compton's property but rather was a transfer of the bank's property. The bankruptcy court entered judgment on the motion on September 10, 1986. Trustee Kellogg appealed this decision to the district court. On December 11, 1986, the district court affirmed the bankruptcy court ruling, holding that the trustee did not establish two necessary elements of a voidable transfer under § 547. The district court agreed with Blue Quail and the bankruptcy court that the trustee could not establish that the funds transferred to Blue Quail were ever property of Compton. Furthermore, the district court held that the transfer of the increased security interest to MBank was a transfer of the debtor's property for the sole benefit of the bank and in no way benefitted Blue Quail. The district court therefore found no voidable preference as to Blue Quail. The trustee is appealing the decision to this Court.

II. *The Letter of Credit*

It is well established that a letter of credit and the proceeds therefrom are not property of the debtor's estate under § 541. * * * When the issuer honors a proper draft under a letter of credit, it does so from its own assets and not from the assets of its customer who caused the letter of credit to be issued. * * * As a result, a bankruptcy trustee is not entitled to enjoin a post petition payment of funds under a letter of credit from the issuer to the beneficiary, because such a payment is not a transfer of debtor's property (a threshold requirement under § 547(b)). A case apparently holding otherwise, In re Twist Cap, Inc., 1 B.R. 284 (Bankr.Fla.1979), has been roundly criticized and otherwise ignored by courts and commentators alike.

Recognizing these characteristics of a letter of credit in a bankruptcy case is necessary in order to maintain the independence principle, the cornerstone of letter of credit law. Under the independence principle, an issuer's obligation to the letter of credit's beneficiary is independent from any obligation between the beneficiary and the issuer's customer. All a beneficiary has to do to receive payment under a letter of credit is to show that it has performed all the duties required by the letter of credit. Any disputes between the beneficiary and the customer do not affect the issuer's obligation to the beneficiary to pay under the letter of credit.

Letters of credit are most commonly arranged by a party who benefits from the provision of goods or services. The party will request a bank to issue a letter of credit which names the provider of the goods or services as the beneficiary. Under a standby letter of credit, the bank becomes primarily liable to the beneficiary upon the default of the bank's customer to pay for the goods or services. The bank charges a fee to issue a letter of credit and to undertake this liability. The shifting of liability to the bank rather than to the services or goods provider is the main purpose of the letter of credit. After all, the bank is in a much better position to assess the risk of its customer's insolvency than is the the service or goods provider. It should be noted, however, that it is the risk of the debtor's insolvency and not the risk of a preference attack that a bank assumes under a letter of credit transaction. Overall, the independence principle is necessary to insure "the certainty of payments for services or goods rendered regardless of any intervening misfortune which may befall the other contracting party." In re North Shore, 30 B.R. at 378.

The trustee in this case accepts this analysis and does not ask us to upset it. The trustee is not attempting to set aside the post petition payments by MBank to Blue Quail under the letter of credit as a preference; nor does the trustee claim the letter of credit itself constitutes debtor's property. The trustee is instead challenging the earlier transfer in which Compton granted MBank an increased security interest in its assets to obtain the letter of credit for the benefit of Blue Quail. Collateral which has been pledged by a debtor as security for a letter of credit is property of the debtor's estate. In re W.L. Mead, 42 B.R. at 59. The trustee claims that the direct transfer to MBank of the increased security interest on May 6, 1982, also constituted an indirect transfer to Blue Quail which occurred one day prior to the filing of the involuntary bankruptcy petition and is voidable as a preference under § 547. This assertion of a preferential transfer is evaluated in Parts III and IV of this opinion.

It is important to note that the irrevocable standby letter of credit in the case at bar was not arranged in connection with Blue Quail's initial decision to sell oil to Compton on credit. Compton arranged for the letter of credit after Blue Quail had shipped the oil and after Compton had defaulted in payment. The letter of credit in this case did not serve its usual function of backing up a contemporaneous credit decision, but instead served as a back up payment guarantee on an extension of credit already in jeopardy. The letter of credit was issued to pay off an antecedent unsecured debt.

This fact was clearly noted on the face of the letter of credit. Blue Quail, the beneficiary of the letter of credit, did not give new value for the issuance of the letter of credit by MBank on May 6, 1982, or for the resulting increased security interest held by MBank. MBank, however, did give new value for the increased security interest it obtained in Compton's collateral: the bank issued the letter of credit.

When a debtor pledges its assets to secure a letter of credit, a transfer of debtor's property has occurred under the provisions of § 547. By subjecting its assets to MBank's reimbursement claim in the event MBank had to pay on the letter of credit, Compton made a transfer of its property. The broad definition of "transfer" under § 101 is clearly designed to cover such a transfer. Overall, the letter of credit itself and the payments thereunder may not be property of debtor, but the collateral pledged as a security interest for the letter of credit is.

Furthermore, in a secured letter of credit transaction, the transfer of debtor's property takes place at the time the letter of credit is issued (when the security interest is granted) and received by the beneficiary, not at the time the issuer pays on the letter of credit. * * *

The transfer to MBank of the increased security interest was a direct transfer which occurred on May 6, 1982, when the bank issued the letter of credit. Under § 547(e)(2)(A), however, such a transfer is deemed to have taken place for purposes of § 547 at the time such transfer "takes effect" between the transferor and transferee if such transfer is perfected within 10 days. The phrase "takes effect" is undefined in the Bankruptcy Code, but under Uniform Commercial Code Article 9 law, a transfer of a security interest "takes effect" when the security interest attaches. Because of the future advances clause in MBank's 1980 security agreement with Compton, the attachment of the MBank's security interest relates back to May 9, 1980, the date the security agreement went into effect. The bottom line is that the direct transfer of the increased security interest to MBank is artificially deemed to have occurred at least by May 7, 1981, the date MBank filed its final financing statement, for purposes of a preference attack against the bank.[4] This date is well before the 90 day window of § 547(b)(4)(A). This would protect the bank from a preference attack by the trustee even if the bank had not given new value at the time it received the increased security interest.[1] MBank is therefore protected from a

4. UCC § 9–312(7) specifies that for purposes of priority among competing secured parties, the security interest for a future advance has the same priority as the security interest for the first advance. Conflicting security interests rank according to priority in time of filing or perfection. UCC § 9–312(5).

1. [Editors' Note: The "relation back" theory of the Court is not supported by the Bankruptcy Code. The Court is correct in stating that the phrase "at the time such

transfer takes effect" in § 547(e)(2)(A) refers to the time the security interest "attaches" under the UCC. The time of attachment is governed by UCC § 9–203. In this case attachment occurred when three events occurred: (1) value was given by MBank; (2) the debtor had rights in the collateral; and (3) the debtor signed a security agreement providing for the security interest. The second and third events occurred before May 6, but MBank did not give value with respect to the transfer challenged by the trustee in bank-

preference attack by the trustee for the increased security interest transfer under either of two theories: under § 547(c)(1) because it gave new value and under the operation of the relation back provision of § 547(e)(2)(A). The bank is also protected from any claims of reimbursement by Blue Quail because the bank received no voidable preference.

The relation back provision of § 547(e)(2)(A), however, applies only to the direct transfer of the increased security interest to MBank. The indirect transfer to Blue Quail that allegedly resulted from the direct transfer to MBank occurred on May 6, 1982, the date of issuance of the letter of credit. The relation back principle of § 547(e)(2)(A) does not apply to this indirect transfer to Blue Quail. Blue Quail was not a party to the security agreement between MBank and Compton. So it will not be able to utilize the relation back provision if it is deemed to have received an indirect transfer resulting from the direct transfer of the increased security interest to MBank. Blue Quail, therefore, cannot assert either of the two defenses to a preference attack which MBank can claim. Blue Quail did not give new value under § 547(c)(1), and it received a transfer within 90 days of the filing of Compton's bankruptcy petition.

III.   *Direct/Indirect Transfer Doctrine*

The federal courts have long recognized that "[t]o constitute a preference, it is not necessary that the transfer be made directly to the creditor." National Bank of Newport v. National Herkimer County Bank, 225 U.S. 178, 184 (1912). "If the bankrupt has made a transfer of his property, the *effect* of which is to enable one of his creditors to obtain a greater percentage of his debt than another creditor of the same class, circuity of arrangement will not avail to save it." Id. (Emphasis added). To combat such circuity, the courts have broken down certain transfers into two transfers, one direct and one indirect. The direct transfer to the third party may be valid and not subject to a preference attack. The indirect transfer, arising from the same action by the debtor, however, may constitute a voidable preference as to the creditor who indirectly benefitted from the direct transfer to the third party.

This is the situation presented in the case before us. The term "transfer" as used in the various bankruptcy statutes through the years has always been broad enough to cover such indirect transfers and to catch

---

ruptcy until the letter of credit was issued on May 6. Thus, under § 547(e)(2)(A), the transfer could not have occurred before May 6. Under UCC § 9–303, the security interest that attached on May 6 was perfected at the time it attached because the filing of a financing statement—the applicable step required for perfection—had already occurred before May 6. Because May 6 is the day of both attachment and perfection, the result under § 547(e)(2)(A) is that the transfer from the debtor to MBank occurred on May 6. It is irrelevant under § 547 that UCC § 9–312(5) and (7) date the priority of MBank with respect to the May 6 transaction from the time MBank filed its financing statement. § 547(e)(2)(A) refers to the time of attachment and perfection, not to the date of priority. There is no avoidable preference in this case, however. The Court correctly holds that the giving of value by MBank and the transfer by the debtor to MBank were a contemporaneous exchange under § 547(c)(1).]

various circuitous arrangements. Katz v. First National Bank of Glen Head, 568 F.2d 964, 969 n. 4, (2d Cir.), cert. denied, 434 U.S. 1069 (1978). The new Bankruptcy Code implicitly adopts this doctrine through its broad definition of "transfer."[2] Examining the case law that has developed since the *National Bank of Newport* case yields an understanding of what types of transfers the direct/indirect doctrine is meant to cover.

In Palmer v. Radio Corporation of America, 453 F.2d 1133 (5th Cir.1971), a third party purchased from the debtor a television station for $40,000 cash and the assumption of certain liabilities of the debtor, including unsecured claims by creditor RCA. This Court found the direct transfer from the debtor to the third party purchaser constituted an indirect preferential transfer to creditor RCA. We found that the assumption by the third party purchaser of the debt owed by the debtor to RCA and the subsequent payments made thereunder constituted a voidable transfer as to RCA. The court noted that such indirect transfers as this had long been held to constitute voidable preferences under bankruptcy laws. 453 F.2d at 1136.

* * *

In Virginia National Bank v. Woodson, 329 F.2d 836 (4th Cir.1964), the debtor had several overdrawn accounts with his bank. The debtor talked his sister into paying off $8,000 of the overdrafts in exchange for an $8,000 promissory note and an assignment of some collateral as security. The debtor's sister made the $8,000 payment directly to the bank. The $8,000 technically was never part of the debtor's estate. The court, however, held that the payment of the $8,000 by the sister to the bank was a preference as to the bank to the extent of the value of the collateral held by the sister. The court noted that the measure of the value of a voidable preference is diminution of the debtor's estate and not the value of the transfer to the creditor.

In the *Woodson* case the sister was secured only to the extent the pledged collateral had value; the remainder of her loan to her brother was unsecured. Swapping one unsecured creditor for another unsecured creditor does not create any kind of preference. The court held that a preference in such a transaction arises only when a secured creditor is swapped for an unsecured creditor. Only then is the pool of assets available for distribution to the general unsecured creditors depleted because the secured creditor has priority over the unsecured creditors. Furthermore, the court held that the bank and not the sister had received the voidable preference and had to pay back to the trustee an amount equal to the value of the collateral.

* * *

2. "Transfer" means every mode, direct or *indirect,* absolute or conditional, voluntary or involuntary, of disposing of or parting with property or with an interest in property, including retention of title as a security interest and foreclosure of the debtor's equity of redemption. § 101 (emphasis added). See also the Notes of the Committee on the Judiciary under 11 U.S.C. 101 ("The definition of transfer is as broad as possible.")

IV. *The Direct/Indirect Doctrine in the Context*
of a Letter of Credit Transaction

The case at bar differs from the cases discussed in Part III supra only by the presence of the letter of credit as the mechanism for paying off the unsecured creditor. Blue Quail's attempt to otherwise distinguish the case from the direct/indirect transfer cases does not withstand scrutiny.

In the letter of credit cases discussed in Part II supra, the letters of credit were issued contemporaneously with the initial extension of credit by the beneficiaries of the letters. In those cases the letters of credit effectively served as security devices for the benefit of the creditor beneficiaries and took the place of formal security interests. The courts in those cases properly found there had been no voidable transfers, direct or indirect, in the letter of credit transactions involved. New value was given contemporaneously with the issuance of the letters of credit in the form of the extensions of credit by the beneficiaries of the letters. As a result, the § 547(c)(1) preference exception was applicable.

The case at bar differs from these other letter of credit cases by one very important fact: the letter of credit in this case was issued to secure an antecedent unsecured debt due the beneficiary of the letter of credit. The unsecured creditor beneficiary gave no new value upon the issuance of the letter of credit. When the issuer paid off the letter of credit and foreclosed on the collateral securing the letter of credit, a preferential transfer had occurred. An unsecured creditor was paid in full and a secured creditor was substituted in its place.

The district court upheld the bankruptcy court in maintaining the validity of the letter of credit issued to cover the antecedent debt. The district court held that MBank, the issuer of the letter of credit, could pay off the letter of credit and foreclose on the collateral securing it. We are in full agreement. But we also look to the impact of the transaction as it affects the situation of Blue Quail in the bankrupt estate. We hold that the bankruptcy trustee can recover from Blue Quail, the beneficiary of the letter of credit, because Blue Quail received an indirect preference. This result preserves the sanctity of letter of credit and carries out the purposes of the Bankruptcy Code by avoiding a preferential transfer. MBank, the issuer of the letter of credit, being just the intermediary through which the preferential transfer was accomplished, completely falls out of the picture and is not involved in this particular legal proceeding.

MBank did not receive any preferential transfer—it gave new value for the security interest. Furthermore, because the direct and indirect transfers are separate and independent, the trustee does not even need to challenge the direct transfer of the increased security interest to MBank, or seek any relief at all from MBank, in order to attack the indirect transfer and recover under § 550 from the indirect transferee Blue Quail.

We hold that a creditor cannot secure payment of an unsecured antecedent debt through a letter of credit transaction when it could not do so through any other type of transaction. The purpose of the letter of credit transaction in this case was to secure payment of an unsecured antecedent debt for the benefit of an unsecured creditor. This is the only proper way to look at such letters of credit in the bankruptcy context. The promised transfer of pledged collateral induced the bank to issue the letter of credit in favor of the creditor. The increased security interest held by the bank clearly benefitted the creditor because the bank would not have issued the letter of credit without this security. A secured creditor was substituted for an unsecured creditor to the detriment of the other unsecured creditors.

* * *

The precise holding in this case needs to be emphasized. We do not hold that payment under a letter of credit, or even a letter of credit itself, constitute preferential transfers under § 547(b) or property of a debtor under § 541. The holding of this case fully allows the letter of credit to function. We preserve its sanctity and the underlying independence doctrine. We do not, however, allow an unsecured creditor to avoid a preference attack by utilizing a letter of credit to secure payment of an antecedent debt. Otherwise the unsecured creditor would receive an indirect preferential transfer from the granting of the security for the letter of credit to the extent of the value of that security. Our holding does not affect the strength of or the proper use of letters of credit. When a letter of credit is issued contemporaneously with a new extension of credit, the creditor beneficiary will not be subject to a preferential attack under the direct/indirect doctrine elaborated in this case because the creditor will have given new value in exchange for the indirect benefit of the secured letter of credit. Only when a creditor receives a secured letter of credit to cover an unsecured antecedent debt will it be subject to a preferential attack under § 547(b).

* * *

NOTE

In *Compton* we see that a debtor who already owes a debt makes a voidable preference to the creditor if it causes a bank to issue a letter of credit to the creditor to secure the debt within 90 days of bankruptcy. If the debtor had paid the creditor or had granted the creditor a security interest in the debtor's property during the 90–day period, there would clearly be a preference. The debtor cannot alter this result by use of a letter of credit. But letters of credit are not normally used to secure antecedent debts. The usual case is one in which the letter of credit is issued to the creditor at the inception of the credit transaction between the beneficiary and applicant. An example is one in which the beneficiary sells goods to the debtor-applicant on credit and takes a standby letter of credit to protect itself against the debtor-applicant's failure to pay. Here the seller-beneficiary gives new value at the time it receives the letter of credit. Is it possible for a preference problem to arise in such a case?

Take two cases:

Case #1. Beneficiary sold goods to Applicant on 60–day credit for $100,000 and demanded a letter of credit to secure it against Applicant's default. Applicant induced Bank to issue the letter of credit by granting Bank a security interest in its property worth in excess of $100,000 to secure its agreement to reimburse Bank. Applicant was unable to pay for the goods at the end of the credit period but induced Beneficiary not to draw on the letter of credit for a month. At the end of the month Applicant, though thoroughly insolvent, paid $100,000 to Beneficiary in satisfaction of the debt. Within 90 days of the payment, Applicant filed in bankruptcy and its trustee sought to recover the payment as a voidable preference. There should be no preference in this case under § 547(b)(5), and it shouldn't matter if payment to Beneficiary came from Bank or Applicant. The transfer of assets from Applicant's estate occurred when the security interest was granted to Bank, and Bank gave new value for that transfer by undertaking to pay Beneficiary. If Bank pays Beneficiary, Bank has a valid secured claim in Applicant's bankruptcy for $100,000. If Applicant pays, Bank's claim to the security is released and, although Applicant's unsecured creditors have lost $100,000 in the cash payment Applicant made to Beneficiary, they have gained the same amount in the release of Bank's claim against Applicant's property. The transfer of assets that depleted Applicant's estate to the detriment of its creditors took place before the beginning of the 90–day period.

Case #2. Difficulties arise when we change only one fact in the case above. Assume that Applicant either granted no security interest in its property to Bank or, more realistically, granted a security interest in property that eventually turned out to be worth much less than $100,000. Let's assume for purposes of discussion that the collateral became worthless. If Bank pays Beneficiary on the letter of credit, there is no preference because Bank's payment does not transfer property of Applicant's estate. Before payment Applicant owed $100,000 to Beneficiary on an unsecured claim; after payment Applicant owes the same amount to Bank on an unsecured claim. The problem arises if Applicant, rather than Bank, pays the Beneficiary. Here $100,000 in cash has been taken from Applicant's estate for the benefit of Beneficiary during the 90–day period. We look at preferences from the point of view of the debtor's unsecured creditors; are they worse off after the transfer than before? True, Applicant has been relieved from Bank's unsecured contingent claim for reimbursement, but that does not put money into the Applicant's estate for the benefit of its creditors. In re Powerine Oil Co., 59 F.3d 969 (9th Cir.1995), held that payment by the Applicant in such a case is preferential, even though payment by the Bank in the same case would not be. Noting that the result of this case makes Beneficiary better off if its debtor, the Applicant, defaults, the court said "Law can be stranger than fiction in the Preference Zone." 59 F.3d at 971. The Bankruptcy Appellate Panel had held that the payment was not a preference because it did not enable the Beneficiary to obtain more than it would in a Chapter 7 bankruptcy. If Applicant hadn't paid it, Bank would have had to. Could you contend that Bank rather than Beneficiary is the recipient of the preference in *Powerine*?

GOOD FAITH PURCHASE AND DOCUMENTS OF TITLE

A. GOOD FAITH PURCHASE

1. GOODS

Under the holder-in-due-course doctrine, a person who purchases a negotiable instrument from a thief can, under some circumstances, acquire title to the instrument free of the claim of the owner from whom the instrument was stolen. § 3–306. There is no comparable common law doctrine applicable to goods. At common law a person without legal title to goods cannot convey legal title to anybody. There is, however, a common law doctrine that allows a person with an imperfect title to goods to convey good title to a bona fide purchaser for value. For example, if X, through fraudulent representations, induced Y to transfer title of goods to X, traditional legal analysis was that X had legal title to the goods, but Y had a right recognized in equity to rescind the transaction and revest title in Y. X's imperfect legal title is referred to as "voidable title." But if X sold the goods to a bona fide purchaser for value having no notice of Y's claim, the BFP got good title free of Y's claim. The transaction of sale between X and the BFP resulted in passage of the legal title to the BFP. Since in equity there was no basis for choosing between Y and BFP, two innocent parties, BFP's legal title was left undisturbed. Y had rights only against X. The common law doctrine is illustrated by Phelps v. McQuade which follows. *Phelps* demonstrates that the common law rule is easy to state but difficult to apply. Section 2–403(1) is a codification of the common law rule with some amplification.

a. VOIDABLE TITLE

Phelps v. McQuade

Court of Appeals of New York, 1917.
220 N.Y. 232, 115 N.E. 441, 1918B, L.R.A. 973.

■ ANDREWS, J. One Walter J. Gwynne falsely represented to the appellants that he was Baldwin J. Gwynne, a man of financial responsibility, residing at Cleveland, Ohio. Relying upon the truth of this statement the appellants delivered to him upon credit a quantity of jewelry. Gwynne in turn sold it to the respondent, who bought it without notice, express or implied, of any defect in title, and for value. Learning of the deception practiced upon them, the appellants began an action in replevin to recover the goods.

The only question before us is whether under such circumstances, the vendor of personal property does or does not retain title thereto after he has parted with possession thereof.

The learned Appellate Division rested their decision upon the definition of common law larceny, holding that where such larceny had been committed the thief acquired no title by his crime; where it had not, at least a voidable title passed. We agree with that statement of the law. But we should prefer to define the rule in another form. Where the vendor of personal property intends to sell his goods to the person with whom he deals, then title passes, even though he be deceived as to that person's identity or responsibility. Otherwise it does not. It is purely a question of the vendor's intention.

The fact that the vendor deals with the person personally rather than by letter is immaterial, except in so far as it bears upon the question of intent.

Where the transaction is a personal one, the seller intends to transfer title to a person of credit, and he supposes the one standing before him to be that person. He is deceived. But in spite of that fact his primary intention is to sell his goods to the person with whom he negotiates.

Where the transaction is by letter the vendor intends to deal with the person whose name is signed to the letter. He knows no one else. He supposes he is dealing with no one else. And while in both cases other facts may be shown that would alter the rule, yet in their absence, in the first, title passes; in the second, it does not. Two cases that illustrate the distinction are Edmunds v. Merchants' Dispatch Transportation Company, 135 Mass. 283, and Cundy v. Lindsay, 3 App.Cas. 463.

In Edmunds v. Merchants' Dispatch Transportation Company a swindler, representing himself to be one Edward Pape, personally bought goods of the plaintiff on credit. The court held that the title passed. "The minds of the parties met and agreed upon all the terms of the sale, the thing sold, the price and time of payment, the person selling and the person buying. The fact that the seller was induced to sell by fraud of the buyer made the sale voidable, but not void. He could not have supposed that he was selling to any other person; his intention was to sell to the person present, and identified by sight and hearing; it does not defeat the sale because the buyer assumed a false name, or practiced any other deceit to induce the vendor to sell."

* * *

In Cundy v. Lindsay one Blenkarn, signing himself Blenkiron & Co., bought goods by letter of Lindsay & Co. The latter shipped the goods to Blenkiron & Co. They knew of the firm of Blenkiron & Son; believed the letter came from that firm and that the goods were shipped to it. Blenkiron & Son were the persons with whom Lindsay & Co., intended to deal and supposed they were dealing. Under those circumstances it was held that, although Blenkarn obtained possession of the goods, he never acquired title thereto.

* * *

Another class of cases such as Hentz v. Miller, 94 N.Y. 64, and Consumers' Ice Company of Buffalo v. E. Webster, Son & Co., 32 App.Div. 592, 53 N.Y.S. 56, illustrate the rule under different circumstances. In them, persons falsely stating that they are the agents or representatives of others fraudulently obtained possession of goods under a pretense of sale to such others. There is no intention on the part of the vendor to sell to the pretended agent or representative and no title passes.

In indictments for larceny, before the definition of that crime was changed by statute, this question of the passing of title was material; and, therefore, discussions as to whether an indictment or conviction could be sustained were relevant in cases where the question was whether or not the title had in fact passed. But in cases of each class the intention of the person having title to the goods and delivering them to another was the ultimate matter to be decided. And although it might be said in the one class of cases that where title did not pass there was no larceny, and in the other that where there was larceny the title did not pass, yet in both the test to be applied was this same intention on the part of the owner of the property.

The judgment of the Appellate Division must be affirmed, with costs.

NOTES

1. In Rogers v. Dutton, 182 Mass. 187, 65 N.E. 56 (1902), a man who identified himself as Simmons fraudulently represented to Seller that he was Buyer's agent and that Buyer wanted to purchase some hay. Induced by these misrepresentations, Seller agreed to sell Buyer the hay and delivered it to Buyer's place of business. Simmons told Buyer that the hay belonged to Simmons. Simmons sold it to Buyer, received payment, and absconded. Seller was allowed to recover the hay. Holmes, C. J., stated: "It is evident on these facts that there was no sale and that plaintiff never parted with his title." 182 Mass. at 188–189, 65 N.E. at 56. In *Rogers* there was a misrepresentation of authority to act for Buyer but no impersonation. Suppose Buyer had an authorized agent named Simmons, that Seller was aware of that fact, and that an impostor represented to Seller that he was Simmons. If all the other facts in *Rogers* were the same, should the result be different?

2. How would § 2–403 apply to the face-to-face impersonation in *Phelps*, the impersonation by letter referred to in *Phelps*, and the misrepresentation of agency in *Rogers*?

3. The third sentence of § 2–403(1) provides that when goods have been delivered under a "transaction of purchase" the purchaser has the power to transfer good title to a good faith purchaser for value in four cases: deception as to identity, receipt of a bad check, cash sale, and fraudulent delivery. Was the use of the quoted phrase a drafting error which might frustrate the purpose of the third sentence? That is, if a jurisdiction's pre-Code case law is that of *Phelps*, has the property been delivered to the defrauder pursuant to a "transaction of purchase" if the seller did not intend to pass title? See the definition of "purchase" in § 1–201(32).

b. ENTRUSTING

Article 2 codifies the common law doctrine of good faith purchase in § 2–403(1), but it goes beyond that doctrine by introducing the concept of "entrusting to a merchant" which may allow a buyer to acquire good title to goods from a seller who had no title whatsoever. This concept is stated in § 2–403(2) and (3).

Canterra Petroleum, Inc. v. Western Drilling & Mining Supply

Supreme Court of North Dakota, 1987.
418 N.W.2d 267.

■ ERICKSTAD, CHIEF JUSTICE.

* * *

This multi-party litigation arises out of various transactions involving a certain quantity of oilfield pipe. The pipe was originally owned by Mitchell Energy Corporation ["Mitchell"]. In late 1981, Mitchell entrusted the pipe to Port Pipe Terminal, Inc. ["Port Pipe"] for storage.

Through paper transactions, two high-ranking employees of Port Pipe succeeded in fraudulently transferring apparent ownership of the pipe to Pharoah, Inc. ["Pharoah"], a "dummy" corporation which they had created to facilitate the fraudulent sale of merchandise stored at Port Pipe's facilities. On March 3, 1982, Pharoah sold the pipe owned by Mitchell to Nickel Supply Company, Inc. ["Nickel"]. On that same date, Nickel sold the pipe to Yamin Oil Supply ["Yamin"]. Five days later Yamin sold the pipe to NorthStar. On March 23, 1982, NorthStar sold it to Western, which a few days later sold it to Canterra Petroleum, Inc. ["Canterra"].

All of these intervening transactions, culminating in the sale to Canterra, were paper transactions only. The pipe never left Port Pipe's storage facility in Houston, Texas, until Canterra had it delivered to Getter Trucking in Dickinson sometime after its purchase in March 1982. The pipe remained stored at Getter Trucking until December 1983, when Canterra relinquished the pipe to Mitchell upon being informed by law enforcement agencies that the pipe was owned by Mitchell.

Canterra sued Western for breach of warranty of title seeking damages of $201,014.39, the price Canterra had paid for the pipe, plus interest. Western commenced a third-party action against NorthStar for breach of warranty of title, and NorthStar commenced a fourth-party action against Yamin.

Canterra moved for and received summary judgment against Western. Western then moved for summary judgment on its third-party claim against NorthStar. The court granted summary judgment to Western, awarding $228,245.72 in damages and interest. NorthStar has appealed from the judgment.

NorthStar contends that it did not breach the warranty of title, and that it presented sufficient evidence to demonstrate that material issues of fact remain to be resolved on the issue of title. * * * NorthStar contends that this case falls within the entrustment provision of * * * U.C.C. § 2–403:

> "2. Any entrusting of possession of goods to a merchant who deals in goods of that kind gives him power to transfer all rights of the entruster to a buyer in ordinary course of business."

In essence, this statute contains three elements: (1) an entrustment of goods, (2) to a merchant who deals in goods of the kind, (3) followed by a sale to a buyer in the ordinary course of business. * * * If all three elements are present, the rights of the entruster are transferred to the buyer in ordinary course of business. NorthStar argues that Mitchell entrusted the pipe to Port Pipe, a merchant who dealt in pipe, and that through Pharoah the pipe was sold to Nickel, a buyer in the ordinary course of business.

The trial court held that, based upon the affidavits presented, there was no factual dispute as to Port Pipe's status and that, as a matter of law, Port Pipe was merely a storage facility and not a merchant which dealt in pipe. * * *

The determination whether a party to a transaction is a "merchant" under the Uniform Commercial Code is a question of fact. * * *

Western contends that there is no dispute as to the facts regarding this issue, and that the court correctly determined as a matter of law that Port Pipe is a storage facility and not a merchant dealing in pipe. Western relies primarily upon the affidavits of Bradley Beers, an assistant district attorney in Texas who prosecuted the two employees responsible for diverting materials stored at Port Pipe's facilities, and Janet Chisholm, former president of Port Pipe. These affidavits state in conclusory terms that Port Pipe was not a "merchant" dealing in oilfield pipe. Chisholm's affidavit, however, goes on to state that "Port Pipe * * * did sell small quantities of pipe from time to time, to clear odd lots, or to sell that pipe remaining after a substantial portion of a lot was sold."

The entrustment statute requires that goods be entrusted to a "merchant who deals in goods of that kind." * * * U.C.C. § 2–403. The requirement that the party "deals in goods" has been construed to mean one who is engaged regularly in selling goods of the kind. * * *

The conclusory statements contained in the affidavits of Beers and Chisholm that Port Pipe was not a merchant which dealt in oilfield pipe are not dispositive of the issue. * * *

The relevant factual inquiry is whether Port Pipe was regularly engaged in selling pipe. The party opposing summary judgment, in this case NorthStar, is entitled to all favorable inferences which can reasonably be drawn from the evidence. * * * Viewing Chisholm's affidavit in the light most favorable to NorthStar, we conclude that it does raise an inference that Port Pipe regularly sold pipe. Chisholm admits that Port Pipe did sell pipe "from time to time." It will be for the factfinder, after presentation of further evidence regarding the frequency and quantity of Port Pipe's sales of pipe, to determine whether Port Pipe regularly engaged in the sale of pipe and therefore was a merchant which dealt in pipe.

* * *

Western also contends that, even if a fact question remains unresolved regarding Port Pipe's merchant status, summary judgment is nevertheless appropriate. Western asserts that the entrustment doctrine of Section 2–403(2) applies only when the merchant who has been entrusted with the goods sells them in the ordinary course of business. Western contends that the doctrine does not apply where the goods are fraudulently transferred to a dummy corporation by employees of the entrustee and subsequently sold through the dummy corporation to a buyer in the ordinary course of business.

This is a troublesome issue, with neither party directing our attention to a case precisely on point. Both sides have, however, cited cases involving somewhat similar circumstances.

Western relies primarily upon * * * Olin Corp. v. Cargo Carriers, Inc., 673 S.W.2d 211 (Tex.Ct.App.1984).

* * *

In *Olin,* Olin had entrusted fertilizer for storage at the warehouse of Cargo Carriers. The superintendent of Cargo Carriers' warehouse, Jerry Dollar, entered into a scheme with Charles Flowers to sell some of Olin's fertilizer. Flowers would represent himself as the owner of the fertilizer, and Dollar would use his authority to release the fertilizer to the buyer. Several loads of fertilizer were sold in this manner to Ragsdale. When Olin sued Dollar, Flowers, Cargo Carriers, and Ragsdale for the misappropriated fertilizer, Ragsdale sought the protection of Section 2–403, U.C.C. The court held that the statute was inapplicable to Ragsdale because (1) his seller, Flowers, had no title,[2] (2) Olin never entrusted the fertilizer to

---

2. We are not certain why Flowers's lack of title was important. The entrustment statute *presupposes* that the seller to the buyer in ordinary course of business has no title to convey. If the seller had title, the buyer would not need the protection afforded by the statute, which allows the title of the entruster to pass to the buyer. Thus, in the classic entrustment example, when an owner entrusts goods to a merchant for repair and the merchant sells them to a buyer in the ordinary course of business, the merchant

Flowers, and (3) Flowers was not a merchant who dealt in the sale of fertilizer. *Olin,* supra, 673 S.W.2d at 216. These circumstances are materially distinguishable from the instant case. Flowers, Ragsdale's seller, was not an employee of Cargo Carriers but an outside party. Of even more significance is the court's finding that Flowers was not a merchant. Under those circumstances, the entrustment doctrine of Section 2–403, U.C.C., was inapplicable.

This case is readily distinguishable * * *. In *Olin,* the court's holding was based upon the intervention of Flowers, who was not a merchant and was a party unrelated to either the entruster or the entrustee. In this case, however, there is no intervention by an unrelated party. The intervention was by two high-ranking employees of Port Pipe, the entrustee, who allegedly sold the pipe through their dummy corporation, Pharoah, to a buyer in the ordinary course of business.

We believe this case to be more closely analogous to Standard Leasing Corp. v. Missouri Rock Co., 693 S.W.2d 232 (Mo.Ct.App.1985). In that case, Standard Leasing had entrusted two trucks to Herco for repair. Herco was a corporation in the business of leasing, selling, and repairing construction equipment. Herco's president, Robert Herring, transferred the trucks to Superior, a sham corporation created by Herring to fraudulently dispose of assets held by Herco. The trucks were sold by Superior to Dean, who in turn sold them to Missouri Rock. Standard Leasing sued Missouri Rock for replevin and conversion, and Missouri Rock claimed title under the entrustment doctrine. The court, in sustaining a jury verdict for Missouri Rock, held that the fraudulent transfer of the trucks from the entrustee, Herco, to a sham corporation controlled by Herco's president did not render the entrustment doctrine inapplicable. The court focused upon the underlying policies of Section 2–403:

> "Our conclusion is consistent with the policy of § 2–403(2) to increase the marketability of goods. See, Padgett, Uniform Commercial Code Section 2–403(2): The Authority of a Bailee to Convey Title, 21 U.Fla.L.Rev. 241, at 251 (1968–69). Section 2–403(2) places a greater burden on bailors than previous uniform commercial statutory enactments to exercise discretion in entrusting their goods to bailees. Id. In our case, both plaintiffs and defendants are innocent victims of fraudulent schemers. But under UCC 2–403(2) Standard took the risk that its bailee might set up a sham corporation to aid it in its unlawful transfer of Standard's property. Where one of two innocent parties must suffer a loss occasioned by a third person, the person who enabled the acts of the wrongdoer must suffer the loss." *Standard Leasing,* supra, 693 S.W.2d at 237.

This rationale has also been expressed in 3 Anderson, Uniform Commercial Code § 2–403:4 (3d ed. 1983) (quoting Sacks v. State, 172 Ind.App. 185, 360 N.E.2d 21 (1977)):

has no title but the title of the entruster   ute.
passes to the buyer by operation of the stat-

" 'Section 2–403 was intended to determine the priorities between two innocent parties: (1) the original owner who parts with his goods through fraudulent conduct of another and (2) an innocent third party who gives value for the goods to the perpetrator of the fraud without knowledge of the fraud. By favoring the innocent third party, the Uniform Commercial Code endeavors to promote the flow of commerce by placing the burden of ascertaining and preventing fraudulent transactions on the one in the best position to prevent them, the original seller.' "

We believe this policy also supports application of the entrustment doctrine to a situation where employees of the entrustee transfer the entrusted goods to their sham corporation, which in turn sells the goods to a buyer in the ordinary course of business. As between the two innocent parties in this case [Mitchell, which entrusted the pipe to Port Pipe, and Nickel, which bought the pipe in the ordinary course of business from Pharoah], the policy of the Code places the risk of the entrustee's employees fraudulently diverting and selling the goods upon the entruster, Mitchell, which had the opportunity to select its entrustee. Applying the doctrine to this case, Nickel would acquire the title of the entruster, Mitchell, and title would have passed on to the subsequent purchasers of the pipe.[3]

We conclude that the trial court erred in holding that, as a matter of law, Port Pipe was not a "merchant" under UCC § 2–403(2) and that the entrustment doctrine was therefore inapplicable. Material issues of fact remain which require resolution upon trial.

* * *

NOTE

Is the analysis in *Canterra* consistent with the language and policy of § 2–403(2)? In *Canterra*, Mitchell entrusted the pipe to Port Pipe. If Port Pipe is a merchant of pipe, § 2–403(2) applies and Port Pipe obtains "power to transfer all rights of the entruster to a buyer in ordinary course of business." Section 2–403(2) is meant to apply to cases in which the merchant to whom goods are entrusted sells the goods to a buyer in

---

3. This scenario presupposes, of course, that Port Pipe was a merchant. As previously noted, that determination will be for the finder of fact at trial. If it is found that Port Pipe was not a merchant, U.C.C. § 2–403 is inapplicable, and Mitchell retained title to the pipe.

Although not addressed by the parties, the "shelter" principle governs subsequent transactions after entrusted goods have been sold and title transferred to a buyer in ordinary course of business. The rule is explained in 3 Anderson, Uniform Commercial Code § 2–403:59 (3d ed. 1983):

"The sale by the entrustee makes a definitive transfer of the entruster's title. Hence, not only the immediate buyer from the entrustee but all successive transferees of the goods hold the title of the entruster. That is, once a buyer acquires title by virtue of UCC § 2–403, subsequent purchasers from him benefit by his title without regard to whether they themselves would qualify as buyers in ordinary course of business."

ordinary course. But in *Canterra*, Port Pipe did not sell the goods to anybody. Rather, "two high-ranking employees of Port Pipe succeeded in fraudulently transferring apparent ownership" of the pipe to Pharoah, a dummy corporation created by the employees. The court does not explain how this "transfer" occurred, but we do know that the pipe remained in the possession of Port Pipe. The court apparently reads the statute to apply not only to a sale by the merchant to whom the goods are entrusted, but also to a sale by an employee of the merchant. But even under that reading, to divest Mitchell of its title it is necessary to find that the employees sold to a buyer in ordinary course. The first purchaser of the pipe was Nickel but it bought from Pharoah. To divest Mitchell's title it is necessary to equate Pharoah and the employees who controlled it. But more is required. Pharoah couldn't give title to Nickel unless Nickel was a buyer in ordinary course. Nickel may have been a bona fide purchaser, but it apparently was not a buyer in ordinary course. As a dummy corporation created for the purpose of carrying out the fraud, Pharoah would not appear to be a "person in the business of selling" pipe as required by § 1–201(9). There may have been entrustment to a merchant and a buyer in ordinary course may have eventually purchased the pipe, but that alone is not enough to divest Mitchell of title.

PROBLEM

Consider the following cases:

Case # 1. Thief stole a diamond watch from Owner and sold it to Jeweler for $2,000.

Case # 2. Owner delivered a diamond watch to Jeweler for the purpose of having certain alterations made to it.

Case # 3. Owner delivered a diamond watch to Jeweler on the following terms: Jeweler was to exhibit it for sale at a price of $5,000; in the event that Jeweler found a purchaser no sale was to be made without Owner's prior consent; and, in the event of sale, Jeweler was to remit the proceeds of sale, less a 25% commission to Owner.

In each case assume the following: Jeweler is engaged in the business of buying, selling, and repairing jewelry and watches, both new and used. Jeweler sold Owner's watch for $3,000 cash to Faith, an ordinary retail customer who bought in good faith without any notice of Owner's rights in the watch. Owner had no prior knowledge of the sale and did not consent to it. Jeweler failed to remit any part of the proceeds of sale to Owner and is insolvent.

What are the rights of Faith under § 2–403(2) and (3) in each case if Owner brings an action for conversion against Faith? Section 2–403 represents a balancing of the interests of Owner and Faith, each of whom may be the victim of the dishonesty of Jeweler. How is the balancing done in each case? Are the equities the same in each case?

2.   DOCUMENTS OF TITLE

Article 7 of the UCC is concerned with documents of title which are divided into two categories: bills of lading and warehouse receipts. A document of title arises out of a transaction in which goods are delivered to a commercial bailee. In the case of a bill of lading, defined in § 1–201(6), the bailee is "a person engaged in the business of transporting or forwarding goods" and is referred to as the carrier. In the case of a warehouse receipt, defined in § 1–201(45), the bailee is "a person engaged in the business of storing goods for hire" and is referred to as the warehouseman. § 7–102(h). A document of title is both an acknowledgment of receipt of the goods by the bailee and a statement of the terms of the bailment contract.

Documents of title can be either negotiable or nonnegotiable, and negotiability is determined by the form of the document. § 7–104(1)(a) and (2). The process by which a negotiable document of title is negotiated is described in § 7–501(1), (2), and (3) and that process is similar to that with respect to negotiable instruments. Negotiation refers to a transfer of the document resulting in the transferee's becoming the holder of the document and can be illustrated by some examples.

If the document calls for delivery of the goods "to bearer," any person in possession of the document is the holder and is entitled to receive delivery of the goods. § 1–201(20) and § 7–403(1) and (4). Suppose a bearer document is issued by the bailee and is delivered to Doe. Doe can negotiate the document to Roe by simply delivering the document to Roe who becomes its holder. § 7–501(2)(a). Or Doe can deliver the document to Roe after indorsing the document by signing it and naming Roe as indorsee. In that case the goods covered by the document are deliverable to Roe and further negotiation of the document requires Roe's indorsement. § 7–501(3).

If the original terms of the document call for delivery of the goods to the order of Doe, negotiation requires the indorsement of Doe. § 7–501(1). Doe's indorsement can name Roe as indorsee as in the previous example, or the indorsement can be "in blank" which means it is simply Doe's signature without designation of an indorsee. In the latter case the document becomes "bearer" paper and further negotiation of the document can be made by delivery alone.

Section 7–501(4) defines when a document is "duly negotiated" and § 7–502(1) states the rights of a holder to whom a document is duly negotiated. Under § 7–502(1) a holder to whom a document is duly negotiated obtains title to the document, title to the goods, and the right to receive the goods from the bailee. Thus, a holder without title to either the document or the goods may be able to transfer good title to both to a holder to whom the document is duly negotiated. But in some cases due negotiation does not give the transferee good title to the goods because rights under § 7–502(1) are subject to important limitations stated in § 7–503(1). These limitations are illustrated in the Problems that follow.

Negotiability with respect to documents of title borrows some elements from the law applicable to negotiable instruments and some elements from the law applicable to goods. The Problems that follow illustrate that fact.

PROBLEMS

1. O, a cotton producer, stored cotton in Public Warehouse which issued to O a warehouse receipt providing that the cotton was deliverable to the bearer of the warehouse receipt. X, an employee of O, stole the warehouse receipt from O and sold and delivered it to Y, a cotton merchant who knew that the warehouse receipt had been stolen. Y then sold and delivered the warehouse receipt to BFP, another cotton merchant who purchased in good faith and without notice that the document was not the property of Y. O later learned all the facts and brought an action against BFP to recover the warehouse receipt and against Public Warehouse for delivery of the cotton represented by the warehouse receipt. Decide the merits of the two actions brought by O. § 7–104(1)(a); § 7–501(2)(a); § 7–501(4); § 1–201(25); § 1–201(20); § 7–502(1) and (2); § 7–403(1) and (4).

2. O, a cotton producer, stored cotton in Public Warehouse which issued to O a warehouse receipt in bearer form. X, an employee of O, stole the warehouse receipt from O and sold and delivered it to Y, a cotton merchant who knew that the warehouse receipt had been stolen. Y then obtained delivery of the cotton from Public Warehouse upon presentation and surrender of the warehouse receipt. Y then sold the cotton to BFP, a cotton merchant who purchased in good faith without any notice of O's claim to the cotton. O, upon learning the facts, brought an action against BFP for conversion of the cotton. Decide the merits of the action. Read the sections cited in Problem 1.

3. O, a cotton producer, was the owner of cotton that was being transported in O's truck to O's customer. X, a hijacker, stole O's truck and the cotton that it contained. X delivered the cotton to Public Warehouse which issued to X a warehouse receipt in bearer form. X sold and delivered the warehouse receipt to Y, a cotton merchant who knew that the warehouse receipt was stolen. Y then sold and delivered the warehouse receipt to BFP, another cotton merchant who purchased in good faith and without notice that the document was not the property of Y. BFP then obtained delivery of the cotton from Public Warehouse upon presentation and surrender of the warehouse receipt. O later learned all of the facts and brought an action against BFP and Public Warehouse for conversion of the cotton. Decide the merits of the two actions brought by O. In addition to the sections cited in Problem 1, read § 7–503(1)(a) and (b); § 7–404. Suppose Public Warehouse had not yet delivered the cotton to anyone. If both O and BFP demand delivery, to whom is Public Warehouse required to deliver? What should Public Warehouse do to protect itself? § 7–603.

4. O, a cotton producer, was the owner of cotton. O, not having any space on its premises to store the cotton, asked Y, a cotton merchant, for permission to store the cotton on Y's premises for a few days while O found a buyer for it. Y agreed and the cotton was delivered to Y. Y received no consideration for storing O's cotton and was not engaged in the business of storing goods for hire. Assume the following two alternative fact situations:

(a) Y, without O's permission or knowledge, sold the cotton to BFP, a cotton merchant who bought the cotton in good faith believing that it was the property of Y.

(b) Y, without O's permission or knowledge, delivered the cotton to Public Warehouse which issued to Y a warehouse receipt in bearer form. Y then sold and delivered the warehouse receipt to BFP, a cotton merchant, who bought in good faith and without notice of O's claim to the cotton. BFP then obtained delivery of the cotton from Public Warehouse upon presentation and surrender of the warehouse receipt.

In each case O, upon learning the facts, brought an action against BFP for conversion of the cotton. Decide the merits of the actions. In addition to the sections cited in Problems 1 and 3, read § 2–403(2).

B.   BILLS OF LADING

1.   USE OF NEGOTIABLE BILLS OF LADING IN DOCUMENTARY SALES

The UCC sets a pattern of inspection-acceptance-payment for a typical sale of goods. Upon acceptance Buyer is obliged to pay the price (§ 2–607) but acceptance presupposes an opportunity by Buyer to inspect the goods (§ 2–606). Thus, unless Seller agrees to give Buyer credit, delivery and acceptance of the goods and payment for the goods take place contemporaneously. In a face-to-face transaction Buyer is protected by the ability to reject the goods if inspection discloses that they are not as warranted, and Seller, who still has possession of the rejected goods, is adequately protected by the ability to dispose of the goods. However, where Buyer and Seller are physically remote from each other, different considerations apply. Buyer's power to reject the goods, whether exercised rightfully or wrongfully, while serving to protect the Buyer's interests can be damaging to the interests of Seller. Seller may be unable to dispose of rejected goods in a distant market in which Seller is not adequately represented. We have seen that § 2–603 deals with this problem by placing on Buyer certain duties with respect to rejected goods, but Seller has no assurances that these duties will be carried out. And, it may be small solace to unpaid Seller to have a cause of action against Buyer for breach of contract for Buyer's failure to perform duties imposed by the UCC. Seller, in some cases, may be willing to give Buyer credit and simply ship the goods. In many cases, however, particularly those involving international sales, Seller may not be willing to take the risk that the goods will be rejected and not paid for when delivered. If Seller has sufficient bargaining power Seller can demand payment prior to shipment, but in that case, Buyer is left to the mercy of Seller. Since Buyer has no assurance of ever getting the goods Buyer may be unwilling to accept these terms. A method of protecting the interests of both Buyer and Seller in this kind of case is provided by the documentary sale.

The documentary sale involves the use of a bill of lading and a sight draft, and usually a third document, a letter of credit. We saw previously that a bill of lading can be either nonnegotiable (a "straight bill") or negotiable (an "order bill" or "bearer bill"). A straight bill acknowledges instructions from the shipper or consignor to deliver the goods to a named consignee at a specified destination. The shipper under a straight bill, however, has control of the goods through the ability to change the destination or the consignee at any time before delivery; the carrier will normally follow those instructions regardless of who has possession of the bill of lading. § 7–303(1)(b). A negotiable bill in this respect is different. Under a negotiable bill the goods are to be delivered only to the holder of the bill of lading and only upon its surrender. § 7–403(1), (3) and (4). Thus, the shipper that retains possession of an order bill has maximum control of the goods, but all control over the goods is lost when the bill is delivered to Buyer. § 7–303(1)(a). A negotiable bill of lading thus represents the right to receive the goods. Because the goods are represented by a negotiable bill, it can be used as a device for giving a security interest in the goods. Possession of a negotiable bill by the holder is for these purposes tantamount to possession of the goods. If Seller ships the goods to Buyer but has a bill of lading issued to Seller's order, the goods represented by the bill of lading in effect become collateral for the obligation of Buyer under the sales contract to pay the price of the goods. A shipment made in this manner is known as a shipment under reservation. § 2–505(1)(a).

The second document used in a documentary sale is the sight draft. A sight draft is an order by the drawer of the draft to the drawee of the draft to pay, on presentation of the draft to the drawee ("on sight"), a stated sum of money to the order of a named payee. In the case of a documentary sale the drawer is Seller, the drawee is Buyer or Buyer's bank, and the payee is usually Seller, or a bank or other financial institution that either is acting as Seller's collecting agent or is acting in its own behalf as purchaser of the draft from Seller.

The object of a documentary sale is to assure Seller of payment for the goods before they arrive at their destination, and to assure Buyer that at the time of payment for the goods Buyer will have effective control of the goods. To carry out these objectives, a negotiable bill of lading is used. Although details of the transaction may vary, the following conforms to the basic pattern of a documentary sale: Seller ships the goods to Buyer and takes from the carrier an order bill of lading. Seller takes the order bill of lading, to which is attached a sight draft for the amount owed by Buyer for the goods, to Seller's bank. The bank is directed to present the draft to Buyer for payment, and upon payment to simultaneously deliver the order bill of lading. Since Buyer is in a distant place the presentation of the draft and the exchange of the bill of lading for the amount of the draft is made by a correspondent bank in Buyer's city that acts as agent of Seller's bank.

Or in some cases, Seller may send the documents directly to Seller's agent in Buyer's city. The proceeds of the draft are remitted through the chain of agents to Seller. Sometimes Seller's bank purchases or "discounts" the draft at the outset and takes the order bill of lading as security for payment of the draft. In that event Seller is paid immediately for the goods and the proceeds of the draft when paid by Buyer are paid to Seller's bank.

Although possession of the order bill of lading assures Buyer of control of the goods, this type of exchange denies to Buyer the right to inspect the goods before payment of the price. At the time the exchange is made the goods normally will not have arrived at their destination. Buyer can look only to the often inadequate description of the goods in the bill of lading as assurance that the goods will be those bargained for.

Although this type of exchange assures Seller of payment for the goods before giving up control of them, it does not guarantee that Buyer in fact will pay the draft when presented. Buyer may not pay either because financially unable to pay, or because Buyer is repudiating the contract. If Buyer doesn't pay, Seller will have to find some other destination for the goods that are at that point in transit to Buyer. A third document, the irrevocable letter of credit, can be used to eliminate this risk. The irrevocable letter of credit, used in a variety of commercial transactions, is usually used in documentary sales involving overseas shipments where the consequences to Seller of nonpayment by Buyer are particularly onerous. The irrevocable letter of credit, in this context, is a document usually issued by a bank ("the issuer") at the request of Buyer ("the customer") in which the issuer undertakes to honor drafts of Seller ("the beneficiary") when those drafts are presented in accordance with conditions stated in the letter of credit, including the presentation of described bills of lading. § 5–103(1)(a). Because the irrevocable letter of credit is for the benefit of the beneficiary, once it has been delivered to the beneficiary or the beneficiary has been advised of its issuance it can't be revoked without the consent of the beneficiary. § 5–106(1) and (2). The letter of credit represents an obligation of the issuer independent of the underlying transaction between the beneficiary and the customer, and if the draft is presented in accordance with the terms of the credit with all supporting documents the issuer must honor it. § 5–114(1). In that case Buyer cannot prevent payment by the issuer even if Seller is in breach of the underlying contract. If the documents appear on their face to comply with the credit the only remedy of Buyer is to enjoin the issuer from paying, but the injunction can be granted only in case of fraud in the transaction, forged documents, or other defect not apparent on the face of the documents. § 5–114(2)(b).

Bills of lading are regulated by many federal and state statutes. State law is found primarily in Article 7 of the UCC but that article has limited application. Section 7–103 makes Article 7 subject to "any [applicable] treaty or statute of the United States, regulatory statute of this State or tariff, classification or regulation filed or issued pursuant thereto." Federal law plays a dominant role in the regulation of bills of lading. The Federal Bills of Lading Act, 49 U.S.C. §§ 81–124, applies to carriages of goods by a common carrier from any state to a foreign country or to another state, or from any state that passes through a foreign country or another state. Coverage of Article 7 is thus limited to carriages of goods in which the goods never leave the state of origin and to shipments of goods from a foreign country to any state. In the latter case, however, if an ocean bill of lading is involved the Carriage of Goods by Sea Act, 46 U.S.C. §§ 1300–15, and the Harter Act, 46 U.S.C. §§ 190–195, apply. With respect to the liability of the carrier for loss or damage to the goods the Carmack Amendment to the Interstate Commerce Act, 49 U.S.C. § 20, applies to interstate shipments. There are numerous other federal and state statutes, as well as regulations of the Interstate Commerce Commission, that may apply to a particular case involving rights under a bill of lading.

Thus, the rights and obligations of parties to a bill of lading are in the majority of cases decided by federal law, principally the Bills of Lading Act. That Act is in most respects consistent with Article 7 and is almost identical to the Uniform Bills of Lading Act which was the applicable state law in a majority of the states before adoption of Article 7.

Banque de Depots v. Ferroligas

Court of Appeal of Louisiana, Fourth Circuit, 1990.
569 So.2d 40.

■ LOBRANO, JUDGE.

* * *

Banque de Depots, a Swiss bank, (Bank) instituted these proceedings against Bozel Mineracao E Ferroligas (Bozel) in the Thirty Fourth Judicial District seeking a money judgment asserting numerous allegations that Bozel fraudulently misused and/or misapplied the Bank's funds. The Bank asserts that Bozel is a foreign corporation existing under the laws of Brazil, is not licensed to do business in Louisiana, and has no designated agent for service of process. Pursuant to the provisions of Code of Civil Procedure Article 3541(5), the Bank sought and obtained a nonresident writ of attachment wherein 1,300 metric tons of calcium silicon were seized. The calcium silicon was shipped by Bozel from Rio de Janeiro to the port of New Orleans for transit to three purchasers, none of whom are located in Louisiana, or do business here. The order of seizure was signed on May 14, 1990, and the property was seized the same day at the facilities of Chalmette Slip in Arabi, Louisiana.

On May 25, 1990 Bozel filed a motion to dissolve the writ of attachment asserting three errors, namely that the verified petition was deficient, that Bozel was not the owner of the goods, and that the cargo was subject to bills of lading and thus UCC § 7–602 prevented their seizure.

* * *

The trial court dismissed Bozel's rule to dissolve the attachment and issued extensive reasons. Bozel seeks relief from this court.

Initially, we note that the only issue for our determination is whether the writ of attachment should be dissolved. * * *

The cargo seized was in transit to three non-Louisiana purchasers. Forty percent (455 metric tons) of the total shipment, represented by bills of lading nos. 71–80, was sold to Picklands Mather Sales Company in Cleveland, Ohio (the Pickland cargo). The remainder of the cargo, represented by bills of lading nos. 70 and 81–94, was sold to Lakeside Metals and Petrochemicals of Geneva, Switzerland, with its ultimate destination to Odermath (USA), and Shieldalloy Metallurgical Corporation (the Lakeside cargo).

The record is clear that the entirety of the cargo was shipped under negotiable bearer bills of lading. With respect to the Pickland cargo, Bozel's bank in Brazil forwarded the bills of lading, and other documentation, to Society National Bank for collection from Pickland. The Lakeside cargo was handled in a similar manner. Payment for that cargo was by letters of credit issued by Banque Bruxelles Lambert. Neither purchaser paid for its cargo prior to the issuance of the attachment, although the record is unclear as to whether all of the Lakeside bills of lading were in the possession of the collecting bank.[1]

For the following reasons we hold that the trial court was in error and that the attachment was erroneously issued. We grant the relief sought, and dissolve the writ of seizure.

Most of the argument between the parties concerns the ownership of the cargo when it reached the dock in Chalmette. Bozel asserts that once the cargo was placed on the ship in Brazil title passed to the purchasers. In support they refer to numerous articles of Article 2 of the U.C.C. with respect to the shipping instructions designated as "F.O.B." and "C.I.F."[2] They further argue that title to the cargo follows the bills of lading, and once those were transferred to the collecting entities, they (Bozel) were no longer the owner of the cargo.

The Bank asserts that ownership must be determined under Louisiana law, and since Article 2 of the U.C.C. has not been adopted in this state, arguments with respect to shipping instructions, i.e. the designations "F.O.B." and "C.I.F.", lack merit. They further urge that only bills of lading which are "duly negotiated" transfer ownership of the goods, citing UCC § 7–502. They contend that the bills of lading may have been transferred to collecting agencies, but they were not "duly negotiated" as contemplated by section 7–502 since there was no value given prior to the attachment, citing UCC § 7–501(4).

1. The forwarding bank is Bozel's bank in Brazil. The collecting banks are the recipients of the delivery documentation.

2. The Picklands cargo was shipped "C.I.F." meaning "Cost Insurance and Freight." The Lakeside cargo was shipped "F.O.B. Rio de Janeiro" meaning "Free on Board in Rio de Janeiro." Under both situations, Bozel argues that responsibility for the cargo and its ownership pass to the purchasers once the cargo is loaded on the carrier.

We agree that Louisiana law governs the ownership of the cargo when it reached Chalmette. Article 2 of the U.C.C. has not been adopted in Louisiana, hence the courts must look to the Civil Code in determining the ownership of movables. However, with respect to movables shipped under a negotiable bill of lading, * * * we deem UCC § 7–602 to be controlling in the instant case.

* * * By adopting UCC § 7–602 Louisiana law makes it clear that irrespective of who may be deemed the owner of the property, if it is shipped pursuant to a negotiable bill of lading, no seizure can be effected unless the document is surrendered to the carrier (depositary) or impounded by a court (i.e. its negotiation enjoined).

The Bank argues, however, that UCC § 7–602 is inapplicable because its intent is to protect the bailee (depositary) from competing claims, rather than shielding a debtor's property from seizure, citing the U.C.C. comment to the statute. They further argue that, even if the statute is applicable, on May 18, 1990 and June 1, 1990, after the attachment issued, they instituted proceedings in Switzerland and Ohio, respectively, to enjoin negotiation of the documents.

The holder of a duly negotiated bill of lading acquires title to the document and title to the goods described therein. UCC § 7–502. It is clear that once a carrier has issued a negotiable bill of lading for goods being placed in commerce, the intent of the law is to protect those who subsequently become holders through "due negotiation." * * * Part and parcel of that intent is the protection afforded the depositary in relinquishing possession of the goods to the holder of the document. Thus, although goods in the possession of a depositary may have been seized, if the document's negotiation has not been enjoined or the document is not in its possession, UCC § 7–602 permits the depositary to surrender the goods to the duly negotiated holder. The law protects that holder from acquiring goods that are subject to a seizure. Any other conclusion would lead to the absurd result of requiring the holder, prior to his purchase of the bill of lading, to check every jurisdiction through which the goods passed to determine if it has been seized by judicial process. This would defeat the purpose of our commercial laws.

The record is clear that on May 14, 1990, the date of the seizure, the negotiable bills of lading were outstanding. They were not in the hands of the carrier and their negotiation had not been enjoined. As discussed supra, the validity of the attachment must be determined as of the date it was issued. The Bank cannot cure this defect by seeking to impound the bills of lading after it obtained the seizure. To hold otherwise would create an impossible contradiction in our commercial laws since the "seized" goods would still be subject to the legal effects of the unimpaired "due negotiation" of the corresponding bills of lading. The legal "capture" of the bills of lading is a prerequisite to the seizure of the goods.

* * * Accordingly, we reverse the trial court and make Bozel's rule absolute. We order that the writ of attachment be dissolved.

2. NONNEGOTIABLE BILLS OF LADING

Clock v. Missouri–Kansas–Texas Railroad Co.

United States District Court, E.D.Missouri, 1976.
407 F.Supp. 448.

■ NANGLE, DISTRICT JUDGE. Plaintiff Gerald Clock brought this action to recover the cost of goods which were allegedly converted by defendant Missouri–Kansas–Texas Railroad Company. By amended complaint, plaintiff added Stanley L. Crawford as defendant. Plaintiff also alleges that defendant Railroad breached its obligation to deliver the goods. Prior to the filing of plaintiff's amended complaint, defendant Railroad filed a third-party complaint against Crawford, alleging that if the Railroad should be liable to plaintiff, third-party defendant would be liable to the Railroad to the extent of the liability to plaintiff. Crawford now being a defendant in this action, defendant Railroad's complaint is in fact a cross-claim and will be treated as such.

* * *

On January 14, 1975, Crawford sold two carloads of bulk ammonium nitrate fertilizer to Buford Cunningham and received two checks in payment therefor. On the same date, the goods were placed in the care and custody of defendant Railroad for shipment from Oklahoma to Eaton Agricultural Center in Indiana. Defendant Railroad issued bills of lading to cover the goods.

* * *

At the time of sale, Crawford knew that Cunningham was going to sell the goods to a third party. Soon after the sale to Cunningham, Cunningham did sell the goods to plaintiff for $30,195.12. At the time of this sale, plaintiff had no knowledge of any infirmities in title, or right to possession, by Cunningham.

On January 23, 1975, the bank notified Crawford that there were insufficient funds in Cunningham's account to cover the checks. Accordingly, they were returned to Crawford.

The goods were still in transit at this point. Crawford instructed the Railroad to hold the railroad cars containing the goods until further instructions from him. Defendant Railroad complied.

On February 3, 1975, Crawford certified to defendant Railroad that he was the true owner of the goods and he issued a reconsignment order on the goods, instructing that they be sent to Farmers Union Coop, instead of Eaton Agricultural Center. Defendant Railroad complied with these instructions.

Plaintiff furnished replacement goods to Eaton Agricultural Center of a like quantity and value, and acquired the right, title and interest of Eaton

Agricultural Center to the goods, by reason of an assignment by Eaton Agricultural Center executed on February 10, 1975.

* * *

The bills of lading involved herein are straight bills of lading. 49 U.S.C.A. §§ 82, 86. It is clear that "[a] straight bill can not be negotiated free from existing equities * * * ". 49 U.S.C.A. § 109. While not negotiable, straight bills are transferable. The transferee stands in the shoes of the transferor, acquiring no additional rights over those held by the transferor. * * *

A carrier may deliver goods to "a person lawfully entitled to the possession of the goods" or to the consignee. 49 U.S.C.A. § 89. The question for determination therefore is whether Crawford was lawfully entitled to possession of the goods. While it is true that title passes to a buyer when the seller completes his performance under the contract, UCC § 2–401, it is equally true that

> where the buyer * * * fails to make a payment due * * * the aggrieved seller may
>
> > (a) withholding delivery of such goods;
> >
> > (b) stop delivery by any bailee * * * ;
> >
> > * * *
> >
> > (d) resell and recover damages * * * ;
> >
> > * * *
> >
> > (f) cancel. UCC § 2–703.

It is the Court's conclusion, therefore, that upon the failure of the checks presented by Cunningham to Crawford, Crawford was "lawfully entitled to the possession of the goods." Plaintiff, as transferee of a straight bill of lading, can not have any greater rights than did Cunningham, and can not have the status of a bona fide purchaser for value. Since Crawford was entitled to possession of the goods, defendant Railroad can not be liable for delivering the goods in accordance with Crawford's instructions. 49 U.S.C.A. § 89. * * *

The applicable provisions of the Commercial Code provide that

> (1) Unless the bill of lading otherwise provides, the carrier may deliver the goods to a person or destination other than that stated in the bill or may otherwise dispose of the goods on instructions from
>
> (b) the consignor on a nonnegotiable bill notwithstanding contrary instructions from the consignee * * * . UCC § 7–303.

Under the facts established herein, Crawford was the consignor, as Crawford was "the person from whom the goods have been received for shipment." UCC § 7–102(c). Since the bills of lading were nonnegotiable, and defendant Railroad delivered the goods pursuant to the instructions of the consignor, there can be no liability. See Comments, UCC §§ 7–303 and 7–504(3).

Under 49 U.S.C.A. § 112, the authority of the shipper to stop shipment in transit and redirect it is well established. * * * The same right is recognized in the Commercial Code. See UCC §§ 2–703 and 2–705. Accordingly there can be no recovery by plaintiff against Crawford.

Plaintiff has claimed that both the Railroad and Crawford converted the shipments in question to their own use. Conversion has been defined as "* * * an *unauthorized* assumption and exercise of the right of ownership over the personal property of another to the exclusion of the owners' right". Carson Union May Stern Co. v. Pennsylvania Railroad Co., 421 S.W.2d 540 (Mo.App.1967) [emphasis in the original]. Having concluded that Crawford was lawfully entitled to possession of the goods, it is clear that recovery for conversion will not lie.

The cases cited by plaintiff are inapposite as they involve a bona fide purchaser for value. Under the authority of 49 U.S.C.A. § 81 et seq., there can not be such status where one is a transferee under a straight bill of lading. North American Van Lines, Inc. v. Heller, 371 F.2d 629 (5th Cir.1967) is equally unavailing since the Court concludes that Crawford was lawfully entitled to possession.

Accordingly, judgment will be for defendants Railroad and Crawford. Since plaintiff will not recover any damages from defendant Railroad, judgment will be for defendant Crawford on the Railroad's cross-claim.

NOTES

1. In *Clock,* when Crawford gave his reconsignment order to Railroad he certified that he was "the true owner of the goods." If we assume that the contract of sale was a shipment contract, who had title to the goods at the time of the reconsignment order? § 2–401(2). Did the right of Crawford to reconsign the goods depend on who had title to the goods at that time? Did the right of Crawford to reconsign the goods depend on who had possession of the bill of lading? § 2–703 and § 2–705. Suppose Crawford wrongfully reconsigned the goods, i.e., assume that the checks of Cunningham had not been returned for insufficient funds. Would Railroad have been liable to Clock, who was the transferee of the bill of lading from Cunningham? § 7–303(1). Would Crawford have been liable to Clock? § 7–504(1). Would Farmers Union Coop, which received the goods on reconsignment, have been liable to Clock? § 7–504(3).

2. How would you have answered the questions asked in Note 1 if, at the time of receipt of Cunningham's checks, Crawford had delivered to Cunningham a negotiable bill of lading to the order of Cunningham rather than a nonnegotiable bill?

C.   WAREHOUSE RECEIPTS

1.   LIABILITY OF WAREHOUSEMAN FOR LOSS OF IDENTIFIED GOODS

I.C.C. Metals, Inc. v. Municipal Warehouse Co.

Court of Appeals of New York, 1980.
50 N.Y.2d 657, 431 N.Y.S.2d 372, 409 N.E.2d 849.

■ GABRIELLI, JUDGE. At issue on this appeal is whether a warehouse which provides no adequate explanation for its failure to return stored property upon a proper demand is entitled to the benefit of a contractual limitation upon its liability. For the reasons discussed below, we conclude that proof of delivery of the stored property to the warehouse and its failure to return that property upon proper demand suffices to establish a prima facie case of conversion and thereby renders inapplicable the liability-limiting provision, unless the warehouse comes forward with evidence sufficient to prove that its failure to return the property is not the result of its conversion of that property to its own use. If the warehouse does proffer such evidence and is able to persuade the trier of facts of the truth of its explanation, then the limitation of liability will be given effect and the bailor will be required to prove the warehouse to be at fault if it is to recover even those limited damages allowed by the provision.

The facts relevant to this appeal are undisputed and may be simply stated. In the autumn of 1974, plaintiff, an international metals trader, delivered three separate lots of an industrial metal called indium to defendant commercial warehouse for safekeeping. The parties have stipulated that the three lots of indium, which had an aggregate weight of some 845 pounds, were worth $100,000. When the metal was delivered to defendant, it supplied plaintiff with warehouse receipts for each lot. Printed on the back of each receipt were the terms and conditions of the bailment, as proposed by defendant. Section 11 of those terms and conditions provided as follows: "Limitation of Liability—Sec. 11. The Liability of the warehouseman as to all articles and items listed on the face of this warehouse receipt is limited to the actual value of each article and item, but the total liability of the warehouseman shall not exceed in any event for damage to any or all the items or articles listed on this warehouse receipt the sum of fifty ($50.00) dollars; provided, however, that such liability may, on written request of the bailor at the time of signing this warehouse receipt or within twenty (20) days after receipt of this warehouse receipt, be increased on part or all of the articles and items hereunder, in which event, increased rates shall be charged based upon such increased valuation, but the warehouseman's maximum liability shall in no event exceed the actual value of any or all of the articles and items in question. In no case shall the liability be extended to include any loss of profit".[1] Plaintiff did not request any increase in defendant's contractual liability, nor did it inform defendant of the value of the metal.

For almost two years, defendant billed plaintiff for storage of each of the three lots by means of monthly invoices that specifically identified the stored metal, and plaintiff duly paid each invoice. Finally, in May of 1976, plaintiff requested the return of one of the three lots of indium. At that point defendant for the first time informed plaintiff that it was unable to locate any of the indium. Plaintiff then commenced this action in conversion, seeking to recover the full value of the indium. In response, defendant contended that the metal had been stolen through no fault of defendant's and that, at any rate, section 11 of the terms printed on each warehouse receipt limited plaintiff's potential recovery to a maximum of $50 per lot of indium.

Special Term granted summary judgment to plaintiff for the full value of the indium. The court found that plaintiff had made out a prima facie case of conversion by proffering undisputed proof that the indium had been delivered to defendant and that defendant had failed to return it upon a proper demand. As to defendant's contention that the metal had been stolen, the court concluded that this allegation was completely speculative and that defendant had failed to raise any question of fact sufficient to warrant a trial on the issue. Finally, Special Term held that the contractual limitation upon defendant's liability was inapplicable to an action in conversion. The Appellate Division, 67 A.D.2d 640, 412 N.Y.S.2d 531, affirmed the judgment in favor of plaintiff and we granted defendant leave to appeal to this court. We now affirm the order appealed from.

Absent an agreement to the contrary, a warehouse is not an insurer of goods and may not be held liable for any injury to or loss of stored property not due to some fault upon its part (Uniform Commercial Code, § 7–204, subd. [1]). As a bailee, however, a warehouse is required both to exercise reasonable care so as to prevent loss of or damage to the property * * * and, a fortiori, to refrain from itself converting materials left in its care * * *. If a warehouse does not convert the goods to its own use and does exercise reasonable care, it may not be held liable for any loss of or damage to the property unless it specifically agrees to accept a higher burden. If, however, the property is lost or damaged as a result of negligence upon the part of the warehouse, it will be liable in negligence. Similarly, should a warehouse actually convert stored property to its own use, it will be liable in conversion. Hence, a warehouse which fails to redeliver goods to the person entitled to their return upon a proper demand, may be liable for either negligence or conversion, depending upon the circumstances * * *.

A warehouse unable to return bailed property either because it has lost the property as a result of its negligence or because it has converted the property will be liable for the full value of the goods at the time of the loss

[1]. In light of our disposition of the main issue presented by this case we need not and accordingly do not determine whether this limitation applies to loss of bailed property as well as damage to that property.

or conversion * * * unless the parties have agreed to limit the warehouse's potential liability. It has long been the law in this State that a warehouse, like a common carrier, may limit its liability for loss of or damage to stored goods even if the injury or loss is the result of the warehouse's negligence, so long as it provides the bailor with an opportunity to increase that potential liability by payment of a higher storage fee * * *. If the warehouse converts the goods, however, strong policy considerations bar enforcement of any such limitation upon its liability * * *. This rule, which has now been codified in subdivision (2) of section 7–204 of the Uniform Commercial Code, is premised on the distinction between an intentional and an unintentional tort. Although public policy will in many situations countenance voluntary prior limitations upon that liability which the law would otherwise impose upon one who acts carelessly * * * such prior limitations may not properly be applied so as to diminish one's liability for injuries resulting from an affirmative and intentional act of misconduct * * *. Any other rule would encourage wrongdoing by allowing the converter to retain the difference between the value of the converted property and the limited amount of liability provided in the agreement of storage. That result would be absurd. To avoid such an anomaly, the law provides that when a warehouse converts bailed property, it thereby ceases to function as a warehouse and thus loses its entitlement to the protections afforded by the agreement of storage * * *. In short, although the merely careless bailee remains a bailee and is entitled to whatever limitations of liability the bailor has agreed to, the converter forsakes his status as bailee completely and accordingly forfeits the protections of such limitations. Hence, in the instant case, whether defendant is entitled to the benefit of the liability-limiting provision of the warehouse receipt turns upon whether plaintiff has proven conversion or merely negligence.

Plaintiff has proffered uncontroverted proof of delivery of the indium to defendant, of a proper demand for its return, and of defendant's failure to honor that demand. Defendant has failed to make a sufficient showing in support of its suggested explanation of the loss to defeat plaintiff's motion for summary judgment. Its unsupported claim that the metal was stolen does not suffice to raise any issue of fact on this point.[3] Upon this record, it is beyond cavil that plaintiff would be entitled to judgment had it elected to

---

3. The explanation proffered by the warehouse in such a case must be supported by sufficient evidence and cannot be merely the product of speculation and conjecture. "The explanation must show with reasonable certainty how the loss occurred, as, by theft or fire * * * It is not enough to show that defendant-bailee used reasonable care in its system of custody if mysterious disappearance is the only 'explanation' given" * * *. In the instant case, defendant offered proof of the following facts in support of its claim that the indium had been stolen: "(1) the storage of the indium in three different locations in two different buildings, and the absence of any indication in [defendant] Municipal's records that the indium was moved, negate the possibility of misdelivery; (2) the storage of the indium without special precautions, because [plaintiff] ICC failed to advise Municipal of its true value, supports the likelihood of theft; (3) the form of the indium (small bars) would have facilitated removal without detection; (4) a recently discharged employee was experienced in 'weighing and sampling' and thus presumably was aware of the value of indium; (5) there was a series of alarms, any one of which could have been caused by a theft; (6) Municipal promptly reported the loss to the police; and (7) ICC reported the

sue defendant in negligence * * *. We now hold that such a record also suffices to sustain plaintiff's action in conversion, thereby rendering inapplicable the contractual limitation upon defendant's liability.[4]

The rule requiring a warehouse to come forward with an explanation for its failure to return bailed goods or be cast in damages in negligence is based upon practical necessity. As is noted above, a warehouse may only be held liable for loss of or damage to bailed goods if the loss or damage is due to the negligence of the warehouse or if the warehouse has converted the property. Hence, in order to recover damages for lost or damaged goods, a bailor must prove either that the warehouse was negligent or that it converted the goods. Since bailed property is in the possession of and under the sole control of the warehouse at the time of injury or loss, however, it is the warehouse which is in the best, if not the only, position to explain the loss of or damage to the property. Indeed, such information normally will be exclusively in the possession of the warehouse and will not be readily accessible to the bailor. Because of this, the law properly refuses to allow a warehouse, which has undertaken for a fee to securely store goods belonging to another, to avoid liability by simply pleading ignorance of the fate of the stored merchandise. To allow the warehouse to so easily escape its responsibilities would be to place the bailor in an untenable position and would serve to encourage both dishonesty and carelessness. Clearly, the temptation to convert stored property would be significantly increased could the warehouse then avoid all civil liability by simply denying all knowledge of the circumstances of the loss and placing upon the bailor the well nigh impossible burden of determining and proving what happened to his property while it was hidden from sight in the depths of the defendant's warehouse. Similarly, such a rule would reward those warehouses with the least efficient inventory control procedures, since they would be most able to honestly plead ignorance of the fate of goods entrusted to their care.

To prevent such absurd results, the law has long placed upon the warehouse the burden of advancing an adequate explanation of the reasons for its failure to properly return stored property * * *. This does not mean

loss to its insurers as a theft and continued to employ Municipal's services, thus negating any suspicion that Municipal had misappropriated the indium or had been grossly negligent in its care." Viewed most favorably to defendant, this evidence would indicate at most that theft by a third party was one possible explanation for the defendant's failure to redeliver the indium to plaintiff. This is simply insufficient, since the warehouse is required to show not merely what might conceivably have happened to the goods, but rather what actually happened to the goods. Defendant proved only that theft was possible, and presented no proof of an actual theft. Hence, the proffered explanation was inadequate as a matter of law.

4. We emphasize at this point that we do not suggest by our holding in this case that proof of negligence will support a recovery in conversion. Rather, our holding is limited to those situations in which the warehouse fails to provide an adequate explanation for its failure to return stored goods. If the warehouse comes forward with an explanation supported by evidentiary proof in admissible form, the plaintiff will then be required to prove that the loss was due to either negligence or conversion, depending on the circumstances. For plaintiff to recover in conversion after the warehouse has established a prima facie explanation for its failure to deliver, the trier of facts must find all the traditional elements of conversion.

that the warehouse is required to prove that it acted properly, nor does this doctrine shift the burden of proof to the warehouse. Rather, the warehouse must come forward and explain the circumstances of the loss of or damage to the bailed goods upon pain of being held liable for negligence. If the warehouse does provide an explanation for the loss or damage, the plaintiff then must prove that the warehouse was at fault if he is to recover * * *. A few illustrations of this principle may be of some assistance. Where the warehouse simply refuses to return bailed property upon a legitimate demand and does not advance any explanation for that refusal, the plaintiff will be entitled to recover without more. Similarly, where the warehouse does suggest an explanation for the loss but is unable to proffer sufficient evidentiary support for that explanation to create a question of fact, as in this case, the plaintiff will be entitled to recover without more. Where, however, the warehouse proffers sufficient evidence supporting its explanation to create a question of fact, the jury must be instructed that if it believes that explanation, the plaintiff must be denied any recovery unless he has proven that the warehouse was at fault (Uniform Commercial Code, § 7–403, subd. [1], par. [b]). In other words, if the jury is persuaded that the goods were accidentally mislaid or destroyed in a fire or accident or stolen by a third party, the plaintiff cannot recover unless he has proven that the loss or the fire or the accident or the theft were the proximate result of either a purposive act or a negligent commission or omission by the warehouse.

Although it has long been settled that this is the rule in an action in negligence, there has been considerable inconsistency and uncertainty as to the application of this principle to an action in conversion. Thus, although we have on occasion declared that a bailor establishes a prima facie case of conversion by simply proving delivery to the bailee and an unexplained failure to return the stored goods upon demand * * * we have at other times indicated that something more is needed to maintain an action in conversion and that a plaintiff will be required to provide positive evidence of an intentional act by the warehouse inconsistent with the plaintiff's interest in the property * * *. We deem it unnecessary to engage in an extended discussion of each of the precedents in this area, for they appear essentially irreconcilable. Rather, we have decided to take this opportunity to re-examine the matter and to determine the most appropriate resolution of this controversy.

We now conclude that there exists no sound reason to apply a different rule to the two types of action where, as here, the bailee comes forward with insufficient proof of its explanation for the loss of the bailed goods. The same policy considerations which prevent a warehouse from avoiding liability in negligence by a declaration of ignorance appear equally applicable to an action in conversion. Indeed, as a practical matter, a bailor will be even less able to prove conversion by a warehouse than he would negligence, since a warehouseman who actually converts stored property will generally strive mightily to prevent knowledge of his malfeasance from coming to light. The possibility of fraud is obvious, for a dishonest warehouseman might well be encouraged to convert bailed property if he could then obtain the benefit of a contractual limitation of liability by the simple expedient of professing ignorance as to the fate of the goods. The rule requiring a warehouse to explain the loss of or damage to the goods lest it be held liable would be severely undermined could a warehouse avoid the bulk of potential liability in such a case by means of a contractual provision.

We note, moreover, that the requirement that a warehouse provide an explanation for loss of property entrusted to it is certainly not overly harsh, nor does it impose a heavy burden upon the warehouse. The warehouse must only offer proof of what actually happened to the goods and need not show that it was free from fault, for once the warehouse makes the initial required showing, the burden of proving the warehouse to be at fault will fall squarely upon the plaintiff. No greater duty of care is created by this rule, nor does it establish any sort of strict liability. Certainly a warehouse may reasonably be required to keep track of goods entrusted to it and to supply an accurate explanation of any loss to the bailor.

Finally, where a warehouse does not explain the cause of the loss, it would appear as reasonable to assume that this profession of ignorance is due to the fact that the warehouse has converted the goods as to presume that it is due to the fact that the warehouse has been negligent. Indeed, one who commits an intentional wrong is more likely to attempt to cover his tracks than one who has been at most negligent, especially in light of the disparity in potential liability created by the insertion of a limitation of liability clause. For all these reasons, we conclude that plaintiff was entitled to summary judgment in its action in conversion. Quite simply, plaintiff proved delivery of the indium to defendant warehouse and defendant's subsequent failure to return the metal, whereas defendant has not come forward with adequate evidentiary proof in admissible form to support its suggested explanation of that failure. That being so, the limitation on liability was inapplicable, and plaintiff was entitled to recover the actual value of the missing indium.

Accordingly, the order appealed from should be affirmed, with costs.

■ JASEN, JUDGE (dissenting). My disagreement with the majority stems from their conclusion that plaintiff is entitled to summary judgment on the theory of conversion absent any proof whatsoever that defendant converted the indium metal to its own use or the use of another. The plaintiff bailor having failed to demonstrate in an evidentiary manner an intentional act by the defendant bailee which worked to deprive the plaintiff of its property, the defendant should not be held liable for the conversion of the stored property.

* * *

Conversion is viewed as requiring "an intentional exercise of dominion or control over a chattel which so seriously interferes with the right of another to control it that the actor may justly be required to pay the other the full value of the chattel." (Restatement, Torts 2d, § 222A * * *.) Thus, one who does not intentionally exercise dominion or control over property is not liable for conversion, even though his act or omission may be said to constitute negligence. As was stated in Magnin v. Dinsmore, 70 N.Y. 410,

417: "A conversion implies a wrongful act, a mis-delivery, a wrongful disposition, or withholding of the property. A mere nondelivery will not constitute a conversion, nor will a refusal to deliver, on demand, if the goods have been lost through negligence, or have been stolen." * * *

While proof of delivery to a bailee, of a demand for the property's return, and of a failure of the bailee to return the goods establishes a prima facie case of negligence, these items of proof do not, in my opinion, constitute a prima facie case of conversion. The majority, obviously recognizing this fact, resorts to a newly created presumption of conversion in order to sustain the judgment rendered plaintiff below. Such legal reasoning is unwarranted.

First, I would consider the law in this commercial area well settled and in accordance with the basic principle that a cause of action sounding in conversion will not be maintainable absent proof of intentional wrongdoing by the bailee. * * * Here, plaintiff has presented no proof whatsoever of an intentional wrongdoing by defendant, and the majority's conclusion that this "record * * * suffices to sustain plaintiff's action in conversion" flies in the face of this established rule that an action for conversion requires an evidentiary showing that defendant bailee *intentionally* acted in a manner so as to deprive plaintiff of its property.

Second, I take issue with the policy reasons cited by the majority to support their obliteration of the distinction between negligence and conversion—that the bailee is in the better position to explain what happened to the goods and, thus, should be required to come forth with such explanation; and that instances of fraud would proliferate if a bailee could merely profess ignorance as to the goods' disappearance and, then, claim as a sanctuary the contractual limitation of liability. While I would agree that a bailee should keep track of goods entrusted to it and that a bailee is in a better position than the bailor to explain what happened to the goods, it does not follow that its failure to produce the stored goods upon demand should serve as the vehicle to thrust upon the bailee the burden traditionally placed upon a plaintiff bailor when suing in conversion to demonstrate an intentional act by the defendant bailee which worked to deprive that plaintiff of its property. As a matter of public policy, I believe the burden of proving a wrongful act such as conversion should remain upon the party claiming it, rather than the one accused of the wrongdoing.

There is simply no rational reason, under the guise of policy considerations, to shift the burden of coming forward with evidence of what "actually happened"[4] to the goods when a cause of action is framed in conversion. If the bailor is seeking to circumvent the contractual limitation on damages, agreed upon by the parties as a condition of the bailment, the bailor should be put to the task of demonstrating that the bailee converted the goods to its own use or the use of another. To hold otherwise is to permit the bailor to have its cake and eat it too. This is so because the bailor, as in this case, need not declare the full value of the goods and, as a result, is required to pay only a *de minimus* bailment fee, rather than a fee

---

4. The majority stresses that their holding is limited to only requiring a ware-

houseman to establish, in the first instance, "a prima facie explanation for its failure to

based on actual value; yet, upon loss of the goods, it may seek compensation for their full value even though it was never disclosed to the bailee.

This, it seems to me, is fundamentally unfair, especially when one considers that plaintiff voluntarily signed as a condition of bailment a contractual limitation of liability ($50) as to each article and item stored, although the true value of the three lots of indium was $100,000. The limitation of liability and the actual value of the stored property were known to plaintiff, and yet it chose not to avail itself of the opportunity to declare the full value of the goods to insure that it would be made whole in case of loss. Plaintiff had only to be candid about the true value of the goods entrusted to defendant and pay a storage rate commensurate with the risk in order to protect itself from any and all loss, whether such loss be precipitated by fraud, conversion, negligence, or otherwise. Having not exercised this option and, thus, having paid a much lower storage fee than what would have been charged had the bailee known the true value of the goods and been responsible for the same, the bailor should be held to the terms of the bailment absent an affirmative evidentiary showing of intentional wrongdoing by the bailee. In this commercial setting, dealing as we are with sophisticated businessmen, we should not reach out and relieve the plaintiff of its failure to protect itself contractually. I can only read the majority's opinion as doing violence to the law, without rhyme or reason.

For the above-stated reasons, I would reverse the order of the Appellate Division and grant summary judgment to defendant.

COOKE, C.J., and JONES, WACHTLER, FUCHSBERG and MEYER, JJ., concur with GABRIELLI, J.

JASEN, J., dissents and votes to reverse in a separate opinion.

Order affirmed.

2.   COMMERCIAL USES OF WAREHOUSE RECEIPTS

Dolan, Good Faith Purchase and Warehouse Receipts: Thoughts on the Interplay of Articles 2, 7, and 9 of the UCC
30 Hast.L.J. 1, 2–3 (1978).

Functions of the Warehouse Receipt

Historically, documents of title such as warehouse receipts facilitated the practice of storing and transporting commodities. More recently, the receipt has taken on significant marketing and financing features.

deliver" the goods [footnote 4]. However, I derive little solace from this qualification, inasmuch as a bailee "is required to show not merely what might conceivably have happened to the goods, but rather what *actually* happened to the goods" [footnote 3] [emphasis added]. Since we are concerned with cases involving unexplained losses, the majority opinion sanctions, for all practical purposes, the imposition of full liability for the value of the goods stored whenever the bailee is unable to deliver the stored goods or explain "what actually happened to the goods." This, I suggest, is an onerous burden upon the warehouseman.

The Marketing Function

For some purchasers, delivery is not an essential part of the purchase transaction. Grain dealers, for example, frequently purchase from producers and sell to industry consumers without moving the grain from the elevators to which the producers delivered it for drying and storing after harvest. Customarily these buyers and sellers effect such transfers by negotiable warehouse receipts. The producer obtains the receipt, which describes the grain according to industry standards; the grain dealer then purchases the receipt and transfers it, perhaps through a series of buyers, to a buyer who desires to ship or otherwise take possession of the grain. This last purchaser then surrenders the receipt to the elevator and takes delivery. The result is that the parties have achieved the marketing of the grain without incurring unnecessary transportation expenses.

Similarly, in the cotton industry a producer will deliver cotton to a gin for processing and storing. The gin will issue a negotiable receipt for the cotton with a sample attached. Brokers then display the samples to buyers who may be located in markets distant from the gin. Upon receipt of a satisfactory offer, the broker forwards the receipt with a draft through banking channels. When the purchaser honors the draft the bank delivers the receipt; the purchaser, unless he desires to resell the cotton without taking possession, will surrender the receipt to the gin and take delivery of the goods. Again, the receipt simplifies the marketing process and saves transportation costs.

The Financing Function

In transactions similar to the foregoing illustrations, market conditions or production schedules may force a buyer to hold a commodity. During that interval the buyer owns a valuable asset but cannot utilize it and, therefore, may seek to borrow against it. Lenders will grant credit on the security of the stored commodity by taking the negotiable warehouse receipt. When the borrower finds a buyer for the commodity or is prepared to use it in its own production process, the borrower will pay off the loan, obtain the receipt from the creditor and surrender the receipt to the warehouse against delivery of the goods.

Some borrowers use nonnegotiable receipts in connection with inventory financing. This form of inventory loan satisfies a lender's policing requirements in situations in which the lender fears his collateral may disappear quickly. The borrower delivers the inventory to a "field warehouse," usually a part of the borrower's premises controlled by an independent, field-warehouse company. The warehouse then issues nonnegotiable receipts to the lender. When the borrower needs inventory to fill customer orders, he will satisfy a portion of the loan; the lender in turn will issue delivery orders to the field warehouse, which will then release part of the inventory to the borrower.

These models illustrate typical patterns through which business people employ warehouse receipts to save transaction costs and to achieve liquidity. The models also forecast the potential conflicts in these commodity paper transactions. With respect to each purchase, for example, there is the classic tension between the purchaser, on the one hand, and the seller's secured lender, on the other. Conflicts between purchasers and lenders claiming an interest in the same goods may also arise because some sellers will enter into a contract of sale with more than one buyer or grant a security interest to more than one lender.

3. WAREHOUSE RECEIPTS FOR FUNGIBLE GOODS

Suppose Farmer delivers 1,000 units of grain to Warehouse Co. for storage in a grain elevator that Warehouse operates. The grain will lose its identity by being added to the mass of similar grain in the grain elevator. The grain in this case is referred to as "fungible goods." § 1–201(17). How do we characterize the transaction if Warehouse issues to Farmer a warehouse receipt for the grain? Conceptually the transaction does not have the normal characteristics of a bailment because Farmer is not entitled to get back the same grain that Farmer deposited. If the transaction is not a bailment, how is it analyzed? We could say that Farmer transferred title to the grain to Warehouse and, in return, Farmer received the obligation of Warehouse to pay on demand the economic equivalent of the deposited grain measured at the time of demand. Thus, if Farmer deposited 1,000 units of grain Farmer is entitled on demand to receive from Warehouse 1,000 units of similar grain or its then market value if Warehouse does not have the grain to deliver. Whether the transaction is characterized in this way or as a bailment is not important so long as Warehouse is solvent. In either case Warehouse is required to deliver grain to Farmer, or if it has no grain to deliver, its value. Characterization of the transaction is important, however, in the case of insolvency of Warehouse.

If Farmer gave up title to the grain in exchange for a claim against Warehouse, Farmer is only an unsecured creditor of Warehouse which is now an insolvent debtor. Grain owned by Warehouse is an asset available for payment of all creditors of Warehouse. If the transaction is treated as a bailment, Farmer has an ownership interest in the grain held by Warehouse for Farmer at the time of the insolvency proceeding. In that case Farmer is asserting a claim to Farmer's grain rather than a creditor's claim against Warehouse.

Section 7–207 deals with this issue. Under the first sentence of subsection (2) Farmer is an owner of the grain held by Warehouse, as a tenant in common with other "persons entitled" to the grain. The extent of Farmer's right to the grain is affected by the question of "overissue" addressed in § 7–402 and the last sentence of § 7–207(2).

Sometimes a warehouseman will fraudulently or mistakenly issue a warehouse receipt for goods which were never deposited in the warehouse. Assume that that occurred with respect to a negotiable warehouse receipt covering goods specifically identified in the receipt rather than fungible goods. The warehouse receipt was then duly negotiated to a bank as collateral for a loan. § 7–501. In the event of default by the debtor the bank's expectation is that it can, under § 7–502 and § 7–403(1), obtain possession of the goods represented by the receipt and use the goods as a source of payment of the debt. But since the warehouse receipt does not in fact represent any goods deposited with the warehouseman, all that the bank has is a claim for damages against the warehouseman. § 7–203. If the warehouseman becomes insolvent the bank's collateral is reduced to an unsecured claim against the warehouseman that may have no value. How is the case changed if the warehouse receipt did not purport to represent specifically identified goods, but rather fungible goods like grain?

Let us return to our original hypothetical case. Assume that originally there was no grain on deposit in the grain elevator of Warehouse. Then, Farmer A and Farmer B each deposited 3,000 units of grain. Warehouse commingled the grain and issued negotiable warehouse receipts for 3,000 units to each of them. Farmer A and Farmer B became tenants in common of the 6,000 units in the grain elevator. § 7–207(2), first sentence. Warehouse then fraudulently issued a negotiable warehouse receipt for 3,000 units of grain to Farmer C who deposited no grain. The receipt purported to give to Farmer C common tenancy ownership rights in grain held by Warehouse. But since the only grain held by Warehouse is that deposited by Farmer A and Farmer B, the receipt issued to Farmer C was an overissue. Warehouse held 6,000 units of grain and issued receipts covering 9,000 units. The normal rule, applicable to goods other than fungible goods, is that if two warehouse receipts have been issued for the same goods the second receipt is not effective to confer any rights to the goods. § 7–402. The issuer is liable for damages caused by the overissue (§ 7–203) but the holder of the second receipt gets no ownership right to the goods. But Article 7 applies a different rule to commingled fungible goods. If Farmer C duly negotiates the warehouse receipt to Bank as collateral for a loan, the apparent result under the second sentence of § 7–207(2) is that Bank acquires common tenancy ownership rights equal to those of Farmer A and Farmer B even though no deposit of grain was made with respect to Bank's warehouse receipt. Before Farmer C duly negotiated the warehouse receipt to Bank, Farmer A and Farmer B owned 3,000 units each. After that event they and Bank each owned 2,000 units. The last sentence of § 7–207(2) is a change from pre-Code law. 1 Hawkland, Transactional Guide to the UCC 367 (1964).

Thus, persons entitled under warehouse receipts (§ 7–403(4)) with respect to commingled grain have ownership rights in the commingled mass but they bear the risk that their interest in the commingled grain may be reduced as the result of overissued receipts that are duly negotiated. This risk is similar to the risk that they take with respect to fraudulent sales by the warehouseman of commingled grain which is not owned by the warehouseman. Frequently, the warehouseman is in the business of buying and selling grain for its own account as well as storing grain for others. In that case, some of the grain in the elevator is owned by the warehouseman and some of the grain is owned by holders of warehouse receipts. If the warehouseman sells and delivers some of the latter grain to a person who is a buyer in ordinary course of business (§ 1–201(9)), that person gets good title to the grain and defeats any ownership claim of the defrauded holders. § 7–205. The rationale of § 7–205 is similar to that of § 2–403(2).

Branch, the case that follows, involved the rights of a bank which took as collateral for a loan fraudulently issued negotiable warehouse receipts which purported to represent grain deposited in the warehouse, but which in fact were issued without any deposit having been made.

Branch Banking & Trust Co. v. Gill

Supreme Court of North Carolina, 1977.
293 N.C. 164, 237 S.E.2d 21.

[Woodcock was the manager of Farmers Grain Elevator at Warsaw ("Elevator"), a public warehouse, and was also Secretary–Treasurer of Southeastern Farmers Grain Association, Inc. ("Southeastern"), which was engaged in the business of buying and selling grain. All warehouse receipts issued by Elevator bore Woodcock's signature. The plaintiff, Branch Banking & Trust Co. ("Bank") loaned money to Southeastern under an agreement which provided that warehouse receipts representing stored grain would be pledged as security for the loans. Bank was aware that Woodcock was employed by both Elevator and Southeastern. Southeastern pledged to Bank 13 negotiable warehouse receipts (numbered 974–986) issued by Elevator as collateral for loans totalling $314,354.38. The 13 warehouse receipts were fraudulently issued by Woodcock. They did not represent any grain deposited by Southeastern with Elevator.]

■ SHARP, CHIEF JUSTICE. In our earlier opinion in this case we held: (1) that the Bank did not take the 13 fraudulent warehouse receipts (Nos. 974–986) by "due negotiation" and thus did not acquire the rights specified in UCC § 7–502; (2) that "nothing else appearing" the Bank was merely a transferee of the negotiable warehouse receipts and thus acquired no greater rights or title than its transferor, Southeastern; * * *

Our prior holding that the Bank did not take the 13 receipts through "due negotiation" is clearly correct.

* * *

By their terms, the grain the 13 warehouse receipts purportedly represented was to be delivered to Southeastern or to its order. These receipts, therefore, were negotiable documents of title. UCC § 1–201(15), UCC § 7–102(1)(e), UCC § 7–104(1)(a). These receipts, however, were not indorsed by Southeastern at the time they were delivered to the Bank. Neither Woodcock, the secretary-treasurer, nor any other officer of Southeastern ever signed the receipts. Upon Bank's request for its indorsement, Southeastern's bookkeeper, Mrs. Carlton, stamped the name "Southeastern Farmers Grain Association, Inc." on the reverse side of the receipts.

As we said in our former opinion, "[T]he affixing of the payee's (or subsequent holder's) name upon the reverse side of a negotiable document of title by rubber stamp is a valid indorsement, if done by a person authorized to indorse for the payee and with intent thereby to indorse. * * * However, the Superior Court found that Mrs. Carlton, who stamped the name of Southeastern upon the reverse side of these receipts, had neither the authority nor the intent thereby to indorse them in the name of Southeastern. The evidence supports these findings and would support no contrary finding." * * * Since the receipts were not properly indorsed to the Bank, they were not negotiated to it. The Bank, therefore, not having acquired the receipts through "due negotiation," did not acquire the rights provided in UCC § 7–502.

Under UCC § 7–506 the Bank could compel Southeastern to supply the lacking indorsement to the 13 receipts. However, the transfer "becomes a negotiation only as of the time the indorsement is supplied." Since the Bank was specifically informed of the fraud surrounding the issuance of the receipts on the evening of 7 May 1970 any subsequent indorsement by Southeastern would be ineffective to make the Bank "a holder to whom a negotiable document of title [was] duly negotiated." UCC § 7–501(4).

Thus, because of the lack of proper negotiation, the Bank became a mere transferee of the 13 warehouse receipts. The status of such a transferee is fixed by UCC § 7–504(1) which provides: "A transferee of a document, whether negotiable or nonnegotiable, to whom the document has been delivered but not duly negotiated, acquires the title and rights which his transferor had or had actual authority to convey." Here Southeastern, the Bank's transferor, had no title by way of the fraudulent receipts to any grain held by Elevator, and it had no rights against Elevator. Woodcock, acting for and on behalf of Southeastern, had fraudulently procured the issuance of these receipts to Southeastern without the deposit of any grain. Then, as Southeastern's manager, he had pledged them to Bank in substitution of 16 previously issued receipts purportedly representing corn deposited in Elevator. However, at least six of these represented no grain at the time they were issued, and between the warehouse examiner's inspections of 10 February 1970 and May 1970,— without requiring the surrender of any receipts—Elevator had delivered to or for the account of Southeastern nearly 113,000 bushels of grain more than Southeastern allegedly had in storage there. Thus, Elevator had no obligation to deliver any grain to Southeastern, and it did not become obligated to Bank merely because Southeastern transferred the receipts.

* * *

The purpose of UCC § 7–203 is to protect specified parties to or purchasers of warehouse receipts by imposing liability upon the warehouseman when either he or his agent fraudulently or mistakenly issues receipts (negotiable or nonnegotiable) for misdescribed or nonexistent goods. This section, coupled with the definition of issuer (UCC § 7–102(1)(g)), clearly places upon the warehouseman the risk that his agent may fraudulently or mistakenly issue improper receipts. The theory of the law is that the warehouseman, being in the best position to prevent the issuance of mistaken or fraudulent receipts, should be obligated to do so; that such receipts are a risk and cost of the business enterprise which the issuer is best able to absorb. * * *

In the Comment to UCC § 7–203 it is said: "The issuer is liable on documents issued by an agent, contrary to instructions of his principal, without receiving goods. No disclaimer of the latter liability is permitted." *Issuer* is defined by UCC § 7–102 as "a bailee who issues a document. * * * Issuer includes any person for whom an agent or employee purports to act in issuing a document if the agent or employee has real or apparent authority to issue documents, notwithstanding that the issuer received no goods or that the goods were misdescribed or that in any other respect the agent or employee violated his instructions." Under these provisions Elevator would clearly be liable to the Bank on the 13 fraudulent receipts issued by its agent Woodcock *provided* the Bank could carry its burden of affirmatively proving that it came within the protection of UCC § 7–203.

* * *

We now consider whether the Bank qualifies for this protection. At the outset of our discussion we note that UCC § 7–203 contains no requirement that the purchaser take negotiable documents through "due negotiation" before he can recover from the issuer. (Compare this section with the analogous U.C.C. provision covering bills of lading, which provides protection to "a consignee of a nonnegotiable bill who has given value in good faith or a holder to whom a negotiable bill has been duly negotiated relying in either case upon the description * * *." UCC § 7–301(1).) Of course, had the Bank met all the requirements of due negotiation it also would have met the requirements of UCC § 7–203.

To be entitled to recover under UCC § 7–203 a claimant has the burden of proving that he (1) is a party to or *purchaser of a document of title* other than a bill of lading; (2) *gave value* for the document; (3) took the document in *good faith;* (4) *relied* to his detriment upon the description of the goods in the document; and (5) took *without notice* that the goods were misdescribed or were never received by the issuer. Many of these terms are defined in Article 1 of the U.C.C., and those definitions are also made applicable to Article 7.

Under UCC § 1–201(33) and UCC § 1–201(32) Bank acquired the 13 negotiable warehouse receipts by purchase. Further, when Bank surrendered to Southeastern its old notes and the 16 receipts securing them, taking in return the new notes secured by the 13 receipts, it gave "value." Under UCC § 1–201(44) a person, *inter alia,* gives "value" for rights if he acquires them "(b) as security for or in total or partial satisfaction of a pre-existing claim; or (d) generally, in return for any consideration sufficient to support a simple contract." It now remains to determine whether Bank, at the time it relinquished the 16 old receipts in return for the 13 receipts, was acting (1) without notice that no goods had been received by the issuer for the 13 receipts, (2) in good faith, and (3) in reliance upon the descriptions in the receipts.

The trial court, after making detailed findings as to facts known to Bank at the time it accepted the 13 receipts, found and concluded the ultimate fact that "the plaintiff Bank did not receive warehouse receipts numbered 974 through 986 in good faith without notice of claims and defenses." This finding, although stated in the negative in order to use the precise language of UCC § 7–501(4), is equivalent to a positive finding that Bank took the 13 receipts with notice that they were spurious. On the same findings the judge also concluded that plaintiff did not come into court with "clean hands." This finding likewise is equivalent in import and meaning to a finding that Bank did not take the 13 receipts in good faith. * * * Upon these findings he held that plaintiff had no cause of action either at law or in equity based on the 13 receipts against either the State Warehouse Superintendent or against the State Treasurer as custodian of the State Indemnity and Guaranty Fund. We must, therefore, determine whether these findings are supported by competent evidence.

Upon our reconsideration of this case we have concluded (1) that the record evidence fully supports the trial judge's findings that Bank did not take the receipts in good faith and without notice that they had been fraudulently issued and (2) that his findings compel his conclusions of law.

[The court's review of the evidence on the issue of good faith is omitted.]

The Code was not designed to permit those dealing in the commercial world to obtain rights by an absence of inquiry under circumstances amounting to an intentional closing of the eyes and mind to defects in or defenses to the transaction. * * * Nor did the General Assembly, when, by G.S. 106–435, it created the State Indemnifying and Guaranty Fund to safeguard the State Warehouse System and to make its receipts acceptable as collateral, intend that it should encourage individuals or financial institutions to engage in transactions from which they would otherwise have recoiled. On the contrary, the fund was created to protect those parties to or purchasers of warehouse receipts who, acting in good faith and without reason to know that the goods described thereon are misdescribed or nonexistent, suffer loss through their acceptance or purchase of the receipt.

The case comes down to this: Plaintiff Bank based its right to recover on the 13 fraudulent warehouse receipts numbered 974–986 for which Elevator received no grain. Its action, if any, was under UCC § 7–203. Therefore, if plaintiff could prove it acquired the receipts in good faith and without notice of the fraud, it was entitled to recover; otherwise, not. The trier of facts, upon sufficient evidence, found that plaintiff did not acquire the receipts in good faith and without notice.

The judgment of the trial court is therefore affirmed as to all defendants and our former decision as reported in 286 N.C. 342, 211 S.E.2d 327 (1975) is withdrawn.

Affirmed.

PROBLEM

Smith is manager of Grain Elevator, a public warehouse which also engages in the business of buying and selling grain. Grain Elevator stores in one common mass both the grain which it owns and the grain deposited by farmers for which it issues warehouse receipts. Smith is authorized to issue warehouse receipts on behalf of Grain Elevator. Smith is also President of Grain Corporation which is engaged in the business of buying and selling grain.

During a six-month period the following transactions occurred: 100 farmers each deposited with Grain Elevator 1,000 units of grain for which Grain Elevator issued negotiable warehouse receipts; Grain Elevator stored in its elevator 10,000 units of grain which it owned; and Grain Elevator sold 40,000 units of grain to various buyers in ordinary course of business. No other withdrawals of grain were made during the period. At the end of the period there were 70,000 units of grain in the elevator and there were outstanding negotiable warehouse receipts covering 100,000 units of grain. At that time Smith, acting on behalf of Grain Elevator, fraudulently issued a negotiable warehouse receipt to Grain Corporation for 20,000 units of grain. No grain was deposited by Grain Corporation. Grain Corporation then negotiated this warehouse receipt to Bank as collateral for a loan made contemporaneously. Bank acted in good faith and had no knowledge of the circumstances surrounding the issuance of the warehouse receipt. It believed that the warehouse receipt represented grain deposited with Grain Elevator by Grain Corporation.

Both Grain Elevator and Grain Corporation are now insolvent. Grain Elevator has in storage the same 70,000 units of grain on hand at the end of the six-month period. There are outstanding warehouse receipts covering 100,000 units of grain deposited by the 100 farmers and 20,000 units covered by the warehouse receipt held by Bank. Bank's loan to Grain Corporation remains unpaid.

Assume that in the insolvency proceedings any person who can prove ownership of the grain in the possession of Grain Elevator is entitled to take delivery free of the claims of the creditors of Grain Elevator.

1. What rights do the 100 farmers have against the customers of Grain Elevator who purchased the 40,000 units of grain during the six-month period? Should it make any difference that some of the farmers deposited grain before the sale of the 40,000 units to buyers in ordinary course while other farmers deposited grain after the sale?

2. What rights do the 100 farmers and Bank have to the grain held by Grain Elevator?

INDEX

†

1–56662–550–5

90000

9 781566 625500